# BRITISH HIT ALBUMS

## PAUL GAMBACCINI
·
## TIM RICE
·
## JONATHAN RICE

GUINNESS PUBLISHING

**Picture Acknowledgements:** Hulton Picture Company;
London Features International; Redferns; Rex Features.

Editor: Honor Head
Art Editor: David Roberts
Picture Editor: Alex Goldberg
GRR Editorial Associate: Tony Brown

First edition 1983, reprinted once
Second edition 1986
Third edition 1988
Fourth edition 1990, reprinted 1991 (twice)

Published in Great Britain by Guinness Publishing Ltd,
33 London Road, Enfield, Middlesex

Typeset in Bembo by
Ace Filmsetting Ltd, Frome, Somerset
Printed and bound in Great Britain by
Hazell Books, Aylesbury

British Library Cataloguing in Publication Data
Gambaccini, Paul
    The Guinness book of British hit albums.—4th ed.
    1. Pop music. Long playing sound discs—Discographies
    I. Title   II. Rice, Tim   III. Rice, Jo
    016.7899'1245
    ISBN 0-85112-397-X

# Introduction

The times they are a-changin'. Sure, Bob Dylan, 1964, number four, but that's not why we mention it. This is no pop quiz. This is *British Hit Albums*, and LPs are most definitely a-changin', changing in the way they are manufactured and the way they are marketed. There is a new breed of artists being bought and the widest range of product being sold since the Beatles claimed the chart for rock in the early Sixties.

Think of the software first. Not since the late sixties have three configurations been competing for the buyer's attention. In those increasingly dim and distant days the vinyl disc held forth against competition from cassette and eight-track cartridge. The latter form was heavily promoted but lost the battle so quickly and completely it is now difficult to explain to younger listeners what an eight-track cartridge even was.

Today vinyl is still fighting the good fight against cassette, but this time it has a new foe in the compact disc. As certain as it seemed to win its war twenty-plus years ago, it now appears doomed to die by the end of the century. Compact disc sales continue to climb, despite pricing controversies. The only reason a bigger percentage of album sales are not on CD is that the majority of the population still do not have compact disc machines. The price of the hardware, unlike the discs, has been steadily falling, so it grows likelier as each year goes by that a larger portion of the public is going to be buying its albums on CD. This will become even more probable as affordable car players are introduced. In America, where the trade is seen to be hastening the death of vinyl, Milli Vanilli's 'All or Nothing' became, in late 1989, the first number one album not to be available on black disc. Further stocks subsequently came onto the market, but this distinction was seen as an omen rather than as a mistake.

Almost without exception music sounds better on CD than on vinyl. The only questionable cases are with old works recorded with what we might call low technology. The enhancement of sound reproduction CD makes possible shows up the limitations of these original recordings. Even so, the amount of vintage material available on compact disc grows every year, and one previous fear, that collectors of obscure early material and minority music might not be catered for by CD, has proven false. In fact, CD has generally proved superior to vinyl for the repackaging of oldies, since more of an artist's work can be put on a CD than a black disc.

The way music is marketed, whatever the configuration, has also altered. In previous editions of this book we noted how first EMI/Virgin and then WEA/CBS came to take a sizeable section of the field with their 'Now' and 'Hits' series of compilations. After a few years the very industry which had started this autocannibalism (for surely making a new or minor artist's hit available with a bunch of proven winners must diminish sales of that act's own album) complained that their sales success distorted the chart. Just look at the growing number of these compilations that went to number one—one in 1983, three in 1984, five in 1985, and so on. In 1988 three of the top thirteen sellers of the year were part of the 'Now That's What I Call Music' series.

The business bosses didn't like the way their new progeny were keeping their prodigies from prominent places in the platter parade. In an attempt to give the highest chart positions back to individual acts, the BPI decided in late 1988 to establish separate charts for compilations and new material. This change is reflected in this book and explained in our introductory remarks to Part 1.

There is a new variety of artists being bought on LP, too. It's easy to miss this when seeing the very obvious high profile of mass appeal artists who sell hundreds of thousands of compact discs. It's also tempting to be captivated by the way availability on CD has spurred purchases of old product by consumers wishing to replace worn vinyl editions. It's thrilling, for example, to see Phil Collins notch up sales of over one million copies of '. . . But Seriously' during the 1989 holiday season alone, and to watch 'Rumours' by Fleetwood Mac continue to add to its all-time longest chart run thanks to CD sales.

But let's not overlook a reality that's hard for the record

industry itself to swallow. The best selling albums of 1988 and 1989 were the first offerings of Kylie Minogue and Jason Donovan, respectively. Because the songwriting/production team Stock-Aitken-Waterman so dominated the singles chart, little attention was given to their album feats. The Osmonds in their various forms dominated the singles chart in 1972–73, but they never had a top three album in any combination. Not since the Beatles, who as well as being critical favourites were originally teen screams, have pin-up singles stars done so well in the album list.

Yet for the first time in many years several young bands taken more seriously by the music press have also made highly placed debut discs. Groups like Happy Mondays, the Stone Roses, the Quireboys and Sundays are making their first appearance in this book, yet they do so with top five entries. Tracy Chapman, who already seems a veteran, wasn't even with us last time around when we included all hits to the end of 1987.

It isn't just rock that is providing breakthroughs. *Aspects of Love*, which bowed at number one, and several recent West End shows have had good long term selling original cast albums. The astonishing Gloria Estefan, who nabbed two of the top five sellers of 1989, has opened a market in Latin-based music as Enya has done for New Age with her 1988 winner, 'Watermark'. House music has done better in its compilations than other recent dance crazes. In short, the album market is fragmented, both in type of album sold and type of configuration in which it is sold. We could be living in interesting times. We are certainly living in changing times.

PAUL GAMBACCINI

TIM RICE

JONATHAN RICE

# Year by Year Review 1958–1989

# 1958

In 1948 CBS introduced the long-playing microgroove recording to America, devised by Peter Goldmark who, it is said, had had enough of getting up several times during one piece of music to change several 78s. He thought there had to be a market for a single disc that could contain an entire symphony or sonata.

The eighteen albums that hit the chart in the last eight weeks of 1958, the first weeks of *Melody Maker*'s Top Ten chart (the first LP chart published in the UK), demonstrated that Goldmark's invention had other applications. None of the eighteen best-sellers was a classical orchestral performance! Thirteen were by adult male performers with wide audience appeal and five were of show business origin – that is, stage, screen or television.

The soundtrack to 'South Pacific' was number one for each of the eight weeks, a prelude to its equally total domination of the 1959 lists. The man with the most LPs to chart was Frank Sinatra, who touched the Top Ten four times. Elvis Presley had the most total weeks on chart, that is to say a sum of the runs of each of his hit LPs. Both 'Elvis' Golden Records' and 'King Creole' were on every one of the eight charts.

The other artists who contributed to the all-male domain were Perry Como, Russ Conway, Mario Lanza, the American satirist Tom Lehrer, and Johnny Mathis. Perhaps Lanza was the closest to what Goldmark had in mind: one side of his disc was the soundtrack to the film about the classical tenor Enrico Caruso, 'The Great Caruso'.

# 1959

It can be whispered in reverent awe or shouted from the rooftops, but the achievement is so great that it cannot be conveyed in casual conversation: the original soundtrack to the film 'South Pacific' was at number one for the entire year 1959. This family favourite led the list for every one of the 52 weeks, a feat which has never been matched, though later discs would surpass it in sales. 'South Pacific' boasted a wide range of memorable music, from the love ballad 'Some Enchanted Evening' (an American number one for Perry Como) to the novelty tune *Happy Talk* (eventually a UK number one for Captain Sensible).

Film soundtracks were still the leading money-spinners in the LP market of 1959. The form was only a decade old, and soundtracks, Broadway cast performances and classical works were still the most logical initial uses of Peter Goldmark's invention, requiring the additional space a long player could provide. The movie versions of 'Gigi' and 'The King And I' were notable winners in 1959, as was the New York stage production of 'West Side Story'.

Rock-and-roll vocalists, previously content with singles, made further inroads into the album field, but Frank Sinatra still scored the most weeks on chart for a solo singer. Elvis Presley was a close second, registering an impressive success with 'Elvis' Golden Records'. The chart appearance of two LPs by Cliff Richard was the best 1959 showing by a young Briton.

'Curtain Up!', a compilation of stars from the London Palladium hosted by Bruce Forsyth, enjoyed a 13-week run, but the most impressive performance by a show business star was that of Peter Sellers, who spent 32 weeks in the Top Ten with two solo LPs and a further five with his colleagues the Goons.

# 1960

'South Pacific' dominated the album charts one more time in 1960, though not to the extent it had in 1959. It was in the best-sellers for every one of the 53 charts of the year, the only title to achieve that run, but it did occasionally let other discs take the top spot. Number one on the very first *Record Retailer* album chart, that of 10 March, was 'The Explosive Freddy Cannon', which fell in fragments the following week after giving Cannon the distinction of being the first rock-and-roll singer to have a number one LP in the UK. Even the second, Elvis Presley, who had been a more likely contender for that honour, only managed one week at the summit, scoring with 'Elvis Is

Back'. The other disc to interrupt the 'South Pacific' streak was 'Down Drury Lane To Memory Lane', a nostalgic effort by the studio group 101 Strings.

Rock-and-roll made great progress in the long playing market in 1960. The previous year only four rockers had charted in the entire 12 months. This time five of the top six acts were rock stars, though the majority of chart artists were still not of this nature. Presley pipped Peter Sellers as the individual with most weeks on the chart, though Sellers would have ranked above Presley if the computation included his additional appearances with the Goons and Sophia Loren, not, one must add, on the same disc.

American guitarist Duane Eddy's surprisingly strong showing in fourth place should not be overlooked.

# 1961

Commercial success does not guarantee artistic immortality, as the George Mitchell Minstrels have proved. Their 'Black And White Minstrel Show' was an enormous success on television, record and stage, but an entire generation has grown up in, shall we say, the dark about their achievements.

'The Black And White Minstrel Show' was the only album to stay in the chart for the whole of 1961. It accumulated seven weeks at number one in four separate visits, while 'Another Black And White Minstrel Show' had a single mighty eight-week run at the top. Mass audiences loved the old-time performances of The Minstrels, many of whom blacked up to sing vintage popular songs. It was the dated nature of their material, as well as increased sophistication concerning racial matters, which spelled an end to large scale interest in the group in the late sixties.

Elvis Presley was the outstanding artist for the second consecutive year, enjoying 22 weeks at number one with the soundtrack to 'GI Blues'. The granddaddy of film favourites, 'South Pacific', put in a final nine weeks at the peak before retiring. It was a bumper year for original cast recordings of stage musicals, with a strong emphasis on the London stage. 'Oliver', 'Sound of Music' and 'Stop the

World I Want To Get Off' all had lengthy runs with British rosters. The year saw hit honours for the well-remembered 'Beyond The Fringe' and the completely forgotten 'King Kong'. Even the London cast of 'Bye Bye Birdie' flew out of the wings and into the charts.

Frank Sinatra continued his series of fine years, entering the Top Twenty with seven titles on four different labels. Cliff Richard had three new top two successes and one happy hangover from 1960, 'Me And My Shadows'. '21 Today' was his first number one, though his mates beat him to the top by six weeks with their debut disc 'The Shadows'.

# 1962

Elvis Presley and the George Mitchell Minstrels overachieved again in 1962. The King of rock-and-roll notched up 18 weeks at number one with his 'Blue Hawaii' soundtrack, more time at the top than any other long player that year, and he ruled the roost for six more weeks with 'Pot Luck'. The Minstrels led the list with their new release, 'On Stage With The George Mitchell Minstrels', and then encored with their 1960 issue, the original 'Black And White Minstrel Show'. Their three albums tallied a total of 109 weeks in the chart, the first time any act had hit the century.

Compared to these two artists the rest of the field failed to flame, though 'South Pacific' again managed to appear in every one of the 52 charts. The new film sensation was 'West Side Story', surpassing its significant stage sales to pace the pack for 12 weeks. Four other multi-media successes were the soundtrack to 'It's Trad Dad', the original cast album of the London production *Blitz*, and two Dorothy Provine sets inspired by her television series 'The Roaring 20s'. Further evidence of the taste for trad was the appearance of a budget album at number one for two weeks, 'The Best of Ball, Barber and Bilk'. Chris Barber and Acker Bilk had appeared together on two fast-selling packages in 1961, sans Kenny Ball.

The Shadows achieved the fabulous feat of nabbing their second number one with their second effort, 'Out Of The Shadows'. They shared credit on Cliff Richard's table-topping 'The Young Ones'. Cliff managed to top the Shads in weeks on chart thanks to his subsequent release, the literally timed and titled '32 Minutes And 17 Seconds'.

# 1963

Beatlemania spread like a flash fire in 1963, and the album chart showed its effects. The Fab Four's 'Please Please Me' seized the top spot on 11 May and held it for 30 consecutive weeks, to be replaced only by 'With the Beatles', which kept clear for a further 21. The Liverpudlians had come from nowhere to hold the premier position for one week shy of a full year. It was nothing short of a musical revolution: from their arrival until 1968, only one non-rock album would have a look in at number one. A field that had been the domain of the soundtrack and cast album overnight became ruled by rock. It was hard to believe that 1963 had begun with 'The Black and White Minstrel Show' still in the lead. With a couple of notable exceptions, the film and stage market dried up.

Cliff Richard was the weeks on chart champ this time, his total fed by three new successes. The second highest figures were achieved equally by Elvis Presley and Buddy Holly. The Pelvis began twitching in anxiety as the soundtracks to three bad films did progressively worse. Holly, dead for four years, had always been a strong album seller, but really surged in 1963 when the poignantly-titled collection 'Reminiscing' joined the list of his other posthumous best-sellers.

Frank Ifield proved a one-year though not a one-hit wonder, reaching number three with two releases. He never came close again. Frank Sinatra rebounded with three top tenners, including a team-up with Count Basie that went to number two.

# 1964

The Beatles and Rolling Stones monopolized the number one position during 1964, making it the purest year for rock music in terms of holding the top spot. The only 12 weeks John, Paul, George and Ringo were not ahead with either 'With The Beatles', 'A Hard Day's Night' or 'Beatles For Sale', their chief competition was in front with the debut disc 'The Rolling Stones'. The fresh triumphs of 'A Hard Day's Night' and 'Beatles For Sale' gave the Beatles four number ones in four releases, a 100 per cent success ratio they maintained through all of their 11 official outings, though two other issues, a compilation and the 'Yellow Submarine' soundtrack on which they played only a part, fell short of the top. No other act has hit number one every time with as many records.

The Fab Four's quartet of hit LPs gave them 104 weeks on chart, the first time a century had been achieved by a rock act. But even they were outdistanced by Jim Reeves. The American country singer had enjoyed two big albums to accompany his two strong singles in the first half of the year. After he died in a plane crash in July, nine further packages made the chart, six in a four-week period. Gentleman Jim accumulated 115 weeks on chart in all, a record that would stand until 1968.

Third in the weeks on chart category was Roy Orbison, who enjoyed the distinction of seeing his 'In Dreams' set on every chart of the year, a feat attained for the second consecutive year by 'West Side Story'. Cliff Richard had only one new album, below average for his early years, and Elvis Presley slipped seriously as none of his three long players reached the top three.

# 1965

For the three middle years of the sixties only the Beatles, Rolling Stones, Bob Dylan and 'The Sound Of Music' reached number one, trading off in a seemingly endless sequence. The first three were the rock artists who came to represent the spirit of the decade, while the last was a show business phenomenon that came, saw, conquered, and wouldn't go away.

The Beatles began the year on top with 'Beatles For Sale' and ended it there with 'Rubber Soul', having spent much of the summer there as well with 'Help'. Bob Dylan had the second highest total of chart-toppers, two, succeeding 'The Freewheelin' Bob Dylan' with his own 'Bringing It All Back Home', but his most impressive statistic was his 112 weeks on chart. Much of his back catalogue charted in late 1964 and 1965. Though primarily considered an album artist, he also logged five top thirty singles in 1965, his peak year.

Dylan's dear friend Joan Baez shared his success, with three charters to follow her 1964 debut. Her winners included 'Joan Baez', 'Joan Baez No. 5' and 'Farewell Angelina', but no sign of Joan Baez Nos. 2, 3 or 4.

Though Miss Baez was the front-running credited female vocalist, Julie Andrews accounted for the greatest grosses with her soundtracks. 'Mary Poppins' spent the most weeks on chart of any 1965 title, 50, and 'The Sound Of Music' began a run to rival that of 'South Pacific', accumulating its first 20 weeks at number one.

Sir Winston Churchill, who had died early in the year, had a posthumous Top Ten LP, 'The Voice Of Sir Winston Churchill'.

# 1966

Cash register tills were still alive to 'The Sound Of Music' in 1966. If the Beatles or Rolling Stones didn't have a new album, the star soundtrack of the sixties kept the number one position warm. It followed 'Rubber Soul' and preceded 'Aftermath'; it moved back in the aftermath of 'Aftermath' and before 'Revolver'. When the latter Beatles album had shot its bolt, Julie Andrews and company skipped back to the top for the last three months of the year.

'The Sound Of Music' was the only album to spend all of 1966 in the best sellers. It was as big an international phenomenon as a UK success. *Time* reported that it had sold seven million copies by Christmas, outmoving all other stage or screen sets, even the legendary 'South Pacific'.

The musical version of the Von Trapp family story was a timely purchase in any season, not linked to fad or fashion. The Beatles' unprecedented popularity, on the other hand, had made every one of their new discs an immediate must purchase. A short period of colossal concentrated sale would then be followed by a chart decline. Hence

'Revolver', a summer number one, was almost gone by Christmas. Parlophone, wanting a Beatles product for the major marketing month of the year, issued 'A Collection Of Beatles Oldies' in December. However, the fans weren't fooled. It peaked at seven, a commercial miscalculation.

The Beach Boys spent more weeks on the chart than anyone in 1966, with five long players accumulating 95 weeks between them. This success reflected their four consecutive top three singles. One album, the classic 'Pet Sounds', did much better in Britain than America, reaching number two.

The other album artist of note was Herb Alpert, who garnered 89 weeks, but while his Tijuana Brass LPs loitered on the list they did not reach the highest chart positions.

# 1967

History remembers 1967 as the year of flower power and psychedelia. The only real evidence of this in the upper echelons of the LP charts was the tremendous success of the Beatles' landmark 'Sergeant Pepper's Lonely Hearts Club Band' and the considerable achievement of 'Are You Experienced?' by the Jimi Hendrix Experience.

'Sergeant Pepper', chosen the best rock album of all time in two international critics' polls, spent exactly half the year at number one. The other 26 weeks were divided between the recurrent 'The Sound of Music' and the first-time sets by the distinctly unpsychedelic Monkees. In a year when they had six hit singles and a cult television show, the 'fabricated four' reached the top with 'The Monkees' and 'More Of The Monkees'.

With only those four albums going all the way in 1967, it was a major achievement to get to number two. Hendrix and band did. Cream did respectably but not quite as well, earning Top Ten placings with their first two cartons of 'Fresh Cream' and 'Disraeli Gears'. The Rolling Stones surprisingly peaked at three with 'Between The Buttons'.

It was a fine year for easy listening and soul. In addition to 'Best Of The Beach Boys', records that rode the roster for all 52 weeks included the soundtracks of 'The Sound Of Music' and 'Dr Zhivago' and 'Going Places' by Herb Alpert and the Tijuana Brass. Alpert led overall by a toot with 101 weeks on chart, though the Beach Boys were a close second with 97. Tom Jones had three Top Ten issues and the Dubliners, Irish singers enjoying a year of British popularity, had two.

This was the best year on record for Geno Washington, an outstanding live soul attraction. Otis Redding and the Four Tops also had strong chart performances, but they would do even better in 1968.

# 1968

The album chart lost its sense of discipline in 1968. In previous years the number of different artists who had reached number one, not counting performers on film soundtracks, could be counted on the fingers of a sawmill operator's hand. This time no fewer than a dozen different acts went all the way, with occasional further appearances by 'The Sound Of Music'.

The nature of the chart-toppers changed, too. Recently the number one spot had been the property of the world's outstanding rock talents. In 1968 Val Doonican, Tom Jones and Andy Williams managed to head the hordes. The Small Faces and Scott Walker enjoyed their only number one LPs, and Simon and Garfunkel their first. The Four Tops, Otis Redding, and Diana Ross and the Supremes broke the all-white stranglehold on the top spot. The only black faces to have been there before were the made-up ones of the George Mitchell Minstrels. Sadly, Redding's number one was achieved posthumously. Four albums charted after his death, two studio sets, a compilation, and a live LP.

For the fifth time in six seasons, the Fab Four had the Christmas number one, this year with the double disc 'The Beatles', often referred to as 'The White Album'. The Rolling Stones could reach no higher than three for the second straight year. Bob Dylan, on the other hand, had a marvellous comeback from his motorcycle mishap, spending 13 weeks at number one with 'John Wesley Harding'.

Tom Jones had 135 weeks on the chart, the highest total yet achieved in any calendar year. Otis Redding also broke the previous high, set by another aeroplane casualty, Jim Reeves, by tallying 121 weeks. In the How Great Thou Were department, Elvis Presley only had one week on the chart in 1968, as did the George Mitchell Minstrels. Even the Mothers of Invention did better than both of them put together.

# 1969

For the third time the Beatles began and ended a year with different albums at number one. Their double LP 'The Beatles' ushered 1969 in and 'Abbey Road' showed it out. The 11 straight weeks the latter disc spent on top just before Christmas was the longest consecutive stint by any record since 'Sergeant Pepper'. 'Abbey Road' returned in the last week of the year, marking the fifth occasion in 1969 when a former number one encored at that position. This statistic demonstrates the instability of the chart during these 12 months.

Familiar faces atop the heap included Bob Dylan, who successfully flirted with country music in 'Nashville Skyline', the Rolling Stones, who managed a week out front with 'Let It Bleed', and Elvis Presley, who scored a glorious comeback with 'From Elvis In Memphis'. Other rock luminaries who led the list included Cream, whose farewell set 'Goodbye' had three separate appearances at number one, the Moody Blues, who scored the first of their three toppers, and Jethro Tull, making their only standout stint with 'Stand Up'.

But one cannot overlook the achievement of the easy listening mogul Ray Conniff, who spent three weeks ahead of the herd without the benefit of a hit single. Jim Reeves astonished all by registering the only number one of his career five years after his death. It should be noted, however, that his 'According To My Heart' was a budget album.

'Best of the Seekers' bested all competition on five separate occasions. The Australians had the most weeks on chart with a comparatively feeble total of 66, three ahead of Simon and Garfunkel, who tallied their total without the benefit of a new release.

One LP most chartologists might not have remembered as a number one which did get there was 'Diana Ross And The Supremes Join The Temptations'. One LP most chartologists might have thought of as a number one which did not get there was the Who's rock opera 'Tommy', which had to settle for the second spot.

# 1970

Simon and Garfunkel were the mighty men of the new decade's first year. Britain's bestselling album of the seventies, 'Bridge Over Troubled Water', dominated the chart, spending 23 weeks at number one. The closest competitors, 'Abbey Road' and 'Led Zeppelin III', managed five weeks each. The S&G catalogue also sold handsomely in the wake of 'Water', giving the duo an astonishing 167 weeks on the chart in a single year, easily smashing Tom Jones' record of 135.

With the exception of the compilations 'Motown Chartbusters Vol 3 & 4' and the Christmas number one, 'Andy Williams' Greatest Hits', every chart-topper was by a rock artist. The Beatles began their break-up year with 'Abbey Road' and parted with their spring smash 'Let It Be'. Fab Four fans obviously didn't want to say goodbye, buying enough various Beatle albums to give the group 122 weeks in the chart, the highest total of any year in their career. In parallel fashion, the greatest American star of the sixties, Bob Dylan, also had his last two number one LPs in 1970, 'Self Portrait' and 'New Morning'.

It was a banner year for what was then called progressive music. The Moody Blues had a number one and an admirable 115 weeks on the chart. Led Zeppelin flew over all followers with both 'II' and 'III'. Pink Floyd exploded with a real mother, 'Atom Heart Mother', and Black Sabbath won hosannas for heavy metal with their powerful 'Paranoid'.

The outstanding performance by an artist in a supporting role was by Johnny Cash. Though he did not get to number one, the former Sun star did notch up 125 weeks on the chart as four albums entered on the heels of his phenomenally successful 'Johnny Cash At San Quentin'.

# 1972

'Bridge Over Troubled Water' was the outstanding album of yet another year, accumulating 17 weeks at number one, more than any other title. It was the only LP to appear on every one of the year's weekly tabulations.

Simon and Garfunkel works spent a total of 102 weeks on the chart during 1971, a sum exceeded only by the product of the prolific Andy Williams. The long-time hitmaker was at the peak of his career courtesy of his popular television series, and two different titles, 'Greatest Hits' and 'Home Loving Man', reached number one for him during the 12-month period. No other artist had more than one chart-topper this year, although three lots of uncredited session singers and instrumentalists did go all the way with budget compilations of cover versions. If anyone was involved with more than one of these productions, they have wisely remained silent.

Two ex-Beatles fronted the flock with solo albums, Paul McCartney with 'Ram' and John Lennon with 'Imagine', though additional credits were given to Linda McCartney and the Plastic Ono Band, respectively. 'Sticky Fingers', the Rolling Stones' first effort on their eponymous label, gave them a one-for-one record. They continued their 100 per cent performance until their 1974 issue, 'It's Only Rock And Roll', only hit number two. The Stones' competitors for the title of the World's Greatest Live Rock and Roll Band, the Who, scored their only chart-topper ever, 'Who's Next', while after a year of dominating the singles scene T. Rex managed an album number one in 'Electric Warrior'. Other acts enjoying outstanding years included Led Zeppelin, Rod Stewart, James Taylor, and the veteran Frank Sinatra. Only the 'My Way' man and Elvis Presley were still going strong from the original crew of 1958.

# 1972

Marc Bolan and a load of other people dominated the album charts in 1972. The T. Rex phenomenon was merely one aspect of genuine fan fervour. The appearance of five Various Artist LPs at number one was a triumph of marketing.

The year began with 'Electric Warrior' retaining the top spot. In May a double re-issue, 'My People Were Fair'/ 'Prophets Seers And Sages', grabbed the glory for a week, bearing the original label credit of Tyrannosaurus Rex. That an artist's old material released under an obsolete name could get to number one indicated the frenzied following T. Rex had at the time. The following set, 'Bolan Boogie', also went all the way. T. Rex were the first act to have three number one albums in one year.

Bolan's boys were one of four attractions to spend between 80 and 90 weeks on the chart in 1972. Cat Stevens did best with 89 in a year when no one hit the century.

Rod Stewart had his second good year as 'Never A Dull Moment' went to number one and 'Every Picture Tells A Story' continued a long run. These were the first two of six consecutive toppers by the leader of the Faces. That group's 'A Nod's as Good as a Wink' reached the second slot in 1972, narrowly missing an unusual double for Stewart. No artist had ever scored number ones as a soloist and a group member in the same year, though Cliff Richard had made it on his own and with the Shadows backing him. Paul Simon came close, touching the top with his solo debut in 1972, but 'Bridge Over Troubled Water' had, by then, finished making occasional appearances at number one.

Outside of the 'Concert For Bangladesh' triple album, the Various Artists compilations that led the list for 27 weeks, over half the year, were assembled by marketing firms for television advertising. This innovation in merchandising started a packaging trend that has stayed strong ever since. Sales of this type of disc generally offered no indication of how popular taste in music was changing, as success was attributable to the impact of the commercial rather than the music itself.

# ·1973

David Bowie and Max Bygraves have never shared the

concert stage, but they certainly were together in the 1973 album charts. The innovatory space rocker had six hit LPs that year, the singalong star five. Two of Bowie's efforts, 'Aladdin Sane' and 'Pin Ups', were number ones, while the resuscitated 'Hunky Dory' soared to three. Bygraves scored three Top Ten entries with his everybody-join-in approach to medleys of old favourites.

'The Rise and Fall of Ziggy Stardust and the Spiders From Mars' had broken Bowie big in '72. Now he ruled the album chart, accumulating an unprecedented 182 weeks on the list during '73 with the six different titles. This sum shattered the mark of 167 weeks set by Simon and Garfunkel in 1970. Ironically, the defunct duo still managed to total 104 weeks in 1973, three years after their break-up, with the potent pairing of 'Greatest Hits' and 'Bridge Over Troubled Water'.

The siblings from the States, the Carpenters, managed 88 weeks in the list to tie Max Bygraves for third, though the positions reached were less impressive. Elton John and Slade both achieved two number ones, Gilbert O'Sullivan his only one and Roxy Music their first. Rod Stewart nabbed one as a soloist and another as a member of the Faces, completing the odd double that had eluded him in 1972.

Perhaps the most telling statistic of the year is that twenty different albums reached number one. This new high suggested that even the outstanding artists were not dominating the charts as firmly as in the sixties, and that marketing departments had learned how to achieve great sales in a limited time period.

# 1974

Two artists who were already strong in 1973, the Carpenters and Elton John, surged in 1974. Richard and Karen accumulated 17 weeks at number one in four summit visits with 'The Singles 1969–73', the highest total since 'Bridge Over Troubled Water'. The bespectacled pianist, who had scored two number ones the previous 12 months, bagged another brace this time, reigning with 'Caribou' and the Christmas number one 'Elton John's Greatest Hits'.

Another keyboard wizard did a double. For the second successive year the previously unknown feat of hitting the heights both as a soloist and a group member was achieved. Rick Wakeman's last album with Yes, 'Tales From Topographic Oceans' was the year's first number one. That spring the synthesizer star topped the table again with his own 'Journey to the Centre of the Earth'.

Dramatic evidence that the album and singles charts had grown far apart was offered in September. Mike Oldfield held the first two long player disc positions with his new release, 'Hergest Ridge', and his 1973 classic, 'Tubular Bells'. Simultaneously the Osmonds were at one and two in the seven-inch stakes with their own 'Love Me For A Reason' and Donny and Marie's 'I'm Leaving It (All) Up To You'. Oldfield and Osmonds – two more contrasting acts could hardly be imagined.

David Bowie narrowly nudged the Carpenters in the weeks on chart table in 1974, 107 to 106. In the process he picked up his third career number one, 'Diamond Dogs'.

The Beatles were close behind with 104, thanks to the year-long persistence of their 1973 compilations, '1962–66' and '1967–70'. Paul McCartney was doubtless more pleased by the seven-week tenure at the top by Wings' 'Band On The Run'.

# 1975

The album and singles charts showed greater similarities in 1975 than in the immediate past. The three best-selling singles of the year were by the Bay City Rollers, Rod Stewart and the Stylistics, and all three artists also achieved number one LPs. 'Best of the Stylistics' spent more weeks in the Top Ten than any other disc, a statistic that startles until one recalls it benefited from a mighty marketing campaign that included considerable television advertising.

Other greatest hits albums that went to the summit courtesy of blurbs on the box included anthologies by Perry Como, Engelbert Humperdinck, Tom Jones and Jim Reeves; mass appeal singers logically benefited most from mass advertising. The one collection that went to number one naturally as a result of the artist's current popularity rather than artificial stimulus was 'Elton John's Greatest Hits'. By landing the laurels for the last five weeks of 1974 and the first five of 1975, the Pinner prodigy matched the Stylistics' ten weeks over two calendar years. Elton was out front on his own with his total of 105 weeks on the chart, approached only by the slow-to-fade Simon and Garfunkel, whose back catalogue stayed around for one hundred more seven-day spells.

The year ended with Queen's 'A Night At The Opera' ruling. It included the Christmas number one single, 'Bohemian Rhapsody'. Status Quo, Led Zeppelin and Pink Floyd all lent the number one spot a heavier touch during the course of '75. Max Boyce translated his Welsh superstardom into disc sales with the first ever comedy number one.

# 1976

Beware of Greeks bearing gift tokens. There must have been a lot of them about in 1976, because Demis Roussos came from out of the Aegean blue to spend more weeks in the album chart than any other artist. The man-mountain scaled the survey with two top five entries, 'Happy to Be' and 'Forever And Ever', in reaching his total of 84 weeks, one more than Queen, two more than John Denver, and three more than Pink Floyd. Roussos also topped the singles chart with his 'Roussos Phenomenon' EP, the first time an Extended Play disc triumphed in that table.

The low magnitude of the leading weeks on chart total suggests that no artist stood out as David Bowie had only recently. This was indeed the case, as only Led Zeppelin zapped two number ones in 1976, both of which stayed on top for only one week. Were there a trend it would appear to have been in greatest hits compilations, with number one packages coming from Perry Como, Roy Orbison, Slim Whitman, Abba, the Beach Boys, and Glen Campbell. The legendary guitar star Bert Weedon actually made it all the way with a set of other people's hits. This information should not suggest that Weedon, Whitman, Como, Campbell or even the Beach Boys were enjoying a renaissance in singles sales, merely that television advertising of the greatest hits LP had reached the peak of its success. Only the 11 weeks spent at number one by 'Abba's Greatest Hits', the highest sum of list leading weeks in 1976, reflected fame on forty-five. Indeed, the SuperSwedes were enjoying their best year on the singles chart.

'Rock Follies' and 'Stupidity' (by Dr Feelgood) both reached the top without benefit of a hit single. For 'Rock Follies' the feat was doubly distinctive: the Andy Mackay–Howard Schuman score was the first television soundtrack ever to top the album chart.

# 1977

Marketing was the main matter when it came to getting to number one in 1977. Clever campaigns, with a heavy emphasis on television advertising, succeeded in helping several artists who had gone cold back to glory.

Slim Whitman, who had registered one hit single in 20 years, was once again brilliantly promoted to the premier long player position by United Artists marketing. The Beatles had their first weeks of supremacy since 'Let It Be' with an extremely after-the-fact live album. Connie Francis and Bread, both of whom had fallen flat for some time, had number one compilations. The roll call of artists who vaulted to Valhalla with TV anthologies reads like a Hall of Fame: Johnny Mathis, Elvis Presley, Cliff Richard, Diana Ross and the Supremes, the Shadows, and Frank Sinatra. By its very nature this plethora of platters could only be issued once, so 1977 was the peak of this kind of catalogue culling.

The only number one greatest hits album that was part of the natural flow of an artist's output was Abba's as it had been in 1976. The SuperSwedes were on top for a total of 10 weeks, more than any other act or compilation. The Sex Pistols made history with their debut disc, 'Never Mind The Bollocks Here's The Sex Pistols', number one for two weeks in November despite some retail reluctance to display the provocative title. It was the first New Wave number one.

Pink Floyd bested Abba for most weeks on chart, 108 to 106, on the basis of their new number two, 'Animals', and their still-selling back list. In the year of his death Elvis Presley accumulated 95 weeks with an unprecedented eighteen titles, almost all re-entries.

# 1978

Two film soundtracks proved it was still possible for albums to achieve lengthy runs at number one, television advertising campaigns and a diverging market notwithstanding. 'Saturday Night Fever' stayed on top for 18 weeks, the longest uninterrupted reign since that of 'Sergeant Pepper's Lonely Hearts Club Band', and indeed there were fewer number one LPs in 1978, eight, than in any year since 1967, the time of the classic Beatles release.

'Grease' was the other movie megahit, spending 13 weeks atop the greasy pole. Since John Travolta starred in both films, one might assume he was on the number one for 31 weeks, the most by any artist since the cast of 'The Sound of Music' achieved the same figure in 1966. But though Travolta was shown on the cover of 'Fever', earning a royalty, he did not figure in the music. The Bee Gees, whose tunes dominated the motion picture, did not appear on the screen. The real winner was the Robert Stigwood Organisation, which issued both films and discs.

Boney M, who enjoyed a pair of chart topping singles in 1978, also enjoyed their most successful LP, 'Nightflight to Venus'. Abba earned seven more number one weeks with 'The Album' and managed 112 weeks on chart during the year, clearly outdistancing all competition. Fleetwood Mac's 'Rumours', America's top record of 1977, finally managed seven days at the summit in Britain.

# 1979

Nineteen different albums played musical chairs with the number one position in 1979, more than twice the total of toppers the previous year. No piece of product could compete with RSO's 1978 soundtracks in terms of length of stay there. 'The Best Disco Album In The World', a Warner Brothers compilation released at the height of the disco craze and supported by television advertising, managed the longest stint, six weeks. Indeed, Warners as a company may have been the sales star of the year, managing to place three consecutive number ones at the top in their first week of release. Certainly the artists involved – Led Zeppelin, Gary Numan and Boney M – could not have been appealing to the same buyers.

The real star performers of 1979 were Abba, Blondie and the Electric Light Orchestra. The first two names each achieved two number ones, spending totals of seven and five weeks ahead respectively. Gary Numan did nab one winner under his own name and another in his group identity, Tubeway Army, but each of those only stayed in the lead for one week.

ELO's mark of merit was the 112 weeks spent on the chart by their various albums, including the number one 'Discovery'. The Jeff Lynne-led ensemble had their finest 12 months, enjoying four Top Ten singles as well. The only act to approach ELO in weeks on chart was Blondie with an exact century; Earth Wind and Fire trailed in third with 68.

'Bat Out of Hell' by Meat Loaf and Jeff Wayne's 'War of the Worlds' each spent the entire year on the chart as they headed for two of the longest runs in recent times. Neither album ever reached number one, but both ultimately outsold almost every disc that did in 1979.

# 1980

Twenty-three different albums led the list at some point during 1980, the most in any single year to date. The number one position was like New England's fabled weather: if you didn't like it, you could stick around for an hour and it would change. Johnny Mathis, Genesis and Rose Royce appeared in quick succession, and if the rapid variation from easy listening to rock to soul wasn't enough for the catholic consumer, Sky followed with a kind of classical and pop hybrid that was impossible to categorize.

With more number one albums in a year than David Bowie has had images in a career, staying in front for even a month was an achievement. The Pretenders made it with their eponymous debut disc, and Roxy Music were champs for four weeks in two stints with 'Flesh And Blood'. The star performers of the year were Police and Abba. The Bleach Boys had their second number one LP, 'Zenyatta Mondatta', and scored 116 on chart in total, far in front of the 70-week sum of runner-up AC/DC. The Scandinavian sensations once again had chart-toppers early and late in a year, registering in January with 'Greatest Hits Volume 2' and beginning a nine-week rule in November with 'Super Trouper'.

An extremely odd circumstance characterized the spring. For the entire season, albums had two-week runs at number one and were then replaced. Seven LPs were in the spring string. The previous record for consecutive two-week reigns had been a mere two, so this development was certainly curious if ultimately unimportant.

# 1981

To find the top album artists of 1981 one didn't have to look far beyond the letter 'A' in alphabetical browser bins. Abba began and ended the year at number one with 'Super Trouper' and 'The Visitors', extending their string of chart-topping LPs to seven. Adam and the Ants were the breakout act of the year, accumulating 12 weeks at the very top with 'Kings Of The Wild Frontier', the longest leading stint. 'Kings' was also one of five long players to stay the course for the entire year. It was joined by previous Adam material and the end-of-year release 'Prince Charming' to give the Ants 87 weeks on the chart, a total topped only by Barry Manilow. The American balladeer bettered the Ant total by five weeks. Personal appearances and heavy promotion gave him a career peak in Britain several years after he had done his best at home.

One had to look hard to find evidence of the growth of technopop, the synthesized sound making great inroads in the singles market. 'Dare' by the Human League was the nation's best-seller for one week, but this was before the fourth single from the set, 'Don't You Want Me', became the year's Christmas number one and propelled its parent back up the charts in 1982. Ultravox, important pioneers of technopop, re-entered for another 48 weeks with

'Vienna' on the strength of the single of the same name.

There were oddities, as always. 'The Royal Wedding' of Prince Charles to Lady Diana Spencer was number one for a fortnight, twice as long as Motorhead managed with their equally live 'No Sleep Till Hammersmith', but the Royals never challenged the heavy metal merchants to a battle of the bands.

# 1982

'Remember my name', Irene Cara advised in the title tune of the film 'Fame', 'I'm gonna live forever.' Well, almost. 'Fame' itself proved to be more enduring than any of the young people in it.

When the BBC began broadcasting the American television series 'Fame', a spin-off from the Alan Parker movie, Cara's original version of the song, a US hit in 1980, zoomed to the top of the UK singles chart. It was actually only the beginning of a phenomenon.

BBC Records' 'The Kids From Fame' television cast collection proceeded to lead the list itself. Fuelled by two Top Ten singles, this album sold over 850,000 copies by December, surpassing even the previous year's 'Royal Wedding' to become the BBC's best-selling long player.

RCA had leased the album because BBC1 could only plug vinyl with the BBC label, and they needed to establish the singing actors as a recording act. Mission accomplished, RCA issued a second TV platter, 'The Kids From Fame Again', and this also made the top three.

The sales success of the 'Kids From Fame' was peculiar to Britain. In contrast, the only LP that outsold theirs in the UK in 1982 was by a worldwide star. 'Love Songs' by Barbra Streisand was the year's best seller. That it did so well was perhaps surprising, since it was a make-do collection with only two new songs assembled in lieu of new product.

ABC distinguished themselves by spending their first-ever week on the chart at number one with 'The Lexicon Of Love'. The debut marked another first, the initial joint number one on the album chart. 'The Lexicon Of Love' shared the spotlight with – yes – 'Fame'.

# 1983

Two of the greatest stars of the early seventies stood out this year, but whereas one, David Bowie, had already set album chart standards, Michael Jackson had previously been best known as a singles artist. He managed to reach number five in 1979 with 'Off The Wall', his solo album start on Epic, but nothing prepared the world for what happened in 1983.

'Thriller' first entered the sweepstakes in December 1982, but by the end of its first month of release had only climbed to fifteen. It was only with the release of the second single from the set, 'Billie Jean', that the platter peaked. It went all the way three times for a total of seven weeks and was the year's best-seller. Michael enjoyed three further weeks at number one when Motown's repackaged '18 Greatest Hits' proved popular during the summer. The llama lover totalled 123 weeks on chart.

This year, however, David Bowie achieved a total eclipse of the chart, setting a new mark with 198. This staggering sum beat his old record of 182, established a full decade earlier in 1973. Nearly all his success this year came in the wake of 'Let's Dance', which entered at number one. Thirteen Bowie titles in all appeared in the fifty-three charts of 1983. Ten Bowie albums were in the week of 16 July, the year's greatest monopoly.

Phil Collins racked up 78 weeks on chart on his own and also did very well with Genesis. Meat Loaf followed closely with 76. Mighty sales figures were accumulated by Paul Young and Lionel Richie. Richard Clayderman, the French pianist cleverly promoted in both print and television, enjoyed two of the year's Top 100 and amassed 66 weeks on chart. He was far and away 1983's most successful instrumentalist.

Thirteen of the year's twenty top albums were by groups. Culture Club were number one for five weeks with 'Colour By Numbers' and Men at Work toiled the same time at the top with 'Business As Usual'. Duran Duran only managed one week ahead of the field with 'Seven And The Ragged Tiger' but did stockpile 105 weeks on chart, more than any group save Dire Straits, who garnered 107 without issuing any new material. Twenty-three different titles reached number one during 1983, more than in any previous calendar year.

Bonnie Tyler was the only female artist to spend even a single week ahead of the field, though Alison 'Alf' Moyet was the featured vocalist with two-week champs Yazoo. Barbra Streisand was the woman winner in weeks on chart with 57, but most of these were the final flings of 1982's list leader, 'Love Songs'. The most noteworthy variety of female achievement from a chart-watcher's point of view was the faddish popularity of a new form – the workout album. Two of the year's Top 100 were of this sort, 'Jane Fonda's Workout Record' and Felicity Kendal's 'Shape Up And Dance (Volume 1)'. Jackie Genova also charted with an exercise exemplar.

# 1984

The face that dominated music advertising on television in George Orwell's dreaded year turned out not to be Big Brother but a pig. The porker was the meaty mascot of the EMI/Virgin anthologies 'Now That's What I Call Music'. The first 'Now' ended 1983 and began 1984 at number one. The second moved into the sty in the sky in April and the third checked in during August. The three double albums spent a total of 15 of the year's 52 weeks on top, more than any individual act managed to achieve. 'Now 4' did well enough in its mere month of release to be one of 1984's Top Ten but was kept out of number one by CBS/ WEA's even more lucrative imitative compilation 'The Hits Album/The Hits Tape'.

Television advertising also played a prominent part in the success of the longest-running number one of the year, the late Bob Marley and the Wailers' 'Legend' (12 weeks). The top-selling album of 1984 was 'Can't Slow Down' by Lionel Richie. Though it was only number one for a fortnight it was near the top most of the year. The Motown marvel was one of an astonishing seven albums to stay on the chart for the entire year along with 'Can't Slow Down', Michael Jackson's 'Thriller', Paul Young's 'No Parlez', Meat Loaf's 'Bat Out Of Hell', Queen's 'Greatest Hits' and U2's 'Live – Under A Blood Red Sky'.

Billy Joel had the most albums on chart in a single week, six. Nik Kershaw managed two of the year's Top Fifty, Elton John two of the Top 100. Michael Jackson also had a brace of best-sellers, 'Off The Wall' continuing its revival. Jackson wound up the year's number two week-wise, with 107 seven-day spells. However, combining the runs of his solo albums and the weeks in residence of Michael Jackson Plus the Jackson Five's '18 Greatest Hits' gave a total of 136. Dire Straits, who accumulated 116 weeks, still enough to place them in the all-time Top Ten for most in a single year, were the year's top weekly act.

Other groups with noteworthy performances included U2, who totalled an even 100 weeks on chart; Queen, who had two of the year's Top Fifty; and Wham!, whose 'Make It Big' was one of the year's Top Five. The Smiths scored two Top Tens on the independent Rough Trade label and 'Welcome To The Pleasuredome' by Frankie Goes To Hollywood gave ZTT its first week at number one.

It was not a great year for female soloists. None reached number one, though women did make the top spot as members of Eurythmics and the Thompson Twins. Sade had the biggest seller by a woman, 'Diamond Life', while Elaine Paige had two of the year's Top 100. Barbra Streisand accumulated 67 weeks on chart to lead the ladies. Instrumentalists fared poorly. Richard Clayderman was the only non-vocalist in the year's Top 100. The independent compilation company Street Sounds attained fifteen charters during the year. The devotional artist Bryn Yemm had three new albums in, more than any other British act. 1984 was itself a star. It was the first year to have three hit LPs named after it.

# 1985

The long distance runner wasn't lonely in 1985. Nine albums remained on the chart for the entire fifty-two weeks, and four acts accumulated totals in excess of one hundred weeks on chart. Astonishing records were set. After a series of UK stadium dates Bruce Springsteen placed his entire catalogue of seven albums in the Top Fifty. Never before had an artist with that large a body of work got the lot that high. Springsteen finished the year with a total of 177 weeks on chart, the third best figure ever. 'Born In The U.S.A.' was one of the nine discs that saw the year through. It wound up the number four seller of 1985. Competing with The Boss for the title of Male Artist of the Year, Phil Collins finished with fewer weeks on chart, a still spectacular 131, but managed to nab the number two spot of the year-end tabulation with 'No Jacket Required'.

Madonna was clearly the female artist of 1985; her 'Like A Virgin' (the third best-selling set of the year) and her retitled first album both entered the Top Fifty. As noteworthy as her own success was the extremely strong showing by female artists in general. Seven of the year's top twenty were either by female soloists or outfits with female vocalists. Sade's two albums both finished in the Top Twenty.

Dire Straits and U2 vied for Group of Year honours. Mark Knopfler's lot put in a special claim with the year's number one, 'Brothers In Arms'. 1985 was the third successive year in which Dire Straits exceeded 100 weeks on chart, a feat previously performed only by Simon and Garfunkel. During the three-year period 1983–85, Mark's men leapt from 33rd to 8th on the all-time list. Despite their achievements they were slightly pipped in weeks on chart by U2, 168 to 158. The Irish band were also on a prolonged hot streak, having vaulted from 20 to 375 weeks on chart in three years.

Richard Clayderman retained his laurels as leading solo instrumentalist, but James Last bounced back as the top orchestra. It was also a good year for what might be called up-market material, with Andrew Lloyd Webber's 'Requiem', Leonard Bernstein's operatic version of 'West Side Story' and the Anderson/Rice/Ulvaeus 'Chess' all in 1985's Top 100.

The most successful broadcasting and charity event of all time, Live Aid, achieved another distinction as the single happening that has most influenced the album chart. In the 27 July chart nine albums by acts in the concert re-entered the Top 100, four after a long absence, and twenty-one previously peaked packages suddenly surged.

The craze of 1984, the TV compilations of recent and current hits, abated only slightly, with three EMI/Virgin 'Now' packages in the year-end Top Ten and two CBS/WEA 'Hits' collections in the Top Twenty.

Meat Loaf's 'Bat Out Of Hell' finally fell from favour but still managed to add 31 weeks to equal 'The Sound Of Music' as the all-time high.

# 1986

Were there a pinball machine of the album chart it would have tilted this year as Dire Straits amassed an unprecedented 217 listed weeks, an average of over four placings per week.

That 'Brothers In Arms' was the year's number two in sales, slipping down just one place from 1985's top spot, was remarkable enough. That Mark Knopfler's band was so popular that a substantial part of Dire Straits' back catalogue resided in the best sellers was astounding.

There was another artist, however, who accounted for three of the Top 100 of 1986. Madonna sold stacks of all three of her releases, and 'True Blue' was the year's number one. All told she spent 125 weeks on chart, by far the highest figure ever achieved by a woman. 1985 debutante Whitney Houston's first album was 1986's number five set of the year.

In the rich-get-richer category old friends Phil Collins and Queen excelled themselves, Collins moving up to third in the annual weeks on chart listing. Though his total fell from 131 to 113 he made amends by sharing Genesis' 28 weeks. Queen broke through the century mark for the first time while staying in the Top Ten artists list for the third consecutive year. Paul Simon's 'Graceland' was the year's number four.

Madonna and Collins were the only two solo artists in the year-end weeks on chart Top Ten. The LP list seemed the province of the big groups in 1986, with Simple Minds enjoying their biggest year and U2 finishing in the charmed circle for the fourth year in succession even though they had no new issues. Talking Heads put in their finest career outing, while A-Ha and Five Star cut impressive figures in their first full year of activity. The 'Now' and 'Hits' series stayed strong.

# 1987

Whatever you thought of the charts in 1987, you had to agree it was a 'Bad' year. Lightning struck a second time for Michael Jackson as he once again achieved a year-end number one. The main difference was that whereas the champ of 1983, 'Thriller', had started slowly in 1982 and grown gradually, 'Bad' was a massive number one in its first week and retained its edge to finish several lengths in front. The new set was only the second package in history to debut at number one in both the UK and US charts. The first was another of this year's giants, 'Whitney', which wound up at number three for 1987.

'Bad', in contrast, seemed to pose no threat to 'Thriller', far and away the most successful LP ever released. Its global sales at about forty million were well ahead of the immediate runners-up, including 'Rumours' by Fleetwood Mac, but that 1977 phenomenon had its own reason to celebrate ten years later. During the course of 1987 it overtook 'Bat Out Of Hell' to become the longest-runner in chart chronicles.

The reappearance of 'Rumours' can be largely attributed to the continued growth of the compact disc market which gave a new lease of life to many classic albums. Collectors who already had black vinyl copies bought CD versions for their superior sound. The Beatles benefited most clearly from this. All of their original studio sets were issued on CD in 1987, and all charted. The 20th anniversary of 'Sergeant Pepper's Lonely Hearts Club Band' attracted massive media attention and boosted the classic package back to the Top Three.

Though Madonna did not have one of the year's Top Ten sellers she was the most charted artist of 1987, her albums making 127 appearances. This tally exceeded the record for a female artist she herself set only the previous year.

U2 and Queen followed the champ with 126 and 117 weeks respectively, both continuing their lengthy run of strong showings and improving on their fine 1986 figures. Dire Straits did well, too, their 84 weeks giving them a career total of exactly 900, the top total of acts still recording.

'The Phantom of the Opera' made history by becoming the first original cast recording to top the UK chart. In this respect 'My Fair Lady' may have been unlucky. In the very first chart of 1958 and peaking at number two, it may have been a number one had its earlier sales been tabulated.

# 1988

For the sixth consecutive year the three acts with the most weeks on chart totalled at least 100. Seven of 1988's ten top stars had been in the charmed circle before, six of them the previous year. Michael Jackson, who paced the pack with 114 weeks, was returning to the leaders for the first time since 1988.

Jacko's joyride came courtesy of 'Bad', on the chart all year, and a variety of back items including 'Thriller' and Motown repackages. In his case the progress from one year to the next looked like a week-to-week sequence, with 1987's number one slipping two places to number three on the 1988 year end tally. 'Bad' was constantly in the public eye thanks to Jackson's personal appearances at open air venues and a steady stream of hit singles. The promotion paid off. Britain was the one major country where 'Bad' outsold 'Thriller', and the artist topped the table of weeks on chart for the first time.

The second place finishers on both the sales and weeks on chart list were vinyl veterans. Cliff Richard, who had the year's number one single, 'Mistletoe and Wine', also had the runner-up album, 'Private Collection'. It was the first time he had finished in the top two in both chart categories. Fleetwood Mac, who had undergone a telephone book's worth of personnel changes since their album chart breakthrough in 1968, scored their first annual century with 107 weeks, second only to Jackson. They, too, were helped by touring, and scored two of the year's 30 best sellers, 'Tango in the Night' and 'Greatest

Hits'. The Pet Shop Boys were the third act to accumulate 100 weeks on chart, doing best with 'Introspective'.

In addition to the two groups mentioned above, U2, Dire Straits, Whitney Houston and Luther Vandross repeated in the year's Top Ten acts. Whitney now had 200 weeks on chart with only two albums for an astonishing average of 100 weeks per release. This was still unlikely to impress U2 and Dire Straits, who continued their winning ways and seemed to guarantee they would finish ahead of Queen as the top album acts of the Eighties.

The most amazing achievement by a new artist belonged to Kylie Minogue. Before January 1988 she had never released an album in Britain. At the end of the year she had the top title of the twelve months, 'Kylie'. This was the first time a solo artist had scored the year's top seller with a debut disc. The teen market didn't just support Stock-Aitken-Waterman acts. The fresh-faced trio Bros wound up at number four with their debut issue, 'Push'. Another new act who came in the Top Ten sellers in famous fashion was Tracy Chapman, whose career took off after she appeared before a live global television audience at the Nelson Mandela Birthday Concert.

Compilations took up so many of the top positions in the album chart that the industry decided they would be segregated in future and have their own list in 1989. This meant that the performance of the 'Now That's What I Call Music' series in placing editions 11, 12 and 13 in the year-end top fifteen would never be repeated. Even compilation soundtracks like the phenomenal 'Dirty Dancing' would be separated out. As the year ended observers wondered if new artists would actually benefit from the new order, in which product by individual acts would overnight chart higher than it would have in 1988. Would the illusion of success become a reality?

# 1989

The cosy feeling old friends gave the album chart in 1988 was displaced by the excitement of new acquaintances a year later. Jason Donovan, a co-star of Kylie Minogue on television's soap opera 'Neighbours', repeated his fellow

Australian's feat of having the best selling LP of the year with a premiere performance. His 'Ten Good Reasons' outshone even Simply Red's long-burning 'A New Flame'.

The continued shift in sales from singles to albums was dramatically underscored this year when four LPs but no 45s sold over a million copies. Including sales in all configurations, the year's number one single, 'Ride On Time' by Black Box, managed 849,116 units. 'Ten Good Reasons' shifted 1,450,500. Indeed, the seven top albums of the year outsold every single. It was thus important financially as well as for image that the young Stock-Aitken-Waterman favourites did well on both sides. Kylie and Jason were each in the 1989 Top Ten on both charts, with Miss Minogue enjoying the year's number six album, 'Enjoy Yourself'.

Kylie was one of eight acts to finish in the year's Top Ten acts who had not been in the previous list. Recalling that in 1988 only four names were non-repeaters gives an indication of the progress of new talent in 1989. Guns N' Roses made the most impressive showing, leading the lot with 85 weeks on chart. This figure, achieved by 'Appetite For Destruction' and 'GN'R Lies', was admittedly below the century, the first time since 1982 that the year's top tally was short of 100. Nonetheless it was a major achievement for a heavy metal act. Strong sellers in this genre usually open strong and fade quickly.

Erasure finished second in the weeks-on-chart sweepstakes, moving up from fourth the year before. Third in the table was what might be called a veteran newcomer, Gloria Estefan. In a masterful piece of public relations her group Miami Sound Machine groomed her as its focal point and then gave her joint and finally sole billing. The strategy succeeded spectacularly with the year's number four seller 'Anything For You' by Gloria Estefan and Miami Sound Machine, and the number five, 'Cuts Both Ways', credited merely to Gloria Estefan.

Another notable newcomer to the top acts list was the Scottish band Deacon Blue, who finished fourth. Bobby Brown, 1989's top singles star, made his album table bow at number ten. The late Roy Orbison experienced a phenomenal posthumous comeback, appearing in the Top Ten acts list for the first time since 1964. A quarter of a century was by far the longest gap between visits to this charmed circle.

The fastest selling work in 1989 was released late in the year. Phil Collins' '. . . But Seriously' managed to chalk up sales of over one million in only six weeks, beginning a long run at number one and setting itself up for continued chart domination in early 1990. Here was a case where the change of decades would be bridged by a single strong record. This had not been the case when the Seventies met the Eighties, when Greatest Hits acts by Abba and Rod Stewart took turns at the top. The *South Pacific* film soundtrack had welded 1959 and 1960 together, and the Beatles' 'Abbey Road' had both seen out 1969 and welcomed 1970. '. . . But Seriously' now joined these giants.

# The Charts

If ever a week went by without a chart being compiled, the previous week's chart was used again for the purposes of all the statistics and information contained in this book. The dates used throughout correspond to the Saturday ending the week in which the chart was published.

The charts used in compiling this book are:

**8 Nov 58**  First album chart published by *Melody Maker*. It is a Top 10.

**27 Jun 59**  Newspaper strike. No chart published until 8 Aug, so the 20 June chart is repeated throughout.

**26 Mar 60**  First *Record Retailer* chart published, a Top 20. We have taken our information from the *Record Retailer* from this date onwards, although the *Melody Maker* chart continued.

**14 Apr 66**  Chart becomes a Top 30.

**8 Dec 66**  Chart becomes a Top 40.

**12 Feb 69**  Chart drops back to a Top 15.

**8 Mar 69**  Incorrect chart published. Correct chart calculated by back-tracking from following week's listings.

**11 Jun 69**  Chart becomes a Top 20 again.

**25 Jun 69**  Chart becomes a Top 40 again.

**9 Aug 69**  Chart is a Top 32 (!) for this one week only.

**11 Oct 69**  Chart drops back to a Top 25.

**8 Nov 69**  Chart varies from a Top 20 to a Top 24 until 24 Jan '70.

**31 Jan 70**  Chart lists from 47 to 77 albums each week until 9 Jan '71.

**9 Jan 71**  *Record Retailer* becomes *Record And Tape Retailer*.

**16 Jan 71**  Chart stabilizes as a Top 50.

**6 Feb 71**  Postal strike means no chart published until 3 Apr '71. 30 Jan chart repeated throughout.

**7 Aug 71**  The Full Price chart (the one we've been using) is combined with the previously separate Budget chart. This means there is a sudden influx of budget label albums onto the chart.

**8 Jan 72**  Chart reverts to a Full Price chart only, so the budget albums disappear as suddenly as they appeared.

**18 Mar 72**  *Record And Tape Retailer* becomes *Music Week*.

**13 Jan 73**  Chart is a Top 24 for this week only.

**5 Jan 74**  Chart is a Top 42 for this week only.

**5 Jul 75**  Chart becomes a Top 60.

**14 Jan 78**  Chart is a Top 30 for this week only.

| 2 Dec 78 | Chart becomes a Top 75. |
| 13 Oct 79 | Two consecutive weeks' charts published simultaneously as a result of speedy new chart compilation system which enables *Music Week* to catch up a week. Until this date, the publication of the chart had been more than a week after the survey period. Both charts of this date are included in our calculations. |
| 8 Aug 81 | Chart becomes a Top 100. |
| 14 Jan 89 | Chart splits in two, and becomes a Top 75 'Artist Albums' and a Top 20 'Compilation Albums'. For this book, the Artist Albums chart is considered the main chart, but we record separately the activities of the Compilations chart. |

# Hit Albums
## alphabetically by artist

The information given in this part of the book is as follows:

**DATE** the album first hit the chart, the album **TITLE**, **LABEL**, **CATALOGUE NUMBER**, the **HIGHEST POSITION** it reached on the chart, and the **TOTAL WEEKS** it remained on the chart. Number One albums are highlighted with a **STAR** ★ and Top 10 albums with a **DOT** ●. A **DAGGER** † indicates the album is still on the charts on 26 December 1989, the final chart included in our calculations for this edition.

For the purposes of this book, an album is considered a re-issue if it hits the chart for a second time with a new catalogue number. From the time when albums began to be produced in both mono and stereo versions (around 1966), we list only the stereo catalogue number. Cassette sales, and since the mid-Eighties CD sales, have become rapidly more significant in the compilation of the albums charts, but we have for consistency's sake listed only the 33⅓ rpm record catalogue number.

Describing a recording act in one sentence is often fraught with danger, but we have attempted to do so above each act's list of hits. although we are aware that many of the 'vocalists' thus described also play an instrument, we have only mentioned this fact where the artist's instrumental skills were an important factor in the album's success.

# *a*

**AARONSON** – *See HAGAR, SCHON, AARONSON, SHRIEVE*

## ABBA
*Sweden/Norway, male/female vocal/instrumental group*     *506 wks*

| | | | |
|---|---|---:|---:|
| 8 Jun 74 | **WATERLOO**   *Epic EPC 80179* ..................... | 28 | 2 wks |
| 31 Jan 76 | **ABBA**   *Epic EPC 80835* ............................. | 13 | 10 wks |
| 10 Apr 76 | ★ **GREATEST HITS**   *Epic EPC 69218* ................. | 1 | 130 wks |
| 27 Nov 76 | ★ **ARRIVAL**   *Epic EPC 86108* ...................... | 1 | 92 wks |
| 4 Feb 78 | ★ **THE ALBUM**   *Epic EPC 86052* ................... | 1 | 61 wks |
| 19 May 79 | ★ **VOULEZ-VOUS**   *Epic EPC 86086* ................. | 1 | 43 wks |
| 10 Nov 79 | ★ **GREATEST HITS VOL.2**   *Epic EPC 10017* ........... | 1 | 63 wks |
| 22 Nov 80 | ★ **SUPER TROUPER**   *Epic EPC 10022* ............. | 1 | 43 wks |
| 19 Dec 81 | ★ **THE VISITORS**   *Epic EPC 10032* ............... | 1 | 21 wks |
| 20 Nov 82 | ★ **THE SINGLES – THE FIRST TEN YEARS**   *Epic ABBA 10* | 1 | 22 wks |
| 19 Nov 83 | **THANK YOU FOR THE MUSIC**   *Epic EPC 10043* ....... | 17 | 12 wks |
| 19 Nov 88 | **ABSOLUTE ABBA**   *Telstar STAR 2329* ............... | 70 | 7 wks |

## Russ ABBOT   *UK, male vocalist*     *16 wks*

| | | | |
|---|---|---:|---:|
| 5 Nov 83 | **RUSS ABBOT'S MADHOUSE**   *Ronco RTL 2096* ........ | 41 | 7 wks |
| 23 Nov 85 | **I LOVE A PARTY**   *K-Tel ONE 1313* ................. | 12 | 9 wks |

## Gregory ABBOTT   *US, male vocalist*     *5 wks*

| | | | |
|---|---|---:|---:|
| 10 Jan 87 | **SHAKE YOU DOWN**   *CBS 450061–1* ................. | 53 | 5 wks |

## ABC   *UK, male vocal/instrumental group*     *77 wks*

| | | | |
|---|---|---:|---:|
| 3 Jul 82 | ★ **THE LEXICON OF LOVE**   *Neutron NTRS 1* ............ | 1 | 50 wks |
| 26 Nov 83 | **BEAUTY STAB**   *Neutron NTRL 2* ..................... | 12 | 13 wks |
| 26 Oct 85 | **HOW TO BE A ZILLIONAIRE**   *Neutron NTRH 3* ....... | 28 | 3 wks |
| 24 Oct 87 | ● **ALPHABET CITY**   *Neutron NTRH 4* ................. | 7 | 10 wks |
| 28 Oct 89 | **UP**   *Neutron 838646 1* ............................. | 58 | 1 wk |

*Group was UK/US, male/female for third album.*

## Paula ABDUL   *US, female vocalist*     *21 wks*

| | | | |
|---|---|---:|---:|
| 15 Apr 89 | ● **FOREVER YOUR GIRL**   *Siren SRNLP 19* ............. | 5 | 21 wks |

## Father ABRAHAM and the SMURFS
*Holland, male vocalist as himself and Smurfs*     *11 wks*

| | | | |
|---|---|---:|---:|
| 25 Nov 78 | **FATHER ABRAHAM IN SMURFLAND**   *Decca SMURF 1* | 19 | 11 wks |

## A.B.'S   *Japan, instrumental group*     *2 wks*

| | | | |
|---|---|---:|---:|
| 14 Apr 84 | **DEJA VU**   *Street Sounds XKHAN 503* ................... | 80 | 2 wks |

## ACADEMY of ANCIENT MUSIC conducted by Christopher HOGWOOD  *UK, male conductor/ instrumentalist – harpsichord, UK chamber orchestra*  *2 wks*

| | | | | |
|---|---|---|---|---|
| 16 Mar 85 | **THE FOUR SEASONS (VIVALDI)** *L'Oiseau Lyre 4101261* | **85** | 2 wks |

**ACADEMY OF ST MARTIN IN THE FIELDS** – *See Neville MARRINER and the ACADEMY OF ST MARTIN IN THE FIELDS*

---

## ACCEPT  *Germany, male vocal/instrumental group*  *5 wks*

| 7 May 83 | **RESTLESS AND WILD** *Heavy Metal Worldwide HMILP 6* .. | **98** | 2 wks |
|---|---|---|---|
| 30 Mar 85 | **METAL HEART** *Portrait PRT 26358* .................. | **50** | 1 wk |
| 15 Feb 86 | **KAIZOKU-BAN** *Portrait PRT 5916* .................. | **91** | 1 wk |
| 3 May 86 | **RUSSIAN ROULETTE** *Portrait PRT 26893* ........... | **80** | 1 wk |

---

## AC/DC  *Australia/UK, male vocal/instrumental group*  *218 wks*

| 5 Nov 77 | **LET THERE BE ROCK** *Atlantic K 50366* .............. | **17** | 5 wks |
|---|---|---|---|
| 20 May 78 | **POWERAGE** *Atlantic K 50483* ....................... | **26** | 9 wks |
| 28 Oct 78 | **IF YOU WANT BLOOD YOU'VE GOT IT** *Atlantic K 50532* ...................................... | **13** | 58 wks |
| 18 Aug 79 | ● **HIGHWAY TO HELL** *Atlantic K 50628* ............. | **8** | 32 wks |
| 9 Aug 80 | ★ **BACK IN BLACK** *Atlantic K 50735* ............... | **1** | 40 wks |
| 5 Dec 81 | ● **FOR THOSE ABOUT TO ROCK** *Atlantic K 50851* ...... | **3** | 29 wks |
| 3 Sep 83 | ● **FLICK OF THE SWITCH** *Atlantic 78–0100–1* .......... | **4** | 9 wks |
| 13 Jul 85 | ● **FLY ON THE WALL** *Atlantic 781263* ................ | **7** | 10 wks |
| 7 Jun 86 | **WHO MADE WHO** *Atlantic WX 57* .................. | **11** | 12 wks |
| 13 Feb 88 | ● **BLOW UP YOUR VIDEO** *Atlantic WX 144* ........... | **2** | 14 wks |

---

## Bryan ADAMS
*Canada, male vocalist/instrumentalist – guitar*  *128 wks*

| 2 Mar 85 | ● **RECKLESS** *A & M AMA 5013* ....................... | **7** | 96 wks |
|---|---|---|---|
| 24 Aug 85 | **YOU WANT IT, YOU GOT IT** *A & M AMLH 64864* ..... | **78** | 5 wks |
| 15 Mar 86 | **CUTS LIKE A KNIFE** *A & M AMLH 64919* ............. | **21** | 6 wks |
| 11 Apr 87 | ● **INTO THE FIRE** *A & M AMA 3907* .................. | **10** | 21 wks |

---

## Cliff ADAMS SINGERS
*UK, male/female vocal group*  *20 wks*

| 16 Apr 60 | **SING SOMETHING SIMPLE** *Pye MPL 28013* .......... | **15** | 4 wks |
|---|---|---|---|
| 24 Nov 62 | **SING SOMETHING SIMPLE** *Pye Golden Guinea GGL 0150* ...................... | **15** | 2 wks |
| 20 Nov 76 | **SING SOMETHING SIMPLE '76** *Warwick WW 5016/17* ........................... | **23** | 8 wks |
| 25 Dec 82 | **SING SOMETHING SIMPLE** *Ronco RTD 2087* ......... | **39** | 6 wks |

*All the identically titled albums are different.*

---

## ADAMSKI  *UK, male multi-instrumentalist/producer*  *1 wk*

| 9 Dec 89 | **LIVE AND DIRECT** *MCA MCL 1900* ................ | **65** | 1 wk |
|---|---|---|---|

---

## King Sunny ADE and his AFRICAN BEATS
*Nigeria, male vocalist and male vocal/instrumental group*  *1 wk*

| 9 Jul 83 | **SYNCHRO SYSTEM** *Island ILPS 9737* ................ | **93** | 1 wk |
|---|---|---|---|

## ADEVA  US, female vocalist

17 wks

| 9 Sep 89 ● **ADEVA**  Cooltempo CTLP 13 | 6† | 17 wks |

## ADICTS  UK, male vocal/instrumental group

1 wk

| 4 Dec 82 **SOUND OF MUSIC**  Razor RAZ 2 | 99 | 1 wk |

## ADVENTURES
UK, male/female vocal/instrumental group

10 wks

| 21 May 88 **THE SEA OF LOVE**  Elektra EKT 45 | 30 | 10 wks |

## ADVERTS  UK, male/female vocal/instrumental group

1 wk

| 11 Mar 78 **CROSSING THE RED SEA WITH THE ADVERTS**  Bright BRL 201 | 38 | 1 wk |

## AEROSMITH  US, male vocal/instrumental group

19 wks

| 5 Sep 87 **PERMANENT VACATION**  Geffen WX 126 | 37 | 8 wks |
| 23 Sep 89 ● **PUMP**  Geffen WX 304 | 3 | 11 wks |

## AFTER THE FIRE  UK, male vocal/instrumental group

4 wks

| 13 Oct 79 **LASER LOVE**  CBS 83795 | 57 | 1 wk |
| 1 Nov 80 **80 F**  Epic EPC 84545 | 69 | 1 wk |
| 3 Apr 82 **BATTERIES NOT INCLUDED**  CBS 85566 | 82 | 2 wks |

**AFRICAN BEATS** – See King Sunny ADE and his AFRICAN BEATS

## A-HA  Norway, male vocal/instrumental group

125 wks

| 9 Nov 85 ● **HUNTING HIGH AND LOW**  Warner Bros. WX 30 | 2 | 77 wks |
| 18 Oct 86 ● **SCOUNDREL DAYS**  Warner Bros. WX 62 | 2 | 29 wks |
| 14 May 88 ● **STAY ON THESE ROADS**  Warner Bros. WX 166 | 2 | 19 wks |

## ALARM  UK, male vocal/instrumental group

26 wks

| 25 Feb 84 ● **DECLARATION**  IRS IRSA 7044 | 6 | 11 wks |
| 26 Oct 85 **STRENGTH**  IRS MIRF 1004 | 18 | 6 wks |
| 14 Nov 87 **EYE OF THE HURRICANE**  IRS MIRG 1023 | 23 | 4 wks |
| 5 Nov 88 **ELECTRIC FOLKLORE LIVE**  IRS MIRMC 5001 | 62 | 2 wks |
| 30 Sep 89 **CHANGE**  IRS EIRSAX 1020 | 13 | 3 wks |

## ALEXANDER BROTHERS  UK, male vocal duo

1 wk

| 10 Dec 66 **THESE ARE MY MOUNTAINS**  Pye GGL 0375 | 29 | 1 wk |

**ALLEN** – See FOSTER and ALLEN

## ALIEN SEX FIEND
UK, male/female vocal/instrumental group

1 wk

| 12 Oct 85 **MAXIMUM SECURITY**  Anagram GRAM 24 | 100 | 1 wk |

## ALL ABOUT EVE
*UK, male/female vocal/instrumental group*                                      *33 wks*

| | | | |
|---|---|---|---|
| 27 Feb 88 | ● ALL ABOUT EVE   *Mercury MERH 119* .................. | 7 | 29 wks |
| 28 Oct 89 | ● SCARLET AND OTHER STORIES   *Mercury 838965 1* ... | 9 | 4 wks |

## Mose ALLISON   *US, male vocalist/instrumentalist – piano*     *1 wk*

| | | | |
|---|---|---|---|
| 4 Jun 66 | MOSE ALIVE   *Atlantic 587–007* ........................ | 30 | 1 wk |

## ALLMAN BROTHERS BAND
*US, male vocal/instrumental group*                                             *4 wks*

| | | | |
|---|---|---|---|
| 6 Oct 73 | BROTHERS AND SISTERS   *Warner Bros. K 47507* ...... | 42 | 3 wks |
| 6 Mar 76 | THE ROAD GOES ON FOREVER   *Capricorn 2637 101* ... | 54 | 1 wk |

## Marc ALMOND   *UK, male vocalist*     *12 wks*

| | | | |
|---|---|---|---|
| 10 Nov 84 | VERMIN IN ERMINE   *Some Bizzare BIZL 8* ........... | 36 | 2 wks |
| 5 Oct 85 | STORIES OF JOHNNY | | |
| | *Some Bizzare FAITH 1* ........................... | 22 | 3 wks |
| 18 Apr 87 | MOTHER FIST AND HER FIVE DAUGHTERS | | |
| | *Some Bizzare FAITH 2* ........................... | 41 | 2 wks |
| 8 Oct 88 | THE STARS WE ARE   *Parlophone PCS 7324* ........... | 41 | 5 wks |

Vermin In Ermine *and* Mother Fist and Her Five Daughters *credited to Marc Almond and the Willing Sinners – UK, male/female vocal/instrumental group. See also Marc and the Mambas.*

## Herb ALPERT and the TIJUANA BRASS
*US, male band leader/instrumentalist – trumpet*                                *309 wks*

| | | | |
|---|---|---|---|
| 29 Jan 66 | ● GOING PLACES   *Pye NPL 28065* ................... | 4 | 138 wks |
| 23 Apr 66 | ● WHIPPED CREAM AND OTHER DELIGHTS | | |
| | *Pye NPL 28058* ........................... | 2 | 42 wks |
| 28 May 66 | WHAT NOW MY LOVE   *Pye NPL 28077* ............. | 18 | 17 wks |
| 11 Feb 67 | ● S.R.O.   *Pye NSPL 28088* ........................ | 5 | 26 wks |
| 15 Jul 67 | SOUNDS LIKE   *A&M AMLS 900* .................... | 21 | 10 wks |
| 3 Feb 68 | NINTH   *A&M AMLS 905* ......................... | 26 | 9 wks |
| 29 Jun 68 | ● BEAT OF THE BRASS   *A&M AMLS 916* ............. | 4 | 21 wks |
| 9 Aug 69 | WARM   *A&M AMLS 937* ......................... | 30 | 4 wks |
| 14 Mar 70 | THE BRASS ARE COMIN'   *A&M AMLS 962* ........... | 40 | 1 wk |
| 30 May 70 | ● GREATEST HITS   *A&M AMLS 980* ................ | 8 | 27 wks |
| 27 Jun 70 | DOWN MEXICO WAY   *A&M AMLS 974* ............. | 64 | 1 wk |
| 13 Nov 71 | AMERICA   *A&M AMLB 1000* ..................... | 45 | 1 wk |
| 12 Nov 77 | 40 GREATEST   *K-Tel NE 1005* ................... | 45 | 2 wks |
| 17 Nov 79 | RISE   *A&M AMLH 64790* ........................ | 37 | 7 wks |
| 4 Apr 87 | KEEP YOUR EYE ON ME   *Breakout AMA 5125* ......... | 79 | 3 wks |

*Last two hits credit only Herb Alpert. On 29 Jun 67* Going Places *and* What Now My Love *changed labels and numbers to A&M AMLS 965 and AMLS 977 respectively.*

## ALTERED IMAGES
*UK, male/female vocal/instrumental group*                                      *40 wks*

| | | | |
|---|---|---|---|
| 19 Sep 81 | HAPPY BIRTHDAY   *Epic EPC 84893* ................ | 26 | 21 wks |
| 15 May 82 | PINKY BLUE   *Epic EPC 85665* ..................... | 12 | 10 wks |
| 25 Jun 83 | BITE   *Epic EPC 25413* ........................... | 16 | 9 wks |

## AMAZULU   *UK, female vocal group*     *1 wk*

| | | | |
|---|---|---|---|
| 6 Dec 88 | AMAZULU   *Island ILPS 9851* ...................... | 97 | 1 wk |

One thing **ABBA** share with Led Zeppelin is the record for the most consecutive number one albums, eight.

**AEROSMITH**, never successful in Britain during their 70s heyday, fared far better when they returned from a lengthy vacation. Lead singer Steve Tyler is shown.

**HERB ALPERT AND THE TIJUANA BRASS** were America's top homegrown album act in 1965–66.

## AMEN CORNER  *UK, male vocal/instrumental group*  8 wks

| | | | | |
|---|---|---|---|---|
| 30 Mar 68 | **ROUND AMEN CORNER**  *Deram SML 1021* .......... | 26 | 7 wks |
| 1 Nov 69 | **EXPLOSIVE COMPANY**  *Immediate IMSP 023* .......... | 19 | 1 wk |

## AMERICA  *US, male vocal/instrumental group*  22 wks

| | | | | |
|---|---|---|---|---|
| 22 Jan 72 | **AMERICA**  *Warner Bros. K 46093* ..................... | 14 | 13 wks |
| 9 Dec 72 | **HOMECOMING**  *Warner Bros. K 46180* ................ | 21 | 5 wks |
| 10 Nov 73 | **HAT TRICK**  *Warner Bros. K 56016* ................. | 41 | 3 wks |
| 7 Feb 76 | **HISTORY – AMERICA'S GREATEST HITS** | | |
| | *Warner Bros. K 56169* ............................ | 60 | 1 wk |

## Ian ANDERSON
*UK, male vocalist/instrumentalist – flute*  1 wk

| | | | |
|---|---|---|---|
| 26 Nov 83 | **WALK INTO LIGHT**  *Chrysalis CDL 1443* .............. | 78 | 1 wk |

## Jon ANDERSON  *UK, male vocalist*  19 wks

| | | | |
|---|---|---|---|
| 24 Jul 76 | ● **OLIAS OF SUNHILLOW**  *Atlantic K 50261* ............. | 8 | 10 wks |
| 15 Nov 80 | **SONG OF SEVEN**  *Atlantic K 50756* ................. | 38 | 3 wks |
| 5 Jun 82 | **ANIMATION**  *Polydor POLD 5044* ................... | 43 | 6 wks |

*See also Jon and Vangelis; Anderson Bruford Wakeman Howe.*

## Laurie ANDERSON
*US, female vocalist/multi-instrumentalist*  8 wks

| | | | |
|---|---|---|---|
| 1 May 82 | **BIG SCIENCE**  *Warner Bros. K 57002* .................. | 29 | 6 wks |
| 10 Mar 84 | **MISTER HEARTBREAK**  *Warner Bros. 92–5077–1* | 93 | 2 wks |

## Lynn ANDERSON  *US, female vocalist*  1 wk

| | | | |
|---|---|---|---|
| 17 Apr 71 | **ROSE GARDEN**  *CBS 64333* ....................... | 45 | 1 wk |

## Moira ANDERSON  *UK, female vocalist*  1 wk

| | | | |
|---|---|---|---|
| 20 Jun 70 | **THESE ARE MY SONGS**  *Decca SKL 5016* ............. | 50 | 1 wk |

*See also Harry Secombe and Moira Anderson.*

## ANDERSON BRUFORD WAKEMAN HOWE
*UK, male vocal/instrumental group*  6 wks

| | | | |
|---|---|---|---|
| 8 Jul 89 | **ANDERSON BRUFORD WAKEMAN HOWE** | | |
| | *Arista 209970* ................................... | 14 | 6 wks |

*See also Jon Anderson; Rick Wakeman; Steve Howe.*

## Julie ANDREWS  *UK, female vocalist*  5 wks

| | | | |
|---|---|---|---|
| 16 Jul 83 | **LOVE ME TENDER**  *Peach River JULIE 1* .............. | 63 | 5 wks |

## ANGELIC UPSTARTS
*UK, male vocal/instrumental group*  20 wks

| | | | |
|---|---|---|---|
| 18 Aug 79 | **TEENAGE WARNING**  *Warner Bros. K 50634* ............ | 29 | 7 wks |
| 12 Apr 80 | **WE'VE GOTTA GET OUT OF THIS PLACE** | | |
| | *Warner Bros. K 56806* ............................ | 54 | 3 wks |
| 7 Jun 81 | **2,000,000 VOICES**  *Zonophone ZONO 104* ............. | 32 | 3 wks |
| 26 Sep 81 | **ANGELIC UPSTARTS**  *Zonophone ZEM 102* .......... | 27 | 7 wks |

## ANIMAL NIGHTLIFE

*UK, male vocal/instrumental group*                                    *6 wks*

| | | | | |
|---|---|---|---|---|
| 24 Aug 85 | **SHANGRI-LA** | *Island ILPS 9830* ..................... | **36** | 6 wks |

## ANIMALS  *UK, male vocal/instrumental group*                         *86 wks*

| | | | | |
|---|---|---|---|---|
| 14 Nov 64 | ● **THE ANIMALS** | *Columbia 33SX 1669* ................. | **6** | 20 wks |
| 22 May 65 | ● **ANIMAL TRACKS** | *Columbia 33SX 1708* ............. | **6** | 26 wks |
| 16 Apr 66 | ● **MOST OF THE ANIMALS** | *Columbia 33SX 6035* ......... | **4** | 20 wks |
| 28 May 66 | ● **ANIMALISMS** | *Decca LK 4797* ...................... | **4** | 17 wks |
| 25 Sep 71 | **MOST OF THE ANIMALS (re-issue)** | *MFP 5218* ......... | **18** | 3 wks |

## Adam ANT  *UK, male vocalist*                                        *139 wks*

| | | | | |
|---|---|---|---|---|
| 15 Nov 80 | ★ **KINGS OF THE WILD FRONTIER** | *CBS 84549* ........ | **1** | 66 wks |
| 17 Jan 81 | **DIRK WEARS WHITE SOX** | *Do It RIDE 3* ........... | **16** | 29 wks |
| 14 Nov 81 | ● **PRINCE CHARMING** | *CBS 85268* ................. | **2** | 21 wks |
| 23 Oct 82 | ● **FRIEND OR FOE** | *CBS 25040* ..................... | **5** | 12 wks |
| 19 Nov 83 | **STRIP** | *CBS 25705* ............................. | **20** | 8 wks |
| 14 Sep 85 | **VIVE LE ROCK** | *CBS 26583* ....................... | **42** | 3 wks |

*All the albums up to and including* Prince Charming *credited to Adam and the Ants – UK, male vocal/instrumental group.*

## ANTHRAX  *US, male vocal/instrumental group*                          *9 wks*

| | | | | |
|---|---|---|---|---|
| 18 Apr 87 | **AMONG THE LIVING** | *Island ILPS 9865* .............. | **18** | 5 wks |
| 24 Sep 88 | **STATE OF EUPHORIA** | *Island ILPS 9916* ............. | **12** | 4 wks |

## ANTI-NOWHERE LEAGUE

*UK, male vocal/instrumental group*                                    *12 wks*

| | | | | |
|---|---|---|---|---|
| 22 May 82 | **WE ARE ... THE LEAGUE** | *WXYZ LMNOP 1* ......... | **24** | 11 wks |
| 5 Nov 83 | **LIVE IN YUGOSLAVIA** | *I.D. NOSE 3* ................ | **88** | 1 wk |

## ANTI-PASTI  *UK, male vocal/instrumental group*                        *7 wks*

| | | | | |
|---|---|---|---|---|
| 15 Aug 81 | **THE LAST CALL** | *Rondelet ABOUT 5* ................. | **31** | 7 wks |

**ANTS** – *See Adam ANT*

**Carmine APPICE** – *See Jeff BECK, Tim BOGERT and Carmine APPICE*

## APRIL WINE  *Canada, male vocal/instrumental group*                    *8 wks*

| | | | | |
|---|---|---|---|---|
| 15 Mar 80 | **HARDER ... FASTER** | *Capitol EST 12013* ............. | **34** | 5 wks |
| 24 Jan 81 | **THE NATURE OF THE BEAST** | *Capitol EST 12125* | **48** | 3 wks |

## ARCADIA  *UK, male vocal/instrumental group*                          *10 wks*

| | | | | |
|---|---|---|---|---|
| 7 Dec 85 | **SO RED THE ROSE** | *Parlophone Odeon PCSD 101* ......... | **30** | 10 wks |

## ARGENT  *UK, male vocal/instrumental group*                            *9 wks*

| | | | | |
|---|---|---|---|---|
| 29 Apr 72 | **ALL TOGETHER NOW** | *Epic EPC 64962* .............. | **13** | 8 wks |
| 31 Mar 73 | **IN DEEP** | *Epic EPC 65475* ........................... | **49** | 1 wk |

## Joan ARMATRADING  *UK, female vocalist*                               *174 wks*

| | | | | |
|---|---|---|---|---|
| 4 Sep 76 | **JOAN ARMATRADING** | *A & M AMLH 64588* .......... | **12** | 27 wks |

| | | | | |
|---|---|---|---|---|
| 1 Oct 77 | ● SHOW SOME EMOTION  A&M AMLH 68433 ......... | 6 | 11 wks |
| 14 Oct 78 | TO THE LIMIT  A&M AMLH 64732 ................. | 13 | 10 wks |
| 24 May 80 | ● ME MYSELF I  A&M AMLH 64809 .............. | 5 | 23 wks |
| 12 Sep 81 | ● WALK UNDER LADDERS  A&M AMLH 64876 ....... | 6 | 29 wks |
| 12 Mar 83 | ● THE KEY  A&M AMLX 64912 ..................... | 10 | 14 wks |
| 26 Nov 83 | TRACK RECORD  A&M JA 2001 ............... | 18 | 32 wks |
| 16 Feb 85 | SECRET SECRETS  A&M AMA 5040 ............ | 14 | 12 wks |
| 24 May 86 | SLEIGHT OF HAND  A&M AMA 5130 ............ | 34 | 6 wks |
| 16 Jul 88 | THE SHOUTING STAGE  A&M AMA 5211 ........... | 28 | 10 wks |

## ARMOURY SHOW
*UK, male vocal/instrumental group*  **1 wk**

| | | | |
|---|---|---|---|
| 21 Sep 85 | **WAITING FOR THE FLOODS**  *Parlophone ARM 1* ...... | 57 | 1 wk |

## Louis ARMSTRONG
*US, male band leader vocalist/instrumentalist – trumpet/cornet*  **14 wks**

| | | | |
|---|---|---|---|
| 22 Oct 60 | **SATCHMO PLAYS KING OLIVER** | | |
| | *Audio Fidelity AFLP 1930* ......................... | 20 | 1 wk |
| 28 Oct 61 | **JAZZ CLASSICS**  *Ace of Hearts AH 7* ............. | 20 | 1 wk |
| 27 Jun 64 | **HELLO DOLLY**  *London HAR 8190* ............... | 11 | 6 wks |
| 16 Nov 68 | **WHAT A WONDERFUL WORLD**  *Stateside SSL 10247* .. | 37 | 3 wks |
| 20 Feb 82 | **THE VERY BEST OF LOUIS ARMSTRONG** | | |
| | *Warwick WW 5112* ............................. | 30 | 3 wks |

## Steve ARRINGTON  *US, male vocalist*  **11 wks**

| | | | |
|---|---|---|---|
| 13 Apr 85 | **DANCIN' IN THE KEY OF LIFE**  *Atlantic 781245* ........ | 41 | 11 wks |

**Davey ARTHUR** – *See FUREYS and Davey ARTHUR*

## ART OF NOISE
*UK, male/female instrumental duo*  **37 wks**

| | | | |
|---|---|---|---|
| 3 Nov 84 | **(WHO'S AFRAID OF) THE ART OF NOISE** | | |
| | *ZTT ZTTIQ 2* ............................... | 27 | 17 wks |
| 26 Apr 86 | **IN VISIBLE SILENCE**  *Chrysalis WOL 2* .............. | 18 | 15 wks |
| 10 Oct 87 | **IN NO SENSE/NONSENSE**  *China WOL 4* ........... | 55 | 2 wks |
| 3 Dec 88 | **THE BEST OF THE ART OF NOISE**  *China 837 367 1* ... | 55 | 3 wks |

*Act was a group for first two albums.*

## ASAP  *UK, male vocal/instrumental group*  **1 wk**

| | | | |
|---|---|---|---|
| 4 Nov 89 | **SILVER AND GOLD**  *EMI EMC 3566* ............... | 70 | 1 wk |

## ASHFORD and SIMPSON
*US, male/female vocal duo*  **6 wks**

| | | | |
|---|---|---|---|
| 16 Feb 85 | **SOLID**  *Capitol SASH 1* .......................... | 42 | 6 wks |

## ASIA  *UK, male vocal/instrumental group*  **50 wks**

| | | | |
|---|---|---|---|
| 10 Apr 82 | **ASIA**  *Geffen GEF 85577* ......................... | 11 | 38 wks |
| 20 Aug 83 | ● **ALPHA**  *Geffen GEF 25508* ..................... | 5 | 11 wks |
| 14 Dec 85 | **ASTRA**  *Geffen GEF 26413* ....................... | 68 | 1 wk |

## ASSOCIATES  *UK, male vocal/instrumental group*  **27 wks**

| | | | |
|---|---|---|---|
| 22 May 82 | ● **SULK**  *Associates ASCL 1* ......................... | 10 | 20 wks |
| 16 Feb 85 | **PERHAPS**  *WEA WX 9* ......................... | 23 | 7 wks |

*Duo for the first album.*

## Rick ASTLEY   *UK, male vocalist*                                      *53 wks*

| 28 Nov 87 | ★ WHENEVER YOU NEED SOMEBODY | | |
|---|---|---|---|
|  | RCA PL 71529 | 1 | 34 wks |
| 10 Dec 88 | ● HOLD ME IN YOUR ARMS   RCA PL 71932 | 8 | 19 wks |

## ASWAD   *UK, male vocal/instrumental group*                           *50 wks*

| 24 Jul 82 | NOT SATISFIED   CBS 85666 | 50 | 6 wks |
|---|---|---|---|
| 10 Dec 83 | LIVE AND DIRECT   Island IMA 6 | 57 | 16 wks |
| 3 Nov 84 | REBEL SOULS   Island ILPS 9780 | 48 | 2 wks |
| 28 Jun 86 | TO THE TOP   Simba SIMBALP 2 | 71 | 3 wks |
| 9 Apr 88 | ● DISTANT THUNDER   Mango ILPS 9895 | 10 | 15 wks |
| 3 Dec 88 | RENAISSANCE   Stylus SMR 866 | 52 | 8 wks |

## ATHLETICO SPIZZ 80
*UK, male vocal/instrumental group*                                      *5 wks*

| 26 Jul 80 | DO A RUNNER   A&M AMLE 68514 | 27 | 5 wks |
|---|---|---|---|

## Chet ATKINS   *US, male instrumentalist – guitar*                      *5 wks*

| 18 Mar 61 | THE OTHER CHET ATKINS   RCA RD 27194 | 20 | 1 wk |
|---|---|---|---|
| 17 Jun 61 | CHET ATKINS' WORKSHOP   RCA RD 27214 | 19 | 1 wk |
| 30 Feb 63 | CARIBBEAN GUITAR   RCA RD 7519 | 17 | 3 wks |

## Rowan ATKINSON   *UK, male comedian*                                   *9 wks*

| 7 Feb 81 | LIVE IN BELFAST   Arista SPART 1150 | 44 | 9 wks |
|---|---|---|---|

## ATLANTIC STARR
*US, male/female vocal/instrumental group*                               *15 wks*

| 15 Jun 85 | AS THE BAND TURNS   A&M AMA 5019 | 64 | 3 wks |
|---|---|---|---|
| 11 Jul 87 | ALL IN THE NAME OF LOVE   WEA WX 115 | 48 | 12 wks |

## ATOMIC ROOSTER
*UK, male vocal/instrumental group*                                      *13 wks*

| 13 Jun 70 | ATOMIC ROOSTER   B&C CAS 1010 | 49 | 1 wk |
|---|---|---|---|
| 16 Jan 71 | DEATH WALKS BEHIND YOU | | |
|  | Charisma CAS 1026 | 12 | 8 wks |
| 21 Aug 71 | IN HEARING OF ATOMIC ROOSTER | | |
|  | Pegasus PEG 1 | 18 | 4 wks |

**ATTRACTIONS** – *See Elvis COSTELLO and the ATTRACTIONS*

## AU PAIRS   *UK, female/male vocal/instrumental group*                  *10 wks*

| 6 Jun 81 | PLAYING WITH A DIFFERENT SEX   Human HUMAN 1 | 33 | 7 wks |
|---|---|---|---|
| 4 Sep 82 | SENSE AND SENSUALITY   Kamera KAM 010 | 79 | 3 wks |

**Brian AUGER TRINITY** – *See Julie DRISCOLL and the Brian AUGER TRINITY*

## Patti AUSTIN   *US, female vocalist*                                   *1 wk*

| 26 Sep 81 | EVERY HOME SHOULD HAVE ONE   Quest K 56931 | 99 | 1 wk |
|---|---|---|---|

## AVERAGE WHITE BAND
*UK, male vocal/instrumental group*                                47 wks

| 1 Mar 75 | ● AVERAGE WHITE BAND  *Atlantic K 50058* .......... | 6 | 14 wks |
|---|---|---|---|
| 5 Jul 75 | CUT THE CAKE  *Atlantic K 50146* ................... | 28 | 4 wks |
| 31 Jul 76 | SOUL SEARCHING TIME  *Atlantic K 50272* .......... | 60 | 1 wk |
| 10 Mar 79 | I FEEL NO FRET  *RCA XL 13063* ................... | 15 | 15 wks |
| 31 May 80 | SHINE  *RCA XL 13123* .......................... | 14 | 13 wks |

## Roy AYERS  *US, male vocalist/instrumentalist – vibraphone*      2 wks

| 26 Oct 85 | YOU MIGHT BE SURPRISED  *CBS 26653* ........... | 91 | 2 wks |
|---|---|---|---|

## Pam AYRES  *UK, female vocalist*                               29 wks

| 27 Mar 76 | SOME OF ME POEMS AND SONGS  *Galaxy GAL 6003* .. | 13 | 23 wks |
|---|---|---|---|
| 11 Dec 76 | SOME MORE OF ME POEMS AND SONGS  *Galaxy GAL 6010* ............................... | 23 | 6 wks |

## Charles AZNAVOUR  *France, male vocalist*                      21 wks

| 29 Jun 74 | AZNAVOUR SINGS AZNAVOUR VOL. 3  *Barclay 80472* . | 23 | 7 wks |
|---|---|---|---|
| 7 Sep 74 | ● A TAPESTRY OF DREAMS  *Barclay 90003* ............. | 9 | 13 wks |
| 2 Aug 80 | HIS GREATEST LOVE SONGS  *K-Tel NE 1078* ........ | 73 | 1 wk |

## AZTEC CAMERA  *UK, male vocal/instrumental group*             67 wks

| 23 Apr 83 | HIGH LAND HARD RAIN  *Rough Trade ROUGH 47* ..... | 22 | 18 wks |
|---|---|---|---|
| 29 Sep 84 | KNIFE  *WEA WX 8* ............................... | 14 | 6 wks |
| 21 Nov 87 | ● LOVE  *WEA WX 128* ............................ | 10 | 43 wks |

# *b*

## Derek B  *UK, male rapper*                                     9 wks

| 28 May 88 | BULLET FROM A GUN  *Tuff Audio DRKLP 1* .......... | 11 | 9 wks |
|---|---|---|---|

## Eric B. and RAKIM  *US, male vocal/instrumental duo*           8 wks

| 12 Sep 87 | PAID IN FULL  *Fourth & Broadway BRLP 514* ............ | 85 | 4 wks |
|---|---|---|---|
| 6 Aug 88 | FOLLOW THE LEADER  *MCA MCG 6031* ............ | 25 | 4 wks |

## B BOYS  *US, male vocal/instrumental group*                    1 wk

| 28 Jan 84 | CUTTIN' HERBIE  *Streetwave X KHAN 501* ............ | 90 | 1 wk |
|---|---|---|---|

## BACCARA  *Spain, female vocal duo*                             6 wks

| 4 Mar 78 | BACCARA  *RCA PL 28316* ......................... | 26 | 6 wks |
|---|---|---|---|

## Burt BACHARACH  *US, orchestra and chorus*                     43 wks

| 22 May 65 | ● HIT MAKER – BURT BACHARACH  *London HAR 8233* . | 3 | 18 wks |
|---|---|---|---|
| 28 Nov 70 | REACH OUT  *A & M AMLS 908* .................... | 52 | 3 wks |
| 3 Apr 71 | ● PORTRAIT IN MUSIC  *A & M AMLS 2010* ........... | 5 | 22 wks |

## BACHELORS *Ireland, male vocal group* 103 wks

| | | | | | | |
|---|---|---|---|---|---|---|
| 27 Jun | 64 | ● THE BACHELORS AND 16 GREAT SONGS | | | 2 | 44 wks |
| | | *Decca LK 4614* | | | | |
| 9 Oct | 65 | MORE GREAT SONG HITS FROM THE BACHELORS | | | 15 | 6 wks |
| | | *Decca LK 4721* | | | 12 | 9 wks |
| 9 Jul | 66 | HITS OF THE SIXTIES | *Decca TXL 102* | | 24 | 8 wks |
| 5 Nov | 66 | BACHELORS' GIRLS | *Decca LK 4827* | | 19 | 7 wks |
| 1 Jul | 67 | GOLDEN ALL TIME HITS | *Decca SKL 4849* | | 8 | 18 wks |
| 14 Jun | 69 | ● WORLD OF THE BACHELORS | *Decca SPA 2* | | 11 | 7 wks |
| 23 Aug | 69 | WORLD OF THE BACHELORS VOL. 2 | *Decca SPA 22* | | 38 | 4 wks |
| 22 Dec | 79 | 25 GOLDEN GREATS | *Warwick WW 5068* | | | |

## BACHMAN-TURNER OVERDRIVE
*Canada, male vocal/instrumental group* 13 wks

| | | | | | | |
|---|---|---|---|---|---|---|
| 14 Dec | 74 | NOT FRAGILE | *Mercury 9100 007* | | 12 | 13 wks |

## BAD COMPANY *UK, male vocal/instrumental group* 87 wks

| | | | | | | |
|---|---|---|---|---|---|---|
| 15 Jun | 74 | ● BAD COMPANY | *Island ILPS 9279* | | 3 | 25 wks |
| 12 Apr | 75 | ● STRAIGHT SHOOTER | *Island ILPS 9304* | | 3 | 27 wks |
| 21 Feb | 76 | ● RUN WITH THE PACK | *Island ILPS 9346* | | 4 | 12 wks |
| 19 Mar | 77 | BURNIN' SKY | *Island ILPS 9441* | | 17 | 8 wks |
| 17 Mar | 79 | ● DESOLATION ANGELS | *Swansong SSK 59408* | | 10 | 9 wks |
| 28 Aug | 82 | ROUGH DIAMONDS | *Swansong SSK 59419* | | 15 | 6 wks |

## BAD ENGLISH *UK/US, male vocal/instrumental group* 1 wk

| | | | | | | |
|---|---|---|---|---|---|---|
| 16 Sep | 89 | BAD ENGLISH | *Epic 463447 1* | | 74 | 1 wk |

**49**

*b*

## BAD MANNERS *UK, male vocal/instrumental group* 44 wks

| | | | | | | |
|---|---|---|---|---|---|---|
| 26 Apr | 80 | SKA 'N' B | *Magnet MAG 5033* | | 34 | 13 wks |
| 29 Nov | 80 | LOONEE TUNES | *Magnet MAG 5038* | | 36 | 12 wks |
| 24 Oct | 81 | GOSH IT'S BAD MANNERS | *Magnet MAGL 5043* | | 18 | 12 wks |
| 27 Nov | 82 | FORGING AHEAD | *Magnet MAGL 5050* | | 78 | 1 wk |
| 7 May | 83 | THE HEIGHT OF BAD MANNERS | *Telstar STAR 2229* | | 23 | 6 wks |

## BAD NEWS *UK, male vocal group* 1 wk

| | | | | | | |
|---|---|---|---|---|---|---|
| 24 Oct | 87 | BAD NEWS | *EMI EMC 3535* | | 69 | 1 wk |

**BAD SEEDS** – *See Nick CAVE featuring the BAD SEEDS*

## BADLANDS *UK, male vocal/instrumental group* 2 wks

| | | | | | | |
|---|---|---|---|---|---|---|
| 24 Jun | 89 | BADLANDS | *WEA 781966 1* | | 39 | 2 wks |

## Joan BAEZ *US, female vocalist* 88 wks

| | | | | | | |
|---|---|---|---|---|---|---|
| 18 Jul | 64 | ● JOAN BAEZ IN CONCERT VOL. 2 | *Fontana TFL 6033* | | 8 | 19 wks |
| 15 May | 65 | ● JOAN BAEZ NO. 5 | *Fontana TFL 6043* | | 3 | 27 wks |
| 19 Jun | 65 | ● JOAN BAEZ | *Fontana TFL 6002* | | 9 | 13 wks |
| 27 Nov | 65 | ● FAREWELL ANGELINA | *Fontana TFL 6058* | | 5 | 23 wks |
| 19 Jul | 69 | JOAN BAEZ ON VANGUARD | *Vanguard SVXL 100* | | 15 | 5 wks |
| 3 Apr | 71 | FIRST TEN YEARS | *Vanguard 6635 003* | | 41 | 1 wk |

## Philip BAILEY *US, male vocalist* 17 wks

| | | | | | | |
|---|---|---|---|---|---|---|
| 30 Mar | 85 | CHINESE WALL | *CBS 26161* | | 29 | 17 wks |

When **THE ANIMALS** regrouped for a tour in the 80s they posed with one of their 60s photos.

**PATTI AUSTIN** (shown below with 'Baby Come to Me' partner James Ingram) believed every home should have one week on chart.

**BURT BACHARACH**, (left) one of the top songwriters of all time, became a hitmaker himself in 1965.

**ANITA BAKER** enraptured listeners in 1986.

## Anita BAKER  *US, female vocalist*                      *67 wks*

| | | | |
|---|---|---|---|
| 3 May 86 | **RAPTURE** *Elektra EKT 37* ......................... | **13** | 47 wks |
| 29 Oct 88 | ● **GIVING YOU THE BEST THAT I GOT**  *Elektra EKT 49* . | **9** | 20 wks |

## BAKER-GURVITZ ARMY
*UK, male vocal/instrumental group*                      *5 wks*

| | | | |
|---|---|---|---|
| 22 Feb 75 | **BAKER-GURVITZ ARMY**  *Vertigo 9103 201* ........... | **22** | 5 wks |

*See also Ginger Baker's Air Force.*

## Ginger BAKER'S AIR FORCE
*UK, male vocal/instrumental group*                      *1 wk*

| | | | |
|---|---|---|---|
| 13 Jun 70 | **GINGER BAKER'S AIR FORCE**  *Polydor 266 2001* ...... | **37** | 1 wk |

*See also Baker-Gurvitz Army.*

## BALAAM AND THE ANGEL
*UK, male/vocal instrumental group*                      *2 wks*

| | | | |
|---|---|---|---|
| 16 Aug 86 | **THE GREATEST STORY EVER TOLD**  *Virgin V 2377* .. | **67** | 2 wks |

## Kenny BALL  *UK, male vocalist/instrumentalist – trumpet*     *26 wks*

| | | | |
|---|---|---|---|
| 7 Sep 63 | ● **KENNY BALL'S GOLDEN HITS** *Pye Golden Guinea GGL 0209* ........................ | **4** | 26 wks |

*See also Kenny Ball, Chris Barber and Acker Bilk.*

## Kenny BALL, Chris BARBER and Acker BILK
*UK, male jazz band leaders/vocalists/instrumentalists – trumpet, trombone and clarinet respectively*                      *24 wks*

| | | | |
|---|---|---|---|
| 25 Aug 62 | ★ **BEST OF BALL, BARBER AND BILK** *Pye Golden Guinea GGL 0131* ........................ | **1** | 24 wks |

*See also Kenny Ball; Chris Barber; Mr Acker Bilk.*

## BANANARAMA  *UK, female vocal group*                  *95 wks*

| | | | |
|---|---|---|---|
| 19 Mar 83 | ● **DEEP SEA SKIVING**  *London RAMA 1* ............... | **7** | 16 wks |
| 28 Apr 84 | **BANANARAMA**  *London RAMA 2* ................... | **16** | 11 wks |
| 19 Jul 86 | **TRUE CONFESSIONS**  *London RAMA 3* ............ | **46** | 5 wks |
| 19 Sep 87 | **WOW!**  *London RAMA 4* ........................ | **27** | 26 wks |
| 22 Oct 88 | ● **THE GREATEST HITS COLLECTION**  *London RAMA 5* . | **3** | 37 wks |

## BAND  *Canada, male vocal/instrumental group*         *18 wks*

| | | | |
|---|---|---|---|
| 31 Jan 70 | **THE BAND**  *Capitol EST 132* ......................... | **25** | 11 wks |
| 3 Oct 70 | **STAGE FRIGHT**  *Capitol EA SW 425* ................ | **15** | 6 wks |
| 27 Nov 71 | **CAHOOTS**  *Capitol EA–ST 651* ...................... | **41** | 1 wk |

## BANGLES  *US, female vocal/instrumental group*        *74 wks*

| | | | |
|---|---|---|---|
| 16 Mar 85 | **ALL OVER THE PLACE**  *CBS 26015* ............... | **86** | 1 wk |
| 15 Mar 86 | ● **DIFFERENT LIGHT**  *CBS 26659* ................... | **3** | 47 wks |
| 10 Dec 88 | ● **EVERYTHING**  *CBS 462979 1* ..................... | **5** | 26 wks |

## Tony BANKS  *UK, male instrumentalist – keyboards*                          *7 wks*

| | | | |
|---|---|---|---|
| 20 Oct 79 | **A CURIOUS FEELING**  *Charisma CAS 1148* ........... | 21 | 5 wks |
| 25 Jun 83 | **THE FUGITIVE**  *Charisma TBLP 1* ................... | 50 | 2 wks |

**BANSHEES** – *See SIOUXSIE and the BANSHEES*

## Chris BARBER
*UK, male vocalist/instrumentalist – trombone*                                *3 wks*

| | | | |
|---|---|---|---|
| 24 Sep 60 | **CHRIS BARBER BAND BOX NO. 2**  *Columbia 33SCX 3277* | 17 | 1 wk |
| 5 Nov 60 | **ELITE SYNCOPATIONS**  *Columbia 33SX 1245* .......... | 18 | 1 wk |
| 12 Nov 60 | **BEST OF CHRIS BARBER**  *Ace Of Clubs ACL 1037* ....... | 17 | 1 wk |

*See also Chris Barber; Mr Acker Bilk; Kenny Ball, Chris Barber and Acker Bilk.*

## Chris BARBER and Acker BILK  *UK, male band*
*leaders/vocalists/instrumentalists – trombone and clarinet*                  *61 wks*

| | | | |
|---|---|---|---|
| 27 May 61 | ● **BEST OF BARBER AND BILK VOL. 1**  *Pye GGL 0075* ... | 4 | 43 wks |
| 11 Nov 61 | ● **BEST OF BARBER AND BILK VOL. 2**  *Pye GGL 0096* ... | 8 | 18 wks |

*See also Chris Barber; Mr Acker Bilk.*

## BARCLAY JAMES HARVEST
*UK, male vocal/instrumental group*                                          *42 wks*

| | | | |
|---|---|---|---|
| 14 Dec 74 | **BARCLAY JAMES HARVEST LIVE**  *Polydor 2683 052* ... | 40 | 2 wks |
| 18 Oct 75 | **TIME HONOURED GHOST**  *Polydor 2383 361* ......... | 32 | 3 wks |
| 23 Oct 76 | **OCTOBERON**  *Polydor 2442 144* .................... | 19 | 4 wks |
| 1 Oct 77 | **GONE TO EARTH**  *Polydor 2442 148* ................ | 30 | 7 wks |
| 21 Oct 78 | **BARCLAY JAMES HARVEST XII**  *Polydor POLD 5006* .. | 31 | 2 wks |
| 23 May 81 | **TURN OF THE TIDE**  *Polydor POLD 5040* ............ | 55 | 2 wks |
| 24 Jul 82 | **A CONCERT FOR THE PEOPLE (BERLIN)** | | |
| | *Polydor POLD 5052* .................................. | 15 | 11 wks |
| 28 May 83 | **RING OF CHANGES**  *Polydor POLH 3* ............... | 36 | 4 wks |
| 14 Apr 84 | **VICTIMS OF CIRCUMSTANCE**  *Polydor POLD 5135* .... | 33 | 6 wks |
| 14 Feb 87 | **FACE TO FACE**  *Polydor POLD 5209* ................ | 65 | 1 wk |

**Daniel BARENBOIM** – *See John WILLIAMS and Daniel BARENBOIM*

## Syd BARRETT  *UK, male vocalist/instrumentalist – guitar*                   *1 wk*

| | | | |
|---|---|---|---|
| 7 Feb 70 | **MADCAP LAUGHS**  *Harvest SHVL 765* ................ | 40 | 1 wk |

**Wild Willy BARRETT** – *See John OTWAY and Wild Willy BARRETT*

## BARRON KNIGHTS  *UK, male vocal/instrumental group*                        *22 wks*

| | | | |
|---|---|---|---|
| 2 Dec 78 | **NIGHT GALLERY**  *Epic EPC 83221* .................. | 15 | 13 wks |
| 1 Dec 79 | **TEACH THE WORLD TO LAUGH**  *Epic EPC 83891* .... | 51 | 4 wks |
| 13 Dec 80 | **JUST A GIGGLE**  *Epic EPC 84550* .................. | 45 | 5 wks |

## John BARRY  *UK, male arranger/conductor*                                   *9 wks*

| | | | |
|---|---|---|---|
| 29 Jan 72 | **THE PERSUADERS**  *CBS 64816* ..................... | 18 | 9 wks |

## Count BASIE  *US, male orchestra leader/instrumentalist – piano*            *1 wk*

| | | | |
|---|---|---|---|
| 16 Apr 60 | **CHAIRMAN OF THE BOARD**  *Columbia 33SX 1209* ..... | 17 | 1 wk |

*See also Frank Sinatra and Count Basie.*

## BASIA  *Poland, female vocalist*                                      3 wks

| | | | | |
|---|---|---|---|---|
| 13 Feb 88 | **TIME AND TIDE** *Portrait 450263 1* .................. | 61 | 3 wks |

## Toni BASIL  *US, female vocalist*                                    16 wks

| | | | | |
|---|---|---|---|---|
| 6 Feb 82 | **WORD OF MOUTH** *Radialchoice BASIL 1* ............. | 15 | 16 wks |

## Shirley BASSEY  *UK, female vocalist*                               259 wks

| | | | | |
|---|---|---|---|---|
| 28 Jan 61 | **FABULOUS SHIRLEY BASSEY** *Columbia 33SX 1178* ... | 12 | 2 wks |
| 25 Feb 61 | ● **SHIRLEY** *Columbia 33SX 1286* ..................... | 9 | 10 wks |
| 17 Feb 62 | **SHIRLEY BASSEY** *Columbia 33SX 1382* ......... | 14 | 11 wks |
| 15 Dec 62 | **LET'S FACE THE MUSIC** *Columbia 33SX 1454* ......... | 12 | 7 wks |
| 4 Dec 65 | **SHIRLEY BASSEY AT THE PIGALLE** | | |
| | *Columbia 33SX 1787* ......................... | 16 | 7 wks |
| 27 Aug 66 | **I'VE GOT A SONG FOR YOU** *United Artists ULP 1142* ... | 26 | 1 wk |
| 17 Feb 68 | **TWELVE OF THOSE SONGS** *Columbia SCX 6204* ...... | 38 | 3 wks |
| 7 Dec 68 | **GOLDEN HITS OF SHIRLEY BASSEY** | | |
| | *Columbia SCX 6294* ..................... | 28 | 40 wks |
| 11 Jul 70 | **LIVE AT THE TALK OF THE TOWN** | | |
| | *United Artists UAS 29095* ......... | 38 | 6 wks |
| 29 Aug 70 | ● **SOMETHING** *United Artists UAS 29100* ............... | 5 | 28 wks |
| 15 May 71 | ● **SOMETHING ELSE** *United Artists UAG 29149* ......... | 7 | 9 wks |
| 2 Oct 71 | **BIG SPENDER** *Sunset SLS 50262* ............... | 27 | 8 wks |
| 30 Oct 71 | **IT'S MAGIC** *Starline SRS 5082* ..................... | 32 | 1 wk |
| 6 Nov 71 | **THE FABULOUS SHIRLEY BASSEY** *MFP 1398* ....... | 48 | 1 wk |
| 4 Dec 71 | **WHAT NOW MY LOVE** *MFP 5230* ................ | 17 | 5 wks |
| 8 Jan 72 | **THE SHIRLEY BASSEY COLLECTION** | | |
| | *United Artists UAD 60013/4* ................... | 37 | 1 wk |
| 19 Feb 72 | **I CAPRICORN** *United Artists UAS 29246* .............. | 13 | 11 wks |
| 29 Nov 72 | **AND I LOVE YOU SO** *United Artists UAS 29385* ......... | 24 | 9 wks |
| 2 Jun 73 | ● **NEVER NEVER NEVER** *United Artists UAG 29471* ..... | 10 | 10 wks |
| 15 Mar 75 | ● **THE SHIRLEY BASSEY SINGLES ALBUM** | | |
| | *United Artists UAS 29728* ..................... | 2 | 23 wks |
| 1 Nov 75 | **GOOD, BAD BUT BEAUTIFUL** *United Artists UAS 29881* . | 13 | 7 wks |
| 15 May 76 | **LOVE, LIFE AND FEELINGS** *United Artists UAS 29944* .. | 13 | 5 wks |
| 4 Dec 76 | **THOUGHTS OF LOVE** *United Artists UAS 30011* ....... | 15 | 9 wks |
| 25 Jun 77 | **YOU TAKE MY HEART AWAY** *United Artists UAS 30037* | 34 | 5 wks |
| 4 Nov 78 | ● **25TH ANNIVERSARY ALBUM** | | |
| | *United Artists SBTV 601 4748* ..................... | 3 | 12 wks |
| 12 May 79 | **THE MAGIC IS YOU** *United Artists UATV 30230* ........ | 40 | 5 wks |
| 17 Jul 82 | **LOVE SONGS** *Applause APKL 1163* ............... | 48 | 5 wks |
| 20 Oct 84 | **I AM WHAT I AM** *Towerbell TOWLP 7* ................ | 25 | 18 wks |

Let's Face The Music *has credit 'with The Nelson Riddle Orchestra'.*

**53**

*b*

## BAUHAUS  *UK, male vocal/instrumental group*                       24 wks

| | | | | |
|---|---|---|---|---|
| 15 Nov 80 | **IN THE FLAT FIELD** *4AD CAD 13* ................... | 72 | 1 wk |
| 24 Oct 81 | **MASK** *Beggars Banquet BEGA 29* ..................... | 30 | 5 wks |
| 30 Oct 82 | ● **THE SKY'S GONE OUT** *Beggars Banquet BEGA 42* ...... | 4 | 6 wks |
| 23 Jul 83 | **BURNING FROM THE INSIDE** *Beggars Banquet BEGA 45* | 13 | 10 wks |
| 30 Nov 85 | **1979–1983** *Beggars Banquet BEGA 64* ............... | 36 | 2 wks |

## BAY CITY ROLLERS  *UK, male vocal/instrumental group*              127 wks

| | | | | |
|---|---|---|---|---|
| 12 Oct 74 | ★ **ROLLIN'** *Bell BELLS 244* ......................... | 1 | 62 wks |
| 3 May 75 | ★ **ONCE UPON A STAR** *Bell SYBEL 8001* ............. | 1 | 37 wks |
| 13 Dec 75 | ● **WOULDN'T YOU LIKE IT** *Bell SYBEL 8002* ......... | 3 | 12 wks |
| 25 Sep 76 | ● **DEDICATION** *Bell SYBEL 8005* ................... | 4 | 12 wks |
| 13 Aug 77 | **IT'S A GAME** *Arista SPARTY 1009* ................. | 18 | 4 wks |

## BBC SYMPHONY ORCHESTRA, SINGERS and CHORUS  *UK, orchestra/choir and audience*  6 wks

| | | | | | |
|---|---|---|---|---|---|
| 4 Oct | 69 | **LAST NIGHT OF THE PROMS**  *Philips SFM 23033* ...... | 36 | 1 wk |
| 11 Dec | 82 | **HIGHLIGHTS – LAST NIGHT OF THE PROMS '82**  *K-Tel NE 1198* .................................. | 69 | 5 wks |

Last Night Of The Proms *was conducted by Colin Davis and* Highlights – Last Night Of The Proms '82 *by James Loughran.*

**BBC WELSH CHORUS** – *See Aled JONES*

## BEACH BOYS  *US, male vocal/instrumental group*  524 wks

| | | | | |
|---|---|---|---|---|
| 25 Sep | 65 | **SURFIN' USA**  *Capitol T 1890* ........................ | 17 | 7 wks |
| 19 Feb | 66 ● | **BEACH BOYS PARTY**  *Capitol T 2398* ............... | 3 | 14 wks |
| 16 Apr | 66 ● | **BEACH BOYS TODAY**  *Capitol T 2269* ............. | 6 | 25 wks |
| 9 Jul | 66 ● | **PET SOUNDS**  *Capitol T 2458* ..................... | 2 | 39 wks |
| 16 Jul | 66 ● | **SUMMER DAYS**  *Capitol T 2354* ................... | 4 | 22 wks |
| 12 Nov | 66 ● | **BEST OF THE BEACH BOYS**  *Capitol T 20865* ......... | 2 | 142 wks |
| 11 Mar | 67 | **SURFER GIRL**  *Capitol T 1981* ................... | 13 | 14 wks |
| 21 Oct | 67 ● | **BEST OF THE BEACH BOYS VOL. 2**  *Capitol ST 20956* .. | 3 | 39 wks |
| 18 Nov | 67 ● | **SMILEY SMILE**  *Capitol ST 9001* ................. | 9 | 8 wks |
| 16 Mar | 68 ● | **WILD HONEY**  *Capitol ST 2859* .................. | 7 | 15 wks |
| 21 Sep | 68 | **FRIENDS**  *Capitol ST 2895* ........................ | 13 | 8 wks |
| 23 Nov | 68 ● | **BEST OF THE BEACH BOYS VOL. 3**  *Capitol ST 21142* .. | 9 | 12 wks |
| 29 Mar | 69 ● | **20/20**  *Capitol EST 133* ........................ | 3 | 10 wks |
| 19 Sep | 70 ● | **GREATEST HITS**  *Capitol ST 21628* ................ | 5 | 30 wks |
| 5 Dec | 70 | **SUNFLOWER**  *Stateside SSL 8251* ................. | 29 | 6 wks |
| 27 Nov | 71 | **SURF'S UP**  *Stateside SLS 10313* ................ | 15 | 7 wks |
| 24 Jun | 72 | **CARL AND THE PASSIONS/SO TOUGH**  *Reprise K 44184* .......................... | 25 | 1 wk |
| 17 Feb | 73 | **HOLLAND**  *Reprise K 54008* ................... | 20 | 7 wks |
| 10 Jul | 76 ★ | **20 GOLDEN GREATS**  *Capitol EMTV 1* .............. | 1 | 86 wks |
| 24 Jul | 76 | **15 BIG ONES**  *Reprise K 54079* ................ | 31 | 3 wks |
| 7 May | 77 | **THE BEACH BOYS LOVE YOU**  *Brother/Reprise K 54087* . | 28 | 1 wk |
| 21 Apr | 79 | **LA (LIGHT ALBUM)**  *Caribou CRB 86081* ............. | 32 | 6 wks |
| 12 Apr | 80 | **KEEPING THE SUMMER ALIVE**  *Caribou CRB 86109* ... | 54 | 3 wks |
| 30 Jul | 83 ★ | **THE VERY BEST OF THE BEACH BOYS**  *Capitol BBTV 1867193* .......................... | 1 | 17 wks |
| 22 Jun | 85 | **THE BEACH BOYS**  *Caribou CRB 26378* ............... | 60 | 2 wks |

**BEAKY** – *See Dave DEE, DOZY, BEAKY, MICK and TICH*

## BEASTIE BOYS  *US, male vocal group*  42 wks

| | | | | |
|---|---|---|---|---|
| 31 Jan | 87 ● | **LICENCE TO ILL**  *Def Jam 450062* ................... | 7 | 40 wks |
| 5 Aug | 89 | **PAUL'S BOUTIQUE**  *Capitol EST 2102* ............... | 44 | 2 wks |

## BEAT  *UK, male vocal/instrumental group*  69 wks

| | | | | |
|---|---|---|---|---|
| 31 May | 80 ● | **JUST CAN'T STOP IT**  *Go-Feet BEAT 001* ............. | 3 | 32 wks |
| 16 May | 81 ● | **WHA'PPEN**  *Go-Feet BEAT 3* ........................ | 3 | 18 wks |
| 9 Oct | 82 | **SPECIAL BEAT SERVICE**  *Go-Feet BEAT 5* ........... | 21 | 6 wks |
| 11 Jun | 83 ● | **WHAT IS BEAT? (THE BEST OF THE BEAT)**  *Go-Feet BEAT 6* .................................. | 10 | 13 wks |

## BEATLES  *UK, male vocal/instrumental group*  1082 wks

| | | | | |
|---|---|---|---|---|
| 6 Apr | 63 ★ | **PLEASE PLEASE ME**  *Parlophone PMC 1202* ........... | 1 | 70 wks |
| 30 Nov | 63 ★ | **WITH THE BEATLES**  *Parlophone PMC 1206* ........... | 1 | 51 wks |
| 18 Jul | 64 ★ | **A HARD DAY'S NIGHT**  *Parlophone PMC 1230* ......... | 1 | 38 wks |
| 12 Dec | 64 ★ | **BEATLES FOR SALE**  *Parlophone PMC 1240* ........... | 1 | 46 wks |
| 14 Aug | 65 ★ | **HELP**  *Parlophone PMC 1255* ..................... | 1 | 37 wks |
| 11 Dec | 65 ★ | **RUBBER SOUL**  *Parlophone PMC 1267* ............... | 1 | 42 wks |
| 13 Aug | 66 ★ | **REVOLVER**  *Parlophone PMC 7009* .................. | 1 | 34 wks |

| Date | Title | Pos | Wks |
|---|---|---|---|
| 10 Dec 66 | ● **A COLLECTION OF BEATLES OLDIES** *Parlophone PMC 7016* | 7 | 34 wks |
| 3 Jun 67 | ★ **SERGEANT PEPPER'S LONELY HEARTS CLUB BAND** *Parlophone PCS 7027* | 1 | 148 wks |
| 13 Jan 68 | **MAGICAL MYSTERY TOUR** (import) *Capitol SMAL 2835* | 31 | 2 wks |
| 7 Dec 68 | ★ **THE BEATLES** *Apple PCS 7067/8* | 1 | 22 wks |
| 1 Feb 69 | ● **YELLOW SUBMARINE** *Apple PCS 7070* | 3 | 10 wks |
| 4 Oct 69 | ★ **ABBEY ROAD** *Apple PCS 7088* | 1 | 81 wks |
| 23 May 70 | ★ **LET IT BE** *Apple PXS 1* | 1 | 59 wks |
| 16 Jan 71 | **A HARD DAY'S NIGHT** (re-issue) *Parlophone PCS 3058* | 30 | 1 wk |
| 24 Jul 71 | **HELP** (re-issue) *Parlophone PCS 3071* | 33 | 2 wks |
| 5 May 73 | ● **THE BEATLES 1967–1970** *Apple PCSP 718* | 2 | 113 wks |
| 5 May 73 | ● **THE BEATLES 1962–1966** *Apple PCSP 717* | 3 | 148 wks |
| 25 Jun 76 | **ROCK 'N' ROLL MUSIC** *Parlophone PCSP 719* | 11 | 15 wks |
| 21 Aug 76 | **THE BEATLES TAPES** *Polydor 2683 068* | 45 | 1 wk |
| 21 May 77 | ★ **THE BEATLES AT THE HOLLYWOOD BOWL** *Parlophone EMTV 4* | 1 | 17 wks |
| 17 Dec 77 | ● **LOVE SONGS** *Parlophone PCSP 721* | 7 | 17 wks |
| 3 Nov 79 | **RARITIES** *Parlophone PCM 1001* | 71 | 1 wk |
| 15 Nov 80 | **BEATLES BALLADS** *Parlophone PCS 7214* | 17 | 16 wks |
| 30 Oct 82 | ● **20 GREATEST HITS** *Parlophone PCTC 260* | 10 | 30 wks |
| 7 Mar 87 | **PLEASE PLEASE ME** (re-issue) *Parlophone CDP 746 435-2* | 32 | 4 wks |
| 7 Mar 87 | **WITH THE BEATLES** (re-issue) *Parlophone CDP 746 436-2* | 40 | 2 wks |
| 7 Mar 87 | **A HARD DAY'S NIGHT** (2nd re-issue) *Parlophone CDP 746 437-2* | 30 | 4 wks |
| 7 Mar 87 | **BEATLES FOR SALE** (re-issue) *Parlophone CDP 746 438-2* | 45 | 2 wks |
| 9 May 87 | **HELP** (2nd re-issue) *Parlophone CDP 746 439-2* | 61 | 2 wks |
| 9 May 87 | **RUBBER SOUL** (re-issue) *Parlophone CDP 746 440-2* | 60 | 3 wks |
| 9 May 87 | **REVOLVER** (re-issue) *Parlophone CDP 746 441-2* | 55 | 5 wks |
| 6 Jun 87 | ● **SERGEANT PEPPER'S LONELY HEARTS CLUB BAND** (re-issue) *Parlophone CDP 746 442-2* | 3 | 16 wks |
| 5 Sep 87 | **THE BEATLES** (re-issue) *Parlophone CDS 746 443-9* | 18 | 2 wks |
| 5 Sep 87 | **YELLOW SUBMARINE** (re-issue) *Parlophone CDP 746 445-2* | 60 | 1 wk |
| 3 Oct 87 | **MAGICAL MYSTERY TOUR** (re-issue) *Parlophone PCTC 255* | 52 | 1 wk |
| 31 Oct 87 | **ABBEY ROAD** (re-issue) *Parlophone CDP 746 446-2* | 30 | 2 wks |
| 31 Oct 87 | **LET IT BE** (re-issue) *Parlophone CDP 746 447-2* | 50 | 1 wk |
| 19 Mar 88 | **PAST MASTERS VOLUME 1** *Parlophone CDBPM 1* | 49 | 1 wk |
| 19 Mar 88 | **PAST MASTERS VOLUME 2** *Parlophone CDBPM 2* | 46 | 1 wk |

Yellow Submarine *featured several tracks by the George Martin Orchestra. The albums recharted in 1987, after being made available as compact discs. The label numbers are the CD catalogue numbers of these re-issues.*

# BEATMASTERS

*UK, male/female instrumental group*  **10 wks**

| | | | |
|---|---|---|---|
| 1 Jul 89 | **ANYWAYAWANNA** *Rhythm King LEFTLP 10* | 30 | 10 wks |

# BEAUTIFUL SOUTH

*UK, male vocal/instrumental group*  **9 wks**

| | | | |
|---|---|---|---|
| 4 Nov 89 | ● **WELCOME TO THE BEAUTIFUL SOUTH** *Go! Discs AGOLP 16* | 2† | 9 wks |

# BE-BOP DELUXE

*UK, male vocal/instrumental group*  **28 wks**

| | | | |
|---|---|---|---|
| 31 Jan 76 | **SUNBURST FINISH** *Harvest SHSP 4053* | 17 | 12 wks |
| 25 Sep 76 | **MODERN MUSIC** *Harvest SHSP 4058* | 12 | 6 wks |
| 6 Aug 77 | ● **LIVE! IN THE AIR AGE** *Harvest SHVL 816* | 10 | 5 wks |
| 25 Feb 78 | **DRASTIC PLASTIC** *Harvest SHSP 4091* | 22 | 5 wks |

## Jeff BECK

*UK, male vocalist/instrumentalist – guitar*                                    *11 wks*

| | | | | | |
|---|---|---|---|---|---|
| 13 Sep | 69 | **BECK-OLA** *Columbia SCX 6351* .................... | **39** | 1 wk |
| 24 Jul | 76 | **WIRED** *CBS 86012* ............................... | **38** | 5 wks |
| 19 Jul | 80 | **THERE AND BACK** *Epic EPC 83288* .............. | **38** | 4 wks |
| 17 Aug | 85 | **FLASH** *Epic EPC 26112* .......................... | **83** | 1 wk |

*See also Jeff Beck, Tim Bogert and Carmine Appice.*


## Jeff BECK, Tim BOGERT and Carmine APPICE

*UK/US, male vocal/instrumental group*                                    *3 wks*

| | | | | |
|---|---|---|---|---|
| 28 Apr | 73 | **JEFF BECK, TIM BOGERT & CARMINE APPICE** *Epic EPC 65455* .................................. | **28** | 3 wks |

*See also Jeff Beck.*


## BEE GEES

*UK/Australia, male vocal/instrumental group*                                    *177 wks*

| | | | | |
|---|---|---|---|---|
| 12 Aug | 67 ● | **BEE GEES FIRST** *Polydor 583–012* ................... | **8** | 26 wks |
| 24 Feb | 68 | **HORIZONTAL** *Polydor 582–020* .................... | **16** | 15 wks |
| 28 Sep | 68 ● | **IDEA** *Polydor 583–036* ........................... | **4** | 18 wks |
| 5 Apr | 69 ● | **ODESSA** *Polydor 583–049/50* ..................... | **10** | 1 wk |
| 8 Nov | 69 ● | **BEST OF THE BEE GEES** *Polydor 583–063* ......... | **7** | 22 wks |
| 9 May | 70 | **CUCUMBER CASTLE** *Polydor 2383–010* ........... | **57** | 2 wks |
| 17 Feb | 79 ★ | **SPIRITS HAVING FLOWN** *RSO RSBG 001* ......... | **1** | 33 wks |
| 10 Nov | 79 ● | **BEE GEES GREATEST** *RSO RSDX 001* ............. | **6** | 25 wks |
| 7 Nov | 81 | **LIVING EYES** *RSO RSBG 002* .................... | **73** | 8 wks |
| 3 Oct | 87 ● | **E.S.P.** *Warner Bros. WX 83* ..................... | **5** | 24 wks |
| 29 Apr | 89 | **ONE** *Warner Bros. WX 252* ...................... | **29** | 3 wks |

*All albums from* Cucumber Castle *onwards group were UK only.*

## Sir Thomas BEECHAM *UK, conductor*                                    *2 wks*

| | | | | |
|---|---|---|---|---|
| 26 Mar | 60 | **CARMEN** *HMV ALP 1762/4* ........................ | **18** | 2 wks |

*Full credit on sleeve reads 'Orchestre National de la Radio Diffusion Francaise, conducted by Sir Thomas Beecham'.*


## BELLAMY BROTHERS *US, male vocal duo*                                    *6 wks*

| | | | | |
|---|---|---|---|---|
| 19 Jun | 76 | **BELLAMY BROTHERS** *Warner Bros. K 56242* ......... | **21** | 6 wks |


## Regina BELLE *US, female vocalist*                                    *5 wks*

| | | | | |
|---|---|---|---|---|
| 1 Aug | 87 | **ALL BY MYSELF** *CBS 450 998–1* .................... | **53** | 4 wks |
| 16 Sep | 89 | **STAY WITH ME** *CBS 465132 1* ...................... | **62** | 1 wk |


## BELLE STARS *UK, female vocal/instrumental group*                                    *12 wks*

| | | | | |
|---|---|---|---|---|
| 5 Feb | 83 | **THE BELLE STARS** *Stiff SEEZ 45* ................... | **15** | 12 wks |


## Pierre BELMONDE

*France, male instrumentalist – panpipes*                                    *10 wks*

| | | | | |
|---|---|---|---|---|
| 7 Jun | 80 | **THEMES FOR DREAMS** *K-Tel ONE 1077* ........... | **13** | 10 wks |

**BELMONTS** – *See DION and the BELMONTS*

## Pat BENATAR  *US, female vocalist*                    *80 wks*

| | | | | | | |
|---|---|---|---|---|---|---|
| 25 Jul | 81 | **PRECIOUS TIME** *Chrysalis CHR 1346* | | **30** | 7 wks |
| 13 Nov | 82 | **GET NERVOUS** *Chrysalis CHR 1396* | | **73** | 6 wks |
| 15 Oct | 83 | **LIVE FROM EARTH** *Chrysalis CHR 1451* | | **60** | 5 wks |
| 17 Nov | 84 | **TROPICO** *Chrysalis CHR 1471* | | **31** | 25 wks |
| 24 Aug | 85 | **IN THE HEAT OF THE NIGHT** *Chrysalis CHR 1236* | | **98** | 1 wk |
| 7 Dec | 85 | **SEVEN THE HARD WAY** *Chrysalis CHR 1507* | | **69** | 4 wks |
| 7 Nov | 87 ● | **BEST SHOTS** *Chrysalis PATV 1* | | **6** | 19 wks |
| 16 Jul | 88 | **WIDE AWAKE IN DREAMLAND** *Chrysalis CDL 1628* | | **11** | 13 wks |

## Cliff BENNETT and the REBEL ROUSERS
*UK, male vocal/instrumental group*                    *3 wks*

| | | | | | |
|---|---|---|---|---|---|
| 22 Oct | 66 | **DRIVIN' ME WILD** *MFP 1121* | | **25** | 3 wks |

## Tony BENNETT  *US, male vocalist*                    *63 wks*

| | | | | | |
|---|---|---|---|---|---|
| 29 May | 65 | **I LEFT MY HEART IN SAN FRANCISCO** *CBS BPG 62201* | **13** | 14 wks |
| 19 Feb | 66 ● | **A STRING OF TONY'S HITS** *CBS DP 66010* | **9** | 13 wks |
| 10 Jun | 67 | **TONY'S GREATEST HITS** *CBS SBPG 62821* | **14** | 24 wks |
| 23 Sep | 67 | **TONY MAKES IT HAPPEN** *CBS SBPG 63055* | **31** | 3 wks |
| 23 Mar | 68 | **FOR ONCE IN MY LIFE** *CBS SBPG 63166* | **29** | 5 wks |
| 26 Feb | 77 | **THE VERY BEST OF TONY BENNETT – 20 GREATEST HITS** *Warwick PA 5021* | **23** | 4 wks |

## George BENSON
*US, male vocalist/instrumentalist – guitar*                    *252 wks*

| | | | | | |
|---|---|---|---|---|---|
| 19 Mar | 77 | **IN FLIGHT** *Warner Bros. K 56237* | **19** | 23 wks |
| 18 Feb | 78 | **WEEKEND IN L.A.** *Warner Bros. K 66074* | **47** | 1 wk |
| 24 Mar | 79 | **LIVING INSIDE YOUR LOVE** *Warner Bros. K 66085* | **24** | 14 wks |
| 26 Jul | 80 ● | **GIVE ME THE NIGHT** *Warner Bros. K 56823* | **3** | 40 wks |
| 14 Nov | 81 | **GEORGE BENSON COLLECTION** *Warner Bros. K 66107* | **19** | 35 wks |
| 11 Jun | 83 ● | **IN YOUR EYES** *Warner Bros. 92-3744-1* | **3** | 53 wks |
| 26 Jan | 85 ● | **20/20** *Warner Bros. 92-5178-1* | **9** | 19 wks |
| 19 Oct | 85 ★ | **THE LOVE SONGS** *K-Tel NE 1308* | **1** | 27 wks |
| 6 Sep | 86 | **WHILE THE CITY SLEEPS...** *Warner Bros. WX 55* | **13** | 27 wks |
| 10 Sep | 88 | **TWICE THE LOVE** *Warner Bros. WX 160* | **16** | 10 wks |
| 8 Jul | 89 | **TENDERLY** *Warner Bros. WX 263* | **52** | 3 wks |

*See also George Benson and Earl Klugh.*

## George BENSON and Earl KLUGH
*US, male instrumental duo – guitars*                    *6 wks*

| | | | | | |
|---|---|---|---|---|---|
| 11 Jul | 87 | **COLLABORATION** *Warner Bros. WX 91* | | **47** | 6 wks |

*See also George Benson.*

## BERLIN
*US, male/female vocal/instrumental group*                    *11 wks*

| | | | | | |
|---|---|---|---|---|---|
| 17 Jan | 87 | **COUNT THREE AND PRAY** *Mercury MER 101* | | **32** | 11 wks |

**BERLIN PHILHARMONIC ORCHESTRA** – *See Herbert VON KARAJAN*

**Leonard BERNSTEIN'S WEST SIDE STORY** – *See Studio Cast Recordings*

## Shelley BERMAN  *US, male vocalist – comedian*                    *4 wks*

| | | | | | |
|---|---|---|---|---|---|
| 19 Nov | 60 | **INSIDE SHELLEY BERMAN** *Capitol CLP 1300* | | **12** | 4 wks |

## Chuck BERRY
*US, male vocalist/instrumentalist – guitar*                                    *53 wks*

| | | | |
|---|---|---|---|
| 25 May 63 | **CHUCK BERRY** *Pye International NPL 28024* .......... | 12 | 16 wks |
| 5 Oct 63 | ● **CHUCK BERRY ON STAGE** *Pye International NPL 28027* . | 6 | 11 wks |
| 7 Dec 63 | ● **MORE CHUCK BERRY** *Pye International NPL 28028* ..... | 9 | 8 wks |
| 30 May 64 | ● **HIS LATEST AND GREATEST** *Pye NPL 28037* ........ | 8 | 7 wks |
| 3 Oct 64 | **YOU NEVER CAN TELL** *Pye NPL 29039* ............ | 18 | 2 wks |
| 12 Feb 77 | ● **MOTORVATIN'** *Chess 9288 690* ................... | 7 | 9 wks |

## Mike BERRY  *UK, male vocalist*                                             *3 wks*

| | | | |
|---|---|---|---|
| 24 Jan 81 | **THE SUNSHINE OF YOUR SMILE** *Polydor 2383 592* ... | 63 | 3 wks |

## Nick BERRY  *UK, male vocalist*                                             *1 wk*

| | | | |
|---|---|---|---|
| 20 Dec 86 | **NICK BERRY** *BBC REB 618* ...................... | 99 | 1 wk |

## BEVERLEY-PHILLIPS ORCHESTRA
*UK, orchestra*                                                                *9 wks*

| | | | |
|---|---|---|---|
| 9 Oct 76 | **GOLD ON SILVER** *Warwick WW 5018* ............... | 22 | 9 wks |

**Frankie BEVERLY** – *See MAZE featuring Frankie BEVERLY*

## B52s  *US, male/female vocal/instrumental group*                            *34 wks*

| | | | |
|---|---|---|---|
| 4 Aug 79 | **B-52s** *Island ILPS 9580* ........................... | 22 | 12 wks |
| 13 Sep 80 | **WILD PLANET** *Island ILPS 9622* ................. | 18 | 4 wks |
| 11 Jul 81 | **THE PARTY MIX ALBUM** *Island IPM 1001* ........... | 36 | 5 wks |
| 27 Feb 82 | **MESOPOTAMIA** *EMI ISSP 4006* ............... | 18 | 6 wks |
| 21 May 83 | **WHAMMY!** *Island ILPS 9759* ................. | 33 | 4 wks |
| 8 Aug 87 | **BOUNCING OFF THE SATELLITES** *Island ILPS 9871* .. | 74 | 2 wks |
| 29 Jul 89 | **COSMIC THING** *Reprise WX 283* ................. | 75 | 1 wk |

## BIBLE  *UK, male vocal/instrumental group*                                  *2 wks*

| | | | |
|---|---|---|---|
| 2 Jan 88 | **EUREKA** *Cooltempo CHR 1646* ...................... | 71 | 1 wk |
| 7 Oct 89 | **THE BIBLE** *Ensign CHEN 12* ...................... | 67 | 1 wk |

## BIG AUDIO DYNAMITE
*UK, male vocal/instrumental group*                                            *41 wks*

| | | | |
|---|---|---|---|
| 16 Nov 85 | **THIS IS BIG AUDIO DYNAMITE** *CBS 26714* .......... | 27 | 27 wks |
| 8 Nov 86 | **No. 10 UPPING STREET** *CBS 450 137–1* ............. | 11 | 8 wks |
| 9 Jul 88 | **TIGHTEN UP VOL. 88** *CBS 461199 1* ............... | 33 | 3 wks |
| 16 Sep 89 | **MEGATOP PHOENIX** *CBS 465790 1* ............... | 26 | 3 wks |

## BIG BEN BANJO BAND
*UK, male instrumental group*                                                  *1 wk*

| | | | |
|---|---|---|---|
| 17 Dec 60 | **MORE MINSTREL MELODIES** *Columbia 33SX 1254* .... | 20 | 1 wk |

## BIG COUNTRY
*UK, male vocal/instrumental group*                                            *123 wks*

| | | | |
|---|---|---|---|
| 6 Aug 83 | ● **THE CROSSING** *Mercury MERH 27* ................. | 3 | 80 wks |
| 27 Oct 84 | ★ **STEELTOWN** *Mercury MERH 49* ................... | 1 | 21 wks |

| 12 Jul | 86 | ● **THE SEER** Mercury MERH 87 ...................... | 2 | 16 wks |
|---|---|---|---|---|
| 8 Oct | 88 | ● **PEACE IN OUR TIME** Mercury MERH 130 ............. | 9 | 6 wks |

## BIG DADDY KANE  US, male vocalist  3 wks

| 30 Sep | 89 | **IT'S A BIG DADDY THING**  Cold Chillin' WX 305 | 37 | 3 wks |
|---|---|---|---|---|

## BIG DISH  UK, male vocal/instrumental group  1 wk

| 11 Oct | 86 | **SWIMMER**  Virgin V 2374 ......................... | 85 | 1 wk |
|---|---|---|---|---|

**BIG ROLL BAND** – See Zoot MONEY and the BIG ROLL BAND

**BIG SOUND** – See Simon DUPREE and the BIG SOUND

## Mr. Acker BILK
### UK, male band leader, vocalist/instrumentalist – clarinet  76 wks

| 19 Mar | 60 | ● **SEVEN AGES OF ACKER**  Columbia 33SX 1205 ......... | 6 | 6 wks |
|---|---|---|---|---|
| 9 Apr | 60 | **ACKER BILK'S OMNIBUS**  Pye NJL 22 ............... | 14 | 3 wks |
| 4 Mar | 61 | **ACKER**  Columbia 33SX 1248 ................... | 17 | 1 wk |
| 1 Apr | 61 | **GOLDEN TREASURY OF BILK**  Columbia 33SX 1304 ..... | 11 | 6 wks |
| 26 May | 62 | ● **STRANGER ON THE SHORE**  Columbia 33SX 1407 ..... | 6 | 28 wks |
| 4 May | 63 | **A TASTE OF HONEY**  Columbia 33SX 1493 ............. | 17 | 4 wks |
| 9 Oct | 76 | **THE ONE FOR ME**  Pye NSPX 41052 ................ | 38 | 6 wks |
| 4 Jun | 77 | ⬤ **SHEER MAGIC**  Warwick WW 5028 ................... | 5 | 8 wks |
| 11 Nov | 78 | **EVERGREEN**  Warwick PW 5045 ................... | 17 | 14 wks |

*See also Kenny Ball, Chris Barber and Acker Bilk; Chris Barber and Acker Bilk.*

## BIRTHDAY PARTY
### Australia, male vocal/instrumental group  3 wks

| 24 Jul | 82 | **JUNKYARD**  4AD CAD 207 ...................... | 73 | 3 wks |
|---|---|---|---|---|

## Stephen BISHOP  US, male instrumentalist – piano  3 wks

| 1 Apr | 72 | **GRIEG AND SCHUMANN PIANO CONCERTOS** Philips 6500 166 .................................. | 34 | 3 wks |
|---|---|---|---|---|

## BLACK  UK, male vocalist/instrumentalist. Colin Vearncombe  27 wks

| 26 Sep | 87 | ● **WONDERFUL LIFE**  A&M AMA 5165 .............. | 3 | 23 wks |
|---|---|---|---|---|
| 29 Oct | 88 | **COMEDY**  A&M AMA 5222 ...................... | 32 | 4 wks |

## Cilla BLACK  UK, female vocalist  61 wks

| 13 Feb | 65 | ● **CILLA**  Parlophone PMC 1243 ...................... | 5 | 11 wks |
|---|---|---|---|---|
| 14 May | 66 | ● **CILLA SINGS A RAINBOW**  Parlophone PMC 7004 ...... | 4 | 15 wks |
| 13 Apr | 68 | ● **SHER-OO**  Parlophone PCS 7041 .................... | 7 | 11 wks |
| 30 Nov | 68 | **BEST OF CILLA BLACK**  Parlophone PCS 7065 .......... | 21 | 11 wks |
| 25 Jul | 70 | **SWEET INSPIRATION**  Parlophone PCS 7103 .......... | 42 | 4 wks |
| 29 Jan | 83 | **THE VERY BEST OF CILLA BLACK**  Parlophone EMTV 38 | 20 | 9 wks |

## BLACK LACE  UK, male vocal/instrumental group  26 wks

| 8 Dec | 84 | ● **PARTY PARTY – 16 GREAT PARTY ICEBREAKERS** Telstar STAR 2250 ................................ | 4 | 14 wks |
|---|---|---|---|---|
| 7 Dec | 85 | **PARTY PARTY 2**  Telstar STAR 2266 ................. | 18 | 6 wks |
| 6 Dec | 86 | **PARTY CRAZY**  Telstar STAR 2288 ................. | 58 | 6 wks |

## BLACK, ROCK and RON  *US, male rap group*  *1 wk*

| 22 Apr 89 | **STOP THE WORLD**  *Supreme SU 5* | 72 | 1 wk |
|---|---|---|---|

## BLACK SABBATH  *UK/US, male vocal/instrumental group*  *206 wks*

| 7 Mar 70 | ● **BLACK SABBATH**  *Vertigo VO 6* | 8 | 42 wks |
|---|---|---|---|
| 26 Sep 70 | ★ **PARANOID**  *Vertigo 6360 011* | 1 | 27 wks |
| 21 Aug 71 | ● **MASTER OF REALITY**  *Vertigo 6360 050* | 5 | 13 wks |
| 30 Sep 72 | ● **BLACK SABBATH VOL. 4**  *Vertigo 6360 071* | 8 | 10 wks |
| 8 Dec 73 | ● **SABBATH BLOODY SABBATH**  *WWA WWA 005* | 4 | 11 wks |
| 27 Sep 75 | ● **SABOTAGE**  *NEMS 9119 001* | 7 | 7 wks |
| 7 Feb 76 | **WE SOLD OUR SOUL FOR ROCK 'N' ROLL**  *NEMS 6641 335* | 35 | 5 wks |
| 6 Nov 76 | **TECHNICAL ECSTASY**  *Vertigo 9102 750* | 13 | 6 wks |
| 14 Oct 78 | **NEVER SAY DIE**  *Vertigo 9102 751* | 12 | 6 wks |
| 26 Apr 80 | ● **HEAVEN AND HELL**  *Vertigo 9102 752* | 9 | 22 wks |
| 5 Jul 80 | ● **BLACK SABBATH LIVE AT LAST**  *NEMS BS 001* | 5 | 15 wks |
| 27 Sep 80 | **PARANOID (re-issue)**  *NEMS NEL 6003* | 54 | 2 wks |
| 14 Nov 81 | **MOB RULES**  *Mercury 6V02119* | 12 | 14 wks |
| 22 Jan 83 | **LIVE EVIL**  *Vertigo SAB 10* | 13 | 11 wks |
| 24 Sep 83 | ● **BORN AGAIN**  *Vertigo VERL 8* | 4 | 7 wks |
| 1 Mar 86 | **SEVENTH STAR**  *Vertigo VERH 29* | 27 | 5 wks |
| 28 Nov 87 | **THE ETERNAL IDOL**  *Vertigo VERH 51* | 66 | 1 wk |
| 29 Apr 89 | **HEADLESS CROSS**  *IRS EIRSA 1002* | 31 | 2 wks |

Seventh Star *credits Black Sabbath featuring Tony Iommi.*

## BLACK UHURU
*Jamaica, male/female vocal/instrumental group*  *22 wks*

| 13 Jun 81 | **RED**  *Island ILPS 9625* | 28 | 13 wks |
|---|---|---|---|
| 22 Aug 81 | **BLACK UHURU**  *Virgin VX 1004* | 81 | 2 wks |
| 19 Jun 82 | **CHILL OUT**  *Island ILPS 9701* | 38 | 6 wks |
| 25 Aug 84 | **ANTHEM**  *Island ILPS 9773* | 90 | 1 wk |

## Band of the BLACK WATCH  *UK, military band*  *13 wks*

| 7 Feb 76 | **SCOTCH ON THE ROCKS**  *Spark SRLM 503* | 11 | 13 wks |
|---|---|---|---|

## BLACK WIDOW  *UK, male vocal/instrumental group*  *2 wks*

| 4 Apr 70 | **SACRIFICE**  *CBS 63948* | 32 | 2 wks |
|---|---|---|---|

## BLACKFOOT  *US, male vocal/instrumental group*  *22 wks*

| 18 Jul 81 | **MARAUDER**  *Atco K 50799* | 38 | 12 wks |
|---|---|---|---|
| 11 Sep 82 | **HIGHWAY SONG – BLACKFOOT LIVE**  *Atco K 50910* | 14 | 6 wks |
| 21 May 83 | **SIOGO**  *Atco 79–0080–1* | 28 | 3 wks |
| 29 Sep 84 | **VERTICAL SMILES**  *Atco 790218* | 82 | 1 wk |

**BLACKHEARTS** – *See Joan JETT and the BLACKHEARTS*

**Ritchie BLACKMORE'S RAINBOW** – *See RAINBOW*

## Howard BLAKE conducting the SINFONIA OF LONDON  *UK, conductor and orchestra*  *12 wks*

| 22 Dec 84 | **THE SNOWMAN**  *CBS 71116* | 54 | 12 wks |
|---|---|---|---|

*Narration by Bernard Cribbins.*

## BLANCMANGE  *UK, male vocal/instrumental duo*  *57 wks*

| 9 Oct 82 | **HAPPY FAMILIES**  *London SH 8552* | 30 | 38 wks |
|---|---|---|---|
| 26 May 84 | ● **MANGE TOUT**  *London SH 8554* | 8 | 17 wks |
| 26 Oct 85 | **BELIEVE YOU ME**  *London LONLP 10* | 54 | 2 wks |

The **BEACH BOYS** pose outside EMI House in London with a pretty wooden excuse for a surfboard.

**JEFF BECK** (left) and Jimmy Page (right) help celebrate electric guitar pioneer Les Paul's 72nd birthday at New York's Hard Rock Cafe.

TONY BENNETT scored with 'For Once In My Life' months before Stevie Wonder's hit version of the title song.

Debbie Harry (far right) fronted BLONDIE in an even 100 weeks on the chart in 1979.

## BLIND FAITH  *UK, male vocal/instrumental group*  10 wks

13 Sep 69 ★ **BLIND FAITH**  *Polydor 583-059* . . . . . . . . . . . . . . . . . . . . . . . . . . . . . . .  **1**  10 wks

## BLITZ  *UK, male vocal/instrumental group*  3 wks

6 Nov 82  **VOICE OF A GENERATION**  *No Future PUNK 1* . . . . . . .  **27**  3 wks

**BLIZZARD OF OZ** – *See Ozzy OSBOURNE*

**BLOCKHEADS** – *See Ian DURY and the BLOCKHEADS*

## BLODWYN PIG  *UK, male vocal/instrumental group*  11 wks

16 Aug 69 ● **AHEAD RINGS OUT**  *Island ILPS 9101* . . . . . . . . . . . . . . .  **9**  4 wks
23 Apr 70 ● **GETTING TO THIS**  *Island ILPS 9122* . . . . . . . . . . . . . . . .  **8**  7 wks

## BLONDIE  *US/UK, female/male vocal/instrumental group*  266 wks

4 Mar 78 ● **PLASTIC LETTERS**  *Chrysalis CHR 1166* . . . . . . . . . . . . .  **10**  54 wks
23 Sep 78 ★ **PARALLEL LINES**  *Chrysalis CDL 1192* . . . . . . . . . . . . . .  **1**  105 wks
10 Mar 79  **BLONDIE**  *Chrysalis CHR 1165* . . . . . . . . . . . . . . . . . . . . . .  **75**  1 wk
13 Oct 79 ★ **EAT TO THE BEAT**  *Chrysalis CDL 1225* . . . . . . . . . . . . .  **1**  38 wks
29 Nov 80 ● **AUTOAMERICAN**  *Chrysalis CDL 1290* . . . . . . . . . . . . .  **3**  16 wks
31 Oct 81 ● **BEST OF BLONDIE**  *Chrysalis CDLTV 1* . . . . . . . . . . . . .  **4**  40 wks
5 Jun 82 ● **THE HUNTER**  *Chrysalis CDL 1384* . . . . . . . . . . . . . . . . . .  **9**  12 wks

## BLOOD SWEAT AND TEARS
*US/Canada, male vocal/instrumental group*  21 wks

13 Jul 68  **CHILD IS FATHER TO THE MAN**  *CBS 63296* . . . . . . . . .  **40**  1 wk
12 Apr 69  **BLOOD SWEAT AND TEARS**  *CBS 63504* . . . . . . . . . . . .  **15**  8 wks
8 Aug 70  **BLOOD SWEAT AND TEARS 3**  *CBS 64024* . . . . . . . . . . .  **14**  12 wks

## BLOW MONKEYS  *UK, male vocal/instrumental group*  27 wks

19 Apr 86  **ANIMAL MAGIC**  *RCA PL 70910* . . . . . . . . . . . . . . . . . . . . .  **21**  8 wks
25 Apr 87  **SHE WAS ONLY A GROCER'S DAUGHTER**
 *RCA PL 71245* . . . . . . . . . . . . . . . . . . . . . . . . . . . . . . . .  **20**  8 wks
11 Feb 89  **WHOOPS! THERE GOES THE NEIGHBOURHOOD**
 *RCA PL 71858* . . . . . . . . . . . . . . . . . . . . . . . . . . . . . . . .  **46**  2 wks
26 Aug 89 ● **CHOICES**  *RCA PL 74191* . . . . . . . . . . . . . . . . . . . . . . . .  **5**  9 wks

## BLUE MURDER  *US, male vocal/instrumental group*  3 wks

6 May 89  **BLUE MURDER**  *Geffen WX 245* . . . . . . . . . . . . . . . . . . . . . .  **45**  3 wks

## BLUE NILE  *UK, male vocal/instrumental group*  6 wks

19 May 84  **A WALK ACROSS THE ROOFTOPS**  *Linn LKH 1* . . . . .  **80**  2 wks
21 Oct 89  **HATS**  *Linn LKH 2* . . . . . . . . . . . . . . . . . . . . . . . . . . . . . . . . . . .  **12**  4 wks

## BLUE OYSTER CULT
*US, male vocal/instrumental group*  40 wks

3 Jul 76  **AGENTS OF FORTUNE**  *CBS 81385* . . . . . . . . . . . . . . . . .  **26**  10 wks
4 Feb 78  **SPECTRES**  *CBS 86050* . . . . . . . . . . . . . . . . . . . . . . . . . . . . . .  **60**  1 wk
28 Oct 78  **SOME ENCHANTED EVENING**  *CBS 86074* . . . . . . . . . .  **18**  4 wks
18 Aug 79  **MIRRORS**  *CBS 86087* . . . . . . . . . . . . . . . . . . . . . . . . . . . . . . .  **46**  5 wks

| 19 Jul | 80 | **CULTOSAURUS ERECTUS** *CBS 86120* ............. | 12 | 7 wks |
| 25 Jul | 81 | **FIRE OF UNKNOWN ORIGIN** *CBS 85137* ........... | 29 | 7 wks |
| 22 May | 82 | **EXTRATERRESTRIAL LIVE** *CBS 22203* ........... | 39 | 5 wks |
| 19 Nov | 83 | **THE REVOLUTION BY NIGHT** *CBS 25686* .......... | 95 | 1 wk |

## BLUE RONDO A LA TURK
*UK, male vocal/instrumental group*                                    *2 wks*

| 6 Nov 82 | **CHEWING THE FAT** *Diable Noir V 2240* ............. | 80 | 2 wks |

## BLUEBELLS  *UK, male vocal/instrumental group*      *10 wks*

| 11 Aug 84 | **SISTERS** *London LONLP 1* ......................... | 22 | 10 wks |

## BLUES BAND  *UK, male vocal/instrumental group*       *18 wks*

| 8 Mar | 80 | **OFFICIAL BOOTLEG ALBUM** *Arista BBBP 101* ........ | 40 | 9 wks |
| 18 Oct | 80 | **READY** *Arista BB 2* ................................. | 36 | 6 wks |
| 17 Oct | 81 | **ITCHY FEET** *Arista BB 3* ........................... | 60 | 3 wks |

## BODINES  *UK, male vocal/instrumental group*       *1 wk*

| 29 Aug 87 | **PLAYED** *Pop BODL 2001* ......................... | 94 | 1 wk |

**Tim BOGERT** – *See Jeff BECK, Tim BOGERT and Carmine APPICE*

**Marc BOLAN** – *See T.REX*

## BOLSHOI  *UK, male vocal/instrumental group*       *1 wk*

| 3 Oct 87 | **LINDY'S PARTY** *Beggars Banquet BEGA 86* ......... | 100 | 1 wk |

## BOMB THE BASS  *UK, male producer. Tim Simenon*       *10 wks*

| 22 Oct 88 | **INTO THE DRAGON** *Rhythm King DOOD 1* ........... | 18 | 10 wks |

## BON JOVI  *US, male vocal/instrumental group*       *133 wks*

| 28 Apr | 84 | **BON JOVI** *Vertigo VERL 14* ......................... | 71 | 3 wks |
| 11 May | 85 | **7800° FAHRENHEIT** *Vertigo VERL 24* ............... | 28 | 12 wks |
| 20 Sep | 86 | ● **SLIPPERY WHEN WET** *Vertigo VERH 38* ........... | 6 | 80 wks |
| 1 Oct | 88 | ★ **NEW JERSEY** *Vertigo VERH 62* ..................... | 1 | 38 wks |

## Graham BOND  *UK, male vocalist/instrumentalist – keyboards*       *2 wks*

| 20 Jun 70 | **SOLID BOND** *Warner Bros. WS 3001* ................. | 40 | 2 wks |

## Gary U.S. BONDS  *US, male vocalist*       *8 wks*

| 22 Aug | 81 | **DEDICATION** *EMI America AML 3017* ............... | 43 | 3 wks |
| 10 Jul | 82 | **ON THE LINE** *EMI America AML 3022* ............... | 55 | 5 wks |

## BONEY M
*Jamaica/Montserrat/Antilles, male/female vocal group*       *130 wks*

| 23 Apr | 77 | **TAKE THE HEAT OFF ME** *Atlantic K 50314* .......... | 40 | 15 wks |
| 6 Aug | 77 | **LOVE FOR SALE** *Atlantic K 50385* ................... | 60 | 1 wk |
| 29 Jul | 78 | ★ **NIGHT FLIGHT TO VENUS** *Atlantic/Hansa K 50498* .... | 1 | 65 wks |

| 29 Sep | 79 | ★ OCEANS OF FANTASY  *Atlantic/Hansa K 50610* ........ | 1 | 18 wks |
| 12 Apr | 80 | ★ THE MAGIC OF BONEY M  *Atlantic/Hansa BMTV 1* ...... | 1 | 26 wks |
| 6 Sep | 86 | THE BEST OF 10 YEARS  *Stylus SMR 621* ............ | 35 | 5 wks |

## BONFIRE  *Germany, male vocal/instrumental group*  1 wk

| 21 Oct | 89 | POINT BLANK  *MSA ZL 74249* ..................... | 74 | 1 wk |

## Graham BONNET  *UK, male vocalist*  3 wks

| 7 Nov | 81 | LINE UP  *Mercury 6302151* ...................... | 62 | 3 wks |

**BONNIE** – *See DELANEY and BONNIE and FRIENDS*

# BONZO DOG DOO-DAH BAND
*UK, male vocal/instrumental group*  4 wks

| 18 Jan | 69 | DOUGHNUT IN GRANNY'S GREENHOUSE  *Liberty LBS 83158* ............................... | 40 | 1 wk |
| 30 Aug | 69 | TADPOLES  *Liberty LBS 83257* ...................... | 36 | 1 wk |
| 22 Jun | 74 | THE HISTORY OF THE BONZOS  *United Artists UAD 60071* .......................... | 41 | 2 wks |

# BOOGIE DOWN PRODUCTIONS  *US, male rapper*  7 wks

| 18 Jan | 88 | BY ALL MEANS NECESSARY  *Jive HIP 63* ........... | 38 | 3 wks |
| 22 Jul | 89 | GHETTO MUSIC  *Jive HIP 80* ..................... | 32 | 4 wks |

# BOOKER T. and the MG'S  *US, male instrumental group*  5 wks

| 25 Jul | 64 | GREEN ONIONS  *London HAK 8182* .................. | 11 | 4 wks |
| 11 Jul | 70 | McLEMORE AVENUE  *Stax SXATS 1031* ............ | 70 | 1 wk |

# BOOMTOWN RATS  *Ireland, male vocal/instrumental group*  93 wks

| 17 Sep | 77 | BOOMTOWN RATS  *Ensign ENVY 1* .................. | 18 | 11 wks |
| 8 Jul | 78 | ● TONIC FOR THE TROOPS  *Ensign ENVY 3* ........... | 8 | 44 wks |
| 3 Nov | 79 | ● THE FINE ART OF SURFACING  *Ensign ENROX 11* .... | 7 | 26 wks |
| 24 Jan | 81 | ● MONDO BONGO  *Mercury 6359 042* ................ | 6 | 7 wks |
| 3 Apr | 82 | V DEEP  *Mercury 6359 082* ...................... | 64 | 5 wks |

## Pat BOONE  *US, male vocalist*  12 wks

| 22 Nov | 58 | ● STARDUST  *London HAD 2127* ..................... | 10 | 1 wk |
| 28 May | 60 | HYMNS WE HAVE LOVED  *London HAD 2228* ........ | 12 | 2 wks |
| 25 Jun | 60 | HYMNS WE LOVE  *London HAD 2092* ............ | 14 | 1 wk |
| 24 Apr | 76 | PAT BOONE ORIGINALS  *ABC ABSD 301* ........... | 16 | 8 wks |

**BOOTZILLA ORCHESTRA** – *See Malcolm McLAREN*

## BOSTON  *US, male vocal/instrumental group*  43 wks

| 5 Feb | 77 | BOSTON  *Epic EPC 81611* .......................... | 11 | 20 wks |
| 9 Sep | 78 | ● DON'T LOOK BACK  *Epic EPC 86057* .............. | 9 | 10 wks |
| 4 Apr | 81 | BOSTON  *Epic EPC 32038* .......................... | 58 | 2 wks |
| 18 Oct | 86 | THIRD STAGE  *MCA MCG 6017* ................... | 37 | 11 wks |

*Both eponymous albums are different.*

## Judy BOUCHER  *UK, female vocalist*  1 wk

| 25 Apr | 87 | CAN'T BE WITH YOU TONIGHT  *Orbitone OLP 024* ... | 95 | 1 wk |

## BOW WOW WOW
*UK, female/male vocal/instrumental group*                    *38 wks*

| | | | | |
|---|---|---|---|---|
| 24 Oct | 81 | **SEE JUNGLE! SEE JUNGLE! GO JOIN YOUR GANG YEAH CITY ALL OVER! GO APE CRAZY** *RCA RCALP 0027 3000* | 26 | 32 wks |
| 7 Aug | 82 | **I WANT CANDY** *EMI EMC 3416* | 26 | 6 wks |

## David BOWIE  *UK, male vocalist*                    *829 wks*

| | | | | |
|---|---|---|---|---|
| 1 Jul | 72 | ● **THE RISE AND FALL OF ZIGGY STARDUST AND THE SPIDERS FROM MARS** *RCA Victor SF 8287* | 5 | 106 wks |
| 23 Sep | 72 | ● **HUNKY DORY** *RCA Victor SF 8244* | 3 | 69 wks |
| 29 Nov | 72 | **SPACE ODDITY** *RCA Victor LSP 4813* | 17 | 37 wks |
| 29 Nov | 72 | **THE MAN WHO SOLD THE WORLD** *RCA Victor LSP 4816* | 26 | 22 wks |
| 5 May | 73 | ★ **ALADDIN SANE** *RCA Victor RS 1001* | 1 | 47 wks |
| 3 Nov | 73 | ★ **PIN-UPS** *RCA Victor RS 1003* | 1 | 21 wks |
| 8 Jun | 74 | ★ **DIAMOND DOGS** *RCA Victor APL1 0576* | 1 | 17 wks |
| 16 Nov | 74 | ● **DAVID LIVE** *RCA Victor APL 2 0771* | 2 | 12 wks |
| 5 Apr | 75 | ● **YOUNG AMERICANS** *RCA Victor RS 1006* | 2 | 12 wks |
| 7 Feb | 76 | ● **STATION TO STATION** *RCA Victor APLI 1327* | 5 | 16 wks |
| 12 Jun | 76 | ● **CHANGESONEBOWIE** *RCA Victor RS 1055* | 2 | 28 wks |
| 29 Jan | 77 | ● **LOW** *RCA Victor PL 12030* | 2 | 18 wks |
| 29 Oct | 77 | ● **HEROES** *RCA Victor PL 12522* | 3 | 18 wks |
| 14 Oct | 78 | ● **STAGE** *RCA Victor PL 02913* | 5 | 10 wks |
| 9 Jun | 79 | ● **LODGER** *RCA BOW LP 1* | 4 | 17 wks |
| 27 Sep | 80 | ★ **SCARY MONSTERS AND SUPER CREEPS** *RCA BOW LP 2* | 1 | 32 wks |
| 10 Jan | 81 | ● **VERY BEST OF DAVID BOWIE** *K-Tel NE 1111* | 3 | 20 wks |
| 17 Jan | 81 | **HUNKY DORY (re-issue)** *RCA International INTS 5064* | 32 | 51 wks |
| 31 Jan | 81 | **THE RISE AND FALL OF ZIGGY STARDUST AND THE SPIDERS FROM MARS (re-issue)** *RCA International INTS 5063* | 33 | 62 wks |
| 28 Nov | 81 | **CHANGESTWOBOWIE** *RCA BOW LP 3* | 24 | 17 wks |
| 6 Mar | 82 | **ALADDIN SANE (re-issue)** *RCA International INTS 5067* | 49 | 24 wks |
| 14 Jan | 83 | **RARE** *RCA PL 45406* | 34 | 11 wks |
| 23 Apr | 83 | ★ **LETS DANCE** *EMI America AML 3029* | 1 | 56 wks |
| 30 Apr | 83 | **PIN-UPS (re-issue)** *RCA International INTS 5236* | 57 | 15 wks |
| 30 Apr | 83 | **THE MAN WHO SOLD THE WORLD (re-issue)** *RCA International INTS 5237* | 64 | 8 wks |
| 14 May | 83 | **DIAMOND DOGS (re-issue)** *RCA International INTS 5068* | 60 | 14 wks |
| 11 Jun | 83 | **HEROES (re-issue)** *RCA International INTS 5066* | 75 | 8 wks |
| 11 Jun | 83 | **LOW (re-issue)** *RCA International INTS 5065* | 85 | 5 wks |
| 20 Aug | 83 | **GOLDEN YEARS** *RCA BOWLP 4* | 33 | 5 wks |
| 5 Nov | 83 | **ZIGGY STARDUST – THE MOTION PICTURE** *RCA PL 84862* | 17 | 6 wks |
| 28 Apr | 84 | **FAME AND FASHION (ALL TIME GREATEST HITS)** *RCA PL 84919* | 40 | 6 wks |
| 19 May | 84 | **LOVE YOU TILL TUESDAY** *Deram BOWIE 1* | 53 | 4 wks |
| 6 Oct | 84 | ★ **TONIGHT** *EMI America DB 1* | 1 | 19 wks |
| 2 May | 87 | ● **NEVER LET ME DOWN** *EMI America AMLS 3117* | 6 | 16 wks |

## BOXCAR WILLIE  *US, male vocalist*                    *12 wks*

| | | | | |
|---|---|---|---|---|
| 31 May | 80 | ● **KING OF THE ROAD** *Warwick WW 5084* | 5 | 12 wks |

## Max BOYCE  *UK, male vocalist/comedian*                    *105 wks*

| | | | | |
|---|---|---|---|---|
| 5 Jul | 75 | **LIVE AT TREORCHY** *One Up OU 2033* | 21 | 32 wks |
| 1 Nov | 75 | ★ **WE ALL HAD DOCTORS' PAPERS** *EMI MB 101* | 1 | 17 wks |
| 20 Nov | 76 | ● **THE INCREDIBLE PLAN** *EMI MB 102* | 9 | 12 wks |
| 7 Jan | 78 | **THE ROAD AND THE MILES** *EMI MB 103* | 50 | 3 wks |
| 11 Mar | 78 | **LIVE AT TREORCHY (re-issue)** *One Up OU 54043* | 42 | 6 wks |
| 27 May | 78 | ● **I KNOW COS I WAS THERE** *EMI MAX 1001* | 6 | 14 wks |
| 13 Oct | 79 | **NOT THAT I'M BIASED** *EMI MAX 1002* | 27 | 13 wks |
| 15 Nov | 80 | **ME AND BILLY WILLIAMS** *EMI MAX 1003* | 37 | 8 wks |

## BOY GEORGE  *UK, male vocalist*  *6 wks*

| 27 Jun 87 | **SOLD**  *Virgin V 2430*  .............................. | 29 | 6 wks |

## BOY MEETS GIRL  *US, male/female vocal/instrumental duo*  *1 wk*

| 4 Feb 89 | **REEL LIFE**  *RCA PL 88414*  ........................ | 74 | 1 wk |

## BOYS  *UK, male vocal/instrumental group*  *1 wk*

| 1 Oct 77 | **THE BOYS**  *NEMS NEL 6001*  ...................... | 50 | 1 wk |

## Billy BRAGG  *UK, male vocalist*  *67 wks*

| 21 Jan 84 | **LIFE'S A RIOT WITH SPY VS SPY** | | |
| | *Go! Discs UTILITY UTIL 1* ......................... | 30 | 30 wks |
| 20 Oct 84 | **BREWING UP WITH BILLY BRAGG** | | |
| | *Go! Discs AGOLP 4*  ................................ | 16 | 21 wks |
| 4 Oct 86 | ● **TALKING WITH THE TAXMAN ABOUT POETRY** | | |
| | *Go! Discs AGOLP 6* ............................. | 8 | 8 wks |
| 13 Jun 87 | **BACK TO BASICS**  *Go! Discs AGOLP 8* ................ | 37 | 4 wks |
| 1 Oct 88 | **WORKERS PLAYTIME**  *Go! Discs AGOLP 15* .......... | 17 | 4 wks |

## Wilfred BRAMBELL and Harry H. CORBETT
*UK, male comic duo*  *34 wks*

| 23 Mar 63 | ● **STEPTOE AND SON**  *Pye NPL 18081* ............... | 4 | 28 wks |
| 11 Mar 64 | **STEPTOE AND SON**  *Pye GGL 0217* ................. | 14 | 5 wks |
| 14 Mar 64 | **MORE JUNK**  *Pye NPL 18090* ...................... | 19 | 1 wk |

*First two albums are different.*

## BRAND X  *UK, male vocal/instrumental group*  *6 wks*

| 21 May 77 | **MOROCCAN ROLL**  *Charisma CAS 1126* .............. | 37 | 5 wks |
| 11 Sep 82 | **IS THERE ANYTHING ABOUT?**  *CBS 85967* .......... | 93 | 1 wk |

## Laura BRANIGAN  *US, female vocalist*  *18 wks*

| 18 Aug 84 | **SELF CONTROL**  *Atlantic 780147* ..................... | 16 | 14 wks |
| 24 Aug 85 | **HOLD ME**  *Atlantic 78–1265–1* ....................... | 64 | 4 wks |

## BRASS CONSTRUCTION
*US, male vocal/instrumental group*  *12 wks*

| 20 Mar 76 | ● **BRASS CONSTRUCTION**  *United Artists UAS 29923* .... | 9 | 11 wks |
| 30 Jun 84 | **RENEGADES**  *Capitol EJ 24 0160* .................... | 94 | 1 wk |

## BREAD  *US, male vocal/instrumental group*  *179 wks*

| 26 Sep 70 | **ON THE WATERS**  *Elektra 2469–005* .................. | 34 | 5 wks |
| 18 Mar 72 | ● **BABY I'M A WANT-YOU**  *Elektra K 42100* ............ | 9 | 19 wks |
| 28 Oct 72 | ● **BEST OF BREAD**  *Elektra K 42115* ............... | 7 | 100 wks |
| 27 Jul 74 | **THE BEST OF BREAD VOL. 2**  *Elektra K 42161* ........ | 48 | 1 wk |
| 29 Jan 77 | **LOST WITHOUT YOUR LOVE**  *Elektra K 52044* ....... | 17 | 6 wks |
| 5 Nov 77 | ★ **THE SOUND OF BREAD**  *Elektra K 52062* ............. | 1 | 46 wks |
| 28 Nov 87 | **THE VERY BEST OF BREAD**  *Telstar STAR 2303* ....... | 84 | 2 wks |

## BREAK MACHINE  *US, male vocal/dance group*  *16 wks*

| 9 Jun 84 | **BREAK MACHINE**  *Record Shack SOHO LP 3* .......... | 17 | 16 wks |

## BREATHE UK, male vocal/instrumental group — 5 wks

| 8 Oct 88 | ALL THAT JAZZ Siren SRNLP 12 ................... | 22 | 5 wks |
|---|---|---|---|

## Adrian BRETT UK, male instrumentalist – flute — 11 wks

| 10 Nov 79 | ECHOES OF GOLD Warwick WW 5062 .............. | 19 | 11 wks |
|---|---|---|---|

## Paul BRETT UK, male instrumentalist – guitar — 7 wks

| 19 Jul 80 | ROMANTIC GUITAR K-Tel ONE 1079 ............. | 24 | 7 wks |
|---|---|---|---|

## Edie BRICKELL and the NEW BOHEMIANS
US, female/male vocal/instrumental group — 17 wks

| 4 Feb 89 | SHOOTING RUBBERBANDS AT THE STARS Geffen WX 215 ................................. | 25 | 17 wks |
|---|---|---|---|

## BRIGHOUSE AND RASTRICK BRASS BAND
UK, male brass band — 11 wks

| 28 Jan 78 | ● FLORAL DANCE Logo 1001 ...................... | 10 | 11 wks |
|---|---|---|---|

## Sarah BRIGHTMAN UK, female vocalist — 2 wks

| 17 Jun 89 | THE SONGS THAT GOT AWAY Really Useful 839116 1 .. | 48 | 2 wks |
|---|---|---|---|

## BRILLIANT UK, male/female vocal/instrumental group — 1 wk

| 20 Sep 86 | KISS THE LIPS OF LIFE Food BRILL 1 .............. | 83 | 1 wk |
|---|---|---|---|

## Johnny BRISTOL US, male vocalist — 7 wks

| 5 Oct 74 | HANG ON IN THERE BABY MGM 2315 303 .......... | 12 | 7 wks |
|---|---|---|---|

## June BRONHILL and Thomas ROUND
Australia/UK, female/male vocal duo — 1 wk

| 18 Jun 60 | LILAC TIME HMV CLP 1248 ...................... | 17 | 1 wk |
|---|---|---|---|

## BRONSKI BEAT UK, male vocal/instrumental group — 65 wks

| 20 Oct 84 | ● THE AGE OF CONSENT Forbidden Fruit BITLP 1 ....... | 4 | 53 wks |
|---|---|---|---|
| 21 Sep 85 | HUNDREDS AND THOUSANDS Forbidden Fruit BITLP 2 | 24 | 6 wks |
| 10 May 86 | TRUTHDARE DOUBLEDARE Forbidden Fruit BITLP 3 | 18 | 6 wks |

## Elkie BROOKS UK, female vocalist — 208 wks

| 18 Jun 77 | TWO DAYS AWAY A&M AMLH 68409 .............. | 16 | 20 wks |
|---|---|---|---|
| 13 May 78 | SHOOTING STAR A&M AMLH 64695 ............. | 20 | 13 wks |
| 13 Oct 79 | LIVE AND LEARN A&M AMLH 68509 ............. | 34 | 6 wks |
| 14 Nov 81 | ● PEARLS A&M ELK 1981 ........................ | 2 | 79 wks |
| 13 Nov 82 | ● PEARLS II A&M ELK 1982 ...................... | 5 | 25 wks |
| 14 Jul 84 | MINUTES A&M AML 68565 .................... | 35 | 7 wks |
| 8 Dec 84 | SCREEN GEMS EMI SCREEN 1 ................. | 35 | 11 wks |
| 6 Dec 86 | ● NO MORE THE FOOL Legend LMA 1 .............. | 5 | 23 wks |
| 27 Dec 86 | ● THE VERY BEST OF ELKIE BROOKS Telstar STAR 2284 | 10 | 18 wks |
| 11 Jun 88 | BOOKBINDER'S KID Legend LMA 3 ................ | 57 | 3 wks |
| 18 Nov 89 | INSPIRATIONS Telstar STAR 2354 .................. | 58 | 3 wks |

The touring philosophy of
**BILLY BRAGG** was to get
back to basics.

**BROS** fared better as a tri
than as a du

# Nigel BROOKS SINGERS
*UK, male/female vocal choir*                                    *17 wks*

| | | | | |
|---|---|---|---|---|
| 29 Nov 75 | ● **SONGS OF JOY**   *K-Tel NE 706* ....................... | **5** | 16 wks |
| 5 Jun 76 | **20 ALL TIME EUROVISION FAVOURITES** | | |
| | *K-Tel NE 712* ................................ | **44** | 1 wk |

# BROS   *UK, male vocal/instrumental duo*                       *64 wks*

| | | | | |
|---|---|---|---|---|
| 9 Apr 88 | ● **PUSH**   *CBS 460629 1* ............................... | **2** | 54 wks |
| 28 Oct 89 | ● **THE TIME**   *CBS 465918 1* .......................... | **4†** | 10 wks |

*Act was a group for first album.*

# BROTHER BEYOND   *UK, male vocal/instrumental group*          *24 wks*

| | | | | |
|---|---|---|---|---|
| 26 Nov 88 | ● **GET EVEN**   *Parlophone PCS 7327* ..................... | **9** | 23 wks |
| 25 Nov 89 | **TRUST**   *Parlophone PCS 7337* ........................ | **60** | 1 wk |

# BROTHERHOOD OF MAN
*UK, male/female vocal group*                                   *40 wks*

| | | | | |
|---|---|---|---|---|
| 24 Apr 76 | **LOVE AND KISSES FROM**   *Pye NSPL 18490* .......... | **20** | 8 wks |
| 12 Aug 78 | **B FOR BROTHERHOOD**   *Pye NSPL 18567* .......... | **18** | 9 wks |
| 7 Oct 78 | ● **BROTHERHOOD OF MAN**   *K-Tel BML 7980* .......... | **6** | 15 wks |
| 29 Nov 80 | **SING 20 NUMBER ONE HITS**   *Warwick WW 5087* ....... | **14** | 8 wks |

# BROTHERS JOHNSON
*US, male vocal/instrumental duo*                               *22 wks*

| | | | | |
|---|---|---|---|---|
| 19 Aug 78 | **BLAM!!**   *A & M AMLH 64714* ....................... | **48** | 8 wks |
| 23 Feb 80 | **LIGHT UP THE NIGHT**   *A & M AMLK 63716* .......... | **22** | 12 wks |
| 18 Jul 81 | **WINNERS**   *A & M AMLK 63724* ..................... | **42** | 2 wks |

# Edgar BROUGHTON BAND
*UK, male vocal/instrumental group*                             *6 wks*

| | | | | |
|---|---|---|---|---|
| 20 Jun 70 | **SING BROTHER SING**   *Harvest SHVL 772* ........... | **18** | 4 wks |
| 5 Jun 71 | **THE EDGAR BROUGHTON BAND** | | |
| | *Harvest SHVL 791* ............................... | **28** | 2 wks |

# Crazy World Of Arthur BROWN
*UK, male vocal/instrumental group*                             *16 wks*

| | | | | |
|---|---|---|---|---|
| 6 Jul 68 | ● **CRAZY WORLD OF ARTHUR BROWN**   *Track 612005* | **2** | 16 wks |

# Bobby BROWN   *US, male vocalist*                             *51 wks*

| | | | | |
|---|---|---|---|---|
| 28 Jan 89 | ● **DON'T BE CRUEL**   *MCA MCF 3425* ................. | **3** | 40 wks |
| 5 Aug 89 | **KING OF STAGE**   *MCA MCL 1886* ................... | **40** | 6 wks |
| 2 Dec 89 | **DANCE!...YA KNOW IT!**   *MCA MCG 6074* .......... | **26†** | 5 wks |

# Dennis BROWN   *Jamaica, male vocalist*                       *6 wks*

| | | | | |
|---|---|---|---|---|
| 26 Jun 82 | **LOVE HAS FOUND ITS WAY**   *A & M AMLH 64886* ..... | **72** | 6 wks |

# James BROWN   *US, male vocalist*                             *29 wks*

| | | | | |
|---|---|---|---|---|
| 18 Oct 86 | **GRAVITY**   *Scotti Bros. SCT 57018* .................... | **85** | 3 wks |

| | | | |
|---|---|---|---|
| 2 Jan 88 | **BEST OF JAMES BROWN – GODFATHER OF SOUL** | | |
| | K-Tel NE 1376 ................................... | 17 | 21 wks |
| 25 Jun 88 | **I'M REAL** Scotti Brothers POLD 5230 ................. | 27 | 5 wks |

## Joe BROWN  UK, male vocalist/instrumentalist – guitar  *47 wks*

| | | | |
|---|---|---|---|
| 1 Sep 62 | ● **A PICTURE OF YOU** Pye Golden Guinea GGL 0146 ....... | 3 | 39 wks |
| 25 May 63 | **JOE BROWN – LIVE** Piccadilly NPL 38006 ............. | 14 | 8 wks |

## Sam BROWN  UK, female vocalist  *18 wks*

| | | | |
|---|---|---|---|
| 11 Mar 89 | ● **STOP** A & M AMA 5195 ......................... | 4 | 18 wks |

## Jackson BROWNE  US, male vocalist  *33 wks*

| | | | |
|---|---|---|---|
| 4 Dec 76 | **THE PRETENDER** Asylum K 53048 ................. | 26 | 5 wks |
| 21 Jan 78 | **RUNNING ON EMPTY** Asylum K 53070 ........... | 28 | 7 wks |
| 12 Jul 80 | **HOLD OUT** Asylum K 52226 ................... | 44 | 5 wks |
| 13 Aug 83 | **LAWYERS IN LOVE** Asylum 96–0268–1 .......... | 37 | 7 wks |
| 8 Mar 86 | **LIVES IN THE BALANCE** Asylum EKT 31 ............ | 36 | 7 wks |
| 17 Jun 89 | **WORLD IN MOTION** Elektra EKT 50 .............. | 39 | 2 wks |

## Dave BRUBECK QUARTET
### US, male instrumental group  *17 wks*

| | | | |
|---|---|---|---|
| 25 Jun 60 | **TIME OUT** Fontana TFL 5085 ..................... | 11 | 1 wk |
| 7 Apr 62 | **TIME FURTHER OUT** Fontana TFL 5161 ............. | 12 | 16 wks |

*Second album just credited to Dave Brubeck.*

## Jack BRUCE
### UK, male vocalist/instrumentalist – bass  *9 wks*

| | | | |
|---|---|---|---|
| 27 Sep 69 | ● **SONGS FOR A TAILOR** Polydor 583–058 ............. | 6 | 9 wks |

**BRUFORD** – See ANDERSON BRUFORD WAKEMAN HOWE

## Peabo BRYSON and Roberta FLACK
### US, male/female vocal duo  *10 wks*

| | | | |
|---|---|---|---|
| 17 Sep 83 | **BORN TO LOVE** Capitol EST 7122841 ............... | 15 | 10 wks |

*See also Roberta Flack.*

## BUCKS FIZZ  UK, male/female vocal group  *80 wks*

| | | | |
|---|---|---|---|
| 8 Aug 81 | **BUCKS FIZZ** RCA RCALP 5050 ................... | 14 | 28 wks |
| 18 May 82 | ● **ARE YOU READY?** RCA RCALP 8000 ........... | 10 | 23 wks |
| 19 Mar 83 | **HAND CUT** RCA RCALP 6100 ................... | 17 | 13 wks |
| 3 Dec 83 | **GREATEST HITS** RCA RCA PL 70022 ............ | 25 | 13 wks |
| 24 Nov 84 | **I HEAR TALK** RCA PL 70397 .................. | 66 | 2 wks |
| 13 Dec 86 | **THE WRITING ON THE WALL** Polydor POHL 30 ...... | 89 | 1 wk |

## Harold BUDD/Liz FRASER/Robin GUTHRIE/ Simon RAYMOND
### UK, male/female vocal/instrumental group  *2 wks*

| | | | |
|---|---|---|---|
| 22 Nov 86 | **THE MOON AND THE MELODIES** 4AD CAD 611 .... | 46 | 2 wks |

## BUDGIE  UK, male vocal/instrumental group  *10 wks*

| | | | |
|---|---|---|---|
| 8 Jun 74 | **IN FOR THE KILL** MCA MCF 2546 .................. | 29 | 3 wks |

| | | | |
|---|---|---|---|
| 27 Sep 75 | **BANDOLIER** *MCA MCF 2723* .................. | 36 | 4 wks |
| 31 Oct 81 | **NIGHT FLIGHT** *RCA RCALP 6003* ................. | 68 | 2 wks |
| 23 Oct 82 | **DELIVER US FROM EVIL** *RCA RCALP 6054* ........ | 62 | 1 wk |

## BUGGLES  *UK, male vocal/instrumental duo*                    *6 wks*

| | | | |
|---|---|---|---|
| 16 Feb 80 | **THE AGE OF PLASTIC** *Island ILPS 9585* ............ | 27 | 6 wks |

**BUNNYMEN** – *See ECHO and the BUNNYMEN*

## Eric BURDON and WAR
*UK, male vocalist and US, male vocal/instrumental group*          *2 wks*

| | | | |
|---|---|---|---|
| 3 Oct 70 | **ERIC BURDON DECLARES WAR** *Polydor 2310–041* .... | 50 | 2 wks |

## Jean-Jacques BURNEL
*UK, male vocalist/instrumentalist – bass guitar*                 *5 wks*

| | | | |
|---|---|---|---|
| 21 Apr 79 | **EUROMAN COMETH** *United Artists UAG 30214* ........ | 40 | 5 wks |

*See also Dave Greenfield and Jean-Jacques Burnel.*

## Kate BUSH  *UK, female vocalist*                     *243 wks*

| | | | |
|---|---|---|---|
| 11 Mar 78 ● | **THE KICK INSIDE** *EMI EMC 3223* ................. | 3 | 70 wks |
| 25 Nov 78 ● | **LIONHEART** *EMI EMA 787* ......................... | 6 | 36 wks |
| 20 Sep 80 ★ | **NEVER FOR EVER** *EMI EMA 7964* ............ | 1 | 23 wks |
| 25 Sep 82 ● | **THE DREAMING** *EMI EMC 3419* ............... | 3 | 9 wks |
| 28 Sep 85 ★ | **HOUNDS OF LOVE** *EMI KAB 1* ............... | 1 | 51 wks |
| 22 Nov 86 ★ | **THE WHOLE STORY** *EMI KBTV 1* ............. | 1 | 44 wks |
| 28 Oct 89 ● | **THE SENSUAL WORLD** *EMI EMD 1010* ............ | 2† | 10 wks |

## Jonathan BUTLER
*South Africa, male vocalist/instrumentalist – guitar*            *14 wks*

| | | | |
|---|---|---|---|
| 12 Sep 87 | **JONATHAN BUTLER** *Jive HIP 46* ................. | 12 | 11 wks |
| 4 Feb 89 | **MORE THAN FRIENDS** *Jive HIP 70* ................ | 29 | 3 wks |

## BUZZCOCKS  *UK, male vocal/instrumental group*          *23 wks*

| | | | |
|---|---|---|---|
| 25 Mar 78 | **ANOTHER MUSIC IN A DIFFERENT KITCHEN** | | |
| | *United Artists UAG 30159* .......................... | 15 | 11 wks |
| 7 Oct 78 | **LOVE BITES** *United Artists UAG 30184* ............... | 13 | 9 wks |
| 6 Oct 79 | **A DIFFERENT KIND OF TENSION** | | |
| | *United Artists UAG 30260* ......................... | 26 | 3 wks |

## BY ALL MEANS  *US, male/female vocal group*          *1 wk*

| | | | |
|---|---|---|---|
| 16 Jul 88 | **BY ALL MEANS** *Fourth & Broadway BRLP 520* .......... | 80 | 1 wk |

## Max BYGRAVES  *UK, male vocalist*                     *176 wks*

| | | | |
|---|---|---|---|
| 23 Sep 72 ● | **SING ALONG WITH MAX** *Pye NSPL 18361* .......... | 4 | 44 wks |
| 2 Dec 72 | **SING ALONG WITH MAX VOL. 2** *Pye NSPL 18383* .... | 11 | 23 wks |
| 5 May 73 ● | **SINGALONGAMAX VOL. 3** *Pye NSPL 18401* .......... | 5 | 30 wks |
| 29 Sep 73 ● | **SINGALONGAMAX VOL. 4** *Pye NSPL 18410* .......... | 7 | 12 wks |
| 15 Dec 73 | **SINGALONGPARTY SONG** *Pye NSPL 18419* .......... | 15 | 6 wks |
| 12 Oct 74 | **YOU MAKE ME FEEL LIKE SINGING A SONG** | | |
| | *Pye NSPL 18436* ................................ | 39 | 3 wks |
| 7 Dec 74 | **SINGALONGAXMAS** *Pye NSPL 18439* .............. | 21 | 6 wks |
| 13 Nov 76 ● | **100 GOLDEN GREATS** *Ronco RTDX 2019* .......... | 3 | 21 wks |
| 28 Oct 78 | **LINGALONGAMAX** *Ronco RPL 2033* ................. | 39 | 5 wks |
| 16 Dec 78 | **THE SONG AND DANCE MEN** *Pye NSPL 18574* ....... | 67 | 1 wk |
| 19 Aug 89 ● | **SINGALONGAWARYEARS** *Parkfield Music PMLP 5001* | 5† | 19 wks |
| 25 Nov 89 | **SINGALONGAWARYEARS VOLUME 2** .............. | | |
| | *Parkfield Music PMLP 5006* ......................... | 33† | 6 wks |

**Charlie BYRD** – *See Stan GETZ and Charlie BYRD*

## Donald BYRD  *US, male vocalist/instrumentalist – trumpet*          *3 wks*

| | | | |
|---|---|---|---|
| 10 Oct 81 | **LOVE BYRD**  *Elektra K 52301* ...................... | 70 | 3 wks |

## BYRDS  *US, male vocal/instrumental group*          *42 wks*

| | | | |
|---|---|---|---|
| 28 Aug 65 | ● **MR. TAMBOURINE MAN**  *CBS BPG 62571* .......... | 7 | 12 wks |
| 9 Apr 66 | **TURN, TURN, TURN**  *CBS BPG 62652* .............. | 11 | 5 wks |
| 1 Oct 66 | **5TH DIMENSION**  *CBS BPG 62783* ................ | 27 | 2 wks |
| 22 Apr 67 | **YOUNGER THAN YESTERDAY**  *CBS SBPG 62988* ... | 37 | 4 wks |
| . 4 May 68 | **THE NOTORIOUS BYRD BROTHERS**  *CBS 63169* .... | 12 | 11 wks |
| 24 May 69 | **DR. BYRDS AND MR. HYDE**  *CBS 63545* ......... | 15 | 1 wk |
| 14 Feb 70 | **BALLAD OF EASY RIDER**  *CBS 63795* ............ | 41 | 1 wk |
| 28 Nov 70 | **UNTITLED**  *CBS 66253* ...................... | 11 | 4 wks |
| 14 Apr 73 | **BYRDS**  *Asylum SYLA 8754* ................ | 31 | 1 wk |
| 19 May 73 | **HISTORY OF THE BYRDS**  *CBS 68242* ............. | 47 | 1 wk |

## David BYRNE  *UK, male vocalist*          *2 wks*

| | | | |
|---|---|---|---|
| 21 Oct 89 | **REI MOMO**  *Warner Bros. WX 319* .................... | 52 | 2 wks |

# C

**Montserrat CABALLE** – *See Freddie MERCURY and Montserrat CABALLE*

## CABARET VOLTAIRE  *UK, male vocal/instrumental group*  *11 wks*

| | | | |
|---|---|---|---|
| 26 Jun 82 | **2 X 45**  *Rough Trade ROUGH 42* ...................... | 98 | 1 wk |
| 13 Aug 83 | **THE CRACKDOWN**  *Some Bizzare CV 1* .............. | 31 | 5 wks |
| 10 Nov 84 | **MICRO-PHONIES**  *Some Bizzare CV 2* ................ | 69 | 1 wk |
| 3 Aug 85 | **DRINKING GASOLINE**  *Some Bizzare CVM 1* .......... | 71 | 2 wks |
| 26 Oct 85 | **THE COVENANT, THE SWORD AND THE ARM OF THE LORD**  *Some Bizzare CV 3* ....................... | 57 | 2 wks |

## CACTUS WORLD NEWS
*Ireland, male vocal/instrumental group*          *2 wks*

| | | | |
|---|---|---|---|
| 24 May 86 | **URBAN BEACHES**  *MCA MCG 6005* ................. | 56 | 2 wks |

## J.J. CALE  *US, male vocalist/instrumentalist – guitar*          *22 wks*

| | | | |
|---|---|---|---|
| 2 Oct 76 | **TROUBADOUR**  *Island ISA 5011* .................... | 53 | 1 wk |
| 25 Aug 79 | **5**  *Shelter ISA 5018* ................................. | 40 | 6 wks |
| 21 Feb 81 | **SHADES**  *Shelter ISA 5021* ........................ | 44 | 7 wks |
| 20 Mar 82 | **GRASSHOPPER**  *Shelter IFA 5022* ................... | 36 | 5 wks |
| 24 Sep 83 | **#8**  *Mercury MERL 22* .............................. | 47 | 3 wks |

## Maria CALLAS  *Greece, female operatic soprano*          *7 wks*

| | | | |
|---|---|---|---|
| 20 Jun 87 | **THE MARIA CALLAS COLLECTION**  *Stylus SMR 732* .. | 50 | 7 wks |

## CAMEL  *UK, male vocal/instrumental group*          *47 wks*

| | | | |
|---|---|---|---|
| 24 May 75 | **THE SNOW GOOSE**  *Decca SKL 5207* ................. | 22 | 13 wks |
| 17 Apr 76 | **MOON MADNESS**  *Decca TXS 115* .................... | 15 | 6 wks |
| 17 Sep 77 | **RAIN DANCES**  *Decca TXS 124* ..................... | 20 | 8 wks |
| 14 Oct 78 | **BREATHLESS**  *Decca TXS 132* .................... | 26 | 1 wk |
| 27 Oct 79 | **I CAN SEE YOUR HOUSE FROM HERE**  *Decca TXS 137* | 45 | 3 wks |
| 31 Jan 81 | **NUDE**  *Decca SKL 5323* ............................ | 34 | 7 wks |
| 15 May 82 | **THE SINGLE FACTOR**  *Decca SKL 5328* ............. | 57 | 5 wks |
| 21 Apr 84 | **STATIONARY TRAVELLER**  *Decca SKL 5334* ......... | 57 | 4 wks |

## CAMEO   *US, male vocal/instrumental group*                     *47 wks*

| 10 Aug 85 |   | SINGLE LIFE | *Club JABH 11* | ........................ | 66 | 12 wks |
|---|---|---|---|---|---|---|
| 18 Oct 86 | ● | WORD UP | *Club JABH 19* | ........................ | 7 | 34 wks |
| 26 Nov 88 |   | MACHISMO | *Club 836002 1* | ........................ | 86 | 1 wk |

## Glen CAMPBELL   *US, male vocalist*                     *183 wks*

| 31 Jan 70 |   | GLEN CAMPBELL LIVE | *Capitol SB 21444* | ............ | 16 | 14 wks |
|---|---|---|---|---|---|---|
| 30 May 70 |   | TRY A LITTLE KINDNESS | *Capitol ESW 389* | ......... | 37 | 10 wks |
| 12 Dec 70 |   | THE GLEN CAMPBELL ALBUM | *Capitol ST 22493* | ..... | 16 | 5 wks |
| 27 Nov 71 | ● | GREATEST HITS | *Capitol ST 21885* | ................. | 8 | 113 wks |
| 25 Oct 75 |   | RHINESTONE COWBOY | *Capitol E-SW 11430* | ........ | 38 | 9 wks |
| 20 Nov 76 | ★ | 20 GOLDEN GREATS | *Capitol EMTV 2* | ............ | 1 | 27 wks |
| 23 Apr 77 |   | SOUTHERN NIGHTS | *Capitol E-ST 11601* | ............ | 51 | 1 wk |
| 22 Jul 89 |   | THE COMPLETE GLEN CAMPBELL | *Stylus SMR 979* | .. | 47 | 4 wks |

*See also Bobbie Gentry and Glen Campbell.*

## CANNED HEAT   *US, male vocal/instrumental group*                     *40 wks*

| 29 Jun 68 | ● | BOOGIE WITH CANNED HEAT | *Liberty LBL 83103* | .... | 5 | 21 wks |
|---|---|---|---|---|---|---|
| 14 Feb 70 | ● | CANNED HEAT COOKBOOK | *Liberty LBS 83303* | | 8 | 12 wks |
| 4 Jul 70 |   | CANNED HEAT '70 CONCERT | *Liberty LBS 83333* | ..... | 15 | 3 wks |
| 10 Oct 70 |   | FUTURE BLUES | *Liberty LBS 83364* | ................. | 27 | 4 wks |

## Freddy CANNON   *US, male vocalist*                     *11 wks*

| 27 Feb 60 | ★ | THE EXPLOSIVE FREDDY CANNON | *Top Rank 25/108* | . | 1 | 11 wks |
|---|---|---|---|---|---|---|

## CAPTAIN and TENNILLE
*US, male instrumentalist – keyboards and female vocalist*                     *6 wks*

| 22 Mar 80 | MAKE YOUR MOVE | *Casablanca CAL 2060* | ............. | 33 | 6 wks |
|---|---|---|---|---|---|

## CAPTAIN BEEFHEART and his MAGIC BAND
*US, male vocal/instrumental group*                     *16 wks*

| 6 Dec 69 | TROUT MASK REPLICA | *Straight STS 1053* | ............ | 21 | 1 wk |
|---|---|---|---|---|---|
| 23 Jan 71 | LICK MY DECALS OFF BABY | *Straight STS 1063* | ........ | 20 | 10 wks |
| 29 May 71 | MIRROR MAN | *Buddah 2365 002* | ..................... | 49 | 1 wk |
| 19 Feb 72 | THE SPOTLIGHT KID | *Reprise K 44162* | ............. | 44 | 2 wks |
| 18 Sep 82 | ICE CREAM FOR CROW | *Virgin V 2337* | ............. | 90 | 2 wks |

## CAPTAIN SENSIBLE   *UK, male vocalist*                     *3 wks*

| 11 Sep 82 | WOMEN AND CAPTAIN FIRST | *A&M AMLH 68548* | .. | 64 | 3 wks |
|---|---|---|---|---|---|

## CARAVAN   *UK, male vocal/instrumental group*                     *2 wks*

| 30 Aug 75 | CUNNING STUNTS | *Decca SKL 5210* | ................. | 50 | 1 wk |
|---|---|---|---|---|---|
| 15 May 76 | BLIND DOG AT ST. DUNSTAN'S | *BTM BTM 1007* | ..... | 53 | 1 wk |

## Belinda CARLISLE   *US, female vocalist*                     *59 wks*

| 2 Jan 88 | ● | HEAVEN ON EARTH | *Virgin V 2496* | ................. | 4 | 50 wks |
|---|---|---|---|---|---|---|
| 4 Nov 89 | ● | RUNAWAY HORSES | *Virgin V 2599* | ................. | 4† | 9 wks |

## CARMEL   *UK, female/male vocal/instrumental group*                     *11 wks*

| 1 Oct 83 | CARMEL | *Red Flame RFM 9* | .......................... | 94 | 2 wks |
|---|---|---|---|---|---|
| 24 Mar 84 | THE DRUM IS EVERYTHING | *London SH 8555* | ........ | 19 | 8 wks |
| 27 Sep 86 | THE FALLING | *London LONLP 17* | ................... | 88 | 1 wk |

## Eric CARMEN    US, male vocalist                                    1 wk

| 15 May 76 | **ERIC CARMEN**    *Arista ARTY 120*   . . . . . . . . . . . . . . . . . . . | 58 | 1 wk |
|---|---|---|---|

## Kim CARNES    US, female vocalist                                 16 wks

| 20 Jun 81 | **MISTAKEN IDENTITY**    *EMI America AML 3018*   . . . . . . . . | 26 | 16 wks |
|---|---|---|---|

## CARPENTERS    US, male/female vocal/instrumental duo        473 wks

| 23 Jan 71 | **CLOSE TO YOU**    *A & M AMLS 998*   . . . . . . . . . . . . . . . . . . | 23 | 82 wks |
|---|---|---|---|
| 30 Oct 71 | **THE CARPENTERS**    *A & M AMLS 63502*   . . . . . . . . . . . . | 12 | 36 wks |
| 15 Apr 72 | **TICKET TO RIDE**    *A & M AMLS 64342*   . . . . . . . . . . . . . | 20 | 3 wks |
| 23 Sep 72 | **A SONG FOR YOU**    *A & M AMLS 63511*   . . . . . . . . . . . | 13 | 37 wks |
| 7 Jul 73 | ● **NOW AND THEN**    *A & M AMLH 63519*   . . . . . . . . . . . | 2 | 65 wks |
| 26 Jan 74 | ★ **THE SINGLES 1969–1973**    *A & M AMLH 63601*   . . . | 1 | 116 wks |
| 28 Jun 75 | ★ **HORIZON**    *A & M AMLK 64530*   . . . . . . . . . . . . . . . . | 1 | 27 wks |
| 23 Aug 75 | **TICKET TO RIDE (re-issue)**    *Hamlet AMLP 8001*   . . . . . . . | 35 | 2 wks |
| 3 Jul 76 | ● **A KIND OF HUSH**    *A & M AMLK 64581*   . . . . . . . . . . | 3 | 15 wks |
| 8 Jan 77 | **LIVE AT THE PALLADIUM**    *A & M   AMLS 68403*   . . . . . . | 28 | 3 wks |
| 8 Oct 77 | **PASSAGE**    *A & M AMLK 64703*   . . . . . . . . . . . . . . . . . . . | 12 | 12 wks |
| 2 Dec 78 | ● **SINGLES 1974–78**    *A & M AMLT 19748*   . . . . . . . . . . | 2 | 20 wks |
| 27 Jun 81 | **MADE IN AMERICA**    *A & M AMLK 63723*   . . . . . . . . . . | 12 | 10 wks |
| 15 Oct 83 | ● **VOICE OF THE HEART**    *A & M AMLX 64954*   . . . . . . . . . | 6 | 19 wks |
| 20 Oct 84 | ● **YESTERDAY ONCE MORE**    *EMI/A & M SING 1*   . . . . . . | 10 | 26 wks |

## Vikki CARR    US, female vocalist                                  12 wks

| 22 Jul 67 | **WAY OF TODAY**    *Liberty SLBY 1331*   . . . . . . . . . . . . . . . | 31 | 2 wks |
|---|---|---|---|
| 12 Aug 67 | **IT MUST BE HIM**    *Liberty LBS 83037*   . . . . . . . . . . . . . | 12 | 10 wks |

## José CARRERAS    Spain, male vocalist                              6 wks

| 1 Oct 88 | **JOSE CARRERAS COLLECTION**    *Stylus SMR 860*   . . . . . | 90 | 4 wks |
|---|---|---|---|
| 23 Dec 89 | **JOSE CARRERAS SINGS ANDREW LLOYD WEBBER** | | |
|  | *WEA WX 325*   . . . . . . . . . . . . . . . . . . . . . . . . . . . . . . . . . . | 42† | 2 wks |

## Jasper CARROTT    UK, male comedian                               66 wks

| 18 Oct 75 | ● **RABBITS ON AND ON**    *DJM DJLPS 462*   . . . . . . . . . . . . . | 10 | 7 wks |
|---|---|---|---|
| 6 Nov 76 | **CARROTT IN NOTTS**    *DJM DJF 20482*   . . . . . . . . . . . . . | 56 | 1 wk |
| 25 Nov 78 | **THE BEST OF JASPER CARROTT**    *DJM DJF 20549*   . . . . | 38 | 13 wks |
| 20 Oct 79 | **THE UNRECORDED JASPER CARROTT** | | |
|  | *DJM DJF 20560*   . . . . . . . . . . . . . . . . . . . . . . . . . . . . . | 19 | 15 wks |
| 19 Sep 81 | **BEAT THE CARROTT**    *DJM DJF 20575*   . . . . . . . . . . . . | 13 | 16 wks |
| 25 Dec 82 | **CARROTT'S LIB**    *DJM DJF 20580*   . . . . . . . . . . . . . . . . | 80 | 3 wks |
| 19 Nov 83 | **THE STUN (CARROTT TELLS ALL)**    *DJF 20582*   . . . . . . | 57 | 8 wks |
| 7 Feb 87 | **COSMIC CARROTT**    *Portrait LAUGH 1*   . . . . . . . . . . . . . | 66 | 3 wks |

## CARS    US, male vocal/instrumental group                         72 wks

| 2 Dec 78 | **CARS**    *Elektra K 52088*   . . . . . . . . . . . . . . . . . . . . . . . . . | 29 | 15 wks |
|---|---|---|---|
| 7 Jul 79 | **CANDY-O**    *Elektra K 52148*   . . . . . . . . . . . . . . . . . . . . | 30 | 6 wks |
| 6 Oct 84 | **HEARTBEAT CITY**    *Elektra 960296*   . . . . . . . . . . . . . . | 25 | 30 wks |
| 9 Nov 85 | **THE CARS GREATEST HITS**    *Elektra EKT 25*   . . . . . . . . . | 27 | 19 wks |
| 5 Sep 87 | **DOOR TO DOOR**    *Elektra EKT 42*   . . . . . . . . . . . . . . . . | 72 | 2 wks |

## Johnny CASH    US, male vocalist                                  285 wks

| 23 Jul 66 | **EVERYBODY LOVES A NUT**    *CBS BPG 62717*   . . . . . . . | 28 | 1 wk |
|---|---|---|---|
| 4 May 68 | **FROM SEA TO SHINING SEA**    *CBS 62972*   . . . . . . . . . . | 40 | 1 wk |
| 6 Jul 68 | **OLD GOLDEN THROAT**    *CBS 63316*   . . . . . . . . . . . . . | 37 | 2 wks |
| 24 Aug 68 | ● **FOLSOM PRISON**    *CBS 63308*   . . . . . . . . . . . . . . . . . . | 8 | 53 wks |

| | | | | |
|---|---|---|---|---|
| 23 Aug 69 | ● JOHNNY CASH AT SAN QUENTIN *CBS 63629* | | 2 | 114 wks |
| 4 Oct 69 | GREATEST HITS VOL. 1 *CBS 63062* | | 23 | 25 wks |
| 7 Mar 70 | ● HELLO I'M JOHNNY CASH *CBS 63796* | | 6 | 16 wks |
| 15 Aug 70 | ● WORLD OF JOHNNY CASH *CBS 66237* | | 5 | 31 wks |
| 12 Dec 70 | THE JOHNNY CASH SHOW *CBS 64089* | | 18 | 6 wks |
| 18 Sep 71 | MAN IN BLACK *CBS 64331* | | 18 | 7 wks |
| 13 Nov 71 | JOHNNY CASH *Hallmark SHM 739* | | 43 | 2 wks |
| 20 May 72 | ● A THING CALLED LOVE *CBS 64898* | | 8 | 11 wks |
| 14 Oct 72 | STAR PORTRAIT *CBS 67201* | | 16 | 7 wks |
| 10 Jul 76 | ONE PIECE AT A TIME *CBS 81416* | | 49 | 3 wks |
| 9 Oct 76 | THE BEST OF JOHNNY CASH *CBS 10000* | | 48 | 2 wks |
| 2 Sep 78 | ITCHY FEET *CBS 10009* | | 36 | 4 wks |

## CASHFLOW *US, male vocal/instrumental group*       *3 wks*

| | | | |
|---|---|---|---|
| 28 Jun 86 | CASHFLOW *Club JABH 17* | 33 | 3 wks |

## CASHMERE *US, male vocal/instrumental group*       *5 wks*

| | | | |
|---|---|---|---|
| 2 Mar 85 | CASHMERE *Fourth & Broadway BRLP 503* | 63 | 5 wks |

## David CASSIDY *US, male vocalist*       *94 wks*

| | | | |
|---|---|---|---|
| 20 May 72 | ● CHERISH *Bell BELLS 210* | 2 | 43 wks |
| 24 Feb 73 | ● ROCK ME BABY *Bell BELLS 218* | 2 | 20 wks |
| 24 Nov 73 | ★ DREAMS ARE NOTHIN' MORE THAN WISHES | | |
| | *Bell BELLS 231* | 1 | 13 wks |
| 3 Aug 74 | ● CASSIDY LIVE *Bell BELLS 243* | 9 | 7 wks |
| 9 Aug 75 | THE HIGHER THEY CLIMB \ *RCA Victor RS 1012* | 22 | 5 wks |
| 8 Jun 85 | ROMANCE *Arista 206 983* | 20 | 6 wks |

## Nick CAVE featuring the BAD SEEDS
*Australia, male vocalist with male vocal/instrumental group*       *6 wks*

| | | | |
|---|---|---|---|
| 2 Jun 84 | FROM HER TO ETERNITY *Mute STUMM 17* | 40 | 3 wks |
| 15 Jun 85 | THE FIRST BORN IS DEAD *Mute STUMM 21* | 53 | 1 wk |
| 30 Aug 86 | KICKING AGAINST THE PRICKS *Mute STUMM 28* | 89 | 1 wk |
| 1 Oct 88 | TENDER PREY *Mute STUMM 52* | 67 | 1 wk |

## C.C.S. *UK, male vocal/instrumental group*       *5 wks*

| | | | |
|---|---|---|---|
| 8 Apr 72 | C.C.S. *RAK SRAK 503* | 23 | 5 wks |

## CENTRAL LINE *UK, male vocal/instrumental group*       *5 wks*

| | | | |
|---|---|---|---|
| 13 Feb 82 | BREAKING POINT *Mercury MERA 001* | 64 | 5 wks |

## CERRONE *France, male producer/multi-instrumentalist*       *1 wk*

| | | | |
|---|---|---|---|
| 30 Sep 78 | SUPERNATURE *Atlantic K 50431* | 60 | 1 wk |

## A CERTAIN RATIO *UK, male vocal/instrumental group*       *3 wks*

| | | | |
|---|---|---|---|
| 30 Jan 82 | SEXTET *Factory FACT 55* | 53 | 3 wks |

## Peter CETERA *US, male vocalist*       *4 wks*

| | | | |
|---|---|---|---|
| 13 Sep 86 | SOLITUDE/SOLITAIRE *Full Moon 925474-1* | 56 | 4 wks |

## Richard CHAMBERLAIN *US, male vocalist* — *8 wks*

| | | | |
|---|---|---|---|
| 16 Mar 63 | ● **RICHARD CHAMBERLAIN SINGS** *MGM C 923* ...... | 8 | 8 wks |

## CHAMELEONS *UK, male vocal/instrumental group* — *4 wks*

| | | | |
|---|---|---|---|
| 25 May 85 | **WHAT DOES ANYTHING MEAN? BASICALLY** *Statik STAT LP 22* ................................. | 60 | 2 wks |
| 20 Sep 86 | **STRANGE TIMES** *Geffen 924 119–1* ................. | 44 | 2 wks |

## CHAMPAIGN *US, male/female vocal/instrumental group* — *4 wks*

| | | | |
|---|---|---|---|
| 27 Jun 81 | **HOW 'BOUT US** *CBS 84927* ....................... | 38 | 4 wks |

## CHANGE *US, male/female vocal/instrumental group* — *23 wks*

| | | | |
|---|---|---|---|
| 19 May 84 | **CHANGE OF HEART** *WEA WX 5* .................. | 34 | 17 wks |
| 27 Apr 85 | **TURN ON THE RADIO** *Cooltempo CHR 1504* ......... | 39 | 6 wks |

## Michael CHAPMAN *UK, male vocalist* — *1 wk*

| | | | |
|---|---|---|---|
| 21 Mar 70 | **FULLY QUALIFIED SURVIVOR** *Harvest SHVL 764* .... | 45 | 1 wk |

## Tracy CHAPMAN *US, female vocalist* — *87 wks*

| | | | |
|---|---|---|---|
| 21 May 88 | ★ **TRACY CHAPMAN** *Elektra EKT 44* ................. | 1 | 75 wks |
| 14 Oct 89 | ★ **CROSSROADS** *Elektra EKT 61* ..................... | 1† | 12 wks |

## CHAQUITO ORCHESTRA
*UK, orchestra arranged and conducted by Johnny Gregory* — *2 wks*

| | | | |
|---|---|---|---|
| 24 Feb 68 | **THIS CHAQUITO** *Fontana SFXL 50* .................. | 36 | 1 wk |
| 4 Mar 72 | **THRILLER THEMES** *Philips 6308 087* ............... | 48 | 1 wk |

*First album credited to Chaquito and Quedo Brass.*

## CHARGE GBH *UK, male vocal/instrumental group* — *6 wks*

| | | | |
|---|---|---|---|
| 14 Aug 82 | **CITY BABY ATTACKED BY RATS** *Clay CLAYLP 4* .... | 17 | 6 wks |

## CHARLENE *US, female vocalist* — *4 wks*

| | | | |
|---|---|---|---|
| 17 Jul 82 | **I'VE NEVER BEEN TO ME** *Motown STML 12171* ....... | 43 | 4 wks |

## Ray CHARLES *US, male vocalist/instrumentalist – piano* — *39 wks*

| | | | |
|---|---|---|---|
| 28 Jul 62 | ● **MODERN SOUNDS IN COUNTRY AND WESTERN MUSIC** *HMV CLP 1580* ......................... | 6 | 16 wks |
| 23 Feb 63 | **MODERN SOUNDS IN COUNTRY AND WESTERN MUSIC VOL. 2** *HMV CLP 1613* .................... | 15 | 5 wks |
| 20 Jul 63 | **GREATEST HITS** *HMV CLP 1626* ................. | 16 | 5 wks |
| 5 Oct 68 | **GREATEST HITS VOL. 2** *Stateside SSL 10241* .......... | 24 | 8 wks |
| 19 Jul 80 | **HEART TO HEART – 20 HOT HITS** *London RAY TV 1* . | 29 | 5 wks |

## Tina CHARLES *UK, female vocalist* — *7 wks*

| | | | |
|---|---|---|---|
| 3 Dec 77 | **HEART 'N' SOUL** *CBS 82180* ...................... | 35 | 7 wks |

**KATE BUSH** is one of the female soloists with the most number one albums (three) along with Madonna and Barbra Streisand.

**RICHARD CHAMBERLAIN** (right), shown as Dr. Kildare with television co-star Raymond Massey, shot up the charts in 1963.

**FREDDY CANNON** (left) had the first number one rock 'n' roll album.

## CHAS and DAVE  *UK, male vocal/instrumental duo*                           *96 wks*

| | | | | |
|---|---|---|---|---|
| 5 Dec 81 | **CHAS AND DAVE'S CHRISTMAS JAMBOREE BAG** | | | |
| | *Warwick WW 5166* ..................... | 25 | 15 wks |
| 17 Apr 82 | **MUSTN'T GRUMBLE** *Rockney 909* .............. | 35 | 11 wks |
| 8 Jan 83 | **JOB LOT** *Rockney ROC 910* ................... | 59 | 15 wks |
| 15 Oct 83 ● | **CHAS AND DAVE'S KNEES UP – JAMBOREE BAG NO 2** | | | |
| | *Rockney ROC 911* .................. | 7 | 17 wks |
| 11 Aug 84 | **WELL PLEASED** *Rockney ROC 912* ........ | 27 | 10 wks |
| 17 Nov 84 | **CHAS AND DAVE'S GREATEST HITS** *Rockney ROC 913* | 16 | 10 wks |
| 15 Dec 84 | **CHAS AND DAVE'S CHRISTMAS JAMBOREE BAG** | | | |
| | **(re-issue)** *Rockney ROCM 001* ............ | 87 | 1 wk |
| 9 Nov 85 | **JAMBOREE BAG NUMBER 3** *Rockney ROC 914* ....... | 15 | 13 wks |
| 13 Dec 86 | **CHAS AND DAVE'S CHRISTMAS CAROL ALBUM** | | | |
| | *Telstar STAR 2293* ........................ | 37 | 4 wks |

## CHEAP TRICK  *US, male vocal/instrumental group*                           *15 wks*

| | | | | |
|---|---|---|---|---|
| 24 Feb 79 | **CHEAP TRICK AT BUDOKAN** *Epic EPC 86083* ....... | 29 | 9 wks |
| 6 Oct 79 | **DREAM POLICE** *Epic EPC 83522* ................. | 41 | 5 wks |
| 5 Jun 82 | **ONE ON ONE** *Epic EPC 85740* ................. | 95 | 1 wk |

## Chubby CHECKER  *US, male vocalist*                           *7 wks*

| | | | | |
|---|---|---|---|---|
| 27 Jan 62 | **TWIST WITH CHUBBY CHECKER** *Columbia 33SX 1315* | 13 | 4 wks |
| 3 Mar 62 | **FOR TWISTERS ONLY** *Columbia 33SX 1341* ......... | 17 | 3 wks |

## CHER  *US, female vocalist*                           *56 wks*

| | | | | |
|---|---|---|---|---|
| 2 Oct 65 ● | **ALL I REALLY WANT TO DO** *Liberty LBY 3058* ....... | 7 | 9 wks |
| 7 May 66 | **SONNY SIDE OF CHER** *Liberty LBY 3072* ........... | 11 | 11 wks |
| 16 Jan 88 | **CHER** *Geffen WX 132* ...................... | 26 | 22 wks |
| 22 Jul 89 | **HEART OF STONE** *Geffen WX 262* .............. | 15† | 14 wks |

*See also Sonny and Cher.*

## CHERELLE  *US, female vocalist*                           *9 wks*

| | | | | |
|---|---|---|---|---|
| 25 Jan 86 | **HIGH PRIORITY** *Tabu TBU 26699* ............... | 17 | 9 wks |

## Neneh CHERRY  *US, female vocalist*                           *24 wks*

| | | | | |
|---|---|---|---|---|
| 17 Jun 89 ● | **RAW LIKE SUSHI** *Circa CIRCA 8* ................ | 2† | 24 wks |

## CHIC  *US, male/female vocal/instrumental group*                           *44 wks*

| | | | | |
|---|---|---|---|---|
| 3 Feb 79 ● | **C'EST CHIC** *Atlantic K 50565* ................. | 2 | 24 wks |
| 18 Aug 79 | **RISQUE** *Atlantic K 50634* ................. | 29 | 12 wks |
| 15 Dec 79 | **THE BEST OF CHIC** *Atlantic K 50686* ........... | 30 | 8 wks |

*See also Chic and Sister Sledge.*

## CHIC and SISTER SLEDGE
*US, male/female vocal/instrumental group and female vocal group*                           *3 wks*

| | | | | |
|---|---|---|---|---|
| 5 Dec 87 | **FREAK OUT** *Telstar STAR 2319* ............ | 72 | 3 wks |

*See also Chic; Sister Sledge.*

## CHICAGO  *US, male vocal/instrumental group*                           *98 wks*

| | | | | |
|---|---|---|---|---|
| 27 Sep 69 ● | **CHICAGO TRANSIT AUTHORITY** *CBS 66221* ....... | 9 | 14 wks |
| 4 Apr 70 ● | **CHICAGO** *CBS 66233* .......................... | 6 | 27 wks |

| | | | |
|---|---|---|---|
| 3 Apr 71 | **CHICAGO 3** *CBS 66260* .......................... | 31 | 1 wk |
| 30 Sep 72 | **CHICAGO 5** *CBS 69108* .......................... | 24 | 2 wks |
| 23 Oct 76 | **CHICAGO X** *CBS 86010* .......................... | 21 | 11 wks |
| 2 Oct 82 | **CHICAGO 16** *Full Moon K 99235* ............... | 44 | 9 wks |
| 4 Dec 82 | **LOVE SONGS** *TV Records TVA 6* ............... | 42 | 8 wks |
| 1 Dec 84 | **CHICAGO 17** *Full Moon 925060* ............... | 24 | 20 wks |
| 25 Nov 89 | **THE HEART OF CHICAGO** *Warner Bros. WX 328* ...... | 15† | 6 wks |

*First album credited to Chicago Transit Authority.*

## CHICKEN SHACK
*UK, male/female vocal/instrumental group*     *9 wks*

| | | | |
|---|---|---|---|
| 22 Jul 68 | **40 BLUE FINGERS FRESHLY PACKED** *Blue Horizon 7–63203* .......................... | 12 | 8 wks |
| 15 Feb 69 | ● **OK KEN?** *Blue Horizon 7–63209* .................... | 9 | 1 wk |

**CHIEFTAINS** – *See James GALWAY and the CHIEFTAINS; Van MORRISON and the CHIEFTAINS*

## Toni CHILDS *US, female vocalist*     *1 wk*

| | | | |
|---|---|---|---|
| 29 Apr 89 | **UNION** *A & M AMA 5175* .......................... | 73 | 1 wk |

## CHINA CRISIS *UK, male vocal/instrumental group*     *64 wks*

| | | | |
|---|---|---|---|
| 20 Nov 82 | **DIFFICULT SHAPES AND PASSIVE RHYTHMS** *Virgin V 2243* .......................... | 21 | 18 wks |
| 12 Nov 83 | **WORKING WITH FIRE AND STEEL – POSSIBLE POP SONGS VOL 2** *Virgin V 2286* .................. | 20 | 16 wks |
| 11 May 85 | ● **FLAUNT THE IMPERFECTION** *Virgin V 2342* ........ | 9 | 22 wks |
| 6 Dec 86 | **WHAT PRICE PARADISE** *Virgin V 2410* ............. | 63 | 6 wks |
| 13 May 89 | **DIARY OF A HOLLOW HORSE** *Virgin V 2567* ........ | 58 | 2 wks |

## CHORDS *UK, male vocal/instrumental group*     *3 wks*

| | | | |
|---|---|---|---|
| 24 May 80 | **SO FAR AWAY** *Polydor POLS 1019* .................. | 30 | 3 wks |

## CHRISTIANS *UK, male vocal/instrumental group*     *68 wks*

| | | | |
|---|---|---|---|
| 31 Oct 87 | ● **THE CHRISTIANS** *Island ILPS 9876* ................ | 2 | 68 wks |

## Tony CHRISTIE *UK, male vocalist*     *10 wks*

| | | | |
|---|---|---|---|
| 24 Jul 71 | **I DID WHAT I DID FOR MARIA** *MCA MKPS 2016* ..... | 37 | 1 wk |
| 17 Feb 73 | **WITH LOVING FEELING** *MCA MUPS 468* ........... | 19 | 2 wks |
| 31 May 75 | **TONY CHRISTIE – LIVE** *MCA MCF 2703* ............ | 33 | 3 wks |
| 6 Nov 76 | **BEST OF TONY CHRISTIE** *MCA MCF 2769* ......... | 28 | 4 wks |

## CHRON GEN *UK, male vocal/instrumental group*     *3 wks*

| | | | |
|---|---|---|---|
| 3 Apr 82 | **CHRONIC GENERATION** *Secret SEC 3* .............. | 53 | 3 wks |

## Sir Winston CHURCHILL *UK, male statesman*     *8 wks*

| | | | |
|---|---|---|---|
| 13 Feb 65 | ● **THE VOICE OF CHURCHILL** *Decca LXT 6200* ........ | 6 | 8 wks |

## CICCONE YOUTH
*US, male/female vocal/instrumental group*     *1 wk*

| | | | |
|---|---|---|---|
| 4 Feb 89 | **THE WHITEY ALBUM** *Blast First BFFP 28* ........... | 63 | 1 wk |

*See also Sonic Youth – they are the same band.*

## CINDERELLA  *US, male vocal/instrumental group*  *6 wks*

| 23 Jul | 88 | **LONG COLD WINTER**  *Vertigo VERH 59* | 30 | 6 wks |

**CITY BEAT BAND** – *See PRINCE CHARLES and the CITY BEAT BAND*

## CLANCY BROTHERS and Tommy MAKEM
*Ireland, male vocal/instrumental group and male vocalist*  *5 wks*

| 16 Apr | 66 | **ISN'T IT GRAND BOYS**  *CBS BPG 62674* | 22 | 5 wks |

## CLANNAD  *Ireland, male/female vocal/instrumental group*  *116 wks*

| 2 Apr | 83 | **MAGICAL RING**  *RCA RCALP 6072* | 26 | 21 wks |
| 12 May | 84 | **LEGEND (MUSIC FROM ROBIN OF SHERWOOD)** *RCA PL 70188* | 15 | 40 wks |
| 2 Jun | 84 | **MAGICAL RING (re-issue)**  *RCA PL 70003* | 91 | 1 wk |
| 26 Oct | 85 | **MACALLA**  *RCA PL 70894* | 33 | 24 wks |
| 7 Nov | 87 | **SIRIUS**  *RCA PL 71513* | 34 | 4 wks |
| 11 Feb | 89 | **ATLANTIC REALM**  *BBC REB 727* | 41 | 3 wks |
| 6 May | 89 | ● **PASTPRESENT**  *RCA PL 74074* | 5 | 23 wks |

## Eric CLAPTON  *UK, male vocalist/instrumentalist – guitar*  *208 wks*

| 5 Sep | 70 | **ERIC CLAPTON**  *Polydor 2383–021* | 17 | 8 wks |
| 26 Aug | 72 | **HISTORY OF ERIC CLAPTON**  *Polydor 2659 2478 027* | 20 | 6 wks |
| 24 Aug | 74 | ● **461 OCEAN BOULEVARD**  *RSO 2479 118* | 3 | 19 wks |
| 12 Apr | 75 | **THERE'S ONE IN EVERY CROWD**  *RSO 2479 132* | 15 | 8 wks |
| 13 Sep | 75 | **E.C. WAS HERE**  *RSO 2394 160* | 14 | 6 wks |
| 11 Sep | 76 | ● **NO REASON TO CRY**  *RSO 2479 179* | 8 | 7 wks |
| 26 Nov | 77 | **SLOWHAND**  *RSO 2479 201* | 23 | 13 wks |
| 9 Dec | 78 | **BACKLESS**  *RSO RSD 5001* | 18 | 12 wks |
| 10 May | 80 | ● **JUST ONE NIGHT**  *RSO RSDX 2* | 3 | 12 wks |
| 7 Mar | 81 | **ANOTHER TICKET**  *RSO RSD 5008* | 18 | 8 wks |
| 24 Apr | 82 | **TIME PIECES – THE BEST OF ERIC CLAPTON** *RSO RSD 5010* | 20 | 13 wks |
| 19 Feb | 83 | **MONEY & CIGARETTES**  *Duck W 3773* | 13 | 17 wks |
| 9 Jun | 84 | **BACKTRACKIN'**  *Starblend ERIC 1* | 29 | 16 wks |
| 23 Mar | 85 | ● **BEHIND THE SUN**  *Duck 92–5166–1* | 8 | 14 wks |
| 6 Dec | 86 | ● **AUGUST**  *Duck WX 71* | 3 | 42 wks |
| 18 Nov | 89 | ● **JOURNEYMAN**  *Duck WX 322* | 3† | 7 wks |

*See also Eric Clapton and Cream; John Mayall and Eric Clapton.*

## Eric CLAPTON and CREAM  *UK, male vocalist/ instrumentalist – guitar and male vocal/instrumental group*  *79 wks*

| 26 Sep | 87 | ● **THE CREAM OF ERIC CLAPTON** *Polydor ECTV 1* | 3 | 79 wks |

*See also Eric Clapton; Cream.*

## Petula CLARK  *UK, female vocalist*  *43 wks*

| 30 Jul | 66 | **I COULDN'T LIVE WITHOUT YOUR LOVE** *Pye NPL 18148* | 11 | 10 wks |
| 4 Feb | 67 | **HIT PARADE**  *Pye NPL 18159* | 18 | 13 wks |
| 18 Feb | 67 | **COLOUR MY WORLD**  *Pye NSPL 18171* | 16 | 9 wks |
| 7 Oct | 67 | **THESE ARE MY SONGS**  *Pye NSPL 18197* | 38 | 3 wks |
| 6 Apr | 68 | **THE OTHER MAN'S GRASS IS ALWAYS GREENER** *Pye NSPL 18211* | 37 | 1 wk |
| 5 Feb | 77 | **20 ALL TIME GREATEST**  *K-Tel NE 945* | 18 | 7 wks |

## Dave CLARK FIVE
*UK, male vocal/instrumental group*      *26 wks*

| | | |
|---|---|---|
| 18 Apr 64 ● **A SESSION WITH THE DAVE CLARK FIVE** | | |
|     *Columbia 33SX 1598* .................................. | **3** | 8 wks |
| 14 Aug 65 ● **CATCH US IF YOU CAN**   *Columbia 33SX 1756* ......... | **8** | 8 wks |
| 4 Mar 78 ● **25 THUMPING GREAT HITS**   *Polydor POLTV 7* ........ | **7** | 10 wks |

**Louis CLARK** – *See ROYAL PHILHARMONIC ORCHESTRA*

## John Cooper CLARKE
*UK, male vocalist*      *9 wks*

| | | |
|---|---|---|
| 19 Apr 80 | **SNAP CRACKLE AND BOP**   *Epic EPC 84083* .......... | **26** | 7 wks |
| 5 Jun 82 | **ZIP STYLE METHOD**   *Epic EPC 85667* .............. | **97** | 2 wks |

## Stanley CLARKE
*US, male vocalist/instrumentalist – bass*      *2 wks*

| | | |
|---|---|---|
| 12 Jul 80 | **ROCKS PEBBLES AND SAND**   *Epic EPC 84342* ........ | **42** | 2 wks |

## CLASH   *UK, male vocal/instrumental group*      *95 wks*

| | | |
|---|---|---|
| 30 Apr 77 | **CLASH**   *CBS 82000* ............................. | **12** | 16 wks |
| 25 Nov 78 ● **GIVE 'EM ENOUGH ROPE**   *CBS 82431* ............. | **2** | 14 wks |
| 22 Dec 79 ● **LONDON CALLING**   *CBS CLASH 3* ............. | **9** | 20 wks |
| 20 Dec 80 | **SANDINISTA**   *CBS FSLN 1* ..................... | **19** | 9 wks |
| 22 May 82 ● **COMBAT ROCK**   *CBS FMLN 2* ................. | **2** | 23 wks |
| 16 Nov 85 | **CUT THE CRAP**   *CBS 26601* ................... | **16** | 3 wks |
| 2 Apr 88 ● **THE STORY OF THE CLASH**   *CBS 460244 1* .......... | **7** | 10 wks |

## CLASSIX NOUVEAUX
*UK, male vocal/instrumental group*      *6 wks*

| | | |
|---|---|---|
| 30 May 81 | **NIGHT PEOPLE**   *Liberty LBG 30325* ................. | **66** | 2 wks |
| 24 Apr 82 | **LA VERITE**   *Liberty LBG 30346* ...................... | **44** | 4 wks |

## Richard CLAYDERMAN
*France, male instrumentalist – piano*      *169 wks*

| | | |
|---|---|---|
| 13 Nov 82 ● **RICHARD CLAYDERMAN**   *Decca SKL 5329* .......... | **2** | 64 wks |
| 8 Oct 83 | **THE MUSIC OF RICHARD CLAYDERMAN** | | |
|     *Decca SKL 5333* .................................. | **21** | 28 wks |
| 24 Nov 84 | **THE MUSIC OF LOVE**   *Decca SKL 5340* ............. | **28** | 21 wks |
| 1 Dec 84 | **CHRISTMAS**   *Decca SKL 5337* ...................... | **53** | 5 wks |
| 23 Nov 85 | **THE CLASSIC TOUCH**   *Decca SKL 5343* ............. | **17** | 18 wks |
| 22 Nov 86 | **HOLLYWOOD AND BROADWAY**   *Decca SKL 5344* .... | **28** | 9 wks |
| 28 Nov 87 | **SONGS OF LOVE**   *Decca SKL 5345* .................. | **19** | 13 wks |
| 3 Dec 88 | **A LITTLE NIGHT MUSIC**   *Decca 8281251* ............. | **52** | 5 wks |
| 25 Nov 89 | **THE LOVE SONGS OF ANDREW LLOYD WEBBER** | | |
|     *Decca 828175 1* ................................... | **18†** | 6 wks |

*The Classic Touch is credited to Richard Clayderman with the Royal Philharmonic Orchestra. See also Royal Philharmonic Orchestra.*

## CLAYTOWN TROUPE   *UK, male vocal/instrumental group*      *1 wk*

| | | |
|---|---|---|
| 21 Oct 89 | **THROUGH THE VEIL**   *Island ILPS 9933* ............. | **72** | 1 wk |

Nelson Mandela Birthday Concert star **TRACY CHAPMAN** provided the first example of an artist breaking worldwide thanks to a global televised performance.

Guitar legend **ERIC CLAPTON** enjoyed his most consistent solo success in the late 80s.

**CHER** and Jon Bon Jovi pose at the 1988 American Music Awards.

## CLIMAX BLUES BAND  UK, male vocal/instrumental group        1 wk

| 13 Nov 76 | **GOLD PLATED**  *BTM 1009* ......................... | 56 | 1 wk |

## CLIMIE FISHER  UK, male vocal/instrumental duo        38 wks

| 13 Feb 88 | **EVERYTHING**  *EMI EMC 3538* .................... | 14 | 36 wks |
| 21 Oct 89 | **COMING IN FOR THE KILL**  *EMI EMC 3565* ......... | 35 | 2 wks |

## Eddie COCHRAN  US, male vocalist/instrumentalist – guitar        47 wks

| 30 Jul 60 | **SINGING TO MY BABY**  *London HAU 2093* ........... | 19 | 1 wk |
| 1 Oct 60 | ● **EDDIE COCHRAN MEMORIAL ALBUM** | | |
| | *London HAG 2267* ........................... | 9 | 12 wks |
| 12 Jan 63 | **CHERISHED MEMORIES**  *Liberty LBY 1109* .......... | 15 | 3 wks |
| 20 Apr 63 | **EDDIE COCHRAN MEMORIAL ALBUM** | | |
| | **(re-issue)**  *Liberty LBY 1127* ...................... | 11 | 18 wks |
| 19 Oct 63 | **SINGING TO MY BABY (re-issue)**  *Liberty LBY 1158* .... | 20 | 1 wk |
| 9 May 70 | **VERY BEST OF EDDIE COCHRAN**  *Liberty LBS 83337* .. | 34 | 3 wks |
| 18 Aug 79 | **THE EDDIE COCHRAN SINGLES ALBUM** | | |
| | *United Artists UAK 30244* .......................... | 39 | 6 wks |
| 16 Apr 88 | **C'MON EVERYBODY**  *Liberty ECR 1* ................ | 53 | 3 wks |

## Joe COCKER  UK, male vocalist        13 wks

| 26 Sep 70 | **MAD DOGS AND ENGLISHMEN**  *A & M AMLS 6002* ... | 16 | 8 wks |
| 6 May 72 | **JOE COCKER/WITH A LITTLE HELP FROM MY** | | |
| | **FRIENDS**  *Double Back TOOFA 1/2* ................. | 29 | 4 wks |
| 30 Jun 84 | **A CIVILISED MAN**  *Capitol EJ 24 0139 1* ............. | 100 | 1 wk |

**COCKNEY REBEL** – *See Steve HARLEY and COCKNEY REBEL*

## COCKNEY REJECTS  UK, male vocal/instrumental group        17 wks

| 15 Mar 80 | **GREATEST HITS VOL. 1**  *Zonophone ZONO 101* ....... | 22 | 11 wks |
| 25 Oct 80 | **GREATEST HITS VOL. 2**  *Zonophone ZONO 102* ....... | 23 | 3 wks |
| 18 Apr 81 | **GREATEST HITS VOL. 3 (LIVE AND LOUD)** | | |
| | *Zonophone ZEM 101* ............................. | 27 | 3 wks |

**COCONUTS** – *See Kid CREOLE and the COCONUTS*

## COCTEAU TWINS  UK, male/female vocal group        34 wks

| 29 Oct 83 | **HEAD OVER HEELS**  *4AD CAD 313* ................ | 51 | 15 wks |
| 24 Nov 84 | **TREASURE**  *4AD CAD 412* ...................... | 29 | 8 wks |
| 26 Apr 86 | ● **VICTORIALAND**  *4AD CAD 602* ................. | 10 | 7 wks |
| 1 Oct 88 | **BLUE BELL KNOLL**  *4AD CAD 807* ................ | 15 | 4 wks |

## Leonard COHEN  Canada, male vocalist        143 wks

| 31 Aug 68 | **SONGS OF LEONARD COHEN**  *CBS 63241* .......... | 13 | 71 wks |
| 3 May 69 | ● **SONGS FROM A ROOM**  *CBS 63587* ............... | 2 | 26 wks |
| 24 Apr 71 | ● **SONGS OF LOVE AND HATE**  *CBS 69004* .......... | 4 | 18 wks |
| 28 Sep 74 | **NEW SKIN FOR THE OLD CEREMONY**  *CBS 69087* ... | 24 | 3 wks |
| 10 Dec 77 | **DEATH OF A LADIES' MAN**  *CBS 86042* ............ | 35 | 5 wks |
| 16 Feb 85 | **VARIOUS POSITIONS**  *CBS 26222* ................. | 52 | 6 wks |
| 27 Feb 88 | **I'M YOUR MAN**  *CBS 460642 1* ................... | 48 | 13 wks |
| 6 Aug 88 | **GREATEST HITS**  *CBS 32644* ..................... | 99 | 1 wk |

## COLDCUT  UK, male production duo        4 wks

| 29 Apr 89 | **WHAT'S THAT NOISE**  *Ahead Of Our Time CCUTLP 1* ... | 20 | 4 wks |

## Lloyd COLE and the COMMOTIONS
*UK, male vocalist and male vocal/instrumental group*                     *75 wks*

| | | | |
|---|---|---|---|
| 20 Oct 84 | **RATTLESNAKES**  *Polydor LCLP 1* ................... | **13** | 30 wks |
| 30 Nov 85 | ● **EASY PIECES**  *Polydor LCLP 2* ...................... | **5** | 18 wks |
| 7 Nov 87 | ● **MAINSTREAM**  *Polydor LCLP 3* ...................... | **9** | 20 wks |
| 8 Apr 89 | **1984–1989**  *Polydor 837736 1* ....................... | **14** | 7 wks |

## Nat 'King' Cole  *US, male vocalist*                     *109 wks*

| | | | |
|---|---|---|---|
| 19 Aug 61 | **STRING ALONG WITH NAT 'KING' COLE** | | |
| | *Encore ENC 102* .................................. | **12** | 9 wks |
| 27 Mar 65 | **UNFORGETTABLE NAT 'KING' COLE**  *Capitol W 20664* | **19** | 8 wks |
| 7 Dec 68 | ● **BEST OF NAT 'KING' COLE**  *Capitol ST 21139* ......... | **5** | 18 wks |
| 5 Dec 70 | **BEST OF NAT 'KING' COLE VOL. 2**  *Capitol ST 21687* .. | **39** | 2 wks |
| 8 Apr 78 | ★ **20 GOLDEN GREATS**  *Capitol EMTV 9* .............. | **1** | 37 wks |
| 20 Nov 82 | ● **GREATEST LOVE SONGS**  *Capitol EMTV 35* .......... | **7** | 26 wks |
| 26 Nov 88 | **CHRISTMAS WITH NAT 'KING' COLE**  *Stylus SMR 868* | **25†** | 9 wks |

*See also Nat 'King' Cole and Dean Martin; Nat 'King' Cole and the George Shearing Quintet.*

## Nat 'King' COLE and Dean MARTIN
*US, male vocalists*                     *1 wk*

| | | | |
|---|---|---|---|
| 27 Nov 71 | **WHITE CHRISTMAS**  *MFP 5224* ................... | **45** | 1 wk |

*See also Nat 'King' Cole; Dean Martin.*

## Nat 'King' COLE and the George SHEARING QUINTET  *US, male vocalist and UK/US instrumental group*                     *7 wks*

| | | | |
|---|---|---|---|
| 20 Oct 62 | ● **NAT 'KING' COLE SINGS AND THE GEORGE** | | |
| | **SHEARING QUINTET PLAYS**  *Capitol W 1675* ....... | **8** | 7 wks |

*See also Nat 'King' Cole; Peggy Lee and George Shearing.*

## Natalie COLE  *US, female vocalist*                     *16 wks*

| | | | |
|---|---|---|---|
| 7 May 88 | **EVERLASTING**  *Manhattan MTL 1012* ................ | **62** | 4 wks |
| 20 May 89 | ● **GOOD TO BE BACK**  *EMI-USA MTL 1042* ........... | **10** | 12 wks |

## Dave and Ansil COLLINS  *Jamaica, male vocal duo*                     *2 wks*

| | | | |
|---|---|---|---|
| 7 Aug 71 | **DOUBLE BARREL**  *Trojan TBL 162* ................. | **41** | 2 wks |

**Joan COLLINS** – *See Anthony NEWLEY, Peter SELLERS, Joan COLLINS*

## Judy COLLINS  *US, female vocalist*                     *18 wks*

| | | | |
|---|---|---|---|
| 10 Apr 71 | **WHALES AND NIGHTINGALES**  *Elektra EKS 75010* ... | **37** | 2 wks |
| 31 May 75 | ● **JUDITH**  *Elektra K 52019* ......................... | **7** | 12 wks |
| 14 Dec 85 | **AMAZING GRACE**  *Telstar STAR 2265* ............... | **34** | 4 wks |

## Phil COLLINS  *UK, male vocalist/instrumentalist – drums*                     *592 wks*

| | | | |
|---|---|---|---|
| 21 Feb 81 | ★ **FACE VALUE**  *Virgin V 2185* ...................... | **1** | 270 wks |
| 13 Nov 82 | ● **HELLO I MUST BE GOING**  *Virgin V 2252* ............ | **2** | 147 wks |
| 2 Mar 85 | ★ **NO JACKET REQUIRED**  *Virgin V 2345* ............ | **1** | 170 wks |
| 2 Dec 89 | ★ **...BUT SERIOUSLY**  *Virgin V 2620* ................. | **1†** | 5 wks |

## Willie COLLINS   US, male vocalist                                    1 wk

| 14 Jun 86 | **WHERE YOU GONNA BE TONIGHT?** |  |  |
|  | Capitol EST 2012 ................................. | 97 | 1 wk |

## COLOSSEUM   UK, male vocal/instrumental group                        14 wks

| 17 May 69 | **COLOSSEUM**   Fontana S 5510 ...................... | 15 | 1 wk |
| 22 Nov 69 | **VALENTYNE SUITE**   Vertigo VO 1 .................. | 15 | 2 wks |
| 5 Dec 70 | **DAUGHTER OF TIME**   Vertigo 6360 017 .............. | 23 | 5 wks |
| 26 Jun 71 | **COLOSSEUM LIVE**   Bronze ICD 1 .................. | 17 | 6 wks |

## COLOURBOX   UK, male vocal/instrumental group                        2 wks

| 24 Aug 85 | **COLOURBOX**   4AD CAD 508 ....................... | 67 | 2 wks |

## COLOUR FIELD   UK, male vocal/instrumental group                     8 wks

| 4 May 85 | **VIRGINS AND PHILISTINES**   Chrysalis CHR 1480 ...... | 12 | 7 wks |
| 4 Apr 87 | **DECEPTION**   Chrysalis CDL 1546 ................... | 95 | 1 wk |

**Alice COLTRANE** – See Carlos SANTANA and Alice COLTRANE

**COMETS** – See Bill HALEY and his COMETS

## COMIC RELIEF   UK, charity ensemble of comedians                     8 wks

| 10 May 86 | ● **UTTERLY UTTERLY LIVE!**   WEA WX 51 .......... | 10 | 8 wks |

## COMMODORES
*US/UK, male vocal/instrumental group*                                  126 wks

| 13 May 78 | **LIVE**   Motown TMSP 6007 ......................... | 60 | 1 wk |
| 10 Jun 78 | ● **NATURAL HIGH**   Motown STML 12087 .............. | 8 | 23 wks |
| 2 Dec 78 | **GREATEST HITS**   Motown STML 12100 .............. | 19 | 16 wks |
| 18 Aug 79 | **MIDNIGHT MAGIC**   Motown STMA 8032 .............. | 15 | 25 wks |
| 28 Jun 80 | **HEROES**   Motown STMA 8034 .................... | 50 | 5 wks |
| 18 Jul 81 | **IN THE POCKET**   Motown STML 12156 ............. | 69 | 5 wks |
| 14 Aug 82 | ● **LOVE SONGS**   K-Tel NE 1171 ..................... | 5 | 28 wks |
| 23 Feb 85 | **NIGHTSHIFT**   Motown ZL 72343 ................. | 13 | 10 wks |
| 9 Nov 85 | **THE VERY BEST OF THE COMMODORES** |  |  |
|  | Telstar STAR 2249 ................................. | 25 | 13 wks |

*Group were US only for first seven albums.*

**COMMOTIONS** – See Lloyd COLE and the COMMOTIONS

## COMMUNARDS   UK, male vocal/instrumental duo                         74 wks

| 2 Aug 86 | ● **COMMUNARDS**   London LONLP 18 ................. | 7 | 45 wks |
| 17 Oct 87 | ● **RED**   London LONLP 39 ............................ | 4 | 29 wks |

## Perry COMO   US, male vocalist                                       191 wks

| 8 Nov 58 | ● **DEAR PERRY**   RCA RD 27078 ..................... | 6 | 5 wks |
| 31 Jan 59 | ● **COMO'S GOLDEN RECORDS**   RCA RD 27100 ........ | 4 | 5 wks |
| 10 Apr 71 | **IT'S IMPOSSIBLE**   RCA Victor SF 8175 .............. | 13 | 13 wks |
| 7 Jul 73 | ★ **AND I LOVE YOU SO**   RCA Victor SF 8360 ............. | 1 | 109 wks |
| 24 Aug 74 | **PERRY**   RCA Victor APL1 0585 ..................... | 26 | 3 wks |

| | | | | |
|---|---|---|---|---|
| 19 Apr 75 | **MEMORIES ARE MADE OF HITS** *RCA Victor RS 1005* .. | 14 | 16 wks |
| 25 Oct 75 | ★ **40 GREATEST HITS** *K-Tel NE 700* ................ | 1 | 34 wks |
| 3 Dec 83 | **FOR THE GOOD TIMES** *Telstar STAR 2235* ........... | 41 | 6 wks |

COMPILATION ALBUMS – *See VARIOUS ARTISTS*

## COMSAT ANGELS *UK, male vocal/instrumental group*     *9 wks*

| | | | | |
|---|---|---|---|---|
| 5 Sep 81 | **SLEEP NO MORE** *Polydor POLS 1038* ............... | 51 | 5 wks |
| 18 Sep 82 | **FICTION** *Polydor POLS 1075* ...................... | 94 | 2 wks |
| 8 Oct 83 | **LAND** *Jive HIP 8* ................................ | 91 | 2 wks |

## Ray CONNIFF *US, male orchestra leader*     *96 wks*

| | | | | |
|---|---|---|---|---|
| 28 May 60 | **IT'S THE TALK OF THE TOWN** *Philips BBL 7354* | 15 | 1 wk |
| 25 Jun 60 | **S'AWFUL NICE** *Philips BBL 7281* ................... | 13 | 1 wk |
| 26 Nov 60 | ● **HI-FI COMPANION ALBUM** *Philips BET 101* .......... | 3 | 44 wks |
| 20 May 61 | **MEMORIES ARE MADE OF THIS** *Philips BBL 7439* .... | 14 | 4 wks |
| 29 Dec 62 | **WE WISH YOU A MERRY CHRISTMAS** *CBS BPG 62092* ......................... | 12 | 1 wk |
| 29 Dec 62 | **'S WONDERFUL 'S MARVELLOUS** *CBS DPG 66001* .. | 18 | 3 wks |
| 16 Apr 66 | **HI-FI COMPANION ALBUM** (re-issue) *CBS DP 66011* . | 24 | 4 wks |
| 9 Sep 67 | **SOMEWHERE MY LOVE** *CBS SBPG 62740* ......... | 34 | 3 wks |
| 21 Jun 69 | ★ **HIS ORCHESTRA, HIS CHORUS, HIS SINGERS, HIS SOUND** *CBS SPR 27* ......................... | 1 | 16 wks |
| 23 May 70 | **BRIDGE OVER TROUBLED WATER** *CBS 64020* ..... | 30 | 14 wks |
| 12 Jun 71 | **LOVE STORY** *CBS 64294* ......................... | 34 | 1 wk |
| 19 Feb 72 | **I'D LIKE TO TEACH THE WORLD TO SING** *CBS 64449* | 17 | 4 wks |

## Billy CONNOLLY *UK, male vocalist*     *108 wks*

| | | | | |
|---|---|---|---|---|
| 20 Jul 74 | ● **SOLO CONCERT** *Transatlantic TRA 279* .............. | 8 | 33 wks |
| 18 Jan 75 | ● **COP YER WHACK OF THIS** *Polydor 2383 310* ........ | 10 | 29 wks |
| 20 Sep 75 | **WORDS AND MUSIC** *Transatlantic TRA SAM 32* | 34 | 10 wks |
| 6 Dec 75 | ● **GET RIGHT INTAE HIM** *Polydor 2383 368* ........... | 6 | 14 wks |
| 11 Dec 76 | **ATLANTIC BRIDGE** *Polydor 2383 419* ............. | 20 | 9 wks |
| 28 Jan 78 | **RAW MEAT FOR THE BALCONY** *Polydor 2383 463* .. | 57 | 3 wks |
| 5 Dec 81 | **PICK OF BILLY CONNOLLY** *Polydor POLTV 15* ....... | 23 | 8 wks |
| 5 Dec 87 | **BILLY AND ALBERT** *10 DIX 65* ................... | 81 | 2 wks |

## Russ CONWAY *UK, male instrumentalist – piano*     *69 wks*

| | | | | |
|---|---|---|---|---|
| 22 Nov 58 | ● **PACK UP YOUR TROUBLES** *Columbia 33SX 1120* ..... | 9 | 5 wks |
| 2 May 59 | ● **SONGS TO SING IN YOUR BATH** *Columbia 33SX 1149* . | 8 | 10 wks |
| 19 Sep 59 | ● **FAMILY FAVOURITES** *Columbia 33SX 1169* .......... | 3 | 16 wks |
| 19 Dec 59 | ● **TIME TO CELEBRATE** *Columbia 33SX 1197* .......... | 3 | 7 wks |
| 26 Mar 60 | ● **MY CONCERTO FOR YOU** *Columbia 33SX 1214* | 5 | 17 wks |
| 17 Dec 60 | ● **PARTY TIME** *Columbia 33SX 1279* ................. | 7 | 11 wks |
| 23 Apr 77 | **RUSS CONWAY PRESENTS 24 PIANO GREATS** *Ronco RTL 2022* ............................... | 25 | 3 wks |

## Ry COODER *US, male vocalist/instrumentalist – guitar*     *30 wks*

| | | | | |
|---|---|---|---|---|
| 11 Aug 79 | **BOP TILL YOU DROP** *Warner Bros. K 56691* ......... | 36 | 9 wks |
| 18 Oct 80 | **BORDER LINE** *Warner Bros. K 56864* .............. | 35 | 6 wks |
| 24 Apr 82 | **THE SLIDE AREA** *Warner Bros. K 56976* ............ | 18 | 12 wks |
| 14 Nov 87 | **GET RHYTHM** *Warner Bros. WX 121* ................. | 75 | 3 wks |

## Peter COOK and Dudley MOORE
*UK, male comedy duo*     *34 wks*

| | | | | |
|---|---|---|---|---|
| 21 May 66 | **ONCE MOORE WITH COOK** *Decca LK 4785* .......... | 25 | 1 wk |
| 18 Sep 76 | **DEREK AND CLIVE LIVE** *Island ILPS 9434* ........... | 12 | 25 wks |
| 24 Dec 77 | **COME AGAIN** *Virgin V 2094* ....................... | 18 | 8 wks |

*See also Dudley Moore.*

## Sam COOKE  *US, male vocalist*                     *27 wks*

26 Apr 86 ● **THE MAN AND HIS MUSIC**   *RCA PL 87127* .......... **8**  27 wks

## COOKIE CREW  *UK, female vocal duo*                 *4 wks*

6 May 89   **BORN THIS WAY!**  *London 828134 1* ................. **24**  4 wks

## Rita COOLIDGE  *US, female vocalist*                *40 wks*

6 Aug 77 ● **ANYTIME ANYWHERE**  *A & M AMLH 64616* ......... **6**  28 wks
8 Jul  78   **LOVE ME AGAIN**  *A & M AMLH 64699* .............. **51**  1 wk
14 Mar 81 ● **VERY BEST OF**  *A & M AMLH 68520* ................ **6**  11 wks

*See also Kris Kristofferson and Rita Coolidge.*

## COOL NOTES  *UK, male/female vocal/instrumental group*   *2 wks*

9 Nov 85   **HAVE A GOOD FOREVER**  *Abstract Dance ADLP 1* ...... **66**  2 wks

## Alice COOPER  *US, male vocalist*                   *115 wks*

5 Feb 72   **KILLER**  *Warner Bros. K 56005* ........................ **27**  18 wks
22 Jul  72 ● **SCHOOL'S OUT**  *Warner Bros. K 56007* ............. **4**  20 wks
9 Sep  72   **LOVE IT TO DEATH**  *Warner Bros. K 46177* ............ **28**  7 wks
24 Mar 73 ★ **BILLION DOLLAR BABIES**  *Warner Bros. K 56013* ...... **1**  23 wks
12 Jan  74   **MUSCLE OF LOVE**  *Warner Bros. K 56018* ............. **34**  4 wks
15 Mar 75   **WELCOME TO MY NIGHTMARE**  *Anchor ANCL 2011* .. **19**  8 wks
24 Jul  76   **ALICE COOPER GOES TO HELL**  *Warner Bros. K 56171* . **23**  7 wks
28 May 77   **LACE AND WHISKY**  *Warner Bros. K 56365* ........... **33**  3 wks
23 Dec 78   **FROM THE INSIDE**  *Warner Bros. K 56577* .......... **68**  3 wks
17 May 80   **FLUSH THE FASHION**  *Warner Bros. K 56805* ......... **56**  3 wks
12 Sep  81   **SPECIAL FORCES**  *Warner Bros. K 56927* ............. **96**  1 wk
12 Nov 83   **DADA**  *Warner Bros. 92–3969–1* ..................... **93**  1 wk
1 Nov  86   **CONSTRICTOR**  *MCA MCF 3341* ................... **41**  2 wks
7 Nov  87   **RAISE YOUR FIST AND YELL**  *MCA MCF 3392* ...... **48**  3 wks
26 Aug 89 ● **TRASH**  *Epic 465130 1* ........................... **2**  12 wks

*Alice Cooper was US, male vocal/instrumental group for first five albums.*

## Julian COPE  *UK, male vocalist*                    *17 wks*

3 Mar 84   **WORLD SHUT YOUR MOUTH**  *Mercury MERL 37* ..... **40**  4 wks
24 Nov 84   **FRIED**  *Mercury MERL 48* ........................ **87**  1 wk
14 Mar 87   **SAINT JULIAN**  *Island ILPS 9861* ................. **11**  10 wks
29 Oct 88   **MY NATION UNDERGROUND**  *Island ILPS 9918* ..... **42**  2 wks

**Harry H. CORBETT** – *See Wilfred BRAMBELL and Harry H. CORBETT*

## Hugh CORNWELL  *UK, male vocalist*                  *1 wk*

18 Jun 88   **WOLF**  *Virgin V 2420* ............................. **98**  1 wk

## CORRIES  *UK, male vocal/instrumental duo*          *5 wks*

9 May 70   **SCOTTISH LOVE SONGS**  *Fontana 6309–004* .......... **46**  4 wks
16 Sep  72   **SOUND OF PIBROCH**  *Columbia SCX 6511* ........... **39**  1 wk

## Elvis COSTELLO and the ATTRACTIONS
*UK, male vocalist and male vocal/instrumental group*      *176 wks*

6 Aug 77   **MY AIM IS TRUE**  *Stiff SEEZ 3* ..................... **14**  12 wks

| | | | | |
|---|---|---|---|---|
| 1 Apr 78 | ● **THIS YEAR'S MODEL** *Radar RAD 3* .............. | 4 | 14 wks |
| 20 Jan 79 | ● **ARMED FORCES** *Radar RAD 14* ................ | 2 | 28 wks |
| 23 Feb 80 | ● **GET HAPPY** *F-Beat XXLP 1* ................. | 2 | 14 wks |
| 31 Jan 81 | ● **TRUST** *F-Beat XXLP 11* ................. | 9 | 7 wks |
| 31 Oct 81 | ● **ALMOST BLUE** *F-Beat XXLP 13* ........... | 7 | 18 wks |
| 10 Jul 82 | ● **IMPERIAL BEDROOM** *F-Beat XXLP 17* ...... | 6 | 12 wks |
| 6 Aug 83 | ● **PUNCH THE CLOCK** *F-Beat XXLP 19* ...... | 3 | 13 wks |
| 7 Jul 84 | ● **GOODBYE CRUEL WORLD** *F-Beat ZL 70317* ........ | 10 | 10 wks |
| 20 Apr 85 | ● **THE BEST OF ELVIS COSTELLO – THE MAN** *Telstar STAR 2247* | 8 | 17 wks |
| 1 May 86 | **KING OF AMERICA** *F-Beat ZL 70496* ......... | 11 | 9 wks |
| 27 Sep 86 | **BLOOD AND CHOCOLATE** *Imp XFIEND 80* ........ | 16 | 5 wks |
| 18 Feb 89 | ● **SPIKE** *Warner Bros. WX 238* ................. | 5 | 16 wks |
| 28 Oct 89 | **GIRLS GIRLS GIRLS** *Demon DFIEND 160* ........... | 67 | 1 wk |

*My Aim Is True, This Year's Model, Trust and The Best of Elvis Costello – The Man are credited to Elvis Costello only. King of America credited to Costello Show – Elvis and a US backing band.*

## Phil COULTER
*Ireland, male orchestra leader/instrumentalist – piano*     *15 wks*

| | | | | |
|---|---|---|---|---|
| 13 Oct 84 | **SEA OF TRANQUILLITY** *K-Tel Ireland KLP 185* ........ | 46 | 14 wks |
| 18 May 85 | **PHIL COULTER'S IRELAND** *K-Tel ONE 1296* ........ | 86 | 1 wk |

## David COVERDALE   *UK, male vocalist*     *1 wk*

| | | | | |
|---|---|---|---|---|
| 27 Feb 82 | **NORTHWINDS** *Purple TTS 3513* ................. | 78 | 1 wk |

## CRAMPS   *US, male/female vocal/instrumental group*     *12 wks*

| | | | | |
|---|---|---|---|---|
| 25 Jun 83 | **OFF THE BONE** *Illegal ILP 012* .................... | 44 | 4 wks |
| 26 Nov 83 | **SMELL OF FEMALE** *Big Beat NED 6* ......... | 74 | 2 wks |
| 1 Mar 86 | **A DATE WITH ELVIS** *Big Beat WIKA 46* ............. | 34 | 6 wks |

## CRASS   *UK, male vocal/instrumental group*     *2 wks*

| | | | | |
|---|---|---|---|---|
| 28 Aug 82 | **CHRIST THE ALBUM** *Crass BOLLOX 2U2* ........... | 26 | 2 wks |

## Michael CRAWFORD   *UK, male vocalist*     *18 wks*

| | | | | |
|---|---|---|---|---|
| 28 Nov 87 | **SONGS FROM THE STAGE AND SCREEN** *Telstar STAR 2308* ............................ | 12 | 13 wks |
| 2 Dec 89 | **WITH LOVE** *Telstar STAR 2340* ................... | 31† | 5 wks |

*Songs From The Stage And Screen credits the London Symphony Orchestra. See also the London Symphony Orchestra.*

## Randy CRAWFORD   *US, female vocalist*     *138 wks*

| | | | | |
|---|---|---|---|---|
| 28 Jun 80 | ● **NOW WE MAY BEGIN** *Warner Bros. K 56791* ........... | 10 | 16 wks |
| 16 May 81 | ● **SECRET COMBINATION** *Warner Bros. K 56904* ........ | 2 | 60 wks |
| 12 Jun 82 | ● **WINDSONG** *Warner Bros. K 57011* ........ | 7 | 17 wks |
| 22 Oct 83 | **NIGHTLINE** *Warner Bros. 92–3976–1* ................. | 37 | 4 wks |
| 13 Oct 84 | ● **MISS RANDY CRAWFORD – THE GREATEST HITS** *K-Tel NE 1281* ............................. | 10 | 17 wks |
| 28 Jun 86 | **ABSTRACT EMOTIONS** *Warner Bros. WX 46* ........... | 14 | 10 wks |
| 10 Oct 87 | **THE LOVE SONGS** *Telstar STAR 2299* ............. | 27 | 13 wks |
| 21 Oct 89 | **RICH AND POOR** *Warner Bros. WX 308* ............... | 63 | 1 wk |

## Robert CRAY BAND   *US, male vocal/instrumental group*     *41 wks*

| | | | | |
|---|---|---|---|---|
| 12 Oct 85 | **FALSE ACCUSATIONS** *Demon FIEND 43* ........... | 68 | 1 wk |
| 15 Nov 86 | **STRONG PERSUADER** *Mercury MERH 97* ........... | 34 | 28 wks |
| 3 Sep 88 | **DON'T BE AFRAID OF THE DARK** *Mercury MERH 129* . | 13 | 12 wks |

*C*

RAY CONNIFF (below) without his orchestra, his chorus, his singers, his sound.

The Canadian singer/songwriter/poet **LEONARD COHEN** had seven hit albums which reached various positions.

**PHIL COLLINS** is shown at home at the time of 'Face Value'.

CRAZY HORSE – *See Neil YOUNG*

CRAZY WORLD – *See Crazy World of Arthur BROWN*

## CREAM  UK, *male vocal/instrumental group*                                  182 wks

| | | | |
|---|---|---|---|
| 24 Dec 66 ● FRESH CREAM  *Reaction 593–001* | | 6 | 17 wks |
| 18 Nov 67 ● DISRAELI GEARS  *Reaction 594–003* | | 5 | 42 wks |
| 17 Aug 68 ● WHEELS OF FIRE  (double)  *Polydor 583–031/2* | | 3 | 26 wks |
| 17 Aug 68 ● WHEELS OF FIRE  (single)  *Polydor 583–033* | | 7 | 13 wks |
| 8 Feb 69 ● FRESH CREAM  (re-issue)  *Reaction 594–001* | | 7 | 2 wks |
| 15 Mar 69 ★ GOODBYE  *Polydor 583–053* | | 1 | 28 wks |
| 8 Nov 69 ● BEST OF CREAM  *Polydor 583–060* | | 6 | 34 wks |
| 4 Jul 70 ● LIVE CREAM  *Polydor 2383–016* | | 4 | 15 wks |
| 24 Jun 72  LIVE CREAM VOL. 2  *Polydor 2383 119* | | 15 | 5 wks |

*See also Eric Clapton and Cream.*

## CREATURES  UK, *male/female vocal/instrumental duo*                       9 wks

| | | | |
|---|---|---|---|
| 28 May 83  FEAST  *Wonderland SHELP 1* | | 17 | 9 wks |

## CREEDENCE CLEARWATER REVIVAL
US, *male vocal/instrumental group*                                           65 wks

| | | | |
|---|---|---|---|
| 24 Jan 70  GREEN RIVER  *Liberty LBS 83273* | | 20 | 6 wks |
| 28 Mar 70 ● WILLY AND THE POOR BOYS  *Liberty LBS 83338* | | 10 | 24 wks |
| 2 May 70  BAYOU COUNTRY  *Liberty LBS 83261* | | 62 | 1 wk |
| 12 Sep 70 ★ COSMO'S FACTORY  *Liberty LBS 83388* | | 1 | 15 wks |
| 23 Jan 71  PENDULUM  *Liberty LBG 83400* | | 23 | 12 wks |
| 30 Jun 79  GREATEST HITS  *Fantasy FT 558* | | 35 | 5 wks |
| 19 Oct 85  THE CREEDENCE COLLECTION  *Impression IMDP 3* | | 68 | 2 wks |

CREME – *See GODLEY and CREME*

## Kid CREOLE and the COCONUTS
US, *male/female vocal/instrumental group*                                    54 wks

| | | | |
|---|---|---|---|
| 22 May 82 ● TROPICAL GANGSTERS  *Ze ILPS 7016* | | 3 | 40 wks |
| 26 Jun 82  FRESH FRUIT IN FOREIGN PLACES  *Ze ILPS 7014* | | 99 | 1 wk |
| 17 Sep 83  DOPPELGANGER  *Island ILPS 9743* | | 21 | 6 wks |
| 15 Sep 84  CRE-OLE  *Island IMA 13* | | 21 | 7 wks |

Bernard CRIBBINS – *See Howard BLAKE conducting the SINFONIA OF LONDON*

## CRICKETS  US, *male vocal/instrumental group*                             7 wks

| | | | |
|---|---|---|---|
| 25 Mar 61  IN STYLE WITH THE CRICKETS  *Coral LVA 9142* | | 13 | 7 wks |

*See also Buddy Holly and the Crickets; Bobby Vee and the Crickets.*

## Bing CROSBY  US, *male vocalist*                                          39 wks

| | | | |
|---|---|---|---|
| 8 Oct 60 ● JOIN BING AND SING ALONG  *Warner Brothers WM 4021* | | 7 | 11 wks |
| 21 Dec 74  WHITE CHRISTMAS  *MCA MCF 2568* | | 45 | 3 wks |
| 20 Sep 75  THAT'S WHAT LIFE IS ALL ABOUT  *United Artists UAG 2973* | | 28 | 6 wks |
| 5 Nov 77  THE BEST OF BING  *MCA MCF 2540* | | 41 | 7 wks |
| 5 Nov 77 ● LIVE AT THE LONDON PALLADIUM  *K-Tel NE 951* | | 9 | 2 wks |
| 17 Dec 77  SEASONS  *Polydor 2442 151* | | 25 | 7 wks |
| 5 May 79  SONGS OF A LIFETIME  *Philips 6641 923* | | 29 | 3 wks |

## Dave CROSBY  US, male vocalist

7 wks

24 Apr 71   **IF ONLY I COULD REMEMBER MY NAME**    12    7 wks
          *Atlantic 2401–005* .....................................

*See also Crosby, Stills and Nash; Crosby, Stills, Nash and Young; Graham Nash and David Crosby.*

---

## CROSBY, STILLS and NASH
*US/UK, male vocal/instrumental group*

14 wks

23 Aug 69   **CROSBY STILLS AND NASH**   *Atlantic 588–189* .........   25    5 wks
9 Jul 77   **CSN**   *Atlantic K 50369* ....................................   23    9 wks

*See also Dave Crosby; Crosby, Stills, Nash and Young; Graham Nash; Stephen Stills.*

---

## CROSBY, STILLS, NASH and YOUNG
*US/UK/Canada, male vocal/instrumental group*

79 wks

30 May 70 ● **DEJA VU**   *Atlantic 2401–001* .......................   5    61 wks
22 May 71 ● **FOUR-WAY STREET**   *Atlantic 2956 004* ..............   5    12 wks
21 Sep 74   **SO FAR**   *Atlantic K 50023* ...........................   25    6 wks

*See also Dave Crosby; Crosby, Stills and Nash; Graham Nash; Stephen Stills; Neil Young.*

---

## CROSS  UK/US, male vocal/instrumental group

2 wks

6 Feb 88   **SHOVE IT**   *Virgin V 2477* ...........................   58    2 wks

---

## Christopher CROSS  US, male vocalist

93 wks

21 Feb 81   **CHRISTOPHER CROSS**   *Warner Bros. K 56789* .........   14    77 wks
19 Feb 83 ● **ANOTHER PAGE**   *Warner Bros. W 3757* ..............   4    16 wks

---

## CROWN HEIGHTS AFFAIR
*US, male vocal/instrumental group*

3 wks

23 Sep 78   **DREAM WORLD**   *Philips 6372 754* ...................   40    3 wks

---

## CRUSADERS  US, male vocal/instrumental group

30 wks

21 Jul 79 ● **STREET LIFE**   *MCA MCF 3008* ......................   10    16 wks
19 Jul 80   **RHAPSODY AND BLUE**   *MCA MCG 4010* ............   40    5 wks
12 Sep 81   **STANDING TALL**   *MCA MCF 3122* ..................   47    5 wks
7 Apr 84   **GHETTO BLASTER**   *MCA MCF 3176* ..............   46    4 wks

---

## Bobby CRUSH  UK, male instrumentalist – piano

12 wks

29 Nov 72   **BOBBY CRUSH**   *Philips 6308 135* ...................   15    7 wks
18 Dec 82   **THE BOBBY CRUSH INCREDIBLE DOUBLE DECKER**
          **PARTY**   *Warwick WW 5126/7* .....................   53    5 wks

**CUDDLES** – *See Keith HARRIS, ORVILLE and CUDDLES*

---

## CULT  UK, male vocal/instrumental group

71 wks

18 Jun 83   **SOUTHERN DEATH CULT**   *Beggars Banquet BEGA 46* ...   43    3 wks
8 Sep 84   **DREAMTIME**   *Beggars Banquet BEGA 57* ..............   21    8 wks

| | | | |
|---|---|---|---|
| 26 Oct 85 ● **LOVE** *Beggars Banquet BEGA 65* | | 4 | 22 wks |
| 18 Apr 87 ● **ELECTRIC** *Beggars Banquet BEGA 80* | | 4 | 22 wks |
| 22 Apr 89 ● **SONIC TEMPLE** *Beggars Banquet BEGA 98* | | 3 | 11 wks |

*First album credited to Southern Death Cult.*

**CULT JAM** – *See LISA LISA and CULT JAM with FULL FORCE*

---

## CULTURE *Jamaica, male vocal/instrumental group*    *1 wk*

| | | | |
|---|---|---|---|
| 1 Apr 78 | **TWO SEVENS CLASH** *Lightning LIP 1* | 60 | 1 wk |

---

## CULTURE CLUB *UK, male vocal/instrumental group*   *144 wks*

| | | | |
|---|---|---|---|
| 16 Oct 82 ● **KISSING TO BE CLEVER** *Virgin V 2232* | | 5 | 59 wks |
| 22 Oct 83 ★ **COLOUR BY NUMBERS** *Virgin V 2285* | | 1 | 56 wks |
| 3 Nov 84 ● **WAKING UP WITH THE HOUSE ON FIRE** | | | |
| *Virgin V 2330* | | 2 | 13 wks |
| 12 Apr 86 ● **FROM LUXURY TO HEARTACHE** *Virgin V 2380* | | 10 | 6 wks |
| 18 Apr 87 ● **THIS TIME** *Virgin VTV 1* | | 8 | 10 wks |

---

## CURE *UK, male vocal/instrumental group*   *150 wks*

| | | | |
|---|---|---|---|
| 2 Jun 79 | **THREE IMAGINARY BOYS** *Fiction FIX 001* | 44 | 3 wks |
| 3 May 80 | **17 SECONDS** *Fiction FIX 004* | 20 | 10 wks |
| 25 Apr 81 | **FAITH** *Fiction FIX 6* | 14 | 8 wks |
| 15 May 82 ● | **PORNOGRAPHY** *Fiction FIX D7* | 8 | 9 wks |
| 3 Sep 83 | **BOYS DON'T CRY** *Fiction SPELP 26* | 71 | 7 wks |
| 24 Dec 83 | **JAPANESE WHISPERS** *Fiction FIXM 8* | 26 | 14 wks |
| 12 May 84 ● | **THE TOP** *Fiction FIXS 9* | 10 | 10 wks |
| 3 Nov 84 | **CONCERT – THE CURE LIVE** *Fiction FIXH 10* | 26 | 4 wks |
| 7 Sep 85 ● | **THE HEAD ON THE DOOR** *Fiction FIXH 11* | 7 | 13 wks |
| 31 May 86 ● | **STANDING ON A BEACH – THE SINGLES** | | |
| | *Fiction FIXH 12* | 4 | 34 wks |
| 6 Jun 87 ● | **KISS ME KISS ME KISS ME** *Fiction FIXH 13* | 6 | 15 wks |
| 13 May 89 ● | **DISINTEGRATION** *Fiction FIXH 14* | 3 | 23 wks |

*The compact disc version of FIXH 12 was titled Staring At The Sea.*

---

## CURIOSITY KILLED THE CAT
*UK, male vocal/instrumental group*   *27 wks*

| | | | |
|---|---|---|---|
| 9 May 87 ★ | **KEEP YOUR DISTANCE** *Mercury CATLP 1* | 1 | 24 wks |
| 4 Oct 89 | **GETAHEAD** *Mercury 842010 1* | 29 | 3 wks |

---

## CURVED AIR *UK, male/female vocal/instrumental group*   *32 wks*

| | | | |
|---|---|---|---|
| 5 Dec 70 ● | **AIR CONDITIONING** *Warner Bros. WSX 3012* | 8 | 21 wks |
| 9 Oct 71 | **CURVED AIR** *Warner Bros. K 46092* | 11 | 6 wks |
| 13 May 72 | **PHANTASMAGORIA** *Reprise K 46158* | 20 | 5 wks |

---

## Adge CUTLER and the WURZELS
*UK, male vocal/instrumental group*   *4 wks*

| | | | |
|---|---|---|---|
| 11 Mar 67 | **ADGE CUTLER AND THE WURZELS** | | |
| | *Columbia SX 6126* | 38 | 4 wks |

*See also the Wurzels.*

---

## CUTTING CREW *UK, male vocal/instrumental group*   *6 wks*

| | | | |
|---|---|---|---|
| 29 Nov 86 | **BROADCAST** *Siren SIRENLP 7* | 41 | 6 wks |

# d

## D. MOB  *UK, male producer. Danny D*  **3 wks**

| 11 Nov 89 | **A LITTLE BIT OF THIS A LITTLE BIT OF THAT**<br>*FFRR 828159 1* . . . . . . . . . . . . . . . . . . . . . . . . . . . . . . | 46 | 3 wks |

**DAINTEES** – *See Martin STEPHENSON and the DAINTEES*

**DAKOTAS** – *See Billy J. KRAMER and the DAKOTAS*

## DALEK I  *UK, male vocal/instrumental group*  **2 wks**

| 9 Aug 80 | **COMPASS KUMPAS**  *Backdoor OPEN 1* . . . . . . . . . . . . . . . | 54 | 2 wks |

## DALI'S CAR  *UK, male vocal/instrumental duo*  **1 wk**

| 1 Dec 84 | **THE WAKING HOUR**  *Paradox DOXLP 1* . . . . . . . . . . . . | 84 | 1 wk |

## Roger DALTREY  *UK, male vocalist*  **24 wks**

| 26 Jul 75 | **RIDE A ROCK HORSE**  *Polydor 2660 111* . . . . . . . . . . . . | 14 | 10 wks |
| 4 Jul 77 | **ONE OF THE BOYS**  *Polydor 2442 146* . . . . . . . . . . . . . . | 45 | 1 wk |
| 23 Aug 80 | **McVICAR (film soundtrack)**  *Polydor POLD 5034* . . . . . . . | 39 | 11 wks |
| 2 Nov 85 | **UNDER A RAGING MOON**  *10 DIX 17* . . . . . . . . . . . . . . | 52 | 2 wks |

## Glen DALY  *UK, male vocalist*  **2 wks**

| 20 Nov 71 | **GLASGOW NIGHT OUT**  *Golden Guinea GGL 0479* . . . . . . | 28 | 2 wks |

## DAMNED  *UK, male vocal/instrumental group*  **54 wks**

| 12 Mar 77 | **DAMNED DAMNED DAMNED**  *Stiff SEEZ 1* . . . . . . . . . | 36 | 10 wks |
| 17 Nov 79 | **MACHINE GUN ETIQUETTE**  *Chiswick CWK 3011* . . . . . | 31 | 5 wks |
| 29 Nov 80 | **THE BLACK ALBUM**  *Chiswick CWK 3015* . . . . . . . . . . . | 29 | 3 wks |
| 28 Nov 81 | **BEST OF**  *Chiswick DAM 1* . . . . . . . . . . . . . . . . . . . . . . . . . | 43 | 12 wks |
| 23 Oct 82 | **STRAWBERRIES**  *Bronze BRON 542* . . . . . . . . . . . . . . . . . | 15 | 4 wks |
| 27 Jul 85 | **PHANTASMAGORIA**  *MCA MCF 3275* . . . . . . . . . . . . . . | 11 | 17 wks |
| 13 Dec 86 | **ANYTHING**  *MCA MCG 6015* . . . . . . . . . . . . . . . . . . . . . | 40 | 2 wks |
| 12 Dec 87 | **LIGHT AT THE END OF THE TUNNEL**<br>*MCA MCSP 312* . . . . . . . . . . . . . . . . . . . . . . . . . . . . . . . . . | 87 | 1 wk |

## Vic DAMONE  *US, male vocalist*  **8 wks**

| 25 Apr 81 | **NOW!**  *RCA INTS 5080* . . . . . . . . . . . . . . . . . . . . . . . . . . . . | 28 | 7 wks |
| 2 Apr 83 | **VIC DAMONE SINGS THE GREAT SONGS**  *CBS 32261* . | 87 | 1 wk |

## DANA  *Ireland, female vocalist*  **2 wks**

| 3 Jan 81 | **EVERYTHING IS BEAUTIFUL**  *Warwick WW 5099* . . . . . | 43 | 2 wks |

## Suzanne DANDO  *UK, female exercise instructor*  **1 wk**

| 17 Mar 84 | **SHAPE UP AND DANCE WITH SUZANNE DANDO**<br>*Lifestyle LEG 21* . . . . . . . . . . . . . . . . . . . . . . . . . . . . . . . . . . | 87 | 1 wk |

## Charlie DANIELS BAND
*US, male vocal/instrumental group*  *1 wk*

| 10 Nov 79 | **MILLION MILE REFLECTIONS** *Epic EPC 83446* ...... | **74** | 1 wk |

## DANNY WILSON *UK, male vocal/instrumental group*  *10 wks*

| 30 Apr 88 | **MEET DANNY WILSON** *Virgin V 2419* ............. | **65** | 5 wks |
| 29 Jul 89 | **BEEBOP MOPTOP** *Virgin V 2594* ................... | **24** | 5 wks |

## DANSE SOCIETY *UK, male vocal/instrumental group*  *4 wks*

| 11 Feb 84 | **HEAVEN IS WAITING** *Society 205 972* ............... | **39** | 4 wks |

## Stephen DANTE *UK, male vocalist*  *1 wk*

| 3 Sep 88 | **FIND OUT** *Cooltempo CTLP 6* ...................... | **87** | 1 wk |

## Terence Trent D'ARBY *US, male vocalist*  *69 wks*

| 25 Jul 87 ★ | **INTRODUCING THE HARDLINE ACCORDING TO TERENCE TRENT D'ARBY** *CBS 450 911-1* ....... | **1** | 65 wks |
| 4 Nov 89 | **NEITHER FISH NOR FLESH** *CBS 465809 1* ......... | **12** | 4 wks |

## Bobby DARIN *US, male vocalist*  *15 wks*

| 19 Mar 60 ● | **THIS IS DARIN** *London HA 2235* .................... | **4** | 8 wks |
| 9 Apr 60 | **THAT'S ALL** *London HAE 2172* .................... | **15** | 1 wk |
| 5 Oct 85 | **THE LEGEND OF BOBBY DARIN – HIS GREATEST HITS** *Stylus SMR 8504* .......................... | **39** | 6 wks |

## DARLING BUDS *UK, male/female vocal/instrumental group*  *3 wks*

| 18 Feb 89 | **POP SAID** *Epic 462894 1* ........................... | **23** | 3 wks |

## DARTS *UK, male/female vocal/instrumental group*  *57 wks*

| 3 Dec 77 ● | **DARTS** *Magnet MAG 5020* ...................... | **9** | 22 wks |
| 3 Jun 78 | **EVERYONE PLAYS DARTS** *Magnet MAG 5022* ....... | **12** | 18 wks |
| 18 Nov 78 ● | **AMAZING DARTS** *K-Tel/Magnet DLP 7981* ............ | **8** | 13 wks |
| 6 Oct 79 | **DART ATTACK** *Magnet MAG 5030* .................. | **38** | 4 wks |

**DAVE** – *See CHAS and DAVE*

**DAVE** – *See SAM and DAVE*

## F.R. DAVID *France, male vocalist*  *6 wks*

| 7 May 83 | **WORDS** *Carrere CAL 145* .......................... | **46** | 6 wks |

**Windsor DAVIES** – *See Don ESTELLE and Windsor DAVIES*

## Miles DAVIS *US, male instrumentalist – trumpet*  *6 wks*

| 11 Jul 70 | **BITCHES BREW** *CBS 66236* ........................ | **71** | 1 wk |
| 15 Jun 85 | **YOU'RE UNDER ARREST** *CBS 26447* ............. | **88** | 1 wk |
| 18 Oct 86 | **TUTU** *Warner Bros. 925490 1* ...................... | **74** | 2 wks |
| 3 Jun 89 | **AMANDLA** *Warner Bros. WX 250* .................. | **49** | 2 wks |

## Sammy DAVIS Jr   *US, male vocalist*                    *1 wk*

13 Apr  63   **SAMMY DAVIS JR. AT THE COCONUT GROVE**
    *Reprise R 6063/2* . . . . . . . . . . . . . . . . . . . . . . . . . . . . . .   **19**   1 wk

## Spencer DAVIS GROUP
*UK, male vocal/instrumental group*                        *47 wks*

8 Jan  66  ● **THEIR 1ST LP**  *Fontana TL 5242* . . . . . . . . . . . . . . . . . . . .   **6**   9 wks
22 Jan  66  ● **THE 2ND LP**  *Fontana TL 5295* . . . . . . . . . . . . . . . . . . . . .   **3**   18 wks
11 Sep  66  ● **AUTUMN '66**  *Fontana TL 5359* . . . . . . . . . . . . . . . . . . . . .   **4**   20 wks

## DAWN   *US, male/female vocal group*                    *2 wks*

4 May 74   **GOLDEN RIBBONS**  *Bell BELLS 236* . . . . . . . . . . . . . . . .   **46**   2 wks

## Doris DAY   *US, female vocalist*                        *19 wks*

6 Jan  79   **20 GOLDEN GREATS**  *Warwick PR 5053* . . . . . . . . . . . . . .   **12**   11 wks
11 Nov 89   **A PORTRAIT OF DORIS DAY**  *Stylus SMR 984* . . . . . . . .   **32†**   8 wks

## Taylor DAYNE   *US, female vocalist*                     *17 wks*

5 Mar 88   **TELL IT TO MY HEART**  *Arista 208898* . . . . . . . . . . . . . . .   **24**   17 wks

## Chris DE BURGH   *Ireland, male vocalist*                *216 wks*

12 Sep  81   **BEST MOVES**  *A & M AMLH 68532* . . . . . . . . . . . . . . . . . . .   **65**   4 wks
9 Oct  82   **THE GETAWAY**  *A & M AMLH 68549* . . . . . . . . . . . . . .   **30**   16 wks
19 May  84   **MAN ON THE LINE**  *A & M AMLX 65002* . . . . . . . . . . . . .   **11**   24 wks
29 Dec  84  ● **THE VERY BEST OF CHRIS DE BURGH**
    *Telstar STAR 2248* . . . . . . . . . . . . . . . . . . . . . . . . . . . . . .   **6**   70 wks
24 Aug  85   **SPANISH TRAIN AND OTHER STORIES**
    *A & M AMLH 68343* . . . . . . . . . . . . . . . . . . . . . . . . . . . . .   **78**   3 wks
7 Jun  86  ● **INTO THE LIGHT**  *A & M AM 5121* . . . . . . . . . . . . . . .   **2**   59 wks
4 Oct  86   **CRUSADER**  *A & M AMLH 64746* . . . . . . . . . . . . . . . .   **72**   1 wk
15 Oct  88  ★ **FLYING COLOURS**  *A & M AMA 5224* . . . . . . . . . . . . .   **1**   30 wks
4 Nov  89  ● **FROM A SPARK TO A FLAME – THE VERY BEST OF**
    **CHRIS DE BURGH**  *A & M CDBLP 100* . . . . . . . . . . . . .   **4†**   9 wks

## DE LA SOUL   *US, male rap/sampling group*              *37 wks*

25 Mar  89   **3 FEET HIGH AND RISING**  *Big Life DLSLP 1* . . . . . . . . . .   **25†**   37 wks

## Waldo DE LOS RIOS   *Argentina, orchestra*              *26 wks*

1 May  71  ● **SYMPHONIES FOR THE SEVENTIES**  *A & M AMLS 2014*  . **6**   26 wks

## Manitas DE PLATA   *Spanish, male instrumentalist – guitar*   *1 wk*

29 Jul   67   **FLAMENCO GUITAR**  *Philips SBL 7786* . . . . . . . . . . . . . .   **40**   1 wk

## DEACON BLUE   *UK, male/female vocal/instrumental group*   *108 wks*

6 Jun  87   **RAINTOWN**  *CBS 450549 1* . . . . . . . . . . . . . . . . . . . . . . .   **14**   74 wks
15 Apr  89  ★ **WHEN THE WORLD KNOWS YOUR NAME**
    *CBS 463321 1* . . . . . . . . . . . . . . . . . . . . . . . . . . . . . . . . .   **1†**   34 wks

Robert Smith (centre) and Lol Tolhurst were the core of **THE CURE**.

Is it **CREEDENCE CLEARWATER REVIVAL** or The Tourists?

**VIC DAMONE** began his album chart career three decades after his number one single.

**TERENCE TRENT D'ARBY** asks what happened to his second album.

## DEAD KENNEDYS   *US, male vocal/instrumental group*                    *8 wks*

| 13 Sep 80 | **FRESH FRUIT FOR ROTTING VEGETABLES** | | |
| | *Cherry Red BRED 10* ................................ | **33** | 6 wks |
| 4 Jul 87 | **GIVE ME CONVENIENCE**  *Alternative Tentacles VIRUS 5* . | **84** | 2 wks |

## DEAD OR ALIVE   *UK, male vocal/instrumental group*                    *22 wks*

| 28 Apr 84 | **SOPHISTICATED BOOM BOOM**  *Epic EPC 25835* ...... | **29** | 3 wks |
| 25 May 85 | ● **YOUTHQUAKE**  *Epic EPC 26420* .................... | **9** | 15 wks |
| 14 Feb 87 | **MAD, BAD AND DANGEROUS TO KNOW** | | |
| | *Epic 450 257–1* ...................................... | **27** | 4 wks |

**DEAN** – *See JAN and DEAN*

## Hazell DEAN   *UK, female vocalist*                    *3 wks*

| 22 Oct 88 | **ALWAYS**  *EMI EMC 3546* ........................ | **38** | 3 wks |

## DeBARGE   *US, male/female vocal group*                    *2 wks*

| 25 May 85 | **RHYTHM OF THE NIGHT**  *Gordy ZL 72340* ........... | **94** | 2 wks |

## Kiki DEE   *UK, female vocalist*                    *9 wks*

| 26 Mar 77 | **KIKI DEE**  *Rocket ROLA 3* .......................... | **24** | 5 wks |
| 18 Jul 81 | **PERFECT TIMING**  *Ariola ARL 5050* ................ | **47** | 4 wks |

## Dave DEE, DOZY, BEAKY, MICK and TICH
*UK, male vocal/instrumental group*                    *15 wks*

| 2 Jul 66 | **DAVE DEE, DOZY, BEAKY, MICK AND TICH** | | |
| | *Fontana STL 5350* ................................. | **11** | 10 wks |
| 7 Jan 67 | **IF MUSIC BE THE FOOD OF LOVE . . . PREPARE FOR** | | |
| | **INDIGESTION**  *Fontana STL 5388* .................. | **27** | 5 wks |

## DEEP PURPLE   *UK, male vocal/instrumental group*                    *269 wks*

| 24 Jan 70 | **CONCERTO FOR GROUP AND ORCHESTRA** | | |
| | *Harvest SHVL 767* .............................. | **26** | 4 wks |
| 20 Jun 70 | ● **DEEP PURPLE IN ROCK**  *Harvest SHVL 777* .......... | **4** | 68 wks |
| 18 Sep 71 | ★ **FIREBALL**  *Harvest SHVL 793* .................... | **1** | 25 wks |
| 15 Apr 72 | ★ **MACHINE HEAD**  *Purple TPSA 7504* ............. | **1** | 24 wks |
| 6 Jan 73 | **MADE IN JAPAN**  *Purple TPSP 351* ................ | **16** | 14 wks |
| 17 Feb 73 | ● **WHO DO WE THINK WE ARE**  *Purple TPSA 7508* ... | **4** | 11 wks |
| 2 Mar 74 | ● **BURN**  *Purple TPA 3505* ...................... | **3** | 21 wks |
| 23 Nov 74 | ● **STORMBRINGER**  *Purple TPS 3508* ............... | **6** | 12 wks |
| 5 Jul 75 | **24 CARAT PURPLE**  *Purple TPSM 2002* ............ | **14** | 17 wks |
| 22 Nov 75 | **COME TASTE THE BAND**  *Purple TPSA 7515* ..... | **19** | 4 wks |
| 27 Nov 76 | **DEEP PURPLE LIVE**  *Purple TPSA 7517* .......... | **12** | 6 wks |
| 21 Apr 79 | **THE MARK II PURPLE SINGLES**  *Purple TPS 3514* ..... | **24** | 6 wks |
| 19 Jul 80 | ★ **DEEPEST PURPLE**  *Harvest EMTV 25* ............ | **1** | 15 wks |
| 13 Dec 80 | **IN CONCERT**  *Harvest SHDW 4121/4122* .......... | **30** | 8 wks |
| 4 Sep 82 | **DEEP PURPLE LIVE IN LONDON**  *Harvest SHSP 4124* . | **23** | 5 wks |
| 10 Nov 84 | ● **PERFECT STRANGERS**  *Polydor POLH 16* ........ | **5** | 15 wks |
| 29 Jun 85 | **THE ANTHOLOGY**  *Harvest PUR 1* ................ | **50** | 3 wks |
| 24 Jan 87 | ● **THE HOUSE OF BLUE LIGHT**  *Polydor POLH 32* ...... | **10** | 9 wks |
| 16 Jul 88 | **NOBODY'S PERFECT**  *Polydor PODV 10* ............. | **38** | 2 wks |

## DEF LEPPARD   *UK, male vocal/instrumental group*                    *119 wks*

| 22 Mar 80 | **ON THROUGH THE NIGHT**  *Vertigo 9102 040* ......... | **15** | 8 wks |
| 25 Jul 81 | **HIGH 'N' DRY**  *Vertigo 6359 045* ................... | **26** | 8 wks |
| 12 Mar 83 | **PYROMANIA**  *Vertigo VERS 2* ................... | **18** | 8 wks |
| 29 Aug 87 | ★ **HYSTERIA**  *Bludgeon Riffola HYSLP 1* ................. | **1** | 95 wks |

## Desmond DEKKER *Jamaica, male vocalist*

*4 wks*

| | | | |
|---|---|---|---|
| 5 Jul 69 | **THIS IS DESMOND DEKKER** *Trojan TTL 4* .......... | 27 | 4 wks |

## DELANEY and BONNIE and FRIENDS
*US/UK, male/female vocal/instrumental group*

*3 wks*

| | | | |
|---|---|---|---|
| 6 Jun 70 | **ON TOUR** *Atlantic 2400–013* ....................... | 39 | 3 wks |

## DEMON *UK, male vocal/instrumental group*

*5 wks*

| | | | |
|---|---|---|---|
| 14 Aug 82 | **THE UNEXPECTED GUEST** *Carrere CAL 139* ......... | 47 | 3 wks |
| 2 Jul 83 | **THE PLAGUE** *Clay CLAY LP 6* .................... | 73 | 2 wks |

## Sandy DENNY *UK, female vocalist*

*2 wks*

| | | | |
|---|---|---|---|
| 2 Oct 71 | **THE NORTH STAR GRASSMAN AND THE RAVENS** *Island ILPS 9165* ................................. | 31 | 2 wks |

## John DENVER *US, male vocalist*

*204 wks*

| | | | |
|---|---|---|---|
| 2 Jun 73 | **POEMS, PRAYERS AND PROMISES** *RCA SF 8219* ................................... | 19 | 5 wks |
| 23 Jun 73 | **RHYMES AND REASONS** *RCA Victor SF 8348* ........ | 21 | 5 wks |
| 30 Mar 74 | ● **THE BEST OF JOHN DENVER** *RCA Victor APLI 0374* .. | 7 | 69 wks |
| 7 Sep 74 | ● **BACK HOME AGAIN** *RCA Victor APLI 0548* .......... | 3 | 29 wks |
| 22 Mar 75 | **AN EVENING WITH JOHN DENVER** *RCA Victor LSA 3211/12* | 31 | 4 wks |
| 11 Oct 75 | **WIND SONG** *RCA Victor APLI 1183* ................. | 14 | 21 wks |
| 15 May 76 | ● **LIVE IN LONDON** *RCA Victor RS 1050* ............. | 2 | 29 wks |
| 4 Sep 76 | ● **SPIRIT** *RCA Victor APLI 1694* ..................... | 9 | 11 wks |
| 19 Mar 77 | ● **BEST OF JOHN DENVER VOL. 2** *RCA Victor PL 42120* .. | 9 | 9 wks |
| 11 Feb 78 | **I WANT TO LIVE** *RCA PL 12561* .................... | 25 | 5 wks |
| 21 Apr 79 | **JOHN DENVER** *RCA Victor PL 13075* ................ | 68 | 1 wk |
| 22 Oct 83 | **IT'S ABOUT TIME** *RCA RCALP 6087* ............... | 90 | 2 wks |
| 1 Dec 84 | **JOHN DENVER COLLECTION** *Telstar STAR 2253* ..... | 20 | 11 wks |
| 23 Aug 86 | **ONE WORLD** *RCA PL 85811* ...................... | 91 | 3 wks |

*See also Placido Domingo and John Denver.*

## Karl DENVER *UK, male vocalist*

*27 wks*

| | | | |
|---|---|---|---|
| 23 Dec 61 | ● **WIMOWEH** *Ace Of Clubs ACL 1098* .................... | 7 | 27 wks |

## DEPECHE MODE *UK, male vocal/instrumental group*

*113 wks*

| | | | |
|---|---|---|---|
| 14 Nov 81 | ● **SPEAK AND SPELL** *Mute STUMM 5* ................. | 10 | 33 wks |
| 9 Oct 82 | ● **A BROKEN FRAME** *Mute STUMM 9* ................. | 8 | 11 wks |
| 3 Sep 83 | ● **CONSTRUCTION TIME AGAIN** *Mute STUMM 13* ..... | 6 | 12 wks |
| 6 Sep 84 | ● **SOME GREAT REWARD** *Mute STUMM 19* .......... | 5 | 12 wks |
| 26 Oct 85 | ● **THE SINGLES 81–85** *Mute MUTEL 1* ............... | 6 | 22 wks |
| 29 Mar 86 | ● **BLACK CELEBRATION** *Mute STUMM 26* ........... | 4 | 11 wks |
| 10 Oct 87 | ● **MUSIC FOR THE MASSES** *Mute STUMM 47* .......... | 10 | 4 wks |
| 25 Mar 89 | ● **101** *Mute STUMM 101* .................................. | 5 | 8 wks |

**DEREK AND CLIVE** – *See Peter COOK and Dudley MOORE*

## DEREK and the DOMINOES
*UK/US, male vocal/instrumental group*

*1 wk*

| | | | |
|---|---|---|---|
| 24 Mar 73 | **IN CONCERT** *RSO 2659 020* ....................... | 36 | 1 wk |

**DESTROYERS** – *See George THOROGOOD and the DESTROYERS*

## DETROIT SPINNERS US, male vocal group   3 wks

| | | | | |
|---|---|---|---|---|
| 14 May 77 | **DETROIT SPINNERS' SMASH HITS** *Atlantic K 50363* .. | 37 | 3 wks |

## Sidney DEVINE UK, male vocalist   11 wks

| | | | |
|---|---|---|---|
| 10 Apr 76 | **DOUBLE DEVINE** *Philips 6625 019* ................. | 14 | 10 wks |
| 11 Dec 76 | **DEVINE TIME** *Philips 6308 283* ..................... | 49 | 1 wk |

## DEVO US, male vocal/instrumental group   22 wks

| | | | |
|---|---|---|---|
| 16 Sep 78 | **Q: ARE WE NOT MEN? A: NO WE ARE DEVO!** *Virgin V 2106* ........................................ | 12 | 7 wks |
| 23 Jun 79 | **DUTY NOW FOR THE FUTURE** *Virgin V 2125* ....... | 49 | 6 wks |
| 24 May 80 | **FREEDOM OF CHOICE** *Virgin V 2162* ............. | 47 | 5 wks |
| 5 Sep 81 | **NEW TRADITIONALISTS** *Virgin V 2191* ............ | 50 | 4 wks |

## Howard DEVOTO UK, male vocalist   2 wks

| | | | |
|---|---|---|---|
| 6 Aug 83 | **JERKY VERSIONS OF THE DREAM** *Virgin V 2272* .... | 57 | 2 wks |

## DEXY'S MIDNIGHT RUNNERS
UK, male/female vocal/instrumental group   64 wks

| | | | |
|---|---|---|---|
| 26 Jul 80 | ● **SEARCHING FOR THE YOUNG SOUL REBELS** *Parlophone PCS 7213* ........................... | 6 | 10 wks |
| 7 Aug 82 | ● **TOO-RYE-AY** *Mercury MERS 5* ..................... | 2 | 46 wks |
| 26 Mar 83 | **GENO** *EMI EMS 1007* ........................... | 79 | 2 wks |
| 21 Sep 85 | **DON'T STAND ME DOWN** *Mercury MERH 56* ......... | 22 | 6 wks |

*Group was all male for first album.*

## Neil DIAMOND US, male vocalist   473 wks

| | | | |
|---|---|---|---|
| 3 Apr 71 | **TAP ROOT MANUSCRIPT** *Uni UNLS 117* ........... | 19 | 12 wks |
| 3 Apr 71 | **GOLD** *Uni UNLS 116* ............................ | 23 | 11 wks |
| 11 Dec 71 | **STONES** *Uni UNLS 121* ......................... | 18 | 14 wks |
| 5 Aug 72 | ● **MOODS** *Uni UNLS 128* ......................... | 7 | 19 wks |
| 12 Jan 74 | **HOT AUGUST NIGHT** *Uni ULD 1* ................ | 32 | 2 wks |
| 16 Feb 74 | **JONATHAN LIVINGSTON SEAGULL** *CBS 69047* ..... | 35 | 1 wk |
| 9 Mar 74 | **RAINBOW** *MCA MCF 2529* ...................... | 39 | 5 wks |
| 29 Jul 74 | **HIS 12 GREATEST HITS** *MCA MCF 2550* ........... | 13 | 78 wks |
| 9 Nov 74 | **SERENADE** *CBS 69067* ........................ | 11 | 14 wks |
| 10 Jul 76 | ● **BEAUTIFUL NOISE** *CBS 86004* ................. | 3 | 26 wks |
| 12 Mar 77 | ● **LOVE AT THE GREEK** *CBS 95001* ............... | 3 | 32 wks |
| 6 Aug 77 | **HOT AUGUST NIGHT (re-issue)** *MCA MCSP 255* ..... | 60 | 1 wk |
| 17 Dec 77 | **I'M GLAD YOU'RE HERE WITH ME TONIGHT** *CBS 86044* ................................. | 16 | 12 wks |
| 25 Nov 78 | ● **20 GOLDEN GREATS** *MCA EMTV 14* ............. | 2 | 26 wks |
| 6 Jan 79 | **YOU DON'T BRING ME FLOWERS** *CBS 86077* ....... | 15 | 23 wks |
| 19 Jan 80 | **SEPTEMBER MORN** *CBS 86096* ................. | 14 | 11 wks |
| 22 Nov 80 | ● **THE JAZZ SINGER** *Capitol EAST 12120* ......... | 3 | 110 wks |
| 28 Feb 81 | **LOVE SONGS** *MCA MCF 3092* ................. | 43 | 6 wks |
| 5 Dec 81 | **THE WAY TO THE SKY** *CBS 85343* ............. | 39 | 13 wks |
| 19 Jun 82 | **12 GREATEST HITS VOL. 2** *CBS 85844* ......... | 32 | 8 wks |
| 13 Nov 82 | **HEARTLIGHT** *CBS 25073* ..................... | 43 | 10 wks |
| 10 Dec 83 | **THE VERY BEST OF NEIL DIAMOND** *K-Tel NE 1265* . | 33 | 11 wks |
| 28 Jul 84 | ● **PRIMITIVE** *CBS 86306* ........................ | 7 | 10 wks |
| 24 May 86 | **HEADED FOR THE FUTURE** *CBS 26952* ............ | 36 | 8 wks |
| 28 Nov 87 | **HOT AUGUST NIGHT 2** *CBS 460 408-1* ............ | 74 | 4 wks |
| 25 Feb 89 | **THE BEST YEARS OF OUR LIVES** *CBS 463201 1* ..... | 42 | 6 wks |

## DIAMOND HEAD  *UK, male vocal/instrumental group*  *9 wks*

| 23 Oct 82 | BORROWED TIME  *MCA DH 1001* ................. | 24 | 5 wks |
| 24 Sep 83 | CANTERBURY  *MCA DH 1002* .................... | 32 | 4 wks |

## DICKIES  *US, male vocal/instrumental group*  *19 wks*

| 17 Feb 79 | THE INCREDIBLE SHRINKING DICKIES | | |
| | *A & M AMLE 64742* ................ | 18 | 17 wks |
| 24 Nov 79 | DAWN OF THE DICKIES  *A & M AMLE 68510* ........ | 60 | 2 wks |

## Barbara DICKSON  *UK, female vocalist*  *126 wks*

| 18 Jun 77 | MORNING COMES QUICKLY  *RSO 2394 188* ........ | 58 | 1 wk |
| 12 Apr 80 | ● THE BARBARA DICKSON ALBUM  *Epic EPC 84088* ... | 7 | 12 wks |
| 16 May 81 | YOU KNOW IT'S ME  *Epic EPC 84551* ........... | 39 | 6 wks |
| 6 Feb 82 | ● ALL FOR A SONG  *Epic 10030* ................ | 3 | 38 wks |
| 24 Sep 83 | TELL ME IT'S NOT TRUE  *Legacy LLM 101* ........... | 100 | 1 wk |
| 23 Jun 84 | HEARTBEATS  *Epic EPC 25706* .................. | 21 | 8 wks |
| 12 Jan 85 | ● THE BARBARA DICKSON SONGBOOK  *K-Tel NE 1287* | 5 | 19 wks |
| 23 Nov 85 | GOLD  *K-Tel ONE 1312* ....................... | 11 | 18 wks |
| 15 Nov 86 | THE VERY BEST OF BARBARA DICKSON | | |
| | *Telstar STAR 2276* ................ | 78 | 8 wks |
| 29 Nov 86 | THE RIGHT MOMENT  *K-Tel ONE 1335* ........... | 39 | 8 wks |
| 6 May 89 | COMING ALIVE AGAIN  *Telstar STAR 2349* .......... | 30 | 7 wks |

Tell Me It's Not True *is a mini-album featuring songs from the musical* Blood Brothers.

## Bo DIDDLEY  *US, male vocalist/instrumentalist – guitar*  *16 wks*

| 5 Oct 63 | BO DIDDLEY  *Pye International NPL 28026* ............. | 11 | 8 wks |
| 9 Oct 63 | BO DIDDLEY IS A GUNSLINGER  *Pye NJL 33* ........ | 20 | 1 wk |
| 30 Nov 63 | BO DIDDLEY RIDES AGAIN  *Pye International NPL 28029* | 19 | 1 wk |
| 15 Feb 64 | BO DIDDLEY'S BEACH PARTY  *Pye NPL 28032* ...... | 13 | 6 wks |

## DIESEL PARK WEST  *UK, male vocal/instrumental group*  *2 wks*

| 11 Feb 89 | SHAKESPEARE ALABAMA  *Food FOODLP 2* ........ | 55 | 2 wks |

## DIFFORD and TILBROOK
*UK, male vocal/instrumental duo*  *3 wks*

| 14 Jul 84 | DIFFORD AND TILBROOK  *A & M AMLX 64985* ...... | 47 | 3 wks |

## Richard DIMBLEBY  *UK, male broadcaster*  *5 wks*

| 4 Jun 66 | VOICE OF RICHARD DIMBLEBY  *MFP 1087* ........ | 14 | 5 wks |

## DIO  *UK/US, male vocal/instrumental group*  *45 wks*

| 11 Jun 83 | HOLY DIVER  *Vertigo VERS 5* .................... | 13 | 15 wks |
| 21 Jul 84 | ● THE LAST IN LINE  *Vertigo VERL 16* ............ | 4 | 14 wks |
| 7 Sep 85 | ● SACRED HEART  *Vertigo VERH 30* ............... | 4 | 6 wks |
| 5 Jul 86 | INTERMISSION  *Vertigo VERB 40* ................ | 22 | 5 wks |
| 22 Aug 87 | ● DREAM EVIL  *Vertigo VERH 46* .................. | 8 | 5 wks |

## DION and the BELMONTS  *US, male vocal group*  *5 wks*

| 12 Apr 80 | 20 GOLDEN GREATS  *K-Tel NE 1057* ................ | 31 | 5 wks |

## DIRE STRAITS  *UK, male vocal/instrumental group*  *1014 wks*

| 22 Jul 78 | ● DIRE STRAITS  *Vertigo 9102 021* .................... | 5 | 130 wks |
| 23 Jun 79 | ● COMMUNIQUE  *Vertigo 9102 031* .................... | 5 | 32 wks |

| 25 Oct 80 | ● MAKIN' MOVIES | Vertigo 6359 034 | 4 | 249 wks |
| 2 Oct 82 | ★ LOVE OVER GOLD | Vertigo 6359 109 | 1 | 198 wks |
| 24 Mar 84 | ● ALCHEMY – DIRE STRAITS LIVE | Vertigo VERY 11 | 3 | 163 wks |
| 25 May 85 | ★ BROTHERS IN ARMS | Vertigo VERH 25 | 1 | 195 wks |
| 29 Oct 88 | ★ MONEY FOR NOTHING | Vertigo VERH 64 | 1 | 47 wks |

## DISCHARGE  UK, male vocal/instrumental group          5 wks

| 15 May 82 | HEAR NOTHING, SEE NOTHING, SAY NOTHING Clay CLAYLP 3 | 40 | 5 wks |

**DISCIPLES OF SOUL** – See LITTLE STEVEN

## Sacha DISTEL  France, male vocalist          14 wks

| 2 May 70 | SACHA DISTEL | Warner Bros. WS 3003 | 21 | 14 wks |

## DJ JAZZY JEFF and FRESH PRINCE
US, male rap duo          3 wks

| 28 Feb 87 | ROCK THE HOUSE | Champion CHAMP 1004 | 97 | 1 wk |
| 21 May 88 | HE'S THE DJ, I'M THE RAPPER | Jive HIP 61 | 68 | 2 wks |

## DOCTOR and the MEDICS
UK, male/female vocal/instrumental group          3 wks

| 21 Jun 86 | LAUGHING AT THE PIECES | MCA MIRG 1010 | 25 | 3 wks |

## DR. FEELGOOD  UK, male vocal/instrumental group          33 wks

| 18 Oct 75 | MALPRACTICE | United Artists UAS 29880 | 17 | 6 wks |
| 2 Oct 76 | ★ STUPIDITY | United Artists UAS 29990 | 1 | 9 wks |
| 4 Jun 77 | ● SNEAKIN' SUSPICION | United Artists UAS 30075 | 10 | 6 wks |
| 8 Oct 77 | BE SEEING YOU | United Artists UAS 30123 | 55 | 3 wks |
| 7 Oct 78 | PRIVATE PRACTICE | United Artists UAG 30184 | 41 | 5 wks |
| 2 Jun 79 | AS IT HAPPENS | United Artists UAK 30239 | 42 | 4 wks |

## DR. HOOK  US, male vocal/instrumental group          130 wks

| 25 Jun 76 | ● A LITTLE BIT MORE | Capitol E-ST 23795 | 5 | 42 wks |
| 29 Oct 77 | MAKING LOVE AND MUSIC | Capitol EST 11632 | 39 | 4 wks |
| 27 Oct 79 | PLEASURE AND PAIN | Capitol EAST 11859 | 47 | 6 wks |
| 17 Nov 79 | SOMETIMES YOU WIN | Capitol EST 12018 | 14 | 44 wks |
| 29 Nov 80 | RISING | Mercury 6302 076 | 44 | 5 wks |
| 6 Dec 80 | ● DR. HOOK'S GREATEST HITS | Capitol EST 26037 | 2 | 28 wks |
| 14 Nov 81 | DR. HOOK LIVE IN THE UK | Capitol EST 26706 | 90 | 1 wk |

## Ken DODD  UK, male vocalist          36 wks

| 25 Dec 65 | ● TEARS OF HAPPINESS | Columbia 33SX 1793 | 6 | 12 wks |
| 23 Jul 66 | HITS FOR NOW AND ALWAYS | Columbia SX 6060 | 14 | 11 wks |
| 14 Jan 67 | FOR SOMEONE SPECIAL | Columbia SCX 6224 | 40 | 1 wk |
| 29 Nov 80 | ● 20 GOLDEN GREATS OF KEN DODD | Warwick WW 5098 | 8 | 12 wks |

## DOGS D'AMOUR  UK, male vocal/instrumental group          8 wks

| 22 Oct 88 | IN THE DYNAMITE JET SALOON | China WOL 8 | 97 | 1 wk |

| | | | |
|---|---|---|---|
| 25 Mar 89 | **A GRAVEYARD OF EMPTY BOTTLES** *China 8390740* . | 16 | 4 wks |
| 30 Sep 89 | **ERROL FLYNN** *China 8397001* ..................... | 22 | 3 wks |

## DOKKEN *US, male vocal/instrumental group*
*1 wk*

| | | | |
|---|---|---|---|
| 21 Nov 87 | **BACK FOR THE ATTACK** *Elektra EKT 43* ........... | 96 | 1 wk |

## Thomas DOLBY
*UK, male vocalist/instrumentalist – keyboards*
*27 wks*

| | | | |
|---|---|---|---|
| 22 May 82 | **THE GOLDEN AGE OF WIRELESS** | | |
| | *Venice In Peril VIP 1001* ........................... | 65 | 10 wks |
| 18 Feb 84 | **THE FLAT EARTH** *Parlophone Odeon PCS 2400341* ...... | 14 | 14 wks |
| 7 May 88 | **ALIENS ATE MY BUICK** *Manhattan MTL 1020* ......... | 30 | 3 wks |

## DOLLAR *UK, male/female vocal duo*
*28 wks*

| | | | |
|---|---|---|---|
| 15 Sep 79 | **SHOOTING STARS** *Carrere CAL 111* ................ | 36 | 8 wks |
| 24 Apr 82 | **THE VERY BEST OF DOLLAR** *Carrere CAL 3001* ...... | 31 | 9 wks |
| 30 Oct 82 | **THE DOLLAR ALBUM** *WEA DTV 1* ............... | 18 | 11 wks |

## Placido DOMINGO *Spain, male vocalist*
*36 wks*

| | | | |
|---|---|---|---|
| 21 May 83 | **MY LIFE FOR A SONG** *CBS 73683* .................. | 31 | 8 wks |
| 27 Dec 86 | **PLACIDO DOMINGO COLLECTION** *Stylus SMR 625* .. | 30 | 14 wks |
| 23 Apr 88 | **GREATEST LOVE SONGS** *CBS 44701* ............... | 63 | 2 wks |
| 17 Jun 89 | **GOYA... A LIFE IN A SONG** *CBS 463294 1* .......... | 36 | 4 wks |
| 17 Jun 89 | **THE ESSENTIAL DOMINGO** | | |
| | *Deutsche Grammophon PDTV 1* ........................ | 20 | 8 wks |

*See also Placido Domingo and John Denver; Andrew Lloyd Webber.*

## Placido DOMINGO and John DENVER
*Spain/US, male vocal duo*
*21 wks*

| | | | |
|---|---|---|---|
| 28 Nov 81 | **PERHAPS LOVE** *CBS 73592* ...................... | 17 | 21 wks |

*See also Placido Domingo; John Denver.*

## Fats DOMINO *US, male vocalist/instrumentalist – piano*
*1 wk*

| | | | |
|---|---|---|---|
| 16 May 70 | **VERY BEST OF FATS DOMINO** *Liberty LBS 83331* ..... | 56 | 1 wk |

**DOMINOES** – *See DEREK and the DOMINOES*

## Lonnie DONEGAN *UK, male vocalist*
*29 wks*

| | | | |
|---|---|---|---|
| 1 Sep 62 ● | **GOLDEN AGE OF DONEGAN** | | |
| | *Pye Golden Guinea GGL 0135* ........................ | 3 | 23 wks |
| 9 Feb 63 | **GOLDEN AGE OF DONEGAN VOL. 2** | | |
| | *Pye Golden Guinea GGL 0170* ........................ | 15 | 3 wks |
| 25 Feb 78 | **PUTTING ON THE STYLE** *Chrysalis CHR 1158* ........ | 51 | 3 wks |

## DONOVAN *UK, male vocalist*
*73 wks*

| | | | |
|---|---|---|---|
| 5 Jun 65 ● | **WHAT'S BIN DID AND WHAT'S BIN HID** | | |
| | *Pye NPL 18117* ..................................... | 3 | 16 wks |
| 6 Nov 65 | **FAIRY TALE** *Pye NPL 18128* ........................ | 20 | 2 wks |
| 8 Jul 67 | **SUNSHINE SUPERMAN** *Pye NPL 18181* ............ | 25 | 7 wks |
| 14 Oct 67 ● | **UNIVERSAL SOLDIER** *Marble Arch MAL 718* .......... | 5 | 18 wks |

| | | | |
|---|---|---|---|
| 11 May 68 | **A GIFT FROM A FLOWER TO A GARDEN** | | |
| | *Pye NSPL 20000* ................. | 13 | 14 wks |
| 12 Sep 70 | **OPEN ROAD** *Dawn DNLS 3009* .................... | 30 | 4 wks |
| 24 Mar 73 | **COSMIC WHEELS** *Epic EPC 65450* ................ | 15 | 12 wks |

## Jason DONOVAN *Australia, male vocalist*     *34 wks*

| | | | |
|---|---|---|---|
| 13 May 89 | ★ **TEN GOOD REASONS** *PWL HF 7* ................. | 1† | 34 wks |

## DOOBIE BROTHERS *US, male vocal/instrumental group*   *30 wks*

| | | | |
|---|---|---|---|
| 30 Mar 74 | **WHAT WERE ONCE VICES ARE NOW HABITS** | | |
| | *Warner Bros. K 56206* ................. | 19 | 10 wks |
| 17 May 75 | **STAMPEDE** *Warner Bros. K 56094* ................ | 14 | 11 wks |
| 10 Apr 76 | **TAKIN' IT TO THE STREETS** *Warner Bros. K 56196* .... | 42 | 2 wks |
| 17 Sep 77 | **LIVING ON THE FAULT LINE** *Warner Bros. K 56383* .... | 25 | 5 wks |
| 11 Oct 80 | **ONE STEP CLOSER** *Warner Bros. K 56824* ............. | 53 | 2 wks |

## DOOLEYS *UK, male/female vocal/instrumental group*   *27 wks*

| | | | |
|---|---|---|---|
| 30 Jun 79 | ● **THE BEST OF THE DOOLEYS** *GTO GTTV 038* ....... | 6 | 21 wks |
| 3 Nov 79 | **THE CHOSEN FEW** *GTO GTLP 040* ............... | 56 | 4 wks |
| 25 Oct 80 | **FULL HOUSE** *GTO GTTV 050* ................... | 54 | 2 wks |

## Val DOONICAN *Ireland, male vocalist*   *164 wks*

| | | | |
|---|---|---|---|
| 12 Dec 64 | ● **LUCKY 13 SHADES OF VAL DOONICAN** | | |
| | *Decca LK 4648* ................................ | 2 | 27 wks |
| 3 Dec 66 | ● **GENTLE SHADES OF VAL DOONICAN** | | |
| | *Decca LK 4831* ................................ | 5 | 52 wks |
| 2 Dec 67 | ★ **VAL DOONICAN ROCKS BUT GENTLY** | | |
| | *Pye NSPL 18204* ............................... | 1 | 23 wks |
| 30 Nov 68 | ● **VAL** *Pye NSPL 18236* ........................ | 6 | 11 wks |
| 14 Jun 69 | ● **WORLD OF VAL DOONICAN** *Decca SPA 3* ........... | 2 | 31 wks |
| 13 Dec 69 | **SOUNDS GENTLE** *Pye NSPL 18321* ............ | 22 | 9 wks |
| 19 Dec 70 | **THE MAGIC OF VAL DOONICAN** *Philips 6642 003* ..... | 34 | 3 wks |
| 27 Nov 71 | **THIS IS VAL DOONICAN** *Philips 6382 017* ........... | 40 | 1 wk |
| 22 Feb 75 | **I LOVE COUNTRY MUSIC** *Philips 9299261* ........... | 37 | 2 wks |
| 21 May 77 | **SOME OF MY BEST FRIENDS ARE SONGS** | | |
| | *Philips 6641 607* ................................ | 29 | 5 wks |

## DOORS *US, male vocal/instrumental group*   *31 wks*

| | | | |
|---|---|---|---|
| 28 Sep 68 | **WAITING FOR THE SUN** *Elektra EKS7 4024* .......... | 16 | 10 wks |
| 11 Apr 70 | **MORRISON HOTEL** *Elektra EKS 75007* .............. | 12 | 8 wks |
| 26 Sep 70 | **ABSOLUTELY LIVE** *Elektra 2665 002* .............. | 69 | 1 wk |
| 31 Jul 71 | **L.A. WOMAN** *Elektra K42090* .................... | 28 | 3 wks |
| 1 Apr 72 | **WEIRD SCENES INSIDE THE GOLD MINE** | | |
| | *Elektra K 62009* ................................ | 50 | 1 wk |
| 29 Oct 83 | **ALIVE, SHE CRIED** *Elektra 96–0269–1* ............... | 36 | 5 wks |
| 4 Jul 87 | **LIVE AT THE HOLLYWOOD BOWL** *Elektra EKT 40* .. | 51 | 3 wks |

## Lee DORSEY *US, male vocalist*   *4 wks*

| | | | |
|---|---|---|---|
| 17 Dec 66 | **NEW LEE DORSEY** *Stateside SSL 10192* .............. | 34 | 4 wks |

## DOUBLE *Switzerland, male vocal/instrumental duo*   *4 wks*

| | | | |
|---|---|---|---|
| 8 Mar 86 | **BLUE** *Polydor POLD 5187* .......................... | 69 | 4 wks |

**DOUBLE TROUBLE** – See Stevie Ray VAUGHAN and DOUBLE TROUBLE

## Craig DOUGLAS *UK, male vocalist*   *2 wks*

| | | | |
|---|---|---|---|
| 6 Aug 60 | **CRAIG DOUGLAS** *Top Rank BUY 049* .............. | 17 | 2 wks |

## Will DOWNING  *US, male vocalist*  *25 wks*

| | | | | |
|---|---|---|---|---|
| 26 Mar 88 | **WILL DOWNING**  *Fourth & Broadway BRLP 518* ......... | 20 | 23 wks |
| 18 Nov 89 | **COME TOGETHER AS ONE**  *Fourth & Broadway BRLP 538* | 36 | 2 wks |

## DREAM ACADEMY
*UK, male/female vocal/instrumental group*  *2 wks*

| | | | | |
|---|---|---|---|---|
| 12 Oct 85 | **THE DREAM ACADEMY**  *blanco y negro BYN 6* ......... | 58 | 2 wks |

**DOZY** – *See Dave DEE, DOZY, BEAKY, MICK and TICH*

**DREAMERS** – *See FREDDIE and the DREAMERS*

## DRIFTERS  *US, male vocal group*  *65 wks*

| | | | | |
|---|---|---|---|---|
| 18 May 68 | **GOLDEN HITS**  *Atlantic 588-103* .................... | 27 | 7 wks |
| 10 Jun 72 | **GOLDEN HITS**  *Atlantic K 40018* ................... | 26 | 8 wks |
| 8 Nov 75 | ● **24 ORIGINAL HITS**  *Atlantic K 60106* ................ | 2 | 34 wks |
| 13 Dec 75 | **LOVE GAMES**  *Bell BELLS 246* .................... | 51 | 1 wk |
| 18 Oct 86 | **THE VERY BEST OF THE DRIFTERS**  *Telstar STAR 2280* | 24 | 15 wks |

*See also Ben E. King.*

## Julie DRISCOLL and the Brian AUGER TRINITY  *UK, female/male vocal/instrumental group*  *13 wks*

| | | | | |
|---|---|---|---|---|
| 8 Jun 68 | **OPEN**  *Marmalade 608-002* ........................... | 12 | 13 wks |

## D-TRAIN  *US, male vocalist/multi-instrumentalist. Hubert Eaves*  *4 wks*

| | | | | |
|---|---|---|---|---|
| 8 May 82 | **D-TRAIN**  *Epic EPC 85683* ...................... | 72 | 4 wks |

## DUBLINERS  *Ireland, male vocal/instrumental group*  *88 wks*

| | | | | |
|---|---|---|---|---|
| 13 May 67 | ● **A DROP OF THE HARD STUFF**  *Major Minor MMLP 3* .. | 5 | 41 wks |
| 9 Sep 67 | **BEST OF THE DUBLINERS**  *Transatlantic TRA 158* ...... | 25 | 11 wks |
| 7 Oct 67 | ● **MORE OF THE HARD STUFF**  *Major Minor MMLP 5* .... | 8 | 23 wks |
| 2 Mar 68 | **DRINKIN' AND COURTIN'**  *Major Minor SMLP 14* ..... | 31 | 3 wks |
| 25 Apr 87 | **THE DUBLINERS 25 YEARS CELEBRATION** *Stylus SMR 731* ................................ | 43 | 10 wks |

## Stephen 'Tin Tin' DUFFY  *UK, male vocalist*  *7 wks*

| | | | | |
|---|---|---|---|---|
| 20 Apr 85 | **THE UPS AND DOWNS**  *10 DIX 5* ................... | 35 | 7 wks |

## George DUKE  *US, male vocalist/instrumentalist – keyboards*  *4 wks*

| | | | | |
|---|---|---|---|---|
| 26 Jul 80 | **BRAZILIAN LOVE AFFAIR**  *Epic EPC 84311* .......... | 33 | 4 wks |

**DUKES** – *See Steve EARLE*

## Simon DUPREE and the BIG SOUND
*UK, male vocal/instrumental group*  *1 wk*

| | | | | |
|---|---|---|---|---|
| 13 Aug 67 | **WITHOUT RESERVATIONS**  *Parlophone PCS 7029* ..... | 39 | 1 wk |

## DURAN DURAN  *UK, male vocal/instrumental group*  *332 wks*

| | | | | |
|---|---|---|---|---|
| 27 Jun 81 | ● **DURAN DURAN**  *EMI EMC 3372* ................... | 3 | 118 wks |
| 22 May 82 | ● **RIO**  *EMI EMC 3411* ................................ | 2 | 109 wks |

Three really was the magic number for rap/scratch/sampling trio **DE LA SOUL**.

**DEACON BLUE** were Scotland's breakout band of the late Eighties.

The multiple keyboard player **THOMAS DOLBY** has a go at the typewriter.

| | | | |
|---|---|---|---|
| 3 Dec 83 | ★ SEVEN AND THE RAGGED TIGER *EMI DD 1* ....... | 1 | 47 wks |
| 24 Nov 84 | ● ARENA *Parlophone DD 2* ................... | 6 | 31 wks |
| 6 Dec 86 | NOTORIOUS *EMI DDN 331* ................. | 16 | 16 wks |
| 29 Oct 88 | BIG THING *EMI DDB 33* ................ | 15 | 5 wks |
| 25 Nov 89 | ● DECADE *EMI DDX 10* ..................... | 5† | 6 wks |

## Deanna DURBIN *Canada, female vocalist* 4 wks

| | | | |
|---|---|---|---|
| 30 Jan 82 | THE BEST OF DEANNA DURBIN | | |
| | *MCA International MCA 1634* ................... | 84 | 4 wks |

## Ian DURY and the BLOCKHEADS
*UK, male vocal/instrumental group* 118 wks

| | | | |
|---|---|---|---|
| 22 Oct 77 | ● NEW BOOTS AND PANTIES!! *Stiff SEEZ 4* ......... | 5 | 90 wks |
| 2 Jun 79 | ● DO IT YOURSELF *Stiff SEEZ 14* ................. | 2 | 18 wks |
| 6 Dec 80 | LAUGHTER *Stiff SEEZ 30* ................. | 48 | 4 wks |
| 10 Oct 81 | LORD UPMINSTER *Polydor POLD 5042* ......... | 53 | 4 wks |
| 4 Feb 84 | 4,000 WEEKS HOLIDAY *Polydor POLD 5112* ......... | 54 | 2 wks |

4,000 Weeks Holiday *credits the Music Students – UK, male vocal/instrumental group.*

## Bob DYLAN *US, male vocalist* 552 wks

| | | | |
|---|---|---|---|
| 23 May 64 | ★ THE FREEWHEELIN' BOB DYLAN *CBS BPG 62193* .. | 1 | 49 wks |
| 11 Jul 64 | ● THE TIMES THEY ARE A-CHANGIN' *CBS BPG 62251* | 4 | 20 wks |
| 21 Nov 64 | ● ANOTHER SIDE OF BOB DYLAN *CBS BPG 62429* .... | 8 | 19 wks |
| 8 May 65 | BOB DYLAN *CBS BPG 62022* ................. | 13 | 6 wks |
| 15 May 65 | ★ BRINGING IT ALL BACK HOME *CBS BPG 62515* ..... | 1 | 29 wks |
| 9 Oct 65 | ★ HIGHWAY 61 REVISITED *CBS BPG 62572* ......... | 4 | 15 wks |
| 20 Aug 66 | ● BLONDE ON BLONDE *CBS DDP 66012* ............. | 3 | 15 wks |
| 14 Jan 67 | ● GREATEST HITS *CBS SBPG 62847* ............ | 6 | 82 wks |
| 2 Mar 68 | ★ JOHN WESLEY HARDING *CBS SBPG 63252* ......... | 1 | 29 wks |
| 17 May 69 | ★ NASHVILLE SKYLINE *CBS 63601* ............. | 1 | 42 wks |
| 11 Jul 70 | ★ SELF PORTRAIT *CBS 66250* ................... | 1 | 15 wks |
| 28 Nov 70 | ★ NEW MORNING *CBS 69001* ................... | 1 | 18 wks |
| 25 Dec 71 | MORE BOB DYLAN GREATEST HITS *CBS 67238/9* ... | 12 | 15 wks |
| 29 Sep 73 | PAT GARRETT AND BILLY THE KID (film soundtrack) | | |
| | *CBS 69042* ................... | 29 | 11 wks |
| 23 Feb 74 | ● PLANET WAVES *Island ILPS 9261* ......... | 7 | 8 wks |
| 13 Jul 74 | ● BEFORE THE FLOOD *Asylum IDBD 1* ......... | 8 | 7 wks |
| 15 Feb 75 | ● BLOOD ON THE TRACKS *CBS 69097* ......... | 4 | 16 wks |
| 26 Jul 75 | ● THE BASEMENT TAPES *CBS 88147* ......... | 8 | 10 wks |
| 31 Jan 76 | ● DESIRE *CBS 86003* ................... | 3 | 35 wks |
| 9 Oct 76 | ● HARD RAIN *CBS 86016* ................. | 3 | 7 wks |
| 1 Jul 78 | ● STREET LEGAL *CBS 86067* ............. | 2 | 20 wks |
| 26 May 79 | ● BOB DYLAN AT BUDOKAN *CBS 96004* ......... | 4 | 19 wks |
| 8 Sep 79 | ● SLOW TRAIN COMING *CBS 86095* ......... | 2 | 13 wks |
| 28 Jun 80 | ● SAVED *CBS 86113* ................... | 3 | 8 wks |
| 29 Aug 81 | ● SHOT OF LOVE *CBS 85178* ............. | 6 | 8 wks |
| 12 Nov 83 | ● INFIDELS *CBS 25539* ................. | 9 | 12 wks |
| 15 Dec 84 | REAL LIVE *CBS 26334* ................. | 54 | 2 wks |
| 22 Jun 85 | EMPIRE BURLESQUE *CBS 86313* ......... | 11 | 6 wks |
| 2 Aug 86 | KNOCKED OUT LOADED *CBS 86326* ......... | 35 | 5 wks |
| 23 Apr 88 | GREATEST HITS *CBS 460907 1* ............. | 99 | 1 wk |
| 25 Jun 88 | DOWN IN THE GROOVE *CBS 460267 1* ............. | 32 | 3 wks |
| 14 Oct 89 | ● OH MERCY *CBS 465800 1* ................. | 6 | 7 wks |

*Both* Greatest Hits *collections are different. See also Bob Dylan and the Grateful Dead.*

## Bob DYLAN and the GRATEFUL DEAD
*US, male vocalist and vocal/instrumental group* 3 wks

| | | | |
|---|---|---|---|
| 18 Feb 89 | DYLAN AND THE DEAD *CBS 463381 1* ............. | 38 | 3 wks |

# e

E STREET BAND – *See Bruce SPRINGSTEEN*

## EAGLES  *US, male vocal/instrumental group*  267 wks

| 27 Apr 74 | ON THE BORDER *Asylum SYL 9016* .................. | 28 | 9 wks |
| 12 Jul 75 | ● ONE OF THESE NIGHTS *Asylum SYLA 8759* .......... | 8 | 40 wks |
| 12 Jul 75 | DESPERADO *Asylum SYLL 9011* ................... | 39 | 9 wks |
| 6 Mar 76 | ● THEIR GREATEST HITS 1971–1975 *Asylum K 53017* .... | 2 | 77 wks |
| 25 Dec 76 | ● HOTEL CALIFORNIA *Asylum K 53051* .............. | 2 | 62 wks |
| 13 Oct 79 | ● THE LONG RUN *Asylum K 52181* .................. | 4 | 16 wks |
| 22 Nov 80 | LIVE *Asylum K 62032* ......................... | 24 | 13 wks |
| 18 May 85 | ● BEST OF THE EAGLES *Asylum EKT 5* .............. | 8 | 41 wks |

## Steve EARLE  *US, male vocalist/instrumentalist – guitar*  10 wks

| 4 Jul 87 | EXIT 0 *MCA MCF 3379* .......................... | 77 | 2 wks |
| 19 Nov 88 | COPPERHEAD ROAD *MCA MCF 3426* ............. | 44 | 8 wks |

Exit 0 *credits The Dukes – US, male instrumental group.*

## EARTH WIND AND FIRE
*US, male vocal/instrumental group*  154 wks

| 21 Jan 78 | ALL 'N' ALL *CBS 86051* .......................... | 13 | 23 wks |
| 16 Dec 78 | ● THE BEST OF EARTH WIND AND FIRE VOL. 1 | | |
| | *CBS 83284* .................................... | 6 | 42 wks |
| 23 Jun 79 | ● I AM *CBS 86084* ............................. | 5 | 41 wks |
| 1 Nov 80 | ● FACES *CBS 88498* ........................... | 10 | 6 wks |
| 14 Nov 81 | RAISE *CBS 85272* ............................. | 14 | 22 wks |
| 19 Feb 83 | POWERLIGHT *CBS 25120* ..................... | 22 | 7 wks |
| 10 May 86 | ● THE COLLECTION *K-Tel NE 1322* ................ | 5 | 13 wks |

## EASTERHOUSE  *UK, male vocal/instrumental group*  1 wk

| 28 Jun 86 | CONTENDERS *Rough Trade ROUGH 94* ............. | 91 | 1 wk |

## EAST OF EDEN  *UK, male vocal/instrumental group*  2 wks

| 14 Mar 70 | SNAFU *Deram SML 1050* ......................... | 29 | 2 wks |

## Sheena EASTON  *UK, female vocalist*  37 wks

| 31 Jan 81 | TAKE MY TIME *EMI EMC 3354* ................... | 17 | 19 wks |
| 3 Oct 81 | YOU COULD HAVE BEEN WITH ME *EMI EMC 3378* . | 33 | 6 wks |
| 25 Sep 82 | MADNESS, MONEY AND MUSIC *EMI EMC 3414* ..... | 44 | 4 wks |
| 15 Oct 83 | BEST KEPT SECRET *EMI EMC 1077951* ............. | 99 | 1 wk |
| 4 Mar 89 | THE LOVER IN ME *MCA MCG 6036* ................ | 30 | 7 wks |

## Clint EASTWOOD and General SAINT
*Jamaica, male vocal duo*  3 wks

| 6 Feb 82 | TWO BAD DJ *Greensleeves GREL 24* ................... | 99 | 2 wks |
| 28 May 83 | STOP THAT TRAIN *Greensleeves GREL 53* ............ | 98 | 1 wk |

Hubert EAVES – *See D-TRAIN*

The three studio albums by the original line-up of **DURAN DURAN** executed a three-stage countdown to number one.

**BOB DYLAN** and Tom Petty toured together shortly before becoming two of the Traveling Wilburys.

**DUKE ELLINGTON**, one of the leading musical figures of the century, had his only UK chart album late in life.

**MANITAS DE PLATA** (left) shows the technique that gave him international renown and one week in the chart.

# ECHO and the BUNNYMEN
*UK, male vocal/instrumental group*                                     *89 wks*

| | | | | |
|---|---|---|---|---|
| 26 Jul | 80 | **CROCODILES** *Korova KODE 1* .................... | 17 | 6 wks |
| 6 Jun | 81 | ● **HEAVEN UP HERE** *Korova KODE 3* ................ | 10 | 16 wks |
| 12 Feb | 83 | ● **PORCUPINE** *Korova KODE 6* .............. | 2 | 17 wks |
| 12 May | 84 | ● **OCEAN RAIN** *Korova KODE 8* .................. | 4 | 26 wks |
| 23 Nov | 85 | ● **SONGS TO LEARN & SING** *Korova KODE 13* ......... | 6 | 15 wks |
| 18 Jul | 87 | ● **ECHO AND THE BUNNYMEN** *WEA WX 108* ........ | 4 | 9 wks |

# EDDIE and the HOT RODS
*UK, male vocal/instrumental group*                                     *5 wks*

| | | | | |
|---|---|---|---|---|
| 18 Dec | 76 | **TEENAGE DEPRESSION** *Island ILPS 9457* ........... | 43 | 1 wk |
| 3 Dec | 77 | **LIFE ON THE LINE** *Island ILPS 9509* ................ | 27 | 3 wks |
| 24 Mar | 79 | **THRILLER** *Island ILPS 9563* .................... | 50 | 1 wk |

# Duane EDDY *US, male instrumentalist – guitar*                       *88 wks*

| | | | | |
|---|---|---|---|---|
| 6 Jun | 59 | ● **HAVE TWANGY GUITAR WILL TRAVEL** | | |
| | | *London HAW 2160* ................................ | 6 | 3 wks |
| 31 Oct | 59 | ● **SPECIALLY FOR YOU** *London HAW 2191* ........... | 6 | 8 wks |
| 19 Mar | 60 | ● **THE TWANG'S THE THANG** *London HAW 2236* ...... | 2 | 25 wks |
| 26 Nov | 60 | **SONGS OF OUR HERITAGE** *London HAW 2285* ........ | 13 | 5 wks |
| 1 Apr | 61 | ● **A MILLION DOLLARS' WORTH OF TWANG** | | |
| | | *London HAW 2325* ................................ | 5 | 19 wks |
| 9 Jun | 62 | **A MILLION DOLLARS' WORTH OF TWANG VOL. 2** | | |
| | | *London HAW 2435* ................................ | 18 | 1 wk |
| 21 Jul | 62 | ● **TWISTIN' AND TWANGIN'** *RCA RD 27264* .......... | 8 | 12 wks |
| 8 Dec | 62 | **TWANGY GUITAR – SILKY STRINGS** *RCA RD 7510* . | 13 | 11 wks |
| 16 Mar | 63 | **DANCE WITH THE GUITAR MAN** *RCA RD 7545* ..... | 14 | 4 wks |

# Dave EDMUNDS *UK, male vocalist/instrumentalist – guitar*            *21 wks*

| | | | | |
|---|---|---|---|---|
| 23 Jun | 79 | **REPEAT WHEN NECESSARY** *Swansong SSK 59409* .... | 39 | 12 wks |
| 18 Apr | 81 | **TWANGIN'** *Swansong SSK 59411* .................... | 37 | 4 wks |
| 3 Apr | 82 | **DE7** *Arista SPART 1184* ......................... | 60 | 3 wks |
| 30 Apr | 83 | **INFORMATION** *Arista 205 348* ..................... | 92 | 2 wks |

# Dennis EDWARDS *US, male vocalist*                                    *1 wk*

| | | | | |
|---|---|---|---|---|
| 14 Apr | 84 | **DON'T LOOK ANY FURTHER** *Gordy ZL 72148* ....... | 91 | 1 wk |

# EEK-A-MOUSE *Jamaica, male vocalist*                                  *3 wks*

| | | | | |
|---|---|---|---|---|
| 14 Aug | 82 | **SKIDIP** *Greensleeves GREL 41* ..................... | 61 | 3 wks |

# 801 *UK, male vocal/instrumental group*                               *2 wks*

| | | | | |
|---|---|---|---|---|
| 20 Nov | 76 | **801 LIVE** *Island ILPS 9444* ..................... | 52 | 2 wks |

# 808 STATE *UK, male instrumental group*                               *1 wk*

| | | | | |
|---|---|---|---|---|
| 16 Dec | 89 | **NINETY** *ZTT ZTT 2* ............................ | 57 | 1 wk |

# EIGHTH WONDER
*UK, male/female vocal/instrumental group*                             *4 wks*

| | | | | |
|---|---|---|---|---|
| 23 Jul | 88 | **FEARLESS** *CBS 460628 1* ......................... | 47 | 4 wks |

## ELECTRIC LIGHT ORCHESTRA

*UK, male vocal/instrumental group*                                         *348 wks*

| | | | |
|---|---|---|---|
| 12 Aug 72 | **ELECTRIC LIGHT ORCHESTRA** *Harvest SHVL 797* ... | 32 | 4 wks |
| 31 Mar 73 | **ELO 2** *Harvest SHVL 806* ........................ | 35 | 1 wk |
| 11 Dec 76 | ● **A NEW WORLD RECORD** *United Artists UAG 30017* ... | 6 | 100 wks |
| 12 Nov 77 | ● **OUT OF THE BLUE** *United Artists UAR 100* ........... | 4 | 108 wks |
| 6 Jan 79 | **THREE LIGHT YEARS** *Jet JET BX 1* .............. | 38 | 9 wks |
| 16 Jun 79 | ★ **DISCOVERY** *Jet JET LX 500* ................... | 1 | 46 wks |
| 1 Dec 79 | ● **ELO'S GREATEST HITS** *Jet JET LX 525* ............. | 7 | 18 wks |
| 8 Aug 81 | ★ **TIME** *Jet JETLP 236* ........................ | 1 | 32 wks |
| 2 Jul 83 | ● **SECRET MESSAGES** *Jet JET LX 527* ................ | 4 | 15 wks |
| 15 Mar 86 | ● **BALANCE OF POWER** *Epic EPC 26467* ............ | 9 | 12 wks |
| 16 Dec 89 | **THE GREATEST HITS** *Telstar STAR 2370* ............ | 23† | 3 wks |

A New World Record *changed to JET LP 200 and* Out Of The Blue *changed label number to JET DP 400 during their chart runs.*


## ELECTRIC WIND ENSEMBLE

*UK, male instrumental group*                                               *9 wks*

| | | | |
|---|---|---|---|
| 18 Feb 84 | **HAUNTING MELODIES** *Nouveau Music NML 1007* ...... | 28 | 9 wks |


## Danny ELFMAN *US, male orchestra leader*                                 *6 wks*

| | | | |
|---|---|---|---|
| 12 Aug 89 | **BATMAN** *Warner Bros. WX 287* ...................... | 45 | 6 wks |


## Duke ELLINGTON *US, orchestra*                                           *2 wks*

| | | | |
|---|---|---|---|
| 8 Apr 61 | **NUT CRACKER SUITE** *Philips BBL 7418* ............. | 11 | 2 wks |


## Ben ELTON *UK, male comedian*                                            *2 wks*

| | | | |
|---|---|---|---|
| 14 Nov 87 | **MOTORMOUTH** *Mercury BENLP 1* ................... | 86 | 2 wks |


## EMERSON, LAKE and PALMER

*UK, male instrumental group*                                               *135 wks*

| | | | |
|---|---|---|---|
| 5 Dec 70 | ● **EMERSON, LAKE AND PALMER** *Island ILPS 9132* .... | 4 | 28 wks |
| 19 Jun 71 | ★ **TARKUS** *Island ILPS 9155* ........................ | 1 | 17 wks |
| 4 Dec 71 | ● **PICTURES AT AN EXHIBITION** *Island HELP 1* ....... | 3 | 5 wks |
| 8 Jul 72 | ● **TRILOGY** *Island ILPS 9186* ...................... | 2 | 29 wks |
| 22 Dec 73 | ● **BRAIN SALAD SURGERY** *Manticore K 53501* ......... | 2 | 17 wks |
| 24 Aug 74 | ● **WELCOME BACK MY FRIENDS TO THE SHOW THAT NEVER ENDS – LADIES AND GENTLEMEN: EMERSON, LAKE AND PALMER** *Manticore K 63500* .................................... | 5 | 5 wks |
| 9 Apr 77 | ● **WORKS** *Atlantic K 80009* ...................... | 9 | 25 wks |
| 10 Dec 77 | **WORKS VOL. 2** *Atlantic K 50422* ................... | 20 | 5 wks |
| 9 Dec 78 | **LOVE BEACH** *Atlantic K 50552* .................... | 48 | 4 wks |

*See also Greg Lake; Emerson, Lake and Powell.*


## EMERSON, LAKE and POWELL

*UK, male vocal/instrumental group*                                         *5 wks*

| | | | |
|---|---|---|---|
| 14 Jun 86 | **EMERSON, LAKE AND POWELL** *Polydor POLD 5191* .. | 35 | 5 wks |

*See also Greg Lake; Cozy Powell; Emerson, Lake and Palmer.*

## ENGLAND FOOTBALL WORLD CUP
**SQUAD** *UK, male football team vocalists*                   *18 wks*

| | | | |
|---|---|---|---|
| 16 May 70 ● | **THE WORLD BEATERS SING THE WORLD BEATERS** | | |
| | *Pye NSPL 18337* .................................... | **4** | 8 wks |
| 15 May 82 | **THIS TIME** *K-Tel NE 1169* ........................ | **37** | 10 wks |

**ENGLISH CHAMBER ORCHESTRA** – *See John WILLIAMS with the ENGLISH CHAMBER ORCHESTRA; Nigel KENNEDY*

---

## ENIGMA *UK, male vocal/instrumental group*                   *3 wks*

| | | | |
|---|---|---|---|
| 5 Sep 81 | **AIN'T NO STOPPIN'** *Creole CRX 1* ................. | **80** | 3 wks |

---

## Brian ENO *UK, male instrumentalist – keyboards*                   *4 wks*

| | | | |
|---|---|---|---|
| 9 Mar 74 | **HERE COME THE WARM JETS** *Island ILPS 9268* ...... | **26** | 2 wks |
| 21 Oct 78 | **MUSIC FOR FILMS** *Polydor 2310 623* ............... | **55** | 1 wk |
| 8 May 82 | **AMBIENT FOUR ON LAND** *EG EGED 20* .......... | **93** | 1 wk |

*See also Brian Eno and David Byrne.*

---

## Brian ENO and David BYRNE
*UK, male instrumentalist – keyboards and UK, male vocalist*                   *8 wks*

| | | | |
|---|---|---|---|
| 21 Feb 81 | **MY LIFE IN THE BUSH OF GHOSTS** *Polydor EGLP 48* .. | **29** | 8 wks |

*See also Brian Eno.*

---

## ENYA *Ireland, female vocalist*                   *59 wks*

| | | | |
|---|---|---|---|
| 6 Jun 87 | **ENYA** *BBC REB 605* ............................. | **69** | 4 wks |
| 15 Oct 88 ● | **WATERMARK** *WEA WX 199* ...................... | **5** | 55 wks |

---

## EQUALS *UK, male vocal/instrumental group*                   *10 wks*

| | | | |
|---|---|---|---|
| 18 Nov 67 ● | **UNEQUALLED EQUALS** *President PTL 1006* .......... | **10** | 9 wks |
| 9 Mar 68 | **EQUALS EXPLOSION** *President PTLS 1015* ........... | **32** | 1 wk |

---

## ERASURE *UK, male vocal/instrumental duo*                   *196 wks*

| | | | |
|---|---|---|---|
| 14 Jun 86 | **WONDERLAND** *Mute STUMM 25* ................... | **71** | 7 wks |
| 11 Apr 87 ● | **THE CIRCUS** *Mute STUMM 35* .................... | **6** | 102 wks |
| 30 Apr 88 ★ | **THE INNOCENTS** *Mute STUMM 55* ................ | **1** | 77 wks |
| 28 Oct 89 ★ | **WILD!** *Mute STUMM 75* ......................... | **1†** | 10 wks |

---

## David ESSEX *UK, male vocalist*                   *137 wks*

| | | | |
|---|---|---|---|
| 24 Nov 73 ● | **ROCK ON** *CBS 65823* ........................... | **7** | 22 wks |
| 19 Oct 74 ● | **DAVID ESSEX** *CBS 69088* ....................... | **2** | 24 wks |
| 27 Sep 75 ● | **ALL THE FUN OF THE FAIR** *CBS 69160* ............ | **3** | 20 wks |
| 5 Jun 76 | **ON TOUR** *CBS 95000* ........................... | **51** | 1 wk |
| 30 Oct 76 | **OUT ON THE STREET** *CBS 86017* ................. | **31** | 9 wks |
| 8 Oct 77 | **GOLD AND IVORY** *CBS 86038* ................... | **29** | 4 wks |
| 6 Jan 79 | **DAVID ESSEX ALBUM** *CBS 10011* ............... | **29** | 7 wks |
| 31 Mar 79 | **IMPERIAL WIZARD** *Mercury 9109 616* ........... | **12** | 9 wks |
| 12 Jun 80 | **HOT LOVE** *Mercury 6359 017* ...................... | **75** | 1 wk |
| 19 Jun 82 | **STAGE-STRUCK** *Mercury MERS 4* ................ | **31** | 4 wks |
| 27 Nov 82 | **THE VERY BEST OF DAVID ESSEX** *TV Records TVA 4* . | **37** | 11 wks |
| 15 Oct 83 | **MUTINY** *Mercury MERH 30* ...................... | **39** | 4 wks |

| 17 Dec 83 | **THE WHISPER** *Mercury MERH 34* | **67** | 6 wks |
|---|---|---|---|
| 6 Dec 86 | **CENTRE STAGE** *K-Tel ONE 1333* | **82** | 4 wks |

*Mutiny is a studio recording of a musical that was not staged until 1985. Both this album and the eventual stage production starred David Essex and Frank Finlay.*

## Gloria ESTEFAN  *US, female vocalist*  *75 wks*

| 19 Nov 88 | ★ **ANYTHING FOR YOU** *Epic 463125 1* | **1** | 53 wks |
|---|---|---|---|
| 5 Aug 89 | ★ **CUTS BOTH WAYS** *Epic 465145 1* | **1†** | 22 wks |

*First album credits the Miami Sound Machine – US, male instrumental group.*

## Don ESTELLE and Windsor DAVIES
*UK, male vocal duo*  *8 wks*

| 10 Jan 76 | ● **SING LOFTY** *EMI EMC 3102* | **10** | 8 wks |
|---|---|---|---|

## Melissa ETHERIDGE  *US, female vocalist*  *1 wk*

| 30 Sep 89 | **BRAVE AND CRAZY** *Island ILPS 9939* | **63** | 1 wk |
|---|---|---|---|

## EUROPE  *Sweden, male vocal/instrumental group*  *42 wks*

| 22 Nov 86 | ● **THE FINAL COUNTDOWN** *Epic EPC 26808* | **9** | 37 wks |
|---|---|---|---|
| 17 Sep 88 | **OUT OF THIS WORLD** *Epic 462449 1* | **12** | 5 wks |

## EUROPEANS  *UK, male vocal/instrumental group*  *1 wk*

| 11 Feb 84 | **LIVE** *A & M SCOT 1* | **100** | 1 wk |
|---|---|---|---|

## EURYTHMICS  *UK, female/male vocal/instrumental group*  *309 wks*

| 12 Feb 83 | ● **SWEET DREAMS (ARE MADE OF THIS)** *RCA RCALP 6063* | **3** | 59 wks |
|---|---|---|---|
| 26 Nov 83 | ★ **TOUCH** *RCA PL 70109* | **1** | 48 wks |
| 9 Jun 84 | **TOUCH DANCE** *RCA PG 70354* | **31** | 5 wks |
| 24 Nov 84 | **1984 (FOR THE LOVE OF BIG BROTHER)** *Virgin V 1984* | **23** | 17 wks |
| 11 May 85 | ● **BE YOURSELF TONIGHT** *RCA PL 70711* | **3** | 80 wks |
| 12 Jul 86 | ● **REVENGE** *RCA PL 71050* | **3** | 52 wks |
| 21 Nov 87 | ● **SAVAGE** *RCA PL 71555* | **7** | 33 wks |
| 23 Sep 89 | ★ **WE TOO ARE ONE** *RCA PL 74251* | **1†** | 15 wks |

## Phil EVERLY  *US, male vocalist*  *1 wk*

| 7 May 83 | **PHIL EVERLY** *Capitol EST 27670* | **61** | 1 wk |
|---|---|---|---|

*See also the Everly Brothers.*

## EVERLY BROTHERS  *US, male vocal duo*  *118 wks*

| 2 Jul 60 | ● **IT'S EVERLY TIME** *Warner Bros. WM 4006* | **2** | 23 wks |
|---|---|---|---|
| 15 Oct 60 | ● **FABULOUS STYLE OF THE EVERLY BROTHERS** *London HAA 2266* | **4** | 11 wks |
| 4 Mar 61 | ● **A DATE WITH THE EVERLY BROTHERS** *Warner Bros. WM 4028* | **3** | 14 wks |
| 21 Jul 62 | **INSTANT PARTY** *Warner Bros. WM 4061* | **20** | 1 wk |
| 12 Sep 70 | ● **ORIGINAL GREATEST HITS** *CBS 66255* | **7** | 16 wks |
| 8 Jun 74 | **THE VERY BEST OF THE EVERLY BROTHERS** *Warner Bros. K 46008* | **43** | 1 wk |
| 29 Nov 75 | ● **WALK RIGHT BACK WITH THE EVERLYS** *Warner Bros. K 56118* | **10** | 10 wks |

| 9 Apr 77 | **LIVING LEGENDS** _Warwick WW 5027_ ............... | 12 | 10 wks |
| 18 Dec 82 | **LOVE HURTS** _K-Tel NE 1197_ ....................... | 31 | 22 wks |
| 7 Jan 84 | **EVERLY BROTHERS REUNION CONCERT** | | |
| | _Impression IMDP 1_ ............................. | 47 | 6 wks |
| 3 Nov 84 | **THE EVERLY BROTHERS** _Mercury MERH 44_ ......... | 36 | 4 wks |

_See also Phil Everly._

## EVERYTHING BUT THE GIRL
_UK, male/female vocal/instrumental group_           _55 wks_

| 16 Jun 84 | **EDEN** _blanco y negro BYN 2_ ..................... | 14 | 22 wks |
| 27 Apr 85 | ● **LOVE NOT MONEY** _blanco y negro BYN 3_ ............. | 10 | 9 wks |
| 6 Sep 86 | **BABY THE STARS SHINE BRIGHT** | | |
| | _blanco y negro BYN 9_ ......................... | 22 | 9 wks |
| 12 Mar 88 | **IDLEWILD** _blanco y negro BYN 14_ ................. | 13 | 9 wks |
| 6 Aug 88 | **IDLEWILD (re-issue)** _blanco y negro BYN 16_ ............ | 21 | 6 wks |

## EXODUS    _US, male vocal/instrumental group_        _1 wk_

| 11 Feb 89 | **FABULOUS DISASTER** _Music For Nations MFN 90_ ...... | 67 | 1 wk |

## EXPLOITED    _UK, male vocal/instrumental group_       _26 wks_

| 16 May 81 | **PUNK'S NOT DEAD** _Secret SEC 1_ ................... | 20 | 11 wks |
| 14 Nov 81 | **EXPLOITED LIVE** _Superville EXPLP 2001_ ............. | 52 | 3 wks |
| 19 Jun 82 | **TROOPS OF TOMORROW** _Secret SEC 8_ ............. | 17 | 12 wks |

# _f_

## FACES    _UK, male vocal/instrumental group_        _56 wks_

| 4 Apr 70 | **FIRST STEP** _Warner Bros. WS 3000_ ................... | 45 | 1 wk |
| 8 May 71 | **LONG PLAYER** _Warner Bros. W 3011_ ................. | 31 | 7 wks |
| 25 Dec 71 | ● **A NOD'S AS GOOD AS A WINK ... TO A BLIND HORSE** | | |
| | _Warner Bros. K 56006_ ............................. | 2 | 22 wks |
| 21 Apr 73 | ★ **OOH-LA-LA** _Warner Bros. K 56011_ ................... | 1 | 13 wks |
| 26 Jan 74 | ● **OVERTURE AND BEGINNERS** _Mercury 9100 001_ ..... | 3 | 7 wks |
| 21 May 77 | **THE BEST OF THE FACES** _Riva RVLP 3_ ............. | 24 | 6 wks |

_Overture And Beginners credited to Rod Stewart and the Faces. See also Rod Stewart._

## Donald FAGEN    _US, male vocalist_        _16 wks_

| 20 Oct 82 | **THE NIGHTFLY** _Warner Bros. 923696_ ................ | 44 | 16 wks |

## FAIRGROUND ATTRACTION
_UK, male/female vocal/instrumental group_        _52 wks_

| 28 May 88 | ● **THE FIRST OF A MILLION KISSES** _RCA PL 71696_ .... | 2 | 52 wks |

## FAIRPORT CONVENTION
_UK, male/female vocal/instrumental group_        _41 wks_

| 2 Aug 69 | **UNHALFBRICKING** _Island ILPS 9102_ ............... | 12 | 8 wks |
| 17 Jan 70 | **LIEGE AND LIEF** _Island ILPS 9115_ ................. | 17 | 15 wks |
| 18 Jul 70 | **FULL HOUSE** _Island ILPS 9130_ ..................... | 13 | 11 wks |
| 3 Jul 71 | ● **ANGEL DELIGHT** _Island ILPS 9162_ ................. | 8 | 5 wks |
| 12 Jul 75 | **RISING FOR THE MOON** _Island ILPS 9313_ ............ | 52 | 1 wk |
| 28 Jan 89 | **RED AND GOLD** _New Routes RUE 002_ ................ | 74 | 1 wk |

## FAITH BROTHERS  *UK, male vocal/instrumental group*  *1 wk*

| 9 Nov 85 | **EVENTIDE**  *Siren SIRENLP 1* | 66 | 1 wk |

## Adam FAITH  *UK, male vocalist*  *44 wks*

| 19 Nov 60 | ● **ADAM**  *Parlophone PMC 1128* | 6 | 36 wks |
| 11 Feb 61 | **BEAT GIRL (film soundtrack)**  *Columbia 33SX 1225* | 11 | 3 wks |
| 24 Mar 62 | **ADAM FAITH**  *Parlophone PMC 1162* | 20 | 1 wk |
| 25 Sep 65 | **FAITH ALIVE**  *Parlophone PMC 1249* | 19 | 1 wk |
| 19 Dec 81 | **20 GOLDEN GREATS**  *Warwick WW 5113* | 61 | 3 wks |

## Marianne FAITHFULL  *UK, female vocalist*  *19 wks*

| 5 Jun 65 | **COME MY WAY**  *Decca LK 4688* | 12 | 7 wks |
| 5 Jun 65 | **MARIANNE FAITHFULL**  *Decca LK 4689* | 15 | 2 wks |
| 24 Nov 79 | **BROKEN ENGLISH**  *Island M1* | 57 | 3 wks |
| 17 Oct 81 | **DANGEROUS ACQUAINTANCES**  *Island ILPS 9648* | 45 | 4 wks |
| 26 Mar 83 | **A CHILD'S ADVENTURE**  *Island ILPS 9734* | 99 | 1 wk |
| 8 Aug 87 | **STRANGE WEATHER**  *Island ILPS 9874* | 78 | 2 wks |

## FALCO  *Austria, male vocalist*  *15 wks*

| 26 Apr 86 | **FALCO 3**  *A & M AMA 5105* | 32 | 15 wks |

## FALL  *UK, male vocal/instrumental group*  *18 wks*

| 20 Mar 82 | **HEX ENDUCTION HOUR**  *Kamera KAM 005* | 71 | 3 wks |
| 20 Oct 84 | **THE WONDERFUL AND FRIGHTENING WORLD OF ...** | | |
| | *Beggars Banquet BEGA 58* | 62 | 2 wks |
| 5 Oct 85 | **THE NATION'S SAVING GRACE** | | |
| | *Beggars Banquet BEGA 67* | 54 | 2 wks |
| 11 Oct 86 | **BEND SINISTER**  *Beggars Banquet BEGA 75* | 36 | 3 wks |
| 12 Mar 88 | **THE FRENZ EXPERIMENT**  *Beggars Banquet BEGA 91* | 19 | 4 wks |
| 12 Nov 88 | **I AM KURIOUS, ORANJ**  *Beggars Banquet BEGA 96* | 54 | 2 wks |
| 8 Jul 89 | **SEMINAL LIVE**  *Beggars Banquet BBL 102* | 40 | 2 wks |

## Agnetha FALTSKOG  *Sweden, female vocalist*  *17 wks*

| 11 Jun 83 | **WRAP YOUR ARMS AROUND ME**  *Epic EPC 25505* | 18 | 13 wks |
| 4 May 85 | **EYES OF A WOMAN**  *Epic EPC 26446* | 38 | 3 wks |
| 12 Mar 88 | **I STAND ALONE**  *WEA WX 150* | 72 | 1 wk |

## Georgie FAME  *UK, male vocalist*  *72 wks*

| 17 Oct 64 | **FAME AT LAST**  *Columbia 33SX 1638* | 15 | 8 wks |
| 14 May 66 | ● **SWEET THINGS**  *Columbia SX 6043* | 6 | 22 wks |
| 15 Oct 66 | ● **SOUND VENTURE**  *Columbia SX 6076* | 9 | 9 wks |
| 11 Mar 67 | **HALL OF FAME**  *Columbia SX 6120* | 12 | 18 wks |
| 1 Jul 67 | **TWO FACES OF FAME**  *CBS SBPG 63018* | 22 | 15 wks |

## FAMILY  *UK, male vocal/instrumental group*  *41 wks*

| 10 Aug 68 | **MUSIC IN THE DOLLS HOUSE**  *Reprise RLP 6312* | 35 | 3 wks |
| 22 Mar 69 | ● **FAMILY ENTERTAINMENT**  *Reprise RSLP 6340* | 6 | 3 wks |
| 7 Feb 70 | ● **A SONG FOR ME**  *Reprise RSLP 9001* | 4 | 13 wks |
| 28 Nov 70 | ● **ANYWAY**  *Reprise RSX 9005* | 7 | 7 wks |
| 20 Nov 71 | **FEARLESS**  *Reprise K 54003* | 14 | 2 wks |
| 30 Sep 72 | **BANDSTAND**  *Reprise K 54006* | 15 | 10 wks |
| 29 Sep 73 | **IT'S ONLY A MOVIE**  *Raft RA 58501* | 30 | 3 wks |

**FAMILY STONE** – *See SLY and the FAMILY STONE*

Andy Bell (right), singer of **ERASURE**, looks at tools of partner Vince Clarke's trade.

**GRACIE FIELDS** is shown performing in her golden years.

The **FINE YOUNG CANNIBALS** really cooked in 1989.

It wasn't only listeners' hearts that **GLORIA ESTEFAN** melted.

## Chris FARLOWE  UK, male vocalist

3 wks

| 2 Apr 66 | 14 THINGS TO THINK ABOUT | Immediate IMLP 005 | .... | 19 | 1 wk |
| 10 Dec 66 | THE ART OF CHRIS FARLOWE | Immediate IMLP 006 | ... | 37 | 2 wks |

## FARMERS BOYS  UK, male vocal/instrumental group

1 wk

| 29 Oct 83 | GET OUT AND WALK | EMI EMC 1077991 | ........... | 49 | 1 wk |

## John FARNHAM  Australia, male vocalist

9 wks

| 11 Jul 87 | WHISPERING JACK | RCA PL 71224 | ................ | 35 | 9 wks |

**FARRAR** – See MARVIN, WELCH and FARRAR

## FASHION  UK, male vocal/instrumental group

17 wks

| 3 Jul 82 | ● FABRIQUE | Arista SPART 1185 | ..................... | 10 | 16 wks |
| 16 Jun 84 | TWILIGHT OF IDOLS | De Stijl EPC 25909 | ........... | 69 | 1 wk |

## FASTER PUSSYCAT  US, male vocal/instrumental group

2 wks

| 16 Sep 89 | WAKE ME WHEN IT'S OVER | Elektra EKT 64 | ......... | 35 | 2 wks |

## FASTWAY  UK, male vocal/instrumental group

2 wks

| 30 Apr 83 | FASTWAY | CBS 25359 | .......................... | 43 | 2 wks |

## FAT BOYS  US, male rap group

5 wks

| 3 Oct 87 | CRUSHIN' | Urban URBLP 3 | ..................... | 49 | 4 wks |
| 30 Jul 88 | COMING BACK HARD AGAIN | Urban URBLP 13 | ...... | 98 | 1 wk |

## FAT LARRY'S BAND  US, male vocal/instrumental group

4 wks

| 9 Oct 82 | BREAKIN' OUT | Virgin V 2229 | ..................... | 58 | 4 wks |

## FATBACK BAND  US, male vocal/instrumental group

7 wks

| 6 Mar 76 | RAISING HELL | Polydor 2391 203 | ..................... | 19 | 6 wks |
| 4 Jul 87 | FATBACK LIVE | Start STL 12 | ..................... | 80 | 1 wk |

**FATHER** – See Steven SMITH and FATHER

**FBI** – See Redhead KINGPIN and the FBI

## Phil FEARON and GALAXY
UK, male/female vocal/instrumental group

9 wks

| 25 Aug 84 | ● PHIL FEARON AND GALAXY | Ensign ENCL 2 | ........ | 8 | 8 wks |
| 14 Feb 85 | THIS KIND OF LOVE | Ensign ENCL 4 | ................ | 98 | 1 wk |

## Wilton FELDER  US, male instrumentalist – tenor sax

3 wks

| 23 Feb 85 | SECRETS | MCA MCF 3237 | ........................ | 77 | 3 wks |

*Also featuring Bobby Womack and introducing Alltrina Grayson.*

## Jose FELICIANO  *US, male vocalist/instrumentalist – guitar*  *40 wks*

| | | | |
|---|---|---|---|
| 2 Nov 68 ● FELICIANO  *RCA Victor SF 7946* .................... | 6 | 36 wks |
| 29 Nov 69  JOSE FELICIANO  *RCA Victor SF 8044* .............. | 29 | 2 wks |
| 14 Feb 70  10 TO 23  *RCA SF 7946* ......................... | 38 | 1 wk |
| 22 Aug 70 , FIREWORKS  *RCA SF 8124* ...................... | 65 | 1 wk |

## Julie FELIX  *US, female vocalist*  *4 wks*

| | | |
|---|---|---|
| 11 Sep 66  CHANGES  *Fontana TL 5368* ........................ | 27 | 4 wks |

## Bryan FERRY  *UK, male vocalist*  *154 wks*

| | | |
|---|---|---|
| 3 Nov 73 ● THESE FOOLISH THINGS  *Island ILPS 9249* .......... | 5 | 42 wks |
| 20 Jul 74 ● ANOTHER TIME, ANOTHER PLACE  *Island ILPS 9284* | 4 | 25 wks |
| 2 Oct 76  LET'S STICK TOGETHER  *Island ILPSX 1* ............ | 19 | 5 wks |
| 5 Mar 77 ● IN YOUR MIND  *Polydor 2302 055* ................... | 5 | 17 wks |
| 30 Sep 78  THE BRIDE STRIPPED BARE  *Polydor POLD 5003* ..... | 13 | 5 wks |
| 15 Jun 85 ★ BOYS AND GIRLS  *EG EGLP 62* ................... | 1 | 44 wks |
| 14 Nov 87 ● BETE NOIRE  *Virgin V 2474* ........................ | 9 | 16 wks |

*See also Bryan Ferry and Roxy Music.*

## Bryan FERRY and ROXY MUSIC
*UK, male vocal/instrumental group*  *104 wks*

| | | |
|---|---|---|
| 26 Apr 86 ★ STREET LIFE – 20 GREAT HITS  *EG EGTV 1* ......... | 1 | 77 wks |
| 19 Nov 88 ● THE ULTIMATE COLLECTION  *EG EGTV 2* ......... | 6 | 27 wks |

*See also Bryan Ferry; Roxy Music.*

**117**

*f*

## Gracie FIELDS  *UK, female vocalist*  *3 wks*

| | | |
|---|---|---|
| 20 Dec 75  THE GOLDEN YEARS  *Warwick WW 5007* ........... | 48 | 3 wks |

## FIELDS OF THE NEPHILIM
*UK, male vocal/instrumental group*  *5 wks*

| | | |
|---|---|---|
| 30 May 87  DAWNRAZOR  *Situation 2 SITU 18* ................. | 62 | 2 wks |
| 17 Sep 88  THE NEPHILIM  *Situation 2 SITU 22* ................ | 14 | 3 wks |

## 52ND STREET  *UK, male/female vocal/instrumental group*  *1 wk*

| | | |
|---|---|---|
| 19 Apr 86  CHILDREN OF THE NIGHT  *10 DIX 25* ............. | 71 | 1 wk |

## FINE YOUNG CANNIBALS
*UK, male vocal/instrumental group*  *71 wks*

| | | |
|---|---|---|
| 21 Dec 85  FINE YOUNG CANNIBALS  *London LONLP 16* ....... | 11 | 25 wks |
| 18 Feb 89 ★ THE RAW AND THE COOKED  *London 828069 1* ...... | 1† | 46 wks |

## FIRM  *UK, male vocal/instrumental group*  *8 wks*

| | | |
|---|---|---|
| 2 Mar 85  THE FIRM  *Atlantic 78-1239-1* ....................... | 15 | 5 wks |
| 5 Apr 86  MEAN BUSINESS  *Atlantic WX 35* .................... | 46 | 3 wks |

## FIRST CIRCLE  *US, male vocal/instrumental group*  *2 wks*

| | | |
|---|---|---|
| 2 May 87  BOYS' NIGHT OUT  *EMI America AML 3118* .......... | 70 | 2 wks |

## FISCHER-Z UK, male vocal/instrumental group

*1 wk*

| | | | | |
|---|---|---|---|---|
| 23 Jun 79 | **WORD SALAD** *United Artists UAG 30232* .............. | 66 | 1 wk |

## Ella FITZGERALD US, female vocalist

*23 wks*

| | | | | |
|---|---|---|---|---|
| 11 Jun 60 | **ELLA SINGS GERSHWIN** *Brunswick LA 8648* .......... | 13 | 3 wks |
| 18 Jun 60 | **ELLA AT THE OPERA HOUSE** *Columbia 3SX 10126* .... | 16 | 1 wk |
| 23 Jul 60 | **ELLA SINGS GERSHWIN VOL. 5** *HMV CLP 1353* ..... | 18 | 2 wks |
| 10 May 80 | **THE INCOMPARABLE ELLA** *Polydor POLTV 9* ........ | 40 | 7 wks |
| 27 Feb 88 | **A PORTRAIT OF ELLA FITZGERALD** *Stylus SMR 847* . | 42 | 10 wks |

## FIVE PENNY PIECE
UK, male/female vocal/instrumental group

*6 wks*

| | | | | |
|---|---|---|---|---|
| 24 Mar 73 | **MAKING TRACKS** *Columbia SCX 6536* .............. | 37 | 1 wk |
| 3 Jul 76 | ● **KING COTTON** *EMI EMC 3129* .................... | 9 | 5 wks |

## FIVE STAR UK, male/female vocal group

*153 wks*

| | | | | |
|---|---|---|---|---|
| 3 Aug 85 | **LUXURY OF LIFE** *Tent PL 70735* .................... | 12 | 70 wks |
| 30 Aug 86 | ★ **SILK AND STEEL** *Tent PL 71100* .................... | 1 | 58 wks |
| 26 Sep 87 | ● **BETWEEN THE LINES** *Tent PL 71505* ............. | 7 | 17 wks |
| 27 Aug 88 | **ROCK THE WORLD** *Tent PL 71747* ................. | 17 | 5 wks |
| 21 Oct 89 | **GREATEST HITS** *Tent PL 74080* ................... | 53 | 3 wks |

## FIXX UK, male vocal/instrumental group

*7 wks*

| | | | | |
|---|---|---|---|---|
| 22 May 82 | **SHUTTERED ROOM** *MCA FX 1001* ................ | 54 | 6 wks |
| 21 May 83 | **REACH THE BEACH** *MCA FX 1002* ............... | 91 | 1 wk |

## Roberta FLACK US, female vocalist

*18 wks*

| | | | | |
|---|---|---|---|---|
| 15 Jul 72 | **FIRST TAKE** *Atlantic K 40040* ...................... | 47 | 2 wks |
| 13 Oct 73 | **KILLING ME SOFTLY** *Atlantic K 50021* ............. | 40 | 2 wks |
| 31 Mar 84 | **GREATEST HITS** *K-Tel NE 1269* ................... | 35 | 14 wks |

*See also Roberta Flack and Donny Hathaway; Peabo Bryson and Roberta Flack.*

## Roberta FLACK and Donny HATHAWAY
US, female/male vocal duo

*7 wks*

| | | | | |
|---|---|---|---|---|
| 7 Jun 80 | **ROBERTA FLACK AND DONNY HATHAWAY** *Atlantic K 50696* ................................... | 31 | 7 wks |

*See also Roberta Flack.*

## FLASH AND THE PAN
Australia, male vocal/instrumental group

*2 wks*

| | | | | |
|---|---|---|---|---|
| 16 Jul 83 | **PAN-ORAMA** *Easy Beat EASLP 100* ................. | 69 | 2 wks |

## FLEETWOOD MAC
UK/US, male/female vocal/instrumental group

*744 wks*

| | | | | |
|---|---|---|---|---|
| 2 Mar 68 | ● **FLEETWOOD MAC** *Blue Horizon BPG 7–63200* ......... | 4 | 37 wks |
| 7 Sep 68 | ● **MR. WONDERFUL** *Blue Horizon 7–63205* ............. | 10 | 11 wks |
| 30 Aug 69 | **PIOUS BIRD OF GOOD OMEN** *Blue Horizon 7–63215* .... | 18 | 4 wks |
| 4 Oct 69 | ● **THEN PLAY ON** *Reprise RSLP 9000* ................. | 6 | 11 wks |
| 10 Oct 70 | **KILN HOUSE** *Reprise RSLP 9004* ................... | 39 | 2 wks |

| 19 Feb 72 | **GREATEST HITS** *CBS 6901* ....................... | **36** | 12 wks |
| 6 Nov 76 | **FLEETWOOD MAC** *Reprise K 54043* ................. | **23** | 20 wks |
| 26 Feb 77 | ★ **RUMOURS** *Warner Bros. K 56344* ..................... | **1** | 443 wks |
| 27 Oct 79 | ★ **TUSK** *Warner Bros. K 66088* .......................... | **1** | 26 wks |
| 13 Dec 80 | **FLEETWOOD MAC LIVE** *Warner Bros. K 66097* ........ | **31** | 9 wks |
| 10 Jul 82 | ● **MIRAGE** *Warner Bros. K 56592* ...................... | **5** | 39 wks |
| 25 Apr 87 | ★ **TANGO IN THE NIGHT** *Warner Bros. WX 65* .......... | **1** | 99 wks |
| 3 Dec 88 | ● **GREATEST HITS** *Warner Bros. WX 221* .............. | **3** | 31 wks |

*Group were UK and male only for first 6 albums. All the above albums are different, although some are identically titled.*

## Berni FLINT   *UK, male vocalist*                    *6 wks*

| 2 Jul 77 | **I DON'T WANT TO PUT A HOLD ON YOU** *EMI EMC 3184* ................................. | **37** | 6 wks |

## FLOATERS   *US, male vocal/instrumental group*          *8 wks*

| 20 Aug 77 | **FLOATERS** *ABC ABCL 5229* ....................... | **17** | 8 wks |

## FLOCK   *UK, male vocal/instrumental group*           *2 wks*

| 2 May 70 | **FLOCK** *CBS 63733* ............................... | **59** | 2 wks |

## A FLOCK OF SEAGULLS
*UK, male vocal/instrumental group*                    *59 wks*

| 17 Apr 82 | **A FLOCK OF SEAGULLS** *Jive HOP 201* .............. | **32** | 44 wks |
| 7 May 83 | **LISTEN** *Jive HIP 4* ............................ | **16** | 10 wks |
| 1 Sep 84 | **THE STORY OF A YOUNG HEART** *Jive HIP 14* ...... | **30** | 5 wks |

**f**

## Eddie FLOYD   *US, male vocalist*                    *5 wks*

| 29 Apr 67 | **KNOCK ON WOOD** *Stax 589-006* ................... | **36** | 5 wks |

## A FLUX OF PINK INDIANS
*UK, male vocal/instrumental group*                    *2 wks*

| 5 Feb 83 | **STRIVE TO SURVIVE CAUSING LEAST SUFFERING POSSIBLE** *Spiderleg SDL 8* ...................... | **79** | 2 wks |

## FLYING LIZARDS   *UK, male/female vocal/instrumental group*   *3 wks*

| 16 Feb 80 | **FLYING LIZARDS** *Virgin V 2150* ................... | **60** | 3 wks |

## FLYING PICKETS   *UK, male vocal group*          *22 wks*

| 17 Dec 83 | **LIVE AT THE ALBANY EMPIRE** *AVM AVMLP 0001* ... | **48** | 11 wks |
| 9 Jun 84 | **LOST BOYS** *10 DIX 4* ........................... | **11** | 11 wks |

## FM   *UK, male vocal/instrumental group*          *3 wk*

| 20 Sep 86 | **INDISCREET** *Portrait PRT 26827* ................... | **76** | 1 wk |
| 14 Oct 89 | **TOUGH IT OUT** *Epic 465589 1* ..................... | **34** | 2 wks |

## FOCUS  *Holland, male instrumental group*  65 wks

| | | | |
|---|---|---|---|
| 11 Nov 72 | ● **MOVING WAVES**  *Polydor 2931 002* .................. | 2 | 34 wks |
| 2 Dec 72 | ● **FOCUS 3**  *Polydor 2383 016* .................. | 6 | 15 wks |
| 20 Oct 73 | **FOCUS AT THE RAINBOW**  *Polydor 2442 118* ........ | 23 | 5 wks |
| 25 May 74 | **HAMBURGER CONCERTO**  *Polydor 2442 124* ......... | 20 | 5 wks |
| 9 Aug 75 | **FOCUS**  *Polydor 2384 070* .......................... | 23 | 6 wks |

## Dan FOGELBERG  *US, male vocalist*  3 wks

| | | | |
|---|---|---|---|
| 29 Mar 80 | **PHOENIX**  *Epic EPC 83317* ......................... | 42 | 3 wks |

## John FOGERTY  *US, male vocalist/instrumentalist – guitar*  11 wks

| | | | |
|---|---|---|---|
| 16 Feb 85 | **CENTERFIELD**  *Warner Bros. 92–5203–1* ............. | 48 | 11 wks |

## Ellen FOLEY  *US, female vocalist*  3 wks

| | | | |
|---|---|---|---|
| 17 Nov 79 | **NIGHT OUT**  *Epic EPC 83718* ...................... | 68 | 1 wk |
| 4 Apr 81 | **SPIRIT OF ST. LOUIS**  *Epic EPC 84809* ............. | 57 | 2 wks |

## Jane FONDA  *US, female exercise instructor*  51 wks

| | | | |
|---|---|---|---|
| 29 Jan 83 | ● **JANE FONDA'S WORKOUT RECORD**  *CBS 88581* .... | 7 | 47 wks |
| 22 Sep 84 | **JANE FONDA'S WORKOUT RECORD: NEW AND IMPROVED**  *CBS 88640* ......................... | 60 | 4 wks |

## Wayne FONTANA and the MINDBENDERS
*UK, male vocalist and male vocal/instrumental group*  1 wk

| | | | |
|---|---|---|---|
| 20 Feb 65 | **WAYNE FONTANA AND THE MINDBENDERS**  *Fontana TL 5230* ................................... | 18 | 1 wk |

*See also the Mindbenders.*

## Steve FORBERT  *US, male vocalist*  3 wks

| | | | |
|---|---|---|---|
| 9 Jun 79 | **ALIVE ON ARRIVAL**  *Epic EPC 83308* .............. | 56 | 1 wk |
| 24 Nov 79 | **JACK RABBIT SLIM**  *Epic EPC 83879* ................ | 54 | 2 wks |

## Clinton FORD  *UK, male vocalist*  4 wks

| | | | |
|---|---|---|---|
| 26 May 62 | **CLINTON FORD**  *Oriole PS 40021* ................... | 16 | 4 wks |

## Lita FORD  *UK, female vocalist*  1 wk

| | | | |
|---|---|---|---|
| 26 May 84 | **DANCIN' ON THE EDGE**  *Vertigo VERL 13* ............ | 96 | 1 wk |

## Julia FORDHAM  *UK, female vocalist*  27 wks

| | | | |
|---|---|---|---|
| 18 Jun 88 | **JULIA FORDHAM**  *Circa CIRCA 4* ................... | 20 | 22 wks |
| 21 Oct 89 | **PORCELAIN**  *Circa CIRCA 10* ..................... | 13 | 5 wks |

## FOREIGNER  *UK/US, male vocal/instrumental group*  117 wks

| | | | |
|---|---|---|---|
| 26 Aug 78 | **DOUBLE VISION**  *Atlantic K 50476* ................. | 32 | 5 wks |
| 25 Jul 81 | ● **4**  *Atlantic K 50796* ................................. | 5 | 62 wks |
| 18 Dec 82 | **RECORDS**  *Atlantic A 0999* ........................ | 58 | 11 wks |
| 22 Dec 84 | ★ **AGENT PROVOCATEUR**  *Atlantic 78–1999–1* .......... | 1 | 32 wks |
| 19 Dec 87 | **INSIDE INFORMATION**  *Atlantic WX 143* ............. | 64 | 7 wks |

## FOSTER and ALLEN  *Ireland, male vocal duo*                    93 wks

| | | | |
|---|---|---|---|
| 14 May 83 | **MAGGIE**  *Ritz RITZLP 0012* .......................... | 72 | 6 wks |
| 5 Nov 83 | **I WILL LOVE YOU ALL OF MY LIFE**  *Ritz RITZLP 0015* | 71 | 6 wks |
| 17 Nov 84 | **THE VERY BEST OF FOSTER AND ALLEN** | | |
| | *Ritz RITZ LP TV 1* ............................... | 18 | 18 wks |
| 29 Mar 86 | **AFTER ALL THESE YEARS**  *Ritz RITZLP 0032* ........ | 82 | 2 wks |
| 25 Oct 86 | **REMINISCING**  *Stylus SMR 623* ..................... | 11 | 15 wks |
| 27 Jun 87 | **LOVE SONGS – THE VERY BEST OF FOSTER AND** | | |
| | **ALLEN VOL 2**  *Ritz RITZLP 0036* .................. | 92 | 1 wk |
| 10 Oct 87 | **REFLECTIONS**  *Stylus SMR 739* ..................... | 16 | 16 wks |
| 30 Apr 88 | **REMEMBER YOU'RE MINE**  *Stylus SMR 853* ......... | 16 | 15 wks |
| 28 Oct 89 | **THE MAGIC OF FOSTER AND ALLEN**  *Stylus SMR 989* . | 29† | 10 wks |
| 9 Dec 89 | **THE FOSTER AND ALLEN CHRISTMAS ALBUM** | | |
| | *Stylus SMR 995* .................................... | 40† | 4 wks |

## FOTHERINGAY  *UK, male/female vocal/instrumental group*       6 wks

| | | | |
|---|---|---|---|
| 11 Jul 70 | **FOTHERINGAY**  *Island ILPS 9125* .................. | 18 | 6 wks |

## FOUR PENNIES  *UK, male vocal/instrumental group*             5 wks

| | | | |
|---|---|---|---|
| 7 Nov 64 | **TWO SIDES OF FOUR PENNIES**  *Philips BL 7642* ...... | 13 | 5 wks |

## FOUR SEASONS  *US, male vocal group*                          49 wks

| | | | |
|---|---|---|---|
| 6 Jul 63 | **SHERRY**  *Stateside SL 10033* ...................... | 20 | 1 wk |
| 10 Apr 71 | **EDIZIONE D'ORO**  *Philips 6640–002* ................ | 11 | 7 wks |
| 20 Nov 71 | **THE BIG ONES**  *Philips 6336–208* .................. | 37 | 1 wk |
| 6 Mar 76 | **THE FOUR SEASONS STORY**  *Private Stock DAPS 1001* . | 20 | 8 wks |
| 6 Mar 76 | **WHO LOVES YOU**  *Warner Bros. K 56179* ............ | 12 | 17 wks |
| 20 Nov 76 | ● **GREATEST HITS**  *K-Tel NE 942* .................. | 4 | 6 wks |
| 21 May 88 | **THE COLLECTION**  *Telstar STAR 2320* .............. | 38 | 9 wks |

*Last two albums credited to Frankie Valli and the Four Seasons.*

## 4-SKINS  *UK, male vocal/instrumental group*                  4 wks

| | | | |
|---|---|---|---|
| 17 Apr 82 | **THE GOOD, THE BAD AND THE 4-SKINS** | | |
| | *Secret SEC 4* ....................................... | 80 | 4 wks |

## FOUR TOPS  *US, male vocal group*                             233 wks

| | | | |
|---|---|---|---|
| 19 Nov 66 | ● **FOUR TOPS ON TOP**  *Tamla Motown TML 11037* ....... | 9 | 23 wks |
| 11 Feb 67 | ● **FOUR TOPS LIVE!**  *Tamla Motown STML 11041* ......... | 4 | 72 wks |
| 25 Nov 67 | ● **REACH OUT**  *Tamla Motown STML 11056* ............. | 4 | 34 wks |
| 20 Jan 68 | ★ **GREATEST HITS**  *Tamla Motown STML 11061* .......... | 1 | 67 wks |
| 8 Feb 69 | **YESTERDAY'S DREAMS**  *Tamla Motown STML 11087* ... | 37 | 1 wk |
| 27 Jun 70 | **STILL WATERS RUN DEEP** | | |
| | *Tamla Motown STML 11149* ......................... | 29 | 8 wks |
| 27 Nov 71 | **FOUR TOPS' GREATEST HITS VOL. 2** | | |
| | *Tamla Motown STML 11195* ......................... | 25 | 10 wks |
| 10 Nov 73 | **THE FOUR TOPS STORY 1964–72** | | |
| | *Tamla Motown TMSP 11241/2* ...................... | 35 | 5 wks |
| 13 Feb 82 | **THE BEST OF THE FOUR TOPS**  *K-Tel NE 1160* ....... | 13 | 13 wks |

*See also Supremes and Four Tops.*

## FOX  *UK, male/female vocal instrumental group*               8 wks

| | | | |
|---|---|---|---|
| 17 May 75 | ● **FOX**  *GTO GTLP 001* ........................... | 7 | 8 wks |

## Samantha FOX  *UK, female vocalist*                           18 wks

| | | | |
|---|---|---|---|
| 26 Jul 86 | **TOUCH ME**  *Jive HIP 39* .......................... | 17 | 10 wks |
| 1 Aug 87 | **SAMANTHA FOX**  *Jive HIP 48* ..................... | 22 | 6 wks |
| 18 Feb 89 | **I WANNA HAVE SOME FUN**  *Jive HIP 72* ............ | 46 | 2 wks |

## Bruce FOXTON  *UK, male vocalist*                    *4 wks*

| 12 May 84 | **TOUCH SENSITIVE**  *Arista 206 251* | 68 | 4 wks |
|---|---|---|---|

## John FOXX  *UK, male vocalist*                    *17 wks*

| 2 Feb 80 | **METAMATIX**  *Metalbeat V 2146* | 18 | 7 wks |
|---|---|---|---|
| 3 Oct 81 | **THE GARDEN**  *Virgin V 2194* | 24 | 6 wks |
| 8 Oct 83 | **THE GOLDEN SECTION**  *Virgin V 2233* | 27 | 3 wks |
| 5 Oct 85 | **IN MYSTERIOUS WAYS**  *Virgin V 2355* | 85 | 1 wk |

## FRAGGLES  *UK/US puppets*                    *4 wks*

| 21 Apr 84 | **FRAGGLE ROCK**  *RCA PL 70221* | 38 | 4 wks |
|---|---|---|---|

## Peter FRAMPTON
*UK, male vocalist/instrumentalist – guitar*                    *49 wks*

| 22 May 76 | ● **FRAMPTON COMES ALIVE**  *A & M AMLM 63703* | 6 | 39 wks |
|---|---|---|---|
| 18 Jun 77 | **I'M IN YOU**  *A & M AMLK 64039* | 19 | 10 wks |

## Connie FRANCIS  *US, female vocalist*                    *26 wks*

| 26 Mar 60 | **ROCK 'N' ROLL MILLION SELLERS**  *MGM C 804* | 12 | 1 wk |
|---|---|---|---|
| 11 Feb 61 | **CONNIE'S GREATEST HITS**  *MGM C 831* | 16 | 3 wks |
| 18 Jun 77 | ★ **20 ALL TIME GREATS**  *Polydor 2391 290* | 1 | 22 wks |

## FRANKIE GOES TO HOLLYWOOD
*UK, male vocal/instrumental group*                    *71 wks*

| 10 Nov 84 | ★ **WELCOME TO THE PLEASUREDOME**  *ZTT ZTTIQ 1* | 1 | 58 wks |
|---|---|---|---|
| 1 Nov 86 | ● **LIVERPOOL**  *ZTT ZTTIQ 8* | 5 | 13 wks |

## Aretha FRANKLIN  *US, female vocalist*                    *58 wks*

| 12 Aug 67 | **I NEVER LOVED A MAN**  *Atlantic 587–006* | 36 | 2 wks |
|---|---|---|---|
| 13 Apr 68 | **LADY SOUL**  *Atlantic 588–099* | 25 | 18 wks |
| 14 Sep 68 | ● **ARETHA NOW**  *Atlantic 588–114* | 6 | 11 wks |
| 18 Jan 86 | **WHO'S ZOOMIN' WHO?**  *Arista 2072 02* | 49 | 12 wks |
| 24 May 86 | **THE FIRST LADY OF SOUL**  *Stylus SMR 8506* | 89 | 1 wk |
| 8 Nov 86 | **ARETHA**  *Arista 208 020* | 51 | 13 wks |
| 3 Jun 89 | **THROUGH THE STORM**  *Arista 209842* | 46 | 1 wk |

## Rodney FRANKLIN  *US, male instrumentalist – piano*                    *2 wks*

| 24 May 80 | **YOU'LL NEVER KNOW**  *CBS 83812* | 64 | 2 wks |
|---|---|---|---|

**Liz FRASER** – *See Harold BUDD/Liz FRASER/Robin GUTHRIE/Simon RAYMOND*

## FRAZIER CHORUS
*UK, male/female vocal/instrumental group*                    *1 wk*

| 20 May 89 | **SUE**  *Virgin V 2578* | 56 | 1 wk |
|---|---|---|---|

## FREDDIE and the DREAMERS
*UK, male vocal/instrumental group*                               *26 wks*

| | | | |
|---|---|---|---|
| 9 Nov 63 | ● **FREDDIE AND THE DREAMERS** *Columbia 33SX 1577* . | **5** | 26 wks |

**FREDERICK** – *See NINA and FREDERICK*

## FREE  *UK, male vocal/instrumental group*                      *62 wks*

| | | | |
|---|---|---|---|
| 11 Jul ·70 | ● **FIRE AND WATER** *Island ILPS 9120* ................ | **2** | 18 wks |
| 23 Jan 71 | **HIGHWAY** *Island ILPS 9138* ..................... | **41** | 10 wks |
| 26 Jun 71 | ● **FREE LIVE!** *Island ILPS 9160* .................... | **4** | 12 wks |
| 17 Jun 72 | ● **FREE AT LAST** *Island ILPS 9192* .................... | **9** | 9 wks |
| 3 Feb 73 | ● **HEARTBREAKER** *Island ILPS 9217* ............... | **9** | 7 wks |
| 16 Mar 74 | ● **THE FREE STORY** *Island ISLD 4* ................. | **2** | 6 wks |

## FREEEZ  *UK, male vocal/instrumental group*                    *18 wks*

| | | | |
|---|---|---|---|
| 7 Feb 81 | **SOUTHERN FREEEZ** *Beggars Banquet BEGA 22* ........ | **17** | 15 wks |
| 22 Oct 83 | **GONNA GET YOU** *Beggars Banquet BEGA 48* .......... | **46** | 3 wks |

## FREHLEY'S COMET  *US, male vocal/instrumental group*           *1 wk*

| | | | |
|---|---|---|---|
| 18 Jun 88 | **SECOND SIGHT** *Atlantic 781862 1* ................. | **79** | 1 wk |

**FRESH PRINCE** – *See DJ JAZZY JEFF and FRESH PRINCE*

## Glenn FREY  *US, male vocalist*                                *9 wks*

| | | | |
|---|---|---|---|
| 6 Jul 85 | **THE ALLNIGHTER** *MCA MCF 3277* ............... | **31** | 9 wks |

## FRIDA  *Norway, female vocalist*                               *8 wks*

| | | | |
|---|---|---|---|
| 18 Sep 82 | **SOMETHING'S GOING ON** *Epic EPC 85966* .......... | **18** | 7 wks |
| 20 Oct 84 | **SHINE** *Epic EPC 26178* ........................... | **67** | 1 wk |

## Dean FRIEDMAN  *US, male vocalist*                             *14 wks*

| | | | |
|---|---|---|---|
| 21 Oct 78 | **WELL, WELL, SAID THE ROCKING CHAIR** *Lifesong LSLP 6019* ............................... | **21** | 14 wks |

**FRIENDS** – *See DELANEY and BONNIE and FRIENDS*

**FRIENDS** – *See Richard HAVEY and FRIENDS*

**FRIENDS** – *See Brian MAY and FRIENDS*

## Robert FRIPP  *UK, male vocalist/instrumentalist – guitar*     *1 wk*

| | | | |
|---|---|---|---|
| 12 May 79 | **EXPOSURE** *Polydor EGLP 101* ..................... | **71** | 1 wk |

**FULL FORCE** – *See LISA LISA and CULT JAM with FULL FORCE*

## FUN BOY THREE  *UK, male vocal/instrumental group*            *40 wks*

| | | | |
|---|---|---|---|
| 20 Mar 82 | ● **FUN BOY THREE** *Chrysalis CHR 1383* ............... | **7** | 20 wks |
| 19 Feb 83 | **WAITING** *Chrysalis CHR 1417* ...................... | **14** | 20 wks |

**FUNK FEDERATION** – *See Arlene PHILLIPS*

## FUNKADELIC  *US, male vocal/instrumental group*    *5 wks*

| 23 Dec 78 | **ONE NATION UNDER A GROOVE**  *Warner Bros. K 56539* | 56 | 5 wks |
|---|---|---|---|

## FUREYS and Davey ARTHUR
*Ireland/UK, male vocal/instrumental group*    *38 wks*

| 8 May 82 | **WHEN YOU WERE SWEET SIXTEEN** *Ritz RITZLP 0004* | 99 | 1 wk |
|---|---|---|---|
| 10 Nov 84 | **GOLDEN DAYS**  *K-Tel ONE 1283* | 17 | 19 wks |
| 26 Oct 85 | **AT THE END OF THE DAY**  *K-Tel ONE 1310* | 35 | 11 wks |
| 21 Nov 87 | **FUREYS FINEST**  *Telstar HSTAR 2311* | 65 | 7 wks |

**FURIOUS FIVE** – *See GRANDMASTER FLASH and the FURIOUS FIVE*

## Billy FURY  *UK, male vocalist*    *51 wks*

| 4 Jun 60 | **THE SOUND OF FURY**  *Decca LF 1329* | 18 | 2 wks |
|---|---|---|---|
| 23 Sep 61 | ● **HALFWAY TO PARADISE**  *Ace Of Clubs ACL 1083* | 5 | 9 wks |
| 11 May 63 | ● **BILLY**  *Decca LK 4533* | 6 | 21 wks |
| 26 Oct 63 | **WE WANT BILLY**  *Decca LK 4548* | 14 | 2 wks |
| 19 Feb 83 | **HIT PARADE**  *Decca TAB 37* | 44 | 15 wks |
| 26 Mar 83 | **THE ONE AND ONLY**  *Polydor POLD 5069* | 54 | 2 wks |

**FUZZBOX** – *See WE'VE GOT A FUZZBOX AND WE'RE GONNA USE IT*

**124**

*g*

# *g*

## Kenny G  *US, male instrumentalist – saxophone*    *10 wks*

| 17 Mar 84 | **G FORCE**  *Arista 206 168* | 56 | 5 wks |
|---|---|---|---|
| 8 Aug 87 | **DUOTONES**  *Arista 207 792* | 28 | 5 wks |

## Peter GABRIEL  *UK, male vocalist*    *154 wks*

| 12 Mar 77 | ● **PETER GABRIEL**  *Charisma CDS 4006* | 7 | 19 wks |
|---|---|---|---|
| 17 Jun 78 | ● **PETER GABRIEL**  *Charisma CDS 4013* | 10 | 8 wks |
| 7 Jun 80 | ★ **PETER GABRIEL**  *Charisma CDS 4019* | 1 | 18 wks |
| 18 Sep 82 | ● **PETER GABRIEL**  *Charisma PG 4* | 6 | 16 wks |
| 18 Jun 83 | ● **PETER GABRIEL PLAYS LIVE**  *Charisma PGDL 1* | 8 | 9 wks |
| 30 Apr 85 | **BIRDY – MUSIC FROM THE FILM** *Charisma CAS 1167* | 51 | 3 wks |
| 31 May 86 | ★ **SO**  *Virgin PG 5* | 1 | 76 wks |
| 17 Jun 89 | **PASSION**  *Virgin RWLP 1* | 29 | 5 wks |

*First four albums are different.*

**GALAXY** – *See Phil FEARON and GALAXY*

## GALLAGHER and LYLE
*UK, male vocal/instrumental duo*    *44 wks*

| 28 Feb 76 | ● **BREAKAWAY**  *A & M AMLH 68348* | 6 | 35 wks |
|---|---|---|---|
| 29 Jan 77 | **LOVE ON THE AIRWAYS**  *A & M AMLH 64620* | 19 | 9 wks |

## Rory GALLAGHER
*UK, male vocalist/instrumentalist – guitar*　　　　　　　　　*43 wks*

| | | | | |
|---|---|---|---|---|
| 29 May 71 | **RORY GALLAGHER** *Polydor 2383–044* | | 32 | 2 wks |
| 4 Dec 71 | **DEUCE** *Polydor 2383–076* | | 39 | 1 wk |
| 20 May 72 ● | **LIVE IN EUROPE** *Polydor 2383 112* | | 9 | 15 wks |
| 24 Feb 73 | **BLUE PRINT** *Polydor 2383 189* | | 12 | 7 wks |
| 17 Nov 73 | **TATTOO** *Polydor 2383 230* | | 32 | 3 wks |
| 27 Jul 74 | **IRISH TOUR '74** *Polydor 2659 031* | | 36 | 2 wks |
| 30 Oct 76 | **CALLING CARD** *Chrysalis CHR 1124* | | 32 | 1 wk |
| 22 Sep 79 | **TOP PRIORITY** *Chrysalis CHR 1235* | | 56 | 4 wks |
| 8 Nov 80 | **STAGE STRUCK** *Chrysalis CHR 1280* | | 40 | 3 wks |
| 8 May 82 | **JINX** *Chrysalis CHR 1359* | | 68 | 5 wks |

## James GALWAY *UK, male instrumentalist – flute*　　　*63 wks*

| | | | |
|---|---|---|---|
| 27 May 78 | **THE MAGIC FLUTE OF JAMES GALWAY** *RCA Red Seal LRL1 5131* | 43 | 6 wks |
| 1 Jul 78 | **THE MAN WITH THE GOLDEN FLUTE** *RCA Red Seal LRL1 5127* | 52 | 3 wks |
| 9 Sep 78 ● | **JAMES GALWAY PLAYS SONGS FOR ANNIE** *RCA Red Seal RL 25163* | 7 | 40 wks |
| 15 Dec 79 | **SONGS OF THE SEASHORE** *Solar RL 25253* | 39 | 6 wks |
| 18 Dec 82 | **THE JAMES GALWAY COLLECTION** *Telstar STAR 2224* | 41 | 8 wks |

*See also James Galway and the Chieftains; James Galway and Henry Mancini; Cleo Laine and James Galway.*

## James GALWAY and Henry MANCINI with the NATIONAL PHILHARMONIC ORCHESTRA
*UK, male instrumentalist – flute, US conductor with UK orchestra*　　*6 wks*

| | | | |
|---|---|---|---|
| 8 Dec 84 | **IN THE PINK** *RCA Red Seal RL 85315* | 62 | 6 wks |

*See also James Galway; Henry Mancini.*

## James GALWAY and the CHIEFTAINS
*UK, male instrumentalist – flute with Ireland, male instrumental group*　　*5 wks*

| | | | |
|---|---|---|---|
| 28 Mar 87 | **JAMES GALWAY AND THE CHIEFTAINS IN IRELAND** *RCA Red Seal RL 85798* | 32 | 5 wks |

*See also James Galway.*

## GANG OF FOUR *UK, male vocal/instrumental group*　　*9 wks*

| | | | |
|---|---|---|---|
| 13 Oct 79 | **ENTERTAINMENT** *EMI EMC 3313* | 45 | 3 wks |
| 21 Mar 81 | **SOLID GOLD** *EMI EMC 3364* | 52 | 2 wks |
| 29 May 82 | **SONGS OF THE FREE** *EMI EMC 3412* | 61 | 4 wks |

## GAP BAND *US, male vocal/instrumental group*　　*3 wks*

| | | | |
|---|---|---|---|
| 7 Feb 87 ● | **GAP BAND 8** *Total Experience FL 89992* | 47 | 3 wks |

## Art GARFUNKEL *US, male vocalist*　　*58 wks*

| | | | |
|---|---|---|---|
| 13 Oct 73 | **ANGEL CLARE** *CBS 69021* | 14 | 7 wks |
| 1 Nov 75 ● | **BREAKAWAY** *CBS 86002* | 7 | 10 wks |
| 18 Mar 78 | **WATER MARK** *CBS 86054* | 25 | 5 wks |
| 21 Apr 79 ● | **FATE FOR BREAKFAST** *CBS 86082* | 2 | 20 wks |
| 19 Sep 81 | **SCISSORS CUT** *CBS 85259* | 51 | 3 wks |
| 17 Nov 84 | **THE ART GARFUNKEL ALBUM** *CBS 10046* | 12 | 13 wks |

*See also Simon and Garfunkel.*

The long-term success of **GENESIS** seems too much for lead singer Phil Collins

**JAMES GALWAY AND HENRY MANCINI** play a flute duet.

The **GIPSY KINGS** charted and played the Royal Albert Hall in 1989.

## Judy GARLAND  *US, female vocalist*                    *3 wks*

| | | | | |
|---|---|---|---|---|
| 3 Mar 62 | **JUDY AT CARNEGIE HALL**  *Capitol W 1569* .......... | 13 | 3 wks |

## Errol GARNER  *US, male instrumentalist – piano*       *1 wk*

| | | | | |
|---|---|---|---|---|
| 14 Jul 62 | **CLOSE UP IN SWING**  *Philips BBL 7579* .............. | 20 | 1 wk |

## David GATES  *US, male vocalist*                        *4 wks*

| | | | | |
|---|---|---|---|---|
| 31 May 75 | **NEVER LET HER GO**  *Elektra K 52012* ................ | 32 | 1 wk |
| 29 Jul 78 | **GOODBYE GIRL**  *Elektra K 52091* ................... | 28 | 3 wks |

## Marvin GAYE  *US, male vocalist*                        *93 wks*

| | | | | |
|---|---|---|---|---|
| 16 Mar 68 | **GREATEST HITS**  *Tamla Motown STML 11065* .......... | 40 | 1 wk |
| 10 Nov 73 | **LET'S GET IT ON**  *Tamla Motown STMA 8013* ........... | 39 | 1 wk |
| 15 May 76 | **I WANT YOU**  *Tamla Motown STML 12025* ............. | 22 | 5 wks |
| 30 Oct 76 | **THE BEST OF MARVIN GAYE**  *Tamla Motown STML 12042* | 56 | 1 wk |
| 28 Feb 81 | **IN OUR LIFETIME**  *Motown STML 12149* .............. | 48 | 4 wks |
| 20 Nov 82 | ● **MIDNIGHT LOVE**  *CBS 85977* ..................... | 10 | 16 wks |
| 12 Nov 83 | **GREATEST HITS**  *Telstar STAR 2234* ............. | 13 | 61 wks |
| 15 Jun 85 | **DREAM OF A LIFETIME**  *CBS 26239* ................ | 46 | 4 wks |

*See also Marvin Gaye and Tammi Terrell; Diana Ross and Marvin Gaye.*

## Marvin GAYE and Smokey ROBINSON
*US, male vocal duo*                                        *9 wks*

| | | | | |
|---|---|---|---|---|
| 12 Nov 88 | **LOVE SONGS**  *Telstar STAR 2331* .................... | 69 | 9 wks |

*See also Marvin Gaye; Smokey Robinson.*

## Marvin GAYE and Tammi TERRELL
*US male/female vocal duo*                                  *4 wks*

| | | | | |
|---|---|---|---|---|
| 22 Aug 70 | **GREATEST HITS**  *Tamla Motown STML 11153* .......... | 60 | 4 wks |

*See also Marvin Gaye.*

## GAYE BYKERS ON ACID
*UK, male vocal/instrumental group*                         *1 wk*

| | | | | |
|---|---|---|---|---|
| 14 Nov 87 | **DRILL YOUR OWN HOLE**  *Virgin V 2478* ............ | 95 | 1 wk |

## Crystal GAYLE  *US, female vocalist*                     *25 wks*

| | | | | |
|---|---|---|---|---|
| 21 Jan 78 | **WE MUST BELIEVE IN MAGIC**  *United Artists UAG 30108* | 15 | 7 wks |
| 23 Sep 78 | **WHEN I DREAM**  *United Artists UAG 30169* ............ | 25 | 8 wks |
| 22 Mar 80 | ● **THE CRYSTAL GAYLE SINGLES ALBUM** *United Artists UAG 30287* ...................... | 7 | 10 wks |

## Gloria GAYNOR  *US, female vocalist*                     *17 wks*

| | | | | |
|---|---|---|---|---|
| 8 Mar 75 | **NEVER CAN SAY GOODBYE**  *MGM 2315 321* ........ | 32 | 8 wks |
| 24 Mar 79 | **LOVE TRACKS**  *Polydor 2391 385* ................... | 31 | 7 wks |
| 16 Aug 86 | **THE POWER OF GLORIA GAYNOR**  *Stylus SMR 618* .. | 81 | 2 wks |

## J. GEILS BAND  *US, male vocal/instrumental group*       *15 wks*

| | | | | |
|---|---|---|---|---|
| 27 Feb 82 | **FREEZE FRAME**  *EMI America AML 3020* ............. | 12 | 15 wks |

## Bob GELDOF  *Ireland, male vocalist*

**1 wk**

| | | | | |
|---|---|---|---|---|
| 6 Dec 86 | **DEEP IN THE HEART OF NOWHERE** | *Mercury BOBLP 1* | 79 | 1 wk |

## GENE LOVES JEZEBEL
*UK, male vocal/instrumental group*

**5 wks**

| | | | | |
|---|---|---|---|---|
| 19 Jul 87 | **DISCOVER** | *Beggars Banquet BEGA 73* | 32 | 4 wks |
| 24 Oct 87 | **HOUSE OF DOLLS** | *Beggars Banquet BEGA 87* | 81 | 1 wk |

## GENERATION X  *UK, male vocal/instrumental group*

**9 wks**

| | | | | |
|---|---|---|---|---|
| 8 Apr 78 | **GENERATION X** | *Chrysalis CHR 1169* | 29 | 4 wks |
| 17 Feb 79 | **VALLEY OF THE DOLLS** | *Chrysalis CHR 1193* | 51 | 5 wks |

## GENESIS  *UK, male vocal/instrumental group*

**379 wks**

| | | | | |
|---|---|---|---|---|
| 14 Oct 72 | **FOXTROT** *Charisma CAS 1058* | | 12 | 7 wks |
| 11 Aug 73 | ● **GENESIS LIVE** *Charisma CLASS 1* | | 9 | 10 wks |
| 20 Oct 73 | ● **SELLING ENGLAND BY THE POUND** *Charisma CAS 1074* | | 3 | 21 wks |
| 11 May 74 | **NURSERY CRYME** *Charisma CAS 1052* | | 39 | 1 wk |
| 7 Dec 74 | ● **THE LAMB LIES DOWN ON BROADWAY** *Charisma CGS 101* | | 10 | 6 wks |
| 28 Feb 76 | ● **A TRICK OF THE TRAIL** *Charisma CDS 4001* | | 3 | 39 wks |
| 15 Jan 77 | ● **WIND AND WUTHERING** *Charisma CDS 4005* | | 7 | 22 wks |
| 29 Oct 77 | ● **SECONDS OUT** *Charisma GE 2001* | | 4 | 17 wks |
| 15 Apr 78 | ● **AND THEN THERE WERE THREE** *Charisma CDS 4010* | | 3 | 32 wks |
| 5 Apr 80 | ★ **DUKE** *Charisma CBR 101* | | 1 | 30 wks |
| 26 Sep 81 | ★ **ABACAB** *Charisma CBR 102* | | 1 | 27 wks |
| 12 Jun 82 | ● **3 SIDES LIVE** *Charisma GE 2002* | | 2 | 19 wks |
| 15 Oct 83 | ★ **GENESIS** *Charisma GENLP 1* | | 1 | 51 wks |
| 31 Mar 84 | **NURSERY CRYME (re-issue)** *Charisma CHC 22* | | 68 | 1 wk |
| 21 Apr 84 | **TRESPASS** *Charisma CHC 12* | | 98 | 1 wk |
| 21 Jun 86 | ★ **INVISIBLE TOUCH** *Charisma GENLP 2* | | 1 | 95 wks |

## Jackie GENOVA  *UK, female exercise instructor*

**2 wks**

| | | | | |
|---|---|---|---|---|
| 21 May 83 | **WORK THAT BODY** | *Island ILPS 9732* | 74 | 2 wks |

## Bobbie GENTRY  *US, female vocalist*

**1 wk**

| | | | | |
|---|---|---|---|---|
| 25 Oct 69 | **TOUCH 'EM WITH LOVE** | *Capitol EST 155* | 21 | 1 wk |

*See also Bobbie Gentry and Glen Campbell.*

## Bobbie GENTRY and Glen CAMPBELL
*US, female/male vocal duo*

**1 wk**

| | | | | |
|---|---|---|---|---|
| 28 Feb 70 | **BOBBIE GENTRY AND GLEN CAMPBELL** *Capitol ST 2928* | | 50 | 1 wk |

*See also Bobbie Gentry; Glen Campbell.*

## Lowell GEORGE  *US, male vocalist/instrumentalist – guitar*

**1 wk**

| | | | | |
|---|---|---|---|---|
| 21 Apr 79 | **THANKS BUT I'LL EAT IT HERE** | *Warner Bros. K 56487* | 71 | 1 wk |

## Robin GEORGE  *UK, male vocalist/instrumentalist – guitar*

**3 wks**

| | | | | |
|---|---|---|---|---|
| 2 Mar 85 | **DANGEROUS MUSIC** | *Bronze BRON 554* | 65 | 3 wks |

## GEORGIA SATELLITES
*US, male vocal/instrumental group*                                    *9 wks*

| 7 Feb 87 | **GEORGIA SATELLITES** *Elektra 980 496-1* ........... | 52 | 7 wks |
| 2 Jul 88 | **OPEN ALL NIGHT** *Elektra EKT 47* ................... | 39 | 2 wks |

## GERRY and the PACEMAKERS
*UK, male vocal/instrumental group*                                   *29 wks*

| 26 Oct 63 | ● **HOW DO YOU LIKE IT?** *Columbia 33SX 1546* ......... | 2 | 28 wks |
| 6 Feb 65 | **FERRY CROSS THE MERSEY** *Columbia 33SX 1676* .... | 19 | 1 wk |

## Stan GETZ and Charlie BYRD
*US, male instrumental duo – saxophone and guitar*                     *7 wks*

| 23 Feb 63 | **JAZZ SAMBA** *Verve SULP 9013* ..................... | 15 | 7 wks |

## Andy GIBB  *UK, male vocalist*                                      *9 wks*

| 19 Aug 78 | **SHADOW DANCING** *RSO RSS 0001* ............... | 15 | 9 wks |

## Barry GIBB  *UK, male vocalist*                                     *2 wks*

| 20 Oct 84 | **NOW VOYAGER** *Polydor POLH 14* ................ | 85 | 2 wks |

## Steve GIBBONS BAND  *UK, male vocal/instrumental group*             *3 wks*

| 22 Oct 77 | **CAUGHT IN THE ACT** *Polydor 2478 112* ............. | 22 | 3 wks |

## Debbie GIBSON  *US, female vocalist*                                *51 wks*

| 30 Jan 88 | **OUT OF THE BLUE** *Atlantic WX 139* ................ | 28 | 35 wks |
| 11 Feb 89 | ● **ELECTRIC YOUTH** *Atlantic WX 231* ................ | 8 | 16 wks |

## Don GIBSON  *US, male vocalist*                                     *10 wks*

| 22 Mar 80 | **COUNTRY NUMBER ONE** *Warwick WW 5079* ........ | 13 | 10 wks |

## GIBSON BROTHERS
*Martinique, male vocal/instrumental group*                            *3 wks*

| 30 Aug 80 | **ON THE RIVIERA** *Island ILPS 9620* ................. | 50 | 3 wks |

## GILLAN  *UK, male vocal/instrumental group*                         *53 wks*

| 17 Jul 76 | **CHILD IN TIME** *Polydor 2490 136* ................... | 55 | 1 wk |
| 20 Oct 79 | **MR. UNIVERSE** *Acrobat ACRO 3* ................... | 11 | 6 wks |
| 16 Aug 80 | ● **GLORY ROAD** *Virgin V 2171* ...................... | 3 | 12 wks |
| 25 Apr 81 | ● **FUTURE SHOCK** *Virgin VK 2196* ................... | 2 | 13 wks |
| 7 Nov 81 | **DOUBLE TROUBLE** *Virgin VGD 3506* ............. | 12 | 15 wks |
| 2 Oct 82 | **MAGIC** *Virgin V 2238* ............................ | 17 | 6 wks |

*Child In Time credited to Ian Gillan Band.*

## David GILMOUR  *UK, male instrumentalist – guitar*                  *18 wks*

| 10 Jun 78 | **DAVID GILMOUR** *Harvest SHVL 817* ............... | 17 | 9 wks |
| 17 Mar 84 | **ABOUT FACE** *Harvest SHSP 2400791* ............... | 21 | 9 wks |

## Gordon GILTRAP  *UK, male instrumentalist – guitar*    *7 wks*

| | | | |
|---|---|---|---|
| 18 Feb 78 | **PERILOUS JOURNEY** *Electric TRIX 4* ............... | 29 | 7 wks |

## GIPSY KINGS  *France, male vocal/instrumental group*    *35 wks*

| | | | |
|---|---|---|---|
| 15 Apr 89 | **GIPSY KINGS** *Telstar STAR 2355* ................. | 16 | 29 wks |
| 25 Nov 89 | **MOSAIQUE** *Telstar STAR 2398* ................. | 27† | 6 wks |

## GIRL  *UK, male vocal/instrumental group*    *6 wks*

| | | | |
|---|---|---|---|
| 9 Feb 80 | **SHEER GREED** *Jet JETLP 224* ................. | 33 | 5 wks |
| 23 Jan 82 | **WASTED YOUTH** *Jet JETLP 238* ................. | 92 | 1 wk |

## GIRLS AT OUR BEST
*UK, male/female vocal/instrumental group*    *3 wks*

| | | | |
|---|---|---|---|
| 7 Nov 81 | **PLEASURE** *Happy Birthday RVLP 1* ................. | 60 | 3 wks |

## GIRLSCHOOL  *UK, female vocal/instrumental group*    *23 wks*

| | | | |
|---|---|---|---|
| 5 Jul 80 | **DEMOLITION** *Bronze BRON 525* ................. | 28 | 10 wks |
| 25 Apr 81 | ● **HIT 'N' RUN** *Bronze BRON 534* ................. | 5 | 6 wks |
| 12 Jun 82 | **SCREAMING BLUE MURDER** *Bronze BRON 541* ...... | 27 | 6 wks |
| 12 Nov 83 | **PLAY DIRTY** *Bronze BRON 548* ................. | 66 | 1 wk |

## Gary GLITTER  *UK, male vocalist*    *92 wks*

| | | | |
|---|---|---|---|
| 21 Oct 72 | ● **GLITTER** *Bell BELLS 216* ................. | 8 | 40 wks |
| 16 Jun 73 | ● **TOUCH ME** *Bell BELLS 222* ................. | 2 | 33 wks |
| 29 Jun 74 | ● **REMEMBER ME THIS WAY** *Bell BELLS 237* .......... | 5 | 14 wks |
| 27 Mar 76 | **GARY GLITTER'S GREATEST HITS** *Bell BELLS 262* .. | 33 | 5 wks |

## GLITTER BAND  *UK, male vocal/instrumental group*    *17 wks*

| | | | |
|---|---|---|---|
| 14 Sep 74 | **HEY** *Bell BELLS 241* ................. | 13 | 12 wks |
| 3 May 75 | **ROCK 'N' ROLL DUDES** *Bell BELLS 253* ............. | 17 | 4 wks |
| 19 Jun 76 | **GREATEST HITS** *Bell BELLS 264* ................. | 52 | 1 wk |

## GLOVE  *UK, male vocal/instrumental group*    *3 wks*

| | | | |
|---|---|---|---|
| 17 Sep 83 | **BLUE SUNSHINE** *Wonderland SHELP 2* ............. | 35 | 3 wks |

## GO WEST  *UK, male vocal/instrumental group*    *88 wks*

| | | | |
|---|---|---|---|
| 13 Apr 85 | ● **GO WEST/BANGS AND CRASHES** *Chrysalis CHR 1495* ................. | 8 | 83 wks |
| 6 Jun 87 | **DANCING ON THE COUCH** *Chrysalis CDL 1550* ....... | 19 | 5 wks |

Bangs and Crashes *is an album of remixed versions of Go West tracks and some new material. From 31 May 1986 both records were available together as a double album.*

## GO-BETWEENS
*Australia, male/female vocal/instrumental group*    *2 wks*

| | | | |
|---|---|---|---|
| 13 Jun 87 | **TALLULAH** *Beggars Banquet BEGA 81* ................. | 91 | 1 wk |
| 10 Sep 88 | **16 LOVERS LANE** *Beggars Banquet BEGA 95* ............ | 81 | 1 wk |

## GODFATHERS  UK, male vocal/instrumental group                    3 wks

| 13 Feb 88 | **BIRTH SCHOOL WORK DEATH**  Epic 460263 1 ......⁵ | 80 | 2 wks |
| 20 May 89 | **MORE SONGS ABOUT LOVE AND HATE** | | |
| | Epic 463394 1 .................................... | 49 | 1 wk |

## GODLEY and CREME  UK, male vocal/instrumental duo        16 wks

| 19 Nov 77 | **CONSEQUENCES**  Mercury CONS 017 ............... | 52 | 1 wk |
| 9 Sep 78 | **L**  Mercury 9109 611 ............................ | 47 | 2 wks |
| 17 Oct 81 | **ISMISM**  Polydor POLD 5043 ....................... | 29 | 13 wks |

Consequences credited to Kevin Godley and Lol Creme. See also 10 C.C. and Godley and Creme.

## GO-GOs  US, female vocal/instrumental group                  3 wks

| 21 Aug 82 | **VACATION**  IRS SP 70031 ........................ | 75 | 3 wks |

## Andrew GOLD  US, male vocalist/instrumentalist – piano        7 wks

| 15 Apr 78 | **ALL THIS AND HEAVEN TOO**  Asylum K 53072  ....... | 31 | 7 wks |

## GOLDEN EARRING  Holland, male vocal/instrumental group      4 wks

| 2 Feb 74 | **MOONTAN**  Track 2406 112 ...................... | 24 | 4 wks |

## Glen GOLDSMITH  UK, male vocalist                         9 wks

| 23 Jul 88 | **WHAT YOU SEE IS WHAT YOU GET**  RCA PL 71750 ... | 14 | 9 wks |

## GOODBYE MR. MACKENZIE
UK, male/female vocal/instrumental group                       3 wks

| 22 Apr 89 | **GOOD DEEDS AND DIRTY RAGS**  Capitol EST 2089 .... | 26 ‹ | 3 wks |

## GOODIES  UK, male vocal group                             11 wks

| 8 Nov 75 | **THE NEW GOODIES LP**  Bradley's BRADL 1010  ........ | 25 | 11 wks |

## Benny GOODMAN  US, male instrumentalist – clarinet        1 wk

| 3 Apr 71 | **BENNY GOODMAN TODAY**  Decca DDS 3 ........... | 49 | 1 wk |

## Ron GOODWIN  UK, orchestra                                1 wk

| 2 May 70 | **LEGEND OF THE GLASS MOUNTAIN** | | |
| | Studio two TWO 220 ............................... | 49 | 1 wk |

## GOOMBAY DANCE BAND
Germany/Montserrat, male/female vocal group                    9 wks

| 10 Apr 82 | **SEVEN TEARS**  Epic EPC 85702 .................... | 16 | 9 wks |

## GOONS  UK, male comic group                                              31 wks

| 28 Nov 59 | ● BEST OF THE GOON SHOWS  *Parlophone PMC 1108* .... | **8** | 14 wks |
| 17 Dec 60 | BEST OF THE GOON SHOWS VOL. 2 | | |
| | *Parlophone PMC 1129* ............................. | **12** | 6 wks |
| 4 Nov 72 | ● LAST GOON SHOW OF ALL | | |
| | *BBC Radio Enterprises REB 142* ...................... | **8** | 11 wks |

**GORDON** – *See PETER and GORDON*

## Martin L. GORE  UK, male vocalist/instrumentalist – keyboards          1 wk

| 24 Jun 89 | COUNTERFEIT E.P.  *Mute STUMM 67* .............. | **51** | 1 wk |

## Jaki GRAHAM  UK, female vocalist                                      10 wks

| 14 Sep 85 | HEAVEN KNOWS  *EMI JK 1* ...................... | **48** | 5 wks |
| 20 Sep 86 | BREAKING AWAY  *EMI EMC 3514* ................ | **25** | 5 wks |

## GRAND PRIX  UK, male vocal/instrumental group                          2 wks

| 18 Jun 83 | SAMURAI  *Chrysalis CHR 1430* ...................... | **65** | 2 wks |

## GRANDMASTER FLASH and the FURIOUS FIVE  US, male vocalist and male vocal group          20 wks

| 23 Oct 82 | THE MESSAGE  *Sugar Hill SHLP 1007* ................ | **77** | 3 wks |
| 23 Jun 84 | GREATEST MESSAGES  *Sugar Hill SHLP 5552* ......... | **41** | 16 wks |
| 23 Feb 85 | THEY SAID IT COULDN'T BE DONE  *Elektra 9–60389–1* | **95** | 1 wk |

## GRANDMASTER MELLE MEL  US, male vocalist                               5 wks

| 20 Oct 84 | WORK PARTY  *Sugar Hill SHLP 5553* ................ | **45** | 5 wks |

## David GRANT  UK, male vocalist                                         7 wks

| 5 Nov 83 | DAVID GRANT  *Chrysalis CHR 1448* ................ | **32** | 6 wks |
| 18 May 85 | HOPES AND DREAMS  *Chrysalis CHR 1483* .......... | **96** | 1 wk |

## Eddy GRANT  Guyana, male vocalist/multi-instrumentalist                47 wks

| 30 May 81 | CAN'T GET ENOUGH  *Ice ICELP 21* ............... | **39** | 6 wks |
| 27 Nov 82 | ● KILLER ON THE RAMPAGE  *Ice ICELP 3023* ......... | **7** | 23 wks |
| 17 Nov 84 | ALL THE HITS  *K-Tel NE 1284* .................... | **23** | 10 wks |
| 1 Jul 89 | WALKING ON SUNSHINE (THE BEST OF EDDY | | |
| | GRANT)  *Parlophone PCSD 108* .................... | **20** | 8 wks |

## GRATEFUL DEAD  US, male vocal/instrumental group                       9 wks

| 19 Sep 70 | WORKINGMAN'S DEAD  *Warner Bros. WS 1869* ....... | **69** | 2 wks |
| 3 Aug 74 | GRATEFUL DEAD FROM THE MARS HOTEL | | |
| | *Atlantic K 59302* ................................. | **47** | 1 wk |
| 1 Nov 75 | BLUES FOR ALLAH  *United Artists UAS 29895* .......... | **45** | 1 wk |
| 4 Sep 76 | STEAL YOUR FACE  *United Artists UAS 60131/2* ........ | **42** | 1 wk |
| 20 Aug 77 | TERRAPIN STATION  *Arista SPARTY 1016* .......... | **30** | 1 wk |
| 19 Sep 87 | IN THE DARK  *Arista 208 564* ...................... | **57** | 3 wks |

*See also Bob Dylan and the Grateful Dead.*

## David GRAY and Tommy TYCHO
*UK, male arrangers*                                                     *6 wks*

| 16 Oct 76 | **ARMCHAIR MELODIES**  *K-Tel NE 927* . . . . . . . . . . . . | 21 | 6 wks |

**Alltrina GRAYSON** – *See Wilton FELDER*

## Al GREEN  *US, male vocalist*                                         *23 wks*

| 26 Apr 75 | **AL GREEN'S GREATEST HITS**  *London SHU 8481* . . . . . | 18 | 16 wks |
| 1 Oct 88 | **HI LIFE – THE BEST OF AL GREEN**  *K-Tel NE 1420* . . . . | 34 | 7 wks |

## Peter GREEN  *UK, male vocalist/instrumentalist – guitar*            *17 wks*

| 9 Jul 79 | **IN THE SKIES**  *Creole PULS 101* . . . . . . . . . . . . . . . . . . . . | 32 | 13 wks |
| 24 May 80 | **LITTLE DREAMER**  *PUK PULS 102* . . . . . . . . . . . . . . . | 34 | 4 wks |

## GREEN ON RED  *US, male vocal/instrumental group*                     *1 wk*

| 26 Oct 85 | **NO FREE LUNCH**  *Mercury MERM 78* . . . . . . . . . . . . . . | 99 | 1 wk |

## Dave GREENFIELD and Jean-Jacques BURNEL
*UK, male vocal/instrumental duo*                                        *1 wk*

| 3 Dec 83 | **FIRE AND WATER**  *Epic EPC 25707* . . . . . . . . . . . . . . . | 94 | 1 wk |

*See also Jean-Jacques Burnel.*

## GREENSLADE  *UK, male vocal/instrumental group*                       *3 wks*

| 14 Sep 74 | **SPYGLASS GUEST**  *Warner Bros. K 56055* . . . . . . . . . . . . . | 34 | 3 wks |

## Christina GREGG  *UK, female exercise instructor*                     *1 wk*

| 27 May 78 | **MUSIC 'N' MOTION**  *Warwick WW 5041* . . . . . . . . . . . . | 51 | 1 wk |

## Nanci GRIFFITH  *US, female vocalist*                                 *4 wks*

| 28 Mar 88 | **LITTLE LOVE AFFAIRS**  *MCA MCF 3413* . . . . . . . . . . . | 78 | 1 wk |
| 23 Sep 89 | **STORMS**  *MCA MCG 6066* . . . . . . . . . . . . . . . . . . . . . . . | 38 | 3 wks |

## GROUNDHOGS  *UK, male vocal/instrumental group*                       *50 wks*

| 6 Jun 70 | ● **THANK CHRIST FOR THE BOMB**  *Liberty LBS 83295* . . . | 9 | 13 wks |
| 3 Apr 71 | ● **SPLIT**  *Liberty LBG 83401* . . . . . . . . . . . . . . . . . . . . . . . . | 5 | 27 wks |
| 18 Mar 72 | ● **WHO WILL SAVE THE WORLD** |  |  |
|  | *United Artists UAG 29237* . . . . . . . . . . . . . . . . . . . . . . . . | 8 | 9 wks |
| 13 Jul 74 | **SOLID**  *WWA WWA 004* . . . . . . . . . . . . . . . . . . . . . . . . . | 31 | 1 wk |

## GTR  *UK, male vocal/instrumental group*                              *4 wks*

| 19 Jul 86 | **GTR**  *Arista 207 716* . . . . . . . . . . . . . . . . . . . . . . . . . . . | 41 | 4 wks |

## GUILDFORD CATHEDRAL CHOIR  *UK, choir*                                 *4 wks*

| 10 Dec 66 | **CHRISTMAS CAROLS FROM GUILDFORD CATHEDRAL** |  |  |
|  | *MFP 1104* . . . . . . . . . . . . . . . . . . . . . . . . . . . . . . . . . . . . | 24 | 4 wks |

*Record credits Barry Rose as conductor.*

## GUN  *UK, male vocal/instrumental group*  *10 wks*

| | | | |
|---|---|---|---|
| 22 Jul 89 | **TAKING ON THE WORLD**  *A & M AMA 7007*  ........ | **44** | 10 wks |

## David GUNSON  *UK, male after dinner speaker*  *2 wks*

| | | | |
|---|---|---|---|
| 25 Dec 82 | **WHAT GOES UP MIGHT COME DOWN**  *Big Ben BB 0012* | **92** | 2 wks |

## GUNS N' ROSES  *US, male vocal/instrumental group*  *108 wks*

| | | | |
|---|---|---|---|
| 1 Aug 87 | ● **APPETITE FOR DESTRUCTION**  *Geffen WX 125* ...... | **5†** | 69 wks |
| 17 Dec 88 | **G N' R LIES...**  *Geffen WX 218*  ..................... | **22** | 39 wks |

## G.U.S. (FOOTWEAR) BAND and the MORRISTOWN ORPHEUS CHOIR
*UK, male instrumental group and male/female vocal group*  *1 wk*

| | | | |
|---|---|---|---|
| 3 Oct 70 | **LAND OF HOPE AND GLORY**  *Columbia SCX 6406* ..... | **54** | 1 wk |

## Arlo GUTHRIE  *US, male vocalist*  *1 wk*

| | | | |
|---|---|---|---|
| 7 Mar 70 | **ALICE'S RESTAURANT**  *Reprise RSLP 6267* .......... | **44** | 1 wk |

## Gwen GUTHRIE  *US, female vocalist*  *14 wks*

| | | | |
|---|---|---|---|
| 23 Aug 86 | **GOOD TO GO LOVER**  *Boiling Point POLD 5201* ....... | **42** | 14 wks |

**Robin GUTHRIE** – *See Harold BUDD/Liz FRASER/Robin GUTHRIE/Simon RAYMOND*

## GUYS 'N' DOLLS  *UK, male/female vocal group*  *1 wk*

| | | | |
|---|---|---|---|
| 31 May 75 | **GUYS 'N' DOLLS**  *Magnet MAG 5005* ................. | **43** | 1 wk |

**GWENT CHORALE** – *See Bryn YEMM*

# *h*

## Steve HACKETT
*UK, male vocalist/instrumentalist – guitar*  *38 wks*

| | | | |
|---|---|---|---|
| 1 Nov 75 | **VOYAGE OF THE ACOLYTE**  *Charisma CAS 1111* ...... | **26** | 4 wks |
| 6 May 78 | **PLEASE DON'T TOUCH**  *Charisma CDS 4012* .......... | **38** | 5 wks |
| 26 May 79 | **SPECTRAL MORNINGS**  *Charisma CDS 4017* .......... | **22** | 11 wks |
| 21 Jun 80 | ● **DEFECTOR**  *Charisma CDS 4018* ..................... | **9** | 7 wks |
| 29 Aug 81 | **CURED**  *Charisma CDS 4021* ........................ | **15** | 5 wks |
| 30 Apr 83 | **HIGHLY STRUNG**  *Charisma HACK 1* ................ | **16** | 3 wks |
| 19 Nov 83 | **BAY OF KINGS**  *Lamborghini LMGLP 3000* ............. | **70** | 1 wk |
| 22 Sep 84 | **TILL WE HAVE FACES**  *Lamborghini LMGLP 4000* ....... | **54** | 2 wks |

## Sammy HAGAR  *US, male vocalist/instrumentalist – guitar*  *19 wks*

| | | | |
|---|---|---|---|
| 29 Sep 79 | **STREET MACHINE**  *Capitol EST 11983* .............. | **38** | 4 wks |
| 22 Mar 80 | **LOUD AND CLEAR**  *Capitol EST 25330* .............. | **12** | 8 wks |

| 7 Jun 80 | **DANGER ZONE** *Capitol EST 12069* ................. | 25 | 3 wks |
| 13 Feb 82 | **STANDING HAMPTON** *Geffen GEF 85456* .......... | 84 | 2 wks |
| 4 Jul 87 | **SAMMY HAGAR** *Geffen WX 114* .................... | 86 | 2 wks |

*See also Hagar, Schon, Aaronson, Shrieve.*

## HAGAR, SCHON, AARONSON, SHRIEVE
*US, male vocal/instrumental group*     *1 wk*

| 19 May 84 | **THROUGH THE FIRE** *Geffen GEF 25893* ............ | 92 | 1 wk |

*See also Sammy Hagar.*

## Paul HAIG   *UK, male vocalist*     *2 wks*

| 22 Oct 83 | **RHYTHM OF LIFE** *Crepuscule ILPS 9742* ............. | 82 | 2 wks |

## HAIRCUT 100   *UK, male vocal/instrumental group*     *34 wks*

| 6 Mar 82 ● | **PELICAN WEST** *Arista HCC 100* ................... | 2 | 34 wks |

## Bill HALEY and his COMETS
*US, male vocal/instrumental group*     *5 wks*

| 18 May 68 | **ROCK AROUND THE CLOCK** *Ace Of Hearts AH 13* .... | 34 | 5 wks |

## HALF MAN HALF BISCUIT
*UK, male vocal/instrumental group*     *14 wks*

| 8 Feb 86 | **BACK IN THE DHSS** *Probe Plus PROBE 4* ............ | 59 | 14 wks |

## Daryl HALL   *US, male vocalist*     *5 wks*

| 23 Aug 86 | **THREE HEARTS IN THE HAPPY ENDING MACHINE** *RCA PL 87196* ................................. | 26 | 5 wks |

*See also Daryl Hall and John Oates.*

## Daryl HALL and John OATES   *US, male vocal duo*     *132 wks*

| 3 Jul 76 | **HALL AND OATES** *RCA Victor APL1 1144* ............ | 56 | 1 wk |
| 18 Sep 76 | **BIGGER THAN BOTH OF US** *RCA Victor APL1 1467* .... | 25 | 7 wks |
| 15 Oct 77 | **BEAUTY ON A BACK STREET** *RCA PL 12300* ........ | 40 | 2 wks |
| 6 Feb 82 ● | **PRIVATE EYES** *RCA RCALP 6001* ................. | 8 | 21 wks |
| 23 Oct 82 | **H2O** *RCA RCALP 6056* .......................... | 24 | 35 wks |
| 29 Oct 83 | **ROCK 'N' SOUL (PART 1)** *RCA PL 84858* ............ | 16 | 45 wks |
| 27 Oct 84 | **BIG BAM BOOM** *RCA PL 85309* .................... | 28 | 13 wks |
| 28 Sep 85 | **LIVE AT THE APOLLO WITH DAVID RUFFIN AND EDDIE KENDRICK** *RCA PL 87035* ................... | 32 | 5 wks |
| 18 Jun 88 | **OOH YEAH!** *RCA 208895* ........................ | 52 | 3 wks |

*See also Daryl Hall.*

## HAMBURG STUDENTS' CHOIR
*Germany, male vocal group*     *6 wks*

| 17 Dec 60 | **HARK THE HERALD ANGELS SING** *Pye GGL 0023* .. | 11 | 6 wks |

## George HAMILTON IV   *US, male vocalist*     *11 wks*

| 10 Apr 71 | **CANADIAN PACIFIC** *RCA SF 8062* ................ | 45 | 1 wk |
| 10 Feb 79 | **REFLECTIONS** *Lotus WH 5008* .................... | 25 | 9 wks |
| 13 Nov 82 | **SONGS FOR A WINTER'S NIGHT** *Ronco RTL 2082* .... | 94 | 1 wk |

The long-stand
popularity of T
**GOONS** (lef
right: Ha
Secombe, Mic
Bentine, P
Sellers and Sp
Milligan) m
theirs the m
successful serie
radio recordi
ever. Most of th
radio success ca
after Bentine l

W. Axl Rose (right) of **GUNS N' ROSES**, the heavy heroes of 1989.

**TED HAWKINS** became a chart artist after extensive broadcast support from disc jockey Andy Kershaw.

**HEART** had hits on four labels before finding one on which they had consistent success.

## Jan HAMMER  *Czechoslovakia, male instrumentalist – keyboards*  *12 wks*

| 14 Nov 87 | **ESCAPE FROM TV**  *MCA MCF 3407* .................. | 34 | 12 wks |

## Herbie HANCOCK
*US, male vocalist/instrumentalist – keyboards*  *24 wks*

| 9 Sep 78 | **SUNLIGHT**  *CBS 82240* ........................... | 27 | 6 wks |
| 24 Feb 79 | **FEETS DON'T FAIL ME NOW**  *CBS 83491* ........... | 28 | 8 wks |
| 27 Aug 83 | **FUTURE SHOCK**  *CBS 25540* ...................... | 27 | 10 wks |

## Tony HANCOCK  *UK, male comedian*  *42 wks*

| 9 Apr 60 | ● **THIS IS HANCOCK**  *Pye NPL 10845* ................ | 2 | 22 wks |
| 12 Nov 60 | **PIECES OF HANCOCK**  *Pye NPL 18054* .............. | 17 | 2 wks |
| 3 Mar 62 | **HANCOCK**  *Pye NPL 18068* ....................... | 12 | 14 wks |
| 14 Sep 63 | **THIS IS HANCOCK (re-issue)** | | |
| | *Pye Golden Guinea GGL 0206* ...................... | 16 | 4 wks |

**Vernon HANDLEY** – *See Nigel KENNEDY*

## Bo HANNSON  *Sweden, multi-instrumentalist*  *2 wks*

| 18 Nov 72 | **LORD OF THE RINGS**  *Charisma CAS 1059* ........... | 34 | 2 wks |

## HANOI ROCKS
*Finland/UK, male vocal/instrumental group*  *4 wks*

| 11 Jun 83 | **BACK TO MYSTERY CITY**  *Lick LICLP 1* ............. | 87 | 1 wk |
| 20 Oct 84 | **TWO STEPS FROM THE MOVE**  *CBS 26066* .......... | 28 | 3 wks |

## John HANSON  *UK, male vocalist*  *12 wks*

| 23 Apr 60 | **THE STUDENT PRINCE**  *Pye NPL 18046* ............. | 17 | 1 wk |
| 2 Sep 61 | ● **THE STUDENT PRINCE/VAGABOND KING** | | |
| | *Pye GGL 0086* ................................... | 9 | 7 wks |
| 10 Dec 77 | **JOHN HANSON SINGS 20 SHOWTIME GREATS** | | |
| | *K-Tel NE 1002* .................................. | 16 | 4 wks |

## Paul HARDCASTLE
*UK, male producer/instrumentalist – synthesizer*  *5 wks*

| 30 Nov 85 | **PAUL HARDCASTLE**  *Chrysalis CHR 1517* ........... | 53 | 5 wks |

## Mike HARDING  *UK, male comedian*  *24 wks*

| 30 Aug 75 | **MRS 'ARDIN'S KID**  *Rubber RUB 011* ................ | 24 | 6 wks |
| 10 Jul 76 | **ONE MAN SHOW**  *Philips 6625 022* ................. | 19 | 10 wks |
| 11 Jun 77 | **OLD FOUR EYES IS BACK**  *Philips 6308 290* .......... | 31 | 6 wks |
| 24 Jun 78 | **CAPTAIN PARALYTIC AND THE BROWN ALE COWBOY** | | |
| | *Philips 6641 798* ................................. | 60 | 2 wks |

**HARDY** – *See LAUREL and HARDY*

## Steve HARLEY and COCKNEY REBEL
*UK, male vocalist and male vocal/instrumental group*  *52 wks*

| 22 Jun 74 | ● **THE PSYCHOMODO**  *EMI EMC 3033* .............. | 8 | 20 wks |
| 22 Mar 75 | ● **THE BEST YEARS OF OUR LIVES**  *EMI EMC 3068* .... | 4 | 19 wks |
| 14 Feb 76 | **TIMELESS FLIGHT**  *EMI EMA 775* ................. | 18 | 6 wks |
| 27 Nov 76 | **LOVE'S A PRIMA DONNA**  *EMI EMC 3156* .......... | 28 | 3 wks |

30 Jul 77 **FACE TO FACE – A LIVE RECORDING**
EMI EMSP 320 ................................. **40** 4 wks

*First album credited to Cockney Rebel.*

## Roy HARPER *UK, male vocalist/instrumentalist – guitar* *5 wks*

| | | | |
|---|---|---|---|
| 9 Mar 74 | **VALENTINE** *Harvest SHSP 4027* ................... | **27** | 1 wk |
| 21 Jun 75 | **H.Q.** *Harvest SHSP 4046* ........................... | **31** | 2 wks |
| 12 Mar 77 | **BULLINAMINGVASE** *Harvest SHSP 4060* ........... | **25** | 2 wks |

*See also Roy Harper and Jimmy Page.*

## Roy HARPER and Jimmy PAGE

*UK, male vocal/instrumental duo* *4 wks*

| | | | |
|---|---|---|---|
| 16 Mar 85 | **WHATEVER HAPPENED TO JUGULA?** | | |
| | *Beggars Banquet BEGA 60* ......................... | **44** | 4 wks |

*See also Roy Harper; Jimmy Page.*

## Anita HARRIS *UK, female vocalist* *5 wks*

| | | | |
|---|---|---|---|
| 27 Jan 68 | **JUST LOVING YOU** *CBS SBPG 63182* .............. | **29** | 5 wks |

## Emmylou HARRIS *US, female vocalist* *29 wks*

| | | | |
|---|---|---|---|
| 14 Feb 76 | **ELITE HOTEL** *Reprise K 54060* ................... | **17** | 11 wks |
| 29 Jan 77 | **LUXURY LINER** *Warner Bros. K 56344* .............. | **17** | 6 wks |
| 4 Feb 78 | **QUARTER MOON IN A TEN CENT TOWN** | | |
| | *Warner Bros. K 56433* ........................... | **40** | 5 wks |
| 29 Mar 80 | **HER BEST SONGS** *K-Tel NE 1058* ................. | **36** | 3 wks |
| 14 Feb 81 | **EVANGELINE** *Warner Bros. K 56880* ................ | **53** | 4 wks |

*See also Dolly Parton/Linda Ronstadt/Emmylou Harris.*

## Keith HARRIS, ORVILLE and CUDDLES

*UK, male ventriloquist vocalist with dummies* *1 wk*

| | | | |
|---|---|---|---|
| 4 Jun 83 | **AT THE END OF THE RAINBOW** *BBC REH 465* ...... | **92** | 1 wk |

## George HARRISON

*UK, male vocalist/instrumentalist – guitar* *76 wks*

| | | | |
|---|---|---|---|
| 26 Dec 70 | ● **ALL THINGS MUST PASS** *Apple STCH 639* ........... | **4** | 24 wks |
| 7 Jul 73 | ● **LIVING IN THE MATERIAL WORLD** *Apple PAS 10006* | **2** | 12 wks |
| 18 Oct 75 | **EXTRA TEXTURE (READ ALL ABOUT IT)** | | |
| | *Apple PAS 10009* ................................. | **16** | 4 wks |
| 18 Dec 76 | **THIRTY THREE AND A THIRD** *Dark Horse K 56319* ... | **35** | 4 wks |
| 17 Mar 79 | **GEORGE HARRISON** *Dark Horse K 56562* ........... | **39** | 5 wks |
| 13 Jun 81 | **SOMEWHERE IN ENGLAND** *Dark Horse K 56870* ...... | **13** | 4 wks |
| 14 Nov 87 | ● **CLOUD NINE** *Dark Horse WX 123* ................... | **10** | 23 wks |

## Jane HARRISON *UK, female operatic vocalist* *1 wk*

| | | | |
|---|---|---|---|
| 4 Feb 89 | **NEW DAY** *Stylus SMR 869* ......................... | **70** | 1 wk |

## Debbie HARRY *US, female vocalist* *25 wks*

| | | | |
|---|---|---|---|
| 8 Aug 81 | ● **KOO KOO** *Chrysalis CHR 1347* .................... | **6** | 7 wks |
| 29 Nov 86 | **ROCKBIRD** *Chrysalis CHR 1540* .................... | **31** | 11 wks |
| 28 Oct 89 | **DEF DUMB AND BLONDE** *Chrysalis CHR 1650* ........ | **12** | 7 wks |

*Act known as Deborah Harry on third album. See also Debbie Harry and Blondie.*

## Debbie HARRY and BLONDIE
*US, female vocalist and UK/US, male/female vocal/instrumental group*    *4 wks*

17 Dec 88   **ONCE MORE INTO THE BLEACH**  *Chrysalis CJB 2* ..... 50   4 wks
*See also Debbie Harry; Blondie.*

## Keef HARTLEY BAND   *UK, male vocal/instrumental group*   *3 wks*

5 Sep 70   **THE TIME IS NEAR**  *Deram SML 1071* ............... 41   3 wks

## Richard HARVEY and FRIENDS
*UK, male instrumental group*                                   *1 wk*

6 May 89   **EVENING FALLS**  *Telstar STAR 2350* ................ 72   1 wk

## HATFIELD AND THE NORTH
*UK, male/female vocal/instrumental group*                      *1 wk*

29 Mar 75   **ROTTERS CLUB**  *Virgin V 2030* .................... 43   1 wk

**Donny HATHAWAY** – *See Roberta FLACK and Donny HATHAWAY*

## Ted HAWKINS   *US, male vocalist/instrumentalist – guitar*   *1 wk*

18 Apr 87   **HAPPY HOUR**  *Windows On The World WOLP 2* ........ 82   1 wk

## HAWKWIND   *UK, male vocal/instrumental group*   *98 wks*

| | | | |
|---|---|---|---|
| 6 Nov 71 | **IN SEARCH OF SPACE**  *United Artists UAS 29202* ....... | 18 | 19 wks |
| 23 Dec 72 | **DOREMI FASOL LATIDO**  *United Artists UAS 29364* ..... | 14 | 5 wks |
| 2 Jun 73 ● | **SPACE RITUAL ALIVE**  *United Artists UAD 60037/8* ..... | 9 | 5 wks |
| 21 Sep 74 | **HALL OF THE MOUNTAIN GRILL** | | |
| | *United Artists UAG 29672* .......................... | 16 | 5 wks |
| 31 May 75 | **WARRIOR ON THE EDGE OF TIME** | | |
| | *United Artists UAG 29766* .......................... | 13 | 7 wks |
| 24 Apr 76 | **ROAD HAWKS**  *United Artists UAK 29919* ............. | 34 | 4 wks |
| 18 Sep 76 | **ASTONISHING SOUNDS, AMAZING MUSIC** | | |
| | *Charisma CDS 4004* ................................ | 33 | 5 wks |
| 9 Jul 77 | **QUARK STRANGENESS AND CHARM** | | |
| | *Charisma CDS 4008* ................................ | 30 | 6 wks |
| 21 Oct 78 | **25 YEARS ON**  *Charisma CD 4014* .................... | 48 | 3 wks |
| 30 Jun 79 | **PXR 5**  *Charisma CDS 4016* ......................... | 59 | 5 wks |
| 9 Aug 80 | **LIVE 1979**  *Bronze BRON 527* ....................... | 15 | 7 wks |
| 8 Nov 80 | **LEVITATION**  *Bronze BRON 530* ..................... | 21 | 4 wks |
| 24 Oct 81 | **SONIC ATTACK**  *RCA RCALP 5004* ................... | 19 | 5 wks |
| 22 May 82 | **CHURCH OF HAWKWIND**  *RCA RCALP 9004* ........ | 26 | 6 wks |
| 23 Oct 82 | **CHOOSE YOUR MASQUES**  *RCA RCALP 6055* ....... | 29 | 5 wks |
| 5 Nov 83 | **ZONES**  *Flicknife SHARP 014* ....................... | 57 | 2 wks |
| 25 Feb 84 | **HAWKWIND**  *Liberty SLS 1972921* ................... | 75 | 1 wk |
| 16 Nov 85 | **CHRONICLE OF THE BLACK SWORD** | | |
| | *Flicknife SHARP 033* ............................... | 65 | 2 wks |
| 14 May 88 | **THE XENON CODEX**  *GWR GWLP 26* .............. | 79 | 2 wks |

*25 Years On credited to Hawklords, a pseudonym for Hawkwind.*

## Isaac HAYES   *US, male vocalist/multi-instrumentalist*   *14 wks*

18 Dec 71   **SHAFT**  *Polydor 2659 007* .......................... 17   13 wks
12 Feb 72   **BLACK MOSES**  *Stax 2628 004* ..................... 38   1 wk

## HAYSI FANTAYZEE  *UK, male/female vocal duo*    *5 wks*

| 26 Feb 83 | **BATTLE HYMNS FOR CHILDREN SINGING**<br>*Regard RGLP 6000* .............................. | **53** | 5 wks |

## Justin HAYWARD  *UK, male vocalist* .    *10 wks*

| 5 Mar 77 | **SONGWRITER**  *Deram SDL 15* ..................... | **28** | 5 wks |
| 19 Jul 80 | **NIGHT FLIGHT**  *Decca TXS 138* ................... | **41** | 4 wks |
| 19 Oct 85 | **MOVING MOUNTAINS**  *Towerbell TOWLP 15* .......... | **78** | 1 wk |

*See also Justin Hayward and John Lodge; Justin Hayward, Mike Batt and the London Philharmonic Orchestra.*

## Justin HAYWARD, Mike BATT and the LONDON PHILHARMONIC ORCHESTRA
*UK, male vocalist, male producer and orchestra*    *7 wks*

| 28 Oct 89 | **CLASSIC BLUE**  *Trax MODEM 1040* ................. | **47** | 7 wks |

*See also Justin Hayward; London Philharmonic Orchestra.*

## Justin HAYWARD and John LODGE
*UK, male vocal/instrumental duo*    *18 wks*

| 29 Mar 75 | ● **BLUE JAYS**  *Threshold THS 12* ....................... | **4** | 18 wks |

*See also Justin Hayward; John Lodge; Justin Hayward, Mike Batt and the London Philharmonic Orchestra.*

**Lee HAZLEWOOD** – *See Nancy SINATRA and Lee HAZLEWOOD*

## Jeff HEALEY BAND  *US, male vocal/instrumental group*    *7 wks*

| 14 Jan 89 | **SEE THE LIGHT**  *Arista 209441* ..................... | **58** | 7 wks |

## HEART  *US, female/male vocal/instrumental group*    *113 wks*

| 22 Jan 77 | **DREAMBOAT ANNIE**  *Arista ARTY 139* .............. | **36** | 8 wks |
| 23 Jul 77 | **LITTLE QUEEN**  *Portrait PRT 82075* .................. | **34** | 4 wks |
| 19 Jun 82 | **PRIVATE AUDITION**  *Epic EPC 85792* .............. | **77** | 2 wks |
| 26 Oct 85 | **HEART**  *Capitol EJ 24-0372-1* ....................... | **19** | 43 wks |
| 6 Jun 87 | ● **BAD ANIMALS**  *Capitol ESTU 2032* ................. | **7** | 56 wks |

*Heart changed label number during its chart run to Capitol LOVE 1.*

## HEARTBREAKERS  *US, male vocal/instrumental group*    *1 wk*

| 5 Nov 77 | **L.A.M.F.**  *Track 2409 218* .......................... | **55** | 1 wk |

## Ted HEATH AND HIS MUSIC
*UK, conductor and orchestra*    *5 wks*

| 21 Apr 62 | **BIG BAND PERCUSSION**  *Decca PFM 24004* .......... | **17** | 5 wks |

## HEATWAVE  *UK/US, male vocal/instrumental group*    *26 wks*

| 11 Jun 77 | **TOO HOT TO HANDLE**  *GTO GTLP 013* ............. | **46** | 2 wks |
| 6 May 78 | **CENTRAL HEATING**  *GTO GTLP 027* .............. | **26** | 15 wks |
| 14 Feb 81 | **CANDLES**  *GTO GTLP 047* ........................ | **29** | 9 wks |

## HEAVEN 17  *UK, male vocal/instrumental group*          *126 wks*

| 26 Sep 81 | PENTHOUSE AND PAVEMENT  *Virgin V 2208* ........ | 14 | 76 wks |
| 7 May 83 | ● THE LUXURY GAP  *Virgin V 2253* ................. | 4 | 36 wks |
| 6 Oct 84 | HOW MEN ARE  *B.E.F. V 2326* ..................... | 12 | 11 wks |
| 12 Jul 86 | ENDLESS  *Virgin TCVB/CDV 2383* ................. | 70 | 2 wks |
| 29 Nov 86 | PLEASURE ONE  *Virgin V 2400* ................... | 78 | 1 wk |

*Endless was available only on cassette and CD.*

## HEAVY PETTIN'  *UK, male vocal/instrumental group*          *4 wks*

| 29 Oct 83 | LETTIN' LOOSE  *Polydor HEPLP 1* ................. | 55 | 2 wks |
| 13 Jul 85 | ROCK AIN'T DEAD  *Polydor HEPLP 2* ............... | 81 | 2 wks |

## HELLOWEEN  *Germany, male vocal/instrumental group*          *7 wks*

| 17 Sep 88 | KEEPER OF THE SEVEN KEYS PART 2 | | |
| | *Noise International NUK 117* ......................... | 24 | 5 wks |
| 15 Apr 89 | LIVE IN THE UK  *EMI EMC 3558* ................... | 26 | 2 wks |

## Jimi HENDRIX  *US, male vocalist/instrumentalist – guitar*          *193 wks*

| 27 May 67 | ● ARE YOU EXPERIENCED  *Track 612–001* ............. | 2 | 33 wks |
| 16 Dec 67 | ● AXIS: BOLD AS LOVE  *Track 613–003* ............... | 5 | 16 wks |
| 27 Apr 68 | ● SMASH HITS  *Track 613–004* ...................... | 4 | 25 wks |
| 16 Nov 68 | ● ELECTRIC LADYLAND  *Track 613–008/9* ............. | 6 | 12 wks |
| 4 Jul 70 | ● BAND OF GYPSIES  *Track 2406–001* ................ | 6 | 30 wks |
| 3 Apr 71 | ● CRY OF LOVE  *Track 2408–101* .................... | 2 | 14 wks |
| 28 Aug 71 | ● EXPERIENCE  *Ember NR 5057* ..................... | 9 | 6 wks |
| 20 Nov 71 | JIMI HENDRIX AT THE ISLE OF WIGHT | | |
| | *Track 2302 016* .................................. | 17 | 2 wks |
| 4 Dec 71 | RAINBOW BRIDGE  *Reprise K 44159* ................. | 16 | 8 wks |
| 5 Feb 72 | ● HENDRIX IN THE WEST  *Polydor 2302 018* ........... | 7 | 14 wks |
| 11 Dec 72 | WAR HEROES  *Polydor 2302 020* .................... | 23 | 3 wks |
| 21 Jul 73 | SOUNDTRACK RECORDINGS FROM THE FILM 'JIMI | | |
| | HENDRIX'  *Warner Bros. K 64017* ................... | 37 | 1 wk |
| 29 Mar 75 | JIMI HENDRIX  *Polydor 2343 080* ................... | 35 | 4 wks |
| 30 Aug 75 | CRASH LANDING  *Polydor 2310 398* ................. | 35 | 3 wks |
| 29 Nov 75 | MIDNIGHT LIGHTNING  *Polydor 2310 415* ............ | 46 | 1 wk |
| 14 Aug 82 | THE JIMI HENDRIX CONCERTS  *CBS 88592* ......... | 16 | 11 wks |
| 19 Feb 83 | THE SINGLES ALBUM  *Polydor PODV 6* ............. | 77 | 4 wks |
| 11 Mar 89 | RADIO ONE  *Castle Collectors CCSLP 212* ............. | 30 | 6 wks |

*See also Jimi Hendrix and Curtis Knight. Act billed as Jimi Hendrix Experience, US/UK, male vocal/instrumental group, for first four hits.*

## Jimi HENDRIX and Curtis KNIGHT
*US, male vocal/instrumental duo*          *2 wks*

| 18 May 68 | GET THAT FEELING  *London HA 8349* .............. | 39 | 2 wks |

*See also Jimi Hendrix.*

## Don HENLEY  *US, male vocalist*          *27 wks*

| 9 Mar 85 | BUILDING THE PERFECT BEAST  *Geffen GEF 25939* .. | 14 | 11 wks |
| 8 Jul 89 | THE END OF INNOCENCE  *Geffen WX 253* ........... | 17 | 16 wks |

## Band and Chorus of HER MAJESTY'S
## GUARDS DIVISION  *UK, military band*          *4 wks*

| 22 Nov 75 | 30 SMASH HITS OF THE WAR YEARS | | |
| | *Warwick WW 5006* ................................. | 38 | 4 wks |

## HERD  *UK, male vocal/instrumental group*                                        *1 wk*

24 Feb 68   **PARADISE LOST**   *Fontana STL 5458* .................   **38**   1 wk

## HERMAN'S HERMITS  *UK, male vocal/instrumental group*   *11 wks*

18 Sep 65   **HERMAN'S HERMITS**   *Columbia 33SX 1727* ..........   **16**   2 wks
25 Sep 71   **THE MOST OF HERMAN'S HERMITS**   *MFP 5216* .....   **14**   5 wks
8 Oct 77    **GREATEST HITS**   *K-Tel NE 1001* ..................   **37**   4 wks

## Nick HEYWARD  *UK, male vocalist*                                *13 wks*

29 Oct 83 ● **NORTH OF A MIRACLE**   *Arista NORTH 1* ...........   **10**   13 wks

## HI TENSION  *UK, male vocal/instrumental group*                 *4 wks*

6 Jan 79   **HI TENSION**   *Island ILPS 9564* ......................   **74**   4 wks

## Benny HILL  *UK, male vocalist*                                 *8 wks*

11 Dec 71 ● **WORDS AND MUSIC**   *Columbia SCX 6479* ...........   **9**   8 wks

## Vince HILL  *UK, male vocalist*                                *10 wks*

20 May 67   **EDELWEISS**   *Columbia SCX 6141* ...................   **23**   9 wks
29 Apr 78   **THAT LOVING FEELING**   *K-Tel NE 1017* ...........   **51**   1 wk

## Steve HILLAGE  *UK, male vocalist/instrumentalist – guitar*   *41 wks*

3 May 75    **FISH RISING**   *Virgin V 2031* .......................   **33**   3 wks
16 Oct 76 ● **L**   *Virgin V 2066* ..................................   **10**   12 wks
22 Oct 77   **MOTIVATION RADIO**   *Virgin V 2777* ................   **28**   5 wks
29 Apr 78   **GREEN VIRGIN**   *V 2098* .........................   **30**   8 wks
17 Feb 79   **LIVE HERALD**   *Virgin VGD 3502* ................   **54**   5 wks
5 May 79    **RAINBOW DOME MUSIC**   *Virgin VR 1* .............   **52**   5 wks
27 Oct 79   **OPEN**   *Virgin V 2135* ...........................   **71**   1 wk
5 Mar 83    **FOR TO NEXT**   *Virgin V 2244* .....................   **48**   2 wks

## HIPSWAY  *UK, male vocal/instrumental group*                   *23 wks*

19 Apr 86   **HIPSWAY**   *Mercury MERH 85* .........................   **42**   23 wks

## Roger HODGSON  *UK, male vocalist*                             *4 wks*

20 Oct 84   **IN THE EYE OF THE STORM**
            *A & M AMA 5004* ..............................   **70**   4 wks

## Gerard HOFFNUNG  *UK, male vocal/instrumental group*   *19 wks*

3 Sep 60 ● **AT THE OXFORD UNION**   *Decca LF 1330* ...........   **4**   19 wks

**Christopher HOGWOOD** – *See ACADEMY OF ANCIENT MUSIC conducted by Christopher HOGWOOD*

## Billie HOLIDAY  *US, female vocalist*                          *10 wks*

16 Nov 85   **THE LEGEND OF BILLIE HOLIDAY**   *MCA BHTV 1* ...   **60**   10 wks

## HOLLIES *UK, male vocal/instrumental group* 143 wks

| | | | |
|---|---|---:|---|
| 15 Feb 64 ● **STAY WITH THE HOLLIES** *Parlophone PMC 1220* ...... | 2 | 25 wks |
| 2 Oct 65 ● **HOLLIES** *Parlophone PMC 1261* ...................... | 8 | 14 wks |
| 16 Jul 66 **WOULD YOU BELIEVE** *Parlophone PMC 7008* ......... | 16 | 8 wks |
| 17 Dec 66 **FOR CERTAIN BECAUSE** *Parlophone PCS 17011* ....... | 23 | 7 wks |
| 17 Jun 67 **EVOLUTION** *Parlophone PCS 7022* .................. | 13 | 10 wks |
| 17 Aug 68 ★ **GREATEST HITS** *Parlophone PCS 7057* ............... | 1 | 27 wks |
| 17 May 69 ● **HOLLIES SING DYLAN** *Parlophone PCS 7078* .......... | 3 | 7 wks |
| 28 Nov 70 **CONFESSIONS OF THE MIND** *Parlophone PCS 7117* .... | 30 | 5 wks |
| 16 Mar 74 **HOLLIES** *Polydor 2383 262* ......................... | 38 | 3 wks |
| 19 Mar 77 ● **HOLLIES LIVE HITS** *Polydor 2383 428* ............... | 4 | 12 wks |
| 22 Jul 78 ● **20 GOLDEN GREATS** *EMI EMTV 11* ............... | 2 | 20 wks |
| 1 Oct 88 **ALL THE HITS AND MORE** *EMI EM 1301* .......... | 51 | 5 wks |

*The two albums titled Hollies are different.*

## Buddy HOLLY and the CRICKETS
*US, male vocalist, male vocal/instrumental group* 319 wks

| | | | |
|---|---|---:|---|
| 2 May 59 ● **BUDDY HOLLY STORY** *Coral LVA 9105* ............. | 2 | 156 wks |
| 15 Oct 60 ● **BUDDY HOLLY STORY VOL. 2** *Coral LVA 9127* ...... | 7 | 14 wks |
| 21 Oct 61 ● **THAT'LL BE THE DAY** *Ace Of Hearts AH 3* ............ | 5 | 14 wks |
| 6 Apr 63 ● **REMINISCING** *Coral LVA 9212* ................... | 2 | 31 wks |
| 13 Jun 64 ● **BUDDY HOLLY SHOWCASE** *Coral LVA 9222* ........ | 3 | 16 wks |
| 26 Jun 65 **HOLLY IN THE HILLS** *Coral LVA 9227* ............. | 13 | 6 wks |
| 15 Jul 67 ● **BUDDY HOLLY'S GREATEST HITS** | | |
| *Ace Of Hearts AH 148* ............................. | 9 | 40 wks |
| 12 Apr 69 **GIANT** *MCA MUPS 371* ........................ | 13 | 1 wk |
| 21 Aug 71 **BUDDY HOLLY'S GREATEST HITS (re-issue)** | | |
| *Coral CP 8* ..................................... | 32 | 6 wks |
| 12 Jul 75 **BUDDY HOLLY'S GREATEST HITS (2nd re-issue)** | | |
| *Coral CDLM 8007* ............................... | 42 | 3 wks |
| 11 Mar 78 ★ **20 GOLDEN GREATS** *MCA EMTV 8* ............... | 1 | 20 wks |
| 8 Sep 84 **GREATEST HITS (3rd re-issue)** *MCA MCL 1618* ....... | 100 | 1 wk |
| 18 Feb 89 ● **TRUE LOVE WAYS** *Telstar STAR 2339* .............. | 8 | 11 wks |

*Most albums feature the Crickets on at least some tracks. See also The Crickets.*

## John HOLT *Jamaica, male vocalist* 2 wks

| | | | |
|---|---|---:|---|
| 1 Feb 75 **A THOUSAND VOLTS OF HOLT** *Trojan TRLS 75* ...... | 42 | 2 wks |

## HOME *UK, male vocal/instrumental group* 1 wk

| | | | |
|---|---|---:|---|
| 11 Nov 72 **DREAMER** *CBS 67522* ........................... | 41 | 1 wk |

## HONEYDRIPPERS
*UK/US, male vocal/instrumental group* 10 wks

| | | | |
|---|---|---:|---|
| 1 Dec 84 **THE HONEYDRIPPERS VOLUME 1** *Es Paranza 790220* . | 56 | 10 wks |

## John Lee HOOKER *US, male vocalist* 3 wks

| | | | |
|---|---|---:|---|
| 4 Feb 67 **HOUSE OF THE BLUES** *Marble Arch MAL 663* ........ | 34 | 2 wks |
| 11 Nov 89 **THE HEALER** *Silvertone ORELP 508* ................ | 75 | 1 wk |

## Mary HOPKIN *UK, female vocalist* 9 wks

| | | | |
|---|---|---:|---|
| 1 Mar 69 ● **POSTCARD** *Apple SAPCOR 5* ..................... | 3 | 9 wks |

## Bruce HORNSBY and the RANGE
*US, male vocal/instrumental group*                                         *44 wks*

| | | | |
|---|---|---|---|
| 13 Sep 86 | **THE WAY IT IS** *RCA PL 89901* | 16 | 26 wks |
| 14 May 88 | **SCENES FROM THE SOUTHSIDE** *RCA PL 86686* | 18 | 18 wks |

## HORSLIPS *Ireland, male vocal/instrumental group*                       *3 wks*

| | | | |
|---|---|---|---|
| 30 Apr 77 | **THE BOOK OF INVASIONS – A CELTIC SYMPHONY** *DJM DJF 20498* | 39 | 3 wks |

## HOT CHOCOLATE
*UK, male vocal/instrumental group*                                         *111 wks*

| | | | |
|---|---|---|---|
| 15 Nov 75 | **HOT CHOCOLATE** *RAK SRAK 516* | 34 | 7 wks |
| 7 Aug 76 | **MAN TO MAN** *RAK SRAK 522* | 32 | 7 wks |
| 20 Nov 76 | ● **GREATEST HITS** *RAK SRAK 524* | 6 | 35 wks |
| 8 Apr 78 | **EVERY 1'S A WINNER** *RAK SRAK 531* | 30 | 8 wks |
| 15 Dec 79 | ● **20 HOTTEST HITS** *RAK EMTV 22* | 3 | 19 wks |
| 25 Sep 82 | **MYSTERY** *RAK SRAK 549* | 24 | 7 wks |
| 21 Feb 87 | ★ **THE VERY BEST OF HOT CHOCOLATE** *RAK EMTV 42* | 1 | 28 wks |

**HOT RODS** – *See EDDIE and the HOT RODS*

## HOTHOUSE FLOWERS
*Ireland, male vocal/instrumental group*                                    *19 wks*

| | | | |
|---|---|---|---|
| 18 Jun 88 | ● **PEOPLE** *London LONLP 58* | 2 | 19 wks |

## HOUSEMARTINS *UK, male vocal/instrumental group*                         *70 wks*

| | | | |
|---|---|---|---|
| 5 Jul 86 | ● **LONDON 0 HULL 4** *Go! Discs AGOLP 7* | 3 | 41 wks |
| 27 Dec 86 | **HOUSEMARTINS' CHRISTMAS SINGLES BOX** *Go! Discs GOD 816* | 84 | 1 wk |
| 3 Oct 87 | ● **THE PEOPLE WHO GRINNED THEMSELVES TO DEATH** *Go! Discs AGOLP 9* | 9 | 18 wks |
| 21 May 88 | ● **NOW THAT'S WHAT I CALL QUITE GOOD!** *Go! Discs AGOLP 11* | 8 | 10 wks |

## Whitney HOUSTON *US, female vocalist*                                     *220 wks*

| | | | |
|---|---|---|---|
| 14 Dec 85 | ● **WHITNEY HOUSTON** *Arista 206978* | 2 | 119 wks |
| 13 Jun 87 | ★ **WHITNEY** *Arista 208141* | 1 | 101 wks |

## Steve HOWE *UK, male vocalist/instrumentalist – guitar*                   *6 wks*

| | | | |
|---|---|---|---|
| 15 Nov 75 | **BEGINNINGS** *Atlantic K 50151* | 22 | 4 wks |
| 24 Nov 79 | **STEVE HOWE ALBUM** *Atlantic K 50621* | 68 | 2 wks |

*See also Anderson Bruford Wakeman Howe.*

## HUDDERSFIELD CHORAL SOCIETY
*UK, choir*                                                                 *14 wks*

| | | | |
|---|---|---|---|
| 15 Mar 86 | ● **THE HYMNS ALBUM** *HMV EMTV 40* | 8 | 10 wks |
| 13 Dec 86 | **THE CAROLS ALBUM** *EMI EMTV 43* | 29 | 4 wks |

## HUE AND CRY *UK, male vocal/instrumental duo*                             *54 wks*

| | | | |
|---|---|---|---|
| 7 Nov 87 | **SEDUCED AND ABANDONED** *Circa CIRCA 2* | 22 | 11 wks |
| 10 Dec 88 | ● **REMOTE** *Circa CIRCA 6* | 10† | 43 wks |

*Remote re-entered the chart on 16 Dec 89 when it was made available with a free album* The Bitter Suite.

## Alan HULL    UK, male vocalist                                      3 wks

| | | | | | |
|---|---|---|---|---|---|
| 28 Jul | 73 | **PIPEDREAM**  *Charisma CAS 1069* .................. | **29** | 3 wks |

## HUMAN LEAGUE
*UK, male/female vocal/instrumental group*                             179 wks

| | | | | |
|---|---|---|---|---|
| 31 May 80 | **TRAVELOGUE**  *Virgin V 2160* ...................... | **16** | 42 wks |
| 22 Aug 81 | **REPRODUCTION**  *Virgin V 2133* ................... | **49** | 23 wks |
| 24 Oct 81 | ★ **DARE**  *Virgin V 2192* ............................. | **1** | 71 wks |
| 19 May 84 | ● **HYSTERIA**  *Virgin V 2315* ........................ | **3** | 18 wks |
| 20 Sept 86 | ● **CRASH**  *Virgin V 2391* ........................... | **7** | 6 wks |
| 12 Nov 88 | ● **GREATEST HITS**  *Virgin HLTV 1* ................... | **3** | 19 wks |

## HUMBLE PIE    UK, male vocal/instrumental group                     10 wks

| | | | | |
|---|---|---|---|---|
| 6 Sep | 69 | **AS SAFE AS YESTERDAY IS**  *Immediate IMSP 025* ...... | **32** | 1 wk |
| 22 Jan | 72 | **ROCKING AT THE FILLMORE**  *A & M AMLH 63506* ... | **32** | 2 wks |
| 15 Apr | 72 | **SMOKIN'**  *A & M AMLS 64342* ...................... | **28** | 5 wks |
| 7 Apr | 73 | **EAT IT**  *A & M AMLS 6004* ........................ | **34** | 2 wks |

## Engelbert HUMPERDINCK    UK, male vocalist                          233 wks

| | | | | |
|---|---|---|---|---|
| 20 May 67 | ● **RELEASE ME**  *Decca SKL 4868* ...................... | **6** | 58 wks |
| 25 Nov 67 | ● **THE LAST WALTZ**  *Decca SKL 4901* ................. | **3** | 33 wks |
| 3 Aug 68 | ● **A MAN WITHOUT LOVE**  *Decca SKL 4939* ............ | **3** | 45 wks |
| 1 Mar 69 | ● **ENGELBERT**  *Decca SKL 4985* ...................... | **3** | 8 wks |
| 6 Dec 69 | ● **ENGELBERT HUMPERDINCK**  *Decca SKL 5030* ....... | **5** | 23 wks |
| 11 Jul 70 | **WE MADE IT HAPPEN**  *Decca SKL 5054* .............. | **17** | 11 wks |
| 18 Sep 71 | **ANOTHER TIME, ANOTHER PLACE**  *Decca SKL 5097* . | **48** | 1 wk |
| 26 Feb 72 | **LIVE AT THE RIVIERA LAS VEGAS**  *Decca TXS 105* ... | **45** | 1 wk |
| 21 Dec 74 | ★ **ENGELBERT HUMPERDINCK – HIS GREATEST HITS** | | |
| | *Decca SKL 5198* ................................ | **1** | 34 wks |
| 4 May 85 | **GETTING SENTIMENTAL**  *Telstar STAR 2254* ......... | **35** | 10 wks |
| 4 Apr 87 | **THE ENGELBERT HUMPERDINCK COLLECTION** | | |
| | *Telstar STAR 2294* ............................... | **35** | 9 wks |

## Ian HUNTER    UK, male vocalist                                     26 wks

| | | | | |
|---|---|---|---|---|
| 12 Apr 75 | **IAN HUNTER**  *CBS 80710* ......................... | **21** | 15 wks |
| 29 May 76 | **ALL AMERICAN ALIEN BOY**  *CBS 81310* ............ | **29** | 4 wks |
| 5 May 79 | **YOU'RE NEVER ALONE WITH A SCHIZOPHRENIC** | | |
| | *Chrysalis CHR 1214* ............................ | **49** | 3 wks |
| 26 Apr 80 | **WELCOME TO THE CLUB**  *Chrysalis CJT 6* ........... | **61** | 2 wks |
| 29 Aug 81 | **SHORT BACK AND SIDES**  *Chrysalis CHR 1326* ........ | **79** | 2 wks |

## HURRAH!    UK, male vocal/instrumental group                        1 wk

| | | | |
|---|---|---|---|
| 28 Feb 87 | **TELL GOD I'M HERE**  *Kitchenware 208 201* ............. | **71** | 1 wk |

HURRICANES – See JOHNNY and the HURRICANES

## HÜSKER DÜ    US, male vocal/instrumental group                      1 wk

| | | | |
|---|---|---|---|
| 14 Feb 87 | **WAREHOUSE: SONGS AND STORIES** | | |
| | *Warner Bros. 925 544–1* ........................... | **72** | 1 wk |

## Phyllis HYMAN    US, female vocalist                                1 wk

| | | | |
|---|---|---|---|
| 20 Sep 86 | **LIVING ALL ALONE** | | |
| | *Philadelphia International PHIL 4001* .................... | **97** | 1 wk |

**HOUSEMARTINS** 4 all out.

Torvill and Dean got the medal, **RICHARD HARTLEY AND THE MICHAEL REED ORCHESTRA** got the hit.

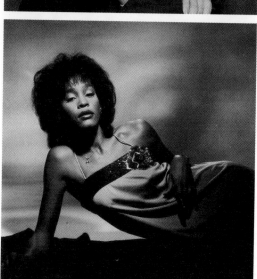

**WHITNEY HOUSTON** has sold more copies of her first two albums than any other artist.

'Kick' by **INXS** had a short chart run before re-entering for the group's British breakout.

# *i*

## ICEHOUSE
*Australia/New Zealand male vocal/instrumental group*       *6 wks*

| | | | | |
|---|---|---|---|---|
| 5 Mar 83 | **LOVE IN MOTION** *Chrysalis CHR 1390* .............. | **64** | 6 wks |
| 2 Apr 88 | **MAN OF COLOURS** *Chrysalis CHR 1592* ............. | **93** | 1 wk |

## ICE-T *US, male rapper*       *2 wks*

| | | | | |
|---|---|---|---|---|
| 21 Oct 89 | **THE ICEBERG/FREEDOM OF SPEECH** | | |
| | *Warner Bros. WX 316* ........................... | **42** | 2 wks |

## ICICLE WORKS *UK, male vocal/instrumental group*       *18 wks*

| | | | | |
|---|---|---|---|---|
| 31 Mar 84 | **THE ICICLE WORKS** *Beggars Banquet BEGA 50* ......... | **24** | 6 wks |
| 28 Sep 85 | **THE SMALL PRICE OF A BICYCLE** | | |
| | *Beggars Banquet BEGA 61* .......................... | **55** | 3 wks |
| 1 Mar 86 | **SEVEN SINGLES DEEP** *Beggars Banquet BEGA 71* ....... | **52** | 2 wks |
| 21 Mar 87 | **IF YOU WANT TO DEFEAT YOUR ENEMY SING HIS SONG** | | |
| | *Beggars Banquet BEGA 78* .......................... | **28** | 4 wks |
| 14 May 88 | **BLIND** *Beggars Banquet IWA 2* ...................... | **40** | 3 wks |

## Billy IDOL *UK, male vocalist*       *90 wks*

| | | | | |
|---|---|---|---|---|
| 8 Jun 85 | ● **VITAL IDOL** *Chrysalis CUX 1502* ..................... | **7** | 34 wks |
| 28 Sep 85 | **REBEL YELL** *Chrysalis CHR 1450* ................... | **36** | 11 wks |
| 1 Nov 86 | ● **WHIPLASH SMILE** *Chrysalis CDL 1514* .............. | **8** | 20 wks |
| 2 Jul 88 | ● **IDOL SONGS: 11 OF THE BEST** *Chrysalis BILTVD 1* .... | **2** | 25 wks |

**147**

*i*

## Frank IFIELD *UK, male vocalist*       *83 wks*

| | | | | |
|---|---|---|---|---|
| 16 Feb 63 | ● **I'LL REMEMBER YOU** *Columbia 33SX 1467* ........... | **3** | 36 wks |
| 21 Sep 63 | ● **BORN FREE** *Columbia 33SX 1462* ................... | **3** | 32 wks |
| 28 Mar 64 | ● **BLUE SKIES** *Columbia 55SX 1588* .................. | **10** | 12 wks |
| 19 Dec 64 | ● **GREATEST HITS** *Columbia 33SX 1633* ............... | **9** | 3 wks |

## Julio IGLESIAS *Spain, male vocalist*       *96 wks*

| | | | | |
|---|---|---|---|---|
| 7 Nov 81 | **DE NINA A MUJER** *CBS 85063* ..................... | **43** | 5 wks |
| 28 Nov 81 | ● **BEGIN THE BEGUINE** *CBS 85462* ................... | **5** | 28 wks |
| 16 Oct 82 | **AMOR** *CBS 25103* .............................. | **14** | 14 wks |
| 2 Jul 83 | ● **JULIO** *CBS 10038* .............................. | **5** | 17 wks |
| 1 Sep 84 | **1100 BEL AIR PLACE** *CBS 86308* ................... | **14** | 14 wks |
| 19 Oct 85 | **LIBRA** *CBS 26623* ............................. | **61** | 4 wks |
| 3 Sep 88 | **NON STOP** *CBS 460990 1* ........................ | **33** | 14 wks |

## I-LEVEL *UK, male vocal/instrumental group*       *4 wks*

| | | | | |
|---|---|---|---|---|
| 9 Jul 83 | **I-LEVEL** *Virgin V 2270* ........................... | **50** | 4 wks |

## IMAGINATION *UK, male vocal group*       *122 wks*

| | | | | |
|---|---|---|---|---|
| 24 Oct 81 | **BODY TALK** *R & B RBLP 1001* ....................... | **20** | 53 wks |
| 11 Sep 82 | ● **IN THE HEAT OF THE NIGHT** *R & B RBLP 1002* ...... | **7** | 29 wks |
| 14 May 83 | ● **NIGHT DUBBING** *R & B RBDUB 1* ................. | **9** | 20 wks |
| 12 Nov 83 | **SCANDALOUS** *R & B RBLP 1004* ................... | **25** | 8 wks |
| 12 Aug 89 | ● **IMAGINATION** *Stylus SMR 985* ................... | **7** | 12 wks |

## IMMACULATE FOOLS   UK, male vocal/instrumental group   2 wks

| 11 May 85 | HEARTS OF FORTUNE   A&M AMA 5030 ........... | 65 | 2 wks |

## INCANTATION   UK, male instrumental group   52 wks

| 11 Dec 82 | ● CACHARPAYA (PANPIPES OF THE ANDES) Beggars Banquet BEGA 39 ........................... | 9 | 26 wks |
| 17 Dec 83 | DANCE OF THE FLAMES   Beggars Banquet BEGA 49 ..... | 61 | 7 wks |
| 28 Dec 85 | BEST OF INCANTATION – MUSIC FROM THE ANDES West Five CODA 19 ............................. | 28 | 19 wks |

## INCOGNITO   France, male instrumental group   8 wks

| 18 Apr 81 | JAZZ FUNK   Ensign ENVY 504 ..................... | 28 | 8 wks |

## INCREDIBLE STRING BAND
UK, male/female vocal/instrumental group   36 wks

| 21 Oct 67 | 5,000 SPIRITS OR THE LAYERS OF THE ONION Elektra EUKS 257 ............................. | 26 | 4 wks |
| 6 Apr 68 | ● HANGMAN'S BEAUTIFUL DAUGHTER Elektra EVKS7 258 .......................... | 5 | 21 wks |
| 20 Jul 68 | INCREDIBLE STRING BAND   Elektra EKL 254 ........ | 34 | 3 wks |
| 24 Jan 70 | CHANGING HORSES   Elektra EKS 74057 ............. | 30 | 1 wk |
| 9 May 70 | I LOOKED UP   Elektra 2469–002 ................... | 30 | 4 wks |
| 31 Oct 70 | U   Elektra 2665–001 ............................. | 34 | 2 wks |
| 30 Oct 71 | LIQUID ACROBAT AS REGARDS THE AIR Island ILPS 9172 .............................. | 46 | 1 wk |

## INFA RIOT   UK, male vocal/instrumental group   4 wks

| 7 Aug 82 | STILL OUT OF ORDER   Secret SEC 7 ............... | 42 | 4 wks |

## James INGRAM   US, male vocalist   19 wks

| 31 Mar 84 | IT'S YOUR NIGHT   Qwest 9239701 .................. | 25 | 17 wks |
| 30 Aug 86 | NEVER FELT SO GOOD   Qwest WX 44 .............. | 72 | 2 wks |

## INNER CITY   US, male/female vocal/instrumental duo   25 wks

| 20 May 89 | ● PARADISE   10 DIX 81 ........................... | 3† | 25 wks |

## INSPIRATIONAL CHOIR   US, male/female choir   4 wks

| 18 Jan 86 | SWEET INSPIRATION   Portrait PRT 10048 ........... | 59 | 4 wks |

## INTI ILLIMANI-GUAMARY
Chile, male vocal/instrumental group – panpipes   7 wks

| 17 Dec 83 | THE FLIGHT OF THE CONDOR – ORIGINAL TV SOUNDTRACK   BBC REB 440 ................... | 62 | 7 wks |

INVISIBLE GIRLS – See Pauline MURRAY and the INVISIBLE GIRLS

## INXS   Australia, male vocal/instrumental group   111 wks

| 8 Feb 86 | LISTEN LIKE THIEVES   Mercury MERH 82 ........... | 48 | 15 wks |
| 28 Nov 87 | ● KICK   Mercury MERH 114 ........................ | 9 | 96 wks |

## IQ  *UK, male vocal/instrumental group*      *1 wk*

| | | | | |
|---|---|---|---|---|
| 22 Jun | 85 | **THE WAKE**  *Sahara SAH 136* ........................ | 72 | 1 wk |

## IRON MAIDEN  *UK, male vocal/instrumental group*      *131 wks*

| | | | | |
|---|---|---|---|---|
| 26 Apr | 80 | ● **IRON MAIDEN**  *EMI EMC 3330* .................... | 4 | 15 wks |
| 28 Feb | 81 | **KILLERS**  *EMI EMC 3357* .......................... | 12 | 8 wks |
| 10 Apr | 82 | ★ **THE NUMBER OF THE BEAST**  *EMI EMC 3400* ....... | 1 | 31 wks |
| 28 May | 83 | ● **PIECE OF MIND**  *EMI EMA 800* ................... | 3 | 18 wks |
| 15 Sep | 84 | ● **POWERSLAVE**  *EMI POWER 1* .................... | 2 | 13 wks |
| 15 Jun | 85 | **IRON MAIDEN (re-issue)**  *Fame FA 41–3121–1* ......... | 71 | 2 wks |
| 26 Oct | 85 | ● **LIVE AFTER DEATH**  *EMI RIP 1* ................... | 2 | 14 wks |
| 11 Oct | 86 | ● **SOMEWHERE IN TIME**  *EMI EMC 3512* ............. | 3 | 11 wks |
| 20 Jun | 87 | **THE NUMBER OF THE BEAST (re-issue)**  *Fame FA 3178* | 98 | 1 wk |
| 23 Apr | 88 | ★ **SEVENTH SON OF A SEVENTH SON**  *EMI EMD 1006* . | 1 | 18 wks |

## Gregory ISAACS  *Jamaica, male vocalist*      *6 wks*

| | | | | |
|---|---|---|---|---|
| 12 Sep | 81 | **MORE GREGORY**  *Charisma PREX 9* ................. | 93 | 1 wk |
| 4 Sep | 82 | **NIGHT NURSE**  *Island ILPS 9721* .................... | 32 | 5 wks |

## ISLEY BROTHERS  *US, male vocal/instrumental group*      *24 wks*

| | | | | |
|---|---|---|---|---|
| 14 Dec | 68 | **THIS OLD HEART OF MINE**  *Tamla Motown STML 11034* . | 23 | 6 wks |
| 14 Aug | 76 | **HARVEST FOR THE WORLD**  *Epic EPC 81268* ........ | 50 | 5 wks |
| 14 May | 77 | **GO FOR YOUR GUNS**  *Epic EPC 86027* .............. | 46 | 2 wks |
| 24 Jun | 78 | **SHOWDOWN**  *Epic EPC 86039* ..................... | 50 | 1 wk |
| 5 Mar | 88 | **GREATEST HITS**  *Telstar STAR 2306* ................. | 41 | 10 wks |

## IT BITES  *UK, male vocal/instrumental group*      *11 wks*

| | | | | |
|---|---|---|---|---|
| 6 Sep | 86 | **THE BIG LAD IN THE WINDMILL**  *Virgin V 2378* ...... | 35 | 5 wks |
| 2 Apr | 88 | **ONCE AROUND THE WORLD**  *Virgin V 2456* ........ | 43 | 3 wks |
| 24 Jun | 89 | **EAT ME IN ST. LOUIS**  *Virgin V 2591* ................ | 40 | 3 wks |

## IT'S A BEAUTIFUL DAY
*US, male/female vocal/instrumental group*      *3 wks*

| | | | | |
|---|---|---|---|---|
| 23 May | 70 | **IT'S A BEAUTIFUL DAY**  *CBS 63722* ................ | 58 | 1 wk |
| 18 Jul | 70 | **MARRYING MAIDEN**  *CBS 66236* ................... | 45 | 2 wks |

## IT'S IMMATERIAL  *UK, male vocal/instrumental group*      *3 wks*

| | | | | |
|---|---|---|---|---|
| 27 Sep | 86 | **LIFE'S HARD AND THEN YOU DIE**  *Siren SIRENLP 4* . | 62 | 3 wks |

# *j*

## Freddie JACKSON  *US, male vocalist*      *46 wks*

| | | | | |
|---|---|---|---|---|
| 18 May | 85 | **ROCK ME TONIGHT**  *Capitol EJ 2440316–1* ............ | 27 | 22 wks |
| 8 Nov | 86 | **JUST LIKE THE FIRST TIME**  *Capitol EST 2023* ....... | 30 | 15 wks |
| 30 Jul | 88 | **DON'T LET LOVE SLIP AWAY**  *Capitol EST 2067* ...... | 24 | 9 wks |

## Janet JACKSON  US, female vocalist  *98 wks*

| | | | | | |
|---|---|---|---|---|---|
| 5 Apr | 86 | ● CONTROL  *A & M AMA 5016* ...................... | 8 | 72 wks |
| 14 Nov | 87 | CONTROL – THE REMIXES  *Breakout MIXLP 1* ........ | 20 | 14 wks |
| 30 Sep | 89 | ● RHYTHM NATION 1814  *A & M AMA 3920* ........... | 4 | 12 wks |

## Jermaine JACKSON  US, male vocalist  *12 wks*

| | | | | |
|---|---|---|---|---|
| 31 May | 80 | LET'S GET SERIOUS  *Motown STML 12127* ........... | 22 | 6 wks |
| 12 May | 84 | DYNAMITE  *Arista 206 317* ........................ | 57 | 6 wks |

*See also Jacksons.*

## Joe JACKSON  UK, male vocalist  *95 wks*

| | | | | |
|---|---|---|---|---|
| 17 Mar | 79 | LOOK SHARP  *A & M AMLH 64743* ................. | 40 | 11 wks |
| 13 Oct | 79 | I'M THE MAN  *A & M AMLH 64794* ................. | 12 | 16 wks |
| 18 Oct | 80 | BEAT CRAZY  *A & M AMLH 64837* ................. | 42 | 3 wks |
| 4 Jul | 81 | JUMPIN' JIVE  *A & M AMLH 68530* ................. | 14 | 14 wks |
| 3 Jul | 82 | ● NIGHT AND DAY  *A & M AMLH 64906* ........... | 3 | 27 wks |
| 7 Apr | 84 | BODY AND SOUL  *A & M AMLX 65000* ........... | 14 | 14 wks |
| 5 Apr | 86 | BIG WORLD  *A & M JWA 3* ...................... | 41 | 5 wks |
| 7 May | 88 | LIVE 1980–1986  *A & M AMA 6706* ............... | 66 | 2 wks |
| 29 Apr | 89 | BLAZE OF GLORY  *A & M AMA 5249* ............... | 36 | 3 wks |

*Jumpin' Jive credited to Joe Jackson's Jumpin' Jive.*

## Michael JACKSON  US, male vocalist  *533 wks*

| | | | | |
|---|---|---|---|---|
| 3 Jun | 72 | GOT TO BE THERE  *Tamla Motown STML 11205* ........ | 37 | 5 wks |
| 13 Jan | 73 | BEN  *Tamla Motown STML 11220* ................. | 17 | 7 wks |
| 29 Sep | 79 | ● OFF THE WALL  *Epic EPC 83468* ................. | 5 | 173 wks |
| 4 Jul | 81 | BEST OF MICHAEL JACKSON  *Motown STMR 9009* .... | 11 | 18 wks |
| 18 Jul | 81 | ONE DAY IN YOUR LIFE  *Motown STML 12158* ........ | 29 | 8 wks |
| 11 Dec | 82 | ★ THRILLER  *Epic EPC 85930* ................. | 1 | 168 wks |
| 12 Feb | 83 | E.T. THE EXTRA TERRESTRIAL  *MCA 7000* ......... | 82 | 2 wks |
| 3 Dec | 83 | MICHAEL JACKSON 9 SINGLE PACK  *Epic MJ1* ........ | 66 | 3 wks |
| 9 Jun | 84 | ● FAREWELL MY SUMMER LOVE  *Motown ZL 72227* ... | 9 | 14 wks |
| 12 Sep | 87 | ★ BAD  *Epic EPC 450 291–1* ................. | 1 | 109 wks |
| 26 Dec | 87 | THE MICHAEL JACKSON MIX  *Stylus SMR 745* ........ | 27 | 25 wks |
| 30 Jul | 88 | SOUVENIR SINGLES PACK  *Epic MJ 5* .............. | 91 | 1 wk |

*See also the Jacksons; Diana Ross/Michael Jackson/Gladys Knight/Stevie Wonder.*

## Millie JACKSON  US, female vocalist  *7 wks*

| | | | | |
|---|---|---|---|---|
| 18 Feb | 84 | E.S.P.  *Sire 250382* ................................ | 59 | 5 wks |
| 6 Apr | 85 | LIVE AND UNCENSORED  *Important TADLP 001* ...... | 81 | 2 wks |

## JACKSONS  US, male vocal group  *140 wks*

| | | | | |
|---|---|---|---|---|
| 21 Mar | 70 | DIANA ROSS PRESENTS THE JACKSON FIVE  *Tamla Motown STML 11142* ................... | 16 | 4 wks |
| 15 Aug | 70 | ABC  *Tamla Motown STML 11153* ................. | 22 | 6 wks |
| 7 Oct | 72 | GREATEST HITS  *Tamla Motown STML 11212* .......... | 26 | 14 wks |
| 18 Nov | 72 | LOOKIN' THROUGH THE WINDOWS  *Tamla Motown STML 11214* .................... | 16 | 8 wks |
| 16 Jul | 77 | THE JACKSONS  *Epic EPC 86009* ................. | 54 | 1 wk |
| 3 Dec | 77 | GOIN' PLACES  *Epic EPC 86035* ................. | 45 | 1 wk |
| 5 May | 79 | DESTINY  *Epic EPC 83200* ................. | 33 | 7 wks |
| 11 Oct | 80 | TRIUMPH  *Epic EPC 86112* ................. | 13 | 16 wks |
| 12 Dec | 81 | THE JACKSONS  *Epic EPC 88562* ................. | 53 | 9 wks |
| 9 Jul | 83 | ★ 18 GREATEST HITS  *Telstar STAR 2232* ............... | 1 | 58 wks |

Choreographer and subsequent hitmaker Paula Abdul leads
**JANET JACKSON** (right) through a routine.

**MICK JAGGER**, shown here leading the Rolling Stones, found
his second solo project got a cool reception.

iller' by **MICHAEL JACKSON** is the world's all-time
ber one album, but 'Bad' outsold it in Britain.

| 21 Jul 84 ● **VICTORY** Epic EPC 86303 | 3 | 13 wks |
|---|---|---|
| 1 Jul 89 **2300 JACKSON ST** Epic 463352 1 | 39 | 3 wks |

*First four albums credited to Jackson Five. 18 Greatest Hits, credited to Michael Jackson plus the Jackson Five, contains hits by both acts. All other albums credited to the Jacksons. Jermaine Jackson appeared on the first four albums. See also Michael Jackson; Jermaine Jackson.*

## Mick JAGGER *UK, male vocalist*   *16 wks*

| 16 Mar 85 ● **SHE'S THE BOSS** CBS 86310 | 6 | 11 wks |
|---|---|---|
| 26 Sep 87 **PRIMITIVE COOL** CBS 460 123–1 | 26 | 5 wks |

## JAM *UK, male vocal/instrumental group*   *148 wks*

| 28 May 77 **IN THE CITY** Polydor 2383 447 | 20 | 18 wks |
|---|---|---|
| 26 Nov 77 **THIS IS THE MODERN WORLD** Polydor 2383 475 | 22 | 5 wks |
| 11 Nov 78 ● **ALL MOD CONS** Polydor POLD 5008 | 6 | 17 wks |
| 24 Nov 79 ● **SETTING SONS** Polydor POLD 5028 | 4 | 19 wks |
| 6 Dec 80 ● **SOUND AFFECTS** Polydor POLD 5035 | 2 | 19 wks |
| 20 Mar 82 ★ **THE GIFT** Polydor POLD 5055 | 1 | 24 wks |
| 18 Dec 82 ● **DIG THE NEW BREED** Polydor POLD 5075 | 2 | 15 wks |
| 27 Aug 83 **IN THE CITY (re-issue)** Polydor SPELP 27 | 100 | 1 wk |
| 22 Oct 83 ● **SNAP** Polydor SNAP 1 | 2 | 30 wks |

## JAMES *UK, male vocal/instrumental group*   *3 wks*

| 2 Aug 86 **STUTTER** blanco y negro JIMLP 1 | 68 | 2 wks |
|---|---|---|
| 8 Oct 88 **STRIP MINE** Sire JIMLP 2 | 90 | 1 wk |

## Rick JAMES *US, male vocalist*   *2 wks*

| 24 Jul 82 **THROWIN' DOWN** Motown STML 12167 | 93 | 2 wks |
|---|---|---|

## JAN and DEAN *US, male vocal duo*   *2 wks*

| 12 Jul 80 **THE JAN AND DEAN STORY** K-Tel NE 1084 | 67 | 2 wks |
|---|---|---|

## JAPAN *UK, male vocal/instrumental group*   *136 wks*

| 9 Feb 80 **QUIET LIFE** Ariola Hansa AHAL 8011 | 53 | 8 wks |
|---|---|---|
| 15 Nov 80 **GENTLEMEN TAKE POLAROIDS** Virgin V 2180 | 45 | 10 wks |
| 26 Sep 81 **ASSEMBLAGE** Hansa HANLP 1 | 26 | 46 wks |
| 28 Nov 81 **TIN DRUM** Virgin V 2209 | 12 | 50 wks |
| 18 Jun 83 ● **OIL ON CANVAS** Virgin VD 2513 | 5 | 14 wks |
| 8 Dec 84 **EXORCISING GHOSTS** Virgin VGD 3510 | 45 | 8 wks |

## Jeff JARRATT and Don REEDMAN
*UK, male producers*   *8 wks*

| 22 Nov 80 **MASTERWORKS** K-Tel ONE 1093 | 39 | 8 wks |
|---|---|---|

## Jean-Michel JARRE *France, male instrumentalist/producer*   *196 wks*

| 20 Aug 77 ● **OXYGENE** Polydor 2310 555 | 2 | 24 wks |
|---|---|---|
| 16 Dec 78 **EQUINOXE** Polydor POLD 5007 | 11 | 26 wks |
| 6 Jun 81 ● **MAGNETIC FIELDS** Polydor POLS 1033 | 6 | 17 wks |
| 15 May 82 ● **THE CONCERTS IN CHINA** Polydor PODV 3 | 6 | 17 wks |
| 12 Nov 83 **THE ESSENTIAL JEAN MICHEL JARRE** Polystar PROLP 3 | 14 | 29 wks |
| 24 Nov 84 **ZOOLOOK** Polydor POLH 15 | 47 | 14 wks |
| 12 Apr 86 ● **RENDEZ-VOUS** Polydor POLH 27 | 9 | 37 wks |

| | | | | | |
|---|---|---|---|---|---|
| 18 Jul | 87 | IN CONCERT LYONS/HOUSTON *Polydor POLH 36* ... | | 18 | 15 wks |
| 8 Oct | 88 | ● REVOLUTIONS *Polydor POLH 45* ................ | | 2 | 13 wks |
| 14 Oct | 89 | JARRE LIVE *Polydor 841258 1* .................... | | 16 | 4 wks |

## AI JARREAU  *US, male vocalist*      *37 wks*

| | | | | | |
|---|---|---|---|---|---|
| 5 Sep | 81 | BREAKING AWAY *Warner Bros. K 56917* ............ | | 60 | 8 wks |
| 30 Apr | 83 | JARREAU *WEA International U 0070* ............... | | 39 | 18 wks |
| 17 Nov | 84 | HIGH CRIME *WEA 250807* ...................... | | 81 | 1 wk |
| 13 Sep | 86 | L IS FOR LOVER *WEA International 253 080–1* ......... | | 45 | 10 wks |

## JEFFERSON AIRPLANE
*US/UK, female vocal/instrumental group*      *10 wks*

| | | | | | |
|---|---|---|---|---|---|
| 28 Jun | 69 | BLESS ITS POINTED LITTLE HEAD *RCA SF 8019* .... | | 38 | 1 wk |
| 7 Mar | 70 | VOLUNTEERS *RCA SF 8076* .................... | | 34 | 7 wks |
| 2 Oct | 71 | BARK *Grunt FTR 1001* ......................... | | 42 | 1 wk |
| 2 Sep | 72 | LONG JOHN SILVER *Grunt FTR 1007* ............. | | 30 | 1 wk |

*See also Jefferson Starship; Starship – later incarnations of Jefferson Airplane.*

## JEFFERSON STARSHIP
*US, male vocal/instrumental group*      *13 wks*

| | | | | | |
|---|---|---|---|---|---|
| 31 Jul | 76 | SPITFIRE *Grunt RFL 1557* ........................ | | 30 | 2 wks |
| 9 Feb | 80 | FREEDOM AT POINT ZERO *Grunt FL 13452* ........ | | 22 | 11 wks |

*See also Jefferson Airplane; Starship.*

## JELLYBEAN  *US, male instrumentalist/producer*      *35 wks*

| | | | | | |
|---|---|---|---|---|---|
| 31 Oct | 87 | JUST VISITING THIS PLANET *Chrysalis CHR 1569* ..... | | 15 | 28 wks |
| 3 Sep | 88 | ROCKS THE HOUSE! *Chrysalis CJB 1* ............... | | 16 | 7 wks |

## JESUS AND MARY CHAIN
*UK, male vocal/instrumental group*      *28 wks*

| | | | | | |
|---|---|---|---|---|---|
| 30 Nov | 85 | PSYCHOCANDY *blanco y negro BYN 7* ............... | | 31 | 10 wks |
| 12 Sep | 87 | ● DARKLANDS *blanco y negro BYN 11* ............... | | 5 | 7 wks |
| 30 Apr | 88 | ● BARBED WIRE KISSES *blanco y negro BYN 15* ......... | | 9 | 7 wks |
| 21 Oct | 89 | AUTOMATIC *blanco y negro BYN 20* ................ | | 11 | 4 wks |

## JESUS JONES  *UK, male vocal/instrumental group*      *3 wks*

| | | | | | |
|---|---|---|---|---|---|
| 14 Oct | 89 | LIQUIDIZER *Food FOODLP 3* ..................... | | 32 | 3 wks |

## JETHRO TULL  *UK, male vocal/instrumental group*      *226 wks*

| | | | | | |
|---|---|---|---|---|---|
| 2 Nov | 68 | ● THIS WAS *Island ILPS 9085* ...................... | | 10 | 22 wks |
| 9 Aug | 69 | ★ STAND UP *Island ILPS 9103* ...................... | | 1 | 29 wks |
| 9 May | 70 | ● BENEFIT *Island ILPS 9123* ...................... | | 3 | 13 wks |
| 3 Apr | 71 | ● AQUALUNG *Island ILPS 9145* ................... | | 4 | 21 wks |
| 18 Mar | 72 | ● THICK AS A BRICK *Chrysalis CHR 1003* ............. | | 5 | 14 wks |
| 15 Jul | 72 | ● LIVING IN THE PAST *Chrysalis CJT 1* ............... | | 8 | 11 wks |
| 28 Jul | 73 | A PASSION PLAY *Chrysalis CHR 1040* .............. | | 13 | 8 wks |
| 2 Nov | 74 | WAR CHILD *Chrysalis CHR 1067* ................ | | 14 | 4 wks |
| 27 Sep | 75 | MINSTREL IN THE GALLERY *Chrysalis CHR 1082* .... | | 20 | 6 wks |
| 31 Jan | 76 | M.U. THE BEST OF JETHRO TULL *Chrysalis CHR 1078* | | 44 | 5 wks |
| 15 May | 76 | TOO OLD TO ROCK 'N' ROLL TOO YOUNG TO DIE | | | |
| | | *Chrysalis CHR 1111* ......................... | | 25 | 10 wks |
| 19 Feb | 77 | SONGS FROM THE WOOD *Chrysalis CHR 1132* ....... | | 13 | 12 wks |
| 29 Apr | 78 | HEAVY HORSES *Chrysalis CHR 1175* .............. | | 20 | 10 wks |
| 14 Oct | 78 | LIVE BURSTING OUT *Chrysalis CJT 4* ............. | | 17 | 8 wks |

| | | | |
|---|---|---|---|
| 6 Oct 79 | **STORM WATCH** *Chrysalis CDL 1238* ............. | **27** | 4 wks |
| 6 Sep 80 | **A** *Chrysalis CDL 1301* ............................ | **25** | 5 wks |
| 17 Apr 82 | **BROADSWORD AND THE BEAST** *Chrysalis CDL 1380* . | **27** | 19 wks |
| 15 Sep 84 | **UNDER WRAPS** *Chrysalis CDL 1461* ............. | **18** | 5 wks |
| 2 Nov 85 | **ORIGINAL MASTERS** *Chrysalis JTTV 1* ............. | **63** | 3 wks |
| 19 Sep 87 | **CREST OF A KNAVE** *Chrysalis CDL 1590* ........ | **19** | 10 wks |
| 9 Jul 88 | **20 YEARS OF JETHRO TULL** *Chrysalis TBOX 1* ........ | **78** | 1 wk |
| 2 Sep 89 | **ROCK ISLAND** *Chrysalis CHR 1708* ............. | **18** | 6 wks |

## JETS  *UK, male vocal/instrumental group*  *6 wks*

| | | | |
|---|---|---|---|
| 10 Apr 82 | **100 PERCENT COTTON** *EMI EMC 3399* ............. | **30** | 6 wks |

## JETS  *US, male/female vocal/instrumental group*  *4 wks*

| | | | |
|---|---|---|---|
| 11 Apr 87 | **CRUSH ON YOU** *MCA MCF 3312* ................. | **57** | 4 wks |

## Joan JETT and the BLACKHEARTS
*US, female/male vocal/instrumental group*  *7 wks*

| | | | |
|---|---|---|---|
| 8 May 82 | **I LOVE ROCK 'N' ROLL** *Epic EPC 85686* ............. | **25** | 7 wks |

## JIVE BUNNY and the MASTERMIXERS
*UK, male production/mixing group*  *4 wks*

| | | | |
|---|---|---|---|
| 9 Dec 89 | ● **JIVE BUNNY – THE ALBUM** *Telstar STAR 2390* ........ | **2†** | 4 wks |

## 154

*j*

## JO BOXERS  *UK, male vocal/instrumental group*  *5 wks*

| | | | |
|---|---|---|---|
| 24 Sep 83 | **LIKE GANGBUSTERS** *RCA BOXXLP 1* ............. | **18** | 5 wks |

## Billy JOEL  *US, male vocalist*  *273 wks*

| | | | |
|---|---|---|---|
| 25 Mar 78 | **THE STRANGER** *CBS 82311* ..................... | **25** | 40 wks |
| 25 Nov 78 | ● **52ND STREET** *CBS 83181* ..................... | **10** | 43 wks |
| 22 Mar 80 | ● **GLASS HOUSES** *CBS 86108* ..................... | **9** | 24 wks |
| 10 Oct 81 | **SONGS IN THE ATTIC** *CBS 85273* ............. | **57** | 3 wks |
| 2 Oct 82 | **NYLON CURTAIN** *CBS 85959* ............. | **27** | 8 wks |
| 10 Sep 83 | ● **AN INNOCENT MAN** *CBS 25554* ............. | **2** | 94 wks |
| 4 Feb 84 | **COLD SPRING HARBOUR** *CBS 32400* ............. | **95** | 1 wk |
| 23 Jun 84 | **PIANO MAN** *CBS 32002* ..................... | **98** | 1 wk |
| 20 Jul 85 | ● **GREATEST HITS VOLUME I & VOLUME II** *CBS 88666* | **7** | 39 wks |
| 16 Aug 86 | **THE BRIDGE** *CBS 86323* ..................... | **38** | 10 wks |
| 28 Nov 87 | **KOHYEPT – LIVE IN LENINGRAD** *CBS 460 407–1* ... | **92** | 1 wk |
| 4 Nov 89 | ● **STORM FRONT** *CBS 465658 1* ................... | **5†** | 9 wks |

## Elton JOHN  *UK, male vocalist/instrumentalist – piano*  *617 wks*

| | | | |
|---|---|---|---|
| 23 May 70 | **ELTON JOHN** *DJM DJLPS 406* ................... | **11** | 14 wks |
| 16 Jan 71 | ● **TUMBLEWEED CONNECTION** *DJM DJLPS 410* ..... | **6** | 20 wks |
| 1 May 71 | **THE ELTON JOHN LIVE ALBUM 17-11-70** *DJM DJLPS 414* ....................... | **20** | 2 wks |
| 20 May 72 | **MADMAN ACROSS THE WATER** *DJM DJLPH 420* ... | **41** | 2 wks |
| 3 Jun 72 | ● **HONKY CHATEAU** *DJM DJLPH 423* ............. | **2** | 23 wks |
| 10 Feb 73 | ★ **DON'T SHOOT ME I'M ONLY THE PIANO PLAYER** *DJM DJLPH 427* ................. | **1** | 42 wks |
| 3 Nov 73 | ★ **GOODBYE YELLOW BRICK ROAD** *DJM DJLPO 1001* | **1** | 84 wks |
| 13 Jul 74 | ★ **CARIBOU** *DJM DJLPH 439* ................... | **1** | 18 wks |
| 23 Nov 74 | ★ **ELTON JOHN'S GREATEST HITS** *DJM DJLPH 442* ... | **1** | 84 wks |
| 7 Jun 75 | ● **CAPTAIN FANTASTIC AND THE BROWN DIRT COWBOY** *DJM DJLPX 1* ................. | **2** | 24 wks |
| 8 Nov 75 | ● **ROCK OF THE WESTIES** *DJM DJLPH 464* ......... | **5** | 12 wks |

| | | | |
|---|---|---|---|
| 15 May 76 ● | HERE AND THERE  *DJM DJLPH 473* .............. | 6 | 9 wks |
| 6 Nov 76 ● | BLUE MOVES  *Rocket ROSP 1* ...................... | 3 | 15 wks |
| 15 Oct 77 ● | GREATEST HITS VOL. 2  *DJM DJH 20520* .......... | 6 | 24 wks |
| 4 Nov 78 ● | A SINGLE MAN  *Rocket TRAIN 1* .................. | 8 | 26 wks |
| 20 Oct 79 | VICTIM OF LOVE  *Rocket HISPD 125* ............... | 41 | 3 wks |
| 8 Mar 80 | LADY SAMANTHA  *DJM 22085* ................... | 56 | 2 wks |
| 31 May 80 | 21 AT 33  *Rocket HISPD 126* .................... | 12 | 13 wks |
| 25 Oct 80 | THE VERY BEST OF ELTON JOHN  *K-Tel NE 1094* .... | 24 | 13 wks |
| 30 May 81 | THE FOX  *Rocket TRAIN 16* ..................... | 12 | 12 wks |
| 17 Apr 82 | JUMP UP  *Rocket HISPD 127* .................... | 13 | 12 wks |
| 6 Nov 82 | LOVE SONGS  *TV Records TVA 3* .................. | 39 | 13 wks |
| 11 Jun 83 ● | TOO LOW FOR ZERO  *Rocket HISPD 24* ........... | 7 | 73 wks |
| 30 Jun 84 ● | BREAKING HEARTS  *Rocket HISPD 25* ............ | 2 | 23 wks |
| 16 Nov 85 ● | ICE ON FIRE  *Rocket HISPD 26* .................. | 3 | 23 wks |
| 15 Nov 86 | LEATHER JACKETS  *Rocket EJLP 1* .............. | 24 | 9 wks |
| 12 Sep 87 | LIVE IN AUSTRALIA  *Rocket EJBXL 1* ............ | 43 | 7 wks |
| 16 Jul 88 | REG STRIKES BACK  *Rocket EJLP 3* ............. | 18 | 6 wks |
| 23 Sep 89 ● | SLEEPING WITH THE PAST  *Rocket 838839 1* ........ | 6 | 9 wks |

Live In Australia *credits Elton John and the Melbourne Symphony Orchestra. It reappeared in 1988 as EJLP 2; EJBXL 1 was the original 'de luxe' version.*

## JOHNNY and the HURRICANES

*US, male instrumental group*  5 wks

| | | | |
|---|---|---|---|
| 3 Dec 60 | STORMSVILLE  *London HAI 2269* ................... | 18 | 1 wk |
| 1 Apr 61 | BIG SOUND OF JOHNNY AND THE HURRICANES | | |
| | *London HAK 2322* ................................ | 14 | 4 wks |

## JOHNNY HATES JAZZ

*UK, male vocal/instrumental group*  39 wks

| | | | |
|---|---|---|---|
| 23 Jan 88 ★ | TURN BACK THE CLOCK  *Virgin V 2475* ............ | 1 | 39 wks |

## Holly JOHNSON  *UK, male vocalist*

17 wks

| | | | |
|---|---|---|---|
| 6 May 89 ★ | BLAST  *MCA MCG 6042* ......................... | 1 | 17 wks |

## Linton Kwesi JOHNSON  *Jamaica, male poet*

8 wks

| | | | |
|---|---|---|---|
| 30 Jun 79 | FORCE OF VICTORY  *Island ILPS 9566* .............. | 66 | 1 wk |
| 31 Oct 80 | BASS CULTURE  *Island ILPS 9605* ................... | 46 | 5 wks |
| 10 Mar 84 | MAKING HISTORY  *Island ILPS 9770* .............. | 73 | 2 wks |

## Paul JOHNSON  *UK, male vocalist*

3 wks

| | | | |
|---|---|---|---|
| 4 Jul 87 | PAUL JOHNSON  *CBS 450640 1* ..................... | 63 | 2 wks |
| 16 Sep 89 | PERSONAL  *CBS 463284 1* ...................... | 70 | 1 wk |

## Al JOLSON  *US, male vocalist*

11 wks

| | | | |
|---|---|---|---|
| 14 Mar 81 | 20 GOLDEN GREATS  *MCA MCTV 4* ............... | 18 | 7 wks |
| 17 Dec 83 | THE AL JOLSON COLLECTION  *Ronco RON LP 5* ..... | 67 | 4 wks |

## JON and VANGELIS

*UK, male vocalist and Greece, male instrumentalist – keyboards*  53 wks

| | | | |
|---|---|---|---|
| 26 Jan 80 ● | SHORT STORIES  *Polydor POLD 5030* ............... | 4 | 11 wks |
| 11 Jul 81 ● | THE FRIENDS OF MR. CAIRO  *Polydor POLD 5039* .... | 17 | 8 wks |
| 23 Jan 82 ● | THE FRIENDS OF MR. CAIRO (re-issue) | | |
| | *Polydor POLD 5053* .......................... | 6 | 15 wks |
| 2 Jul 83 | PRIVATE COLLECTION  *Polydor POLH 4* ........... | 22 | 10 wks |
| 11 Aug 84 | THE BEST OF JON AND VANGELIS  *Polydor POLH 6* .. | 42 | 9 wks |

*See also Jon Anderson; Vangelis.*

## Aled JONES  *UK, male chorister*

140 wks

| | | | | | | |
|---|---|---|---|---|---|---|
| 27 Apr | 85 | ● VOICES FROM THE HOLY LAND  *BBC REC 564* ..... | 6 | 43 wks |
| 29 Jun | 85 | ● ALL THROUGH THE NIGHT  *BBC REH 569* ......... | 2 | 43 wks |
| 23 Nov | 85 | ALED JONES WITH THE BBC WELSH CHORUS  *10/BBC AJ 1* ......... | 11 | 10 wks |
| 22 Feb | 86 | WHERE E'ER YOU WALK  *10 DIX 21* ............... | 36 | 6 wks |
| 12 Jul | 86 | PIE JESU  *10 AJ 2* | 25 | 16 wks |
| 29 Nov | 86 | AN ALBUM OF HYMNS  *Telstar STAR 2272* ............ | 18 | 11 wks |
| 14 Mar | 87 | ALED (MUSIC FROM THE TV SERIES)  *10 AJ 3* ...... | 52 | 6 wks |
| 5 Dec | 87 | THE BEST OF ALED JONES  *10 AJ 5* ............... | 59 | 5 wks |

*First three albums credit the BBC Welsh Chorus.*

## Glenn JONES  *US, male vocalist*

1 wk

| | | | | | |
|---|---|---|---|---|---|
| 31 Oct | 87 | GLENN JONES  *Jive HIP 51* ...................... | 62 | 1 wk |

## Grace JONES  *US, female vocalist*

80 wks

| | | | | | |
|---|---|---|---|---|---|
| 30 Aug | 80 | WARM LEATHERETTE  *Island ILPS 9592* ........... | 45 | 2 wks |
| 23 May | 81 | NIGHTCLUBBING  *Island ILPS 9624* ................ | 35 | 16 wks |
| 20 Nov | 82 | LIVING MY LIFE  *Island ILPS 9722* | 15 | 22 wks |
| 9 Nov | 85 | SLAVE TO THE RHYTHM  *ZTT GRACE 1* ......... | 12 | 8 wks |
| 14 Dec | 85 | ● ISLAND LIFE  *Island GJ 1* | 4 | 30 wks |
| 29 Nov | 86 | INSIDE STORY  *Manhattan MTL 1007* ................ | 61 | 2 wks |

## Howard JONES  *UK, male vocalist*

120 wks

| | | | | | |
|---|---|---|---|---|---|
| 17 Mar | 84 | ★ HUMAN'S LIB  *WEA WX 1* ...................... | 1 | 57 wks |
| 8 Dec | 84 | THE 12″ ALBUM  *WEA WX 14* ................... | 15 | 33 wks |
| 23 Mar | 85 | ● DREAM INTO ACTION  *WEA WX 15* ......... | 2 | 25 wks |
| 25 Oct | 86 | ● ONE TO ONE  *WEA WX 68* ..................... | 10 | 4 wks |
| 1 Apr | 89 | CROSS THAT LINE  *WEA WX 225* ................. | 64 | 1 wk |

## Jack JONES  *US, male vocalist*

70 wks

| | | | | | |
|---|---|---|---|---|---|
| 29 Apr | 72 | ● A SONG FOR YOU  *RCA Victor SF 8228* ............... | 9 | 6 wks |
| 3 Jun | 72 | ● BREAD WINNERS  *RCA Victor SF 8280* ............ | 7 | 36 wks |
| 7 Apr | 73 | ● TOGETHER  *RCA Victor SF 8342* ................... | 8 | 10 wks |
| 23 Feb | 74 | ● HARBOUR  *RCA Victor APLI 0408* ............. | 10 | 5 wks |
| 19 Feb | 77 | THE FULL LIFE  *RCA Victor PL 12067* ......... | 41 | 5 wks |
| 21 May | 77 | ALL TO YOURSELF  *RCA TVL 2* ............. | 10 | 8 wks |

## Quincy JONES

*US, male arranger/instrumentalist – keyboards*

29 wks

| | | | | | |
|---|---|---|---|---|---|
| 18 Apr | 81 | THE DUDE  *A & M AMLK 63721* ................... | 19 | 25 wks |
| 20 Mar | 82 | THE BEST  *A & M AMLH 68542* ...................... | 41 | 4 wks |

## Rickie Lee JONES  *US, female vocalist*

39 wks

| | | | | | |
|---|---|---|---|---|---|
| 16 Jun | 79 | RICKIE LEE JONES  *Warner Bros. K 56628* ............. | 18 | 19 wks |
| 8 Aug | 81 | PIRATES  *Warner Bros. K 56816* ...................... | 37 | 11 wks |
| 2 Jul | 83 | GIRL AT HER VOLCANO  *Warner Bros. 92–3805–1* ...... | 51 | 3 wks |
| 13 Oct | 84 | THE MAGAZINE  *Warner Bros. 925117* ................ | 40 | 4 wks |
| 7 Oct | 89 | FLYING COWBOYS  *Geffen WX 309* ................. | 50 | 2 wks |

## Tammy JONES  *UK, female vocalist*                              5 wks

| | | | | |
|---|---|---|---|---|
| 12 Jul | 75 | **LET ME TRY AGAIN**  *Epic EPC 80853* | 38 | 5 wks |

## Tom JONES  *UK, male vocalist*                                  411 wks

| | | | | |
|---|---|---|---|---|
| 5 Jun | 65 | **ALONG CAME JONES**  *Decca LK 6693* | 11 | 5 wks |
| 8 Oct | 66 | **FROM THE HEART**  *Decca LK 4814* | 23 | 8 wks |
| 8 Apr | 67 | ● **GREEN GREEN GRASS OF HOME**  *Decca SKL 4855* | 3 | 49 wks |
| 24 Jun | 67 | ● **LIVE AT THE TALK OF THE TOWN**  *Decca SKL 4874* | 6 | 90 wks |
| 30 Dec | 67 | ● **13 SMASH HITS**  *Decca SKL 4909* | 5 | 49 wks |
| 27 Jul | 68 | ★ **DELILAH**  *Decca SKL 4946* | 1 | 29 wks |
| 21 Dec | 68 | ● **HELP YOURSELF**  *Decca SKL 4982* | 4 | 9 wks |
| 28 Jun | 69 | ● **THIS IS TOM JONES**  *Decca SKL 5007* | 2 | 20 wks |
| 15 Nov | 69 | ● **TOM JONES LIVE IN LAS VEGAS**  *Decca SKL 5032* | 3 | 45 wks |
| 25 Apr | 70 | ● **TOM**  *Decca SKL 5045* | 4 | 18 wks |
| 14 Nov | 70 | ● **I WHO HAVE NOTHING**  *Decca SKL 5072* | 10 | 10 wks |
| 29 May | 71 | ● **SHE'S A LADY**  *Decca SKL 5089* | 9 | 7 wks |
| 27 Nov | 71 | **LIVE AT CAESAR'S PALACE**  *Decca 1/1–1/2* | 27 | 5 wks |
| 24 Jun | 72 | **CLOSE UP**  *Decca SKL 5132* | 17 | 4 wks |
| 23 Jun | 73 | **THE BODY AND SOUL OF TOM JONES**  *Decca SKL 5162* | 31 | 1 wk |
| 5 Jan | 74 | **GREATEST HITS**  *Decca SKL 5176* | 15 | 13 wks |
| 22 Mar | 75 | ★ **20 GREATEST HITS**  *Decca TJD 1/11/2* | 1 | 21 wks |
| 7 Oct | 78 | **I'M COMING HOME**  *Lotus WH 5001* | 12 | 9 wks |
| 16 May | 87 | **THE GREATEST HITS**  *Telstar STAR 2296* | 16 | 12 wks |
| 13 May | 89 | **AT THIS MOMENT**  *Jive TOMTV 1* | 34 | 3 wks |
| 8 Jul | 89 | **AFTER DARK**  *Stylus SMR 978* | 46 | 4 wks |

## Janis JOPLIN  *US, female vocalist*                             7 wks

| | | | | |
|---|---|---|---|---|
| 17 Apr | 71 | **PEARL**  *CBS 64188* | 50 | 1 wk |
| 22 Jul | 72 | **JANIS JOPLIN IN CONCERT**  *CBS 67241* | 30 | 6 wks |

## JOURNEY  *US, male vocal/instrumental group*                  30 wks

| | | | | |
|---|---|---|---|---|
| 20 Mar | 82 | **ESCAPE**  *CBS 85138* | 32 | 16 wks |
| 19 Feb | 83 | ● **FRONTIERS**  *CBS 25261* | 6 | 8 wks |
| 6 Aug | 83 | **EVOLUTION**  *CBS 32342* | 100 | 1 wk |
| 24 May | 86 | **RAISED ON RADIO**  *CBS 26902* | 22 | 5 wks |

## JOY DIVISION  *UK, male vocal/instrumental group*              29 wks

| | | | | |
|---|---|---|---|---|
| 26 Jul | 80 | ● **CLOSER**  *Factory FACT 25* | 6 | 8 wks |
| 30 Aug | 80 | **UNKNOWN PLEASURES**  *Factory FACT 10* | 71 | 1 wk |
| 17 Oct | 81 | ● **STILL**  *Factory FACT 40* | 5 | 12 wks |
| 23 Jul | 88 | ● **1977–1980 SUBSTANCE**  *Factory FAC 250* | 7 | 8 wks |

## JUDAS PRIEST  *UK, male vocal/instrumental group*              75 wks

| | | | | |
|---|---|---|---|---|
| 14 May | 77 | **SIN AFTER SIN**  *CBS 82008* | 23 | 6 wks |
| 25 Feb | 78 | **STAINED GLASS**  *CBS 82430* | 27 | 5 wks |
| 11 Nov | 78 | **KILLING MACHINE**  *CBS 83135* | 32 | 9 wks |
| 6 Oct | 79 | ● **UNLEASHED IN THE EAST**  *CBS 83852* | 10 | 8 wks |
| 19 Apr | 80 | ● **BRITISH STEEL**  *CBS 84160* | 4 | 17 wks |
| 7 Mar | 81 | **POINT OF ENTRY**  *CBS 84834* | 14 | 5 wks |
| 17 Jul | 82 | **SCREAMING FOR VENGEANCE**  *CBS 85941* | 11 | 9 wks |
| 28 Jan | 84 | **DEFENDERS OF THE FAITH**  *CBS 25713* | 19 | 5 wks |
| 19 Apr | 86 | **TURBO**  *CBS 26641* | 33 | 4 wks |
| 13 Jun | 87 | **PRIEST LIVE**  *CBS 450 639–1* | 47 | 2 wks |
| 28 May | 88 | **RAM IT DOWN**  *CBS 461108 1* | 24 | 5 wks |

## JUDGE DREAD  *UK, male vocalist*                                14 wks

| | | | | |
|---|---|---|---|---|
| 6 Dec | 75 | **BEDTIME STORIES**  *Cactus CTLP 113* | 26 | 12 wks |
| 7 Mar | 81 | **40 BIG ONES**  *Creole BIG 1* | 51 | 2 wks |

AL JARREAU broke into the chart in 1981.

Only Elvis Presley tops **ELTON JOHN** for the longest active streak of successive years in the chart.

**BILLY JOEL** (right) asks Mark Knopfler what he has to do to get a UK number one album.

## JUICY LUCY  *UK, male vocal/instrumental group*                                   *5 wks*

| | | | | | |
|---|---|---|---|---|---|
| 18 Apr 70 | **JUICY LUCY** | *Vertigo VO 2* | ........................ | 41 | 4 wks |
| 21 Nov 70 | **LIE BACK AND ENJOY IT** | *Vertigo 6360 014* | .......... | 53 | 1 wk |

## JULUKA  *South Africa, male/female vocal/instrumental group*          *3 wks*

| | | | | | |
|---|---|---|---|---|---|
| 23 Jul 83 | **SCATTERLINGS** | *Safari SHAKA 1* | ................... | 50 | 3 wks |

## JUNIOR  *UK, male vocalist*                                                        *14 wks*

| | | | | | |
|---|---|---|---|---|---|
| 5 Jun 82 | **JI** | *Mercury MERS 3* | ................................ | 28 | 14 wks |

# *k*

## Bert KAEMPFERT  *Germany, orchestra*                                      *104 wks*

| | | | | | |
|---|---|---|---|---|---|
| 5 Mar 66 | ● **BYE BYE BLUES** | *Polydor BM 84086* | ................. | 4 | 22 wks |
| 16 Apr 66 | **BEST OF BERT KAEMPFERT** | *Polydor 84–012* | | 27 | 1 wk |
| 28 May 66 | **SWINGING SAFARI** | *Polydor LPHM 46–384* | ........... | 20 | 15 wks |
| 30 Jul 66 | **STRANGERS IN THE NIGHT** | *Polydor LPHM 84–053* | ... | 13 | 26 wks |
| 4 Feb 67 | **RELAXING SOUND OF BERT KAEMPFERT** | | | | |
| | *Polydor 583–501* | | ...................... | 33 | 3 wks |
| 18 Feb 67 | **BERT KAEMPFERT – BEST SELLER** | *Polydor 583–551* . | | 25 | 18 wks |
| 29 Apr 67 | **HOLD ME** | *Polydor 184–072* | ........................ | 36 | 5 wks |
| 26 Aug 67 | **KAEMPFERT SPECIAL** | *Polydor 236–207* | ............. | 24 | 5 wks |
| 19 Jun 71 | **ORANGE COLOURED SKY** | *Polydor 2310–091* | ......... | 49 | 1 wk |
| 5 Jul 80 | **SOUNDS SENSATIONAL** | *Polydor POLTB 10* | .......... | 17 | 8 wks |

## KAJAGOOGOO  *UK, male vocal/instrumental group*                  *23 wks*

| | | | | | |
|---|---|---|---|---|---|
| 30 Apr 83 | ● **WHITE FEATHERS** | *EMI EMC 3433* | ................. | 5 | 20 wks |
| 26 May 84 | **ISLANDS** | *EMI KAJA 1* | ........................... | 35 | 3 wks |

## Nick KAMEN  *UK, male vocalist*                                               *7 wks*

| | | | | | |
|---|---|---|---|---|---|
| 18 Apr 87 | **NICK KAMEN** | *WEA WX 84* | ...................... | 34 | 7 wks |

## KANE GANG  *UK, male vocal/instrumental group*                    *12 wks*

| | | | | | |
|---|---|---|---|---|---|
| 23 Feb 85 | **THE BAD AND LOWDOWN WORLD OF THE KANE GANG** | | | | |
| | *Kitchenware KWLP 2* | ...................... | 21 | 8 wks |
| 8 Aug 87 | **MIRACLE** | *Kitchenware KWLP 7* | ..................... | 41 | 4 wks |

## Mick KARN  *UK, male vocalist/instrumentalist – bass*              *4 wks*

| | | | | | |
|---|---|---|---|---|---|
| 20 Nov 82 | **TITLES** | *Virgin V 2249* | .......................... | 74 | 3 wks |
| 28 Feb 87 | **DREAMS OF REASON PRODUCE MONSTERS** | | | | |
| | *Virgin V 2389* | ..................................... | 89 | 1 wk |

## KATRINA and the WAVES
*UK/US, female/male vocal/instrumental group*                            *7 wks*

| | | | | | |
|---|---|---|---|---|---|
| 8 Jun 85 | **KATRINA AND THE WAVES** | *Capitol KTW 1* | ......... | 28 | 6 wks |
| 10 May 86 | **WAVES** | *Capitol EST 2010* | ......................... | 70 | 1 wk |

## K.C. and the SUNSHINE BAND
*US, male vocal/instrumental group*       *17 wks*

| | | | |
|---|---|---|---|
| 30 Aug 75 | **K.C. AND THE SUNSHINE BAND**   *Jayboy JSL 9* ....... | 26 | 7 wks |
| 1 Mar 80 | ● **GREATEST HITS**   *TK TKR 83385* ................... | 10 | 6 wks |
| 27 Aug 83 | **ALL IN A NIGHT'S WORK**   *Epic EPC 85847* .......... | 46 | 4 wks |

## KEEL   *US, male vocal/instrumental group*     *2 wks*

| | | | |
|---|---|---|---|
| 17 May 86 | **THE FINAL FRONTIER**   *Vertigo VERH 33* ............ | 83 | 2 wks |

## Howard KEEL   *US, male vocalist*     *36 wks*

| | | | |
|---|---|---|---|
| 14 Apr 84 | ● **AND I LOVE YOU SO**   *Warwick WW 5137* ............ | 6 | 19 wks |
| 9 Nov 85 | **REMINISCING – THE HOWARD KEEL COLLECTION** *Telstar STAR 2259* ............................... | 20 | 12 wks |
| 28 Mar 88 | **JUST FOR YOU**   *Telstar STAR 2318* .................. | 51 | 5 wks |

## Felicity KENDAL   *UK, female exercise instructor*     *47 wks*

| | | | |
|---|---|---|---|
| 19 Jun 82 | **SHAPE UP AND DANCE (VOL. 1)**   *Lifestyle LEG 1* ...... | 29 | 47 wks |

**Eddie KENDRICK** – *See Daryl HALL and John OATES.*

## Nigel KENNEDY   *UK, male instrumentalist – violin*     *9 wks*

| | | | |
|---|---|---|---|
| 1 Mar 86 | **ELGAR VIOLIN CONCERTO**   *EMI EMX 4120581* ...... | 97 | 1 wk |
| 7 Oct 89 | **VIVALDI FOUR SEASONS**   *EMI NIGE 2* ............ | 42† | 8 wks |

*Elgar Violin Concerto was with the London Philharmonic Orchestra, conducted by Vernon Handley. Vivaldi Four Seasons was with the English Chamber Orchestra. See also London Philharmonic Orchestra.*

## KENNY   *UK, male vocal/instrumental group*     *1 wk*

| | | | |
|---|---|---|---|
| 17 Jan 76 | **THE SOUND OF SUPER K**   *RAK SRAK 518* ........... | 56 | 1 wk |

## Gerard KENNY   *US, male vocalist*     *4 wks*

| | | | |
|---|---|---|---|
| 21 Jul 79 | **MADE IT THROUGH THE RAIN**   *RCA Victor PL 25218* . | 19 | 4 wks |

## Nik KERSHAW   *UK, male vocalist*     *100 wks*

| | | | |
|---|---|---|---|
| 10 Mar 84 | ● **HUMAN RACING**   *MCA MCF 3197* ................. | 5 | 61 wks |
| 1 Dec 84 | ● **THE RIDDLE**   *MCA MCF 3245* ..................... | 8 | 36 wks |
| 8 Nov 86 | **RADIO MUSICOLA**   *MCA MCG 6016* ............... | 47 | 3 wks |

## Chaka KHAN   *US, female vocalist*     *39 wks*

| | | | |
|---|---|---|---|
| 20 Oct 84 | **I FEEL FOR YOU**   *Warner Bros. 925 162* ................ | 15 | 22 wks |
| 9 Aug 86 | **DESTINY**   *Warner Bros. WX 45* ..................... | 77 | 2 wks |
| 3 Jun 89 | **LIFE IS A DANCE – THE REMIX PROJECT** *Warner Bros. WX 268* ............................ | 14 | 15 wks |

*See also Rufus and Chaka Khan.*

## Aram KHATCHATURIAN/VIENNA PHILMARMONIC ORCHESTRA

*Russia, male conductor/Austria, orchestra*                           *15 wks*

22 Jan  72   **SPARTACUS**  *Decca SXL 6000* ...................... 16   15 wks

## KIDS FROM FAME

*US, male/female vocal/instrumental group*                     *117 wks*

24 Jul  82 ★ **KIDS FROM FAME**  *BBC REP 447* ................... 1   45 wks
16 Oct  82 ● **KIDS FROM FAME AGAIN**  *RCA RCALP 6057* ......... 2   21 wks
26 Feb  83 ● **THE KIDS FROM FAME LIVE**  *BBC KIDLP 003* ........ 8   28 wks
14 May  83   **THE KIDS FROM FAME SONGS**  *BBC KIDLP 004* ..... 14   16 wks
20 Aug  83   **SING FOR YOU**  *BBC KIDLP 005* ................... 28   7 wks

## KILLING JOKE   *UK, male vocal/instrumental group*            *30 wks*

25 Oct  80   **KILLING JOKE**  *Polydor EGMD 545* ................... 39   4 wks
20 Jun  81   **WHAT'S THIS FOR**  *Malicious Damage EGMD 550* ....... 42   4 wks
 8 May  82   **REVELATIONS**  *Malicious Damage EGMD 3* ............. 12   6 wks
27 Nov  82   **'HA' – KILLING JOKE LIVE**  *EG EGMDT 4* .......... 66   2 wks
23 Jul  83   **FIRE DANCES**  *EG EGMD 5* ....................... 29   3 wks
 9 Mar  85   **NIGHT TIME**  *EG EGLP 61* ...................... 11   9 wks
22 Nov  86   **BRIGHTER THAN A THOUSAND SUNS**  *EG EGLP 66*   54   1 wk
 9 Jul  88   **OUTSIDE THE GATE**  *EG EGLP 73* ................ 92   1 wk

**KIM** – *See MEL and KIM*

## KIMERA with the LONDON SYMPHONY ORCHESTRA   *Korea, female vocalist with UK, orchestra*   *4 wks*

26 Oct  85   **HITS ON OPERA**  *Stylus SMR 8505* ................... 38   4 wks
*See also London Symphony Orchestra.*

## KING   *UK, male vocal/instrumental group*                     *32 wks*

 9 Feb  85 ● **STEPS IN TIME**  *CBS 26095* ........................ 6   21 wks
23 Nov  85   **BITTER SWEET**  *CBS 86320* ....................... 16   11 wks

## B.B. KING   *US, male vocalist/instrumentalist – guitar*        *5 wks*

25 Aug  79   **TAKE IT HOME**  *MCA MCF 3010* ................... 60   5 wks

## Ben E. KING   *UK, male vocalist*                               *11 wks*

 1 Jul  67   **SPANISH HARLEM**  *Atlantic 590–001* ............... 30   3 wks
14 Mar  87   **STAND BY ME (THE ULTIMATE COLLECTION)**
             *Atlantic WX 90* .................................. 14   8 wks
*Stand By Me features tracks by the Drifters. See also the Drifters.*

## Carole KING   *US, female vocalist/instrumentalist – piano*     *102 wks*

24 Jul  71 ● **TAPESTRY**  *A&M AMLS 2025* ..................... 4   90 wks
15 Jan  72   **MUSIC**  *A&M AMLH 67013* ...................... 18   10 wks
 2 Dec  72   **RHYMES AND REASONS**  *Ode 77016* .............. 40   2 wks

## Evelyn KING   *US, female vocalist*                     *9 wks*

| 11 Sep 82 | **GET LOOSE**   *RCA RCALP 3093* ..................... | 35 | 9 wks |

## Mark KING   *UK, male vocalist/instrumentalist – bass*                     *2 wks*

| 21 Jul 84 | **INFLUENCES**   *Polydor MKLP 1* ..................... | 77 | 2 wks |

## Solomon KING   *US, male vocalist*                     *1 wk*

| 22 Jun 68 | **SHE WEARS MY RING**   *Columbia SCX 6250* ........... | 40 | 1 wk |

## KING CRIMSON   *UK, male vocal/instrumental group*                     *53 wks*

| 1 Nov 69 | ● **IN THE COURT OF THE CRIMSON KING** *Island ILPS 9111* ................................. | 5 | 18 wks |
| 30 May 70 | ● **IN THE WAKE OF POSEIDON**   *Island ILPS 9127* ....... | 4 | 13 wks |
| 16 Jan 71 | **LIZARD**   *Island ILPS 9141* ......................... | 30 | 1 wk |
| 8 Jan 72 | **ISLANDS**   *Island ILPS 9175* ....................... | 30 | 1 wk |
| 7 Apr 73 | **LARKS' TONGUES IN ASPIC**   *Island ILPS 9230* ...... | 20 | 4 wks |
| 13 Apr 74 | **STARLESS AND BIBLE BLACK**   *Island ILPS 9275* ...... | 28 | 2 wks |
| 26 Oct 74 | **RED**   *Island ILPS 9308* ........................... | 45 | 1 wk |
| 10 Oct 81 | **DISCIPLINE**   *EG EGLP 49* ........................ | 41 | 4 wks |
| 26 Jun 82 | **BEAT**   *EG EGLP 51* ............................... | 39 | 5 wks |
| 31 Mar 84 | **THREE OF A PERFECT PAIR**   *EG EGLP 55* .......... | 30 | 4 wks |

## KING KURT   *UK, male vocal/instrumental group*                     *5 wks*

| 10 Dec 83 | **OOH WALLAH WALLAH**   *Stiff SEEZ 52* ............. | 99 | 1 wk |
| 8 Mar 86 | **BIG COCK**   *Stiff SEEZ 62* ......................... | 50 | 4 wks |

## KINGDOM COME   *US, male vocal/instrumental group*                     *10 wks*

| 28 Mar 88 | **KINGDOM COME**   *Polydor KCLP 1* ................... | 43 | 6 wks |
| 13 May 89 | **IN YOUR FACE**   *Polydor 839192 1* ................... | 25 | 4 wks |

## Redhead KINGPIN and the FBI   *US, male vocalist*                     *3 wks*

| 9 Sep 89 | **A SHADE OF RED**   *10 DIX 85* ...................... | 35 | 3 wks |

## The Choir of KING'S COLLEGE, CAMBRIDGE
*UK, choir*                     *3 wks*

| 11 Dec 71 | **THE WORLD OF CHRISTMAS**   *Argo SPAA 104* ....... | 38 | 3 wks |

## KINGS OF SWING ORCHESTRA
*Australia, orchestra*                     *11 wks*

| 29 May 82 | **SWITCHED ON SWING**   *K-Tel ONE 1166* ............ | 28 | 11 wks |

## KINGS X   *US, male vocal/instrumental group*                     *1 wk*

| 1 Jul 89 | **GRETCHEN GOES TO NEBRASKA**   *Atlantic WX 279* ... | 52 | 1 wk |

NTON KWESI JOHNSON was the top-charting poet of the 80s.

A supergroup of chart-making Jones Boys would include Aled, Glenn, Howard, Quincy, Tom and **JACK JONES**.

'Tapestry' by **CAROLE KING** was the world's all-time best-selling album by a woman for fifteen years before being eclipsed by 'Whitney Houston'.

Red Wedge stars performing for Labour in 1987 included (left to right) Paul Weller, Jimmy Somerville, Sarah Jane Morris, Billy Bragg and **JUNIOR**.

## KINKS  UK, male vocal/instrumental group  123 wks

| | | | | |
|---|---|---|---|---|
| 17 Oct 64 | ● **KINKS**  Pye NPL 18096 | | 3 | 25 wks |
| 13 Mar 65 | ● **KINDA KINKS**  Pye NPL 18112 | | 3 | 15 wks |
| 4 Dec 65 | ● **KINKS KONTROVERSY**  Pye NPL 18131 | | 9 | 12 wks |
| 11 Sep 66 | ● **WELL RESPECTED KINKS**  Marble Arch MAL 612 | | 5 | 31 wks |
| 5 Nov 66 | **FACE TO FACE**  Pye NPL 18149 | | 12 | 11 wks |
| 14 Oct 67 | **SOMETHING ELSE**  Pye NSPL 18193 | | 35 | 2 wks |
| 2 Dec 67 | ● **SUNNY AFTERNOON**  Marble Arch MAL 716 | | 9 | 11 wks |
| 23 Oct 71 | **GOLDEN HOUR OF THE KINKS**  Golden Hour GH 501 | | 21 | 4 wks |
| 14 Oct 78 | **20 GOLDEN GREATS**  Ronco RPL 2031 | | 19 | 6 wks |
| 5 Nov 83 | **KINKS GREATEST HITS – DEAD END STREET**  PRT KINK 1 | | 96 | 1 wk |
| 16 Sep 89 | **THE ULTIMATE COLLECTION**  Castle Communications CTVLP 001 | | 35 | 5 wks |

## Kathy KIRBY  UK, female vocalist  8 wks

| | | | | |
|---|---|---|---|---|
| 4 Jan 64 | **16 HITS FROM STARS AND GARTERS**  Decca LK 5475 | | 11 | 8 wks |

## KISS  US, male vocal/instrumental group  62 wks

| | | | | |
|---|---|---|---|---|
| 29 May 76 | **DESTROYER**  Casablanca CBSP 4008 | | 22 | 5 wks |
| 25 Jun 76 | **ALIVE!**  Casablanca CBSP 401 | | 49 | 2 wks |
| 17 Dec 77 | **ALIVE**  Casablanca CALD 5004 | | 60 | 1 wk |
| 7 Jul 79 | **DYNASTY**  Casablanca CALH 2051 | | 50 | 6 wks |
| 28 Jun 80 | **UNMASKED**  Mercury 6302 032 | | 48 | 3 wks |
| 5 Dec 81 | **THE ELDER**  Casablanca 6302 163 | | 51 | 3 wks |
| 26 Jun 82 | **KILLERS**  Casablanca CANL 1 | | 42 | 6 wks |
| 6 Nov 82 | **CREATURES OF THE NIGHT**  Casablanca CANL 4 | | 22 | 4 wks |
| 8 Oct 83 | ● **LICK IT UP**  Vertigo VERL 9 | | 7 | 7 wks |
| 6 Oct 84 | **ANIMALISE**  Vertigo VERL 18 | | 11 | 4 wks |
| 5 Oct 85 | **ASYLUM**  Vertigo VERH 32 | | 12 | 3 wks |
| 7 Nov 87 | ● **CRAZY NIGHTS**  Vertigo VERH 49 | | 4 | 14 wks |
| 10 Dec 88 | **SMASHES, THRASHES AND HITS**  Vertigo 836759 1 | | 62 | 2 wks |
| 4 Nov 89 | **HOT IN THE SHADE**  Fontana 838913 1 | | 35 | 2 wks |

k

## KISSING THE PINK
### UK, male/female vocal/instrumental group  5 wks

| | | | | |
|---|---|---|---|---|
| 4 Jun 83 | **NAKED**  Magnet KTPL 1001 | | 54 | 5 wks |

## Eartha KITT  US, female vocalist  1 wk

| | | | | |
|---|---|---|---|---|
| 11 Feb 61 | **REVISITED**  London HA 2296 | | 17 | 1 wk |

## KLEEER  US, male vocal/instrumental group  1 wk

| | | | | |
|---|---|---|---|---|
| 6 Jul 85 | **SEEKRET**  Atlantic 78–1254–1 | | 96 | 1 wk |

**Earl KLUGH** – See George BENSON and Earl KLUGH

## KNACK  US, male vocal/instrumental group  2 wks

| | | | | |
|---|---|---|---|---|
| 4 Aug 79 | **GET THE KNACK**  Capitol EST 11948 | | 65 | 2 wks |

**Curtis KNIGHT** – See Jimi HENDRIX and Curtis KNIGHT

## Gladys KNIGHT and the PIPS
*US, female vocalist/male vocal backing group*                    *105 wks*

| | | | | |
|---|---|---|---|---|
| 31 May 75 | **I FEEL A SONG** *Buddah BDLP 4030* ............ | 20 | 15 wks |
| 28 Feb 76 ● | **THE BEST OF GLADYS KNIGHT AND THE PIPS** | | |
| | *Buddah BDLH 5013* ............................... | 6 | 43 wks |
| 16 Jul 77 | **STILL TOGETHER** *Buddah BDLH 5014* ........... | 42 | 3 wks |
| 12 Nov 77 ● | **30 GREATEST** *K-Tel NE 1004* .................. | 3 | 22 wks |
| 4 Oct 80 | **A TOUCH OF LOVE** *K-Tel NE 1090* ............. | 16 | 6 wks |
| 4 Feb 84 | **THE COLLECTION – 20 GREATEST HITS** | | |
| | *Starblend NITE 1* ............................... | 43 | 5 wks |
| 27 Feb 88 | **ALL OUR LOVE** *MCA MCF 3409* ............... | 80 | 1 wk |
| 28 Oct 89 | **THE SINGLES ALBUM** *Polygram GKTV 1* ........ | 13† | 10 wks |

*See also Diana Ross/Michael Jackson/Gladys Knight/Stevie Wonder.*


## KNIGHTSBRIDGE STRINGS  *UK, male orchestra*      *1 wk*

| | | | | |
|---|---|---|---|---|
| 25 Jun 60 | **STRING SWAY** *Top Rank BUY 017* ............. | 20 | 1 wk |


## David KNOPFLER
*UK, male vocalist/instrumentalist – guitar*                      *1 wk*

| | | | | |
|---|---|---|---|---|
| 19 Nov 83 | **RELEASE** *Peach River DAVID 1* .............. | 82 | 1 wk |


## Mark KNOPFLER
*UK, male vocalist/instrumentalist*                               *14 wks*

| | | | | |
|---|---|---|---|---|
| 16 Apr 83 | **LOCAL HERO** *Vertigo VERL 4* ............... | 14 | 11 wks |
| 20 Oct 84 | **CAL – MUSIC FROM THE FILM** *Vertigo VERH 17* ..... | 65 | 3 wks |


## John KONGOS
*South Africa, male vocalist/multi-instrumentalist*              *2 wks*

| | | | | |
|---|---|---|---|---|
| 15 Jan 72 | **KONGOS** *Fly HIFLY 7* ...................... | 29 | 2 wks |


## KOOL AND THE GANG
*US, male vocal/instrumental group*                               *114 wks*

| | | | | |
|---|---|---|---|---|
| 21 Nov 81 ● | **SOMETHING SPECIAL** *De-Lite DSR 001* ......... | 10 | 20 wks |
| 2 Oct 82 | **AS ONE** *De-Lite DSR 3* ..................... | 49 | 10 wks |
| 7 May 83 ● | **TWICE AS KOOL** *De-Lite PROLP 2* ............ | 4 | 23 wks |
| 14 Jan 84 | **IN THE HEART** *De-Lite DSR 4* ............... | 18 | 23 wks |
| 15 Dec 84 | **EMERGENCY** *De-Lite DSR 6* ................. | 47 | 25 wks |
| 12 Nov 88 | **THE SINGLES COLLECTION** *De-Lite KGTV 1* ........ | 28 | 13 wks |


## KORGIS  *UK, male vocal/instrumental duo*      *4 wks*

| | | | | |
|---|---|---|---|---|
| 26 Jul 80 | **DUMB WAITERS** *Rialto TENOR 104* ............. | 40 | 4 wks |


## KRAFTWERK  *Germany, male vocal/instrumental group*      *65 wks*

| | | | | |
|---|---|---|---|---|
| 17 May 75 ● | **AUTOBAHN** *Vertigo 6360 620* ................ | 4 | 18 wks |
| 20 May 78 ● | **THE MAN-MACHINE** *Capitol EST 11728* ......... | 9 | 13 wks |
| 23 May 81 | **COMPUTER WORLD** *EMI EMC 3370* ............. | 15 | 22 wks |
| 6 Feb 82 | **TRANS-EUROPE EXPRESS** *Capitol EST 11603* ....... | 49 | 7 wks |
| 22 Jun 85 | **AUTOBAHN (re-issue)** *Parlophone AUTO 1* ............ | 61 | 3 wks |
| 15 Nov 86 | **ELECTRIC CAFE** *EMI EMD 1001* .................. | 58 | 2 wks |

## Billy J. KRAMER and the DAKOTAS
*UK, male vocalist, male instrumental backing group* **17 wks**

| 16 Nov 63 | **LISTEN TO BILLY J. KRAMER** *Parlophone PMC 1209* | 11 | 17 wks |
|---|---|---|---|

## Kris KRISTOFFERSON and Rita COOLIDGE
*US, male/female vocal duo* **4 wks**

| 6 May 78 | **NATURAL ACT** *A & M AMLH 64690* | 35 | 4 wks |
|---|---|---|---|

*See also Rita Coolidge.*

## KROKUS *Switzerland/Malta, male vocal/instrumental group* **11 wks**

| 21 Feb 81 | **HARDWARE** *Ariola ARL 5064* | 44 | 4 wks |
|---|---|---|---|
| 20 Feb 82 | **ONE VICE AT A TIME** *Arista SPART 1189* | 28 | 5 wks |
| 16 Apr 83 | **HEADHUNTER** *Arista 205 255* | 74 | 2 wks |

## Charlie KUNZ *US, male instrumentalist – piano* **11 wks**

| 14 Jun 69 | ● **THE WORLD OF CHARLIE KUNZ** *Decca SPA 15* | 9 | 11 wks |
|---|---|---|---|

**166**
**l**

*l*

## L.A. GUNS *US, male/female vocal/instrumental group* **3 wks**

| 5 Mar 88 | **L.A. GUNS** *Vertigo VERH 55* | 73 | 1 wk |
|---|---|---|---|
| 30 Sep 89 | **COCKED AND LOADED** *Vertigo 838592 1* | 45 | 2 wks |

## Patti LaBELLE *US, female vocalist* **17 wks**

| 24 May 86 | **THE WINNER IN YOU** *MCA MCF 3319* | 30 | 17 wks |
|---|---|---|---|

## LADYSMITH BLACK MAMBAZO
*South Africa, male vocal group* **11 wks**

| 11 Apr 87 | **SHAKA ZULU** *Warner Bros. WX 94* | 34 | 11 wks |
|---|---|---|---|

## Cleo LAINE *UK, female vocalist* **1 wk**

| 2 Dec 78 | **CLEO** *Arcade ADEP 37* | 68 | 1 wk |
|---|---|---|---|

*See also Cleo Laine and John Williams; Cleo Laine and James Galway.*

## Cleo LAINE and James GALWAY
*UK, female vocalist and male instrumentalist – flute* **14 wks**

| 31 May 80 | **SOMETIMES WHEN WE TOUCH** *RCA PL 25296* | 15 | 14 wks |
|---|---|---|---|

*See also Cleo Laine; James Galway.*

## Cleo LAINE and John WILLIAMS
*UK, female vocalist and male instrumentalist – guitar*                    *22 wks*

7 Jan 78   **BEST OF FRIENDS**   *RCA RS 1094* ...................   **18**   22 wks
*See also Cleo Laine; John Williams.*


## Frankie LAINE   *US, male vocalist*       *29 wks*

24 Jun 61  ● **HELL BENT FOR LEATHER**   *Philips BBL 7468* ........   **7**   23 wks
24 Sep 77  ● **THE VERY BEST OF FRANKIE LAINE**   *Warwick PR 5032*   **7**   6 wks


## Greg LAKE   *UK, male vocalist*       *3 wks*

17 Oct 81   **GREG LAKE**   *Chrysalis CHR 1357* ....................   **62**   3 wks
*See also Emerson, Lake and Palmer; Emerson, Lake and Powell.*


## Annabel LAMB   *UK, female vocalist*       *1 wk*

28 Apr 84   **THE FLAME**   *A & M AMLX 68564* ...................   **84**   1 wk


## LAMBRETTAS   *UK, male vocal/instrumental group*       *8 wks*

5 Jul 80   **BEAT BOYS IN THE JET AGE**   *Rocket TRAIN 10* .......   **28**   8 wks


## LANDSCAPE   *UK, male vocal/instrumental group*       *12 wks*

21 Mar 81   **FROM THE TEAROOMS OF MARS TO THE HELLHOLES**
             **OF URANUS**   *RCA RCALP 5003* ..................   **13**   12 wks


## Ronnie LANE and the Band SLIM CHANCE
*UK, male vocal/instrumental group*                    *1 wk*

17 Aug 74   **ANYMORE FOR ANYMORE**   *GM GML 1013* ........   **48**   1 wk
*See also Pete Townshend and Ronnie Lane.*


## Thomas LANG   *UK, male vocalist*       *1 wk*

20 Feb 88   **SCALLYWAGJAZ**   *Epic 450996 1* ....................   **92**   1 wk


## Mario LANZA   *US, male vocalist*       *56 wks*

6 Dec 58  ● **THE STUDENT PRINCE/THE GREAT CARUSO**
             *RCA RB 16113* .....................................   **4**   21 wks
23 Jul 60  ● **THE GREAT CARUSO**   *RCA RB 16112* .............   **3**   15 wks
9 Jan 71   **HIS GREATEST HITS VOL. 1**   *RCA LSB 4000* ........   **39**   1 wk
5 Sep 81   **THE LEGEND OF MARIO LANZA**   *K-Tel NE 1110* .....   **29**   11 wks
14 Nov 87   **A PORTRAIT OF MARIO LANZA**   *Stylus SMR 741* .....   **49**   8 wks

*The Great Caruso side of the first album is a film soundtrack.*


## James LAST   *Germany, male orchestra leader*       *364 wks*

15 Apr 67  ● **THIS IS JAMES LAST**   *Polydor 104-678* .................   **6**   48 wks
22 Jul 67   **HAMMOND A-GO-GO**   *Polydor 249-043* ..............   **27**   10 wks
26 Aug 67   **NON-STOP DANCING**   *Polydor 236-203* .............   **35**   1 wk
26 Aug 67   **LOVE THIS IS MY SONG**   *Polydor 583-553* ............   **32**   2 wks
22 Jun 68   **JAMES LAST GOES POP**   *Polydor 249-160* .............   **32**   3 wks

| Date | Title | Pos | Weeks |
|---|---|---|---|
| 8 Feb 69 | **DANCING '68 VOL. 1** *Polydor 249–216* .............. | **40** | 1 wk |
| 31 May 69 | **TRUMPET A-GO-GO** *Polydor 249–239* .............. | **13** | 1 wk |
| 9 Aug 69 | **NON-STOP DANCING '69** *Polydor 249–294* ........... | **26** | 1 wk |
| 24 Jan 70 | **NON-STOP DANCING '69/2** *Polydor 249/354* .......... | **27** | 3 wks |
| 23 May 70 | **NON-STOP EVERGREENS** · *Polydor 249–370* .......... | **26** | 1 wk |
| 11 Jul 70 | **CLASSICS UP TO DATE** *Polydor 249–371* ............ | **44** | 1 wk |
| 11 Jul 70 | **NON-STOP DANCING '70** *Polydor 2371–04* ........... | **67** | 1 wk |
| 24 Oct 70 | **VERY BEST OF JAMES LAST** *Polydor 2371–054* ........ | **45** | 4 wks |
| 8 May 71 | **NON-STOP DANCING '71** *Polydor 2371–111* .......... | **21** | 4 wks |
| 26 Jun 71 | **SUMMER HAPPENING** *Polydor 2371–133* ............. | **38** | 1 wk |
| 18 Sep 71 | **BEACH PARTY 2** *Polydor 2371–211* ................ | **47** | 1 wk |
| 2 Oct 71 | **YESTERDAY'S MEMORIES** *Contour 2870–117* ......... | **17** | 14 wks |
| 16 Oct 71 | **NON-STOP DANCING 12** *Polydor 2371–141* ........... | **30** | 3 wks |
| 19 Feb 72 | **NON-STOP DANCING 13** *Polydor 2371–189* ........... | **32** | 2 wks |
| 4 Mar 72 | **POLKA PARTY** *Polydor 2371–190* ................. | **22** | 3 wks |
| 29 Apr 72 | **JAMES LAST IN CONCERT** *Polydor 2371–191* .......... | **13** | 6 wks |
| 24 Jun 72 | **VOODOO PARTY** *Polydor 2371–235* ................. | **45** | 1 wk |
| 16 Sep 72 | **CLASSICS UP TO DATE VOL. 2** *Polydor 184–061* ....... | **49** | 1 wk |
| 30 Sep 72 | **LOVE MUST BE THE REASON** *Polydor 2371–281* ....... | **32** | 2 wks |
| 27 Jan 73 | **THE MUSIC OF JAMES LAST** *Polydor 2683 010* ........ | **19** | 12 wks |
| 24 Feb 73 | **JAMES LAST IN RUSSIA** *Polydor 2371 293* ........... | **12** | 9 wks |
| 24 Feb 73 | **NON-STOP DANCING VOL. 14** *Polydor 2371–319* ....... | **27** | 3 wks |
| 28 Jul 73 | **OLE** *Polydor 2371 384* ........................ | **24** | 5 wks |
| 1 Sep 73 | **NON-STOP DANCING VOL. 15** *Polydor 2371–376* ....... | **34** | 2 wks |
| 20 Apr 74 | **NON-STOP DANCING VOL. 16** *Polydor 2371–444* ....... | **43** | 2 wks |
| 29 Jun 74 | **IN CONCERT VOL. 2** *Polydor 2371–320* ............. | **49** | 1 wk |
| 23 Nov 74 | **GOLDEN MEMORIES** *Polydor 2371–472* ............. | **39** | 2 wks |
| 26 Jul 75 | ● **TEN YEARS NON-STOP JUBILEE** *Polydor 2660–111* .... | **5** | 16 wks |
| 2 Aug 75 | **VIOLINS IN LOVE** *K-Tel /* ...................... | **60** | 1 wk |
| 22 Nov 75 | ● **MAKE THE PARTY LAST** *Polydor 2371–612* .......... | **3** | 19 wks |
| 8 May 76 | **CLASSICS UP TO DATE VOL. 3** *2371–538* ............. | **54** | 1 wk |
| 6 May 78 | **EAST TO WEST** *Polydor 2630–092* ................. | **49** | 4 wks |
| 14 Apr 79 | ● **LAST THE WHOLE NIGHT LONG** *Polydor PTD 001* ... | **2** | 45 wks |
| 23 Aug 80 | **THE BEST FROM 150 GOLD RECORDS** *Polydor 2681 211* | **56** | 3 wks |
| 1 Nov 80 | **CLASSICS FOR DREAMING** *Polydor POLTV 11* ........ | **12** | 18 wks |
| 14 Feb 81 | **ROSES FROM THE SOUTH** *Polydor 2372 051* ......... | **41** | 5 wks |
| 21 Nov 81 | **HANSIMANIA** *Polydor POLTV 14* ................. | **18** | 13 wks |
| 28 Nov 81 | **LAST FOREVER** *Polydor 2630 135* ................. | **88** | 2 wks |
| 5 Mar 83 | **BLUEBIRD** *Polydor 5072* ....................... | **57** | 3 wks |
| 30 Apr 83 | **THE BEST OF MY GOLD RECORDS** *Polydor PODV 7* .. | **42** | 5 wks |
| 30 Apr 83 | **NON-STOP DANCING '83 – PARTY POWER** *Polydor POLD 5094* ............................ | **56** | 2 wks |
| 3 Dec 83 | **THE GREATEST SONGS OF THE BEATLES** *Polydor POLD 5119* ............................ | **52** | 8 wks |
| 24 Mar 84 | **THE ROSE OF TRALEE AND OTHER IRISH FAVOURITES** *Polydor POLD 5131* ............................ | **21** | 11 wks |
| 13 Oct 84 | **PARADISE** *Polydor POLD 5163* .................. | **74** | 2 wks |
| 8 Dec 84 | **JAMES LAST IN SCOTLAND** *Polydor POLD 5166* ...... | **68** | 9 wks |
| 14 Sep 85 | **LEAVE THE BEST TO LAST** *Polydor PROLP 7* ......... | **11** | 27 wks |
| 18 Apr 87 | **BY REQUEST** *Polydor POLH 34* .................. | **22** | 11 wks |
| 26 Nov 88 | **DANCE DANCE DANCE** *Polydor JLTV 1* .............. | **38** | 8 wks |

## LATIN QUARTER  *UK, male/female vocal/instrumental group*  *3 wks*

| Date | Title | Pos | Weeks |
|---|---|---|---|
| 1 Mar 86 | **MODERN TIMES** *Rockin' Horse RHLP 1* .............. | **91** | 2 wks |
| 6 Jun 87 | **MICK AND CAROLINE** *Rockin' Horse 208 142* .......... | **96** | 1 wk |

## Cyndi LAUPER  *US, female vocalist*  *56 wks*

| Date | Title | Pos | Weeks |
|---|---|---|---|
| 18 Feb 84 | **SHE'S SO UNUSUAL** *Portrait PRT 25792* .............. | **16** | 32 wks |
| 11 Oct 86 | **TRUE COLOURS** *Portrait PRT 26948* ................. | **25** | 12 wks |
| 1 Jul 89 | ● **A NIGHT TO REMEMBER** *Epic 462499 1* ............. | **9** | 12 wks |

## LAUREL and HARDY  *UK/US, male comic duo*  *4 wks*

| Date | Title | Pos | Weeks |
|---|---|---|---|
| 6 Dec 75 | **THE GOLDEN AGE OF HOLLYWOOD COMEDY** *United Artists UAG 29676* .......................... | **55** | 4 wks |

## Syd LAWRENCE  *UK, orchestra*  *9 wks*

| | | | | |
|---|---|---|---|---|
| 8 Aug 70 | **MORE MILLER AND OTHER BIG BAND MAGIC** | | | |
| | *Philips 6642 001* ................................ | 14 | 4 wks |
| 25 Dec 71 | **SYD LAWRENCE WITH THE GLENN MILLER SOUND** | | | |
| | *Fontana SFL 13178* .............................. | 31 | 2 wks |
| 25 Dec 71 | **MUSIC OF GLENN MILLER IN SUPER STEREO** | | | |
| | *Philips 6641–017* ............................... | 43 | 2 wks |
| 26 Feb 72 | **SOMETHING OLD, SOMETHING NEW**  *Philips 6308 090* | 34 | 1 wk |

## Ronnie LAWS  *US, male vocalist/instrumentalist – saxophone*  *1 wk*

| | | | | |
|---|---|---|---|---|
| 17 Oct 81 | **SOLID GROUND**  *Liberty LBG 30336* ................ | 100 | 1 wk |

## LEAGUE UNLIMITED ORCHESTRA
*UK, male/female instrumental/vocal group*  *52 wks*

| | | | | |
|---|---|---|---|---|
| 17 Jul  82 | ● **LOVE AND DANCING**  *Virgin OVED 6* .............. | 3 | 52 wks |

*This album is a predominantly instrumental version of previously recorded Human League songs re-mixed by UK producer Martin Rushent.*

## LED ZEPPELIN  *UK, male vocal/instrumental group*  *411 wks*

| | | | | |
|---|---|---|---|---|
| 12 Apr 69 | ● **LED ZEPPELIN**  *Atlantic 588–171* .................... | 6 | 79 wks |
| 8 Nov 69 | ★ **LED ZEPPELIN 2**  *Atlantic 588–198* .................... | 1 | 138 wks |
| 7 Nov 70 | ★ **LED ZEPPELIN 3**  *Atlantic 2401–002* .................. | 1 | 40 wks |
| 27 Nov 71 | ★ **FOUR SYMBOLS**  *Atlantic 2401–012* ................... | 1 | 62 wks |
| 14 Apr 73 | ★ **HOUSES OF THE HOLY**  *Atlantic K 50014* ............. | 1 | 13 wks |
| 15 Mar 75 | ★ **PHYSICAL GRAFFITI**  *Swan Song SSK 89400* .......... | 1 | 27 wks |
| 24 Apr 76 | ★ **PRESENCE**  *Swan Song SSK 59402* .................. | 1 | 14 wks |
| 6 Nov 76 | ★ **THE SONG REMAINS THE SAME**  *Swan Song SSK 89402* | 1 | 15 wks |
| 8 Sep 79 | ★ **IN THROUGH THE OUT DOOR**  *Swan Song SSK 59410* . | 1 | 16 wks |
| 4 Dec 82 | ● **CODA**  *Swan Song A 0051* .......................... | 4 | 7 wks |

*Led Zeppelin 2 changed label/number to Atlantic K 40037, Four Symbols changed to Atlantic K 50008 during their runs. The fourth Led Zeppelin album appeared in the chart under various guises: The Fourth Led Zeppelin Album, Runes, The New Led Zeppelin Album, Led Zeppelin 4 and Four Symbols.*

**LEE** – *See PETERS and LEE*

## Brenda LEE  *US, female vocalist*  *57 wks*

| | | | | |
|---|---|---|---|---|
| 24 Nov 62 | **ALL THE WAY**  *Brunswick LAT 8383* .................. | 20 | 2 wks |
| 16 Feb 63 | **BRENDA – THAT'S ALL**  *Brunswick LAT 8516* .......... | 13 | 9 wks |
| 13 Apr 63 | ● **ALL ALONE AM I**  *Brunswick LAT 8530* ............. | 8 | 20 wks |
| 16 Jul 66 | **BYE BYE BLUES**  *Brunswick LAT 8649* ................ | 21 | 2 wks |
| 1 Nov 80 | **LITTLE MISS DYNAMITE**  *Warwick WW 5083* ......... | 15 | 11 wks |
| 7 Jan 84 | **25TH ANNIVERSARY**  *MCA MCLD 609* ............. | 65 | 4 wks |
| 30 Mar 85 | **THE VERY BEST OF BRENDA LEE**  *MCA LETV 1* .... | 16 | 9 wks |

## Peggy LEE  *US, female vocalist*  *17 wks*

| | | | | |
|---|---|---|---|---|
| 4 Jun 60 | ● **LATIN A LA LEE**  *Capitol T 1290* ................... | 8 | 15 wks |
| 20 May 61 | **BEST OF PEGGY LEE VOL. 2**  *Brunswick LAT 8355* ...... | 18 | 1 wk |
| 21 Oct 61 | **BLACK COFFEE**  *Ace of Hearts AH 5* ................. | 20 | 1 wk |

*See also Peggy Lee and George Shearing.*

## Peggy LEE and George SHEARING
*US, female vocalist and UK, male instrumentalist – piano*  *6 wks*

| | | | | |
|---|---|---|---|---|
| 11 Jun 60 | **BEAUTY AND THE BEAT**  *Capitol T 1219* ............ | 16 | 6 wks |

*See also Peggy Lee.*

## Raymond LEFEVRE  *France, orchestra*  *9 wks*

| | | | | |
|---|---|---|---|---|
| 7 Oct 67 ● **RAYMOND LEFEVRE**  *Major Minor  MMLP  4*  .......... | **10** | 7 wks |
| 17 Feb 68 **RAYMOND LEFEVRE VOL. 2**  *Major Minor  SMLP  13*  .... | **37** | 2 wks |

## Tom LEHRER  *US, male comic vocalist*  *26 wks*

| | | | |
|---|---|---|---|
| 8 Nov 58 ● **SONGS BY TOM LEHRER**  *Decca  LF  1311*  ............ | **7** | 19 wks |
| 25 Jun 60 ● **AN EVENING WASTED WITH TOM LEHRER**  *Decca  LK  4332*  .................................. | **7** | 7 wks |

## John LENNON  *UK, male vocalist*  *297 wks*

| | | | |
|---|---|---|---|
| 16 Jan 71 **JOHN LENNON AND THE PLASTIC ONO BAND**  *Apple  PCS  7124*  .................................. | **11** | 11 wks |
| 30 Oct 71 ★ **IMAGINE**  *Apple  PAS  10004*  ...................... | **1** | 101 wks |
| 14 Oct 72 **SOMETIME IN NEW YORK CITY**  *Apple  PCSP  716*  .... | **11** | 6 wks |
| 8 Dec 73 **MIND GAMES**  *Apple  PCS  7165*  ................... | **13** | 12 wks |
| 19 Oct 74 ● **WALLS AND BRIDGES**  *Apple  PCTC  253*  .......... | **6** | 10 wks |
| 8 Mar 75 ● **ROCK 'N' ROLL**  *Apple  PCS  7169*  .............. | **6** | 28 wks |
| 8 Nov 75 ● **SHAVED FISH**  *Apple  PCS  7173*  ................... | **8** | 29 wks |
| 22 Nov 80 ★ **DOUBLE FANTASY**  *Geffen  K  99131*  ............... | **1** | 36 wks |
| 20 Nov 82 ★ **THE JOHN LENNON COLLECTION**  *Parlophone  EMTV  37*  ........................... | **1** | 42 wks |
| 4 Feb 84 ● **MILK AND HONEY**  *Polydor  POLH  5*  ............. | **3** | 13 wks |
| 8 Mar 86 **LIVE IN NEW YORK CITY**  *Parlophone  PCS  7031*  ....... | **55** | 3 wks |
| 22 Oct 88 **IMAGINE – MUSIC FROM THE MOTION PICTURE**  *Parlophone  PCSP  722*  ............................ | **64** | 6 wks |

Imagine *changed its label credit to Parlophone PAS 10004 between its initial chart run and later runs.* John Lennon and the Plastic Ono Band *is credited to John Lennon and the Plastic Ono Band.* Imagine *is credited to John Lennon and the Plastic Ono Band with the Flux Fiddlers.* Sometime In New York City *is credited to John and Yoko Lennon with the Plastic Ono Band and Elephant's Memory.* Double Fantasy *and* Milk And Honey *are credited to John Lennon and Yoko Ono.* Shaved Fish *and* The John Lennon Collection *are compilations and so have various credits.* Imagine – Music From The Motion Picture *includes tracks by the Beatles. See also Beatles; Yoko Ono.*

## Julian LENNON  *UK, male vocalist*  *16 wks*

| | | | |
|---|---|---|---|
| 3 Nov 84 **VALOTTE**  *Charisma  JLLP  1*  ........................ | **20** | 15 wks |
| 5 Apr 86 **THE SECRET VALUE OF DAYDREAMING**  *Charisma  CAS  1171*  .............................. | **93** | 1 wk |

## Deke LEONARD  *UK, male vocalist/instrumentalist – guitar*  *1 wk*

| | | | |
|---|---|---|---|
| 13 Apr 74 **KAMIKAZE**  *United Artists  UAG  29544*  ................. | **50** | 1 wk |

## Paul LEONI  *UK, male instrumentalist – pan flute*  *19 wks*

| | | | |
|---|---|---|---|
| 24 Sep 83 **FLIGHTS OF FANCY**  *Nouveau Music  NML  1002*  ......... | **17** | 19 wks |

## LEVEL 42  *UK, male vocal/instrumental group*  *210 wks*

| | | | |
|---|---|---|---|
| 29 Aug 81 **LEVEL 42**  *Polydor  POLS  1036*  ........................ | **20** | 18 wks |
| 10 Apr 82 **THE EARLY TAPES JULY–AUGUST 1980**  *Polydor  POLS  1064*  ................................ | **46** | 6 wks |
| 18 Sep 82 **THE PURSUIT OF ACCIDENTS**  *Polydor  POLD  5067*  ... | **17** | 16 wks |
| 3 Sep 83 ● **STANDING IN THE LIGHT**  *Polydor  POLD  5110*  ....... | **9** | 13 wks |
| 13 Oct 84 **TRUE COLOURS**  *Polydor  POLH  10*  ............... | **14** | 8 wks |
| 6 Jul 85 **A PHYSICAL PRESENCE**  *Polydor  POLH  23*  .......... | **28** | 5 wks |
| 26 Oct 85 ● **WORLD MACHINE**  *Polydor  POLH  25*  .............. | **3** | 72 wks |
| 28 Mar 87 ● **RUNNING IN THE FAMILY**  *Polydor  POLH  42*  ......... | **2** | 54 wks |
| 1 Oct 88 ● **STARING AT THE SUN**  *Polydor  POLH  50*  ............ | **2** | 11 wks |
| 18 Nov 89 ● **LEVEL BEST**  *Polydor  LEVTV  1*  ................... | **5†** | 7 wks |

## LEVERT  *UK, male vocal group*                                    *1 wk*

| 29 Aug 87 | **THE BIG THROWDOWN**  *Atlantic 781773–1* .......... | 86 | 1 wk |

## Huey LEWIS and the NEWS
*US, male vocal/instrumental group*                                  *84 wks*

| 14 Sep 85 | **SPORTS**  *Chrysalis CHR 1412* ..................... | 23 | 24 wks |
| 20 Sep 86 | ● **FORE!**  *Chrysalis CDL 1534* ................... | 8 | 52 wks |
| 6 Aug 88 | **SMALL WORLD**  *Chrysalis CDL 1622* ............... | 12 | 8 wks |

## Jerry Lee LEWIS  *US, male vocalist/instrumentalist – piano*      *6 wks*

| 2 Jun 62 | **JERRY LEE LEWIS VOL. 2**  *London HA 2440* .......... | 14 | 6 wks |

## Linda LEWIS  *UK, female vocalist*                                *4 wks*

| 9 Aug 75 | **NOT A LITTLE GIRL ANYMORE**  *Arista ARTY 109* .... | 40 | 4 wks |

## Ramsey LEWIS TRIO
*US, male vocal/instrumental trio*                                   *4 wks*

| 21 May 66 | **HANG ON RAMSEY**  *Chess CRL 4520* ............... | 20 | 4 wks |

## LIGHT OF THE WORLD
*UK, male vocal/instrumental group*                                  *1 wk*

| 24 Jan 81 | **ROUND TRIP**  *Ensign ENVY 14* ..................... | 73 | 1 wk |

## Gordon LIGHTFOOT  *Canada, male vocalist*                         *2 wks*

| 20 May 72 | **DON QUIXOTE**  *Reprise K 44166* ..................... | 44 | 1 wk |
| 17 Aug 74 | **SUNDOWN**  *Reprise K 54020* ....................... | 45 | 1 wk |

## LIL LOUIS  *US, male producer*                                    *5 wks*

| 26 Aug 89 | **FRENCH KISSES**  *FFRR 828170 1* .................. | 35 | 5 wks |

## LIMAHL  *UK, male vocalist*                                       *3 wks*

| 1 Dec 84 | **DON'T SUPPOSE**  *EMI PLML 1* .................... | 63 | 3 wks |

## LINDISFARNE  *UK, male vocal/instrumental group*                  *118 wks*

| 30 Oct 71 | ★ **FOG ON THE TYNE**  *Charisma CAS 1050* ............. | 1 | 56 wks |
| 15 Jan 72 | ● **NICELY OUT OF TUNE**  *Charisma CAS 1025* ........... | 8 | 30 wks |
| 30 Sep 72 | ● **DINGLY DELL**  *Charisma CAS 1057* .................. | 5 | 10 wks |
| 11 Aug 73 | **LINDISFARNE LIVE**  *Charisma CLASS 2* ............. | 25 | 6 wks |
| 18 Oct 75 | **FINEST HOUR**  *Charisma CAS 1108* ................ | 55 | 1 wk |
| 24 Jun 78 | **BACK AND FOURTH**  *Mercury 9109 609* ............. | 22 | 11 wks |
| 9 Dec 78 | **MAGIC IN THE AIR**  *Mercury 6641 877* ............. | 71 | 1 wk |
| 23 Oct 82 | **SLEEPLESS NIGHT**  *LMP GET 1* ................... | 59 | 3 wks |

## LINX  *UK, male vocal/instrumental duo*                           *23 wks*

| 28 Mar 81 | ● **INTUITION**  *Chrysalis CHR 1332* .................. | 8 | 19 wks |
| 31 Oct 81 | **GO AHEAD**  *Chrysalis CHR 1358* ..................... | 35 | 4 wks |

## LIQUID GOLD  *UK, male/female vocal/instrumental group*  *3 wks*

16 Aug 80 **LIQUID GOLD**  *Polo POLP 101* . . . . . . . . . . . . . . . . . . . . . . **34** 3 wks

**LISA** – *See WENDY and LISA*

## LISA LISA and CULT JAM with FULL FORCE
*US, female vocalist with two US, male vocal/instrumental groups*  *1 wk*

21 Sep 85 **LISA LISA AND CULT JAM WITH FULL FORCE**
CBS 26593 . . . . . . . . . . . . . . . . . . . . . . . . . . . . . . . . **96** 1 wk

## LITTLE FEAT  *US, male vocal/instrumental group*  *19 wks*

| | | | |
|---|---|---|---|
| 6 Dec 75 | **THE LAST RECORD ALBUM**  *Warner Bros. K 56156* . . . . . | **36** | 3 wks |
| 21 May 77 | ● **TIME LOVES A HERO**  *Warner Bros. K 56349* . . . . . . . . . . | **8** | 11 wks |
| 11 Mar 78 | **WAITING FOR COLUMBUS**  *Warner Bros. K 66075* . . . . . | **43** | 1 wk |
| 1 Dec 79 | **DOWN ON THE FARM**  *Warner Bros. K 56667* . . . . . . . . . . | **46** | 3 wks |
| 8 Aug 81 | **HOY HOY**  *Warner Bros. K 666100* . . . . . . . . . . . . . . . . . . | **76** | 1 wk |

## LITTLE STEVEN  *US, male vocalist/instrumentalist – guitar*  *4 wks*

6 Nov 82 **MEN WITHOUT WOMEN**  *EMI America 3027* . . . . . . . . . . **73** 2 wks
6 Jun 87 **FREEDOM NO COMPROMISE**  *Manhattan MTL 1010* . . . **52** 2 wks
*First album credited to Little Steven and the Disciples of Soul.*

## LIVING IN A BOX  *UK, male vocal/instrumental group*  *32 wks*

9 May 87 **LIVING IN A BOX**  *Chrysalis CDL 1547* . . . . . . . . . . . . . . . **25** 19 wks
8 Jul 89 **GATECRASHING**  *Chrysalis CDI 1676* . . . . . . . . . . . . . . . **21†** 13 wks

## LL COOL J  *US, male rapper*  *23 wks*

15 Feb 86 **RADIO**  *Def Jam DEF 26745* . . . . . . . . . . . . . . . . . . . . . . . . **71** 1 wk
13 Jun 87 **BIGGER AND DEFFER**  *Def Jam 450 515–1* . . . . . . . . . . . . **54** 19 wks
8 Jul 89 **WALKING WITH A PANTHER**  *Def Jam 465112 1* . . . . . . **43** 3 wks

## Andrew LLOYD WEBBER
*UK, male composer/producer*  *37 wks*

11 Feb 78 ● **VARIATIONS**  *MCA MCF 2824* . . . . . . . . . . . . . . . . . . . . **2** 19 wks
23 Mar 85 ● **REQUIEM**  *HMV ALW 1* . . . . . . . . . . . . . . . . . . . . . . . . . . **4** 18 wks
*Variations features cellist Julian Lloyd Webber. Requiem credits Placido Domingo, Sarah Brightman, Paul Miles-Kingston, Winchester Cathedral Choir and the English Chamber Orchestra conducted by Lorin Maazel.*

## Julian LLOYD WEBBER and the LONDON SYMPHONY ORCHESTRA
*UK, male instrumentalist  – cello with UK, orchestra*  *6 wks*

14 Sep 85 **PIECES**  *Polydor PROLP 6* . . . . . . . . . . . . . . . . . . . . . . . . **59** 5 wks
21 Feb 87 **ELGAR CELLO CONCERTO**  *Philips 416 354–1* . . . . . . . . **94** 1 wk
*See also the London Symphony Orchestra; Andrew Lloyd Webber.*

## Los LOBOS  *US, male vocal/instrumental group*  *9 wks*

6 Apr 85 **HOW WILL THE WOLF SURVIVE?**  *Slash SLMP 3* . . . . **77** 6 wks
7 Feb 87 **BY THE LIGHT OF THE MOON**  *Slash SLAP 13* . . . . . . . . **77** 3 wks

## Tone LOC  *US, male rapper*  **16 wks**

25 Mar 89  **LOC'ED AFTER DARK**  *Delicious BRLP 526* ............  **22**  16 wks

## Josef LOCKE  *Ireland, male vocalist*  **1 wk**

28 Jun 69  **THE WORLD OF JOSEF LOCKE TODAY**  *Decca SPA 21*  **29**  1 wk

## John LODGE  *UK, male vocalist/instrumentalist – guitar*  **2 wks**

19 Feb 77  **NATURAL AVENUE**  *Decca TXS 120* ................  **38**  2 wks
*See also Justin Hayward and John Lodge.*

## Nils LOFGREN  *US, male vocalist/instrumentalist – guitar*  **29 wks**

17 Apr 76 ● **CRY TOUGH**  *A & M AMLH 64573* ..................  **8**  11 wks
26 Mar 77  **I CAME TO DANCE**  *A & M AMLH 64628* ............  **30**  4 wks
5 Nov 77  **NIGHT AFTER NIGHT**  *A & M AMLH 68439* ..........  **38**  2 wks
26 Sep 81  **NIGHT FADES AWAY**  *Backstreet MCF 3121* ..........  **50**  3 wks
1 May 82  **A RHYTHM ROMANCE**  *A & M AMLH 68543* .........  **100**  1 wk
6 Jul 85  **FLIP**  *Towerbell TOWLP 11* .........................  **36**  7 wks
5 Apr 86  **CODE OF THE ROAD**  *Towerbell TOWDLP 17* ..........  **86**  1 wk

## Johnny LOGAN  *Ireland, male vocalist*  **1 wk**

22 Aug 87  **HOLD ME NOW**  *CBS 451 073–1* ...................  **83**  1 wk

## LONDON BOYS  *UK, male vocal duo*  **23 wks**

29 Jul  89 ● **THE TWELVE COMMANDMENTS OF DANCE**
   *WEA WX 278* ...................................  **2†**  23 wks

## LONDON PHILHARMONIC CHOIR  *UK, choir*  **17 wks**

3 Dec 60 ● **THE MESSIAH**  *Pye Golden Guinea GGL 0062* ............  **10**  7 wks
13 Nov 76 ● **SOUND OF GLORY**  *Arcade ADEP 25* ................  **10**  10 wks
*The Messiah credits the London Orchestra conducted by Walter Susskind. Sound Of Glory credits the National Philharmonic Orchestra and conductor John Aldiss.*

## LONDON PHILHARMONIC ORCHESTRA
*UK, orchestra*  **5 wks**

23 Apr 60  **RAVEL'S BOLERO**  *London HAV 2189* ...............  **15**  4 wks
8 Apr 61  **VICTORY AT SEA**  *Pye GGL 0073* ..................  **12**  1 wk
*See also Nigel Kennedy; Ennio Morricone; Justin Hayward, Mike Batt and the London Philharmonic Orchestra.*

## LONDON SYMPHONY ORCHESTRA
*UK, orchestra*  **173 wks**

18 Mar 72  **TOP TV THEMES**  *Studio Two STWO 372* .............  **13**  7 wks
16 Dec 72 ● **THE STRAUSS FAMILY**  *Polydor 2659 014* ............  **2**  21 wks
5 Jul 75  **MUSIC FROM 'EDWARD VII'**  *Polydor 2659 041* .......  **52**  1 wk
21 Jan 78  **STAR WARS (soundtrack)**  *20th Century BTD 541*  **21**  12 wks
8 Jul 78 ● **CLASSIC ROCK**  *K-Tel ONE 1009* ..................  **3**  39 wks
10 Feb 79  **CLASSIC ROCK – THE SECOND MOVEMENT**
   *K-Tel NE 1039* ...............................  **26**  8 wks
5 Jan 80  **RHAPSODY IN BLACK**  *K-Tel ONE 1063* ............  **34**  5 wks
1 Aug 81 ● **CLASSIC ROCK – ROCK CLASSICS**  *K-Tel ONE 1123*  **5**  23 wks
27 Nov 82  **THE BEST OF CLASSIC ROCK**  *K-Tel ONE 1080* ......  **35**  11 wks
27 Aug 83  **ROCK SYMPHONIES**  *K-Tel ONE 1243* .............  **40**  9 wks

| 16 Nov 85 | **THE POWER OF CLASSIC ROCK** *Portrait PRT 10049* .. | 13 | 15 wks |
|---|---|---|---|
| 14 Nov 87 | **CLASSIC ROCK COUNTDOWN** *CBS MOOD 3* ...... | 32 | 16 wks |
| 18 Nov 89 | **CLASSIC ROCK – THE LIVING YEARS** *CBS MOOD 9* | 51 | 6 wks |

The Strauss Family *was conducted by Cyril Ornadel. See also Michael Crawford; Kimera; Julian Lloyd Webber; Cyril Ornadel, all with the London Symphony Orchestra; Spike Milligan.*

## LONDON WELSH MALE VOICE CHOIR
*UK, male choir*        *10 wks*

| 5 Sep 81 | **SONGS OF THE VALLEYS** *K-Tel NE 1117* ........... | 61 | 10 wks |
|---|---|---|---|

## LONE JUSTICE  *US, male/female vocal/instrumental group*   *5 wks*

| 6 Jul 85 | **LONE JUSTICE** *Geffen GEF 26288* ................... | 49 | 2 wks |
|---|---|---|---|
| 8 Nov 86 | **SHELTER** *Geffen WX 73* ......................... | 84 | 3 wks |

## LONE STAR  *UK, male vocal/instrumental group*   *7 wks*

| 2 Oct 76 | **LONE STAR** *Epic EPC 81545* ....................... | 47 | 1 wk |
|---|---|---|---|
| 17 Sep 77 | **FIRING ON ALL SIX** *CBS 82213* .................... | 36 | 6 wks |

## LONG RYDERS  *US, male vocal/instrumental group*   *1 wk*

| 16 Nov 85 | **STATE OF OUR UNION** *Island ILPS 9802* ............. | 66 | 1 wk |
|---|---|---|---|

## Joe LONGTHORNE  *UK, male vocalist – impersonator*   *26 wks*

| 3 Dec 88 | **THE JOE LONGTHORNE SONGBOOK** *Telstar STAR 2353* ............................. | 16 | 12 wks |
|---|---|---|---|
| 29 Jul 89 | **ESPECIALLY FOR YOU** *Telstar STAR 2365* ........... | 22 | 10 wks |
| 9 Dec 89 | **THE JOE LONGTHORNE CHRISTMAS ALBUM** *Telstar STAR 2385* ............................... | 44† | 4 wks |

## LOOP  *UK, male vocal/instrumental group*   *1 wk*

| 4 Feb 89 | **FADE OUT** *Chapter 22 CHAPLP 34* .................. | 51 | 1 wk |
|---|---|---|---|

## LOOSE ENDS  *UK, male/female vocal/instrumental group*   *34 wks*

| 21 Apr 84 | **A LITTLE SPICE** *Virgin V 2301* ..................... | 46 | 9 wks |
|---|---|---|---|
| 20 Apr 85 | **SO WHERE ARE YOU?** *Virgin V 2340* ............... | 13 | 13 wks |
| 18 Oct 86 | **ZAGORA** *Virgin V 2384* ......................... | 15 | 8 wks |
| 2 Jul 88 | **THE REAL CHUCKEEBOO** *Virgin V 2528* ........... | 52 | 4 wks |

## Trini LOPEZ  *US, male vocalist*   *42 wks*

| 26 Oct 63 | ● **TRINI LOPEZ AT P.J.'S** *Reprise R 6093* ............. | 7 | 25 wks |
|---|---|---|---|
| 25 Mar 67 | ● **TRINI LOPEZ IN LONDON** *Reprise RSLP 6238* ........ | 6 | 17 wks |

## Jeff LORBER  *US, male vocalist/instrumentalist – keyboards*   *2 wks*

| 18 May 85 | **STEP BY STEP** *Club JABH 9* ...................... | 97 | 2 wks |
|---|---|---|---|

**Sophia LOREN** – *See Peter SELLERS and Sophia LOREN*

## Joe LOSS  *UK, orchestra*   *10 wks*

| 30 Oct 71 | **ALL-TIME PARTY HITS** *MFP 5227* .................. | 24 | 10 wks |
|---|---|---|---|

*See also the George Mitchell Minstrels.*

## LOTUS EATERS  *UK, male vocal/instrumental group*       *1 wk*

| 16 Jun 84 | **NO SENSE OF SIN** *Sylvan 206 263* .................. | 96 | 1 wk |

## Jacques LOUSSIER  *France, male instrumentalist – piano*       *3 wks*

| 30 Mar 85 | **THE BEST OF PLAY BACH** *Start STL 1* ............. | 58 | 3 wks |

## LOVE  *US, male vocal/instrumental group*       *8 wks*

| 24 Feb 68 | **FOREVER CHANGES** *Elektra EKS7 4013* ............. | 24 | 6 wks |
| 16 May 70 | **OUT HERE** *Harvest Show 3/4* ........................ | 29 | 2 wks |

## Geoff LOVE  *UK, orchestra*       *28 wks*

| 7 Aug 71 | **BIG WAR MOVIE THEMES** *MFP 5171* ............... | 11 | 20 wks |
| 21 Aug 71 | **BIG WESTERN MOVIE THEMES** *MFP 5204* .......... | 38 | 3 wks |
| 30 Oct 71 | **BIG LOVE MOVIE THEMES** *MFP 5221* .............. | 28 | 5 wks |

*See also Manuel and his Music of the Mountains.*

## LOVE AND MONEY  *UK, male vocal/instrumental group*       *1 wk*

| 29 Oct 88 | **STRANGE KIND OF LOVE** *Fontana SFLP 7* .......... | 71 | 1 wk |

## Lene LOVICH  *US, female vocalist*       *17 wks*

| 17 Mar 79 | **STATELESS** *Stiff SEEZ 7* ........................ | 35 | 11 wks |
| 2 Feb 80 | **FLEX** *Stiff SEEZ 19* ............................ | 19 | 6 wks |

## LOVIN' SPOONFUL
*US/Canada, male vocal/instrumental group*       *11 wks*

| 7 May 66 | ● **DAYDREAM** *Pye NPL 28078* ...................... | 8 | 11 wks |

## Nick LOWE  *UK, male vocalist*       *17 wks*

| 11 Mar 78 | **THE JESUS OF COOL** *Radar RAD 1* ................. | 22 | 9 wks |
| 23 Jun 79 | **LABOUR OF LUST** *Radar RAD 21* .................. | 43 | 6 wks |
| 20 Feb 82 | **NICK THE KNIFE** *F.Beat XXLP 14* ................. | 99 | 2 wks |

## LULU  *UK, female vocalist*       *6 wks*

| 25 Sep 71 | **THE MOST OF LULU** *MFP 5215* ................... | 15 | 6 wks |

## Bob LUMAN  *US, male vocalist*       *1 wk*

| 14 Jan 61 | **LET'S THINK ABOUT LIVING** *Warner Bros. WM 4025* .. | 18 | 1 wk |

## LURKERS  *UK, male vocal/instrumental group*       *1 wk*

| 1 Jul 78 | **FULHAM FALLOUT** *Beggars Banquet BEGA 2* ......... | 57 | 1 wk |

**LYLE** – *See GALLAGHER and LYLE*

## Vera LYNN  *UK, female vocalist*  *15 wks*

| 21 Nov 81 | **20 FAMILY FAVOURITES**  *EMI EMTV 28*  . . . . . . . . . . . | **25** | 12 wks |
| 9 Sep 89 | **WE'LL MEET AGAIN**  *Telstar STAR 2369*  . . . . . . . . . . . . . | **44** | 3 wks |

## Philip LYNOTT  *Ireland, male vocalist*  *6 wks*

| 26 Apr 80 | **SOLO IN SOHO**  *Vertigo 9102 038*  . . . . . . . . . . . . . . . . . . . . | **28** | 6 wks |

*See also Phil Lynott and Thin Lizzy.*

## Phil LYNOTT and THIN LIZZY
*Ireland/UK/US, male vocal/instrumental group*  *10 wks*

| 14 Nov 87 | **SOLDIER OF FORTUNE – THE BEST OF PHIL LYNOTT AND THIN LIZZY**  *Telstar STAR 2300*  . . . . . . . . . . . . . | **55** | 10 wks |

*See also Phil Lynott and Thin Lizzy.*

## LYNYRD SKYNYRD  *US, male vocal/instrumental group*  *19 wks*

| 3 May 75 | **NUTHIN' FANCY**  *MCA MCF 2700*  . . . . . . . . . . . . . . . . . | **43** | 1 wk |
| 28 Feb 76 | **GIMME BACK MY BULLETS**  *MCA MCF 2744*  . . . . . . . . | **34** | 5 wks |
| 6 Nov 76 | **ONE MORE FOR THE ROAD**  *MCA MCPS 279*  . . . . . . . | **17** | 4 wks |
| 12 Nov 77 | **STREET SURVIVORS**  *MCA MCG 3525*  . . . . . . . . . . . . | **13** | 4 wks |
| 4 Nov 78 | **SKYNYRD'S FIRST AND LAST**  *MCA MCG 3529*  . . . . . | **50** | 1 wk |
| 9 Feb 80 | **GOLD AND PLATINUM**  *MCA MCSP 308*  . . . . . . . . . . . . | **49** | 4 wks |

# m

**Lorin MAAZEL** – *See Andrew LLOYD WEBBER*

## MAC BAND featuring the McCAMPBELL BROTHERS  *US, male vocal group*  *3 wks*

| 20 Aug 88 | **THE MAC BAND**  *MCA MCG 6032*  . . . . . . . . . . . . . . . . . . | **61** | 3 wks |

## Frankie McBRIDE  *Ireland, male vocalist*  *3 wks*

| 17 Feb 68 | **FRANKIE McBRIDE**  *Emerald SLD 28*  . . . . . . . . . . . . . . . | **29** | 3 wks |

## MACC LADS  *UK, male vocal/instrumental group*  *1 wk*

| 7 Oct 89 | **FROM BEER TO ETERNITY**  *Hectic House HHLP 12*  . . . . | **72** | 1 wk |

**McCAMPBELL BROTHERS** – *See MAC BAND featuring the McCAMPBELL BROTHERS*

## Paul McCARTNEY  *UK, male vocalist/multi-instrumentalist*  *497 wks*

| 2 May 70 | ● **McCARTNEY**  *Apple PCS 7102*  . . . . . . . . . . . . . . . . . . . . . . | **2** | 32 wks |
| 5 Jun 71 | ★ **RAM**  *Apple PAS 10003*  . . . . . . . . . . . . . . . . . . . . . . . . . . . . . | **1** | 24 wks |
| 18 Dec 71 | **WILD LIFE**  *Apple PCS 7142*  . . . . . . . . . . . . . . . . . . . . . . . . . | **11** | 9 wks |
| 19 May 73 | ● **RED ROSE SPEEDWAY**  *Apple PCTC 251*  . . . . . . . . . . . . | **5** | 16 wks |
| 15 Dec 73 | ★ **BAND ON THE RUN**  *Apple PAS 10007*  . . . . . . . . . . . . . | **1** | 124 wks |
| 21 Jun 75 | ★ **VENUS AND MARS**  *Apple PCTC 254*  . . . . . . . . . . . . . . | **1** | 29 wks |
| 17 Apr 76 | ● **WINGS AT THE SPEED OF SOUND**  *Apple PAS 10010* . . | **2** | 35 wks |
| 15 Jan 77 | ● **WINGS OVER AMERICA**  *Parlophone PAS 720*  . . . . . . . . | **8** | 22 wks |
| 15 Apr 78 | ● **LONDON TOWN**  *Parlophone PAS 10012*  . . . . . . . . . . . . | **4** | 23 wks |
| 16 Dec 78 | ● **WINGS GREATEST HITS**  *Parlophone PCTC 256*  . . . . . . | **5** | 32 wks |
| 23 Jun 79 | ● **BACK TO THE EGG**  *Parlophone PCTC 257*  . . . . . . . . . . . | **6** | 15 wks |

| | | |
|---|---|---|
| 31 May 80 ★ **McCARTNEY II** *Parlophone PCTC 258* ................ | **1** | 18 wks |
| 7 Mar 81 **McCARTNEY INTERVIEW** *EMI CHAT 1* ........... | **34** | 4 wks |
| 8 May 82 ★ **TUG OF WAR** *Parlophone PCTC 259* .................. | **1** | 27 wks |
| 12 Nov 83 ● **PIPES OF PEACE** *Parlophone PCTC 1652301* ........... | **4** | 23 wks |
| 3 Nov 84 ★ **GIVE MY REGARDS TO BROAD STREET** | | |
| *Parlophone PCTC 2* ................................ | **1** | 21 wks |
| 13 Sep 86 ● **PRESS TO PLAY** *Parlophone PCSD 103* ................ | **8** | 6 wks |
| 14 Nov 87 ● **ALL THE BEST!** *Parlophone PMTV 1* .................. | **2** | 21 wks |
| 17 Jun 89 ★ **FLOWERS IN THE DIRT** *Parlophone PCSD 106* ........ | **1** | 16 wks |

Ram *credited to Paul and Linda McCartney.* Red Rose Speedway *and* Band On The Run *credited to Paul McCartney and Wings.* Wild Life *and the five albums from* Venus and Mars *to* Wings Greatest Hits *inclusive credited to Wings. All other albums credited to Paul McCartney.*

## Kirsty MacCOLL  *UK, female vocalist*  **12 wks**

| | | |
|---|---|---|
| 20 May 89 **KITE** *Virgin KMLP 1* ............................. | **34** | 12 wks |

## Van McCOY and the SOUL CITY SYMPHONY
*US, orchestra*  **11 wks**

| | | |
|---|---|---|
| 5 Jul 75 **DISCO BABY** *Avco 9109 004* ...................... | **32** | 11 wks |

## George McCRAE  *US, male vocalist*  **29 wks**

| | | |
|---|---|---|
| 3 Aug 74 **ROCK YOUR BABY** *Jayboy JSL 3* ................... | **13** | 28 wks |
| 13 Sep 75 **GEORGE McCRAE** *Jayboy JSL 10* .................. | **54** | 1 wk |

## Ian McCULLOCH  *UK, male vocalist*  **3 wks**

| | | |
|---|---|---|
| 7 Oct 89 **CANDLELAND** *WEA WX 303* ..................... | **18** | 3 wks |

## Michael McDONALD  *US, male vocalist*  **35 wks**

| | | |
|---|---|---|
| 22 Nov 86 ● **SWEET FREEDOM: BEST OF MICHAEL McDONALD** | | |
| *Warner Bros. WX 67* ............................. | **6** | 35 wks |

## Bobby McFERRIN  *US, male vocalist*  **1 wk**

| | | |
|---|---|---|
| 29 Oct 88 **SIMPLE PLEASURES** *Manhattan MTL 1018* ........... | **92** | 1 wk |

## Kate and Anna McGARRIGLE
*Canada, female vocal duo*  **4 wks**

| | | |
|---|---|---|
| 26 Feb 77 **DANCER WITH BRUISED KNEES** | | |
| *Warner Bros. K 56356* .......................... | **35** | 4 wks |

## Mary MacGREGOR  *US, female vocalist*  **1 wk**

| | | |
|---|---|---|
| 23 Apr 77 **TORN BETWEEN TWO LOVERS** | | |
| *Ariola America AAS 1504* ...................... | **59** | 1 wk |

## McGUINNESS FLINT  *UK, male vocal/instrumental group*  **10 wks**

| | | |
|---|---|---|
| 23 Jan 71 ● **McGUINNESS FLINT** *Capitol EA-ST 22625* ........... | **9** | 10 wks |

## Maria McKEE  *US, female vocalist*  **3 wks**

| | | |
|---|---|---|
| 24 Jun 89 **MARIA McKEE** *Geffen WX 270* ...................... | **49** | 3 wks |

## Kenneth McKELLAR  *UK, male vocalist*  *10 wks*

| | | | | | |
|---|---|---|---|---|---|
| 28 Jun 69 | THE WORLD OF KENNETH McKELLAR | *Decca SPA 11* | | 27 | 7 wks |
| 31 Jan 70 | ECCO DI NAPOLI  *Decca SKL 5018* | | | 45 | 3 wks |

## Malcolm McLAREN  *UK, male vocalist*  *40 wks*

| | | | | | |
|---|---|---|---|---|---|
| 4 Jun 83 | DUCK ROCK  *Charisma MMLP 1* | | | 18 | 17 wks |
| 26 May 84 | WOULD YA LIKE MORE SCRATCHIN'  *Charisma CLAM 1* | | | 44 | 4 wks |
| 29 Dec 84 | FANS  *Charisma MMDL 2* | | | 47 | 8 wks |
| 15 Jul 89 | WALTZ DANCING  *Epic 460736 1* | | | 30 | 11 wks |

*Would Ya Like More Scratchin' is credited to Malcolm McLaren and the World's Famous Supreme Team Show. Waltz Dancing credits the Bootzilla Orchestra.*

## Don McLEAN  *US, male vocalist*  *89 wks*

| | | | | | |
|---|---|---|---|---|---|
| 11 Mar 72 | ● AMERICAN PIE  *United Artists UAS 29285* | | | 3 | 54 wks |
| 17 Jun 72 | TAPESTRY  *United Artists UAS 29350* | | | 16 | 12 wks |
| 24 Nov 73 | PLAYIN' FAVORITES  *United Artists UAG 29528* | | | 42 | 2 wks |
| 14 Jun 80 | CHAIN LIGHTNING  *EMI International INS 3025* | | | 19 | 9 wks |
| 27 Sep 80 | ● THE VERY BEST OF DON McLEAN  *United Artists UAG 30314* | | | 4 | 12 wks |

## Ralph McTELL  *UK, male vocalist*  *17 wks*

| | | | | | |
|---|---|---|---|---|---|
| 18 Nov 72 | NOT TILL TOMORROW  *Reprise K 44210* | | | 36 | 1 wk |
| 2 Mar 74 | EASY  *Reprise K 54013* | | | 31 | 4 wks |
| 15 Feb 75 | STREETS  *Warner Bros. K 56105* | | | 13 | 12 wks |

## Christine McVIE  *UK, female vocalist*  *4 wks*

| | | | | | |
|---|---|---|---|---|---|
| 11 Feb 84 | CHRISTINE McVIE  *Warner Bros. 92 5059* | | | 58 | 4 wks |

## David McWILLIAMS  *UK, male vocalist*  *9 wks*

| | | | | | |
|---|---|---|---|---|---|
| 10 Jun 67 | DAVID McWILLIAMS SINGS  *Major Minor MMLP 2* | | | 38 | 2 wks |
| 4 Nov 67 | DAVID McWILLIAMS VOL. 2  *Major Minor MMLP 10* | | | 23 | 6 wks |
| 9 Mar 68 | DAVID McWILLIAMS VOL. 3  *Major Minor MMLP 11* | | | 39 | 1 wk |

## MADNESS  *UK, male vocal/instrumental group*  *300 wks*

| | | | | | |
|---|---|---|---|---|---|
| 3 Nov 79 | ● ONE STEP BEYOND  *Stiff SEEZ 17* | | | 2 | 78 wks |
| 4 Oct 80 | ● ABSOLUTELY  *Stiff SEEZ 29* | | | 2 | 46 wks |
| 10 Oct 81 | ● MADNESS 7  *Stiff SEEZ 39* | | | 5 | 29 wks |
| 1 May 82 | ★ COMPLETE MADNESS  *Stiff HIT-TV 1* | | | 1 | 88 wks |
| 13 Nov 82 | ● THE RISE AND FALL  *Stiff SEEZ 46* | | | 10 | 22 wks |
| 3 Mar 84 | ● KEEP MOVING  *Stiff SEEZ 53* | | | 6 | 19 wks |
| 12 Oct 85 | MAD NOT MAD  *Zarjazz JZLP 1* | | | 16 | 9 wks |
| 6 Dec 86 | UTTER MADNESS  *Zarjazz JZLP 2* | | | 29 | 8 wks |
| 7 May 88 | THE MADNESS  *Virgin V 2507* | | | 65 | 1 wk |

## MADONNA  *US, female vocalist*  *409 wks*

| | | | | | |
|---|---|---|---|---|---|
| 11 Feb 84 | ● MADONNA/THE FIRST ALBUM  *Sire 923867* | | | 6 | 123 wks |
| 24 Nov 84 | ★ LIKE A VIRGIN  *Sire 925157* | | | 1 | 151 wks |
| 12 Jul 86 | ★ TRUE BLUE  *Sire WX 54* | | | 1 | 81 wks |
| 28 Nov 87 | ● YOU CAN DANCE  *Sire WX 76* | | | 5 | 14 wks |
| 1 Apr 89 | ★ LIKE A PRAYER  *Sire WX 239* | | | 1† | 40 wks |

*From 22 Aug 85 Madonna was repackaged and was available as The First Album SIRE WX 22. Like A Virgin changed label number during its chart run to SIRE WX 20.*

## MAGAZINE   UK, male vocal/instrumental group

24 wks

| | | | | |
|---|---|---|---|---|
| 24 Jun 78 | **REAL LIFE**   *Virgin V 2100* | | 29 | 8 wks |
| 14 Apr 79 | **SECONDHAND DAYLIGHT**   *Virgin V 2121* | | 38 | 8 wks |
| 10 May 80 | **CORRECT USE OF SOAP**   *Virgin V 2156* | | 28 | 4 wks |
| 13 Dec 80 | **PLAY**   *Virgin V 2184* | | 69 | 1 wk |
| 27 Jun 81 | **MAGIC, MURDER AND THE WEATHER** *Virgin V 2200* | | 39 | 3 wks |

**MAGIC BAND** – *See CAPTAIN BEEFHEART and his MAGIC BAND*

## MAGNA CARTA   UK, male vocal/instrumental group

2 wks

| | | | | |
|---|---|---|---|---|
| 8 Aug 70 | **SEASONS**   *Vertigo 6360 003* | | 55 | 2 wks |

## MAGNUM   UK, male vocal/instrumental group

38 wks

| | | | | |
|---|---|---|---|---|
| 16 Sep 78 | **KINGDOM OF MADNESS**   *Jet JETLP 210* | | 58 | 1 wk |
| 19 Apr 80 | **MARAUDER**   *Jet JETLP 230* | | 34 | 5 wks |
| 6 Mar 82 | **CHASE THE DRAGON**   *Jet JETLP 235* | | 17 | 7 wks |
| 21 May 83 | **THE ELEVENTH HOUR**   *Jet JETLP 240* | | 38 | 4 wks |
| 25 May 85 | **ON A STORYTELLER'S NIGHT**   *FM WKFM LP 34* | | 24 | 7 wks |
| 4 Oct 86 | **VIGILANTE**   *Polydor POLD 5198* | | 24 | 5 wks |
| 9 Apr 88 | ● **WINGS OF HEAVEN**   *Polydor POLD 5221* | | 5 | 9 wks |

## MAHAVISHNU ORCHESTRA
*UK/US, male instrumental group*

5 wks

| | | | | |
|---|---|---|---|---|
| 31 Mar 73 | **BIRDS OF FIRE**   *CBS 65321* | | 20 | 5 wks |

*See also Carlos Santana and Mahavishnu John McLaughlin.*

## MAI TAI   Holland, female vocal group

1 wk

| | | | | |
|---|---|---|---|---|
| 6 Jul 85 | **HISTORY**   *Virgin V 2359* | | 91 | 1 wk |

## MAJESTICS   UK, male/female vocal group

4 wks

| | | | | |
|---|---|---|---|---|
| 4 Apr 87 | **TUTTI FRUTTI**   *BBC REN 629* | | 64 | 4 wks |

**Tommy MAKEM** – *See CLANCY BROTHERS and Tommy MAKEM*

## Yngwie J. MALMSTEEN
*Sweden, male instrumentalist – guitar*

8 wks

| | | | | |
|---|---|---|---|---|
| 21 May 88 | **ODYSSEY**   *Polydor POLD 5224* | | 27 | 7 wks |
| 4 Nov 89 | **TRIAL BY FIRE – LIVE IN LENINGRAD** *Polydor 839726 1* | | 65 | 1 wk |

## MAMA'S BOYS   Ireland, male vocal/instrumental group

4 wks

| | | | | |
|---|---|---|---|---|
| 6 Apr 85 | **POWER AND PASSION**   *Jive HIP 24* | | 55 | 4 wks |

## MAMAS and PAPAS   US, male/female vocal group

61 wks

| | | | | |
|---|---|---|---|---|
| 25 Jun 66 | ● **THE MAMAS AND PAPAS**   *RCA Victor RD 7803* | | 3 | 18 wks |
| 28 Jan 67 | **CASS, JOHN, MICHELLE, DENNY** *RCA Victor SF 7639* | | 24 | 6 wks |
| 24 Jun 67 | ● **MAMAS AND PAPAS DELIVER**   *RCA Victor SF 7880* | | 4 | 22 wks |
| 26 Apr 69 | ● **HITS OF GOLD**   *Stateside S 5007* | | 7 | 2 wks |
| 18 Jun 77 | ● **THE BEST OF THE MAMAS AND PAPAS** *Arcade ADEP 30* | | 6 | 13 wks |

**MAMBAS** – See MARC and the MAMBAS

## MAN  UK, male vocal/instrumental group
11 wks

| | | | | |
|---|---|---|---|---|
| 20 Oct 73 | **BACK INTO THE FUTURE**  United Artists UAD 60053/4 .. | 23 | 3 wks |
| 25 May 74 | **RHINOS WINOS AND LUNATICS**  United Artists UAG 29631 ............................ | 24 | 4 wks |
| 11 Oct 75 | **MAXIMUM DARKNESS**  United Artists UAG 29872 ...... | 25 | 2 wks |
| 17 Apr 76 | **WELSH CONNECTION**  MCA MCF 2753 ............ | 40 | 2 wks |

## MANCHESTER BOYS CHOIR  UK, male choir
2 wks

| | | | |
|---|---|---|---|
| 21 Dec 85 | **THE NEW SOUND OF CHRISTMAS**  K-Tel ONE 1314 . | 80 | 2 wks |

## Henry MANCINI  US, orchestra/chorus
8 wks

| | | | |
|---|---|---|---|
| 16 Oct 76 | **HENRY MANCINI**  Arcade ADEP 24 ................. | 26 | 8 wks |

See also James Galway and Henry Mancini; Johnny Mathis and Henry Mancini; Luciano Pavarotti with the Henry Mancini Orchestra.

## MANFRED MANN
### South Africa/UK, male vocal/instrumental group
72 wks

| | | | |
|---|---|---|---|
| 19 Sep 64 ● | **FIVE FACES OF MANFRED MANN**  HMV CLP 1731 ... | 3 | 24 wks |
| 23 Oct 65 ● | **MANN MADE**  HMV CLP 1911 ................. | 7 | 11 wks |
| 17 Sep 66 | **MANN MADE HITS**  HMV CLP 3559 ............... | 11 | 18 wks |
| 29 Oct 66 | **AS IS**  Fontana TL 5377 ...................... | 22 | 4 wks |
| 21 Jan 67 | **SOUL OF MANN**  HMV CSD 3594 ............... | 40 | 1 wk |
| 15 Sep 79 ● | **SEMI-DETACHED SUBURBAN**  EMI EMTV 19 ....... | 9 | 14 wks |

See also Manfred Mann's Earth Band.

## MANHATTAN TRANSFER
### US, male/female vocal group
85 wks

| | | | |
|---|---|---|---|
| 12 Mar 77 | **COMING OUT**  Atlantic K 50291 .................... | 12 | 20 wks |
| 19 Mar 77 | **MANHATTAN TRANSFER**  Atlantic K 50138 .......... | 49 | 7 wks |
| 25 Feb 78 ● | **PASTICHE**  Atlantic K 50444 ........................ | 10 | 34 wks |
| 11 Nov 78 ● | **LIVE**  Atlantic K 50540 ......................... | 4 | 17 wks |
| 17 Nov 79 | **EXTENSIONS**  Atlantic K 50674 ................... | 63 | 3 wks |
| 18 Feb 84 | **BODIES AND SOULS**  Atlantic 780104 ............... | 53 | 4 wks |

## MANHATTANS  US, male vocal group
3 wks

| | | | |
|---|---|---|---|
| 14 Aug 76 | **MANHATTANS**  CBS 81513 ...................... | 37 | 3 wks |

## Barry MANILOW  US, male vocalist
308 wks

| | | | |
|---|---|---|---|
| 23 Sep 78 | **EVEN NOW**  Arista SPART 1047  .................... | 12 | 28 wks |
| 3 Mar 79 ● | **MANILOW MAGIC**  Arista ARTV 2 .................. | 3 | 151 wks |
| 20 Oct 79 | **ONE VOICE**  Arista SPART 1106 .................. | 18 | 7 wks |
| 29 Nov 80 ● | **BARRY**  Arista DLART 2 ....................... | 5 | 34 wks |
| 25 Apr 81 | **GIFT SET**  Arista BOX 1 ...................... | 62 | 1 wk |
| 3 Oct 81 ● | **IF I SHOULD LOVE AGAIN**  Arista BMAN 1 ........... | 5 | 26 wks |
| 1 May 82 ★ | **BARRY LIVE IN BRITAIN**  Arista ARTV 4 .......... | 1 | 23 wks |
| 27 Nov 82 ● | **I WANNA DO IT WITH YOU**  Arista BMAN 2 ......... | 7 | 9 wks |
| 8 Oct 83 ● | **A TOUCH MORE MAGIC**  Arista BMAN 3 ............ | 10 | 12 wks |
| 1 Dec 84 | **2.00 AM PARADISE CAFE**  Arista 206 496 ............. | 28 | 6 wks |
| 16 Nov 85 | **MANILOW**  RCA PL 87044 ....................... | 40 | 6 wks |
| 20 Feb 88 | **SWING STREET**  Arista 208860 .................... | 81 | 1 wk |
| 20 May 89 | **SONGS TO MAKE THE WHOLE WORLD SING**  Arista 209927 ................................... | 20 | 4 wks |

## Roberto MANN  *UK, male orchestra leader*                 *9 wks*

| | | | | |
|---|---|---|---|---|
| 9 Dec 67 | **GREAT WALTZES**  *Deram SML 1010* ................. | 19 | 9 wks |

## Shelley MANNE  *US, male instrumentalist – drums*        *1 wk*

| | | | | |
|---|---|---|---|---|
| 18 Jun 60 | **MY FAIR LADY**  *Vogue LAC 12100* ................... | 20 | 1 wk |

## Manfred MANN'S EARTH BAND
*South Africa/UK, male vocal/instrumental group*             *24 wks*

| | | | | |
|---|---|---|---|---|
| 18 Sep 76 | ● **THE ROARING SILENCE**  *Bronze ILPS 9357* .......... | 10 | 9 wks |
| 17 Jun 78 | **WATCH**  *Bronze BRON 507* ...................... | 33 | 6 wks |
| 24 Mar 79 | **ANGEL STATION**  *Bronze BRON 516* ................ | 30 | 8 wks |
| 26 Feb 83 | **SOMEWHERE IN AFRIKA**  *Bronze BRON 543* ......... | 87 | 1 wk |

*See also Manfred Mann.*

## MANOWAR  *US, male vocal/instrumental group*             *3 wks*

| | | | | |
|---|---|---|---|---|
| 18 Feb 84 | **HAIL TO ENGLAND**  *Music For Nations MFN 19* ......... | 83 | 2 wks |
| 6 Oct 84 | **SIGN OF THE HAMMER**  *10 DIX 10* ................ | 73 | 1 wk |

## MANTOVANI  *UK, orchestra*                               *151 wks*

| | | | | |
|---|---|---|---|---|
| 21 Feb 59 | ● **CONTINENTAL ENCORES**  *Decca LK 4298* ........... | 4 | 12 wks |
| 18 Feb 61 | **CONCERT SPECTACULAR**  *Decca LK 4377* ........... | 16 | 2 wks |
| 16 Apr 66 | ● **MANTOVANI MAGIC**  *Decca LK 7949* ............... | 3 | 15 wks |
| 15 Oct 66 | **MR MUSIC – MANTOVANI**  *Decca LK 4809* ......... | 24 | 3 wks |
| 14 Jan 67 | ● **MANTOVANI'S GOLDEN HITS**  *Decca SKL 4818* ...... | 10 | 43 wks |
| 30 Sep 67 | **HOLLYWOOD**  *Decca SKL 4887* ................... | 37 | 1 wk |
| 14 Jun 69 | ● **THE WORLD OF MANTOVANI**  *Decca SPA 1* ...... | 6 | 31 wks |
| 4 Oct 69 | ● **THE WORLD OF MANTOVANI VOL. 2**  *Decca SPA 36* .. | 4 | 19 wks |
| 16 May 70 | **MANTOVANI TODAY**  *Decca SKL 5003* .............. | 16 | 8 wks |
| 26 Feb 72 | **TO LOVERS EVERYWHERE**  *Decca SKL 5112* ........ | 44 | 1 wk |
| 3 Nov 79 | ● **20 GOLDEN GREATS**  *Warwick WW 5067* ............ | 9 | 13 wks |
| 16 Mar 85 | **MANTOVANI MAGIC**  *Telstar STAR 2237* ............ | 52 | 3 wks |

*Mantovani Magic on Telstar conducted by Roland Shaw.*

## MANTRONIX  *Jamaica/US, male vocal/instrumental duo*     *9 wks*

| | | | | |
|---|---|---|---|---|
| 29 Mar 86 | **THE ALBUM**  *10 DIX 37* ........................... | 45 | 3 wks |
| 13 Dec 86 | **MUSICAL MADNESS**  *10 DIX 50* ................... | 66 | 3 wks |
| 2 Apr 88 | **IN FULL EFFECT**  *10 DIX 74* ...................... | 39 | 3 wks |

## MANUEL and his MUSIC OF THE MOUNTAINS
*UK, orchestra, leader Geoff Love*                          *38 wks*

| | | | | |
|---|---|---|---|---|
| 10 Sep 60 | **MUSIC OF THE MOUNTAINS**  *Columbia 33SX 1212* ..... | 17 | 1 wk |
| 7 Aug 71 | **THIS IS MANUEL**  *Studio Two STWO 5* ............... | 18 | 19 wks |
| 31 Jan 76 | ● **CARNIVAL**  *Studio Two TWO 337* ................... | 3 | 18 wks |

*See also Geoff Love.*

## Phil MANZANERA  *UK, male vocalist/instrumentalist – guitar*   *1 wk*

| | | | | |
|---|---|---|---|---|
| 24 May 75 | **DIAMOND HEAD**  *Island ILPS 9315* ................ | 40 | 1 wk |

## MARC and the MAMBAS
*UK, male/female vocal/instrumental group*                  *9 wks*

| | | | | |
|---|---|---|---|---|
| 16 Oct 82 | **UNTITLED**  *Some Bizzare BZA 13* ................... | 42 | 4 wks |
| 20 Aug 83 | **TORMENT AND TOREROS**  *Some Bizzare BIZL 4* ...... | 28 | 5 wks |

*See also Marc Almond.*

## MARILLION  *UK, male vocal/instrumental group*  144 wks

| | | | | | | |
|---|---|---|---|---|---|---|
| 26 Mar | 83 ● | SCRIPT FOR A JESTER'S TEAR | *EMI EMC 3429* | ...... | 7 | 31 wks |
| 24 Mar | 84 ● | FUGAZI | *EMI EMC 2400851* | ..................... | 5 | 20 wks |
| 17 Nov | 84 ● | REAL TO REEL | *EMI JEST 1* | ..................... | 8 | 21 wks |
| 29 Jun | 85 ★ | MISPLACED CHILDHOOD | *EMI MRL 2* | ........... | 1 | 41 wks |
| 4 Jul | 87 ● | CLUTCHING AT STRAWS | *EMI EMD 1002* | .......... | 2 | 15 wks |
| 23 Jul | 88 | B SIDES THEMSELVES | *EMI EMS 1295* | ............ | 64 | 6 wks |
| 10 Dec | 88 | THE THIEVING MAGPIE | *EMI MARIL 1* | ........... | 25 | 6 wks |
| 7 Oct | 89 ● | SEASON'S END | *EMI EMD 1011* | ................ | 7 | 4 wks |

## Yannis MARKOPOULOS  *Greece, orchestra*  8 wks

| | | | | | | |
|---|---|---|---|---|---|---|
| 26 Aug | 78 | WHO PAYS THE FERRYMAN | *BBC REB 315* | ........ | 22 | 8 wks |

## Bob MARLEY and the WAILERS
*Jamaica, male vocal/instrumental group*  271 wks

| | | | | | | |
|---|---|---|---|---|---|---|
| 4 Oct | 75 | NATTY DREAD | *Island ILPS 9281* | ................ | 43 | 5 wks |
| 20 Dec | 75 | LIVE | *Island ILPS 9376* | ........................ | 38 | 11 wks |
| 8 May | 76 | RASTAMAN VIBRATION | *Island ILPS 9383* | ....... | 15 | 13 wks |
| 11 Jun | 77 ● | EXODUS | *Island ILPS 9498* | .................... | 8 | 56 wks |
| 1 Apr | 78 ● | KAYA | *Island ILPS 9517* | ...................... | 4 | 24 wks |
| 16 Dec | 78 | BABYLON BY BUS | *Island ISLD 11* | .............. | 40 | 11 wks |
| 13 Oct | 79 | SURVIVAL | *Island ILPS 9542* | ................... | 20 | 6 wks |
| 28 Jun | 80 ● | UPRISING | *Island ILPS 9596* | ................... | 6 | 17 wks |
| 28 May | 83 ● | CONFRONTATION | *Island ILPS 9760* | ........... | 5 | 19 wks |
| 19 May | 84 ★ | LEGEND | *Island BMW 1* | ..................... | 1 | 106 wks |
| 28 Jul | 86 | REBEL MUSIC | *Island ILPS 9843* | ................ | 54 | 3 wks |

Live *Island ILPS 9376 returned to the chart in 1981 under the title* Live At The Lyceum.

## Neville MARRINER and the ACADEMY OF ST MARTIN IN THE FIELDS
*UK, male conductor with chamber orchestra*  6 wks

| | | | | | |
|---|---|---|---|---|---|
| 6 Apr | 85 | AMADEUS – ORIGINAL SOUNDTRACK *London LONDP 6* | ................................ | 64 | 6 wks |

## Bernie MARSDEN  *UK, male vocalist/instrumentalist – guitar*  2 wks

| | | | | | | |
|---|---|---|---|---|---|---|
| 5 Sep | 81 | LOOK AT ME NOW | *Parlophone PCF 7217* | ............ | 71 | 2 wks |

## Lena MARTELL  *UK, female vocalist*  71 wks

| | | | | | |
|---|---|---|---|---|---|
| 25 May | 74 | THAT WONDERFUL SOUND OF LENA MARTELL *Pye SPL 18427* | ...................................... | 35 | 2 wks |
| 8 Jan | 77 | THE BEST OF LENA MARTELL *Pye NSPL 18506* | ...... | 13 | 16 wks |
| 27 May | 78 | THE LENA MARTELL COLLECTION *Ronco RTL 2028* | . | 12 | 19 wks |
| 20 Oct | 79 ● | LENA'S MUSIC ALBUM *Pye N 123* | .................... | 5 | 18 wks |
| 19 Apr | 80 ● | BY REQUEST *Ronco RTL 2046* | .................... | 9 | 9 wks |
| 29 Nov | 80 | BEAUTIFUL SUNDAY *Ronco RTL 2052* | ............. | 23 | 7 wks |

## MARTHA and the MUFFINS
*Canada, male/female vocal/instrumental group*  6 wks

| | | | | | |
|---|---|---|---|---|---|
| 15 Mar | 80 | METRO MUSIC | *DinDisc DID 1* | ................... | 34 | 6 wks |

## MARTIKA  *US, female vocalist*  16 wks

| | | | | | |
|---|---|---|---|---|---|
| 16 Sep | 89 | MARTIKA | *CBS 463355 1* | ........................ | 24† | 16 wks |

the late 70s **LENA MARTELL** took one year at a time.

**MICHAEL McDONALD** is shown with his wife at the 1988 ASCAP Awards in Los Angeles.

**GLENN MILLER**, shown leading his band, has had more hit albums than any other artist who died before the chart began.

## Dean MARTIN  *US, male vocalist*      *24 wks*

| | | | |
|---|---|---|---|
| 13 May 61 | **THIS TIME I'M SWINGING**  *Capitol T 1442* ............ | 18 | 1 wk |
| 25 Feb 67 | **AT EASE WITH DEAN**  *Reprise RSLP 6322* ............ | 35 | 1 wk |
| 4 Nov 67 | **WELCOME TO MY WORLD**  *Philips DBL 001* ......... | 39 | 1 wk |
| 12 Oct 68 | **GREATEST HITS VOL. 1**  *Reprise RSLP 6301* ........... | 40 | 1 wk |
| 22 Feb 69 | ● **BEST OF DEAN MARTIN**  *Capitol ST 21194* ...... | 9 | 1 wk |
| 22 Feb 69 | ● **GENTLE ON MY MIND**  *Reprise RSLP 6330* ............ | 9 | 8 wks |
| 13 Nov 76 | ● **20 ORIGINAL DEAN MARTIN HITS**  *Reprise K 54066* ... | 7 | 11 wks |

*See also Nat 'King' Cole and Dean Martin.*

## Juan MARTIN and the ROYAL PHILHARMONIC ORCHESTRA
*Spain, male instrumentalist – guitar with UK, orchestra*     *9 wks*

| | | | |
|---|---|---|---|
| 11 Feb 84 | **SERENADE**  *K-Tel NE 1267* ........................ | 21 | 9 wks |

*See also Royal Philharmonic Orchestra.*

## John MARTYN  *UK, male vocalist/instrumentalist – guitar*      *23 wks*

| | | | |
|---|---|---|---|
| 4 Feb 78 | **ONE WORLD**  *Island ILPS 9492* .................... | 54 | 1 wk |
| 1 Nov 80 | **GRACE AND DANGER**  *Island ILPS 9560* ............ | 54 | 2 wks |
| 26 Sep 81 | **GLORIOUS FOOL**  *Geffen K 99178* .................. | 25 | 7 wks |
| 4 Sep 82 | **WELL KEPT SECRET**  *WEA K 99255* .............. | 20 | 7 wks |
| 17 Nov 84 | **SAPPHIRE**  *Island ILPS 9779* .................... | 57 | 2 wks |
| 8 Mar 86 | **PIECE BY PIECE**  *Island ILPS 9807* .............. | 28 | 4 wks |

## Hank MARVIN  *UK, male vocalist/instrumentalist – guitar*      *5 wks*

| | | | |
|---|---|---|---|
| 22 Nov 69 | **HANK MARVIN**  *Columbia SCX 6352* ................. | 14 | 2 wks |
| 20 Mar 82 | **WORDS AND MUSIC**  *Polydor POLD 5054* ............. | 66 | 3 wks |

*See also Marvin, Welch and Farrar.*

## MARVIN, WELCH and FARRAR
*UK, male vocal/instrumental group*     *4 wks*

| | | | |
|---|---|---|---|
| 3 Apr 71 | **MARVIN, WELCH AND FARRAR**  *Regal Zonophone SRZA 8502* ........................ | 30 | 4 wks |

*See also Hank Marvin.*

## MARY JANE GIRLS  *US, female vocal group*      *9 wks*

| | | | |
|---|---|---|---|
| 28 May 83 | **MARY JANE GIRLS**  *Gordy STML 12189* .............. | 51 | 9 wks |

**MARY** – *See* PETER, PAUL *and* MARY

## Richard MARX  *US, male vocalist*      *14 wks*

| | | | |
|---|---|---|---|
| 9 Apr 88 | **RICHARD MARX**  *Manhattan MTL 1017* .............. | 68 | 2 wks |
| 20 May 89 | ● **REPEAT OFFENDER**  *EMI-USA MTL 1043* ........... | 8 | 12 wks |

## MASSED WELSH CHOIRS  *UK, male voice choir*      *7 wks*

| | | | |
|---|---|---|---|
| 9 Aug 69 | ● **CYMANSA GANN**  *BBC REC 53 M* .................. | 5 | 7 wks |

**MASTERMIXERS** – *See* JIVE BUNNY *and the* MASTERMIXERS

## MATCHBOX  *UK, male vocal/instrumental group*      *14 wks*

| | | | |
|---|---|---|---|
| 2 Feb 80 | **MATCHBOX**  *Magnet MAG 5031* .................... | 44 | 5 wks |
| 11 Oct 80 | **MIDNITE DYNAMOS**  *Magnet MAG 5036* ............. | 23 | 9 wks |

## Mireille MATHIEU  *France, female vocalist*          *1 wk*

| | | | |
|---|---|---|---|
| 2 Mar 68 | **MIREILLE MATHIEU**  *Columbia SCX 6210* ............ | 39 | 1 wk |

## Johnny MATHIS  *US, male vocalist*          *193 wks*

| | | | |
|---|---|---|---|
| 8 Nov 58 | ● **WARM**  *Fontana TBA TFL 5015* ...................... | 6 | 2 wks |
| 24 Jan 59 | ● **SWING SOFTLY**  *Fontana TBA TFL 5039* .............. | 10 | 1 wk |
| 13 Feb 60 | ● **RIDE ON A RAINBOW**  *Fontana TFL 5061* ........... | 10 | 2 wks |
| 10 Dec 60 | ● **RHYTHMS AND BALLADS OF BROADWAY** | | |
| | *Fontana SET 101*  ........ | 6 | 10 wks |
| 17 Jun 61 | **I'LL BUY YOU A STAR**  *Fontana TFL 5143* ........... | 18 | 1 wk |
| 16 May 70 | **RAINDROPS KEEP FALLING ON MY HEAD** | | |
| | *CBS 63587* ................ | 23 | 10 wks |
| 3 Apr 71 | **LOVE STORY**  *CBS 64334* ..................... | 27 | 5 wks |
| 9 Sep 72 | **FIRST TIME EVER I SAW YOUR FACE** | | |
| | *CBS 64930* ..................... | 40 | 3 wks |
| 16 Dec 72 | **MAKE IT EASY ON YOURSELF**  *CBS 65161* .......... | 49 | 1 wk |
| 8 Mar 75 | **I'M COMING HOME**  *CBS 65690* ................. | 18 | 11 wks |
| 5 Apr 75 | **THE HEART OF A WOMAN**  *CBS 80533* ............ | 39 | 2 wks |
| 26 Jul 75 | **WHEN WILL I SEE YOU AGAIN**  *CBS 80738* ...... | 13 | 10 wks |
| 3 Jul 76 | **I ONLY HAVE EYES FOR YOU**  *CBS 81329* ........... | 14 | 12 wks |
| 19 Feb 77 | **GREATEST HITS VOL. IV**  *CBS 86022* .............. | 31 | 5 wks |
| 18 Jun 77 | ★ **THE JOHNNY MATHIS COLLECTION**  *CBS 10003* .... | 1 | 40 wks |
| 17 Dec 77 | **SWEET SURRENDER**  *CBS 86036* .................. | 55 | 1 wk |
| 29 Apr 78 | ● **YOU LIGHT UP MY LIFE**  *CBS 86055* ........... | 3 | 19 wks |
| 7 Apr 79 | **THE BEST DAYS OF MY LIFE**  *CBS 86080* ........... | 38 | 5 wks |
| 3 Nov 79 | **MATHIS MAGIC**  *CBS 86103* ................. | 59 | 4 wks |
| 8 Mar 80 | ★ **TEARS AND LAUGHTER**  *CBS 10019* ........... | 1 | 15 wks |
| 12 Jul 80 | **ALL FOR YOU**  *CBS 86115* ................. | 20 | 8 wks |
| 19 Sep 81 | ● **CELEBRATION**  *CBS 10028* ................ | 9 | 16 wks |
| 15 May 82 | **FRIENDS IN LOVE**  *CBS 85652* ................. | 34 | 7 wks |
| 15 Sep 84 | **A SPECIAL PART OF ME**  *CBS 25475* ................ | 45 | 3 wks |

*See also Johnny Mathis and Natalie Cole; Johnny Mathis and Henry Mancini; Johnny Mathis and Deniece Williams.*

## Johnny MATHIS and Natalie COLE
*US, male/female vocal duo*          *16 wks*

| | | | |
|---|---|---|---|
| 17 Sep 83 | ● **UNFORGETTABLE: A MUSICAL TRIBUTE TO NAT KING** | | |
| | **COLE**  *CBS 10042* ............................. | 5 | 16 wks |

*See also Johnny Mathis; Natalie Cole.*

## Johnny MATHIS and Henry MANCINI
*US, male vocalist with US, orchestra*          *8 wks*

| | | | |
|---|---|---|---|
| 13 Dec 86 | **THE HOLLYWOOD MUSICALS**  *CBS 450 258-1* ...... | 46 | 8 wks |

*See also Johnny Mathis; Henry Mancini.*

## Johnny MATHIS and Deniece WILLIAMS
*US, male/female vocal duo*          *11 wks*

| | | | |
|---|---|---|---|
| 26 Aug 78 | **THAT'S WHAT FRIENDS ARE FOR**  *CBS 86068* ...... | 16 | 11 wks |

*See also Johnny Mathis; Deniece Williams.*

## MATT BIANCO  *UK, male vocalist, Mark Riley*          *65 wks*

| | | | |
|---|---|---|---|
| 8 Sep 84 | **WHOSE SIDE ARE YOU ON**  *WEA WX 7* ............ | 35 | 39 wks |
| 22 Mar 86 | **MATT BIANCO**  *WEA WX 35* ...................... | 26 | 13 wks |
| 9 Jul 88 | **INDIGO**  *WEA WX 181* ........................... | 23 | 13 wks |

*For first album, act was a UK/Poland, male/female vocal/instrumental group.*

## MATTHEWS' SOUTHERN COMFORT
*UK, male vocal/instrumental group*     *4 wks*

| | | | |
|---|---|---|---|
| 25 Jul 70 | **SECOND SPRING** *Uni UNLS 112* ................. | 52 | 4 wks |

## MAX Q *Australia, male vocal/instrumental duo*     *1 wk*

| | | | |
|---|---|---|---|
| 4 Nov 89 | **MAX Q** *Mercury 838942 1* ........................... | 69 | 1 wk |

## Brian MAY and FRIENDS *UK, male vocalist/instrumentalist – guitar, and UK/US, male instrumental group*     *4 wks*

| | | | |
|---|---|---|---|
| 12 Nov 83 | **STAR FLEET PROJECT** *EMI SFLT 1078061* .......... | 35 | 4 wks |

## Simon MAY ORCHESTRA *UK, orchestra*     *7 wks*

| | | | |
|---|---|---|---|
| 27 Sep 86 | **SIMON'S WAY** *BBC REB 594* ...................... | 59 | 7 wks |

## John MAYALL *UK, male vocalist*     *97 wks*

| | | | |
|---|---|---|---|
| 4 Mar 67 | ● **A HARD ROAD** *Decca SKL 4853* .................... | 10 | 19 wks |
| 23 Sep 67 | ● **CRUSADE** *Decca SKL 4890* ...................... | 8 | 14 wks |
| 25 Nov 67 | **BLUES ALONE** *Ace Of Clubs SCL 1243* .............. | 24 | 5 wks |
| 16 Mar 68 | **DIARY OF A BAND VOL. 1** *Decca SKL 4918* .......... | 27 | 9 wks |
| 16 Mar 68 | **DIARY OF A BAND VOL. 2** *Decca SKL 4919* .......... | 28 | 5 wks |
| 20 Jul 68 | ● **BARE WIRES** *Decca SKL 4945* .................... | 3 | 17 wks |
| 18 Jan 69 | **BLUES FROM LAUREL CANYON** *Decca SKL 4972* .... | 33 | 3 wks |
| 23 Aug 69 | **LOOKING BACK** *Decca SKL 5010* ................. | 14 | 7 wks |
| 15 Nov 69 | **TURNING POINT** *Polydor 583–571* ................. | 11 | 7 wks |
| 11 Apr 70 | ● **EMPTY ROOMS** *Polydor 583–580* ................. | 9 | 8 wks |
| 12 Dec 70 | **U.S.A. UNION** *Polydor 2425–020* ................. | 50 | 1 wk |
| 26 Jun 71 | **BACK TO THE ROOTS** *Polydor 2657–005* ............. | 31 | 2 wks |

*First four Decca albums credited to John Mayall's Bluesbreakers. See also John Mayall and Eric Clapton.*

## John MAYALL and Eric CLAPTON
*UK, male vocal/instrumental duo*     *17 wks*

| | | | |
|---|---|---|---|
| 30 Jul 66 | ● **BLUES BREAKERS** *Decca LK 4804* ................. | 6 | 17 wks |

*See also John Mayall; Eric Clapton.*

## Curtis MAYFIELD *US, male vocalist*     *2 wks*

| | | | |
|---|---|---|---|
| 31 Mar 73 | **SUPERFLY** *Buddah 2318 065* ...................... | 26 | 2 wks |

## MAZE featuring Frankie BEVERLY
*US, male vocalist and male vocal/instrumental group*     *25 wks*

| | | | |
|---|---|---|---|
| 7 May 83 | **WE ARE ONE** *Capitol EST 12262* .................... | 38 | 6 wks |
| 9 Mar 85 | **CAN'T STOP THE LOVE** *Capitol MAZE 1* .......... | 41 | 12 wks |
| 27 Sep 86 | **LIVE IN LOS ANGELES** *Capitol ESTSP 24* .......... | 70 | 2 wks |
| 16 Sep 89 | **SILKY SOUL** *Warner Bros. WX 301* ................. | 43 | 5 wks |

## Vaughn MEADER *US, male comedian*     *8 wks*

| | | | |
|---|---|---|---|
| 29 Dec 62 | **THE FIRST FAMILY** *London HAA 8048* .............. | 12 | 8 wks |

## MEAT LOAF  *US, male vocalist*  525 wks

| | | | |
|---|---|---|---|
| 11 Mar 78 | ● BAT OUT OF HELL  *Epic EPC 82419* ................ | 9 | 395 wks |
| 12 Sep 81 | ★ DEAD RINGER  *Epic EPC 83645* .................... | 1 | 46 wks |
| 7 May 83 | ● MIDNIGHT AT THE LOST AND FOUND  *Epic EPC 25243* .................................. | 7 | 23 wks |
| 10 Nov 84 | ● BAD ATTITUDE  *Arista 206 619* .................... | 8 | 16 wks |
| 26 Jan 85 | ● HITS OUT OF HELL  *Epic EPC 26156* ................ | 2 | 37 wks |
| 11 Oct 86 | BLIND BEFORE I STOP  *Arista 207 741* ............... | 28 | 6 wks |
| 7 Nov 87 | LIVE AT WEMBLEY  *RCA 208599* ................. | 60 | 2 wks |

**MECHANICS** – *See MIKE and the MECHANICS*

## Glenn MEDEIROS  *US, male vocalist*  2 wks

| | | | |
|---|---|---|---|
| 8 Oct 88 | NOT ME  *London LONLP 68* ......................... | 63 | 2 wks |

**MEDICS** – *See DOCTOR and the MEDICS*

## MEGACITY FOUR  *UK, male vocal/instrumental group*  1 wk

| | | | |
|---|---|---|---|
| 17 Jun 89 | TRANZOPHOBIA  *Decoy DYL 3* ..................... | 67 | 1 wk |

## MEGADETH  *US, male vocal/instrumental group*  5 wks

| | | | |
|---|---|---|---|
| 26 Mar 88 | SO FAR SO GOOD ... SO WHAT!  *Capitol EST 2053* .... | 18 | 5 wks |

## MEL and KIM  *UK, female vocal duo*  25 wks

| | | | |
|---|---|---|---|
| 25 Apr 87 | ● F.L.M.  *Supreme SU 2* ............................. | 3 | 25 wks |

## MELANIE  *US, female vocalist*  69 wks

| | | | |
|---|---|---|---|
| 19 Sep 70 | ● CANDLES IN THE RAIN  *Buddah 2318-009* ........... | 5 | 27 wks |
| 16 Jan 71 | LEFTOVER WINE  *Buddah 2318-011* ................. | 22 | 11 wks |
| 29 May 71 | ● GOOD BOOK  *Buddah 2322 001* .................... | 9 | 9 wks |
| 8 Jan 72 | GATHER ME  *Buddah 2322 002* ................... | 14 | 14 wks |
| 1 Apr 72 | GARDEN IN THE CITY  *Buddah 2318 054* ............. | 19 | 6 wks |
| 7 Oct 72 | THE FOUR SIDES OF MELANIE  *Buddah 2659 013* ..... | 23 | 2 wks |

**MELBOURNE SYMPHONY ORCHESTRA** – *See Elton JOHN*

## John Cougar MELLENCAMP  *US, male vocalist*  23 wks

| | | | |
|---|---|---|---|
| 6 Nov 82 | AMERICAN FOOL  *Riva RVLP 16* ................... | 37 | 6 wks |
| 3 Mar 84 | UH-HUH  *Riva RIVL 1* ........................... | 92 | 1 wk |
| 3 Oct 87 | THE LONESOME JUBILEE  *Mercury MERH 109* ........ | 31 | 12 wks |
| 27 May 89 | BIG DADDY  *Mercury MERH 838220 1* ............... | 25 | 4 wks |

American Fool *credited to John Cougar.*

## MEN AT WORK  *Australia, male vocal/instrumental group*  71 wks

| | | | |
|---|---|---|---|
| 15 Jan 83 | ★ BUSINESS AS USUAL  *Epic EPC 85669* .............. | 1 | 44 wks |
| 30 Apr 83 | ● CARGO  *Epic EPC 25372* ........................... | 8 | 27 wks |

## MEN THEY COULDN'T HANG
*UK, male vocal/instrumental group*  8 wks

| | | | |
|---|---|---|---|
| 27 Jul 85 | NIGHT OF A THOUSAND CANDLES  *Imp FIEND 50* .. | 91 | 2 wks |
| 8 Nov 86 | HOW GREEN IS THE VALLEY  *MCA MCF 3337* ...... | 68 | 2 wks |
| 23 Apr 88 | WAITING FOR BONAPARTE  *Magnet MAGL 5075* ..... | 41 | 2 wks |
| 6 May 89 | SILVER TOWN  *Silvertone ORELP 503* ............... | 39 | 2 wks |

## MEN WITHOUT HATS
*Canada, male vocal/instrumental group*      *1 wk*

12 Nov 83   **RHYTHM OF YOUTH**   *Statik STATLP 10* ............   **96**   1 wk

## MEMBERS   *UK, male vocal/instrumental group*     *5 wks*

28 Apr 79   **AT THE CHELSEA NIGHTCLUB**   *Virgin V 2120* .......   **45**   5 wks

## Freddie MERCURY   *UK, male vocalist*     *23 wks*

11 May 85  ● **MR BAD GUY**   *CBS 86312* .....................   **6**   23 wks
*See also Freddie Mercury and Montserrat Caballe.*

## Freddie MERCURY and Montserrat CABALLE
*UK/Spain, male/female vocal duo*     *4 wks*

22 Oct 88   **BARCELONA**   *Polydor POLH 44* ...................   **25**   4 wks
*See also Freddie Mercury.*

## MERLE and ROY   *UK, female/male vocal/instrumental duo*     *5 wks*

26 Sep 87   **REQUESTS**   *Mynod Mawr RMBR 8713* ...............   **74**   5 wks

## MERSEYBEATS   *UK, male vocal/instrumental group*     *9 wks*

20 Jun 64   **THE MERSEYBEATS**   *Fontana TL 5210* .............   **12**   9 wks

## METALLICA   *US/Denmark, male vocal/instrumental group*     *12 wks*

11 Aug 84   **RIDE THE LIGHTNING**   *Music For Nations MFN 27* ......   **87**   2 wks
15 Mar 86   **MASTER OF PUPPETS**   *Music For Nations MFN 60* .......   **41**   4 wks
17 Sep 88  ● **... AND JUSTICE FOR ALL**   *Vertigo VERH 61* ..........   **4**   6 wks

## METEORS   *UK, male vocal/instrumental group*     *3 wks*

26 Feb 83   **WRECKIN' CREW**   *I.D. NOSE 1* ...................   **53**   3 wks

## MEZZOFORTE   *Iceland, male instrumental group*     *10 wks*

5 Mar 83   **SURPRISE SURPRISE**   *Steinar STELP 02* ............   **23**   9 wks
2 Jul 83   **CATCHING UP WITH MEZZOFORTE**   *Steinar STELP 03*   **95**   1 wk

**MG'S** – *See Booker T. and the MG's*

**MIAMI SOUND MACHINE** – *See Gloria ESTEFAN*

## George MICHAEL   *UK, male vocalist*     *69 wks*

14 Nov 87  ★ **FAITH**   *Epic 460 000–1* ...........................   **1**   69 wks

## Keith MICHELL   *Australia, male vocalist*     *12 wks*

9 Feb 80   **CAPTAIN BEAKY AND HIS BAND**   *Polydor 238 3462* ...   **28**   12 wks

**MICK** – *See Dave DEE, DOZY BEAKY, MICK and TICH*

## Bette MIDLER   *US, female vocalist*     *9 wks*

15 Jul 89   **BEACHES**   *Atlantic 781993 1* ........................   **21**   9 wks

## MIDNIGHT OIL  *Australia, male vocal/instrumental group*  *16 wks*

| | | | |
|---|---|---|---|
| 25 Jun 88 | **DIESEL AND DUST**  *CBS 460005 1* ................ | 19 | 16 wks |

## MIDNIGHT STAR
*US, male/female vocal/instrumental group*  *6 wks*

| | | | |
|---|---|---|---|
| 2 Feb 85 | **PLANETARY INVASION**  *Solar MCF 3251* ........... | 85 | 2 wks |
| 5 Jul 86 | **HEADLINES**  *Solar MCF 3322* ...................... | 42 | 4 wks |

## MIGHTY LEMON DROPS
*UK, male vocal/instrumental group*  *5 wks*

| | | | |
|---|---|---|---|
| 4 Oct 86 | **HAPPY HEAD**  *Blue Guitar AZLP 1* .................. | 58 | 2 wks |
| 27 Feb 88 | **THE WORLD WITHOUT END**  *Blue Guitar AZLP 4* .... | 34 | 3 wks |

## MIGHTY WAH  *UK, male vocal/instrumental group*  *11 wks*

| | | | |
|---|---|---|---|
| 18 Jul 81 | **NAH—POO=THE ART OF BLUFF**  *Eternal CLASSIC 1* .. | 33 | 5 wks |
| 4 Aug 84 | **A WORD TO THE WISE GUY**  *Beggars Banquet BEGA 54* . | 28 | 6 wks |

*First album credited to Wah!*

## MIKE and the MECHANICS
*UK, male vocal/instrumental group*  *22 wks*

| | | | |
|---|---|---|---|
| 15 Mar 86 | **MIKE AND THE MECHANICS**  *WEA WX 49* .......... | 78 | 3 wks |
| 26 Nov 88 | ● **THE LIVING YEARS**  *WEA WX 203* ................ | 2 | 19 wks |

*See also Mike Rutherford.*

**Buddy MILES** – *See Carlos SANTANA and Buddy MILES*

## John MILES  *UK, male vocalist/multi-instrumentalist*  *25 wks*

| | | | |
|---|---|---|---|
| 27 Mar 76 | ● **REBEL**  *Decca SKL 5231* ............................ | 9 | 10 wks |
| 26 Feb 77 | **STRANGER IN THE CITY**  *Decca TXS 118* ............ | 37 | 3 wks |
| 1 Apr 78 | **ZARAGON**  *Decca TXS 126* ........................... | 43 | 5 wks |
| 21 Apr 79 | **MORE MILES PER HOUR**  *Decca TXS 135* ........... | 46 | 5 wks |
| 29 Aug 81 | **MILES HIGH**  *EMI EMC 3374* ...................... | 96 | 2 wks |

**Paul MILES-KINGSTON** – *See Andrew LLOYD WEBBER*

## Frankie MILLER  *UK, male vocalist*  *1 wk*

| | | | |
|---|---|---|---|
| 14 Apr 79 | **FALLING IN LOVE**  *Chrysalis CHR 1220* .............. | 54 | 1 wk |

## Glenn MILLER  *US, orchestra*  *68 wks*

| | | | |
|---|---|---|---|
| 28 Jan 61 | ● **GLENN MILLER PLAYS SELECTIONS FROM 'THE GLENN MILLER STORY' AND OTHER HITS**  *RCA RD 27068 0023* ............................ | 10 | 18 wks |
| 5 Jul 69 | ● **THE BEST OF GLENN MILLER**  *RCA International 1002* ............................ | 5 | 14 wks |
| 6 Sep 69 | **NEARNESS OF YOU**  *RCA International INTS 1019* ...... | 30 | 2 wks |
| 25 Apr 70 | **A MEMORIAL 1944–1969**  *RCA GM 1* ................ | 18 | 17 wks |
| 25 Dec 71 | **THE REAL GLENN MILLER AND HIS ORCHESTRA PLAY THE ORIGINAL MUSIC OF THE FILM 'THE GLENN MILLER STORY' AND OTHER HITS**  *RCA International INTS 1157* ...................... | 28 | 2 wks |
| 14 Feb 76 | **A LEGENDARY PERFORMER**  *RCA Victor DPM 2065* .. | 41 | 5 wks |
| 14 Feb 76 | **A LEGENDARY PERFORMER VOL. 2**  *RCA Victor CPL 11349* ......................... | 53 | 2 wks |
| 9 Apr 77 | ● **THE UNFORGETTABLE GLENN MILLER**  *RCA Victor TVL 1* ................................ | 4 | 8 wks |

*The Real Glenn Miller And His Orchestra Play . . . is a re-titled re-issue of the first album.*

## Steve MILLER BAND  US, male vocal/instrumental group    47 wks

| | | | |
|---|---|---|---|
| 12 Jun 76 | **FLY LIKE AN EAGLE**  Mercury 9286 177 .............. | **11** | 17 wks |
| 4 Jun 77 | **BOOK OF DREAMS**  Mercury 9286 456 ................ | **12** | 12 wks |
| 19 Jun 82 | ● **ABRACADABRA**  Mercury 6302 204 ................ | **10** | 16 wks |
| 7 May 83 | **STEVE MILLER BAND LIVE!**  Mercury MERL 18 ....... | **79** | 2 wks |

## MILLICAN and NESBIT  UK, male vocal duo    24 wks

| | | | |
|---|---|---|---|
| 23 Mar 74 | ● **MILLICAN AND NESBIT**  Pye NSPL 18428 ............ | **3** | 21 wks |
| 4 Jan 75 | **EVERYBODY KNOWS MILLICAN AND NESBIT** | | |
| | Pye NSPL 18446  ................................. | **23** | 3 wks |

## Spike MILLIGAN  UK, male comedian    5 wks

| | | | |
|---|---|---|---|
| 25 Nov 61 | **MILLIGAN PRESERVED**  Parlophone PMC 1152 ........ | **11** | 4 wks |
| 18 Dec 76 | **THE SNOW GOOSE**  RCA RS 1088 .................. | **49** | 1 wk |

*Second album credits the London Symphony Orchestra. See also Harry Secombe, Peter Sellers and Spike Milligan; London Symphony Orchestra.*

## MILLI VANILLI  France/Germany, male vocal duo    16 wks

| | | | |
|---|---|---|---|
| 21 Jan 89 | ● **ALL OR NOTHING/2X2**  Cooltempo CTLP 11 ........... | **7†** | 16 wks |

*All Or Nothing was repackaged and available with a free re-mix album, 2X2, from 16 Oct 89 onwards.*

## Mrs. MILLS  UK, female instrumentalist – piano    13 wks

| | | | |
|---|---|---|---|
| 10 Dec 66 | **COME TO MY PARTY**  Parlophone PMC 7010 ........... | **17** | 7 wks |
| 28 Dec 68 | **MRS. MILLS' PARTY PIECES**  Parlophone PCS 7066 ..... | **32** | 3 wks |
| 13 Dec 69 | **LET'S HAVE ANOTHER PARTY**  Parlophone PCS 7035 . | **23** | 2 wks |
| 6 Nov 71 | **I'M MIGHTY GLAD**  MFP 5225 .................... | **49** | 1 wk |

## MINDBENDERS  UK, male vocal/instrumental group    4 wks

| | | | |
|---|---|---|---|
| 25 Jun 66 | **THE MINDBENDERS**  Fontana TL 5324 .............. | **28** | 4 wks |

*See also Wayne Fontana and the Mindbenders.*

## Zodiac MINDWARP and the LOVE REACTION
UK, male vocal/instrumental group    5 wks

| | | | |
|---|---|---|---|
| 5 Mar 88 | **TATTOOED BEAT MESSIAH**  Mercury ZODLP 1 ....... | **20** | 5 wks |

## Liza MINNELLI  US, female vocalist    24 wks

| | | | |
|---|---|---|---|
| 7 Apr 73 | ● **LIZA WITH A 'Z'**  CBS 65212 ........................ | **9** | 15 wks |
| 16 Jun 73 | **THE SINGER**  CBS 65555 .......................... | **45** | 1 wk |
| 21 Oct 89 | ● **RESULTS**  Epic 465511 1 ......................... | **6** | 8 wks |

## MINIPOPS  UK, male/female vocal group    12 wks

| | | | |
|---|---|---|---|
| 26 Dec 81 | **MINIPOPS**  K-Tel NE 1102 ......................... | **63** | 7 wks |
| 19 Feb 83 | **WE'RE THE MINIPOPS**  K-Tel ONE 1187 ............. | **54** | 5 wks |

## Kylie MINOGUE  Australia, female vocalist    78 wks

| | | | |
|---|---|---|---|
| 16 Jul 88 | ★ **KYLIE**  PWL HF 3 ............................... | **1** | 67 wks |
| 21 Oct 89 | ★ **ENJOY YOURSELF**  PWL HF 9 .................... | **1†** | 11 wks |

**KYLIE MINOGUE**'s debut is the biggest selling album by an Australian act.

## MIRAGE  *UK, male/female vocal/instrumental group*    *33 wks*

| | | | | | |
|---|---|---|---|---|---|
| 26 Dec | 87 | ● THE BEST OF MIRAGE JACK MIX '88  *Stylus SMR 746* .. | 7 | 15 wks |
| 25 Jun | 88 | ● JACK MIX IN FULL EFFECT  *Stylus SMR 856* .......... | 7 | 12 wks |
| 7 Jan | 89 | ROYAL MIX '89  *Stylus SMR 871* .................... | 34 | 6 wks |

## MISSION  *UK, male vocal/instrumental group*    *33 wks*

| | | | | |
|---|---|---|---|---|
| 22 Nov | 86 | GOD'S OWN MEDICINE  *Mercury MERH 102* .......... | 14 | 20 wks |
| 4 Jul | 87 | THE FIRST CHAPTER  *Mercury MISH 1* ............. | 35 | 4 wks |
| 12 Mar | 88 | ● LITTLE CHILDREN  *Mercury MISH 2* ............... | 2 | 9 wks |

## MR. BIG  *US, male vocal/instrumental group*    *1 wk*

| | | | | |
|---|---|---|---|---|
| 22 Jul | 89 | MR. BIG  *Atlantic 781990 1* ....................... | 60 | 1 wk |

## Joni MITCHELL  *Canada, female vocalist*    *108 wks*

| | | | | |
|---|---|---|---|---|
| 6 Jun | 70 | ● LADIES OF THE CANYON  *Reprise RSLP 6376* ......... | 8 | 25 wks |
| 24 Jul | 71 | ● BLUE  *Reprise K 44128* ......................... | 3 | 18 wks |
| 16 Mar | 74 | COURT AND SPARK  *Asylum SYLA 8756* ............. | 14 | 11 wks |
| 1 Feb | 75 | MILES OF AISLES  *Asylum SYSP 902* ................ | 34 | 4 wks |
| 27 Dec | 75 | THE HISSING OF SUMMER LAWNS  *Asylum SYLA 8763* ............................. | 14 | 10 wks |
| 11 Dec | 76 | HEJIRA  *Asylum K 53063* ......................... | 11 | 5 wks |
| 21 Jan | 78 | DON JUAN'S RECKLESS DAUGHTER  *Asylum K 63003* ................................. | 20 | 7 wks |
| 14 Jul | 79 | MINGUS  *Asylum K 53091* ......................... | 24 | 7 wks |
| 4 Oct | 80 | SHADOWS AND LIGHT  *Elektra K 62030* ............. | 63 | 3 wks |
| 4 Dec | 82 | WILD THINGS RUN FAST  *Geffen GEF 25102* ........ | 32 | 8 wks |
| 30 Nov | 85 | DOG EAT DOG  *Geffen GEF 26455* ................. | 57 | 3 wks |
| 2 Apr | 88 | CHALK MARK IN A RAIN STORM  *Geffen WX 141*...... | 26 | 7 wks |

## George MITCHELL MINSTRELS
*UK, male/female vocal group*    *240 wks*

| | | | | |
|---|---|---|---|---|
| 26 Nov | 60 | ★ THE BLACK AND WHITE MINSTREL SHOW  *HMV CLP 1399* ................................... | 1 | 90 wks |
| 21 Oct | 61 | ★ ANOTHER BLACK AND WHITE MINSTREL SHOW  *HMV CLP 1460* ................................... | 1 | 64 wks |
| 20 Oct | 62 | ★ ON STAGE WITH THE GEORGE MITCHELL  MINSTRELS  *HMV CLP 1599* ................... | 1 | 26 wks |
| 2 Nov | 63 | ● ON TOUR WITH THE GEORGE MITCHELL  MINSTRELS  *HMV CLP 1667* ................. | 6 | 18 wks |
| 12 Dec | 64 | ● SPOTLIGHT ON THE GEORGE MITCHELL  MINSTRELS  *HMV CLP 1803* ................. | 6 | 7 wks |
| 4 Dec | 65 | ● MAGIC OF THE MINSTRELS  *HMV CLP 1917* ........ | 9 | 7 wks |
| 26 Nov | 66 | HERE COME THE MINSTRELS  *HMV CLP 3579* ...... | 11 | 11 wks |
| 16 Dec | 67 | SHOWTIME  *HMV CSD 3642* ...................... | 26 | 2 wks |
| 14 Dec | 68 | SING THE IRVING BERLIN SONGBOOK  *Columbia SCX 6267* .............................. | 33 | 1 wk |
| 19 Dec | 70 | THE MAGIC OF CHRISTMAS  *Columbia SCX 6431* ...... | 32 | 4 wks |
| 19 Nov | 77 | ● 30 GOLDEN GREATS  *EMI EMTV 7* ................ | 10 | 10 wks |

30 Golden Greats *also credits the Joe Loss Orchestra. See also Joe Loss.*

## MODERN EON  *UK, male vocal/instrumental group*    *1 wk*

| | | | | |
|---|---|---|---|---|
| 13 Jun | 81 | FICTION TALES  *DinDisc DID 11* ................... | 65 | 1 wk |

**MODERN LOVERS** – *See Jonathan RICHMAN and the MODERN LOVERS*

## MODERN ROMANCE  *UK, male vocal/instrumental group*    *13 wks*

| | | | | |
|---|---|---|---|---|
| 16 Apr | 83 | TRICK OF THE LIGHT  *WEA X 0127* ............... | 53 | 7 wks |
| 3 Dec | 83 | PARTY TONIGHT  *Ronco RON LP 3* ................ | 45 | 6 wks |

## MODERN TALKING  *Germany, male vocal/instrumental group*  *3 wks*

| | | | | | |
|---|---|---|---|---|---|
| 11 Oct 86 | **READY FOR ROMANCE** | *RCA PL 71133* | ............ | 76 | 3 wks |

## MOLLY HATCHET  *US, male vocal/instrumental group*  *1 wk*

| | | | | | |
|---|---|---|---|---|---|
| 25 Jan 86 | **DOUBLE TROUBLE – LIVE** | *Epic EPC 88670* | ......... | 94 | 1 wk |

## Zoot MONEY and the BIG ROLL BAND
*UK, male vocalist and male instrumental backing group*  *3 wks*

| | | | | | |
|---|---|---|---|---|---|
| 15 Oct 66 | **ZOOT** | *Columbia SX 6075* | ........................ | 23 | 3 wks |

## MONKEES  *US/UK, male vocal/instrumental group*  *101 wks*

| | | | | | |
|---|---|---|---|---|---|
| 28 Jan 67 | ★ **THE MONKEES** | *RCA Victor SF 7844* | ................ | 1 | 36 wks |
| 15 Apr 67 | ★ **MORE OF THE MONKEES** | *RCA Victor SF 7868* | ........ | 1 | 25 wks |
| 8 Jul 67 | ● **HEADQUARTERS** | *RCA Victor SF 7886* | ............. | 2 | 19 wks |
| 13 Jan 68 | ● **PISCES, AQUARIUS, CAPRICORN & JONES LTD.** | | | | |
| | | *RCA Victor SF 7912* | ............................ | 5 | 11 wks |
| 28 Nov 81 | **THE MONKEES** | *Arista DARTY 12* | .................. | 99 | 1 wk |
| 15 Apr 89 | **HEY HEY IT'S THE MONKEES – GREATEST HITS** | | | | |
| | | *K-Tel NE 1432* | ................................ | 12 | 9 wks |

*The two albums titled* The Monkees *are different.*

## MONOCHROME SET  *UK, male vocal/instrumental group*  *4 wks*

| | | | | | |
|---|---|---|---|---|---|
| 3 May 80 | **STRANGE BOUTIQUE** | *Dindisc DID 4* | ............... | 62 | 4 wks |

## Tony MONOPOLY  *Australia, male vocalist*  *4 wks*

| | | | | | |
|---|---|---|---|---|---|
| 12 Jun 76 | **TONY MONOPOLY** | *BUK BULP 2000* | ............... | 25 | 4 wks |

## Matt MONRO  *UK, male vocalist*  *15 wks*

| | | | | | |
|---|---|---|---|---|---|
| 7 Aug 65 | **I HAVE DREAMED** | *Parlophone PMC 1250* | ............. | 20 | 1 wk |
| 17 Sep 66 | **THIS IS THE LIFE** | *Capitol T 2540* | ................... | 25 | 2 wks |
| 26 Aug 67 | **INVITATION TO THE MOVIES** | *Capitol ST 2730* | ....... | 30 | 1 wk |
| 15 Mar 80 | ● **HEARTBREAKERS** | *EMI EMTV 23* | ............... | 5 | 11 wks |

## MONTROSE  *US, male vocal/instrumental group*  *1 wk*

| | | | | | |
|---|---|---|---|---|---|
| 15 Jun 74 | **MONTROSE** | *Warner Bros. K 46276* | .................. | 43 | 1 wk |

## MONTY PYTHON'S FLYING CIRCUS
*UK, male comedy group*  *31 wks*

| | | | | | |
|---|---|---|---|---|---|
| 30 Oct 71 | **ANOTHER MONTY PYTHON RECORD** | | | | |
| | *Charisma CAS 1049* | ............................. | | 26 | 3 wks |
| 27 Jan 73 | **MONTY PYTHON'S PREVIOUS ALBUM** | | | | |
| | *Charisma CAS 1063* | ............................. | | 39 | 3 wks |
| 23 Feb 74 | **MATCHING TIE AND HANDKERCHIEF** | | | | |
| | *Charisma CAS 1080* | ............................. | | 49 | 2 wks |
| 27 Jul 74 | **LIVE AT DRURY LANE** | *Charisma CLASS 4* | ........... | 19 | 8 wks |
| 9 Aug 75 | **MONTY PYTHON** | *Charisma CAS 1003* | .......... | 45 | 4 wks |
| 24 Nov 79 | **THE LIFE OF BRIAN** | *Warner Bros. K 56751* | ........... | 63 | 3 wks |
| 18 Oct 80 | **CONTRACTUAL OBLIGATION ALBUM** | | | | |
| | *Charisma CAS 1152* | ............................. | | 13 | 8 wks |

## MOODY BLUES  *UK, male vocal/instrumental group*  *307 wks*

| | | | |
|---|---|---|---|
| 27 Jan 68 | **DAYS OF FUTURE PASSED** *Deram SML 707* ......... | 27 | 16 wks |
| 3 Aug 68 | ● **IN SEARCH OF THE LOST CHORD** *Deram SML 711* ... | 5 | 32 wks |
| 3 May 69 | ★ **ON THE THRESHOLD OF A DREAM** *Deram SML 1035* | 1 | 73 wks |
| 6 Dec 69 | ● **TO OUR CHILDREN'S CHILDREN'S CHILDREN** *Threshold THS 1* .................................... | 2 | 44 wks |
| 15 Aug 70 | ★ **A QUESTION OF BALANCE** *Threshold THS 3* ......... | 1 | 19 wks |
| 7 Aug 71 | ★ **EVERY GOOD BOY DESERVES FAVOUR** *Threshold THS 5* .................................... | 1 | 21 wks |
| 2 Dec 72 | ● **SEVENTH SOJOURN** *Threshold THS 7* ............. | 5 | 18 wks |
| 16 Nov 74 | **THIS IS THE MOODY BLUES** *Threshold MB 1/2* ........ | 14 | 18 wks |
| 24 Jun 78 | ● **OCTAVE** *Decca TXS 129* ........................... | 6 | 18 wks |
| 10 Nov 79 | **OUT OF THIS WORLD** *K-Tel NE 1051* ............... | 15 | 10 wks |
| 23 May 81 | ● **LONG DISTANCE VOYAGER** *Threshold TXS 139* ...... | 7 | 19 wks |
| 10 Sep 83 | **THE PRESENT** *Threshold TXS 140* .................. | 15 | 8 wks |
| 10 May 86 | **THE OTHER SIDE OF LIFE** *Threshold POLD 5190* ....... | 24 | 6 wks |
| 25 Jun 88 | **SUR LA MER** *Polydor POLH 43* ...................... | 21 | 5 wks |

## Dudley MOORE  *UK, male instrumentalist – piano*  *19 wks*

| | | | |
|---|---|---|---|
| 4 Dec 65 | **THE OTHER SIDE OF DUDLEY MOORE** *Decca LK 4732* ................................... | 11 | 9 wks |
| 11 Jun 66 | **GENUINE DUD** *Decca LK 4788* ...................... | 13 | 10 wks |

*Second album credited to the Dudley Moore Trio. See also Peter Cook and Dudley Moore.*

## Gary MOORE  *UK, male vocalist/instrumentalist – guitar*  *45 wks*

| | | | |
|---|---|---|---|
| 3 Feb 79 | **BACK ON THE STREETS** *MCA MCF 2853* ........... | 70 | 1 wk |
| 16 Oct 82 | **CORRIDORS OF POWER** *Virgin V 2245* ........... | 30 | 6 wks |
| 18 Feb 84 | **VICTIMS OF THE FUTURE** *10 DIX 2* ............. | 12 | 7 wks |
| 13 Oct 84 | **WE WANT MOORE!** *10 GMDL 1* .................. | 32 | 3 wks |
| 14 Sep 85 | **RUN FOR COVER** *10 DIX 16* .................... | 12 | 8 wks |
| 12 Jul 86 | **ROCKIN' EVERY NIGHT** *10 XID 1* .............. | 99 | 1 wk |
| 14 Mar 87 | ● **WILD FRONTIER** *10 DIX 56* ...................... | 8 | 14 wks |
| 11 Feb 89 | **AFTER THE WAR** *Virgin V 2575* .................. | 23 | 5 wks |

## Patrick MORAZ

*Switzerland, male instrumentalist – keyboards*  *8 wks*

| | | | |
|---|---|---|---|
| 10 Apr 76 | **PATRICK MORAZ** *Charisma CDS 4002* .............. | 28 | 7 wks |
| 23 Jul 77 | **OUT IN THE SUN** *Charisma CDS 4007* ............... | 44 | 1 wk |

**Giorgio MORODER** – *See Philip OAKEY and Giorgio MORODER*

**Joseph MOROVITZ** – *See SOUTH BANK ORCHESTRA*

## Ennio MORRICONE  *Italy, orchestra*  *15 wks*

| | | | |
|---|---|---|---|
| 2 May 81 | **THIS IS ENNIO MORRICONE** *EMI THIS 33* ......... | 23 | 5 wks |
| 9 May 81 | **CHI MAI** *BBC REH 414* ........................... | 29 | 6 wks |
| 7 Mar 87 | **THE MISSION – ORIGINAL SOUNDTRACK** *Virgin V 2402* ..................................... | 73 | 4 wks |

*The Mission credits the London Philharmonic Orchestra. See also London Philharmonic Orchestra.*

## Van MORRISON  *UK, male vocalist*  *92 wks*

| | | | |
|---|---|---|---|
| 18 Apr 70 | **MOONDANCE** *Warner Bros. WS 1835* ................ | 32 | 2 wks |
| 11 Aug 73 | **HARD NOSE THE HIGHWAY** *Warner Bros. K 46242* .... | 22 | 3 wks |
| 16 Nov 74 | **VEEDON FLEECE** *Warner Bros. K 56068* .......... | 41 | 1 wk |
| 7 May 77 | **A PERIOD OF TRANSITION** *Warner Bros. K 56322* ..... | 23 | 5 wks |
| 21 Oct 78 | **WAVELENGTH** *Warner Bros. K 56526* ............. | 27 | 6 wks |
| 8 Sep 79 | **INTO THE MUSIC** *Vertigo 9120 852* ............. | 21 | 9 wks |
| 20 Sep 80 | **THE COMMON ONE** *Mercury 6302 001* ............... | 53 | 3 wks |
| 27 Feb 82 | **BEAUTIFUL VISION** *Mercury 6302 122* .............. | 31 | 14 wks |
| 26 Mar 83 | **INARTICULATE SPEECH OF THE HEART** *Mercury MERL 16* ................................. | 14 | 8 wks |

| | | | |
|---|---|---|---|
| 3 Mar 84 | **LIVE AT THE GRAND OPERA HOUSE** | | |
| | Mercury MERL 36 .................... | 47 | 4 wks |
| 9 Feb 85 | **A SENSE OF WONDER** Mercury MERH 54 ........... | 25 | 5 wks |
| 2 Aug 86 | **NO GURU, NO METHOD, NO TEACHER** | | |
| | Mercury MERH 94 ..................... | 27 | 5 wks |
| 19 Sep 87 | **POETIC CHAMPIONS COMPOSE** Mercury MERH 110 .. | 26 | 6 wks |
| 2 Jul 88 | **IRISH HEARTBEAT** Mercury MERH 124 ............. | 18 | 7 wks |
| 10 Jun 89 | **AVALON SUNSET** Polydor 839262 1 ................. | 13 | 14 wks |

Irish Heartbeat credits The Chieftains, Ireland, male instrumental group. See also James Galway and the Chieftains.

## MORRISSEY  UK, male vocalist

20 wks

| | | | |
|---|---|---|---|
| 26 Mar 88 | ★ **VIVA HATE** HMV CSD 3787 ..................... | 1 | 20 wks |

## MORRISSEY MULLEN

UK, male vocal/instrumental duo

11 wks

| | | | |
|---|---|---|---|
| 18 Jul 81 | **BADNESS** Beggars Banquet BEGA 27 ................... | 43 | 5 wks |
| 3 Apr 82 | **LIFE ON THE WIRE** Beggars Banquet BEGA 33 .......... | 47 | 5 wks |
| 23 Apr 83 | **IT'S ABOUT TIME** Beggars Banquet BEGA 44 .......... | 95 | 1 wk |

**MORRISTOWN ORPHEUS CHOIR** – See G.U.S. (FOOTWEAR) BAND and the MORRISTOWN ORPHEUS CHOIR

## MOTHERS OF INVENTION

US, male vocal/instrumental group

12 wks

| | | | |
|---|---|---|---|
| 29 Jun 68 | **WE'RE ONLY IN IT FOR THE MONEY** Verve SVLP 9199 | 32 | 5 wks |
| 28 Mar 70 | **BURNT WEENY SANDWICH** Reprise RSLP 6370 ...... | 17 | 3 wks |
| 3 Oct 70 | **WEASELS RIPPED MY FLESH** Reprise RSLP 2028 ..... | 28 | 4 wks |

## MOTLEY CRUE  US, male vocal/instrumental group

21 wks

| | | | |
|---|---|---|---|
| 13 Jul 85 | **THEATRE OF PAIN** Elektra EKT 8 ................. | 36 | 3 wks |
| 30 May 87 | **GIRLS GIRLS GIRLS** Elektra EKT 39 ................ | 14 | 11 wks |
| 16 Sep 89 | ● **DR. FEELGOOD** Elektra EKT 59 ................... | 4 | 7 wks |

## MOTORHEAD  UK, male vocal/instrumental group

97 wks

| | | | |
|---|---|---|---|
| 24 Sep 77 | **MOTORHEAD** Chiswick WIK 2 .................... | 43 | 5 wks |
| 24 Mar 79 | **OVERKILL** Bronze BRON 515 ..................... | 24 | 11 wks |
| 27 Oct 79 | **BOMBER** Bronze BRON 523 ...................... | 12 | 13 wks |
| 8 Dec 79 | **ON PARADE** United Artists LBR 1004 ............... | 65 | 2 wks |
| 8 Nov 80 | ● **ACE OF SPADES** Bronze BRON 531 ............... | 4 | 16 wks |
| 27 Jun 81 | ★ **NO SLEEP TILL HAMMERSMITH** Bronze BRON 535 .. | 1 | 21 wks |
| 17 Apr 82 | ● **IRONFIST** Bronze BRNA 539 ...................... | 6 | 9 wks |
| 26 Feb 83 | **WHAT'S WORDS WORTH** Big Beat NED 2 .......... | 71 | 2 wks |
| 4 Jun 83 | **ANOTHER PERFECT DAY** Bronze BRON 546 ........ | 20 | 4 wks |
| 15 Sep 84 | **NO REMORSE** Bronze PROTV MOTOR 1 ............ | 14 | 6 wks |
| 9 Aug 86 | **ORGASMATRON** GWR GWLP 1 ................... | 21 | 4 wks |
| 5 Sep 87 | **ROCK 'N' ROLL** GWR GWLP 14 ................... | 34 | 3 wks |
| 15 Oct 88 | **NO SLEEP AT ALL** GWR GWR 31 ................. | 79 | 1 wk |

## MOTORS  UK, male vocal/instrumental group

6 wks

| | | | |
|---|---|---|---|
| 15 Oct 77 | **THE MOTORS** Virgin V 2089 ..................... | 46 | 5 wks |
| 3 Jun 78 | **APPROVED BY THE MOTORS** Virgin V 2101 ......... | 60 | 1 wk |

## MOTT THE HOOPLE

UK, male vocal/instrumental group

32 wks

| | | | |
|---|---|---|---|
| 2 May 70 | **MOTT THE HOOPLE** Island ILPS 9108 .............. | 66 | 1 wk |

| Date | Title | Pos | Weeks |
|------|-------|-----|-------|
| 17 Oct 70 | **MAD SHADOWS** *Island ILPS 9119* ................. | 48 | 2 wks |
| 17 Apr 71 | **WILD LIFE** *Island ILPS 9144* ..................... | 44 | 2 wks |
| 23 Sep 72 | **ALL THE YOUNG DUDES** *CBS 65184* ....... | 21 | 4 wks |
| 11 Aug 73 | ● **MOTT** *CBS 69038* ............................... | 7 | 15 wks |
| 13 Apr 74 | **THE HOOPLE** *CBS 69062* ....................... | 11 | 5 wks |
| 23 Nov 74 | **LIVE** *CBS 69093* ................................... | 32 | 2 wks |
| 4 Oct 75 | **DRIVE ON** *CBS 69154* ............................ | 45 | 1 wk |

## MOUNTAIN  *US/Canada, male vocal/instrumental group*  4 wks

| Date | Title | Pos | Weeks |
|------|-------|-----|-------|
| 5 Jun 71 | **NANTUCKET SLEIGHRIDE** *Island ILPS 9148* ........ | 43 | 1 wk |
| 8 Jul 72 | **THE ROAD GOES EVER ON** *Island ILPS 9199* ........ | 21 | 3 wks |

## Nana MOUSKOURI  *Greece, female vocalist*  208 wks

| Date | Title | Pos | Weeks |
|------|-------|-----|-------|
| 7 Jun 69 | ● **OVER AND OVER** *Fontana S 5511* ................. | 10 | 105 wks |
| 4 Apr 70 | ● **THE EXQUISITE NANA MOUSKOURI** *Fontana STL 5536* ............................... | 10 | 25 wks |
| 10 Oct 70 | **RECITAL '70** *Fontana 6312 003* ................. | 68 | 1 wk |
| 3 Apr 71 | **TURN ON THE SUN** *Fontana 6312 008* ............... | 16 | 15 wks |
| 29 Jul 72 | **BRITISH CONCERT** *Fontana 6651 003* ............. | 29 | 11 wks |
| 28 Apr 73 | **SONGS FROM HER TV SERIES** *Fontana 6312 036* ..... | 29 | 11 wks |
| 28 Sep 74 | **SPOTLIGHT ON NANA MOUSKOURI** *Fontana 6641 197* .......................... | 38 | 6 wks |
| 10 Jul 76 | ● **PASSPORT** *Philips 9101 061* .................. | 3 | 16 wks |
| 22 Feb 86 | **ALONE** *Philips PHH 3* .......................... | 19 | 10 wks |
| 8 Oct 88 | **THE MAGIC OF NANA MOUSKOURI** *Philips NMTV 1* . | 44 | 8 wks |

## MOVE  *UK, male vocal/instrumental group*  9 wks

| Date | Title | Pos | Weeks |
|------|-------|-----|-------|
| 13 Apr 68 | **MOVE** *Regal Zonophone SLPZ 1002* ................... | 15 | 9 wks |

## Alison MOYET  *UK, female vocalist*  136 wks

| Date | Title | Pos | Weeks |
|------|-------|-----|-------|
| 17 Nov 84 | ★ **ALF** *CBS 26229* ................................. | 1 | 84 wks |
| 18 Apr 87 | ● **RAINDANCING** *CBS 450 152-1* ................... | 2 | 52 wks |

## MR. MISTER  *US, male vocal/instrumental group*  24 wks

| | | | |
|------|-------|-----|-------|
| 15 Feb 86 | ● **WELCOME TO THE REAL WORLD** *RCA PL 89647* ... | 6 | 24 wks |

## MSG  *Germany/UK, male vocal/instrumental group*  2 wks

| | | | |
|------|-------|-----|-------|
| 24 Oct 87 | **PERFECT TIMING** *EMI EMC 3539* ................. | 65 | 2 wks |

*MSG is the Michael Schenker Group with Robin McAuley in place of Michael Schenker.*
*See also Michael Schenker Group.*

## MTUME  *US, male/female vocal/instrumental group*  1 wk

| Date | Title | Pos | Weeks |
|------|-------|-----|-------|
| 6 Oct 84 | **YOU, ME AND HE** *Epic EPC 26077* ................. | 85 | 1 wk |

## MUD  *UK, male vocal/instrumental group*  58 wks

| | | | |
|------|-------|-----|-------|
| 28 Sep 74 | ● **MUD ROCK** *RAK SRAK 508* ....................... | 8 | 35 wks |
| 26 Jul 75 | ● **MUD ROCK VOL. 2** *RAK SRAK 513* ................. | 6 | 12 wks |
| 1 Nov 75 | **MUD'S GREATEST HITS** *RAK SRAK 6755* ........... | 25 | 6 wks |
| 27 Dec 75 | **USE YOUR IMAGINATION** *Private Stock PVLP 1003* .... | 33 | 5 wks |

MUFFINS – *See MARTHA and the MUFFINS*

## Gerry MULLIGAN and Ben WEBSTER
*US, male instrumental duo – baritone and tenor sax*  *1 wk*

| | | | |
|---|---|---|---|
| 24 Sep 60 | **GERRY MULLIGAN MEETS BEN WEBSTER** *HMV CLP 1373* | 15 | 1 wk |

## MUNGO JERRY  *UK, male vocal/instrumental group*  *14 wks*

| | | | |
|---|---|---|---|
| 8 Aug 70 | **MUNGO JERRY** *Dawn DNLS 3008* | 13 | 6 wks |
| 10 Apr 71 | **ELECTRONICALLY TESTED** *Dawn DNLS 3020* | 14 | 8 wks |

## MUPPETS  *US, puppets*  *45 wks*

| | | | |
|---|---|---|---|
| 11 Jun 77 | ★ **THE MUPPET SHOW** *Pye NSPH 19* | 1 | 35 wks |
| 25 Feb 78 | **THE MUPPET SHOW VOL. 2** *Pye NSPH 21* | 16 | 10 wks |

## Peter MURPHY  *UK, male vocalist*  *1 wk*

| | | | |
|---|---|---|---|
| 26 Jul 86 | **SHOULD THE WORLD FAIL TO FALL APART** *Beggars Banquet BEGA 69* | 82 | 1 wk |

## Anne MURRAY  *Canada, female vocalist*  *10 wks*

| | | | |
|---|---|---|---|
| 3 Oct 81 | **VERY BEST OF ANNE MURRAY** *Capitol EMTV 31* | 14 | 10 wks |

## Pauline MURRAY and the INVISIBLE GIRLS
*UK, female vocalist with male vocal/instrumental group*  *4 wks*

| | | | |
|---|---|---|---|
| 11 Oct 80 | **PAULINE MURRAY AND THE INVISIBLE GIRLS** *Elusive 2394 227* | 25 | 4 wks |

**MUSIC OF THE MOUNTAINS** – *See MANUEL and his MUSIC OF THE MOUNTAINS*

## MUSICAL YOUTH  *UK, male vocal/instrumental group*  *22 wks*

| | | | |
|---|---|---|---|
| 4 Dec 82 | **THE YOUTH OF TODAY** *MCA YOULP 1* | 24 | 22 wks |

**MUSIC STUDENTS** – *See Ian DURY*

# *n*

## NARADA  *US, male vocalist/instrumentalist/producer*  *5 wks*

| | | | |
|---|---|---|---|
| 14 May 88 | **DIVINE EMOTION** *Reprise WX 172* | 60 | 5 wks |

## Graham NASH  *UK, male vocalist*  *8 wks*

| | | | |
|---|---|---|---|
| 26 Jun 71 | **SONGS FOR BEGINNERS** *Atlantic 2401–011* | 13 | 8 wks |

*See also Crosby, Stills and Nash; Crosby, Stills, Nash and Young; Graham Nash and David Crosby.*

## Graham NASH and David CROSBY
*UK/US, male vocal duo*                                                  *5 wks*

| | | | |
|---|---|---|---|
| 13 May 72 | **GRAHAM NASH AND DAVID CROSBY** *Atlantic K 50011* | 13 | 5 wks |

*See also Graham Nash; Dave Crosby.*

## Johnny NASH  *US, male vocalist*                                      *17 wks*

| | | | |
|---|---|---|---|
| 5 Aug 72 | **I CAN SEE CLEARLY NOW** *CBS 64860* ............. | 39 | 6 wks |
| 10 Dec 77 | **JOHNNY NASH COLLECTION** *Epic EPC 10008* ....... | 18 | 11 wks |

## NASH THE SLASH
*Canada, male vocalist/multi-instrumentalist*                            *1 wk*

| | | | |
|---|---|---|---|
| 21 Feb 81 | **CHILDREN OF THE NIGHT** *DinDisc DID 9* .......... | 61 | 1 wk |

## NATASHA  *UK, female vocalist*                                        *3 wks*

| | | | |
|---|---|---|---|
| 9 Oct 82 | **CAPTURED** *Towerbell TOWLP 2* ................... | 53 | 3 wks |

## NATIONAL BRASS BAND  *UK, orchestra*                                   *10 wks*

| | | | |
|---|---|---|---|
| 10 May 80 | **GOLDEN MELODIES** *K-Tel ONE 1075* .............. | 15 | 10 wks |

**NATIONAL PHILHARMONIC ORCHESTRA** – *See LONDON PHILHARMONIC CHOIR*

## NAZARETH  *UK, male vocal/instrumental group*                          *51 wks*

| | | | |
|---|---|---|---|
| 26 May 73 | **RAZAMANAZ** *Mooncrest CREST 1* ................. | 11 | 25 wks |
| 24 Nov 73 ● | **LOUD 'N' PROUD** *Mooncrest CREST 4* .............. | 10 | 7 wks |
| 18 May 74 | **RAMPANT** *Mooncrest CREST 15* .................... | 13 | 3 wks |
| 13 Dec 75 | **GREATEST HITS** *Mountain TOPS 108* .............. | 54 | 1 wk |
| 3 Feb 79 | **NO MEAN CITY** *Mountain TOPS 123* ............... | 34 | 9 wks |
| 28 Feb 81 | **THE FOOL CIRCLE** *NEMS NEL 6019* ............... | 60 | 3 wks |
| 3 Oct 81 | **NAZARETH LIVE** *NEMS NELD 102* ................ | 78 | 3 wks |

## Bill NELSON  *UK, male vocalist/multi-instrumentalist*                 *21 wks*

| | | | |
|---|---|---|---|
| 24 Feb 79 | **SOUND ON SOUND** *Harvest SHSP 4095* ............. | 33 | 5 wks |
| 23 May 81 ● | **QUIT DREAMING AND GET ON THE BEAM** *Mercury 6359 055* .................................. | 7 | 6 wks |
| 3 Jul 82 | **THE LOVE THAT WHIRLS (DIARY OF A THINKING HEART)** *Mercury WHIRL 3* ...................... | 28 | 4 wks |
| 14 May 83 | **CHIMERA** *Mercury MERB 19* .................... | 30 | 5 wks |
| 3 May 86 | **GETTING THE HOLY GHOST ACROSS** *Portrait PRT 26602* .............................. | 91 | 1 wk |

*First album credited to Bill Nelson's Red Noise – UK, male vocal/instrumental group.*

## Phyllis NELSON  *US, female vocalist*                                  *10 wks*

| | | | |
|---|---|---|---|
| 20 Apr 85 | **MOVE CLOSER** *Carrere CAL 203* ................... | 29 | 10 wks |

## NENA  *Germany, female/male vocal/instrumental group*                  *5 wks*

| | | | |
|---|---|---|---|
| 24 Mar 84 | **NENA** *Epic EPC 25925* ........................... | 31 | 5 wks |

**NESBIT** – *See MILLICAN and NESBIT*

## Robbie NEVIL  *US, male vocalist*                                      *1 wk*

| | | | |
|---|---|---|---|
| 13 Jun 87 | **C'EST LA VIE** *Manhattan MTL 1006* .................. | 93 | 1 wk |

Aaron **NEVILLE** – *See Linda RONSTADT*

**NEW BOHEMIANS** – *See Edie BRICKELL and the NEW BOHEMIANS*

## NEW KIDS ON THE BLOCK  US, male vocal group        *4 wks*

| | | | |
|---|---|---|---|
| 9 Dec 89 | ● **HANGIN' TOUGH**  CBS 460874 1 .................. | 8† | 4 wks |

## NEW MODEL ARMY  UK, male vocal/instrumental group        *14 wks*

| | | | |
|---|---|---|---|
| 12 May 84 | **VENGEANCE**  *Abstract ABT 008* ..................... | 73 | 5 wks |
| 25 May 85 | **NO REST FOR THE WICKED**  *EMI NMAL 1* ......... | 22 | 3 wks |
| 11 Oct 86 | **THE GHOST OF CAIN**  *EMI EMC 3516* .............. | 45 | 3 wks |
| 18 Feb 89 | **THUNDER AND CONSOLATION**  *EMI EMC 3552* .... | 20 | 3 wks |

## NEW MUSIK  UK, male vocal/instrumental group        *11 wks*

| | | | |
|---|---|---|---|
| 17 May 80 | **FROM A TO B**  *GTO GTLP 041* ..................... | 35 | 9 wks |
| 14 Mar 81 | **ANYWHERE**  *GTO GTLP 044* ..................... | 68 | 2 wks |

## NEW ORDER  UK, male/female vocal/instrumental group        *105 wks*

| | | | |
|---|---|---|---|
| 28 Nov 81 | **MOVEMENT**  *Factory FACT 50* ..................... | 30 | 10 wks |
| 14 May 83 | ● **POWER, CORRUPTION AND LIES**  *Factory FACT 75* .. | 4 | 29 wks |
| 25 May 85 | ● **LOW-LIFE**  *Factory FACT 100* ..................... | 7 | 10 wks |
| 11 Oct 86 | ● **BROTHERHOOD**  *Factory FACT 150* ................ | 9 | 5 wks |
| 29 Aug 87 | ● **SUBSTANCE**  *Factory FACT 200* ................... | 3 | 37 wks |
| 11 Feb 89 | ★ **TECHNIQUE**  *Factory FACT 275* ................... | 1 | 14 wks |

## NEW SEEKERS  UK, male/female vocal/instrumental group        *49 wks*

| | | | |
|---|---|---|---|
| 5 Feb 72 | **NEW COLOURS**  *Polydor 2383 066* ................. | 40 | 4 wks |
| 1 Apr 72 | ● **WE'D LIKE TO TEACH THE WORLD TO SING** | | |
| | *Polydor 2883 103* ................................. | 2 | 25 wks |
| 12 Aug 72 | **NEVER ENDING SONG OF LOVE**  *Polydor 2383 126* ..... | 35 | 4 wks |
| 14 Oct 72 | **CIRCLES**  *Polydor 2442 102* ........................ | 23 | 5 wks |
| 21 Apr 73 | **NOW**  *Polydor 2383 195* ........................... | 47 | 2 wks |
| 30 Mar 74 | **TOGETHER**  *Polydor 2383 264* ..................... | 12 | 9 wks |

## NEW WORLD THEATRE ORCHESTRA
*UK, orchestra*        *1 wk*

| | | | |
|---|---|---|---|
| 24 Dec 60 | **LET'S DANCE TO THE HITS OF THE 30'S AND 40'S** | | |
| | *Pye Golden Guinea GGL 0026* ....................... | 20 | 1 wk |

## NEWCLEUS  US, male vocal/instrumental group        *2 wks*

| | | | |
|---|---|---|---|
| 25 Aug 84 | **JAM ON REVENGE**  *Sunnyview SVLP 6600* ............ | 84 | 2 wks |

## Bob NEWHART  US, male comedian        *37 wks*

| | | | |
|---|---|---|---|
| 1 Oct 60 | ● **BUTTON-DOWN MIND OF BOB NEWHART** | | |
| | *Warner Bros. WM 4010* ............................ | 2 | 37 wks |

## Anthony NEWLEY  UK, male vocalist        *14 wks*

| | | | |
|---|---|---|---|
| 14 May 60 | **LOVE IS A NOW AND THEN THING**  *Decca LK 4343* ... | 19 | 2 wks |
| 8 Jul 61 | ● **TONY**  *Decca LK 4406* ........................... | 5 | 12 wks |

*See also Anthony Newley, Peter Sellers, Joan Collins.*

**LIZA MINNELLI** had her first hit in sixteen years with production help from the Pet Shop Boys.

**BOB NEWHART**
the most successful alb
by an Amer
comed

The **MOTHERS OF INVENTION** tower over the mentor who later outgrew them, Frank Zappa.

## Anthony NEWLEY, Peter SELLERS, Joan COLLINS
*UK, male/female vocalists*                                    *10 wks*

| | | | |
|---|---|---|---|
| 28 Sep 63 | ● **FOOL BRITANNIA** *Ember CEL 902* | 10 | 10 wks |

*See also Anthony Newley; Peter Sellers.*

**NEWS** – *See Huey LEWIS and the NEWS*

## Olivia NEWTON-JOHN  *UK, female vocalist*                   *93 wks*

| | | | |
|---|---|---|---|
| 2 Mar 74 | **MUSIC MAKES MY DAY** *Pye NSPL 28186* | 37 | 3 wks |
| 29 Jun 74 | **LONG LIVE LOVE** *EMI EMC 3028* | 40 | 2 wks |
| 26 Apr 75 | **HAVE YOU NEVER BEEN MELLOW** *EMI EMC 3069* | 37 | 2 wks |
| 29 May 76 | **COME ON OVER** *EMI EMC 3124* | 49 | 4 wks |
| 27 Aug 77 | **MAKING A GOOD THING BETTER** *EMI EMC 3192* | 60 | 1 wk |
| 21 Jan 78 | **GREATEST HITS** *EMI EMA 785* | 19 | 9 wks |
| 9 Dec 78 | **TOTALLY HOT** *EMI EMA 789* | 30 | 9 wks |
| 31 Oct 81 | **PHYSICAL** *EMI EMC 3386* | 11 | 22 wks |
| 23 Oct 82 | ● **GREATEST HITS** *EMI EMTV 36* | 8 | 38 wks |
| 8 Mar 86 | **SOUL KISS** *Mercury MERH 77* | 66 | 3 wks |

## NICE  *UK, male instrumental group*                         *38 wks*

| | | | |
|---|---|---|---|
| 13 Sep 69 | ● **NICE** *Immediate IMSP 026* | 3 | 6 wks |
| 27 Jun 70 | ● **FIVE BRIDGES** *Charisma CAS 1014* | 2 | 21 wks |
| 17 Apr 71 | ● **ELEGY** *Charisma CAS 1030* | 5 | 11 wks |

## Paul NICHOLAS  *UK, male vocalist*                          *8 wks*

| | | | |
|---|---|---|---|
| 29 Nov 86 | **JUST GOOD FRIENDS** *K-Tel ONE 1334* | 30 | 8 wks |

## Stevie NICKS  *US, female vocalist*                         *71 wks*

| | | | |
|---|---|---|---|
| 8 Aug 81 | **BELLA DONNA** *WEA K 99169* | 11 | 16 wks |
| 2 Jul 83 | **THE WILD HEART** *WEA 25-0071-1* | 28 | 19 wks |
| 14 Dec 85 | **ROCK A LITTLE** *Modern PCS 7300* | 30 | 22 wks |
| 10 Jun 89 | ● **THE OTHER SIDE OF THE MIRROR** *EMI EMD 1008* | 3 | 14 wks |

## Hector NICOL  *UK, male vocalist*                           *1 wk*

| | | | |
|---|---|---|---|
| 28 Apr 84 | **BRAVO JULIET** *Klub KLP 42* | 92 | 1 wk |

## NICOLE  *Germany, female vocalist*                          *2 wks*

| | | | |
|---|---|---|---|
| 2 Oct 82 | **A LITTLE PEACE** *CBS 85011* | 85 | 2 wks |

## NILSSON  *US, male vocalist*                                *43 wks*

| | | | |
|---|---|---|---|
| 29 Jan 72 | **THE POINT** *RCA Victor SF 8166* | 46 | 1 wk |
| 5 Feb 72 | ● **NILSSON SCHMILSSON** *RCA Victor SF 8242* | 4 | 22 wks |
| 19 Aug 72 | **SON OF SCHMILSSON** *RCA Victor SF 8297* | 41 | 1 wk |
| 28 Jul 73 | **A LITTLE TOUCH OF SCHMILSSON IN THE NIGHT** *RCA Victor SF 8371* | 20 | 19 wks |

## NINA and FREDERICK  *Denmark, male/female vocal duo*        *6 wks*

| | | | |
|---|---|---|---|
| 13 Feb 60 | ● **NINA AND FREDERICK** *Pye NPT 19023* | 9 | 2 wks |
| 29 Apr 61 | **NINA AND FREDERICK** *Columbia COL 1314* | 11 | 4 wks |

*These two albums, although identically named, are different.*

## 9 BELOW ZERO  *UK, male vocal/instrumental group*  *12 wks*

| | | | | |
|---|---|---|---|---|
| 14 Mar 81 | **DON'T POINT YOUR FINGER**  *A & M  AMLH 68521*  ... | 56 | 6 wks |
| 20 Mar 82 | **THIRD DEGREE**  *A & M  AMLH 68537* ................ | 38 | 6 wks |

## 999  *UK, male vocal/instrumental group*  *1 wk*

| | | | | |
|---|---|---|---|---|
| 25 Mar 78 | **999**  *United Artists UAG 30199* ....................... | 53 | 1 wk |

## NOLANS  *Ireland, female vocal group*  *84 wks*

| | | | | |
|---|---|---|---|---|
| 20 Jul 78 | ● **20 GIANT HITS**  *Target TGS 502* ..................... | 3 | 12 wks |
| 19 Jan 80 | **NOLANS**  *Epic EPC 83892* .......................... | 15 | 13 wks |
| 25 Oct 80 | **MAKING WAVES**  *Epic EPC 10023* ................. | 11 | 33 wks |
| 27 Mar 82 | ● **PORTRAIT**  *Epic EPC 10033* ..................... | 7 | 10 wks |
| 20 Nov 82 | **ALTOGETHER**  *Epic EPC 10037* ................... | 52 | 8 wks |
| 17 Nov 84 | **GIRLS JUST WANNA HAVE FUN**  *Towerbell TOWLP 10* . | 39 | 8 wks |

*First album credited to Nolan Sisters.*

## NOT THE 9 O'CLOCK NEWS CAST
*UK/New Zealand, male/female TV cast*  *51 wks*

| | | | | |
|---|---|---|---|---|
| 8 Nov 80 | ● **NOT THE 9 O'CLOCK NEWS**  *BBC REB 400* .......... | 5 | 23 wks |
| 17 Oct 81 | ● **HEDGEHOG SANDWICH**  *BBC REB 421* ............. | 5 | 24 wks |
| 23 Oct 82 | **THE MEMORY KINDA LINGERS**  *BBC REF 453* ...... | 63 | 4 wks |

## NU SHOOZ  *US, male/female vocal duo*  *8 wks*

| | | | | |
|---|---|---|---|---|
| 14 Jun 86 | **POOLSIDE**  *Atlantic WX 60* ......................... | 32 | 8 wks |

## NUCLEAR ASSAULT  *US, male vocal/instrumental group*  *1 wk*

| | | | | |
|---|---|---|---|---|
| 7 Oct 89 | **HANDLE WITH CARE**  *Under One Flag FLAG 35* ....... | 60 | 1 wk |

## NUCLEUS  *UK, male instrumental group*  *1 wk*

| | | | | |
|---|---|---|---|---|
| 11 Jul 70 | **ELASTIC ROCK**  *Vertigo 6360 006* ................... | 46 | 1 wk |

## Ted NUGENT
*US, male vocalist/instrumentalist – guitar*  *14 wks*

| | | | | |
|---|---|---|---|---|
| 4 Sep 76 | **TED NUGENT**  *Epic EPC 81268* ..................... | 56 | 1 wk |
| 30 Oct 76 | **FREE FOR ALL**  *Epic EPC 81397* ............. | 33 | 2 wks |
| 2 Jul 77 | **CAT SCRATCH FEVER**  *Epic EPC 82010* ............. | 28 | 5 wks |
| 11 Mar 78 | **DOUBLE LIVE GONZO**  *Epic EPC 88282* ............. | 47 | 2 wks |
| 14 Jun 80 | **SCREAM DREAM**  *Epic EPC 86111* ................... | 37 | 3 wks |
| 25 Apr 81 | **IN 10 CITIES**  *Epic EPC 84917* ....................... | 75 | 1 wk |

## Gary NUMAN  *UK, male vocalist*  *135 wks*

| | | | | |
|---|---|---|---|---|
| 9 Jun 79 | ★ **REPLICAS**  *Beggars Banquet BEGA 7* ............. | 1 | 31 wks |
| 25 Aug 79 | **TUBEWAY ARMY**  *Beggars Banquet BEGA 4* ......... | 14 | 10 wks |
| 22 Sep 79 | ★ **THE PLEASURE PRINCIPLE**  *Beggars Banquet BEGA 10* . | 1 | 21 wks |
| 13 Sep 80 | ★ **TELEKON**  *Beggars Banquet BEGA 19* ................ | 1 | 11 wks |
| 2 May 81 | ● **LIVING ORNAMENTS 1979–1980** | | |
| | *Beggars Banquet BOX 1* | 2 | 4 wks |
| 2 May 81 | **LIVING ORNAMENTS 1979**  *Beggars Banquet BEGA 24* ... | 47 | 3 wks |
| 2 May 81 | **LIVING ORNAMENTS 1980**  *Beggars Banquet BEGA 25* ... | 39 | 3 wks |
| 12 Sep 81 | ● **DANCE**  *Beggars Banquet BEGA 28* .................... | 3 | 8 wks |
| 18 Sep 82 | ● **I, ASSASSIN**  *Beggars Banquet BEGA 40* ................ | 8 | 6 wks |

| | | | | |
|---|---|---|---|---|
| 27 Nov 82 | **NEW MAN NUMAN – THE BEST OF GARY NUMAN** | | | |
| | *TV Records TVA 7* ................................ | **45** | 7 wks | |
| 24 Sep 83 | **WARRIORS** *Beggars Banquet BEGA 47* ............... | **12** | 6 wks | |
| 6 Oct 84 | **THE PLAN** *Beggars Banquet BEGA 55* ................. | **29** | 4 wks | |
| 24 Nov 84 | **BERSERKER** *Numa NUMA 1001* .................... | **45** | 3 wks | |
| 13 Apr 85 | **WHITE NOISE – LIVE** *Numa NUMAD 1002* .......... | **29** | 5 wks | |
| 28 Sep 85 | **THE FURY** *Numa NUMA 1003* .................... | **24** | 5 wks | |
| 8 Nov 86 | **STRANGE CHARM** *Numa NUMA 1005* .............. | **59** | 2 wks | |
| 3 Oct 87 | **EXHIBITION** *Beggars Banquet BEGA 88* ............ | **43** | 3 wks | |
| 8 Oct 88 | **METAL RHYTHM** *Illegal ILP 035* ................ | **48** | 2 wks | |
| 28 Oct 89 | **SKIN MECHANIC** *IRS EIRSA 1019* ................ | **55** | 1 wk | |

*First two albums credited to Tubeway Army. The Plan is credited to Tubeway Army and Gary Numan. All other albums are credited to Gary Numan. Living Ornaments 1979–1980 is a boxed set of Living Ornaments 1979 and Living Ornaments 1980. See also Sharpe and Numan.*

## N.W.A. *US, male rap group*      *3 wks*

| | | | | |
|---|---|---|---|---|
| 30 Sep 89 | **STRAIGHT OUTTA COMPTON** | | | |
| | *Fourth & Broadway BRLP 534* ........................ | **41** | 3 wks | |

# *O*

## Philip OAKEY and Giorgio MORODER
*UK/Italy, male vocal/instrumental duo*      *5 wks*

*O*

| | | | | |
|---|---|---|---|---|
| 10 Aug 85 | **PHILIP OAKEY AND GIORGIO MORODER** | | | |
| | *Virgin V 2351* ................................ | **52** | 5 wks | |

## OASIS *UK, male/female vocal group*      *14 wks*

| | | | | |
|---|---|---|---|---|
| 28 Apr 84 | **OASIS** *WEA WX 3* ............................ | **23** | 14 wks | |

**John OATES** – *See Daryl HALL and John OATES*

## Billy OCEAN *UK, male vocalist*      *114 wks*

| | | | | |
|---|---|---|---|---|
| 24 Nov 84 | ● **SUDDENLY** *Jive JIP 12* ......................... | **9** | 59 wks | |
| 17 May 86 | ● **LOVE ZONE** *Jive HIP 35* ....................... | **2** | 32 wks | |
| 19 Mar 88 | ● **TEAR DOWN THESE WALLS** *Jive HIP 57* .......... | **3** | 13 wks | |
| 28 Oct 89 | ● **GREATEST HITS** *Jive BOTV 1* .................... | **4†** | 10 wks | |

## Des O'CONNOR *UK, male vocalist*      *41 wks*

| | | | | |
|---|---|---|---|---|
| 7 Dec 68 | ● **I PRETEND** *Columbia SCX 6295* ................. | **8** | 10 wks | |
| 5 Dec 70 | **WITH LOVE** *Columbia SCX 6417* .................. | **40** | 4 wks | |
| 2 Dec 72 | **SING A FAVOURITE SONG** *Pye NSPL 18390* ........ | **25** | 6 wks | |
| 2 Feb 80 | **JUST FOR YOU** *Warwick WW 5071* ................ | **17** | 7 wks | |
| 13 Oct 84 | **DES O'CONNOR NOW** *Telstar STAR 2245* ........... | **24** | 14 wks | |

## Hazel O'CONNOR *UK, female vocalist*      *45 wks*

| | | | | |
|---|---|---|---|---|
| 9 Aug 80 | ● **BREAKING GLASS (film soundtrack)** | | | |
| | *A & M AMLH 64820* ........................... | **5** | 38 wks | |
| 12 Sep 81 | **COVER PLUS** *Albion ALB 108* .................... | **32** | 7 wks | |

## Sinéad O'CONNOR
*Ireland, female vocalist*                                                   *13 wks*

| | | | | | |
|---|---|---|---|---|---|
| 23 Jan | 88 | **THE LION AND THE COBRA** *Ensign CHEN 7* ........ | 27 | 13 wks |

## Daniel O'DONNELL  *Ireland, male vocalist*                  *22 wks*

| | | | | | |
|---|---|---|---|---|---|
| 15 Oct | 88 | **FROM THE HEART** *Telstar STAR 2327* .............. | 56 | 12 wks |
| 28 Oct | 89 | **THOUGHTS OF HOME** *Telstar STAR 2372* ........... | 43† | 10 wks |

## ODYSSEY  *US, male/female vocal group*                    *32 wks*

| | | | | | |
|---|---|---|---|---|---|
| 16 Aug | 80 | **HANG TOGETHER** *RCA PL 13526* ................... | 38 | 3 wks |
| 4 Jul | 81 | **I'VE GOT THE MELODY** *RCA RCALP 5028* .......... | 29 | 7 wks |
| 3 Jul | 82 | **HAPPY TOGETHER** *RCA RCALP 6036* ............. | 21 | 9 wks |
| 20 Nov | 82 | **THE MAGIC TOUCH OF ODYSSEY** *Telstar STAR 2223* . | 69 | 5 wks |
| 26 Sep | 87 | **THE GREATEST HITS** *Stylus SMR 735* .............. | 26 | 8 wks |

## Esther and Abi OFARIM
*Israel, female/male vocal duo*                                        *24 wks*

| | | | | | |
|---|---|---|---|---|---|
| 24 Feb | 68 | ● **2 IN 3** *Philips SBL 7825* ........................... | 6 | 20 wks |
| 12 Jul | 69 | **OFARIM CONCERT – LIVE '69** *Philips XL 4* .......... | 29 | 4 wks |

## Mary O'HARA
*UK, female vocalist/instrumentalist – harp*                 *12 wks*

| | | | | | |
|---|---|---|---|---|---|
| 8 Apr | 78 | **MARY O'HARA AT THE ROYAL FESTIVAL HALL** *Chrysalis CHR 1159* ........................... | 37 | 3 wks |
| 1 Dec | 79 | **TRANQUILLITY** *Warwick WW 5072* ............... | 12 | 9 wks |

**204**

*O*

## Mike OLDFIELD
*UK, male multi-instrumentalist/vocalist*                   *471 wks*

| | | | | | |
|---|---|---|---|---|---|
| 14 Jul | 73 | ★ **TUBULAR BELLS** *Virgin V 2001* .................... | 1 | 264 wks |
| 14 Sep | 74 | ★ **HERGEST RIDGE** *Virgin V 2013* ................... | 1 | 17 wks |
| 8 Feb | 75 | **THE ORCHESTRAL TUBULAR BELLS** *Virgin V 2026* . | 17 | 7 wks |
| 15 Nov | 75 | ● **OMMADAWN** *Virgin V 2043* ...................... | 4 | 23 wks |
| 20 Nov | 76 | **BOXED** *Virgin V BOX 1* ......................... | 22 | 13 wks |
| 9 Dec | 78 | **INCANTATIONS** *Virgin VDT 101* ................ | 14 | 17 wks |
| 11 Aug | 79 | **EXPOSED** *Virgin VD 2511* ...................... | 16 | 9 wks |
| 8 Dec | 79 | **PLATINUM** *Virgin V 2141* .................... | 24 | 9 wks |
| 8 Nov | 80 | **QE 2** *Virgin V 2181* ......................... | 27 | 12 wks |
| 27 Mar | 82 | **FIVE MILES OUT** *Virgin V 2222* ................... | 7 | 27 wks |
| 4 Jun | 83 | ● **CRISES** *Virgin V 2262* ........................ | 6 | 29 wks |
| 7 Jul | 84 | **DISCOVERY** *Virgin V 2308* ..................... | 15 | 16 wks |
| 15 Dec | 84 | **THE KILLING FIELDS** *Virgin V 2328* .............. | 97 | 1 wk |
| 2 Nov | 85 | **THE COMPLETE MIKE OLDFIELD** *Virgin MOC 1* ..... | 36 | 17 wks |
| 10 Oct | 87 | **ISLANDS** *Virgin V 2466* ....................... | 29 | 5 wks |
| 22 Jul | 89 | **EARTH MOVING** *Virgin V 2610* ................... | 30 | 5 wks |

The Orchestral Tubular Bells *is with the Royal Philharmonic Orchestra. See also Royal Philharmonic Orchestra.*

## ONE HUNDRED & ONE STRINGS
*Germany, orchestra*                                                    *35 wks*

| | | | | | |
|---|---|---|---|---|---|
| 26 Sep | 59 | ● **GYPSY CAMPFIRES** *Pye GGL 0009* ................ | 9 | 7 wks |
| 26 Mar | 60 | **SOUL OF SPAIN** *Pye GGL 0017* .................... | 17 | 1 wk |
| 16 Apr | 60 | ● **GRAND CANYON SUITE** *Pye GGL 0048* ............. | 10 | 1 wk |
| 27 Aug | 60 | ★ **DOWN DRURY LANE TO MEMORY LANE** *Pye GGL 0061* ................................. | 1 | 21 wks |
| 15 Oct | 83 | **MORNING, NOON AND NIGHT** *Ronco RTL 2094* ...... | 32 | 5 wks |

*The orchestra was American based for last album.*

## Alexander O'NEAL   *US, male vocalist*                              *122 wks*

| 1 Jun 85 | **ALEXANDER O'NEAL**   *Tabu TBU 26485* .............. | 19 | 18 wks |
| 8 Aug 87 | ● **HEARSAY/ALL MIXED UP**   *Tabu 450 936-1* .......... | 4† | 101 wks |
| 17 Dec 88 | **MY GIFT TO YOU**   *Tabu 463152 1* ................... | 53 | 3 wks |

All Mixed Up, *a re-mixed album of* Hearsay *was listed with* Hearsay *from 15 Jul 89.*

## ONLY ONES   *UK, male vocal/instrumental group*                    *8 wks*

| 3 Jun 78 | **THE ONLY ONES**   *CBS 82830* ...................... | 56 | 1 wk |
| 31 Mar 79 | **EVEN SERPENTS SHINE**   *CBS 83451* .............. | 42 | 2 wks |
| 3 May 80 | **BABY'S GOT A GUN**   *CBS 84089* .................. | 37 | 5 wks |

## Yoko ONO   *Japan, female vocalist*                                 *2 wks*

| 20 Jun 81 | **SEASON OF GLASS**   *Geffen K 99164* ................. | 47 | 2 wks |

*See also John Lennon.*

## ONSLAUGHT   *UK, male vocal/instrumental group*                    *2 wks*

| 20 May 89 | **IN SEARCH OF SANITY**   *London 828142 1* ............ | 46 | 2 wks |

## ORANGE JUICE   *UK, male vocal/instrumental group*                 *18 wks*

| 6 Mar 82 | **YOU CAN'T HIDE YOUR LOVE FOREVER** | | |
| | *Polydor POLS 1057* ................................ | 21 | 6 wks |
| 20 Nov 82 | **RIP IT UP**   *Holden Caulfield Universal   POLS 1076* ......... | 39 | 8 wks |
| 10 Mar 84 | **TEXAS FEVER**   *Polydor OJMLP 1* ................... | 34 | 4 wks |

## Roy ORBISON   *US, male vocalist*                                  *208 wks*

| 8 Jun 63 | **LONELY AND BLUE**   *London HAU 2342* .............. | 15 | 8 wks |
| 29 Jun 63 | **CRYING**   *London HAU 2437* ...................... | 17 | 3 wks |
| 30 Nov 63 | ● **IN DREAMS**   *London HAU 8108* .................. | 6 | 57 wks |
| 25 Jul 64 | **EXCITING SOUNDS OF ROY ORBISON**   *Ember NR 5013* | 17 | 2 wks |
| 5 Dec 64 | ● **OH PRETTY WOMAN**   *London HAU 8207* ............ | 4 | 16 wks |
| 25 Sep 65 | ● **THERE IS ONLY ONE ROY ORBISON** | | |
| | *London HAU 8252* ............................... | 10 | 12 wks |
| 26 Feb 66 | **THE ORBISON WAY**   *London HAU 8279* ............. | 11 | 10 wks |
| 24 Sep 66 | **THE CLASSIC ROY ORBISON**   *London HAU 8297* ..... | 12 | 8 wks |
| 22 Jul 67 | **ORBISONGS**   *Monument SMO 5004* .................. | 40 | 1 wk |
| 30 Sep 67 | **ROY ORBISON'S GREATEST HITS** | | |
| | *Monument SMO 5007* .......................... | 40 | 1 wk |
| 27 Jan 73 | **ALL-TIME GREATEST HITS**   *Monument MNT 67290* .... | 39 | 3 wks |
| 29 Nov 75 | ★ **THE BEST OF ROY ORBISON**   *Arcade ADEP 19* ....... | 1 | 20 wks |
| 18 Jul 81 | **GOLDEN DAYS**   *CBS 10026* ...................... | 63 | 1 wk |
| 4 Jul 87 | **IN DREAMS: THE GREATEST HITS**   *Virgin VGD 3514* . | 86 | 2 wks |
| 29 Oct 88 | ★ **THE LEGENDARY ROY ORBISON**   *Telstar STAR 2330* . | 1† | 38 wks |
| 11 Feb 89 | ● **MYSTERY GIRL**   *Virgin V 2576* ...................... | 2 | 23 wks |
| 25 Nov 89 | **A BLACK AND WHITE NIGHT**   *Virgin V 2601* ......... | 51 | 3 wks |

## ORCHESTRAL MANOEUVRES IN THE DARK
*UK, male vocal/instrumental duo*                                    *182 wks*

| 1 Mar 80 | **ORCHESTRAL MANOEUVRES IN THE DARK** | | |
| | *DinDisc DID 2* ................................... | 27 | 29 wks |
| 1 Nov 80 | ● **ORGANISATION**   *DinDisc DID 6* .................... | 6 | 25 wks |
| 14 Nov 81 | ● **ARCHITECTURE AND MORALITY**   *DinDisc DID 12* .. | 3 | 39 wks |
| 12 Mar 83 | ● **DAZZLE SHIPS**   *Telegraph V 2261* .................. | 5 | 13 wks |
| 12 May 84 | ● **JUNK CULTURE**   *Virgin V 2310* ................... | 9 | 27 wks |
| 29 Jun 85 | **CRUSH**   *Virgin V 2349* ......................... | 13 | 12 wks |
| 11 Oct 86 | **THE PACIFIC AGE**   *Virgin V 2398* .................. | 15 | 7 wks |
| 12 Mar 88 | ● **THE BEST OF O.M.D.**   *Virgin OMD 1* ................ | 2 | 30 wks |

## L'ORCHESTRE ELECTRONIQUE
*UK, male synthesized orchestra*                                    *1 wk*

| | | | | |
|---|---|---|---|---|
| 29 Oct 83 | **SOUND WAVES** *Nouveau Musique NML 1005* .......... | 75 | 1 wk |

**Cyril ORNADEL** – *See LONDON SYMPHONY ORCHESTRA*

**ORVILLE** – *See Keith HARRIS, ORVILLE and CUDDLES*

## Jeffrey OSBORNE  *US, male vocalist*                           *10 wks*

| | | | |
|---|---|---|---|
| 5 May 84 | **STAY WITH ME TONIGHT** *A & M AMLX 64940* ....... | 56 | 7 wks |
| 13 Oct 84 | **DON'T STOP** *A & M AMA 5017* .................... | 59 | 3 wks |

## Ozzy OSBOURNE  *UK, male vocalist*                            *53 wks*

| | | | |
|---|---|---|---|
| 20 Sep 80 | ● **OZZY OSBOURNE'S BLIZZARD OF OZ** *Jet JETLP 234* ................................. | 7 | 8 wks |
| 7 Nov 81 | **DIARY OF A MADMAN** *Jet JETLP 237* .............. | 14 | 12 wks |
| 27 Nov 82 | **TALK OF THE DEVIL** *Jet JETDP 401* ............. | 21 | 6 wks |
| 10 Dec 83 | **BARK AT THE MOON** *Epic EPC 25739* ............. | 24 | 7 wks |
| 22 Feb 86 | ● **THE ULTIMATE SIN** *Epic EPC 26404* ............. | 8 | 10 wks |
| 23 May 87 | **TRIBUTE** *Epic 450 475–1* ......................... | 13 | 6 wks |
| 22 Oct 88 | **NO REST FOR THE WICKED** *Epic 462581 1* .......... | 23 | 4 wks |

*Ozzy Osbourne's Blizzard Of Oz are a UK/US male vocal/instrumental group.*

## OSIBISA  *Ghana/Nigeria, male vocal/instrumental group*      *17 wks*

| | | | |
|---|---|---|---|
| 22 May 71 | **OSIBISA** *MCA MDKS 8001* ......................... | 11 | 10 wks |
| 5 Feb 72 | **WOYAYA** *MCA MDKS 8005* ......................... | 11 | 7 wks |

## Donny OSMOND  *US, male vocalist*                            *104 wks*

| | | | |
|---|---|---|---|
| 23 Sep 72 | ● **PORTRAIT OF DONNY** *MGM 2315 108* ............. | 5 | 43 wks |
| 16 Dec 72 | ● **TOO YOUNG** *MGM 2315 113* ..................... | 7 | 24 wks |
| 26 May 73 | ● **ALONE TOGETHER** *MGM 2315 210* ................ | 6 | 19 wks |
| 15 Dec 73 | ● **A TIME FOR US** *MGM 2315 273* .................... | 4 | 13 wks |
| 8 Feb 75 | **DONNY** *MGM 2315 314* ......................... | 16 | 4 wks |
| 2 Oct 76 | **DISCOTRAIN** *Polydor 2391 226* .................... | 59 | 1 wk |

*See also Osmonds; Donny and Marie Osmond.*

## Donny and Marie OSMOND
*US, male/female vocal duo*                                       *19 wks*

| | | | |
|---|---|---|---|
| 2 Nov 74 | **I'M LEAVING IT ALL UP TO YOU** *MGM 2315 307* ..... | 13 | 15 wks |
| 26 Jul 75 | **MAKE THE WORLD GO AWAY** *MGM 2315 343* ...... | 30 | 3 wks |
| 5 Jun 76 | **DEEP PURPLE** *Polydor 2391 220* .................... | 48 | 1 wk |

*See also Donny Osmond; Marie Osmond.*

## Little Jimmy OSMOND  *US, male vocalist*                      *12 wks*

| | | | |
|---|---|---|---|
| 17 Feb 73 | **KILLER JOE** *MGM 2315 157* ........................ | 20 | 12 wks |

## Marie OSMOND  *US, female vocalist*                           *1 wk*

| | | | |
|---|---|---|---|
| 9 Feb 74 | **PAPER ROSES** *MGM 2315 262* .................... | 46 | 1 wk |

*See also Donny and Marie Osmond.*

It's hearsay, but **ALEXANDER O'NEAL** had two hit albums with only one LP's vocal performance.

**ORCHESTRAL MANOEUVRES IN THE DARK** (Andy McCluskey and Paul Humphreys) were the most successful act on DinDisc.

**ROBERT PALMER** finally ripped open the Top Ten in 1985.

## OSMONDS  *US, male vocal/instrumental group*  *103 wks*

| 18 Nov 72 | **OSMONDS LIVE**  *MGM 2315 117* ................. | 13 | 22 wks |
|---|---|---|---|
| 16 Dec 72 | ● **CRAZY HORSES**  *MGM 2315 123* ................ | 9 | 19 wks |
| 25 Aug 73 | ● **THE PLAN**  *MGM 2315 251* ..................... | 6 | 25 wks |
| 17 Aug 74 | ● **OUR BEST TO YOU**  *MGM 2315 300* ........... | 5 | 20 wks |
| 7 Dec 74 | **LOVE ME FOR A REASON**  *MGM 2315 312* .......... | 13 | 9 wks |
| 14 Jun 75 | **I'M STILL GONNA NEED YOU**  *MGM 2315 342* ....... | 19 | 7 wks |
| 10 Jan 76 | **AROUND THE WORLD – LIVE IN CONCERT** | | |
| | *MGM 2659 044* ................................. | 41 | 1 wk |

*See also Donny Osmond.*

## Gilbert O'SULLIVAN  *UK, male vocalist*  *191 wks*

| 25 Sep 71 | ● **HIMSELF**  *MAM 501* ............................ | 5 | 82 wks |
|---|---|---|---|
| 18 Nov 72 | ★ **BACK TO FRONT**  *MAM 502* .................. | 1 | 64 wks |
| 6 Oct 73 | ● **I'M A WRITER NOT A FIGHTER**  *MAMS 505* ........ | 2 | 25 wks |
| 26 Oct 74 | ● **STRANGER IN MY OWN BACK YARD** | | |
| | *MAM MAMS 506* ................................ | 9 | 8 wks |
| 18 Dec 76 | **GREATEST HITS**  *MAM MAMA 2003* ................ | 13 | 11 wks |
| 12 Sep 81 | **20 GOLDEN GREATS**  *K-Tel NE 1133* ................ | 98 | 1 wk |

## John OTWAY and Wild Willy BARRETT
*UK, male vocal/instrumental duo*  *1 wk*

| 1 Jul 78 | **DEEP AND MEANINGLESS**  *Polydor 2382 501* ......... | 44 | 1 wk |
|---|---|---|---|

## OVERLORD X  *UK, male rapper*  *1 wk*

| 4 Feb 89 | **WEAPON IS MY LYRIC**  *Mango Street ILPS 9924* ........ | 68 | 1 wk |
|---|---|---|---|

*p*

PACEMAKERS – *See GERRY and the PACEMAKERS*

## Jimmy PAGE  *UK, male instrumentalist – guitar*  *10 wks*

| 27 Feb 82 | **DEATHWISH II (film soundtrack)**  *Swansong SSK 59415* . | 40 | 4 wks |
|---|---|---|---|
| 2 Jul 88 | **OUTRIDER**  *Geffen WX 155* ....................... | 27 | 6 wks |

*See also Roy Harper with Jimmy Page.*

## Elaine PAIGE  *UK, female vocalist*  *128 wks*

| 1 May 82 | **ELAINE PAIGE**  *WEA K 58385* ................... | 56 | 6 wks |
|---|---|---|---|
| 5 Nov 83 | ● **STAGES**  *K-Tel NE 1262* ........................ | 2 | 48 wks |
| 20 Oct 84 | **CINEMA**  *K-Tel NE 1282* ........................ | 12 | 25 wks |
| 16 Nov 85 | ● **LOVE HURTS**  *WEA WX 28* ..................... | 8 | 20 wks |
| 29 Nov 86 | **CHRISTMAS**  *WEA WX 80* ..................... | 27 | 6 wks |
| 5 Dec 87 | **MEMORIES – THE BEST OF ELAINE PAIGE** | | |
| | *Telstar STAR 2313* ............................ | 14 | 15 wks |
| 19 Nov 88 | **THE QUEEN ALBUM**  *Siren SRNLP 22* .............. | 51 | 8 wks |

## PALE FOUNTAINS  *UK, male vocal/instrumental group*  *3 wks*

| 10 Mar 84 | **PACIFIC STREET**  *Virgin V 2274* .................... | 85 | 2 wks |
|---|---|---|---|
| 16 Feb 85 | **FROM ACROSS THE KITCHEN TABLE**  *Virgin V 2333* . | 94 | 1 wk |

## PALLAS  UK, male vocal/instrumental group                      4 wks

| 25 Feb 84 | **SENTINEL**  Harvest SHSP 2400121 | 41 | 3 wks |
| 22 Feb 86 | **THE WEDGE**  Harvest SHVL 850 | 70 | 1 wk |

## Robert PALMER  UK, male vocalist                      98 wks

| 6 Nov 76 | **SOME PEOPLE CAN DO WHAT THEY LIKE** | | |
| | Island ILPS 9420 | 46 | 1 wk |
| 14 Jul 79 | **SECRETS**  Island ILPS 9544 | 54 | 4 wks |
| 6 Sep 80 | **CLUES**  Island ILPS 9595 | 31 | 8 wks |
| 3 Apr 82 | **MAYBE IT'S LIVE**  Island ILPS 9665 | 32 | 6 wks |
| 23 Apr 83 | **PRIDE**  Island ILPS 9720 | 37 | 9 wks |
| 16 Nov 85 | ● **RIPTIDE**  Island ILPS 9801 | 5 | 37 wks |
| 9 Jul 88 | **HEAVY NOVA**  EMI EMD 1007 | 17 | 25 wks |
| 11 Nov 89 | ● **ADDICTIONS VOLUME 1**  Island ILPS 9944 | 7† | 8 wks |

**PAPAS** – See MAMAS and PAPAS

## Mica PARIS  UK, female vocalist                      32 wks

| 3 Sep 88 | ● **SO GOOD**  Fourth & Broadway BRLP 525 | 6 | 32 wks |

## Graham PARKER and the RUMOUR
UK, male vocal/instrumental group                      35 wks

| 27 Nov 76 | **HEAT TREATMENT**  Vertigo 6360 137 | 52 | 2 wks |
| 12 Nov 77 | **STICK TO ME**  Vertigo 9102 017 | 19 | 4 wks |
| 27 May 78 | **PARKERILLA**  Vertigo 6641 797 | 14 | 5 wks |
| 7 Apr 79 | **SQUEEZING OUT SPARKS**  Vertigo 9102 030 | 18 | 8 wks |
| 7 Jun 80 | **THE UP ESCALATOR**  Stiff SEEZ 23 | 11 | 10 wks |
| 27 Mar 82 | **ANOTHER GREY AREA**  RCA RCALP 6029 | 40 | 6 wks |

Another Grey Area credited to Graham Parker.

## Ray PARKER Jr.  US, male vocalist                      7 wks

| 10 Oct 87 | **AFTER DARK**  WEA WX 122 | 40 | 7 wks |

## John PARR  UK, male vocalist                      2 wks

| 2 Nov 85 | **JOHN PARR**  London LONLP 12 | 60 | 2 wks |

## Alan PARSONS PROJECT
UK, male vocal/instrumental group                      38 wks

| 28 Aug 76 | **TALES OF MYSTERY AND IMAGINATION** | | |
| | Charisma CDS 4003 | 56 | 1 wk |
| 13 Aug 77 | **I ROBOT**  Arista SPARTY 1016 | 30 | 1 wk |
| 10 Jun 78 | **PYRAMID**  Arista SPART 1054 | 49 | 4 wks |
| 29 Sep 79 | **EVE**  Arista SPARTY 1100 | 74 | 1 wk |
| 15 Nov 80 | **THE TURN OF A FRIENDLY CARD**  Arista DLART 1 | 38 | 4 wks |
| 29 May 82 | **EYE IN THE SKY**  Arista 204 666 | 27 | 11 wks |
| 26 Nov 83 | **THE BEST OF THE ALAN PARSONS PROJECT** | | |
| | Arista APP 1 | 99 | 1 wk |
| 3 Mar 84 | **AMMONIA AVENUE**  Arista 206 100 | 24 | 8 wks |
| 23 Feb 85 | **VULTURE CULTURE**  Arista 206 577 | 40 | 5 wks |
| 14 Feb 87 | **GAUDI**  Arista 208 084 | 66 | 2 wks |

## PARTISANS  UK, male vocal/instrumental group                      1 wk

| 19 Feb 83 | **THE PARTISANS**  No Future PUNK 4 | 94 | 1 wk |

## Dolly PARTON  *US, female vocalist*                    *13 wks*

| | | | | |
|---|---|---|---|---|
| 25 Nov 78 | **BOTH SIDES**  *Lotus WH 5006* ........................ | 45 | 12 wks |
| 7 Sep 85 | **GREATEST HITS**  *RCA PL 84422* ................... | 74 | 1 wk |

*See also Dolly Parton/Linda Ronstadt/Emmylou Harris.*


## Dolly PARTON/Linda RONSTADT/Emmylou HARRIS  *US, female vocal trio*                    *4 wks*

| | | | | |
|---|---|---|---|---|
| 14 Mar 87 | **TRIO**  *Warner Bros. 925 491–1* ...................... | 60 | 4 wks |

*See also Dolly Parton; Linda Ronstadt; Emmylou Harris.*


## PARTRIDGE FAMILY  *US, male/female vocal group*                    *13 wks*

| | | | | |
|---|---|---|---|---|
| 8 Jan 72 | **UP TO DATE**  *Bell SBLL 143* ...................... | 46 | 2 wks |
| 22 Apr 72 | **THE PARTRIDGE FAMILY SOUND MAGAZINE** *Bell BELLS 206* ................................ | 14 | 7 wks |
| 30 Sep 72 | **SHOPPING BAG**  *Bell BELLS 212* ................... | 28 | 3 wks |
| 9 Dec 72 | **CHRISTMAS CARD**  *Bell BELLS 214* ............... | 45 | 1 wk |


## PASADENAS  *UK, male vocal group*                    *21 wks*

| | | | | |
|---|---|---|---|---|
| 22 Oct 88 | ● **TO WHOM IT MAY CONCERN**  *CBS 462877 1* ........ | 3 | 21 wks |


## PASSIONS  *UK, male/female vocal/instrumental group*                    *1 wk*

| | | | | |
|---|---|---|---|---|
| 3 Oct 81 | **THIRTY THOUSAND FEET OVER CHINA** *Polydor POLS 1041* ............................. | 92 | 1 wk |

**PAUL** – *See PETER, PAUL and MARY*


## Luciano PAVAROTTI  *Italy, male vocalist*                    *42 wks*

| | | | | |
|---|---|---|---|---|
| 15 May 82 | **PAVAROTTI'S GREATEST HITS**  *Decca D 2362* ....... | 95 | 1 wk |
| 9 Aug 86 | **THE PAVAROTTI COLLECTION**  *Stylus SMR 8617* .... | 12 | 34 wks |
| 16 Jul 88 | **THE NEW PAVAROTTI COLLECTION LIVE!** *Stylus SMR 857* ................................. | 63 | 7 wks |

*See also Luciano Pavarotti with the Henry Mancini Orchestra.*


## Luciano PAVAROTTI with the Henry MANCINI ORCHESTRA  *Italy, male vocalist with US, conductor/orchestra*                    *1 wk*

| | | | | |
|---|---|---|---|---|
| 30 Jun 84 | **MAMMA**  *Decca 411959* ........................... | 96 | 1 wk |

*See also Luciano Pavarotti; Henry Mancini.*


## Tom PAXTON  *US, male vocalist*                    *10 wks*

| | | | | |
|---|---|---|---|---|
| 13 Jun 70 | **NO. 6**  *Elektra 2469–003* ............................... | 23 | 5 wks |
| 3 Apr 71 | **THE COMPLEAT TOM PAXTON**  *Elektra EKD 2003* .... | 18 | 4 wks |
| 1 Jul 72 | **PEACE WILL COME**  *Reprise K 44182* ................ | 47 | 1 wk |


## David PEASTON  *UK, male vocalist*                    *1 wk*

| | | | | |
|---|---|---|---|---|
| 26 Aug 89 | **INTRODUCING...DAVID PEASTON**  *Geffen 924228 1* | 66 | 1 wk |

**PEBBLES**  *US, female vocalist*  *4 wks*

14 May 88   **PEBBLES**  *MCA MCF 3418*  . . . . . . . . . . . . . . . . . . . . . . .  56   4 wks

---

**PEDDLERS**  *UK, male vocal/instrumental group*  *16 wks*

16 Mar 68   **FREE WHEELERS**  *CBS SBPG 63183*  . . . . . . . . . . . . . . .  27   13 wks
7 Feb 70   **BIRTHDAY**  *CBS 63682*  . . . . . . . . . . . . . . . . . . . . . . . . . .  16   3 wks

---

**Kevin PEEK**  *UK, male instrumentalist – guitar*  *2 wks*

21 Mar 81   **AWAKENING**  *Ariola ARL 5065*  . . . . . . . . . . . . . . . . . . . .  52   2 wks
*See also Kevin Peek and Rick Wakeman.*

---

## Kevin PEEK and Rick WAKEMAN
*UK, male instrumental duo – guitar and keyboards*  *6 wks*

13 Oct 84   **BEYOND THE PLANETS**  *Telstar STAR 2244*  . . . . . . . . . .  64   6 wks

*Beyond the Planets also features Jeff Wayne with narration by Patrick Allen. See also Kevin Peek; Rick Wakeman; Jeff Wayne.*

---

**Teddy PENDERGRASS**  *US, male vocalist*  *8 wks*

21 May 88   **JOY**  *Elektra 960775 1*  . . . . . . . . . . . . . . . . . . . . . . . . . . .  45   8 wks

---

**PENETRATION**  *UK, male/female vocal/instrumental group*  *8 wks*

28 Oct 78   **MOVING TARGETS**  *Virgin V 2109*  . . . . . . . . . . . . . . . . .  22   4 wks
6 Oct 79   **COMING UP FOR AIR**  *Virgin V 2131*  . . . . . . . . . . . . . . . .  36   4 wks

---

## PENGUIN CAFE ORCHESTRA
*UK, male instrumental group*  *5 wks*

4 Apr 87   **SIGNS OF LIFE**  *Edition EG EGED 50*  . . . . . . . . . . . . . . . .  49   5 wks

---

**PENTANGLE**  *UK, male/female vocal/instrumental group*  *39 wks*

15 Jun 68   **THE PENTANGLE**  *Transatlantic TRA 162*  . . . . . . . . . . . . .  21   9 wks
1 Nov 69 ● **BASKET OF LIGHT**  *Transatlantic TRA 205*  . . . . . . . . . . . .  5   28 wks
12 Dec 70   **CRUEL SISTER**  *Transatlantic TRA 228*  . . . . . . . . . . . . . .  51   2 wks

**PEPA** – *See SALT 'N' PEPA*

---

**PEPSI and SHIRLIE**  *UK, female vocal duo*  *2 wks*

7 Nov 87   **ALL RIGHT NOW**  *Polydor POLH 38*  . . . . . . . . . . . . . . . . .  69   2 wks

---

**Carl PERKINS**  *US, male vocalist*  *3 wks*

15 Apr 78   **OL' BLUE SUEDES IS BACK**  *Jet UATV 30146*  . . . . . . . . .  38   3 wks

---

**Steve PERRY**  *US, male vocalist*  *2 wks*

14 Jul 84   **STREET TALK**  *CBS 25967*  . . . . . . . . . . . . . . . . . . . . . . . . .  59   2 wks

## PESTALOZZI CHILDREN'S CHOIR

*International, male/female vocal group*                                    *2 wks*

| | | | |
|---|---|---|---|
| 26 Dec 81 | **SONGS OF JOY**  *K-Tel NE 1140* ..................... | 65 | 2 wks |

## PETER and GORDON  *UK, male vocal duo*                              *1 wk*

| | | | |
|---|---|---|---|
| 20 Jun 64 | **PETER AND GORDON**  *Columbia 33SX 1630* .......... | 18 | 1 wk |

## PETER, PAUL and MARY

*US, male/female vocal/instrumental group*                               *26 wks*

| | | | |
|---|---|---|---|
| 4 Jan 64 | **PETER PAUL AND MARY**  *Warner Bros. WM 4064* ...... | 18 | 1 wk |
| 21 Mar 64 | **IN THE WIND**  *Warner Bros. WM 8142* ................ | 11 | 19 wks |
| 13 Feb 65 | **IN CONCERT VOL. 1**  *Warner Bros. WM 8158* .......... | 20 | 2 wks |
| 5 Sep 70 | **TEN YEARS TOGETHER**  *Warner Bros. WS 2552* ....... | 60 | 4 wks |

## PETERS and LEE  *UK, male/female vocal duo*                       *166 wks*

| | | | |
|---|---|---|---|
| 30 Jun 73 | ★ **WE CAN MAKE IT**  *Philips 6308 165* ............... | 1 | 55 wks |
| 22 Dec 73 | ● **BY YOUR SIDE**  *Philips 6308 192* ................... | 9 | 48 wks |
| 21 Sep 74 | ● **RAINBOW**  *Philips 6308 208* ...................... | 6 | 27 wks |
| 4 Oct 75 | ● **FAVOURITES**  *Philips 9109 205* ................... | 2 | 32 wks |
| 18 Dec 76 | **INVITATION**  *Philips 9101 027* ..................... | 44 | 4 wks |

## PET SHOP BOYS  *UK, male vocal/instrumental duo*                *252 wks*

| | | | |
|---|---|---|---|
| 5 Apr 86 | ● **PLEASE**  *Parlophone PSB 1* ......................... | 3 | 82 wks |
| 29 Nov 86 | **DISCO**  *EMI PRG 1001* ........................... | 15 | 72 wks |
| 19 Sep 87 | ● **PET SHOP BOYS ACTUALLY**  *Parlophone PCSD 104* .... | 2 | 59 wks |
| 22 Oct 88 | ● **INTROSPECTIVE**  *Parlophone PCS 7325* .............. | 2 | 39 wks |

## Tom PETTY and the HEARTBREAKERS

*US, male vocal/instrumental group*                                      *54 wks*

| | | | |
|---|---|---|---|
| 4 Jun 77 | **TOM PETTY AND THE HEARTBREAKERS**  *Shelter ISA 5014* ................................. | 24 | 12 wks |
| 1 Jul 78 | **YOU'RE GONNA GET IT**  *Island ISA 5017* ............ | 34 | 5 wks |
| 17 Nov 79 | **DAMN THE TORPEDOES**  *MCA MCF 3044* ........ | 57 | 4 wks |
| 23 May 81 | **HARD PROMISES**  *MCA MCF 3098* ................ | 32 | 5 wks |
| 20 Nov 82 | **LONG AFTER DARK**  *MCA MCF 3155* ............. | 45 | 4 wks |
| 20 Apr 85 | **SOUTHERN ACCENTS**  *MCA MCF 3260* ............ | 23 | 6 wks |
| 2 May 87 | **LET ME UP (I'VE HAD ENOUGH)**  *MCA MCG 6014* ... | 59 | 2 wks |
| 8 Jul 89 | ● **FULL MOON FEVER**  *MCA MCG 6034* .............. | 8 | 16 wks |

Full Moon Fever *credited simply to Tom Petty.*

## PhD  *UK, male vocal/instrumental duo*                              *8 wks*

| | | | |
|---|---|---|---|
| 1 May 82 | **PhD**  *WEA K 99150* ........................... | 33 | 8 wks |

## PHENOMENA  *UK, male vocal/instrumental group*                  *2 wks*

| | | | |
|---|---|---|---|
| 6 Jul 85 | **PHENOMENA**  *Bronze PM 1* ....................... | 63 | 2 wks |

## Arlene PHILLIPS  *UK, female exercise instructor*                 *24 wks*

| | | | |
|---|---|---|---|
| 28 Aug 82 | **KEEP IN SHAPE SYSTEM**  *Supershape SUP 01* .......... | 41 | 23 wks |
| 18 Feb 84 | **KEEP IN SHAPE SYSTEM VOL. 2**  *Supershape SUP 2* .... | 100 | 1 wk |

Keep In Shape System *features music by Funk Federation.*

## PHOTOS UK, male/female vocal/instrumental group          9 wks

21 Jun 80 ● **THE PHOTOS**  CBS PHOTO 5 ..................... **4**   9 wks


## Edith PIAF  France, female vocalist          5 wks

26 Sep 87   **HEART AND SOUL**  Stylus SMR 736  ................ **58**   5 wks


## PIGBAG  UK, male instrumental group          14 wks

13 Mar 82   **DR HECKLE AND MR JIVE**  Y Y 17 ................ **18**   14 wks


## PILOT  UK, male vocal/instrumental group          1 wk

31 May 75   **SECOND FLIGHT**  EMI EMC 3075 ................. **48**   1 wk


## Courtney PINE  UK, male instrumentalist – saxophone          13 wks

25 Oct 86   **JOURNEY TO THE URGE WITHIN**  Island ILPS 9846 .. **39**   11 wks
6 Feb 88   **DESTINY'S SONGS**  Antilles AN 8275 ............... **54**   2 wks


## PINK FAIRIES  UK, male vocal/instrumental group          1 wk

29 Jul 72   **WHAT A BUNCH OF SWEETIES**  Polydor 2383 132 ..... **48**   1 wk


## PINK FLOYD  UK, male vocal/instrumental group          736 wks

19 Aug 67 ● **PIPER AT THE GATES OF DAWN**  Columbia SCX 6157 .   **6**   14 wks
13 Jul  68 ● **SAUCERFUL OF SECRETS**  Columbia SCX 6258 .......   **9**   11 wks
28 Jun 69 ● **MORE (film soundtrack)**  Columbia SCX 6346 ..........   **9**   5 wks
15 Nov 69 ● **UMMAGUMMA**  Harvest SHDW 1/2 .................   **5**   21 wks
24 Oct 70 ★ **ATOM HEART MOTHER**  Harvest SHVL 781 ..........   **1**   23 wks
7 Aug 71   **RELICS**  Starline SRS 5071 ........................  **32**   6 wks
20 Nov 71 ● **MEDDLE**  Harvest SHVL 795 ....................   **3**   82 wks
17 Jun  72 ● **OBSCURED BY CLOUDS (film soundtrack)**
                   Harvest SHSP 4020 .............................   **6**   14 wks
31 Mar 73 ● **DARK SIDE OF THE MOON**  Harvest SHVL 804 ........   **2**  296 wks
19 Jan  74   **A NICE PAIR (double re-issue)**  Harvest SHDW 403 .....  **21**   20 wks
27 Sep 75 ★ **WISH YOU WERE HERE**  Harvest SHVL 814 ..........   **1**   84 wks
19 Feb 77 ● **ANIMALS**  Harvest SHVL 815 ....................   **2**   33 wks
8 Dec 79 ● **THE WALL**  Harvest SHDW 411 ....................   **3**   46 wks
5 Dec 81   **A COLLECTION OF GREAT DANCE SONGS**
                   Harvest SHVL 822 .............................  **37**   10 wks
2 Apr 83 ★ **THE FINAL CUT**  Harvest SHPF 1983 .................   **1**   25 wks
19 Sep 87 ● **A MOMENTARY LAPSE OF REASON**
                   EMI EMD 1003 ................................   **3**   34 wks
3 Dec 88   **DELICATE SOUND OF THUNDER**  EMI EQ 5009 ....  **11**   12 wks

A Nice Pair is a double re-issue of the first two albums.


**PIPS** – See Gladys KNIGHT and the PIPS


## PIRANHAS  UK, male vocal/instrumental group          3 wks

20 Sep 80   **PIRANHAS**  Sire SRK 6098 ........................  **69**   3 wks


## PIRATES  UK, male vocal/instrumental group          3 wks

19 Nov 77   **OUT OF THEIR SKULLS**  Warner Bros. K 56411 ........  **57**   3 wks

He looks like a middle-aged George Michael, but it's really **LUCIANO PAVAROTTI**.

The **PET SHOP BOYS** actually don't look that pleased with their tremendous disco success.

**PETER, PAUL AND MARY** puffed their way into the chart in 1964.

## Gene PITNEY  US, male vocalist

66 wks

| | | | | | |
|---|---|---|---|---|---|
| 11 Apr | 64 ● | **BLUE GENE** *United Artists ULP 1061* ................. | 7 | 11 wks |
| 6 Feb | 65 | **GENE PITNEY'S BIG 16** *Stateside SL 10118* ........... | 12 | 6 wks |
| 20 Mar | 65 | **I'M GONNA BE STRONG** *Stateside SL 10120* .......... | 15 | 2 wks |
| 20 Nov | 65 | **LOOKIN' THRU THE EYES OF LOVE** *Stateside SL 10148* | 15 | 5 wks |
| 17 Sep | 66 | **NOBODY NEEDS YOUR LOVE** *Stateside SL 10183* ..... | 13 | 17 wks |
| 4 Mar | 67 | **YOUNG WARM AND WONDERFUL** *Stateside SSL 10194* | 39 | 1 wk |
| 22 Apr | 67 | **GENE PITNEY'S BIG SIXTEEN** *Stateside SSL 10199* .... | 40 | 1 wk |
| 20 Sep | 69 ● | **BEST OF GENE PITNEY** *Stateside SSL 10286* .......... | 8 | 9 wks |
| 2 Oct | 76 ● | **HIS 20 GREATEST HITS** *Arcade ADEP 22* ............. | 6 | 14 wks |

## PIXIES  US, male/female vocal/instrumental group

9 wks

| | | | | | |
|---|---|---|---|---|---|
| 29 Apr | 89 ● | **DOOLITTLE** *4AD CAD 905* ...................... | 8 | 9 wks |

## Robert PLANT  UK, male vocalist

40 wks

| | | | | | |
|---|---|---|---|---|---|
| 10 Jul | 82 ● | **PICTURES AT ELEVEN** *Swansong SSK 59418* ......... | 2 | 15 wks |
| 23 Jul | 83 ● | **THE PRINCIPLES OF MOMENTS** *WEA 7901011* ...... | 7 | 14 wks |
| 1 Jun | 85 | **SHAKEN 'N' STIRRED** *Es Paranza 79-0265-1* .......... | 19 | 4 wks |
| 12 Feb | 88 ● | **NOW AND ZEN** *Es Paranza WX 149* ................. | 10 | 7 wks |

## PLASMATICS  US, male/female vocal/instrumental group

3 wks

| | | | | | |
|---|---|---|---|---|---|
| 11 Oct | 80 | **NEW HOPE FOR THE WRETCHED** *Stiff SEEZ 24* .... | 55 | 3 wks |

**PLASTIC ONO BAND** – *See John LENNON*

## PLATTERS  US, male/female vocal group

13 wks

| | | | | | |
|---|---|---|---|---|---|
| 8 Apr | 78 ● | **20 CLASSIC HITS** *Mercury 9100 049* ................. | 8 | 13 wks |

## PLAYERS ASSOCIATION
US, male/female vocal/instrumental group

4 wks

| | | | | | |
|---|---|---|---|---|---|
| 17 Mar | 79 | **TURN THE MUSIC UP** *Vanguard VSD 79421* ........... | 54 | 4 wks |

## PLAYN JAYN  UK, male vocal/instrumental group

1 wk

| | | | | | |
|---|---|---|---|---|---|
| 1 Sep | 84 | **FRIDAY THE 13TH (AT THE MARQUEE CLUB)** *A&M JAYN 13* ................................ | 93 | 1 wk |

## POGUES  Ireland, male vocal/instrumental group

39 wks

| | | | | | |
|---|---|---|---|---|---|
| 3 Nov | 84 | **RED ROSES FOR ME** *Stiff SEEZ 55* ................. | 89 | 1 wk |
| 17 Aug | 85 | **RUM, SODOMY AND THE LASH** *Stiff SEEZ 58* ...... | 13 | 14 wks |
| 30 Jan | 88 ● | **IF I SHOULD FALL FROM GRACE WITH GOD** *Stiff NYR 1* ................................... | 3 | 16 wks |
| 29 Jul | 89 ● | **PEACE AND LOVE** *WEA WX 247* .................. | 5 | 8 wks |

*Group was male/female for first two albums.*

## POINTER SISTERS  US, female vocal group

88 wks

| | | | | | |
|---|---|---|---|---|---|
| 29 Aug | 81 | **BLACK AND WHITE** *Planet K 52300* ................ | 21 | 13 wks |
| 5 May | 84 ● | **BREAK OUT** *Planet PL 84705* ...................... | 9 | 58 wks |
| 27 Jul | 85 | **CONTACT** *Planet PL 85457* ....................... | 34 | 7 wks |
| 29 Jul | 89 | **JUMP – THE BEST OF THE POINTER SISTERS** *RCA PL 90319* ................................ | 11 | 10 wks |

## POISON  US, male vocal/instrumental group

21 wks

| | | | | | |
|---|---|---|---|---|---|
| 21 May | 88 | **OPEN UP AND SAY ... AAH!** *Capitol EST 2059* ........ | 18 | 21 wks |

## POLECATS
UK, male vocal/instrumental group — 2 wks

| 4 Jul 81 | **POLECATS** *Vertigo 6359 057* | 28 | 2 wks |
|----------|------|----|----|

## POLICE
UK, male vocal/instrumental group — 327 wks

| 21 Apr 79 | ● **OUTLANDOS D'AMOUR** *A&M AMLH 68502* | 6 | 96 wks |
|----------|------|----|----|
| 13 Oct 79 | ★ **REGGATTA DE BLANC** *A&M AMLH 64792* | 1 | 74 wks |
| 11 Oct 80 | ★ **ZENYATTA MONDATTA** *A&M AMLH 64831* | 1 | 31 wks |
| 10 Oct 81 | ★ **GHOST IN THE MACHINE** *A&M AMLH 63730* | 1 | 27 wks |
| 25 Jun 83 | ★ **SYNCHRONICITY** *A&M AMLX 63735* | 1 | 48 wks |
| 8 Nov 86 | ★ **EVERY BREATH YOU TAKE – THE SINGLES** *A&M EVERY 1* | 1 | 51 wks |

## Su POLLARD
UK, female vocalist — 3 wks

| 22 Nov 86 | **SU** *K-Tel NE 1327* | 86 | 3 wks |
|----------|------|----|----|

## Iggy POP
US, male vocalist — 24 wks

| 9 Apr 77 | **THE IDIOT** *RCA Victor PL 12275* | 30 | 3 wks |
|----------|------|----|----|
| 4 Jun 77 | **RAW POWER** *Embassy 31464* | 44 | 2 wks |
| 1 Oct 77 | **LUST FOR LIFE** *RCA PL 12488* | 28 | 5 wks |
| 19 May 79 | **NEW VALUES** *Arista SPART 1092* | 60 | 4 wks |
| 16 Feb 80 | **SOLDIER** *Arista SPART 1117* | 62 | 2 wks |
| 11 Oct 86 | **BLAH-BLAH-BLAH** *A&M AMA 5145* | 43 | 7 wks |
| 2 Jul 88 | **INSTINCT** *A&M AMA 5198* | 61 | 1 wk |

Raw Power *credited to Iggy and the Stooges.*

## POP WILL EAT ITSELF
UK, male vocal/instrumental group — 2 wks

| 13 May 89 | **THIS IS THE DAY, THIS IS THE HOUR** *RCA PL 74141* | 24 | 2 wks |
|----------|------|----|----|

**Nick PORTLOCK** – *See ROYAL PHILHARMONIC ORCHESTRA*

## Sandy POSEY
US, female vocalist — 1 wk

| 11 Mar 67 | **BORN A WOMAN** *MGM MGMCS 8035* | 39 | 1 wk |
|----------|------|----|----|

## Frank POURCEL
France, male vocalist — 7 wks

| 20 Nov 71 | ● **THIS IS POURCEL** *Studio Two STWO 7* | 8 | 7 wks |
|----------|------|----|----|

## Cozy POWELL
UK, male instrumentalist – drums — 8 wks

| 26 Jan 80 | **OVER THE TOP** *Ariola ARL 5038* | 34 | 3 wks |
|----------|------|----|----|
| 19 Sep 81 | **TILT** *Polydor POLD 5047* | 58 | 4 wks |
| 28 May 83 | **OCTOPUSS** *Polydor POLD 5093* | 86 | 1 wk |

*See also Emerson, Lake and Powell.*

## Peter POWELL
UK, male exercise instructor — 13 wks

| 20 Mar 82 | ● **KEEP FIT AND DANCE** *K-Tel NE 1167* | 9 | 13 wks |
|----------|------|----|----|

## POWER STATION
UK/US, male vocal/instrumental group — 23 wks

| 6 Apr 85 | **THE POWER STATION** *Parlophone POST 1* | 12 | 23 wks |
|----------|------|----|----|

## PRAYING MANTIS  *UK, male vocal/instrumental group*    2 wks

| 11 Apr 81 | **TIME TELLS NO LIES**  *Arista SPART 1153* ............. | 60 | 2 wks |

## PREFAB SPROUT  *UK, male/female vocal/instrumental group*   70 wks

| 17 Mar 84 | **SWOON**  *Kitchenware KWLP 1* ...................... | 22 | 7 wks |
| 22 Jun 85 | **STEVE McQUEEN**  *Kitchenware KWLP 3* .............. | 21 | 35 wks |
| 26 Mar 88 | ● **FROM LANGLEY PARK TO MEMPHIS** | | |
| | *Kitchenware KWLP 9* ................................ | 5 | 24 wks |
| 1 Jul 89 | **PROTEST SONGS**  *Kitchenware KWLP 4* .............. | 18 | 4 wks |

## Elvis PRESLEY  *US, male vocalist*    1023 wks

| 8 Nov 58 | ● **ELVIS' GOLDEN RECORDS**  *RCA RB 16069* ......... | 3 | 44 wks |
| 8 Nov 58 | ● **KING CREOLE** (film soundtrack)  *RCA RD 27086* ..... | 4 | 14 wks |
| 4 Apr 59 | ● **ELVIS (ROCK 'N' ROLL NO. 1)**  *HMV CLP 1093* ....... | 4 | 9 wks |
| 8 Aug 59 | ● **A DATE WITH ELVIS**  *RCA RD 27128* ............... | 4 | 15 wks |
| 18 Jun 60 | ★ **ELVIS IS BACK**  *RCA RD 27171* ................... | 1 | 27 wks |
| 18 Jun 60 | ● **ELVIS' GOLDEN RECORDS VOL. 2**  *RCA RD 27159* ... | 4 | 20 wks |
| 10 Dec 60 | ★ **G.I. BLUES** (film soundtrack)  *RCA RD 27192* ......... | 1 | 55 wks |
| 20 May 61 | ● **HIS HAND IN MINE**  *RCA RD 27211* ................ | 3 | 25 wks |
| 4 Nov 61 | ● **SOMETHING FOR EVERYBODY**  *RCA RD 27224* ..... | 2 | 18 wks |
| 9 Dec 61 | ★ **BLUE HAWAII** (film soundtrack)  *RCA RD 27238* ...... | 1 | 65 wks |
| 7 Jul 62 | ★ **POT LUCK**  *RCA RD 27265* ....................... | 1 | 25 wks |
| 8 Dec 62 | ● **ROCK 'N' ROLL NO. 2**  *RCA RD 7528* ............. | 3 | 17 wks |
| 26 Jan 63 | ● **GIRLS! GIRLS! GIRLS!** (film soundtrack)  *RCA RD 7534* | 2 | 21 wks |
| 11 May 63 | ● **IT HAPPENED AT THE WORLD'S FAIR** (film soundtrack) | | |
| | *RCA RD 7565* .................................. | 4 | 21 wks |
| 28 Dec 63 | ● **FUN IN ACAPULCO** (film soundtrack)  *RCA RD 7609* .. | 9 | 14 wks |
| 11 Apr 64 | ● **ELVIS' GOLDEN RECORDS VOL. 3**  *RCA RD 7630* .... | 6 | 13 wks |
| 4 Jul 64 | ● **KISSIN' COUSINS** (film soundtrack)  *RCA RD 7645* ... | 5 | 17 wks |
| 9 Jan 65 | **ROUSTABOUT** (film soundtrack)  *RCA RD 7678* ..... | 12 | 4 wks |
| 1 May 65 | ● **GIRL HAPPY** (film soundtrack)  *RCA RD 7714* ........ | 8 | 18 wks |
| 25 Sep 65 | **FLAMING STAR AND SUMMER KISSES**  *RCA RD 7723* | 11 | 4 wks |
| 4 Dec 65 | ● **ELVIS FOR EVERYBODY**  *RCA RD 7782* ............ | 8 | 8 wks |
| 15 Jan 66 | **HAREM HOLIDAY** (film soundtrack)  *RCA RD 7767* ... | 11 | 5 wks |
| 30 Apr 66 | **FRANKIE AND JOHNNY** (film soundtrack) | | |
| | *RCA RD 7793* ................................... | 11 | 5 wks |
| 6 Aug 66 | ● **PARADISE HAWAIIAN STYLE** (film soundtrack) | | |
| | *RCA Victor RD 7810* ................................ | 7 | 9 wks |
| 26 Nov 66 | **CALIFORNIA HOLIDAY** (film soundtrack) | | |
| | *RCA Victor RD 7820* ................................ | 17 | 6 wks |
| 8 Apr 67 | **HOW GREAT THOU ART**  *RCA Victor SF 7867* ........ | 11 | 14 wks |
| 2 Sep 67 | **DOUBLE TROUBLE** (film soundtrack) | | |
| | *RCA Victor SF 7892* ................................ | 34 | 1 wk |
| 20 Apr 68 | **CLAMBAKE** (film soundtrack)  *RCA Victor SD 7917* ..... | 39 | 1 wk |
| 3 May 69 | ● **ELVIS – NBC TV SPECIAL**  *RCA RD 8011* ............ | 2 | 26 wks |
| 5 Jul 69 | **FLAMING STAR**  *RCA International INTS 1012* .......... | 2 | 14 wks |
| 23 Aug 69 | ★ **FROM ELVIS IN MEMPHIS**  *RCA SF 8029* ........... | 1 | 13 wks |
| 28 Feb 70 | **PORTRAIT IN MUSIC** (import)  *RCA 558* ............ | 36 | 1 wk |
| 14 Mar 70 | **FROM MEMPHIS TO VEGAS – FROM VEGAS TO** | | |
| | **MEMPHIS**  *RCA SF 8080/1* ...................... | 3 | 16 wks |
| 1 Aug 70 | ● **ON STAGE**  *RCA SF 8128* ........................ | 2 | 18 wks |
| 5 Dec 70 | **ELVIS' GOLDEN RECORDS VOL. 1** (re-issue) | | |
| | *RCA SF 8129* ..................................... | 21 | 11 wks |
| 12 Dec 70 | **WORLDWIDE 50 GOLD AWARD HITS VOL. 1** | | |
| | *RCA LPM 6401* ................................... | 49 | 2 wks |
| 30 Jan 71 | **THAT'S THE WAY IT IS**  *RCA SF 8162* .............. | 12 | 41 wks |
| 10 Apr 71 | ● **ELVIS COUNTRY**  *RCA SF 8172* ................... | 6 | 9 wks |
| 24 Jul 71 | **LOVE LETTERS FROM ELVIS**  *RCA SF 8202* .......... | 7 | 5 wks |
| 7 Aug 71 | ● **C'MON EVERYBODY**  *RCA International INTS 1286* ..... | 5 | 21 wks |
| 7 Aug 71 | **YOU'LL NEVER WALK ALONE**  *RCA Camden CDM 1088* | 20 | 4 wks |
| 25 Sep 71 | **ALMOST IN LOVE**  *RCA International INTS 1206* ........ | 38 | 2 wks |
| 4 Dec 71 | ● **ELVIS' CHRISTMAS ALBUM**  *RCA International INTS 1126* | 7 | 5 wks |
| 18 Dec 71 | **I GOT LUCKY**  *RCA International INTS 1322* ............ | 26 | 3 wks |

| Date | Title / Catalogue | Pos | Wks |
|---|---|---|---|
| 27 May 72 | **ELVIS NOW** *RCA Victor SF 8266* | 12 | 8 wks |
| 3 Jun 72 | **ROCK AND ROLL (re-issue of ROCK 'N' ROLL NO. 1)** *RCA Victor SF 8233* | 34 | 4 wks |
| 3 Jun 72 | **ELVIS FOR EVERYONE** *RCA Victor SF 8232* | 48 | 1 wk |
| 15 Jul 72 | ● **ELVIS AT MADISON SQUARE GARDEN** *RCA Victor SF 8296* | 3 | 20 wks |
| 12 Aug 72 | **HE TOUCHED ME** *RCA Victor SF 8275* | 38 | 3 wks |
| 24 Feb 73 | **ALOHA FROM HAWAII VIA SATELLITE** *RCA Victor DPS 2040* | 11 | 10 wks |
| 15 Sep 73 | **ELVIS** *RCA Victor SF 8378* | 16 | 4 wks |
| 2 Mar 74 | **A LEGENDARY PERFORMER VOL. 1** *RCA Victor CPLI 0341* | 20 | 3 wks |
| 25 May 74 | **GOOD TIMES** *RCA Victor APLI 0475* | 42 | 1 wk |
| 7 Sep 74 | **ELVIS PRESLEY LIVE ON STAGE IN MEMPHIS** *RCA Victor APLI 0606* | 44 | 1 wk |
| 22 Feb 75 | **PROMISED LAND** *RCA Victor APLI 0873* | 21 | 4 wks |
| 14 Jun 75 | **TODAY** *RCA Victor RS 1011* | 48 | 3 wks |
| 5 Jul 75 | ★ **40 GREATEST HITS** *Arcade ADEP 12* | 1 | 38 wks |
| 6 Sep 75 | **THE ELVIS PRESLEY SUN COLLECTION** *RCA Starcall HY 1001* | 16 | 13 wks |
| 19 Jun 76 | **FROM ELVIS PRESLEY BOULEVARD, MEMPHIS, TENNESSEE** *RCA Victor RS 1060* | 29 | 5 wks |
| 19 Feb 77 | **ELVIS IN DEMAND** *RCA Victor PL 42003* | 12 | 11 wks |
| 27 Aug 77 | ● **MOODY BLUE** *RCA PL 12428* | 3 | 15 wks |
| 3 Sep 77 | ● **WELCOME TO MY WORLD** *RCA PL 12274* | 7 | 9 wks |
| 3 Sep 77 | **G.I. BLUES (re-issue)** *RCA SF 5078* | 14 | 10 wks |
| 10 Sep 77 | **ELVIS' GOLDEN RECORDS VOL. 2 (re-issue)** *RCA SF 8151* | 27 | 4 wks |
| 10 Sep 77 | **HITS OF THE 70'S** *RCA LPLI 7527* | 30 | 4 wks |
| 10 Sep 77 | **BLUE HAWAII (re-issue)** *RCA SF 8145* | 26 | 6 wks |
| 10 Sep 77 | **ELVIS' GOLDEN RECORDS VOL. 3 (re-issue)** *RCA SF 7630* | 49 | 2 wks |
| 10 Sep 77 | **PICTURES OF ELVIS** *RCA Starcall HY 1023* | 52 | 1 wk |
| 8 Oct 77 | **THE SUN YEARS** *Charly SUN 1001* | 31 | 2 wks |
| 15 Oct 77 | **LOVING YOU** *RCA PL 42358* | 24 | 3 wks |
| 19 Nov 77 | **ELVIS IN CONCERT** *RCA PL 02578* | 13 | 11 wks |
| 22 Apr 78 | **HE WALKS BESIDE ME** *RCA PL 12772* | 37 | 1 wk |
| 3 Jun 78 | **THE '56 SESSIONS VOL. 1** *RCA PL 42101* | 47 | 4 wks |
| 2 Sep 78 | **TV SPECIAL** *RCA PL 42370* | 50 | 2 wks |
| 11 Nov 78 | **40 GREATEST HITS (re-issue)** *RCA PL 42691* | 40 | 14 wks |
| 3 Feb 79 | **A LEGENDARY PERFORMER VOL. 3** *RCA PL 13082* | 43 | 3 wks |
| 5 May 79 | **OUR MEMORIES OF ELVIS** *RCA PL 13279* | 72 | 1 wk |
| 24 Nov 79 | ● **LOVE SONGS** *K-Tel NE 1062* | 4 | 13 wks |
| 21 Jun 80 | **ELVIS PRESLEY SINGS LIEBER AND STOLLER** *RCA International INTS 5031* | 32 | 5 wks |
| 23 Aug 80 | **ELVIS ARON PRESLEY** *RCA ELVIS 25* | 21 | 4 wks |
| 23 Aug 80 | **PARADISE HAWAIIAN STYLE (re-issue)** *RCA International INTS 5037* | 53 | 2 wks |
| 29 Nov 80 | ● **INSPIRATION** *K-Tel NE 1101* | 6 | 8 wks |
| 14 Mar 81 | **GUITAR MAN** *RCA RCALP 5010* | 33 | 5 wks |
| 9 May 81 | **THIS IS ELVIS PRESLEY** *RCA RCALP 5029* | 47 | 4 wks |
| 28 Nov 81 | **THE ULTIMATE PERFORMANCE** *K-Tel NE 1141* | 45 | 6 wks |
| 13 Feb 82 | **THE SOUND OF YOUR CRY** *RCA RCALP 3060* | 31 | 12 wks |
| 6 Mar 82 | **ELVIS PRESLEY EP PACK** *RCA EP1* | 97 | 1 wk |
| 21 Aug 82 | **ROMANTIC ELVIS/ROCKIN' ELVIS** *RCA RCALP 1000/1* | 62 | 5 wks |
| 18 Dec 82 | **IT WON'T SEEM LIKE CHRISTMAS WITHOUT YOU** *RCA INTS 5235* | 80 | 1 wk |
| 30 Apr 83 | **JAILHOUSE ROCK/LOVE IN LAS VEGAS** *RCA RCALP 9020* | 40 | 2 wks |
| 20 Aug 83 | **I WAS THE ONE** *RCA RCALP 3105* | 83 | 1 wk |
| 3 Dec 83 | **A LEGENDARY PERFORMER VOL. 4** *RCA PL 84848* | 91 | 1 wk |
| 7 Apr 84 | **I CAN HELP** *RCA PL 89287* | 71 | 3 wks |
| 21 Jul 84 | **THE FIRST LIVE RECORDINGS** *RCA International PG 89387* | 69 | 2 wks |
| 26 Jan 85 | **20 GREATEST HITS VOLUME 2** *RCA International NL 89168* | 98 | 1 wk |
| 25 May 85 | **RECONSIDER BABY** *RCA PL 85418* | 92 | 1 wk |
| 12 Oct 85 | **BALLADS** *Telstar STAR 2264* | 23 | 17 wks |
| 29 Aug 87 | ● **PRESLEY – THE ALL TIME GREATEST HITS** *RCA PL 90100* | 4 | 20 wks |
| 28 Jan 89 | **STEREO '57 (ESSENTIAL ELVIS VOL. 2)** *RCA PL 90250* | 60 | 2 wks |

## PRETTERS

*UK/US, male/female vocal/instrumental group*  131 wks

| | | | | | |
|---|---|---|---|---|---|
| 19 Jan | 80 | ★ **PRETENDERS** *Real RAL 3* | | **1** | 35 wks |
| 15 Aug | 81 | ● **PRETENDERS II** *Real SRK 3572* | | **7** | 27 wks |
| 21 Jan | 84 | **LEARNING TO CRAWL** *Real WX 2* | | **11** | 16 wks |
| 1 Nov | 86 | ● **GET CLOSE** *WEA WX 64* | | **6** | 28 wks |
| 7 Nov | 87 | ● **THE SINGLES** *WEA WX 135* | | **6** | 25 wks |

## PRETTY THINGS *UK, male vocal/instrumental group*  13 wks

| | | | | | |
|---|---|---|---|---|---|
| 27 Mar | 65 | ● **PRETTY THINGS** *Fontana TL 5239* | | **6** | 10 wks |
| 27 Jun | 70 | **PARACHUTE** *Harvest SHVL 774* | | **43** | 3 wks |

## Alan PRICE *UK, male vocalist/instrumentalist – keyboards*  10 wks

| | | | | | |
|---|---|---|---|---|---|
| 8 Jun | 74 | ● **BETWEEN TODAY AND YESTERDAY** *Warner Bros. K 56032* | | **9** | 10 wks |

## Charley PRIDE *US, male vocalist*  17 wks

| | | | | | |
|---|---|---|---|---|---|
| 10 Apr | 71 | **CHARLEY PRIDE SPECIAL** *RCA SF 8171* | | **29** | 1 wk |
| 28 May | 77 | **SHE'S JUST AN OLD LOVE TURNED MEMORY** *RCA Victor PL 12261* | | **34** | 2 wks |
| 3 Jun | 78 | **SOMEONE LOVES YOU HONEY** *RCA PL 12478* | | **48** | 2 wks |
| 26 Jan | 80 | ● **GOLDEN COLLECTION** *K-Tel NE 1056* | | **6** | 12 wks |

## Maxi PRIEST *UK, male vocalist*  16 wks

| | | | | | |
|---|---|---|---|---|---|
| 6 Dec | 86 | **INTENTIONS** *10 DIX 32* | | **96** | 1 wk |
| 5 Dec | 87 | **MAXI** *10 DIX 64* | | **25** | 15 wks |

## PRIMAL SCREAM *UK, male vocal/instrumental group*  1 wk

| | | | | | |
|---|---|---|---|---|---|
| 17 Oct | 87 | **SONIC FLOWER GROOVE** *Elevation ELV 2* | | **62** | 1 wk |

## PRIMITIVES *UK, male/female vocal/instrumental group*  13 wks

| | | | | | |
|---|---|---|---|---|---|
| 9 Apr | 88 | ● **LOVELY** *RCA PL 71688* | | **6** | 10 wks |
| 2 Sep | 89 | **LAZY 86–88** *Lazy 15* | | **73** | 1 wk |
| 28 Oct | 89 | **PURE** *RCA PL 74252* | | **33** | 2 wks |

## PRINCE *US, male vocalist*  230 wks

| | | | | | |
|---|---|---|---|---|---|
| 21 Jul | 84 | ● **PURPLE RAIN – MUSIC FROM THE MOTION PICTURE** *Warner Bros. 925110* | | **7** | 81 wks |
| 8 Sep | 84 | **1999** *Warner Bros. 923720* | | **30** | 21 wks |
| 4 May | 85 | ● **AROUND THE WORLD IN A DAY** *Warner Bros. 92-5286-1* | | **5** | 20 wks |
| 12 Apr | 86 | ● **PARADE – MUSIC FROM 'UNDER THE CHERRY MOON'** *Warner Bros. WX 39* | | **4** | 26 wks |
| 11 Apr | 87 | ● **SIGN 'O' THE TIMES** *Paisley Park WX 88* | | **4** | 32 wks |
| 21 May | 88 | ★ **LOVESEXY** *Paisley Park WX 164* | | **1** | 30 wks |
| 1 Jul | 89 | ★ **BATMAN** *Warner Bros. WX 281* | | **1** | 20 wks |

Purple Rain, Around The World In A Day *and* Parade *credit The Revolution, US, male/female vocal/instrumental group.*

## PRINCE CHARLES and the CITY BEAT BAND
*US, male vocalist with male vocal/instrumental group*     *1 wk*

| 30 Apr 83 | **STONE KILLERS** *Virgin V 2271* .................... | 84 | 1 wk |

## PRINCESS *UK, female vocalist*     *14 wks*

| 17 May 86 | **PRINCESS** *Supreme SU1* ........................... | 15 | 14 wks |

## P.J. PROBY *US, male vocalist*     *3 wks*

| 27 Feb 65 | **I'M P.J. PROBY** *Liberty LBY 1235* .................. | 16 | 3 wks |

## PROCLAIMERS *UK, male vocal/instrumental duo*     *48 wks*

| 9 May 87 | **THIS IS THE STORY** *Chrysalis CHR 1602* ............. | 23 | 21 wks |
| 24 Sep 88 | ● **SUNSHINE ON LEITH** *Chrysalis CHR 1668* ........... | 6 | 27 wks |

## PROCOL HARUM *UK, male vocal/instrumental group*     *11 wks*

| 19 Jul 69 | **A SALTY DOG** *Regal Zonophone SLRZ 1009* ............ | 27 | 2 wks |
| 27 Jun 70 | **HOME** *Regal Zonophone SLRZ 1014* ................... | 49 | 1 wk |
| 3 Jul 71 | **BROKEN BARRICADES** *Island ILPS 9158* ............. | 42 | 1 wk |
| 6 May 72 | **A WHITER SHADE OF PALE/A SALTY DOG (double re-issue)** *Fly Double Back TOOFA 7/8* ................ | 26 | 4 wks |
| 6 May 72 | **PROCOL HARUM IN CONCERT WITH THE EDMONTON SYMPHONY ORCHESTRA** *Chrysalis CHR 1004* ..... | 48 | 1 wk |
| 30 Aug 75 | **PROCOL'S NINTH** *Chrysalis CHR 1080* .............. | 41 | 2 wks |

*A Whiter Shade Of Pale/A Salty Dog is a double re-issue although A Whiter Shade Of Pale was not previously a hit. The Edmonton Symphony Orchestra is a Canadian orchestra.*

## PROPAGANDA
*Germany, male/female vocal/instrumental group*     *14 wks*

| 13 Jul 85 | **A SECRET WISH** *ZTT ZTTIQ 3* ................... | 16 | 12 wks |
| 23 Nov 85 | **WISHFUL THINKING** *ZTT ZTTIQ 20* .............. | 82 | 2 wks |

## Dorothy PROVINE *US, female vocalist*     *49 wks*

| 2 Dec 61 | ● **THE ROARING TWENTIES—SONGS FROM THE TV SERIES** *Warner Bros. WM 4035* .................... | 3 | 42 wks |
| 10 Feb 62 | ● **VAMP OF THE ROARING TWENTIES** *Warner Bros. WM 4053* ......................... | 9 | 7 wks |

## PSYCHEDELIC FURS *UK, male vocal/instrumental group*     *37 wks*

| 15 Mar 80 | **PSYCHEDELIC FURS** *CBS 84084* ................... | 18 | 6 wks |
| 23 May 81 | **TALK TALK TALK** *CBS 84892* ..................... | 30 | 9 wks |
| 2 Oct 82 | **FOREVER NOW** *CBS 85909* ..................... | 20 | 6 wks |
| 19 May 84 | **MIRROR MOVES** *CBS 25950* ................... | 15 | 9 wks |
| 14 Feb 87 | **MIDNIGHT TO MIDNIGHT** *CBS 450 256–1* .......... | 12 | 4 wks |
| 13 Aug 88 | **ALL OF THIS AND NOTHING** *CBS 461101* .......... | 67 | 2 wks |
| 18 Nov 89 | **BOOK OF DAYS** *CBS 465982 1* .................. | 74 | 1 wk |

## PUBLIC ENEMY *US, male rap group*     *9 wks*

| 30 Jul 88 | ● **IT TAKES A NATION OF MILLIONS TO HOLD US BACK** *Def Jam 462415 1* ................................. | 8 | 9 wks |

## PUBLIC IMAGE LTD. *UK, male vocal/instrumental group* 46 wks

| | | | |
|---|---|---|---|
| 23 Dec 78 | **PUBLIC IMAGE** *Virgin V 2114* | 22 | 11 wks |
| 8 Dec 79 | **METAL BOX** *Virgin METAL 1* | 18 | 8 wks |
| 8 Mar 80 | **SECOND EDITION OF PIL** *Virgin VD 2512* | 46 | 2 wks |
| 22 Nov 80 | **PARIS IN THE SPRING** *Virgin V 2183* | 61 | 2 wks |
| 18 Apr 81 | **FLOWERS OF ROMANCE** *Virgin V 2189* | 11 | 5 wks |
| 8 Oct 83 | **LIVE IN TOKYO** *Virgin VGD 3508* | 28 | 6 wks |
| 21 Jul 84 | **THIS IS WHAT YOU WANT . . . THIS IS WHAT YOU GET** *Virgin V 2309* | 56 | 2 wks |
| 15 Feb 86 | **ALBUM/CASSETTE** *Virgin V 2366* | 14 | 6 wks |
| 26 Sep 87 | **HAPPY?** *Virgin V 2455* | 40 | 2 wks |
| 10 Jun 89 | **9** *Virgin V 2588* | 36 | 2 wks |

## Gary PUCKETT and the UNION GAP
*US, male vocalist, male vocal/instrumental group* 4 wks

| | | | |
|---|---|---|---|
| 29 Jun 68 | **UNION GAP** *CBS 63342* | 24 | 4 wks |

# q

## Q-TIPS *UK, male vocal/instrumental group* 1 wk

| | | | |
|---|---|---|---|
| 30 Aug 80 | **Q-TIPS** *Chrysalis CHR 1255* | 50 | 1 wk |

## Suzi QUATRO *US, female vocalist/instrumentalist – guitar* 13 wks

| | | | |
|---|---|---|---|
| 13 Oct 73 | **SUZI QUATRO** *RAK SRAK 505* | 32 | 4 wks |
| 26 Apr 80 | ● **SUZI QUATRO'S GREATEST HITS** *RAK EMTV 24* | 4 | 9 wks |

## QUEEN *UK, male vocal/instrumental group* 841 wks

| | | | |
|---|---|---|---|
| 23 Mar 74 | ● **QUEEN 2** *EMI EMA 767* | 5 | 29 wks |
| 30 Mar 74 | **QUEEN** *EMI EMC 3006* | 24 | 18 wks |
| 23 Nov 74 | ● **SHEER HEART ATTACK** *EMI EMC 3061* | 2 | 42 wks |
| 13 Dec 75 | ★ **A NIGHT AT THE OPERA** *EMI EMTC 103* | 1 | 50 wks |
| 25 Dec 76 | ★ **A DAY AT THE RACES** *EMI EMTC 104* | 1 | 24 wks |
| 12 Nov 77 | ● **NEWS OF THE WORLD** *EMI EMA 784* | 4 | 20 wks |
| 25 Nov 78 | ● **JAZZ** *EMI EMA 788* | 2 | 27 wks |
| 7 Jul 79 | ● **LIVE KILLERS** *EMI EMSP 330* | 3 | 27 wks |
| 12 Jul 80 | ★ **THE GAME** *EMI EMA 795* | 1 | 18 wks |
| 20 Dec 80 | ● **FLASH GORDON (film soundtrack)** *EMI EMC 3351* | 10 | 15 wks |
| 7 Nov 81 | ★ **GREATEST HITS** *EMI EMTV 30* | 1 | 326 wks |
| 15 May 82 | ● **HOT SPACE** *EMI EMA 797* | 4 | 19 wks |
| 10 Mar 84 | ● **THE WORKS** *EMI EMC 240014* | 2 | 93 wks |
| 14 Jun 86 | ★ **A KIND OF MAGIC** *EMI EU 3509* | 1 | 62 wks |
| 13 Dec 86 | ● **LIVE MAGIC** *EMI EMC 3519* | 3 | 40 wks |
| 3 Jun 89 | ★ **THE MIRACLE** *Parlophone PCSD 107* | 1† | 30 wks |
| 16 Dec 89 | **QUEEN AT THE BEEB** *Band Of Joy BOJLP 001* | 67 | 1 wk |

The Works *changed label number during its run to EMI WORK 1.*

## QUEENSRYCHE *US, male vocal/instrumental group* 5 wks

| | | | |
|---|---|---|---|
| 29 Sep 84 | **THE WARNING** *EMI America EJ 2402201* | 100 | 1 wk |
| 26 Jul 86 | **RAGE FOR ORDER** *EMI America AML 3105* | 66 | 1 wk |
| 4 Jun 88 | **OPERATION MINDCRIME** *Manhattan MTL 1023* | 58 | 3 wks |

## QUIET RIOT   US, male vocal/instrumental group

*1 wk*

| | | | | |
|---|---|---|---|---|
| 4 Aug 84 | **CONDITION CRITICAL**   Epic EPC 26075 ............ | **71** | 1 wk |

## QUINTESSENCE
*UK/Australia, male vocal/instrumental group*

*6 wks*

| | | | |
|---|---|---|---|
| 27 Jun 70 | **QUINTESSENCE** Island ILPS 9128 ................... | **22** | 4 wks |
| 3 Apr 71 | **DIVE DEEP**  Island ILPS 9143 ...................... | **43** | 1 wk |
| 27 May 72 | **SELF**  RCA Victor SF 8273 ...................... | **50** | 1 wk |

**QUIVER** – *See SUTHERLAND BROTHERS and QUIVER*


# *r*


Harry **RABINOWITZ** – *See ROYAL PHILHARMONIC ORCHESTRA*

## RACING CARS   UK, male vocal/instrumental group

*6 wks*

| | | | |
|---|---|---|---|
| 19 Feb 77 | **DOWNTOWN TONIGHT**   Chrysalis CHR 1099 ........ | **39** | 6 wks |

## Gerry RAFFERTY   UK, male vocalist

*78 wks*

| | | | |
|---|---|---|---|
| 25 Feb 78 ● | **CITY TO CITY**   United Artists UAS 30104 .............. | **6** | 37 wks |
| 2 Jun 79 ● | **NIGHT OWL**   United Artists UAK 30238 ............... | **9** | 24 wks |
| 26 Apr 80 | **SNAKES AND LADDERS**   United Artists UAK 30298 ..... | **15** | 9 wks |
| 25 Sep 82 | **SLEEPWALKING**   Liberty LBG 30352 ................. | **39** | 4 wks |
| 21 May 88 | **NORTH AND SOUTH**   London LONLP 55 ............ | **43** | 4 wks |

## RAH BAND   UK, male/female vocal/instrumental group

*6 wks*

| | | | |
|---|---|---|---|
| 6 Apr 85 | **MYSTERY**   RCA PL 70640 ........................ | **60** | 6 wks |

## RAILWAY CHILDREN
*UK, male vocal/instrumental group*

*1 wk*

| | | | |
|---|---|---|---|
| 21 May 88 | **RECURRENCE**   Virgin V 2525 ..................... | **96** | 1 wk |

## RAINBOW   UK, male vocal/instrumental group

*163 wks*

| | | | |
|---|---|---|---|
| 13 Sep 75 | **RITCHIE BLACKMORE'S RAINBOW**  Oyster OYA 2001 ............................... | **11** | 6 wks |
| 5 Jun 76 | **RAINBOW RISING**   Polydor 2490 137 ................ | **11** | 33 wks |
| 30 Jul 77 ● | **ON STAGE**   Polydor 2657 016 ...................... | **7** | 10 wks |
| 6 May 78 ● | **LONG LIVE ROCK 'N' ROLL**   Polydor POLD 5002 ...... | **7** | 12 wks |
| 18 Aug 79 ● | **DOWN TO EARTH**   Polydor POLD 5023 ............. | **6** | 37 wks |
| 21 Feb 81 ● | **DIFFICULT TO CURE**   Polydor POLD 5036 ......... | **3** | 22 wks |
| 8 Aug 81 | **RITCHIE BLACKMORE'S RAINBOW (re-issue)**  Polydor 2490 141 ................................. | **91** | 2 wks |
| 21 Nov 81 | **BEST OF RAINBOW**   Polydor POLDV 2 ............. | **14** | 17 wks |
| 24 Apr 82 ● | **STRAIGHT BETWEEN THE EYES**   Polydor POLD 5056 . | **5** | 14 wks |
| 17 Sep 83 | **BENT OUT OF SHAPE**   Polydor POLD 5116 ........... | **11** | 6 wks |
| 8 Mar 86 | **FINYL VINYL**   Polydor PODV 8 .................... | **31** | 4 wks |

*First two albums and re-issue of first album credited to Ritchie Blackmore's Rainbow.*

American country legend **CHARLEY PRIDE** has had more hit albums than singles in Britain.

**SCRITTI POLITTI** were led by Green Gartside (right).

**QUEEN** pose during the making of the video for *I Want to Break Free* from 'The Works'.

## RAIN PARADE  *US, male vocal/instrumental group*　　　*1 wk*

| 29 Jun 85 | **BEYOND THE SUNSET**  *Island IMA 17* .............. | 78 | 1 wk |

**RAKIM** – *See Eric B. and RAKIM*

## RAMONES  *US, male vocal/instrumental group*　　　*28 wks*

| 23 Apr 77 | **LEAVE HOME**  *Philips 9103 254* .................... | 45 | 1 wk |
| 24 Dec 77 | **ROCKET TO RUSSIA**  *Sire 9103 255* ................ | 60 | 2 wks |
| 7 Oct 78 | **ROAD TO RUIN**  *Sire SRK 6063* ................... | 32 | 2 wks |
| 16 Jun 79 | **IT'S ALIVE**  *Sire SRK 26074* ..................... | 27 | 8 wks |
| 19 Jan 80 | **END OF THE CENTURY**  *Sire SRK 6077* ............. | 14 | 8 wks |
| 26 Jan 85 | **TOO TOUGH TO DIE**  *Beggars Banquet BEGA 59* ........ | 63 | 3 wks |
| 31 May 86 | **ANIMAL BOY**  *Beggars Banquet BEGA 70* .............. | 38 | 2 wks |
| 10 Oct 87 | **HALFWAY TO SANITY**  *Beggars Banquet BEGA 89* ...... | 78 | 1 wk |
| 19 Aug 89 | **BRAIN DRAIN**  *Chrysalis CHR 1725* .................. | 75 | 1 wk |

**RANGE** – *See Bruce HORNSBY and the RANGE*

## Roland RAT SUPERSTAR  *UK, male rat vocalist*　　　*3 wks*

| 15 Dec 84 | **THE CASSETTE OF THE ALBUM**  *Rodent RATL 1001* ... | 67 | 3 wks |

## RATT  *US, male vocal/instrumental group*　　　*4 wks*

| 13 Jul 85 | **INVASION OF YOUR PRIVACY**  *Atlantic 78–1257–1* .... | 50 | 2 wks |
| 25 Oct 86 | **DANCING UNDERCOVER**  *Atlantic 781 683–1* ........ | 51 | 1 wk |
| 12 Nov 88 | **REACH FOR THE SKY**  *Atlantic 781929* .............. | 82 | 1 wk |

## RAVEN  *UK, male vocal/instrumental group*　　　*3 wks*

| 17 Oct 81 | **ROCK UNTIL YOU DROP**  *Neat NEAT 1001* .......... | 63 | 3 wks |

**Simon RAYMOND** – *See Harold BUDD/Liz FRASER/Robin GUTHRIE/Simon RAYMOND*

## Chris REA  *UK, male vocalist*　　　*172 wks*

| 28 Apr 79 | **DELTICS**  *Magnet MAG 5028* ...................... | 54 | 3 wks |
| 12 Apr 80 | **TENNIS**  *Magnet MAG 5032* ...................... | 60 | 1 wk |
| 3 Apr 82 | **CHRIS REA**  *Magnet MAGL 5040* .................... | 52 | 4 wks |
| 18 Jun 83 | **WATER SIGN**  *Magnet MAGL 5048* .................. | 64 | 2 wks |
| 21 Apr 84 | **WIRED TO THE MOON**  *Magnet MAGL 5057* .......... | 35 | 7 wks |
| 25 May 85 | **SHAMROCK DIARIES**  *Magnet MAGL 5062* ........... | 15 | 14 wks |
| 26 Apr 86 | **ON THE BEACH**  *Magnet MAGL 5069* ................ | 11 | 37 wks |
| 26 Sep 87 | ● **DANCING WITH STRANGERS**  *Magnet MAGL 5071* ... | 2 | 46 wks |
| 13 Aug 88 | **ON THE BEACH**  (re-issue)  *WEA WX 191* ........... | 37 | 10 wks |
| 29 Oct 88 | ● **NEW LIGHT THROUGH OLD WINDOWS** | | |
| | *WEA WX 200* ...................................... | 5 | 40 wks |
| 11 Nov 89 | ★ **THE ROAD TO HELL**  *WEA WX 317* ................ | 1† | 8 wks |

## REAL THING  *UK, male vocal/instrumental group*　　　*17 wks*

| 6 Nov 76 | **REAL THING**  *Pye NSPL 18507* ...................... | 34 | 3 wks |
| 7 Apr 79 | **CAN YOU FEEL THE FORCE**  *Pye NSPH 18601* ....... | 73 | 1 wk |
| 10 May 80 | **20 GREATEST HITS**  *K-Tel NE 1073* ................ | 56 | 2 wks |
| 12 Jul 86 | **BEST OF THE REAL THING**  *West Five NRT 1* ......... | 24 | 11 wks |

**REBEL ROUSERS** – *See Cliff BENNETT and the REBEL ROUSERS*

## RED BOX  *UK, male vocal/instrumental duo*　　　*4 wks*

| 6 Dec 86 | **THE CIRCLE AND THE SQUARE**  *Sire WX 79* ........ | 73 | 4 wks |

## Sharon REDD   *US, female vocalist*                              5 wks

| 23 Oct 82 | **REDD HOTT**   *Prelude PRL 25056* ..................... | 59 | 5 wks |
|---|---|---|---|

## Otis REDDING   *US, male vocalist*                              192 wks

| 19 Feb 66 ● | **OTIS BLUE**   *Atlantic ATL 5041* ...................... | 6 | 21 wks |
|---|---|---|---|
| 23 Apr 66 | **SOUL BALLADS**   *Atlantic ATL 5029* ................. | 30 | 1 wk |
| 23 Jul 66 | **SOUL ALBUM**   *Atlantic 587–011* ..................... | 22 | 9 wks |
| 21 Jan 67 | **OTIS REDDING'S DICTIONARY OF SOUL** | | |
| | *Atlantic 588–050* ................................ | 23 | 16 wks |
| 21 Jan 67 ● | **OTIS BLUE (re-issue)**   *Atlantic 587–036* ............... | 7 | 54 wks |
| 29 Apr 67 | **PAIN IN MY HEART**   *Atlantic 587–042* ............. | 28 | 9 wks |
| 10 Feb 68 ● | **HISTORY OF OTIS REDDING**   *Volt S 418* ............ | 2 | 43 wks |
| 30 Mar 68 | **OTIS REDDING IN EUROPE**   *Stax 589–016* .......... | 14 | 16 wks |
| 1 Jun 68 ★ | **DOCK OF THE BAY**   *Stax 231–001* .................. | 1 | 15 wks |
| 12 Oct 68 | **IMMORTAL OTIS REDDING**   *Atlantic 588–113* ......... | 19 | 8 wks |

*See also Otis Redding and Carla Thomas.*

## Otis REDDING and Carla THOMAS
*US, male/female vocal duo*                              17 wks

| 1 Jul 67 | **KING AND QUEEN**   *Atlantic 589–007* ................. | 18 | 17 wks |
|---|---|---|---|

*See also Otis Redding.*

## Helen REDDY   *Australia, female vocalist*                       27 wks

| 8 Feb 75 | **FREE AND EASY**   *Capitol E-ST 11348* ................ | 17 | 9 wks |
|---|---|---|---|
| 14 Feb 76 ● | **THE BEST OF HELEN REDDY**   *Capitol E-ST 11467* .... | 5 | 18 wks |

## REDSKINS   *UK, male vocal/instrumental duo*                    4 wks

| 22 Mar 86 | **NEITHER WASHINGTON, NOR MOSCOW** | | |
|---|---|---|---|
| | *Decca FLP 1* ................................... | 31 | 4 wks |

## Dan REED NETWORK   *US, male vocal/instrumental group*   1 wk

| 4 Nov 89 | **SLAM**   *Mercury 838868 1* ........................... | 66 | 1 wk |
|---|---|---|---|

## Lou REED   *US, male vocalist*                              63 wks

| 21 Apr 73 | **TRANSFORMER**   *RCA Victor LSP 4807* .............. | 13 | 25 wks |
|---|---|---|---|
| 20 Oct 73 ● | **BERLIN**   *RCA Victor RS 1002* ...................... | 7 | 5 wks |
| 16 Mar 74 | **ROCK 'N' ROLL ANIMAL**   *RCA Victor APLI 0472* ....... | 26 | 1 wk |
| 14 Feb 76 | **CONEY ISLAND BABY**   *RCA Victor RS 1035* .......... | 52 | 1 wk |
| 3 Jul 82 | **TRANSFORMER (re-issue)**   *RCA INTS 5061* ......... | 91 | 2 wks |
| 9 Jun 84 | **NEW SENSATIONS**   *RCA PL 84998* ................. | 92 | 1 wk |
| 24 May 86 | **MISTRIAL**   *RCA PL 87190* ........................ | 69 | 1 wk |
| 28 Jan 89 | **NEW YORK**   *Sire WX 246* ........................ | 14 | 22 wks |
| 7 Oct 89 | **RETRO**   *RCA PL 90389* ......................... | 29 | 5 wks |

**Don REEDMAN** – *See Jeff JARRATT and Don REEDMAN*

## Jim REEVES   *US, male vocalist*                              381 wks

| 28 Mar 64 ● | **GOOD 'N' COUNTRY**   *RCA Camden CDN 5114* ........ | 10 | 35 wks |
|---|---|---|---|
| 9 May 64 ● | **GENTLEMAN JIM**   *RCA RD 7541* ................... | 3 | 23 wks |
| 15 Aug 64 ● | **A TOUCH OF VELVET**   *RCA RD 7521* .............. | 8 | 9 wks |
| 15 Aug 64 | **INTERNATIONAL JIM REEVES**   *RCA RD 7577* ....... | 11 | 15 wks |
| 22 Aug 64 | **HE'LL HAVE TO GO**   *RCA RD 27176* ............... | 16 | 4 wks |
| 29 Aug 64 | **THE INTIMATE JIM REEVES**   *RCA RD 27193* ......... | 12 | 4 wks |

## Neil REID  *UK, male vocalist*  *18 wks*

## R.E.M.  *US, male vocal/instrumental group*  *37 wks*

## RENAISSANCE
*UK, male/female vocal/instrumental group*  *10 wks*

## RENATO  *Italy, male vocalist*  *14 wks*

## REO SPEEDWAGON
*US, male vocal/instrumental group*  *36 wks*

REVOLUTION – *See PRINCE*

## REZILLOS  *UK, male/female vocal/instrumental group*     *15 wks*

| | | | | |
|---|---|---|---|---|
| 5 Aug 78 | ● CAN'T STAND THE REZILLOS  *Sire  WEA K 56530*  ... | 16 | 10 wks |
| 28 Apr 79 | MISSION ACCOMPLISHED BUT THE BEAT GOES ON | | |
| | *Sire SRK 6069* .................................. | 30 | 5 wks |

## Charlie RICH  *US, male vocalist*     *28 wks*

| | | | |
|---|---|---|---|
| 23 Mar 74 | ● BEHIND CLOSED DOORS  *Epic 65716* .............. | 4 | 26 wks |
| 13 Jul 74 | VERY SPECIAL LOVE SONGS  *Epic 80031* ............ | 34 | 2 wks |

## Richie RICH  *UK, male vocalist*     *1 wk*

| | | | |
|---|---|---|---|
| 22 Jul 89 | I CAN MAKE YOU DANCE  *Gee St. GEEA 3* .......... | 65 | 1 wk |

## RICH KIDS  *UK, male vocal/instrumental group*     *1 wk*

| | | | |
|---|---|---|---|
| 7 Oct 78 | GHOST OF PRINCES IN TOWERS  *EMI EMC 3263*  ... | 51 | 1 wk |

## Cliff RICHARD  *UK, male vocalist*     *684 wks*

| | | | |
|---|---|---|---|
| 18 Apr 59 | ● CLIFF  *Columbia 33SX 1147* ......................... | 4 | 31 wks |
| 14 Nov 59 | ● CLIFF SINGS  *Columbia 33SX 1192* ................... | 2 | 36 wks |
| 15 Oct 60 | ● ME AND MY SHADOWS  *Columbia 33SX 1261* .......... | 2 | 33 wks |
| 22 Apr 61 | ● LISTEN TO CLIFF  *Columbia 33SX 1320* .............. | 2 | 28 wks |
| 21 Oct 61 | ★ 21 TODAY  *Columbia 33SX 1368* .................... | 1 | 16 wks |
| 23 Dec 61 | ★ THE YOUNG ONES (film soundtrack) | | |
| | *Columbia 33SX 1384* ............................ | 1 | 42 wks |
| 29 Sep 62 | ● 32 MINUTES AND 17 SECONDS  *Columbia 33SX 1431*  ... | 3 | 21 wks |
| 26 Jan 63 | ★ SUMMER HOLIDAY (film soundtrack) | | |
| | *Columbia 33SX 1472* ............................ | 1 | 36 wks |
| 13 Jul 63 | ● CLIFF'S HIT ALBUM  *Columbia 33SX 1512* ............ | 2 | 19 wks |
| 28 Sep 63 | ● WHEN IN SPAIN  *Columbia 33SX 1541* ............... | 8 | 10 wks |
| 11 Jul 64 | ● WONDERFUL LIFE (film soundtrack) | | |
| | *Columbia 33SX 1628* ............................ | 2 | 23 wks |
| 9 Jan 65 | ALADDIN (pantomime)  *Columbia 33SX 1676* .......... | 13 | 5 wks |
| 17 Apr 65 | ● CLIFF RICHARD  *Columbia 33SX 1709* ............... | 9 | 5 wks |
| 14 Aug 65 | MORE HITS BY CLIFF  *Columbia 33SX 1737* ............ | 20 | 1 wk |
| 8 Jan 66 | LOVE IS FOREVER  *Columbia 33SX 1769* .............. | 19 | 1 wk |
| 21 May 66 | ● KINDA LATIN  *Columbia SX 6039* ................... | 9 | 12 wks |
| 17 Dec 66 | ● FINDERS KEEPERS (film soundtrack) | | |
| | *Columbia SX 6079* .............................. | 6 | 18 wks |
| 7 Jan 67 | CINDERELLA (pantomime)  *Columbia 33SCX 6103* ..... | 30 | 6 wks |
| 15 Apr 67 | DON'T STOP ME NOW ...  *Columbia SCX 6133* ........ | 23 | 9 wks |
| 11 Nov 67 | GOOD NEWS  *Columbia SCX 6167* ................... | 37 | 1 wk |
| 1 Jun 68 | CLIFF IN JAPAN  *Columbia SCX 6244* ................ | 29 | 2 wks |
| 16 Nov 68 | ESTABLISHED 1958  *Columbia SCX 6282* .............. | 30 | 4 wks |
| 12 Jul 69 | ● BEST OF CLIFF  *Columbia SCX 6343* ................ | 5 | 17 wks |
| 27 Sep 69 | SINCERELY  *Columbia SCX 6357* ..................... | 24 | 3 wks |
| 12 Dec 70 | TRACKS 'N' GROOVES  *Columbia SCX 6435* .......... | 37 | 2 wks |
| 23 Dec 72 | BEST OF CLIFF VOL. 2  *Columbia SCX 6519* ............ | 49 | 2 wks |
| 19 Jan 74 | TAKE ME HIGH (film soundtrack) | | |
| | *EMI EMC 3016* .................................. | 41 | 4 wks |
| 29 May 76 | ● I'M NEARLY FAMOUS  *EMI EMC 3122* .............. | 5 | 21 wks |
| 26 Mar 77 | ● EVERY FACE TELLS A STORY  *EMI EMC 3172* ...... | 8 | 10 wks |
| 22 Oct 77 | ★ 40 GOLDEN GREATS  *EMI EMTV 6* ............... | 1 | 19 wks |
| 4 Mar 78 | SMALL CORNERS  *EMI EMC 3219* .................. | 33 | 5 wks |
| 21 Oct 78 | GREEN LIGHT  *EMI EMC 3231* ..................... | 25 | 3 wks |
| 17 Feb 79 | ● THANK YOU VERY MUCH – REUNION CONCERT AT | | |
| | THE LONDON PALLADIUM  *EMI EMTV 15* ......... | 5 | 12 wks |
| 15 Sep 79 | ● ROCK 'N' ROLL JUVENILE  *EMI EMC 3307* .......... | 3 | 22 wks |
| 13 Sep 80 | ● I'M NO HERO  *EMI EMA 796* ..................... | 4 | 12 wks |
| 4 Jul 81 | ★ LOVE SONGS  *EMI EMTV 27* .................... | 1 | 43 wks |
| 26 Sep 81 | ● WIRED FOR SOUND  *EMI EMC 3377* .............. | 4 | 25 wks |
| 4 Sep 82 | ● NOW YOU SEE ME, NOW YOU DON'T  *EMI EMC 3415* | 4 | 14 wks |
| 21 May 83 | ● DRESSED FOR THE OCCASION  *EMI EMC 3432* ..... | 7 | 17 wks |
| 15 Oct 83 | ● SILVER  *EMI EMC 1077871* ...................... | 7 | 24 wks |

| | | | |
|---|---|---|---|
| 14 Jul 84 | **20 ORIGINAL GREATS** *EMI CRS 1* ................ | **43** | 6 wks |
| 1 Dec 84 | **THE ROCK CONNECTION** *EMI CLIF 2* ............ | **43** | 5 wks |
| 26 Sep 87 | ● **ALWAYS GUARANTEED** *EMI EMD 1004* .......... | **5** | 25 wks |
| 19 Nov 88 | ★ **PRIVATE COLLECTION** *EMI CRTV 30* ............ | **1** | 26 wks |
| 11 Nov 89 | ● **STRONGER** *EMI EMD 1012* ..................... | **7†** | 8 wks |

*The Shadows featured on all or some of the tracks of all albums up to and including* Aladdin *and the following subsequent albums:* More Hits By Cliff, Love Is Forever, Finders Keepers, Cinderella, Established 1958, Best Of Cliff, Best Of Cliff Vol. 2, 40 Golden Greats, Thank You Very Much, Love Songs *and* 20 Original Greats. Cliff *credited to* Cliff Richard and the Drifters, *the original name used by the Shadows. See also the Shadows.*

## Keith RICHARDS
*UK, male vocalist/instrumentalist – guitar*          *3 wks*

| | | | |
|---|---|---|---|
| 15 Oct 88 | **TALK IS CHEAP** *Virgin V 2554* ..................... | **37** | 3 wks |

## Lionel RICHIE   *US, male vocalist*      *293 wks*

| | | | |
|---|---|---|---|
| 27 Nov 82 | ● **LIONEL RICHIE** *Motown STMA 8037* ............... | **9** | 86 wks |
| 29 Oct 83 | ★ **CAN'T SLOW DOWN** *Motown STMA 8041* ............ | **1** | 154 wks |
| 23 Aug 86 | ● **DANCING ON THE CEILING** *Motown ZL 72412* ....... | **2** | 53 wks |

## Jonathan RICHMAN and the MODERN LOVERS   *US, male vocal/instrumental group*    *3 wks*

| | | | |
|---|---|---|---|
| 27 Aug 77 | **ROCK 'N' ROLL WITH THE MODERN LOVERS** *Beserkeley BSERK 9* ............................. | **50** | 3 wks |

## RICHMOND STRINGS/MIKE SAMMES SINGERS   *UK, orchestra/male/female vocal group*    *7 wks*

| | | | |
|---|---|---|---|
| 19 Jan 76 | **MUSIC OF AMERICA** *Ronco TRD 2016* ............... | **18** | 7 wks |

**Nelson RIDDLE ORCHESTRA** – *See Shirley* BASSEY; *Linda* RONSTADT; *Kiri* TE KANAWA

## RIP RIG AND PANIC
*UK/US, male/female vocal/instrumental group*      *3 wks*

| | | | |
|---|---|---|---|
| 26 Jun 82 | **I AM GOLD** *Virgin V 2228* ......................... | **67** | 3 wks |

## Minnie RIPERTON   *US, female vocalist*      *3 wks*

| | | | |
|---|---|---|---|
| 17 May 75 | **PERFECT ANGEL** *Epic EPC 80426* ................. | **33** | 3 wks |

## Angela RIPPON   *UK, female exercise instructor*    *26 wks*

| | | | |
|---|---|---|---|
| 17 Apr 82 | ● **SHAPE UP AND DANCE (VOL. II)** *Lifestyle LEG 2* ..... | **8** | 26 wks |

## RIVER DETECTIVES   *UK, male vocal/instrumental duo*    *1 wk*

| | | | |
|---|---|---|---|
| 23 Sep 89 | **SATURDAY NIGHT SUNDAY MORNING** *WEA WX 2955* ................................ | **51** | 1 wk |

## David ROACH
*UK, male vocalist/instrumentalist – saxophone*      *1 wk*

| | | | |
|---|---|---|---|
| 14 Apr 84 | **I LOVE SAX** *Nouveau Music NML 1006* ................ | **73** | 1 wk |

## ROACHFORD  *UK, male vocalist*  *27 wks*

23 Jul 88   **ROACHFORD**  *CBS 460630 1* . . . . . . . . . . . . . . . . . . . . . . .   **18**   27 wks

**ROBBIE** – *See SLY and ROBBIE*

## Marty ROBBINS  *US, male vocalist*  *15 wks*

13 Aug 60   **GUNFIGHTER BALLADS**  *Fontana TFL 5063* . . . . . . . . . .   **20**   1 wk
10 Feb 79  ● **MARTY ROBBINS COLLECTION**  *Lotus WH 5009* . . . . .   **5**   14 wks

## Paddy ROBERTS  *South Africa, male vocalist*  *6 wks*

26 Sep 59  ● **STRICTLY FOR GROWN-UPS**  *Decca LF 1322* . . . . . . . .   **8**   5 wks
17 Sep 60   **PADDY ROBERTS TRIES AGAIN**  *Decca LK 4358* . . . . .   **16**   1 wk

## B.A. ROBERTSON  *UK, male vocalist*  *10 wks*

29 Mar 80   **INITIAL SUCCESS**  *Asylum K 52216* . . . . . . . . . . . . . . . .   **32**   8 wks
4 Apr 81   **BULLY FOR YOU**  *Asylum K 52275* . . . . . . . . . . . . . . . . . .   **61**   2 wks

## Robbie ROBERTSON  *Canada, male vocalist*  *14 wks*

14 Nov 87   **ROBBIE ROBERTSON**  *Geffen WX 133* . . . . . . . . . . . . . .   **23**   14 wks

## Smokey ROBINSON  *US, male vocalist*  *10 wks*

20 Jun 81   **BEING WITH YOU**  *Motown STML 12151* . . . . . . . . . . . . .   **17**   10 wks

## Tom ROBINSON BAND
*UK, male vocal/instrumental group*  *23 wks*

3 Jun 78  ● **POWER IN THE DARKNESS**  *EMI EMC 3226* . . . . . . . .   **4**   12 wks
24 Mar 79   **TRB2**  *EMI EMC 3296* . . . . . . . . . . . . . . . . . . . . . . . . . . . .   **18**   6 wks
29 Sep 84   **HOPE AND GLORY**  *Castaway ZL 70483* . . . . . . . . . . . . .   **21**   5 wks

Hope And Glory *credited simply to Tom Robinson.*

**ROCK** – *See BLACK ROCK and RON*

## ROCK GODDESS  *UK, female vocal/instrumental group*  *3 wks*

12 Mar 83   **ROCK GODDESS**  *A & M AMLH 68554* . . . . . . . . . . . . . .   **65**   2 wks
29 Oct 83   **HELL HATH NO FURY**  *A & M AMLX 68560* . . . . . . . . . .   **84**   1 wk

## ROCKIN' BERRIES  *UK, male vocal/instrumental group*  *1 wk*

19 Jun 65   **IN TOWN**  *Pye NPL 38013* . . . . . . . . . . . . . . . . . . . . . . . .   **15**   1 wk

## ROCKPILE  *UK, male vocal/instrumental group*  *5 wks*

18 Oct 80   **SECONDS OF PLEASURE**  *F-Beat XXLP 7* . . . . . . . . . . . .   **34**   5 wks

## ROCKSTEADY CREW  *US, male/female vocal group*  *1 wk*

16 Jun 84   **READY FOR BATTLE**  *Charisma RSC LP1* . . . . . . . . . . . .   **73**   1 wk

## ROCKWELL  *US, male vocalist*  *5 wks*

25 Feb 84   **SOMEBODY'S WATCHING ME**  *Motown ZL 72147* . . . . .   **52**   5 wks

## Clodagh RODGERS  *Ireland, female vocalist*  *1 wk*

| | | | | |
|---|---|---|---|---|
| 13 Sep 69 | **CLODAGH RODGERS** *RCA SF 8033* .............. | 27 | 1 wk |

## RODS  *US, male vocal/instrumental group*  *4 wks*

| | | | | |
|---|---|---|---|---|
| 24 Jul 82 | **WILD DOGS** *Arista SPART 1196* ................... | 75 | 4 wks |

## Kenny ROGERS  *US, male vocalist*  *93 wks*

| | | | | |
|---|---|---|---|---|
| 18 Jun 77 | **KENNY ROGERS** *United Artists UAS 30046* ........... | 14 | 7 wks |
| 6 Oct 79 | **THE KENNY ROGERS SINGLES ALBUM** | | |
| | *United Artists UAK 30263* ......................... | 12 | 22 wks |
| 9 Feb 80 | ● **KENNY** *United Artists UAG 30273* .................. | 7 | 10 wks |
| 31 Jan 81 | **LADY** *Liberty LBG 30334* ........................ | 40 | 5 wks |
| 1 Oct 83 | **EYES THAT SEE IN THE DARK** *RCA RCALP 6088* .... | 53 | 19 wks |
| 27 Oct 84 | **WHAT ABOUT ME?** *RCA PL 85043* .................. | 97 | 1 wk |
| 27 Jul 85 | ● **THE KENNY ROGERS STORY** *Liberty EMTV 39* ...... | 4 | 29 wks |

## ROLLING STONES  *UK, male vocal/instrumental group*  *650 wks*

| | | | | |
|---|---|---|---|---|
| 25 Apr 64 | ★ **ROLLING STONES** *Decca LK 4805* ................. | 1 | 51 wks |
| 23 Jan 65 | ★ **ROLLING STONES NO. 2** *Decca LK 4661* ............ | 1 | 37 wks |
| 2 Oct 65 | ● **OUT OF OUR HEADS** *Decca LK 4733* ............... | 2 | 24 wks |
| 23 Apr 66 | ● **AFTERMATH** *Decca LK 4786* .................... | 1 | 28 wks |
| 12 Nov 66 | ● **BIG HITS (HIGH TIDE AND GREEN GRASS)** | | |
| | *Decca TXS 101* ................................. | 4 | 43 wks |
| 28 Jan 67 | ● **BETWEEN THE BUTTONS** *Decca SKL 4852* .......... | 3 | 22 wks |
| 23 Dec 67 | ● **THEIR SATANIC MAJESTIES REQUEST** | | |
| | *Decca TXS 103* ................................. | 3 | 13 wks |
| 21 Dec 68 | ● **BEGGARS BANQUET** *Decca SKL 4955* .............. | 3 | 12 wks |
| 27 Sep 69 | ● **THROUGH THE PAST DARKLY (BIG HITS VOL. 2)** | | |
| | *Decca SKL 5019* ................................ | 2 | 37 wks |
| 20 Dec 69 | ★ **LET IT BLEED** *Decca SKL 5025* ................. | 1 | 29 wks |
| 19 Sep 70 | ★ **GET YOUR YA-YAS OUT** *Decca SKL 5065* ...... | 1 | 15 wks |
| 3 Apr 71 | ● **STONE AGE** *Decca SKL 5084* ...................... | 4 | 7 wks |
| 8 May 71 | ★ **STICKY FINGERS** *Rolling Stones COC 59100* ....... | 1 | 25 wks |
| 18 Sep 71 | **GIMME SHELTER** *Decca SKL 5101* ............. | 19 | 5 wks |
| 11 Mar 72 | **MILESTONES** *Decca SKL 5098* ................. | 14 | 8 wks |
| 10 Jun 72 | ★ **EXILE ON MAIN STREET** *Rolling Stones COC 69100* .... | 1 | 16 wks |
| 11 Nov 72 | **ROCK 'N' ROLLING STONES** *Decca SKL 5149* ........ | 41 | 1 wk |
| 22 Sep 73 | ★ **GOAT'S HEAD SOUP** *Rolling Stones COC 59101* ...... | 1 | 14 wks |
| 2 Nov 74 | ● **IT'S ONLY ROCK 'N' ROLL** *Rolling Stones COC 59103* .. | 2 | 9 wks |
| 28 Jun 75 | **MADE IN THE SHADE** *Rolling Stones COC 59104* ....... | 14 | 12 wks |
| 28 Jun 75 | **METAMORPHOSIS** *Decca SKL 5212* ................. | 45 | 1 wk |
| 29 Nov 75 | ● **ROLLED GOLD – THE VERY BEST OF THE ROLLING** | | |
| | **STONES** *Decca ROST 1/2* ...................... | 7 | 50 wks |
| 8 May 76 | ● **BLACK AND BLUE** *Rolling Stones COC 59106* .......... | 2 | 14 wks |
| 8 Oct 77 | ● **LOVE YOU LIVE** *Rolling Stones COC 89101* ............ | 3 | 8 wks |
| 5 Nov 77 | ● **GET STONED** *Arcade ADEP 32* .................. | 8 | 15 wks |
| 24 Jun 78 | ● **SOME GIRLS** *Rolling Stones CUN 39108* ............. | 2 | 25 wks |
| 5 Jul 80 | ★ **EMOTIONAL RESCUE** *Rolling Stones CUN 39111* ...... | 1 | 18 wks |
| 12 Sep 81 | ● **TATTOO YOU** *Rolling Stones CUNS 39114* ............. | 2 | 29 wks |
| 12 Jun 82 | ● **STILL LIFE (AMERICAN CONCERTS 1981)** | | |
| | *Rolling Stones CUN 39115* ......................... | 4 | 18 wks |
| 31 Jul 82 | **IN CONCERT** (import) *Decca (Holland) 6640 037* ........ | 94 | 3 wks |
| 11 Dec 82 | **STORY OF THE STONES** *K-Tel NE 1201* ............. | 24 | 12 wks |
| 19 Nov 83 | ● **UNDERCOVER** *Rolling Stones CUN 1654361* ........... | 3 | 18 wks |
| 7 Jul 84 | **REWIND 1971–1984 (THE BEST OF THE ROLLING** | | |
| | **STONES)** *Rolling Stones CUN 1* ................... | 23 | 13 wks |
| 5 Apr 86 | ● **DIRTY WORK** *Rolling Stones CUN 86321* ............. | 4 | 10 wks |
| 23 Sep 89 | ● **STEEL WHEELS** *CBS 465752 1* ................. | 2 | 8 wks |

## ROMAN HOLIDAY  *UK, male vocal/instrumental group*  *3 wks*

| | | | | |
|---|---|---|---|---|
| 22 Oct 83 | **COOKIN' ON THE ROOF** *Jive HIP 9* .............. | 31 | 3 wks |

## RONDO VENEZIANO
UK, male/female orchestral group                                33 wks

| | | | |
|---|---|---|---|
| 5 Nov 83 | **VENICE IN PERIL** *Ferroway RON 1* | 39 | 13 wks |
| 10 Nov 84 | **THE GENIUS OF VENICE** *Ferroway RON 2* | 60 | 13 wks |
| 9 Jul 88 | **VENICE IN PERIL (re-issue)** *Fanfare RON 1* | 34 | 7 wks |

## Mick RONSON  UK, male vocalist/instrumentalist – guitar      10 wks

| | | | |
|---|---|---|---|
| 16 Mar 74 ● | **SLAUGHTER ON TENTH AVENUE** | | |
| | *RCA Victor APLI 0353* | 9 | 7 wks |
| 8 Mar 75 | **PLAY DON'T WORRY** *RCA Victor APLI 0681* | 29 | 3 wks |

## Linda RONSTADT  UK, female vocalist                          39 wks

| | | | |
|---|---|---|---|
| 4 Sep 76 | **HASTEN DOWN THE WIND** *Asylum K 53045* | 32 | 8 wks |
| 25 Dec 76 | **GREATEST HITS** *Asylum K 53055* | 37 | 9 wks |
| 1 Oct 77 | **SIMPLE DREAMS** *Asylum K 53065* | 15 | 5 wks |
| 14 Oct 78 | **LIVING IN THE USA** *Asylum K 53085* | 39 | 2 wks |
| 8 Mar 80 | **MAD LOVE** *Asylum K 52210* | 65 | 1 wk |
| 28 Jan 84 | **WHAT'S NEW** *Asylum 96 0260* | 31 | 5 wks |
| 19 Jan 85 | **LUSH LIFE** *Asylum 96–0387–1* | 100 | 1 wk |
| 11 Nov 89 | **CRY LIKE A RAINSTORM – HOWL LIKE THE WIND** | | |
| | *Elektra EKT 76* | 43† | 8 wks |

What's New *and* Lush Life *credited to Linda Ronstadt with the Nelson Riddle Orchestra.* Cry Like A Rainstorm *features Aaron Neville. See also Dolly Parton/Linda Ronstadt/Emmylou Harris.*

## ROSE MARIE  UK, female vocalist                              34 wks

| | | | |
|---|---|---|---|
| 13 Apr 85 | **ROSE MARIE SINGS JUST FOR YOU** *A1 RMTV 1* | 30 | 13 wks |
| 24 May 86 | **SO LUCKY** *A1-Spartan RMLP 2* | 62 | 3 wks |
| 14 Nov 87 | **SENTIMENTALLY YOURS** *Telstar STAR 2302* | 22 | 11 wks |
| 19 Nov 88 | **TOGETHER AGAIN** *Telstar STAR 2333* | 52 | 7 wks |

## ROSE ROYCE  US, male/female vocal/instrumental group         62 wks

| | | | |
|---|---|---|---|
| 22 Oct 77 | **IN FULL BLOOM** *Warner Bros. K 56394* | 18 | 13 wks |
| 30 Sep 78 ● | **STRIKES AGAIN** *Whitfield K 56257* | 7 | 11 wks |
| 22 Sep 79 | **RAINBOW CONNECTION IV** *Atlantic K 56714* | 72 | 2 wks |
| 1 Mar 80 ★ | **GREATEST HITS** *Whitfield K RRTV 1* | 1 | 34 wks |
| 13 Oct 84 | **MUSIC MAGIC** *Streetwave MKL 2* | 69 | 2 wks |

## ROSE TATTOO  Australia, male vocal/instrumental group        4 wks

| | | | |
|---|---|---|---|
| 26 Sep 81 | **ASSAULT AND BATTERY** *Carrere CAL 127* | 40 | 4 wks |

## Diana ROSS  US, female vocalist                              368 wks

| | | | |
|---|---|---|---|
| 24 Oct 70 | **DIANA ROSS** *Tamla Motown SFTML 11159* | 14 | 5 wks |
| 19 Jun 71 | **EVERYTHING IS EVERYTHING** | | |
| | *Tamla Motown STML 11178* | 31 | 3 wks |
| 9 Oct 71 ● | **I'M STILL WAITING** *Tamla Motown STML 11193* | 10 | 11 wks |
| 9 Oct 71 | **DIANA** *Tamla Motown STMA 8001* | 43 | 1 wk |
| 11 Nov 72 | **GREATEST HITS** *Tamla Motown STMA 8006* | 34 | 10 wks |
| 1 Sep 73 ● | **TOUCH ME IN THE MORNING** | | |
| | *Tamla Motown STML 11239* | 7 | 35 wks |
| 27 Oct 73 | **LADY SINGS THE BLUES** *Tamla Motown TMSP 1131* | 50 | 1 wk |
| 2 Mar 74 | **LAST TIME I SAW HIM** *Tamla Motown STML 11255* | 41 | 1 wk |
| 8 Jun 74 | **LIVE** *Tamla Motown STML 11248* | 21 | 8 wks |
| 27 Mar 76 ● | **DIANA ROSS** *Tamla Motown STML 12022* | 4 | 26 wks |
| 7 Aug 76 ● | **GREATEST HITS 2** *Tamla Motown STML 12036* | 2 | 29 wks |
| 19 Mar 77 | **AN EVENING WITH DIANA ROSS** | | |
| | *Motown TMSP 6005* | 52 | 1 wk |

The Reconstruction mentioned in an **R.E.M.**
album title refers to the period in the
American South following the Civil War.

Hell was chart heaven for **CHRIS REA**.

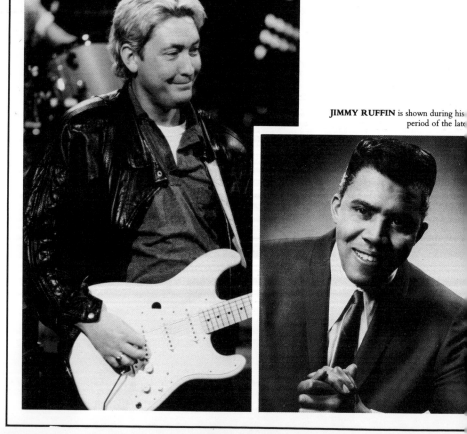

**JIMMY RUFFIN** is shown during his
period of the late

| | | | | |
|---|---|---|---|---|
| 4 Aug 79 | **THE BOSS** *Motown STML 12118* ..................... | 52 | 2 wks |
| 17 Nov 79 | ● **20 GOLDEN GREATS** *Motown EMTV 21* .............. | 2 | 29 wks |
| 21 Jun 80 | **DIANA** *Motown STMA 8033* ........................ | 12 | 32 wks |
| 28 Mar 81 | **TO LOVE AGAIN** *Motown STML 12152* .............. | 26 | 10 wks |
| 7 Nov 81 | **WHY DO FOOLS FALL IN LOVE** *Capitol EST 26733* .... | 17 | 24 wks |
| 21 Nov 81 | **ALL THE GREATEST HITS** *Motown STMA 8036* ....... | 21 | 31 wks |
| 13 Feb 82 | **DIANA ROSS** *Motown STML 12163* ................. | 43 | 6 wks |
| 23 Oct 82 | **SILK ELECTRIC** *Capitol EAST 27313* ............... | 33 | 12 wks |
| 4 Dec 82 | ● **LOVE SONGS** *K-Tel NE 1200* .................... | 5 | 17 wks |
| 19 Jul 83 | **ROSS** *Capitol EST 1867051* ........................ | 44 | 5 wks |
| 24 Dec 83 | ● **PORTRAIT** *Telstar STAR 2238* ................... | 8 | 31 wks |
| 6 Oct 84 | **SWEPT AWAY** *Capitol ROSS 1* .................... | 40 | 5 wks |
| 28 Sep 85 | **EATEN ALIVE** *Capitol ROSS 2* ................... | 11 | 19 wks |
| 30 May 87 | **RED HOT RHYTHM 'N' BLUES** *EMI EMC 3532* ...... | 47 | 4 wks |
| 27 May 89 | **WORKIN' OVERTIME** *EMI EMD 1009* ............. | 23 | 4 wks |
| 25 Nov 89 | **GREATEST HITS LIVE** *EMI EMDC 1001* ........... | 34† | 6 wks |

*See also Diana Ross and Marvin Gaye; Diana Ross and the Supremes with the Temptations; Diana Ross/ Michael Jackson/Gladys Knight/Stevie Wonder; Supremes. The two albums* Diana, *and the three* Diana Ross *titles are all different.*

## Diana ROSS and Marvin GAYE
*US, female/male vocal duo*         *45 wks*

| | | | | |
|---|---|---|---|---|
| 19 Jan 74 | ● **DIANA AND MARVIN** *Tamla Motown STMA 8015* ....... | 6 | 43 wks |
| 29 Aug 81 | **DIANA AND MARVIN** (re-issue) *Motown STMS 5001* .. | 78 | 2 wks |

*See also Marvin Gaye; Diana Ross.*

## Diana ROSS/Michael JACKSON/Gladys KNIGHT/Stevie WONDER *US, female/male vocalists*    *10 wks*

| | | | | |
|---|---|---|---|---|
| 15 Nov 86 | **DIANA ROSS. MICHAEL JACKSON. GLADYS KNIGHT. STEVIE WONDER. THEIR VERY BEST BACK TO BACK** *PrioriTyV PTVR 2* ....................... | 21 | 10 wks |

*See also Diana Ross; Michael Jackson; Gladys Knight and the Pips; Stevie Wonder.*

## Diana ROSS and the SUPREMES with the TEMPTATIONS *US, male/female vocal group*    *31 wks*

| | | | | |
|---|---|---|---|---|
| 25 Jan 69 | ★ **DIANA ROSS AND THE SUPREMES JOIN THE TEMPTATIONS** *Tamla Motown STML 11096* .......... | 1 | 15 wks |
| 28 Jun 69 | **TCB** *Tamla Motown STML 11110* ..................... | 11 | 12 wks |
| 14 Feb 70 | **TOGETHER** *Tamla Motown STML 11122* .............. | 28 | 4 wks |

*See also Supremes; Temptations; Diana Ross; Diana Ross.*

## ROSTAL and SCHAEFER *UK, male instrumental duo*    *2 wks*

| | | | | |
|---|---|---|---|---|
| 14 Jul 79 | **BEATLES CONCERTO** *Parlophone PAS 10014* ......... | 61 | 2 wks |

## David Lee ROTH *US, male vocalist*    *23 wks*

| | | | | |
|---|---|---|---|---|
| 2 Mar 85 | **CRAZY FROM THE HEAT** *Warner Bros. 92–5222–1* ..... | 91 | 2 wks |
| 19 Jul 86 | **EAT 'EM AND SMILE** *Warner Bros. WX 56* ............. | 28 | 9 wks |
| 6 Feb 88 | **SKYSCRAPER** *Warner Bros. 925671 1* ................ | 11 | 12 wks |

## Uli Jon ROTH and ELECTRIC SUN
*Germany, male vocal/instrumental group*    *2 wks*

| | | | | |
|---|---|---|---|---|
| 23 Feb 85 | **BEYOND THE ASTRAL SKIES** *EMI ROTH 1* ......... | 64 | 2 wks |

**Thomas ROUND** – *See June BRONHILL and Thomas ROUND*

## Demis ROUSSOS *Greece, male vocalist* — 143 wks

| | | | | | |
|---|---|---|---|---|---|
| 22 Jun | 74 | ● **FOREVER AND EVER** *Philips 6325 021* .............. | **2** | 68 wks |
| 19 Apr | 75 | **SOUVENIRS** *Philips 6325 201* ....................... | **25** | 18 wks |
| 24 Apr | 76 | ● **HAPPY TO BE** *Philips 9101 027* ..................... | **4** | 34 wks |
| 3 Jul | 76 | **MY ONLY FASCINATION** *Philips 6325 094* ........... | **39** | 6 wks |
| 16 Apr | 77 | **THE MAGIC OF DEMIS ROUSSOS** *Philips 9101 131* .... | **29** | 6 wks |
| 28 Oct | 78 | **LIFE AND LOVE** *Philips 9199 873* ................... | **36** | 11 wks |

## ROXETTE *Sweden, male/female vocal/instrumental duo* — 2 wks

| | | | | | |
|---|---|---|---|---|---|
| 17 Jun | 89 | **LOOK SHARP!** *EMI EMC 3557* .................... | **45** | 2 wks |

## ROXY MUSIC *UK, male vocal/instrumental group* — 293 wks

| | | | | | |
|---|---|---|---|---|---|
| 29 Jul | 72 | ● **ROXY MUSIC** *Island ILPS 9200* ...................... | **10** | 16 wks |
| 7 Apr | 73 | ● **FOR YOUR PLEASURE** *Island ILPS 9232* ............. | **4** | 27 wks |
| 1 Dec | 73 | ★ **STRANDED** *Island ILPS 9252* ...................... | **1** | 17 wks |
| 30 Nov | 74 | ● **COUNTRY LIFE** *Island ILPS 9303* .................. | **3** | 10 wks |
| 8 Nov | 75 | ● **SIREN** *Island ILPS 9344* ......................... | **4** | 17 wks |
| 31 Jul | 76 | ● **VIVA ROXY MUSIC** *Island ILPS 9400* ............... | **6** | 12 wks |
| 19 Nov | 77 | **GREATEST HITS** *Polydor 2302 073* .................. | **20** | 11 wks |
| 24 Mar | 79 | ● **MANIFESTO** *Polydor POLH 001* ................... | **7** | 34 wks |
| 31 May | 80 | ★ **FLESH AND BLOOD** *Polydor POLH 002* ............ | **1** | 60 wks |
| 5 Jun | 82 | ★ **AVALON** *EG EGLP 50* ............................ | **1** | 57 wks |
| 19 Mar | 83 | **THE HIGH ROAD** (import) *EG EGMLP 1* ............ | **26** | 7 wks |
| 12 Nov | 83 | **ATLANTIC YEARS 1973–1980** *EG EGLP 54* ........... | **23** | 25 wks |

*See also Bryan Ferry and Roxy Music.*

**ROY** – *See MERLE and ROY*

## ROYAL PHILHARMONIC ORCHESTRA
*UK, orchestra* — 107 wks

| | | | | | |
|---|---|---|---|---|---|
| 23 Dec | 78 | **CLASSIC GOLD VOL. 2** *Ronco RTD 42032* ............. | **31** | 4 wks |
| 13 Jan | 79 | **CLASSICAL GOLD** *Ronco RTV 42020* ................. | **65** | 1 wk |
| 19 Sep | 81 | ● **HOOKED ON CLASSICS** *K-Tel ONE 1146* ............ | **4** | 43 wks |
| 31 Jul | 82 | **CAN'T STOP THE CLASSICS – HOOKED ON CLASSICS 2** *K-Tel ONE 1173* .................... | **13** | 26 wks |
| 9 Apr | 83 | **JOURNEY THROUGH THE CLASSICS – HOOKED ON CLASSICS 3** *K-Tel ONE 1226* ................. | **19** | 15 wks |
| 8 Oct | 83 | **LOVE CLASSICS** *Nouveau Music NML 1003* ............ | **30** | 9 wks |
| 10 Dec | 83 | **THE BEST OF HOOKED ON CLASSICS** *K-Tel ONE 1266* ................................... | **51** | 6 wks |
| 26 May | 84 | **AS TIME GOES BY** *Telstar STAR 2240* ............... | **95** | 2 wks |
| 26 Nov | 88 | **RHYTHM AND CLASSICS** *Telstar STAR 2344* ......... | **96** | 1 wk |

*All albums conducted by Louis Clark, except Love Classics, by Nick Portlock, and As Time Goes By, by Harry Rabinowitz. See also Juan Martin; Andy Williams, with the Royal Philharmonic Orchestra.*

## RUBETTES *UK, male vocal/instrumental group* — 1 wk

| | | | | | |
|---|---|---|---|---|---|
| 10 May | 75 | **WE CAN DO IT** *State ETAT 001* .................... | **41** | 1 wk |

**David RUFFIN** – *See Darryl HALL and John OATES*

## Jimmy RUFFIN *US, male vocalist* — 10 wks

| | | | | | |
|---|---|---|---|---|---|
| 13 May | 67 | **THE JIMMY RUFFIN WAY** *Tamla Motown STML 11048* .. | **32** | 6 wks |
| 1 Jun | 74 | **GREATEST HITS** *Tamla Motown STML 11259* .......... | **41** | 4 wks |

## RUFUS and Chaka KHAN
*US, male instrumental group and female vocalist*                    *7 wks*

| | | | | |
|---|---|---|---|---|
| 12 Apr 75 | **RUFUSIZED** *ABC ABCL 5063* | 48 | 2 wks |
| 21 Apr 84 | **STOMPIN' AT THE SAVOY** *Warner Bros. 923679* | 64 | 5 wks |

*The first album gave Chaka Khan no separate billing. See also Chaka Khan.*

**RUMOUR** – *See Graham PARKER and the RUMOUR*


## Todd RUNDGREN *US, male vocalist*                    *9 wks*

| | | | | |
|---|---|---|---|---|
| 29 Jan 77 | **RA** *Bearsville K 55514* | 27 | 6 wks |
| 6 May 78 | **HERMIT OF MINK HOLLOW** *Bearsville K 55521* | 42 | 3 wks |


## RUN D.M.C. *US, male rap group*                    *31 wks*

| | | | | |
|---|---|---|---|---|
| 26 Jul 86 | **RAISING HELL** *Profile LONLP 21* | 41 | 26 wks |
| 4 Jun 88 | **TOUGHER THAN LEATHER** *Profile LONLP 38* | 13 | 5 wks |


## RUNRIG *UK, male vocal/instrumental group*                    *6 wks*

| | | | | |
|---|---|---|---|---|
| 26 Nov 88 | **ONCE IN A LIFETIME** *Chrysalis CHR 1695* | 61 | 2 wks |
| 7 Oct 89 | **SEARCHLIGHT** *Chrysalis CHR 1713* | 11 | 4 wks |


## RUSH *Canada, male vocal/instrumental group*                    *86 wks*

| | | | | |
|---|---|---|---|---|
| 8 Oct 77 | **FAREWELL TO KINGS** *Mercury 9100 042* | 22 | 4 wks |
| 25 Nov 78 | **HEMISPHERES** *Mercury 9100 059* | 14 | 6 wks |
| 26 Jan 80 | ● **PERMANENT WAVES** *Mercury 9100 071* | 3 | 16 wks |
| 21 Feb 81 | ● **MOVING PICTURES** *Mercury 6337 160* | 3 | 11 wks |
| 7 Nov 81 | ● **EXIT STAGE LEFT** *Mercury 6619 053* | 6 | 14 wks |
| 18 Sep 82 | ● **SIGNALS** *Mercury 6337 243* | 3 | 9 wks |
| 28 Apr 84 | ● **GRACE UNDER PRESSURE** *Vertigo VERH 12* | 5 | 12 wks |
| 9 Nov 85 | ● **POWER WINDOWS** *Vertigo VERH 31* | 9 | 4 wks |
| 21 Nov 87 | ● **HOLD YOUR FIRE** *Vertigo VERH 47* | 10 | 4 wks |
| 28 Jan 89 | **A SHOW OF HANDS** *Vertigo 836346* | 12 | 4 wks |
| 9 Dec 89 | **PRESTO** *Atlantic WX 327* | 27 | 2 wks |


## Jennifer RUSH *US, female vocalist*                    *43 wks*

| | | | | |
|---|---|---|---|---|
| 16 Nov 85 | ● **JENNIFER RUSH** *CBS 26488* | 7 | 35 wks |
| 3 May 86 | **MOVIN'** *CBS 26710* | 32 | 5 wks |
| 18 Apr 87 | **HEART OVER MIND** *CBS 450 470–1* | 48 | 3 wks |


## Patrice RUSHEN *US, female vocalist*                    *17 wks*

| | | | | |
|---|---|---|---|---|
| 1 May 82 | **STRAIGHT FROM THE HEART** *Elektra K 52352* | 24 | 14 wks |
| 16 Jun 84 | **NOW** *Elektra 960360* | 73 | 3 wks |

**Martin RUSHENT** – *See LEAGUE UNLIMITED ORCHESTRA*


## Brenda RUSSELL *US, female vocalist*                    *4 wks*

| | | | | |
|---|---|---|---|---|
| 23 Apr 88 | **GET HERE** *A & M AMA 5178* | 77 | 4 wks |


## Leon RUSSELL *US, male vocalist*                    *1 wk*

| | | | | |
|---|---|---|---|---|
| 3 Jul 71 | **LEON RUSSELL AND THE SHELTER PEOPLE** *A & M AMLS 65003* | 29 | 1 wk |

## Mike RUTHERFORD
*UK, male vocalist/instrumentalist – guitar*                                    *11 wks*

| | | | |
|---|---|---|---|
| 23 Feb 80 | **SMALLCREEP'S DAY** *Charisma CAS 1149* ........... | 13 | 7 wks |
| 18 Sep 82 | **ACTING VERY STRANGE** *WEA K 99249* ............ | 23 | 4 wks |

*See also Mike and the Mechanics.*

## RUTLES *UK, male vocal/instrumental group*                                  *11 wks*

| | | | |
|---|---|---|---|
| 15 Apr 78 | **THE RUTLES** *Warner Bros. K 56459* ................. | 12 | 11 wks |

## RUTS *UK, male vocal/instrumental group*                                    *10 wks*

| | | | |
|---|---|---|---|
| 13 Oct 79 | **THE CRACK** *Virgin V 2132* ....................... | 16 | 6 wks |
| 18 Oct 80 | **GRIN AND BEAR IT** *Virgin V 2188* ................ | 28 | 4 wks |

*Second album credited to Ruts D.C.*

# S

## S EXPRESS *UK, male/female vocal/instrumental group*                        *9 wks*

| | | | |
|---|---|---|---|
| 1 Apr 89 | ● **ORIGINAL SOUNDTRACK** *Rhythm King LEFTLP 8* .... | 5 | 9 wks |

## SAD CAFE *UK, male vocal/instrumental group*                                *36 wks*

| | | | |
|---|---|---|---|
| 1 Oct 77 | **FANX TA RA** *RCA PL 25101* ....................... | 56 | 1 wk |
| 29 Apr 78 | **MISPLACED IDEALS** *RCA PL 25133* ................ | 50 | 1 wk |
| 29 Sep 79 | ● **FACADES** *RCA PL 25249* ........................ | 8 | 23 wks |
| 25 Oct 80 | **SAD CAFE** *RCA SADLP 4* ......................... | 46 | 5 wks |
| 21 Mar 81 | **LIVE** *RCA SAD LP 5* ............................ | 37 | 4 wks |
| 24 Oct 81 | **OLE** *Polydor POLD 5045* ......................... | 72 | 2 wks |

## SADE *UK, female/male vocal/instrumental group*                            *146 wks*

| | | | |
|---|---|---|---|
| 28 Jul 84 | ● **DIAMOND LIFE** *Epic EPC 26044* ................... | 2 | 98 wks |
| 16 Nov 85 | ★ **PROMISE** *Epic EPC 86318* ....................... | 1 | 31 wks |
| 14 May 88 | ● **STRONGER THAN PRIDE** *Epic 460497 1* ............ | 3 | 17 wks |

## SAILOR *UK, male vocal/instrumental group*                                  *8 wks*

| | | | |
|---|---|---|---|
| 7 Feb 76 | **TROUBLE** *Epic EPC 69192* ....................... | 45 | 8 wks |

**General SAINT** – *See Clint EASTWOOD and General SAINT*

## ST. PAUL'S BOYS' CHOIR *UK, choir*                                          *8 wks*

| | | | |
|---|---|---|---|
| 29 Nov 80 | **REJOICE** *K-Tel NE 1064* .......................... | 36 | 8 wks |

## Ryuichi SAKAMOTO
*Japan, male composer/multi-instrumentalist*                                   *9 wks*

| | | | |
|---|---|---|---|
| 3 Sep 83 | **MERRY CHRISTMAS MR LAWRENCE (film soundtrack)** *Virgin V 2276* ................................... | 36 | 9 wks |

## SALT 'N' PEPA *US, female rap group*                                        *27 wks*

| | | | |
|---|---|---|---|
| 6 Aug 88 | **A SALT WITH A DEADLY PEPA** *FFRR FFRLP 3* ...... | 19 | 27 wks |

## SALVATION ARMY *UK, brass band*                                             *5 wks*

| | | | |
|---|---|---|---|
| 24 Dec 77 | **BY REQUEST** *Warwick WW 5038* ................... | 16 | 5 wks |

## SAM and DAVE  US, male vocal duo                                    20 wks

| 21 Jan | 67 | **HOLD ON I'M COMIN'**  Atlantic 588–045 | 35 | 7 wks |
| 22 Apr | 67 | **DOUBLE DYNAMITE**  Stax 589–003 | 28 | 5 wks |
| 23 Mar | 68 | **SOUL MAN**  Stax 589–015 | 32 | 8 wks |

**Mike SAMMES SINGERS** – *See RICHMOND STRINGS/Mike SAMMES SINGERS*

## SAMSON  UK, male vocal/instrumental group                           6 wks

| 26 Jul | 80 | **HEAD ON**  Gem GEMLP 108 | 34 | 6 wks |

## David SANBORN  US, male instrumentalist – saxophone                 1 wk

| 14 Mar | 87 | **A CHANGE OF HEART**  Warner Bros. 925 479–1 | 86 | 1 wk |

## SANTANA  US, male vocal/instrumental group                          205 wks

| 2 May | 70 | **SANTANA**  CBS 63815 | 26 | 11 wks |
| 28 Nov | 70 | ● **ABRAXAS**  CBS 64807 | 7 | 52 wks |
| 13 Nov | 71 | ● **SANTANA 3**  CBS 69015 | 6 | 14 wks |
| 29 Nov | 72 | ● **CARAVANSERAI**  CBS 65299 | 6 | 11 wks |
| 8 Dec | 73 | ● **WELCOME**  CBS 69040 | 8 | 6 wks |
| 21 Sep | 74 | **GREATEST HITS**  CBS 69081 | 14 | 15 wks |
| 30 Nov | 74 | **BARBOLETTA**  CBS 69084 | 18 | 5 wks |
| 10 Apr | 76 | **AMIGOS**  CBS 86005 | 21 | 9 wks |
| 8 Jan | 77 | **FESTIVAL**  CBS 86020 | 27 | 3 wks |
| 5 Nov | 77 | ● **MOONFLOWER**  CBS 88272 | 7 | 27 wks |
| 11 Nov | 78 | **INNER SECRETS**  CBS 86075 | 17 | 16 wks |
| 24 Mar | 79 | **ONENESS – SILVER DREAMS GOLDEN REALITY**  CBS 86037 | 55 | 4 wks |
| 27 Oct | 79 | **MARATHON**  CBS 86098 | 28 | 5 wks |
| 20 Sep | 80 | **THE SWING OF DELIGHT**  CBS 22075 | 65 | 2 wks |
| 18 Apr | 81 | **ZE BOP**  CBS 84946 | 33 | 4 wks |
| 14 Aug | 82 | **SHANGO**  CBS 85914 | 35 | 7 wks |
| 30 Apr | 83 | **HAVANA MOON**  CBS 25350 | 84 | 3 wks |
| 23 Mar | 85 | **BEYOND APPEARANCES**  CBS 86307 | 58 | 3 wks |
| 15 Nov | 86 | **VIVA! SANTANA – THE VERY BEST**  K-Tel NE 1338 | 50 | 8 wks |

Oneness – Silver Dreams Golden Reality, The Swing Of Delight *and* Havana Moon *are all credited to Carlos Santana, US, male instrumentalist – guitar. See also Carlos Santana and Alice Coltrane; Carlos Santana and Mahavishnu John McLaughlin; Carlos Santana and Buddy Miles.*

## Carlos SANTANA and Alice COLTRANE
US, male/female instrumental duo                                       1 wk

| 2 Nov | 74 | **ILLUMINATIONS**  CBS 69063 | 40 | 1 wk |

*See also Santana.*

## Carlos SANTANA and Mahavishnu John McLAUGHLIN  US, male instrumental duo    9 wks

| 28 Jul | 73 | ● **LOVE DEVOTION SURRENDER**  CBS 69037 | 7 | 9 wks |

*See also Mahavishnu Orchestra; Santana.*

## Carlos SANTANA and Buddy MILES
US, male instrumental duo                                              4 wks

| 26 Aug | 72 | **CARLOS SANTANA AND BUDDY MILES LIVE**  CBS 65142 | 29 | 4 wks |

*See also Santana.*

## Peter SARSTEDT  UK, male vocalist                                    4 wks

| 15 Mar | 69 | ● **PETER SARSTEDT**  United Artists SULP 1219 | 8 | 4 wks |

## Telly SAVALAS  *US, male vocalist*                              *10 wks*

22 Mar 75    **TELLY**   *MCA MCF 2699*  .........................   **12**   10 wks

## SAVOY BROWN  *UK, male vocal/instrumental group*              *1 wk*

28 Nov 70    **LOOKIN' IN**   *Decca SKL 5066*  ......................   **50**   1 wk

## SAXON  *UK, male vocal/instrumental group*                     *97 wks*

| | | | | |
|---|---|---|---|---|
| 12 Apr 80 ● | **WHEELS OF STEEL**  *Carrere CAL 115*  ............... | **5** | 29 wks |
| 15 Nov 80 | **STRONG ARM OF THE LAW**  *Carrere CAL 120*  ........ | **11** | 13 wks |
| 3 Oct 81 ● | **DENIM AND LEATHER**  *Carrere CAL 128*  ............ | **9** | 11 wks |
| 22 May 82 ● | **THE EAGLE HAS LANDED**  *Carrere CAL 157*  ........ | **5** | 19 wks |
| 26 Mar 83 | **POWER AND THE GLORY**  *Carrere CAL 147*  ......... | **15** | 9 wks |
| 11 Feb 84 | **CRUSADER**  *Carrere CAL 200*  ...................... | **18** | 7 wks |
| 14 Sep 85 | **INNOCENCE IS NO EXCUSE**  *Parlophone SAXON 2*  .... | **36** | 4 wks |
| 27 Sep 86 | **ROCK THE NATIONS**  *EMI EMC 3515*  ............... | **34** | 3 wks |
| 9 Apr 88 | **DESTINY**  *EMI EMC 3543*  ........................ | **49** | 2 wks |

## Leo SAYER  *UK, male vocalist*                                 *232 wks*

| | | | | |
|---|---|---|---|---|
| 5 Jan 74 ● | **SILVER BIRD**  *Chrysalis CHR 1050*  .................. | **2** | 22 wks |
| 26 Oct 74 ● | **JUST A BOY**  *Chrysalis CHR 1068*  .................. | **4** | 14 wks |
| 20 Sep 75 ● | **ANOTHER YEAR**  *Chrysalis CHR 1087*  ............... | **8** | 9 wks |
| 27 Nov 76 ● | **ENDLESS FLIGHT**  *Chrysalis CHR 1125*  ............. | **4** | 66 wks |
| 22 Oct 77 ● | **THUNDER IN MY HEART**  *Chrysalis CDL 1154*  ........ | **8** | 16 wks |
| 2 Sep 78 | **LEO SAYER**  *Chrysalis CDL 1198*  ................... | **15** | 25 wks |
| 31 Mar 79 ★ | **THE VERY BEST OF LEO SAYER**  *Chrysalis CDL 1222*  .. | **1** | 37 wks |
| 13 Oct 79 | **HERE**  *Chrysalis CDL 1240*  ...................... | **44** | 4 wks |
| 23 Aug 80 | **LIVING IN A FANTASY**  *Chrysalis CDL 1297*  ........ | **15** | 9 wks |
| 8 May 82 | **WORLD RADIO**  *Chrysalis CDL 1345*  ................ | **30** | 12 wks |
| 12 Nov 83 | **HAVE YOU EVER BEEN IN LOVE**  *Chrysalis LEOTV 1*  .. | **15** | 18 wks |

## Alexei SAYLE  *UK, male comedian*                              *5 wks*

17 Mar 84    **THE FISH PEOPLE TAPES**   *Island IMA 9*  .............   **62**   5 wks

## Boz SCAGGS  *US, male vocalist*                                 *29 wks*

| | | | | |
|---|---|---|---|---|
| 12 Mar 77 | **SILK DEGREES**  *CBS 81193*  ........................ | **37** | 24 wks |
| 17 Dec 77 | **DOWN TWO, THEN LEFT**  *CBS 86036*  .............. | **55** | 1 wk |
| 3 May 80 | **MIDDLE MAN**  *CBS 86094*  ........................ | **52** | 4 wks |

## SCARS  *UK, male vocal/instrumental group*                     *3 wks*

18 Apr 81    **AUTHOR AUTHOR**   *Pre PREX 5*  ...................   **67**   3 wks

**SCHAEFER** – *See ROSTAL and SCHAEFER*

## Michael SCHENKER GROUP
*Germany/UK, male vocal/instrumental group*                       *42 wks*

| | | | | |
|---|---|---|---|---|
| 6 Sep 80 ● | **MICHAEL SCHENKER GROUP**  *Chrysalis CHR 1302*  ... | **8** | 8 wks |
| 19 Sep 81 | **MICHAEL SCHENKER GROUP** (re-issue) | | |
| | *Chrysalis CHR 1336*  ............................. | **14** | 8 wks |
| 13 Mar 82 ● | **ONE NIGHT AT BUDOKAN**  *Chrysalis CTY 1375*  ....... | **5** | 11 wks |
| 23 Oct 82 | **ASSAULT ATTACK**  *Chrysalis CHR 1393*  ............. | **19** | 5 wks |
| 10 Sep 83 | **BUILT TO DESTROY**  *Chrysalis CHR 1441*  ........... | **23** | 5 wks |
| 23 Jun 84 | **ROCK WILL NEVER DIE**  *Chrysalis CUX 1470*  ........ | **24** | 5 wks |

*See also MSG.*

**SCHON** – *See HAGAR, SCHON, AARONSON, SHRIEVE*

**RUSH** have had the most top ten albums by a Canadian act.

**BOZ SCAGGS** first charted in the UK mere months after the British breakthrough of his former colleague Steve Miller.

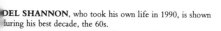

**DEL SHANNON**, who took his own life in 1990, is shown during his best decade, the 60s.

## SCORPIONS *Germany, male vocal/instrumental group*          48 wks

| | | | |
|---|---|---|---|
| 21 Apr 79 | **LOVE DRIVE** *Harvest SHSP 4097* .................... | 36 | 11 wks |
| 3 May 80 | **ANIMAL MAGNETISM** *Harvest SHSP 4113* ............ | 23 | 6 wks |
| 10 Apr 82 | **BLACKOUT** *Harvest SHVL 823* ...................... | 11 | 11 wks |
| 24 Mar 84 | **LOVE AT FIRST STING** *Harvest SHSP 2400071* ........ | 17 | 6 wks |
| 29 Jun 85 | **WORLD WIDE LIVE** *Harvest SCORP 1* .............. | 18 | 8 wks |
| 14 May 88 | **SAVAGE AMUSEMENT** *Harvest SHSP 4125* ........... | 18 | 6 wks |

## SCOTLAND FOOTBALL WORLD CUP
## SQUAD 1974 *UK, male football team vocalists*          9 wks

| | | | |
|---|---|---|---|
| 25 May 74 | ● **EASY EASY** *Polydor 2383 282* ........................ | 3 | 9 wks |

## Band of the SCOTS GUARDS
*UK, military band*          2 wks

| | | | |
|---|---|---|---|
| 28 Jun 69 | **BAND OF THE SCOTS GUARDS** *Fontana SFXL 54* ..... | 25 | 2 wks |

## Jack SCOTT *Canada, male vocalist*          12 wks

| | | | |
|---|---|---|---|
| 7 May 60 | ● **I REMEMBER HANK WILLIAMS** *Top Rank BUY 034* ... | 7 | 11 wks |
| 3 Sep 60 | **WHAT IN THE WORLD'S COME OVER YOU** *Top Rank 25/024* ................................... | 11 | 1 wk |

## SCREAMING BLUE MESSIAHS
*UK, male vocal/instrumental group*          1 wk

| | | | |
|---|---|---|---|
| 17 May 86 | **GUN-SHY** *WEA WX 41* ........................... | 90 | 1 wk |

## SCRITTI POLITTI *UK, male vocal/instrumental group*          37 wks

| | | | |
|---|---|---|---|
| 11 Sep 82 | **SONGS TO REMEMBER** *Rough Trade ROUGH 20* ...... | 12 | 7 wks |
| 22 Jun 85 | ● **CUPID AND PSYCHE 85** *Virgin V 2350* .............. | 5 | 19 wks |
| 18 Jun 88 | ● **PROVISION** *Virgin V 2515* ....................... | 8 | 11 wks |

## SEARCHERS *UK, male vocal/instrumental group*          87 wks

| | | | |
|---|---|---|---|
| 10 Aug 63 | ● **MEET THE SEARCHERS** *Pye NPL 18086* ............ | 2 | 44 wks |
| 16 Nov 63 | ● **SUGAR AND SPICE** *Pye NPL 18089* ................ | 5 | 21 wks |
| 30 May 64 | ● **IT'S THE SEARCHERS** *Pye NPL 18092* .............. | 4 | 17 wks |
| 27 Mar 65 | ● **SOUNDS LIKE THE SEARCHERS** *Pye NPL 18111* .... | 8 | 5 wks |

## Harry SECOMBE *UK, male vocalist*          51 wks

| | | | |
|---|---|---|---|
| 31 Mar 62 | **SACRED SONGS** *Philips RBL 7501* ................... | 16 | 1 wk |
| 22 Apr 67 | ● **SECOMBE'S PERSONAL CHOICE** *Philips BETS 707* ... | 6 | 13 wks |
| 7 Aug 71 | **IF I RULED THE WORLD** *Contour 6870 501* .......... | 17 | 20 wks |
| 16 Dec 78 | ● **20 SONGS OF JOY** *Warwick WW 5052* ........... | 8 | 12 wks |
| 13 Dec 86 | **HIGHWAY OF LIFE** *Telstar STAR 2289* .............. | 45 | 5 wks |

*See also Harry Secombe and Moira Anderson; Harry Secombe, Peter Sellers and Spike Milligan.*

## Harry SECOMBE and Moira ANDERSON
*UK, male/female vocal duo*                                           *5 wks*

| 5 Dec 81 | **GOLDEN MEMORIES** *Warwick WW 5107* ............. | **46** | 5 wks |

*See also Harry Secombe; Moira Anderson.*

## Harry SECOMBE, Peter SELLERS and Spike
## MILLIGAN *UK, male comedy group*                                  *1 wk*

| 18 Apr 64 | **HOW TO WIN AN ELECTION** *Philips AL 3464* ........ | **20** | 1 wk |

*See also Harry Secombe; Peter Sellers; Spike Milligan.*

## SECOND IMAGE
*UK, male vocal/instrumental group*                                   *1 wk*

| 30 Mar 85 | **STRANGE REFLECTIONS** *MCA MCF 3255* .......... | **100** | 1 wk |

## SECRET AFFAIR
*UK, male vocal/instrumental group*                                  *15 wks*

| 1 Dec 79 | **GLORY BOYS** *I-Spy 1* ........................... | **41** | 8 wks |
| 20 Sep 80 | **BEHIND CLOSED DOORS** *I-Spy 2* ................. | **48** | 4 wks |
| 13 Mar 82 | **BUSINESS AS USUAL** *I-Spy 3* .................... | **84** | 3 wks |

## Neil SEDAKA *US, male vocalist*                                   *52 wks*

| 1 Sep 73 | **THE TRA-LA DAYS ARE OVER** *MGM 2315 248* ...... | **13** | 10 wks |
| 22 Jun 74 | **LAUGHTER IN THE RAIN** *Polydor 2383 265* .......... | **17** | 10 wks |
| 23 Nov 74 | **LIVE AT THE ROYAL FESTIVAL HALL** | | |
| | *Polydor 2383 299* ...................................... | **48** | 1 wk |
| 1 Mar 75 | **OVERNIGHT SUCCESS** *Polydor 2442 131* ............. | **31** | 6 wks |
| 10 Jul 76 | ● **LAUGHTER AND TEARS – THE BEST OF NEIL SEDAKA** | | |
| | **TODAY** *Polydor 2383 399* ........................ | **2** | 25 wks |

## SEEKERS *Australia, male/female vocal group*                      *268 wks*

| 3 Jul 65 | ● **A WORLD OF OUR OWN** *Columbia 33SX 1722* ........ | **5** | 36 wks |
| 3 Jul 65 | **THE SEEKERS** *Decca LK 4694* ...................... | **16** | 1 wk |
| 19 Nov 66 | ● **COME THE DAY** *Columbia SCX 6093* ............... | **3** | 67 wks |
| 25 Nov 67 | **SEEKERS – SEEN IN GREEN** *Columbia SCX 6193* ..... | **15** | 10 wks |
| 14 Sep 68 | ● **LIVE AT THE TALK OF THE TOWN** *Columbia SCX 6278* | **2** | 29 wks |
| 16 Nov 68 | ★ **BEST OF THE SEEKERS** *Columbia SCX 6268* .......... | **1** | 125 wks |

## Bob SEGER and the SILVER BULLET BAND
*US, male vocal/instrumental group*                                  *38 wks*

| 3 Jun 78 | **STRANGER IN TOWN** *Capitol EAST 11698* ........... | **31** | 6 wks |
| 15 Mar 80 | **AGAINST THE WIND** *Capitol EAST 12041* ............ | **26** | 6 wks |
| 26 Sep 81 | **NINE TONIGHT** *Capitol ESTSP 23* ................... | **24** | 10 wks |
| 8 Jan 83 | **THE DISTANCE** *Capitol EST 12254* ................. | **45** | 10 wks |
| 26 Apr 86 | **LIKE A ROCK** *Capitol EST 2011* ................... | **35** | 6 wks |

## SELECTER
*UK, male/female vocal/instrumental group*                           *17 wks*

| 23 Feb 80 | ● **TOO MUCH PRESSURE** *2-Tone CDL TT 5002* ........ | **5** | 13 wks |
| 7 Mar 81 | **CELEBRATE THE BULLET** *Chrysalis CHR 1306* ....... | **41** | 4 wks |

## Peter SELLERS
*UK, male vocalist*  84 wks

| | | | | |
|---|---|---|---|---|
| 14 Feb 59 | ● **THE BEST OF SELLERS** | *Parlophone PMD 1069* ......... | 3 | 47 wks |
| 12 Dec 59 | ● **SONGS FOR SWINGING SELLERS** | *Parlophone PMC 1111* | 3 | 37 wks |

*See also Peter Sellers and Sophia Loren; Harry Secombe, Peter Sellers and Spike Milligan; Anthony Newley, Peter Sellers, Joan Collins.*

## Peter SELLERS and Sophia LOREN
*UK/Italy, male/female vocal duo*  18 wks

| | | | | |
|---|---|---|---|---|
| 3 Dec 60 | ● **PETER AND SOPHIA** | *Parlophone PMC 1131* .......... | 5 | 18 wks |

*See also Peter Sellers.*

## SENSATIONAL ALEX HARVEY BAND
*UK, male vocal/instrumental group*  42 wks

| | | | | |
|---|---|---|---|---|
| 26 Oct 74 | **THE IMPOSSIBLE DREAM** | *Vertigo 6360 112* .......... | 16 | 4 wks |
| 10 May 75 | ● **TOMORROW BELONGS TO ME** | *Vertigo 9102 003* ..... | 9 | 10 wks |
| 23 Aug 75 | **NEXT** | *Vertigo 6360 103* ............................. | 37 | 5 wks |
| 27 Sep 75 | **SENSATIONAL ALEX HARVEY BAND LIVE** | | | |
| | | *Vertigo 6360 122* ................................. | 14 | 7 wks |
| 10 Apr 76 | **PENTHOUSE TAPES** | *Vertigo 9102 007* ............. | 14 | 7 wks |
| 31 Jul 76 | **SAHB STORIES** | *Mountain TOPS 112* ................ | 11 | 9 wks |

## Taja SEVELLE  *US, female vocalist*  4 wks

| | | | | |
|---|---|---|---|---|
| 26 Mar 88 | **TAJA SEVELLE** | *Paisley Park WX 165* ................. | 48 | 4 wks |

## SEX PISTOLS
*UK, male vocal/instrumental group*  97 wks

| | | | | |
|---|---|---|---|---|
| 12 Nov 77 | ★ **NEVER MIND THE BOLLOCKS HERE'S THE SEX** | | | |
| | | **PISTOLS** *Virgin V 2086* ......................... | 1 | 48 wks |
| 10 Mar 79 | ● **THE GREAT ROCK 'N' ROLL SWINDLE** | | | |
| | | *Virgin VD 2410* ................................... | 7 | 33 wks |
| 11 Aug 79 | ● **SOME PRODUCT – CARRI ON SEX PISTOLS** | | | |
| | | *Virgin VR 2* ...................................... | 6 | 10 wks |
| 16 Feb 80 | **FLOGGING A DEAD HORSE** | *Virgin V 2142* ........... | 23 | 6 wks |

## SHADOWS  *UK, male instrumental group*  414 wks

| | | | | |
|---|---|---|---|---|
| 16 Sep 61 | ★ **THE SHADOWS** | *Columbia 33SX 1374* ................. | 1 | 57 wks |
| 13 Oct 62 | ★ **OUT OF THE SHADOWS** | *Columbia 33SX 1458* ......... | 1 | 38 wks |
| 22 Jun 63 | ● **GREATEST HITS** | *Columbia 33SX 1522* ............... | 2 | 49 wks |
| 9 May 64 | ● **DANCE WITH THE SHADOWS** | *Columbia 33SX 1619* ... | 2 | 27 wks |
| 17 Jul 65 | ● **SOUND OF THE SHADOWS** | *Columbia 33SX 1736* ...... | 4 | 17 wks |
| 21 May 66 | ● **SHADOW MUSIC** | *Columbia SX 6041* ................ | 5 | 17 wks |
| 15 Jul 67 | ● **JIGSAW** | *Columbia SCX 6148* ...................... | 8 | 16 wks |
| 24 Oct 70 | **SHADES OF ROCK** | *Columbia SCX 6420* ............... | 30 | 4 wks |
| 13 Apr 74 | **ROCKIN' WITH CURLY LEADS** | *EMI EMA 762* ...... | 45 | 1 wk |
| 11 May 74 | **GREATEST HITS (re-issue)** | *Columbia SCX 1522* ........ | 48 | 6 wks |
| 29 Mar 75 | **SPECS APPEAL** | *EMI EMC 3066* ................... | 30 | 5 wks |
| 12 Feb 77 | ★ **20 GOLDEN GREATS** | *EMI EMTV 3* ................ | 1 | 38 wks |
| 15 Sep 79 | ★ **STRING OF HITS** | *EMI EMC 3310* ................. | 1 | 48 wks |
| 26 Jul 80 | **ANOTHER STRING OF HITS** | *EMI EMC 3339* ........ | 16 | 8 wks |
| 13 Sep 80 | **CHANGE OF ADDRESS** | *Polydor 2442 179* ............. | 17 | 6 wks |
| 19 Sep 81 | **HITS RIGHT UP YOUR STREET** | *Polydor POLD 5046* .. | 15 | 16 wks |
| 25 Sep 82 | **LIFE IN THE JUNGLE/LIVE AT ABBEY ROAD** | | | |
| | | *Polydor SHADS 1* .............................. | 24 | 6 wks |
| 22 Oct 83 | **XXV** *Polydor POLD 5120* ........................... | | 34 | 6 wks |
| 17 Nov 84 | **GUARDIAN ANGEL** *Polydor POLD 5169* ............. | | 98 | 1 wk |

| | | | |
|---|---|---|---|
| 24 May 86 | ● **MOONLIGHT SHADOWS** *Polydor PROLP 8* ......... | 6 | 19 wks |
| 24 Oct 87 | **SIMPLY SHADOWS** *Polydor SHAD 1* ................ | 11 | 17 wks |
| 20 May 89 | **STEPPIN' TO THE SHADOWS** *Polydor SHAD 30* ...... | 11 | 9 wks |
| 16 Dec 89 | **AT THEIR VERY BEST** *Polydor 841520 1* ............. | 12† | 3 wks |

*See also Cliff Richard.*

## SHAKATAK  *UK, male/female vocal/instrumental group*  73 wks

| | | | |
|---|---|---|---|
| 30 Jan 82 | **DRIVIN' HARD** *Polydor POLS 1030* ................. | 35 | 17 wks |
| 15 May 82 | ● **NIGHT BIRDS** *Polydor POLS 1059* ................. | 4 | 28 wks |
| 27 Nov 82 | **INVITATIONS** *Polydor POLD 5068* ................. | 30 | 11 wks |
| 22 Oct 83 | **OUT OF THIS WORLD** *Polydor POLD 5115* .......... | 30 | 4 wks |
| 25 Aug 84 | **DOWN ON THE STREET** *Polydor POLD 5148* ........ | 17 | 9 wks |
| 23 Feb 85 | **LIVE!** *Polydor POLH 21* ........................... | 82 | 3 wks |
| 22 Oct 88 | **THE COOLEST CUTS** *K-Tel NE 1422* ............... | 73 | 1 wk |

## SHAKESPEAR'S SISTER
*UK/US, female vocal/instrumental duo*  8 wks

| | | | |
|---|---|---|---|
| 2 Sep 89 | ● **SACRED HEART** *London 828131 1* ................. | 9 | 8 wks |

## SHAKIN' PYRAMIDS  *UK, male vocal/instrumental group*  4 wks

| | | | |
|---|---|---|---|
| 4 Apr 81 | **SKIN 'EM UP** *Cuba Libra V 2199* .................... | 48 | 4 wks |

## SHALAMAR  *US, male/female vocal/instrumental group*  121 wks

| | | | |
|---|---|---|---|
| 27 Mar 82 | ● **FRIENDS** *Solar K 52345* ........................... | 6 | 72 wks |
| 11 Sep 82 | **GREATEST HITS** *Solar SOLA 3001* ................ | 71 | 5 wks |
| 30 Jul 83 | ● **THE LOOK** *Solar 960239* .......................... | 7 | 20 wks |
| 12 Apr 86 | ● **THE GREATEST HITS** *Stylus SMR 8615* ............. | 5 | 24 wks |

## SHAM 69  *UK, male vocal/instrumental group*  27 wks

| | | | |
|---|---|---|---|
| 11 Mar 78 | **TELL US THE TRUTH** *Polydor 2383 491* ............. | 25 | 8 wks |
| 2 Dec 78 | **THAT'S LIFE** *Polydor POLD 5010* ................... | 27 | 11 wks |
| 29 Sep 79 | ● **THE ADVENTURES OF THE HERSHAM BOYS** | | |
| | *Polydor POLD 5025* ............................... | 8 | 8 wks |

## Jimmy SHAND, HIS BAND AND GUESTS
*UK, male instrumentalist – accordion, with male/female
vocal/instrumental dance band*  2 wks

| | | | |
|---|---|---|---|
| 24 Dec 83 | **FIFTY YEARS ON WITH JIMMY SHAND** *Ross WGR 062* | 97 | 2 wks |

## SHANNON  *US, female vocalist*  12 wks

| | | | |
|---|---|---|---|
| 10 Mar 84 | **LET THE MUSIC PLAY** *Club JABL 1* ................. | 52 | 12 wks |

## Del SHANNON  *US, male vocalist*  23 wks

| | | | |
|---|---|---|---|
| 11 May 63 | ● **HATS OFF TO DEL SHANNON** *London HAX 8071* ..... | 9 | 17 wks |
| 2 Nov 63 | **LITTLE TOWN FLIRT** *London HAX 8091* ............. | 15 | 6 wks |

## Helen SHAPIRO  *UK, female vocalist*  25 wks

| | | | |
|---|---|---|---|
| 10 Mar 62 | ● **TOPS WITH ME** *Columbia 33SX 1397* ................ | 2 | 25 wks |

## Feargal SHARKEY  *UK, male vocalist*　　　　　　　　*20 wks*

23 Nov 85　**FEARGAL SHARKEY**　*Virgin V 2360* ................　12　20 wks

## SHARPE and NUMAN  *UK, male vocal/instrumental duo*　　*1 wk*

8 Jul  89　**AUTOMATIC**　*Polydor 839520 1* .....................　59　1 wk
*See also Gary Numan.*

**Roland SHAW** – *See MANTOVANI*

## Sandie SHAW  *UK, female vocalist*　　　　　　　　*13 wks*

6 Mar 65　● **SANDIE**　*Pye NPL 18110* ..........................　3　13 wks

**George SHEARING** – *See Nat 'King' COLE and the George SHEARING QUINTET; Peggy LEE and George SHEARING*

## Pete SHELLEY  *UK, male vocalist*　　　　　　　　*4 wks*

2 Jul  83　**XL-1**　*Genetic XL 1* .................................　42　4 wks

## SHERRICK  *US, male vocalist*　　　　　　　　　　*6 wks*

29 Aug 87　**SHERRICK**　*Warner Bros. WX 118* ....................　27　6 wks

## **244**

### *S*

## Brendon SHINE  *Ireland, male vocalist*　　　　　　*29 wks*

12 Nov 83　**THE BRENDON SHINE COLLECTION**
　　　　　　　*Play PLAYTV 1* ..................................　51　12 wks
3 Nov 84　**WITH LOVE**　*Play PLAYTV 2* .......................　74　4 wks
16 Nov 85　**MEMORIES**　*Play PLAYTV 3* .......................　81　7 wks
18 Nov 89　**MAGIC MOMENTS**　*Stylus SMR 991* .................　62　6 wks

**SHIRLIE** – *See PEPSI and SHIRLIE*

## Michelle SHOCKED  *US, female vocalist*　　　　　　*22 wks*

10 Sep 88　**SHORT SHARP SHOCKED**　*Cooking Vinyl CVLP 1* ......　33　19 wks
18 Nov 89　**CAPTAIN SWING**　*Cooking Vinyl 838878 1* ............　31　3 wks

## SHOP ASSISTANTS
*UK, male/female vocal/instrumental group*　　　　　*1 wk*

29 Nov 86　**SHOP ASSISTANTS**　*Blue Guitar AZLP 2* ..............　100　1 wk

## SHOWADDYWADDY
*UK, male vocal/instrumental group*　　　　　　　　*126 wks*

7 Dec 74　● **SHOWADDYWADDY**　*Bell BELLS 248* ..............　9　19 wks
12 Jul  75　● **STEP TWO**　*Bell BELLS 256* .......................　7　17 wks
29 May 76　**TROCADERO**　*Bell SYBEL 8003* ....................　41　3 wks
25 Dec 76　● **GREATEST HITS**　*Arista ARTY 145* ...............　4　26 wks
3 Dec 77　**RED STAR**　*Arista SPARTY 1023* ...................　20　10 wks
9 Dec 78　★ **GREATEST HITS**　*Arista ARTV 1* ..................　1　17 wks
10 Nov 79　● **CREPES AND DRAPES**　*Arista ARTV 3* .............　8　14 wks
20 Dec 80　**BRIGHT LIGHTS**　*Arista SPART 1142* ...............　54　8 wks
7 Nov 81　**THE VERY BEST OF**　*Arista SPART 1178* .............　33　11 wks
5 Dec 87　**THE BEST STEPS TO HEAVEN**　*Tiger SHTV 1* ........　90　1 wk

## SHRIEKBACK  *UK, male vocal/instrumental group*    *1 wk*

11 Aug 84   **JAM SCIENCE**  *Arista 206 416* ...................    **85**  1 wk

**SHRIEVE** – *See HAGAR, SCHON, AARONSON, SHRIEVE*

## SHY  *UK, male vocal/instrumental group*    *2 wks*

11 Apr 87   **EXCESS ALL AREAS**  *RCA PL 71221* ............    **74**  2 wks

## Labi SIFFRE  *UK, male vocalist*    *2 wks*

24 Jul 71   **SINGER AND THE SONG**  *Pye NSPL 28147* ..........    **47**  1 wk
14 Oct 72   **CRYING, LAUGHING, LOVING, LYING**
            *Pye NSPL 28163* ................................    **46**  1 wk

**SILVER BULLET BAND** – *See Bob SEGER and the SILVER BULLET BAND*

## SIGUE SIGUE SPUTNIK
*UK, male vocal/instrumental group*    *7 wks*

 9 Aug 86  ● **FLAUNT IT**  *Parlophone PCS 7305* ....................    **10**  6 wks
15 Apr 89   **DRESS FOR EXCESS**  *Parlophone PCS 7328* ...........    **53**  1 wk

## SILVER CONVENTION
*Germany/US, female vocal group*    *3 wks*

25 Jun 77   **SILVER CONVENTION: GREATEST HITS**
            *Magnet MAG 6001* ...............................    **34**  3 wks

## Carly SIMON  *US, female vocalist*    *61 wks*

20 Jan 73  ● **NO SECRETS**  *Elektra K 42127* ......................    **3**   26 wks
16 Mar 74   **HOT CAKES**  *Elektra K 52005* .....................    **19**   9 wks
 9 May 87   **COMING AROUND AGAIN**  *Arista 208 140* ...........    **25**  20 wks
 3 Sep 88   **GREATEST HITS LIVE**  *Arista 209196* ...............    **49**   6 wks

## Paul SIMON  *US, male vocalist*    *230 wks*

26 Feb 72  ★ **PAUL SIMON**  *CBS 69007* ..........................    **1**   26 wks
 2 Jun 73  ● **THERE GOES RHYMIN' SIMON**  *CBS 69035* ..........    **4**   22 wks
 1 Nov 75  ● **STILL CRAZY AFTER ALL THESE YEARS**  *CBS 86001*    **6**   31 wks
 3 Dec 77  ● **GREATEST HITS, ETC.**  *CBS 10007* ................    **6**   15 wks
30 Aug 80   **ONE-TRICK PONY**  *Warner Bros. K 56846* ............    **17**  12 wks
12 Nov 83   **HEARTS AND BONES**  *Warner Bros. 92–3942–1* ........    **34**   8 wks
13 Sep 86  ★ **GRACELAND**  *Warner Bros. WX 52* ..................    **1**   99 wks
24 Jan 87   **GREATEST HITS, ETC. (re-issue)**  *CBS 450 166–1* ......    **73**   2 wks
 5 Nov 88   **NEGOTIATIONS AND LOVE SONGS 1971–1986**
            *Warner Bros. WX 223* ...........................    **17**  15 wks

*See also Simon and Garfunkel.*

## SIMON and GARFUNKEL  *US, male vocal duo*    *1034 wks*

16 Apr 66   **SOUNDS OF SILENCE**  *CBS 62690* ..................    **13**  104 wks
 3 Aug 68  ★ **BOOKENDS**  *CBS 63101* ...........................    **1**   77 wks
31 Aug 68   **PARSLEY, SAGE, ROSEMARY AND THYME**
            *CBS 62860* ................................    **13**  66 wks
26 Oct 68  ● **THE GRADUATE (film soundtrack)**  *CBS 70042* .......    **3**   71 wks
 9 Nov 68   **WEDNESDAY MORNING 3 A.M.**  *CBS 63370* .........    **24**   6 wks
21 Feb 70  ★ **BRIDGE OVER TROUBLED WATER**  *CBS 63699* .....    **1**  303 wks
22 Jul 72  ● **GREATEST HITS**  *CBS 69003* ....................    **2**  283 wks

| | | | | |
|---|---|---|---|---|
| 4 Apr 81 | | SOUNDS OF SILENCE (re-issue) *CBS 32020* .......... | 68 | 1 wk |
| 21 Nov 81 | ● | THE SIMON AND GARFUNKEL COLLECTION | | |
| | | *CBS 10029* ...................................... | 4 | 80 wks |
| 20 Mar 82 | ● | THE CONCERT IN CENTRAL PARK *Geffen GEF 96008* | 6 | 43 wks |

*See also Paul Simon; Art Garfunkel.*

## Nina SIMONE  *US, female vocalist*  *12 wks*

| | | | | |
|---|---|---|---|---|
| 24 Jul 65 | | I PUT A SPELL ON YOU *Philips BL 7671* .............. | 18 | 3 wks |
| 15 Feb 69 | | 'NUFF SAID *RCS SF 7979* ......................... | 11 | 1 wk |
| 14 Nov 87 | | MY BABY JUST CARES FOR ME *Charly CR 30217* ..... | 56 | 8 wks |

## SIMPLE MINDS  *UK, male vocal/instrumental group*  *266 wks*

| | | | | |
|---|---|---|---|---|
| 5 May 79 | | A LIFE IN THE DAY *Zoom ZULP 1* .................. | 30 | 6 wks |
| 27 Sep 80 | | EMPIRES AND DANCE *Arista SPART 1140* .......... | 41 | 3 wks |
| 12 Sep 81 | | SONS AND FASCINATIONS/SISTERS FEELINGS CALL | | |
| | | *Virgin V 2207* .................................. | 11 | 7 wks |
| 27 Feb 82 | | CELEBRATION *Arista SPART 1183* ............... | 45 | 7 wks |
| 25 Sep 82 | ● | NEW GOLD DREAM (81, 82, 83, 84) *Virgin V 2230* ...... | 3 | 52 wks |
| 18 Feb 84 | ★ | SPARKLE IN THE RAIN *Virgin V 2300* ........... | 1 | 57 wks |
| 2 Nov 85 | ★ | ONCE UPON A TIME *Virgin V 2364* .............. | 1 | 83 wks |
| 6 Jun 87 | ★ | LIVE IN THE CITY OF LIGHT *Virgin V SMDL 1* ...... | 1 | 26 wks |
| 13 May 89 | ★ | STREET FIGHTING YEARS *Virgin MINDS 1* ......... | 1 | 25 wks |

## SIMPLY RED  *UK, male vocal/instrumental group*  *218 wks*

| | | | | |
|---|---|---|---|---|
| 26 Oct 85 | ● | PICTURE BOOK *Elektra EKT 27* ................... | 2 | 117 wks |
| 21 Mar 87 | ● | MEN AND WOMEN *WEA WX 85* .................... | 2 | 56 wks |
| 25 Feb 89 | ★ | A NEW FLAME *Elektra WX 242* ................... | 1† | 45 wks |

SIMPSON – *See ASHFORD and SIMPSON*

## Joyce SIMS  *US, female vocalist*  *25 wks*

| | | | | |
|---|---|---|---|---|
| 9 Jan 88 | ● | COME INTO MY LIFE *London LONLP 47* .............. | 5 | 24 wks |
| 16 Sep 89 | | ALL ABOUT LOVE *London 828129 1* ................. | 64 | 1 wk |

## Frank SINATRA  *US, male vocalist*  *613 wks*

| | | | | |
|---|---|---|---|---|
| 8 Nov 58 | ● | COME FLY WITH ME *Capitol LCT 6154* .............. | 2 | 18 wks |
| 15 Nov 58 | ● | SONGS FOR SWINGING LOVERS *Capitol LCT 6106* ... | 8 | 8 wks |
| 29 Nov 58 | ● | FRANK SINATRA STORY *Fontana TFL 5030* ......... | 8 | 1 wk |
| 13 Dec 58 | ● | FRANK SINATRA SINGS FOR ONLY THE LONELY | | |
| | | *Capitol LCT 6168* ................................ | 5 | 13 wks |
| 16 May 59 | ● | COME DANCE WITH ME *Capitol LCT 6179* ........... | 2 | 30 wks |
| 22 Aug 59 | ● | LOOK TO YOUR HEART *Capitol LCT 6181* ........... | 5 | 8 wks |
| 11 Jun 60 | ● | COME BACK TO SORRENTO *Fontana TFL 5082* ...... | 6 | 9 wks |
| 29 Oct 60 | ● | SWING EASY *Capitol W 587* ....................... | 5 | 17 wks |
| 21 Jan 61 | ● | NICE 'N EASY *Capitol W 1417* ..................... | 4 | 27 wks |
| 15 Jul 61 | | SINATRA SOUVENIR *Fontana TFL 5138* ............. | 18 | 1 wk |
| 19 Aug 61 | ● | WHEN YOUR LOVER HAS GONE *Encore ENC 101* ... | 6 | 10 wks |
| 23 Sep 61 | ● | SINATRA'S SWINGING SESSION *Capitol W 1491* ..... | 6 | 8 wks |
| 28 Oct 61 | ● | SINATRA SWINGS *Reprise R 1002* .................. | 8 | 8 wks |
| 25 Nov 61 | ● | SINATRA PLUS *Fontana SET 303* ................... | 7 | 9 wks |
| 16 Dec 61 | ● | RING-A-DING-DING *Reprise R 1001* ............... | 8 | 9 wks |
| 17 Feb 62 | | COME SWING WITH ME *Capitol W 1594* ............. | 13 | 4 wks |
| 7 Apr 62 | ● | I REMEMBER TOMMY *Reprise R 1003* .............. | 10 | 12 wks |
| 9 Jun 62 | ● | SINATRA AND STRINGS *Reprise R 1004* ............ | 6 | 20 wks |
| 27 Oct 62 | | GREAT SONGS FROM GREAT BRITAIN *Reprise R 1006* | 12 | 9 wks |
| 29 Dec 62 | | SINATRA WITH SWINGING BRASS *Reprise R 1005* ... | 14 | 11 wks |
| 27 Jul 63 | ● | CONCERT SINATRA *Reprise R 1009* .................. | 8 | 18 wks |

**FRANK SINATRA AND COUNT BASIE**, chart partners in 1963, meet again twenty years later at a charity dinner with Sarah Vaughan and Dionne Warwick.

The **SMITHS** made the top ten with each of their studio albums. Their other LP, 'Louder Than Bombs', was a compilation import that later became available domestically.

| | | | | |
|---|---|---|---|---|
| 5 Oct 63 | ● SINATRA'S SINATRA *Reprise R 1010* ................ | 9 | 24 wks |
| 19 Sep 64 | IT MIGHT AS WELL BE SWING *Reprise R 1012* ........ | 17 | 4 wks |
| 20 Mar 65 | SOFTLY AS I LEAVE YOU *Reprise R 1013* ............ | 20 | 1 wk |
| 22 Jan 66 | ● A MAN AND HIS MUSIC *Reprise R 1016* .......... | 9 | 19 wks |
| 21 May 66 | MOONLIGHT SINATRA *Reprise R 1018* ............ | 18 | 8 wks |
| 2 Jul 66 | ● STRANGERS IN THE NIGHT *Reprise R 1017* .......... | 4 | 18 wks |
| 1 Oct 66 | ● SINATRA AT THE SANDS *Reprise RLP 1019* ........ | 7 | 18 wks |
| 3 Dec 66 | FRANK SINATRA SINGS SONGS FOR PLEASURE *MFP 1120* ..................................... | 26 | 2 wks |
| 25 Feb 67 | THAT'S LIFE *Reprise RSLP 1020* ................. | 22 | 12 wks |
| 7 Oct 67 | FRANK SINATRA *Reprise RSLP 1022* ............... | 28 | 5 wks |
| 19 Oct 68 | ● GREATEST HITS *Reprise RSLP 1025* .............. | 8 | 38 wks |
| 7 Dec 68 | BEST OF FRANK SINATRA *Capitol ST 21140* ........ | 17 | 10 wks |
| 7 Jun 69 | ● MY WAY *Reprise RSLP 1029* ..................... | 2 | 59 wks |
| 4 Oct 69 | A MAN ALONE *Reprise RSLP 1030* ................ | 18 | 7 wks |
| 9 May 70 | WATERTOWN *Reprise RSLP 1031* ................ | 14 | 9 wks |
| 12 Dec 70 | ● GREATEST HITS VOL. 2 *Reprise RSLP 1032* ........ | 6 | 40 wks |
| 5 Jun 71 | ● SINATRA AND COMPANY *Reprise RSLP 1033* ........ | 9 | 9 wks |
| 27 Nov 71 | FRANK SINATRA SINGS RODGERS AND HART *Starline SRS 5083* ................................... | 35 | 1 wk |
| 8 Jan 72 | MY WAY (re-issue) *Reprise K 44015* .................. | 35 | 1 wk |
| 8 Jan 72 | GREATEST HITS VOL. 2 *Reprise K 44018* ............ | 29 | 3 wks |
| 1 Dec 73 | OL' BLUE EYES IS BACK *Warner Bros. K 44249* ...... | 12 | 13 wks |
| 17 Aug 74 | SOME NICE THINGS I'VE MISSED *Reprise K 54020* .... | 35 | 3 wks |
| 15 Feb 75 | THE MAIN EVENT (TV soundtrack) *Reprise K 54031* .... | 30 | 2 wks |
| 14 Jun 75 | THE BEST OF OL' BLUE EYES *Reprise K 54042* ........ | 30 | 3 wks |
| 19 Mar 77 | ★ PORTRAIT OF SINATRA *Reprise K 64039* ............ | 1 | 18 wks |
| 13 May 78 | ● 20 GOLDEN GREATS *Capitol EMTV 10* ............. | 4 | 11 wks |
| 18 Aug 84 | L.A. IS MY LADY *Qwest 925145* .................. | 41 | 8 wks |
| 22 Mar 86 | NEW YORK NEW YORK (GREATEST HITS) *Warner Bros. WX 32* .................................. | 13 | 12 wks |
| 4 Oct 86 | THE FRANK SINATRA COLLECTION *Capitol EMTV 41* ............................... | 40 | 5 wks |

*See also Frank Sinatra and Count Basie.*

## Frank SINATRA and Count BASIE

*US, male vocalist and male orchestra leader/instrumentalist – piano*  *23 wks*

| | | | | |
|---|---|---|---|---|
| 23 Feb 63 | ● SINATRA – BASIE *Reprise R 1008* .................. | 2 | 23 wks |

*See also Count Basie; Frank Sinatra.*

## Nancy SINATRA *US, female vocalist*  *15 wks*

| | | | | |
|---|---|---|---|---|
| 16 Apr 66 | BOOTS *Reprise R 6202* ............................ | 12 | 9 wks |
| 18 Jun 66 | HOW DOES THAT GRAB YOU *Reprise R 6207* ........ | 12 | 3 wks |
| 10 Oct 70 | NANCY'S GREATEST HITS *Reprise RSLP 6409* ........ | 39 | 3 wks |

*See also Nancy Sinatra and Lee Hazlewood.*

## Nancy SINATRA and Lee HAZLEWOOD

*US, female/male vocal duo*  *17 wks*

| | | | | |
|---|---|---|---|---|
| 29 Jun 68 | NANCY AND LEE *Reprise RSLP 6273* ............... | 17 | 12 wks |
| 25 Sep 71 | NANCY AND LEE (re-issue) *Reprise K 44126* ........... | 42 | 1 wk |
| 29 Jan 72 | DID YOU EVER *RCA Victor SF 8240* ................ | 31 | 4 wks |

*See also Nancy Sinatra.*

## SINITTA *US, female vocalist*  *22 wks*

| | | | | |
|---|---|---|---|---|
| 26 Dec 87 | SINITTA! *Fanfare BOYLP 1* ...................... | 34 | 19 wks |
| 9 Dec 89 | WICKED! *Fanfare FARE 2* ........................ | 52 | 3 wks |

**SINFONIA OF LONDON** – *See Howard BLAKE conducting the SINFONIA OF LONDON*

# SIOUXIE and the BANSHEES
*UK, female/male vocal/instrumental group*                                    *111 wks*

| | | | |
|---|---|---|---|
| 2 Dec 78 | **THE SCREAM** *Polydor POLD 5009* | 12 | 11 wks |
| 22 Sep 79 | **JOIN HANDS** *Polydor POLD 5024* | 13 | 5 wks |
| 16 Aug 80 | ● **KALEIDOSCOPE** *Polydor 2442 177* | 5 | 6 wks |
| 27 Jun 81 | ● **JUJU** *Polydor POLS 1034* | 7 | 17 wks |
| 12 Dec 81 | **ONCE UPON A TIME** *Polydor POLS 1056* | 21 | 26 wks |
| 13 Nov 82 | **A KISS IN THE DREAMHOUSE** *Polydor POLD 5064* | 11 | 11 wks |
| 3 Dec 83 | **NOCTURNE** *Wonderland SHAH 1* | 29 | 10 wks |
| 16 Jun 84 | **HYENA** *Wonderland SHELP 2* | 15 | 6 wks |
| 26 Apr 86 | **TINDERBOX** *Wonderland SHELP 3* | 13 | 6 wks |
| 14 Mar 87 | **THROUGH THE LOOKING GLASS** *Wonderland SHELP 4* | 15 | 8 wks |
| 17 Sep 88 | **PEEP SHOW** *Wonderland SHELP 5* | 20 | 5 wks |

# SISTER SLEDGE *US, female vocal group*                                     *50 wks*

| | | | |
|---|---|---|---|
| 12 May 79 | ● **WE ARE FAMILY** *Atlantic K 50587* | 7 | 39 wks |
| 22 Jun 85 | **WHEN THE BOYS MEET THE GIRLS** *Atlantic 78–1255–1* | 19 | 11 wks |

*See also Chic and Sister Sledge.*

# SISTERHOOD *UK, male vocal/instrumental group*                            *1 wk*

| | | | |
|---|---|---|---|
| 26 Jul 86 | **GIFT** *Merciful Release SIS 020* | 90 | 1 wk |

# SISTERS OF MERCY
*UK, male/female vocal/instrumental duo*                                      *28 wks*

| | | | |
|---|---|---|---|
| 23 Mar 85 | **FIRST AND LAST AND ALWAYS** *Merciful Release MR 337 L* | 14 | 8 wks |
| 28 Nov 87 | ● **FLOODLAND** *Merciful Release MR 441 L* | 9 | 20 wks |

*Act was a male-only group for first album.*

# Peter SKELLERN *UK, male vocalist*                                          *28 wks*

| | | | |
|---|---|---|---|
| 9 Sep 78 | **SKELLERN** *Mercury 9109 701* | 48 | 3 wks |
| 8 Dec 79 | **ASTAIRE** *Mercury 9102 702* | 23 | 20 wks |
| 4 Dec 82 | **A STRING OF PEARLS** *Mercury MERL 10* | 67 | 5 wks |

# SKID ROW *UK, male vocal/instrumental group*                               *3 wks*

| | | | |
|---|---|---|---|
| 17 Oct 70 | **SKID** *CBS 63965* | 30 | 3 wks |

# SKID ROW *US, male vocal/instrumental group*                               *3 wks*

| | | | |
|---|---|---|---|
| 2 Sep 89 | **SKID ROW** *Atlantic 781936 1* | 61 | 3 wks |

# SKIDS *UK, male vocal/instrumental group*                                   *20 wks*

| | | | |
|---|---|---|---|
| 17 Mar 79 | **SCARED TO DANCE** *Virgin V 2116* | 19 | 10 wks |
| 27 Oct 79 | **DAYS IN EUROPE** *Virgin V 2138* | 32 | 5 wks |
| 27 Sep 80 | ● **THE ABSOLUTE GAME** *Virgin V 2174* | 9 | 5 wks |

# SKY *UK/Australia, male instrumental group*                                 *202 wks*

| | | | |
|---|---|---|---|
| 2 Jun 79 | ● **SKY** *Ariola ARLH 5022* | 9 | 56 wks |
| 26 Apr 80 | ★ **SKY 2** *Ariola ADSKY 2* | 1 | 53 wks |
| 28 Mar 81 | ● **SKY 3** *Ariola ASKY 3* | 3 | 23 wks |
| 3 Apr 82 | ● **SKY 4 - FORTHCOMING** *Ariola ASKY 4* | 7 | 22 wks |
| 22 Jan 83 | **SKY FIVE LIVE** *Ariola 302 171* | 14 | 14 wks |
| 3 Dec 83 | **CADMIUM** *Ariola 205 885* | 44 | 10 wks |

| | | | |
|---|---|---|---|
| 12 May 84 | **MASTERPIECES – THE VERY BEST OF SKY** | | |
| | Telstar STAR 2241 | 15 | 18 wks |
| 13 Apr 85 | **THE GREAT BALLOON RACE**  Epic EPC 26419 | 63 | 6 wks |

## SKYY  *US, male vocal/instrumental group*  *1 wk*

| | | | |
|---|---|---|---|
| 21 Jun 86 | **FROM THE LEFT SIDE**  Capitol EST 2014 | 85 | 1 wk |

## SLADE  *UK, male vocal/instrumental group*  *202 wks*

| | | | |
|---|---|---|---|
| 8 Apr 72 | ● **SLADE ALIVE**  Polydor 2383 101 | 2 | 58 wks |
| 9 Dec 72 | ★ **SLAYED?**  Polydor 2383 163 | 1 | 34 wks |
| 6 Oct 73 | ★ **SLADEST**  Polydor 2442 119 | 1 | 24 wks |
| 23 Feb 74 | ★ **OLD NEW BORROWED AND BLUE**  Polydor 2383 261 | 1 | 16 wks |
| 14 Dec 74 | ● **SLADE IN FLAME**  Polydor 2442 126 | 6 | 18 wks |
| 27 Mar 76 | **NOBODY'S FOOL**  Polydor 2383 377 | 14 | 4 wks |
| 22 Nov 80 | **SLADE SMASHES**  Polydor POLTV 13 | 21 | 15 wks |
| 21 Mar 81 | **WE'LL BRING THE HOUSE DOWN**  Cheapskate SKATE 1 | 25 | 4 wks |
| 28 Nov 81 | **TILL DEAF US DO PART**  RCA RCALP 6021 | 68 | 2 wks |
| 18 Dec 82 | **SLADE ON STAGE**  RCA RCALP 3107 | 58 | 3 wks |
| 24 Dec 83 | **THE AMAZING KAMIKAZE SYNDROME** | | |
| | RCA PL 70116 | 49 | 13 wks |
| 9 Jun 84 | **SLADE'S GREATS**  Polydor SLAD 1 | 89 | 1 wk |
| 6 Apr 85 | **ROGUES GALLERY**  RCA PL 70604 | 60 | 2 wks |
| 30 Nov 85 | **CRACKERS – THE SLADE CHRISTMAS PARTY ALBUM** | | |
| | Telstar STAR 2271 | 34 | 7 wks |
| 9 May 87 | **YOU BOYZ MAKE BIG NOIZE**  RCA PL 71260 | 98 | 1 wk |

## SLAYER  *US, male vocal/instrumental group*  *7 wks*

| | | | |
|---|---|---|---|
| 2 May 87 | **REIGN IN BLOOD**  Def Jam LONLP 34 | 47 | 3 wks |
| 23 Jul 88 | **SOUTH OF HEAVEN**  London LONLP 63 | 67 | 4 wks |

## Percy SLEDGE  *US, male vocalist*  *4 wks*

| | | | |
|---|---|---|---|
| 14 Mar 87 | **WHEN A MAN LOVES A WOMAN (THE ULTIMATE COLLECTION)**  Atlantic WX 89 | 36 | 4 wks |

## SLEIGHRIDERS  *UK, male vocal/instrumental group*  *1 wk*

| | | | |
|---|---|---|---|
| 17 Dec 83 | **A VERY MERRY DISCO**  Warwick WW 5136 | 100 | 1 wk |

## Grace SLICK  *US, female vocalist*  *6 wks*

| | | | |
|---|---|---|---|
| 31 May 80 | **DREAMS**  RCA PL 13544 | 28 | 6 wks |

## SLIK  *UK, male vocal/instrumental group*  *1 wk*

| | | | |
|---|---|---|---|
| 12 Jun 76 | **SLIK**  Bell SYBEL 8004 | 58 | 1 wk |

**SLIM CHANCE** – See Ronnie LANE and the Band SLIM CHANCE

## SLITS  *UK, female vocal/instrumental group*  *5 wks*

| | | | |
|---|---|---|---|
| 22 Sep 79 | **CUT**  Island ILPS 9573 | 30 | 5 wks |

## SLY and ROBBIE  *Jamaica, male vocal/instrumental duo*  *5 wks*

| | | | |
|---|---|---|---|
| 9 May 87 | **RHYTHM KILLERS**  Fourth & Broadway BRLP 512 | 35 | 5 wks |

# SLY and the FAMILY STONE

US, male/female vocal/instrumental group                     2 wks

| 5 Feb 72 | THERE'S A RIOT GOIN' ON   Epic EPC 64613 | 31 | 2 wks |
|---|---|---|---|

# SMALL FACES   UK, male vocal/instrumental group        66 wks

| 14 May 66 | ● SMALL FACES   Decca LK 4790 | 3 | 25 wks |
|---|---|---|---|
| 17 Jun 67 | FROM THE BEGINNING   Decca LK 4879 | 17 | 5 wks |
| 1 Jul 67 | SMALL FACES   Immediate IMSP 008 | 12 | 17 wks |
| 15 Jun 68 | ★ OGDEN'S NUT GONE FLAKE   Immediate IMLP 012 | 1 | 19 wks |

The two albums titled Small Faces are different.

# Brian SMITH and his HAPPY PIANO

UK, male instrumentalist – piano                             1 wk

| 19 Sep 81 | PLAY IT AGAIN   Deram DS 047 | 97 | 1 wk |
|---|---|---|---|

# Jimmy SMITH   US, male instrumentalist – organ        3 wks

| 18 Jun 66 | GOT MY MOJO WORKING   Verve VLP 912 | 19 | 3 wks |
|---|---|---|---|

# Keely SMITH   US, female vocalist                      9 wks

| 16 Jan 65 | LENNON–McCARTNEY SONGBOOK   Reprise R 6142 | 12 | 9 wks |
|---|---|---|---|

# O.C. SMITH   US, male vocalist                         1 wk

| 17 Aug 68 | HICKORY HOLLER REVISITED   CBS 63362 | 40 | 1 wk |
|---|---|---|---|

# Steven SMITH and FATHER

UK, male instrumental duo                                 3 wks

| 13 May 72 | STEVEN SMITH AND FATHER AND 16 GREAT SONGS   Decca SKL 5128 | 17 | 3 wks |
|---|---|---|---|

# SMITH and JONES   UK, male comedy duo                  8 wks

| 15 Nov 86 | SCRATCH AND SNIFF   10 DIX 51 | 62 | 8 wks |
|---|---|---|---|

# Patti SMITH GROUP

US, female/male vocal/instrumental group                 21 wks

| 1 Apr 78 | EASTER   Arista SPART 1043 | 16 | 14 wks |
|---|---|---|---|
| 19 May 79 | WAVE   Arista SPART 1086 | 41 | 6 wks |
| 16 Jul 88 | DREAM OF LIFE   Arista 209172 | 70 | 1 wks |

Third album credited simply to Patti Smith.

# SMITHS   UK, male vocal/instrumental group            158 wks

| 3 Mar 84 | ● THE SMITHS   Rough Trade ROUGH 61 | 2 | 33 wks |
|---|---|---|---|
| 24 Nov 84 | ● HATFUL OF HOLLOW   Rough Trade ROUGH 76 | 7 | 46 wks |
| 23 Feb 85 | ★ MEAT IS MURDER   Rough Trade ROUGH 81 | 1 | 13 wks |
| 28 Jun 86 | ● THE QUEEN IS DEAD   Rough Trade ROUGH 96 | 2 | 22 wks |
| 7 Mar 87 | ● THE WORLD WON'T LISTEN   Rough Trade ROUGH 101 | 2 | 15 wks |
| 30 May 87 | LOUDER THAN BOMBS   (import) Rough Trade ROUGH 255 | 38 | 5 wks |
| 10 Oct 87 | ● STRANGEWAYS HERE WE COME   Rough Trade ROUGH 106 | 2 | 17 wks |
| 17 Sep 88 | ● RANK   Rough Trade ROUGH 126 | 2 | 7 wks |

## SMOKIE  *UK, male vocal/instrumental group*                    *42 wks*

| | | | |
|---|---|---|---|
| 1 Nov 75 ● | SMOKIE/CHANGING ALL THE TIME  *RAK SRAK 517* . | 18 | 5 wks |
| 30 Apr 77 ● | GREATEST HITS  *RAK SRAK 526* ................. | 6 | 22 wks |
| 4 Nov 78 | THE MONTREUX ALBUM  *RAK SRAK 6757* ......... | 52 | 2 wks |
| 11 Oct 80 | SMOKIE'S HITS  *RAK SRAK 540* .................. | 23 | 13 wks |

**SMURFS** – *See Father ABRAHAM and the SMURFS*

## SOFT CELL  *UK, male vocal/instrumental duo*                    *87 wks*

| | | | |
|---|---|---|---|
| 5 Dec 81 ● | NON-STOP EROTIC CABARET  *Some Bizzare BZLP 2* .. | 5 | 46 wks |
| 26 Jun 82 ● | NON-STOP ECSTATIC DANCING | | |
| | *Some Bizzare BZX 1012* ................... | 6 | 18 wks |
| 22 Jan 83 ● | THE ART OF FALLING APART  *Some Bizzare BIZL 3* ... | 5 | 9 wks |
| 31 Mar 84 | THE LAST NIGHT IN SODOM  *Some Bizzare BIZL 6* .... | 12 | 5 wks |
| 20 Dec 86 | THE SINGLES ALBUM  *Some Bizzare BZLP 3* .......... | 58 | 9 wks |

## SOFT MACHINE  *UK, male vocal/instrumental group*                    *8 wks*

| | | | |
|---|---|---|---|
| 4 Jul 70 | THIRD  *CBS 66246* ........................... | 18 | 6 wks |
| 3 Apr 71 | FOURTH  *CBS 64280* .......................... | 32 | 2 wks |

## SOLID SENDERS  *UK, male vocal/instrumental group*                    *3 wks*

| | | | |
|---|---|---|---|
| 23 Sep 78 | SOLID SENDERS  *Virgin V 2105* ................... | 42 | 3 wks |

## Diane SOLOMON  *UK, female vocalist*                    *6 wks*

| | | | |
|---|---|---|---|
| 9 Aug 75 | TAKE TWO  *Philips 6308 236* ...................... | 26 | 6 wks |

## Jimmy SOMERVILLE  *UK, male vocalist*                    *2 wks*

| | | | |
|---|---|---|---|
| 9 Dec 89 | READ MY LIPS  *London 828166 1* ................... | 66 | 2 wks |

## SONIC YOUTH  *US, male/female vocal/instrumental group*                    *1 wk*

| | | | |
|---|---|---|---|
| 29 Oct 88 | DAYDREAM NATION  *Blast First BFFP 34* ............ | 99 | 1 wk |

## SONNY and CHER  *US, male/female vocal duo*                    *20 wks*

| | | | |
|---|---|---|---|
| 16 Oct 65 ● | LOOK AT US  *Atlantic ATL 5036* ..................... | 7 | 13 wks |
| 14 May 66 | THE WONDROUS WORLD OF SONNY AND CHER | | |
| | *Atlantic 587–006* ................................ | 15 | 7 wks |

*See also Cher.*

## S.O.S. BAND  *US, male/female vocal/instrumental group*                    *19 wks*

| | | | |
|---|---|---|---|
| 1 Sep 84 | JUST THE WAY YOU LIKE IT  *Tabu TBU 26058* ....... | 29 | 10 wks |
| 17 May 86 | SANDS OF TIME  *Tabu TBU 26863* .................. | 15 | 9 wks |

## David SOUL  *US, male vocalist*                    *51 wks*

| | | | |
|---|---|---|---|
| 27 Nov 76 ● | DAVID SOUL  *Private Stock PVLP 1012* ............... | 2 | 28 wks |
| 17 Sep 77 ● | PLAYING TO AN AUDIENCE OF ONE | | |
| | *Private Stock PVLP 1026* .......................... | 8 | 23 wks |

**SOUL CITY SYMPHONY** – *See Van McCOY and the SOUL CITY SYMPHONY*

## SOUL II SOUL

UK, male/female vocal/instrumental group and male producer                 37 wks

22 Apr 89 ★ CLUB CLASSICS VOLUME ONE   10 DIX 82 .......... 1† 37 wks

## SOUNDS ORCHESTRAL   UK, orchestra                 1 wk

12 Jun 65   CAST YOUR FATE TO THE WIND
            Piccadilly NPL 38041 ............................. 17 1 wk

SOUNDTRACKS (films, TV etc) - See VARIOUS ARTISTS

## SOUP DRAGONS   UK, male vocal/instrumental group                 1 wk

7 May 88   THIS IS OUR ART   Sire WX 169 ...................... 60 1 wk

## SOUTH BANK ORCHESTRA   UK, orchestra                 6 wks

2 Dec 78   LILLIE   Sounds MOR 516 ........................... 47 6 wks
This album was conducted by Joseph Morovitz and Laurie Holloway.

SOUTHERN DEATH CULT - See CULT

## SPACE   France, male instrumental group                 9 wks

17 Sep 77   MAGIC FLY   Pye NSPL 28232 ........................ 11 9 wks

## SPANDAU BALLET   UK, male vocal/instrumental group                 247 wks

| | | | |
|---|---|---|---|
| 14 Mar 81 ● JOURNEY TO GLORY   Reformation CHR 1331 ......... | 5 | 29 wks |
| 20 Mar 82   DIAMOND   Reformation CDL 1353 ................... | 15 | 18 wks |
| 12 Mar 83 ★ TRUE   Reformation CDL 1403 ........................ | 1 | 90 wks |
| 7 Jul 84 ● PARADE   Reformation CDL 1473 ...................... | 2 | 39 wks |
| 16 Nov 85 ● THE SINGLES COLLECTION   Chrysalis SBTV 1 ....... | 3 | 49 wks |
| 29 Nov 86 ● THROUGH THE BARRICADES | | |
|             Reformation CBS 450 259-1 ......................... | 7 | 19 wks |
| 30 Sep 89   HEART LIKE A SKY   CBS 4633181 ................... | 31 | 3 wks |

## SPARKS   US/UK, male vocal/instrumental group                 42 wks

1 Jun 74 ● KIMONO MY HOUSE   Island ILPS 9272 .............. 4 24 wks
23 Nov 74 ● PROPAGANDA   Island ILPS 9312 ................... 9 13 wks
18 Oct 75   INDISCREET   Island ILPS 9345 ................... 18 4 wks
8 Sep 79   NUMBER ONE IN HEAVEN   Virgin V 2115 ........... 73 1 wk

## SPEAR OF DESTINY
UK, male vocal/instrumental group                 35 wks

23 Apr 83   GRAPES OF WRATH   Epic EPC 25318 .............. 62 2 wks
28 Apr 84   ONE EYED JACKS   Burning Rome EPC 25836 .......... 22 7 wks
7 Sep 85   WORLD SERVICE   Burning Rome EPC 26514 .......... 11 7 wks
2 May 87   OUTLAND   10 DIX 59 ............................. 16 13 wks
16 May 87   S.O.D. - THE EPIC YEARS   Epic 450 872-1 ......... 53 3 wks
22 Oct 88   THE PRICE YOU PAY   Virgin V 2549 ............... 37 3 wks

## Billie Jo SPEARS   US, female vocalist                 28 wks

11 Sep 76   WHAT I'VE GOT IN MIND   United Artists UAS 29955 .... 47 2 wks
19 May 79 ● THE BILLIE JO SPEARS SINGLES ALBUM
            United Artists UAK 30231 .......................... 7 17 wks
21 Nov 81   COUNTRY GIRL   Warwick WW 5109 ................. 17 9 wks

## SPECIAL A.K.A. *UK, male/female vocal/instrumental group* 70 wks

| | | | | |
|---|---|---|---|---|
| 3 Nov 79 | ● SPECIALS | 2-Tone CDL TT 5001 .................... | 4 | 45 wks |
| 4 Oct 80 | ● MORE SPECIALS | 2-Tone CHR TT 5003 .............. | 5 | 19 wks |
| 23 Jun 84 | IN THE STUDIO | 2-Tone CHR TT 5008 .............. | 34 | 6 wks |

*Group was male only and billed simply as the Specials for the first two albums.*

## Phil SPECTOR *US, male producer* 29 wks

| | | | |
|---|---|---|---|
| 23 Dec 72 | **PHIL SPECTOR'S CHRISTMAS ALBUM** *Apple SAPCOR 24* ................................ | 21 | 3 wks |
| 15 Oct 77 | **PHIL SPECTOR'S ECHOES OF THE 60'S** *Phil Spector International 2307 013* ..................... | 21 | 10 wks |
| 25 Dec 82 | **PHIL SPECTOR'S CHRISTMAS ALBUM (re-issue)** *Phil Spector International/Polydor 2307 005* .............. | 96 | 2 wks |
| 10 Dec 83 | **PHIL SPECTOR'S GREATEST HITS/PHIL SPECTOR'S CHRISTMAS ALBUM (2nd re-issue)** *Impression PSLP 1/2* .............................. | 19 | 8 wks |
| 12 Dec 87 | **PHIL SPECTOR'S CHRISTMAS ALBUM (3rd re-issue)** *Chrysalis CDL 1625* ............................. | 69 | 6 wks |

## SPIDER *UK, male vocal/instrumental group* 2 wks

| | | | |
|---|---|---|---|
| 23 Oct 82 | **ROCK 'N' ROLL GYPSIES** *RCA RCALP 3101* ......... | 75 | 1 wk |
| 7 Apr 84 | **ROUGH JUSTICE** *A & M AMLX 68563* .............. | 96 | 1 wk |

## SPINNERS *UK, male vocal group* 24 wks

| | | | |
|---|---|---|---|
| 5 Sep 70 | **THE SPINNERS ARE IN TOWN** *Fontana 6309 014* ..... | 40 | 5 wks |
| 7 Aug 71 | **SPINNERS LIVE PERFORMANCE** *Contour 6870 502* ... | 14 | 12 wks |
| 13 Nov 71 | **THE SWINGING CITY** *Philips 6382 002* .............. | 20 | 3 wks |
| 8 Apr 72 | **LOVE IS TEASING** *Columbia SCX 6493* .............. | 33 | 4 wks |

## SPIRIT *US, male vocal/instrumental duo* 2 wks

| | | | |
|---|---|---|---|
| 18 Apr 81 | **POTATO LAND** *Beggars Banquet BEGA 23* ............. | 40 | 2 wks |

## SPITTING IMAGE *UK, puppets* 3 wks

| | | | |
|---|---|---|---|
| 18 Oct 86 | **SPIT IN YOUR EAR** *Virgin V 2403* .................. | 55 | 3 wks |

## SPLIT ENZ
*New Zealand/UK, male vocal/instrumental group* 9 wks

| | | | |
|---|---|---|---|
| 30 Aug 80 | **TRUE COLOURS** *A & M AMLH 64822* .............. | 42 | 8 wks |
| 8 May 82 | **TIME AND TIDE** *A & M AMLH 64894* ............... | 71 | 1 wk |

## SPOTNICKS *Sweden, male instrumental group* 1 wk

| | | | |
|---|---|---|---|
| 9 Feb 63 | **OUT-A-SPACE** *Oriole PS 40036* .................... | 20 | 1 wk |

## Dusty SPRINGFIELD *UK, female vocalist* 92 wks

| | | | |
|---|---|---|---|
| 25 Apr 64 | ● **A GIRL CALLED DUSTY** *Philips BL 7594* ............ | 6 | 23 wks |
| 23 Oct 65 | ● **EVERYTHING COMES UP DUSTY** *Philips RBL 1002* .. | 6 | 12 wks |
| 22 Oct 66 | ● **GOLDEN HITS** *Philips BL 7737* ..................... | 2 | 36 wks |
| 11 Nov 67 | **WHERE AM I GOING** *Philips SBL 7820* ............... | 40 | 1 wk |
| 21 Dec 68 | **DUSTY...DEFINITELY** *Philips SBL 7864* ............ | 30 | 6 wks |
| 2 May 70 | **FROM DUSTY WITH LOVE** *Philips SBL 7927* ......... | 35 | 2 wks |
| 4 Mar 78 | **IT BEGINS AGAIN** *Mercury 9109 607* ................ | 41 | 2 wks |
| 30 Jan 88 | **DUSTY – THE SILVER COLLECTION** *Phonogram DUSTV 1* ............................. | 14 | 10 wks |

## Rick SPRINGFIELD  *Australia, male vocalist*                                    8 wks

| 11 Feb 84 | **LIVING IN OZ**  *RCA PL 84660* | 41 | 4 wks |
| 25 May 85 | **TAO**  *RCA PL 85370* | 68 | 3 wks |
| 26 Mar 88 | **ROCK OF LIFE**  *RCA PL 86620* | 80 | 1 wk |

## Bruce SPRINGSTEEN  *US, male vocalist*                                    387 wks

| 1 Nov 75 | **BORN TO RUN**  *CBS 69170* | 17 | 50 wks |
| 17 Jun 78 | **DARKNESS ON THE EDGE OF TOWN**  *CBS 86061* | 16 | 40 wks |
| 25 Oct 80 | ● **THE RIVER**  *CBS 88510* | 2 | 88 wks |
| 2 Oct 82 | ● **NEBRASKA**  *CBS 25100* | 3 | 19 wks |
| 16 Jun 84 | ★ **BORN IN THE USA**  *CBS 86304* | 1 | 126 wks |
| 15 Jun 85 | **THE WILD THE INNOCENT AND THE E STREET SHUFFLE**  *CBS 32363* | 33 | 12 wks |
| 15 Jun 85 | **GREETINGS FROM ASBURY PARK, N.J.**  *CBS 32210* | 41 | 10 wks |
| 22 Nov 86 | ● **LIVE 1975–1985**  *CBS 450 227-1* | 4 | 9 wks |
| 17 Oct 87 | ★ **TUNNEL OF LOVE**  *CBS 460 270-1* | 1 | 33 wks |

Live 1975–1985 *credits the E Street Band.*

## SPYRO GYRA  *US, male instrumental group*                                    23 wks

| 14 Jul 79 | **MORNING DANCE**  *Infinity INS 2003* | 11 | 16 wks |
| 23 Feb 80 | **CATCHING THE SUN**  *MCA MCG 4009* | 31 | 7 wks |

## SQUEEZE  *UK, male vocal/instrumental group*                                    104 wks

| 28 Apr 79 | **COOL FOR CATS**  *A & M AMLH 68503* | 45 | 11 wks |
| 16 Feb 80 | **ARGY BARGY**  *A & M AMLH 64802* | 32 | 15 wks |
| 23 May 81 | **EAST SIDE STORY**  *A & M AMLH 64854* | 19 | 26 wks |
| 15 May 82 | **SWEETS FROM A STRANGER**  *A & M AMLH 64899* | 20 | 7 wks |
| 6 Nov 82 | ● **SINGLES–45'S AND UNDER**  *A & M AMLH 68552* | 3 | 29 wks |
| 7 Sep 85 | **COSI FAN TUTTI FRUTTI**  *A & M AMA 5085* | 31 | 7 wks |
| 19 Sep 87 | **BABYLON AND ON**  *A & M AMA 5161* | 14 | 8 wks |
| 23 Sep 89 | **FRANK**  *A & M AMA 5278* | 58 | 1 wk |

## Chris SQUIRE  *UK, male vocalist/instrumentalist – bass*                                    7 wks

| 6 Dec 75 | **FISH OUT OF WATER**  *Atlantic K 50203* | 25 | 7 wks |

**STAGE CAST RECORDINGS** – *See VARIOUS ARTISTS*

## Lisa STANSFIELD  *UK, female vocalist*                                    5 wks

| 2 Dec 89 | ● **AFFECTION**  *Arista 210379* | 2† | 5 wks |

**Robin STAPLETON** – *See Aled JONES*

## Alvin STARDUST  *UK, male vocalist*                                    17 wks

| 16 Mar 74 | ● **THE UNTOUCHABLE**  *Magnet MAG 5001* | 4 | 12 wks |
| 21 Dec 74 | **ALVIN STARDUST**  *Magnet MAG 5004* | 37 | 3 wks |
| 4 Oct 75 | **ROCK WITH ALVIN**  *Magnet MAG 5007* | 52 | 2 wks |

## Freddie STARR  *UK, male vocalist*                                    7 wks

| 18 Nov 89 | ● **AFTER THE LAUGHTER**  *Dover ADD 10* | 10† | 7 wks |

## Kay STARR  *US, female vocalist*                                    1 wk

| 26 Mar 60 | **MOVIN'**  *Capitol T 1254* | 16 | 1 wk |

## Ringo STARR  *UK, male vocalist*                                    *28 wks*

| | | | | |
|---|---|---|---|---|
| 18 Apr 70 | ● **SENTIMENTAL JOURNEY** *Apple PCS 7101* .......... | **7** | 6 wks |
| 8 Dec 73 | ● **RINGO** *Apple PCTC 252* ........................... | **7** | 20 wks |
| 7 Dec 74 | **GOODNIGHT VIENNA** *Apple PMC 7168* ............. | **30** | 2 wks |

## STARSHIP  *US, male/female vocal/instrumental group*               *5 wks*

| | | | |
|---|---|---|---|
| 18 Jul 87 | **NO PROTECTION** *Grunt FL 86413* ................. | **26** | 5 wks |

*See also Jefferson Airplane; Jefferson Starship.*

## STARSOUND  *Holland, disco aggregation*                            *28 wks*

| | | | |
|---|---|---|---|
| 16 May 81 | ★ **STARS ON 45** *CBS 86132* ........................... | **1** | 21 wks |
| 19 Sep 81 | **STARS ON 45 VOL. 2** *CBS 85181* ................... | **18** | 6 wks |
| 3 Apr 82 | **STARS MEDLEY** *CBS 85651* ...................... | **94** | 1 wk |

## STARTRAX  *UK, disco aggregation*                                  *7 wks*

| | | | |
|---|---|---|---|
| 1 Aug 81 | **STARTRAX CLUB DISCO** *Picksy KSYA 1001* ......... | **26** | 7 wks |

## Candi STATON  *US, female vocalist*                                *3 wks*

| | | | |
|---|---|---|---|
| 24 Jul 76 | **YOUNG HEARTS RUN FREE** *Warner Bros. K 56259* .... | **34** | 3 wks |

## STATUS QUO  *UK, male vocal/instrumental group*                    *399 wks*

| | | | |
|---|---|---|---|
| 20 Jan 73 | ● **PILEDRIVER** *Vertigo 6360 082* .................... | **5** | 37 wks |
| 9 Jun 73 | **THE BEST OF STATUS QUO** *Pye NSPL 18402* ........ | **32** | 7 wks |
| 6 Oct 73 | ★ **HELLO** *Vertigo 6360 098* ......................... | **1** | 28 wks |
| 18 May 74 | ● **QUO** *Vertigo 9102 001* ......................... | **2** | 16 wks |
| 1 Mar 75 | ★ **ON THE LEVEL** *Vertigo 9102 002* ................. | **1** | 27 wks |
| 8 Mar 75 | **DOWN THE DUSTPIPE** *Golden Hour CH 604* .......... | **20** | 6 wks |
| 20 Mar 76 | ★ **BLUE FOR YOU** *Vertigo 9102 006* .................. | **1** | 30 wks |
| 12 Mar 77 | ● **LIVE** *Vertigo 6641 580* ......................... | **3** | 14 wks |
| 26 Nov 77 | ● **ROCKIN' ALL OVER THE WORLD** *Vertigo 9102 014* ... | **5** | 15 wks |
| 11 Nov 78 | ● **CAN'T STAND THE HEAT** *Vertigo 9102 027* .......... | **3** | 14 wks |
| 20 Oct 79 | ● **WHATEVER YOU WANT** *Vertigo 9102 037* ............ | **3** | 14 wks |
| 22 Mar 80 | ● **12 GOLD BARS** *Vertigo QUO TV 1* ................. | **3** | 48 wks |
| 25 Oct 80 | ● **JUST SUPPOSIN'** *Vertigo 6302 057* .................. | **4** | 18 wks |
| 28 Mar 81 | ● **NEVER TOO LATE** *Vertigo 6302 104* ............... | **2** | 13 wks |
| 10 Oct 81 | **FRESH QUOTA** *PRT DOW 2* ...................... | **74** | 1 wk |
| 24 Apr 82 | ★ **1982** *Vertigo 6302 169* ...................... | **1** | 20 wks |
| 13 Nov 82 | ● **FROM THE MAKERS OF ...** *Vertigo PROLP 1* ......... | **4** | 18 wks |
| 3 Dec 83 | ● **BACK TO BACK** *Vertigo VERH 10* ................... | **9** | 22 wks |
| 4 Aug 84 | **STATUS QUO LIVE AT THE NEC** *Vertigo (Holland) 8189 471* ...................... | **83** | 3 wks |
| 1 Dec 84 | **12 GOLD BARS VOLUME 2 (AND 1)** *Vertigo QUO TV 2* ...................... | **12** | 18 wks |
| 6 Sep 86 | ● **IN THE ARMY NOW** *Vertigo VERH 36* ............. | **7** | 23 wks |
| 18 Jun 88 | **AIN'T COMPLAINING** *Vertigo VERH 58* ............. | **12** | 5 wks |
| 2 Dec 89 | **PERFECT REMEDY** *Vertigo 842098 1* ............... | **49** | 2 wks |

## STEEL PULSE  *UK, male vocal/instrumental group*                   *18 wks*

| | | | |
|---|---|---|---|
| 5 Aug 78 | ● **HANDSWORTH REVOLUTION** *Island EMI ILPS 9502* | **9** | 12 wks |
| 14 Jul 79 | **TRIBUTE TO MARTYRS** *Island ILPS 9568* ............. | **42** | 6 wks |

## STEELEYE SPAN
*UK, male/female vocal instrumental group*                            *48 wks*

| | | | |
|---|---|---|---|
| 10 Apr 71 | **PLEASE TO SEE THE KING** *B&C CAS 1029* ......... | **45** | 2 wks |

| | | | | |
|---|---|---|---|---|
| 14 Oct 72 | **BELOW THE SALT** *Chrysalis CHR 1008* .............. | 43 | 1 wk |
| 28 Apr 73 | **PARCEL OF ROGUES** *Chrysalis CHR 1046* ............ | 26 | 5 wks |
| 23 Mar 74 | **NOW WE ARE SIX** *Chrysalis CHR 1053* .............. | 13 | 13 wks |
| 15 Feb 75 | **COMMONER'S CROWN** *Chrysalis CHR 1071* .......... | 21 | 4 wks |
| 25 Oct 75 | ● **ALL AROUND MY HAT** *Chrysalis CHR 1091* ........... | 7 | 20 wks |
| 16 Oct 76 | **ROCKET COTTAGE** *Chrysalis CHR 1123* ............. | 41 | 3 wks |

## STEELY DAN  *US, male vocal/instrumental group*                     77 wks

| | | | | |
|---|---|---|---|---|
| 30 Mar 74 | **PRETZEL LOGIC** *Probe SPBA 6282* .................. | 37 | 2 wks |
| 3 May 75 | **KATY LIED** *ABC ABCL 5094* ...................... | 13 | 6 wks |
| 20 Sep 75 | **CAN'T BUY A THRILL** *ABC ABCL 5024* ............. | 38 | 1 wk |
| 22 May 76 | **ROYAL SCAM** *ABC ABCL 5161* ..................... | 11 | 13 wks |
| 8 Oct 77 | ● **AJA** *ABC ABCL 5225* ........................... | 5 | 10 wks |
| 2 Dec 78 | **GREATEST HITS** *ABC BLD 616* .................... | 41 | 18 wks |
| 29 Nov 80 | **GAUCHO** *MCA MCF 3090* ...................... | 27 | 12 wks |
| 3 Jul 82 | **GOLD** *MCA MCF 3145* ........................... | 44 | 6 wks |
| 26 Oct 85 | **REELIN' IN THE YEARS – THE VERY BEST OF STEELY DAN** *MCA DANTV 1* .......................... | 43 | 5 wks |
| 10 Oct 87 | **DO IT AGAIN – THE VERY BEST OF STEELY DAN** *Telstar STAR 2297* ............................... | 64 | 4 wks |

## Wout STEENHUIS
*Holland, male instrumentalist – guitar*                     7 wks

| | | | | |
|---|---|---|---|---|
| 21 Nov 81 | **HAWAIIAN PARADISE/CHRISTMAS** *Warwick WW 5106* ............................... | 28 | 7 wks |

## Jim STEINMAN  *US, male vocalist*                     24 wks

| | | | | |
|---|---|---|---|---|
| 9 May 81 | ● **BAD FOR GOOD** *Epic EPC 84361* ................... | 7 | 24 wks |

**257**

*S*

## Martin STEPHENSON and the DAINTEES
*UK, male vocal/instrumental group*                     7 wks

| | | | | |
|---|---|---|---|---|
| 17 May 86 | **BOAT TO BOLIVIA** *Kitchenware KWLP 5* .............. | 85 | 3 wks |
| 16 Apr 88 | **GLADSOME, HUMOUR AND BLUE** *Kitchenware KWLP 8* ............................. | 39 | 4 wks |

## STEPPENWOLF  *US, male vocal/instrumental group*                     20 wks

| | | | | |
|---|---|---|---|---|
| 28 Feb 70 | **MONSTER** *Stateside SSL 5021* ...................... | 43 | 4 wks |
| 25 Apr 70 | **STEPPENWOLF** *Stateside SSL 5020* ................. | 59 | 2 wks |
| 4 Jul 70 | **STEPPENWOLF LIVE** *Stateside SSL 5029* ............. | 16 | 14 wks |

## Cat STEVENS  *UK, male vocalist*                     243 wks

| | | | | |
|---|---|---|---|---|
| 25 Mar 67 | ● **MATTHEW AND SON** *Deram SML 1004* .............. | 7 | 16 wks |
| 11 Jul 70 | **MONA BONE JAKON** *Island ILPS 9118* ............. | 63 | 4 wks |
| 28 Nov 70 | **TEA FOR THE TILLERMAN** *Island ILPS 9135* ......... | 20 | 39 wks |
| 2 Oct 71 | ● **TEASER AND THE FIRECAT** *Island ILPS 9154* ........ | 3 | 93 wks |
| 7 Oct 72 | ● **CATCH BULL AT FOUR** *Island ILPS 9206* ........... | 2 | 27 wks |
| 21 Jul 73 | ● **FOREIGNER** *Island ILPS 9240* ................... | 3 | 10 wks |
| 6 Apr 74 | ● **BUDDAH AND THE CHOCOLATE BOX** *Island ILPS 9274* ................................. | 3 | 15 wks |
| 19 Jul 75 | ● **GREATEST HITS** *Island ILPS 9310* ................. | 2 | 24 wks |
| 14 May 77 | **IZITSO** *Island ILPS 9451* ......................... | 18 | 15 wks |

## Ray STEVENS  *US, male vocalist*                     8 wks

| | | | | |
|---|---|---|---|---|
| 26 Sep 70 | **EVERYTHING IS BEAUTIFUL** *CBS 64074* .......... | 62 | 1 wk |
| 13 Sep 75 | **MISTY** *Janus 9109 401* ......................... | 23 | 7 wks |

## Shakin' STEVENS  *UK, male vocalist*  *154 wks*

| | | | | |
|---|---|---|---|---|
| 15 Mar 80 | **TAKE ONE** *Epic EPC 83978* | | 62 | 2 wks |
| 4 Apr 81 | ● **THIS OLE HOUSE** *Epic EPC 84985* | | 2 | 28 wks |
| 8 Aug 81 | **SHAKIN' STEVENS** *Hallmark/Pickwick SHM 3065* | | 34 | 5 wks |
| 19 Sep 81 | ★ **SHAKY** *Epic EPC 10027* | | 1 | 28 wks |
| 9 Oct 82 | ● **GIVE ME YOUR HEART TONIGHT** *Epic EPC 10035* | | 3 | 18 wks |
| 26 Nov 83 | **THE BOP WON'T STOP** *Epic EPC 86301* | | 21 | 27 wks |
| 17 Nov 84 | ● **GREATEST HITS** *Epic EPC 10047* | | 8 | 22 wks |
| 16 Nov 85 | **LIPSTICK POWDER AND PAINT** *Epic EPC 26646* | | 37 | 9 wks |
| 31 Oct 87 | **LET'S BOOGIE** *Epic 460 126–1* | | 59 | 7 wks |
| 19 Nov 88 | **A WHOLE LOTTA SHAKY** *Epic MOOD 5* | | 42 | 8 wks |

## Al STEWART  *UK, male vocalist*  *20 wks*

| | | | | |
|---|---|---|---|---|
| 11 Apr 70 | **ZERO SHE FLIES** *CBS 63848* | | 40 | 4 wks |
| 5 Feb 77 | **YEAR OF THE CAT** *RCA RS 1082* | | 38 | 7 wks |
| 21 Oct 78 | **TIME PASSAGES** *RCA PL 25173* | | 39 | 1 wk |
| 6 Sep 80 | **24 CARAT** *RCA PL 25306* | | 55 | 6 wks |
| 9 Jun 84 | **RUSSIANS AND AMERICANS** *RCA PL 70307* | | 83 | 2 wks |

## Andy STEWART  *UK, male vocalist*  *2 wks*

| | | | | |
|---|---|---|---|---|
| 3 Feb 62 | **ANDY STEWART** *Top Rank 35–116* | | 13 | 2 wks |

## Jermaine STEWART  *US, male vocalist*  *12 wks*

| | | | | |
|---|---|---|---|---|
| 4 Oct 86 | **FRANTIC ROMANTIC** *10 DIX 26* | | 49 | 4 wks |
| 5 Mar 88 | **SAY IT AGAIN** *Siren SRNLP 14* | | 32 | 8 wks |

## Rod STEWART  *UK, male vocalist*  *571 wks*

| | | | | |
|---|---|---|---|---|
| 3 Oct 70 | **GASOLINE ALLEY** *Vertigo 6360 500* | | 62 | 1 wk |
| 24 Jul 71 | ★ **EVERY PICTURE TELLS A STORY** *Mercury 6338 063* | | 1 | 81 wks |
| 5 Aug 72 | ★ **NEVER A DULL MOMENT** *Philips 6499 153* | | 1 | 36 wks |
| 25 Aug 73 | ★ **SING IT AGAIN ROD** *Mercury 6499 484* | | 1 | 30 wks |
| 19 Oct 74 | ★ **SMILER** *Mercury 9104 011* | | 1 | 20 wks |
| 30 Aug 75 | ★ **ATLANTIC CROSSING** *Warner Bros. K 56151* | | 1 | 88 wks |
| 3 Jul 76 | ★ **A NIGHT ON THE TOWN** *Riva RVLP 1* | | 1 | 47 wks |
| 16 Jul 77 | **BEST OF ROD STEWART** *Mercury 6643 030* | | 18 | 22 wks |
| 19 Nov 77 | ● **FOOT LOOSE AND FANCY FREE** *Riva RVLP 5* | | 3 | 26 wks |
| 21 Jan 78 | **ATLANTIC CROSSING (re-issue)** *Riva RVLP 4* | | 60 | 1 wk |
| 9 Dec 78 | ● **BLONDES HAVE MORE FUN** *Riva RVLP 8* | | 3 | 31 wks |
| 10 Nov 79 | ★ **GREATEST HITS** *Riva ROD TV 1* | | 1 | 74 wks |
| 22 Nov 80 | ● **FOOLISH BEHAVIOUR** *Riva RVLP 11* | | 4 | 13 wks |
| 14 Nov 81 | ● **TONIGHT I'M YOURS** *Riva RVLP 14* | | 8 | 21 wks |
| 13 Nov 82 | **ABSOLUTELY LIVE** *Riva RVLP 17* | | 35 | 5 wks |
| 18 Jun 83 | ● **BODY WISHES** *Warner Bros. K 923 8771* | | 5 | 27 wks |
| 23 Jun 84 | ● **CAMOUFLAGE** *Warner Bros. 925095* | | 8 | 17 wks |
| 5 Jul 86 | ● **EVERY BEAT OF MY HEART** *Warner Bros. WX 53* | | 5 | 17 wks |
| 4 Jun 88 | **OUT OF ORDER** *Warner Bros. WX 152* | | 11 | 8 wks |
| 25 Nov 89 | ● **THE BEST OF ROD STEWART** *Warner Bros. WX 314* | | 3† | 6 wks |

*See also the Faces. Greatest Hits changed label/number to Warner Bros. K 56744 during its chart run.*

## STIFF LITTLE FINGERS
*UK, male vocal/instrumental group*  *57 wks*

| | | | | |
|---|---|---|---|---|
| 3 Mar 79 | **INFLAMMABLE MATERIAL** *Rough Trade ROUGH 1* | | 14 | 19 wks |
| 15 Mar 80 | ● **NOBODY'S HEROES** *Chrysalis CHR 1270* | | 8 | 10 wks |
| 20 Sep 80 | ● **HANX** *Chrysalis CHR 1300* | | 9 | 5 wks |
| 25 Apr 81 | **GO FOR IT** *Chrysalis CHX 1339* | | 14 | 8 wks |
| 2 Oct 82 | **NOW THEN** *Chrysalis CHR 1400* | | 24 | 6 wks |
| 12 Feb 83 | **ALL THE BEST** *Chrysalis CTY 1414* | | 19 | 9 wks |

**STATUS QUO** had even more hit albums in the 80s than the 70s.

**ROD STEWART** hit the album chart for fifteen successive years, 1970–84. He went on sabbatical in 1985, during which Billy Idol had his first two solo hits. Here Rod shuts Billy's mouth in a Los Angeles restaurant.

## Stephen STILLS  *US, male vocalist*                    *7 wks*

| | | | | |
|---|---|---|---|---|
| 19 Dec 70 | **STEPHEN STILLS** *Atlantic 2401 004* ................ | 30 | 1 wk |
| 14 Aug 71 | **STEPHEN STILLS 2** *Atlantic 2401 013* ............... | 22 | 3 wks |
| 26 Jul 75 | **STILLS** *CBS 69146* ............................. | 31 | 1 wk |
| 29 May 76 | **ILLEGAL STILLS** *CBS 81330* ...................... | 54 | 2 wks |

*See also Crosby, Stills and Nash; Crosby, Stills, Nash and Young; Stills–Young Band; Stephen Stills' Manassas.*

## Stephen STILLS' MANASSAS
*US, male vocal/instrumental group*                    *7 wks*

| | | | | |
|---|---|---|---|---|
| 20 May 72 | **MANASSAS** *Atlantic K 60021* ..................... | 30 | 5 wks |
| 19 May 73 | **DOWN THE ROAD** *Atlantic K 40440* ............... | 33 | 2 wks |

*See also Stephen Stills.*

## STILLS–YOUNG BAND
*US/Canada, male vocal/instrumental group*                    *5 wks*

| | | | | |
|---|---|---|---|---|
| 9 Oct 76 | **LONG MAY YOU RUN** *Reprise K 54081* ............... | 12 | 5 wks |

*See also Stephen Stills; Neil Young.*

## STING  *UK, male vocalist*                    *123 wks*

| | | | | |
|---|---|---|---|---|
| 29 Jun 85 | ● **THE DREAM OF THE BLUE TURTLES** *A&M DREAM 1* ................................. | 3 | 64 wks |
| 28 Jun 86 | **BRING ON THE NIGHT** *A&M BRING 1* ............. | 16 | 12 wks |
| 24 Oct 87 | ★ **NOTHING LIKE THE SUN** *A&M AMA 6402* ......... | 1 | 47 wks |

## STONE ROSES  *UK, male vocal/instrumental group*                    *22 wks*

| | | | | |
|---|---|---|---|---|
| 13 May 89 | **THE STONE ROSES** *Silvertone ORELP 502* ............ | 32† | 22 wks |

## STONE THE CROWS
*UK, female/male vocal/instrumental group*                    *3 wks*

| | | | | |
|---|---|---|---|---|
| 7 Oct 72 | **ONTINUOUS PERFORMANCE** *Polydor 2391 043* ...... | 33 | 3 wks |

**STOOGES** – *See Iggy POP*

**STORYVILLE JAZZMEN** – *See Bob WALLIS and his STORYVILLE JAZZMEN*

## STRANGLERS  *UK, male vocal/instrumental group*                    *165 wks*

| | | | | |
|---|---|---|---|---|
| 30 Apr 77 | ● **STRANGLERS IV (RATTUS NORVEGICUS)** *United Artists UAG 30045* | 4 | 34 wks |
| 8 Oct 77 | ● **NO MORE HEROES** *United Artists UAG 30200* ......... | 2 | 19 wks |
| 3 Jun 78 | ● **BLACK AND WHITE** *United Artists UAK 30222* ......... | 2 | 18 wks |
| 10 Mar 79 | ● **LIVE (X CERT)** *United Artists UAG 30224* .............. | 7 | 10 wks |
| 6 Oct 79 | ● **THE RAVEN** *United Artists UAG 30262* ............... | 4 | 8 wks |
| 21 Feb 81 | ● **THE MENINBLACK** *Liberty LBG 30313* ............... | 8 | 5 wks |
| 21 Nov 81 | **LA FOLIE** *Liberty LBG 30342* ...................... | 11 | 18 wks |
| 25 Sep 82 | **THE COLLECTION 1977–1982** *Liberty LBS 30353* ....... | 12 | 16 wks |
| 22 Jan 83 | ● **FELINE** *Epic EPC 25237* ......................... | 4 | 11 wks |
| 17 Nov 84 | **AURAL SCULPTURE** *Epic EPC 26220* .............. | 14 | 10 wks |
| 20 Sep 86 | **OFF THE BEATEN TRACK** *Liberty LBG 5001* ......... | 80 | 2 wks |
| 8 Nov 86 | **DREAMTIME** *Epic EPC 26648* ................... | 16 | 6 wks |
| 20 Feb 88 | **ALL LIVE AND ALL OF THE NIGHT** *Epic 465259* ...... | 12 | 6 wks |
| 18 Feb 89 | **THE SINGLES** *EMI EM 1314* ...................... | 57 | 2 wks |

## STRAWBERRY SWITCHBLADE
*UK, female vocal duo*                                                   *4 wks*

| | | | | | |
|---|---|---|---|---|---|
| 13 Apr 85 | **STRAWBERRY SWITCHBLADE** | *Korova KODE 11* .... | 25 | 4 wks |

## STRAWBS   *UK, male vocal/instrumental group*                        *31 wks*

| | | | | |
|---|---|---|---|---|
| 21 Nov 70 | **JUST A COLLECTION OF ANTIQUES AND CURIOS** | | | |
| | *A & M AMLS 994* ................................. | 27 | 2 wks |
| 17 Jul 71 | **FROM THE WITCHWOOD** *A & M AMLH 64304* ...... | 39 | 2 wks |
| 26 Feb 72 | **GRAVE NEW WORLD** *A & M AMLH 68078* .......... | 11 | 12 wks |
| 24 Feb 73 | ● **BURSTING AT THE SEAMS** *A & M AMLH 68144* ...... | 2 | 12 wks |
| 27 Apr 74 | **HERO AND HEROINE** *A & M AMLH 63607* .......... | 35 | 3 wks |

## STRAY CATS   *US, male vocal/instrumental group*                     *32 wks*

| | | | | |
|---|---|---|---|---|
| 28 Feb 81 | ● **STRAY CATS** *Arista STRAY 1* ...................... | 6 | 22 wks |
| 21 Nov 81 | **GONNA BALL** *Arista STRAY 2* ...................... | 48 | 4 wks |
| 3 Sep 83 | **RANT 'N' RAVE WITH THE STRAY CATS** | | | |
| | *Arista STRAY 3* ................................. | 51 | 5 wks |
| 8 Apr 89 | **BLAST OFF** *EMI MTL 1040* ...................... | 58 | 1 wk |

## STREETWALKERS   *UK, male vocal/instrumental group*                  *6 wks*

| | | | | |
|---|---|---|---|---|
| 12 Jun 76 | **RED CARD** *Vertigo 9102 010* ...................... | 16 | 6 wks |

## Barbra STREISAND   *US, female vocalist*                              *377 wks*

| | | | | |
|---|---|---|---|---|
| 22 Jan 66 | ● **MY NAME IS BARBRA, TWO** *CBS BPG 62603* ........ | 6 | 22 wks |
| 4 Apr 70 | **GREATEST HITS** *CBS 63921* ...................... | 44 | 2 wks |
| 17 Apr 71 | **STONEY END** *CBS 64269* ...................... | 28 | 2 wks |
| 15 Jun 74 | **THE WAY WE WERE** *CBS 69057* .................. | 49 | 1 wk |
| 23 Jul 77 | **STREISAND SUPERMAN** *CBS 86030* .............. | 32 | 9 wks |
| 15 Jul 78 | **SONGBIRD** *CBS 86060* .......................... | 50 | 1 wk |
| 17 Mar 79 | ★ **BARBRA STREISAND HITS VOL. 2** *CBS 10012* ....... | 1 | 30 wks |
| 17 Nov 79 | **WET** *CBS 86104* .............................. | 25 | 13 wks |
| 11 Oct 80 | ★ **GUILTY** *CBS 86122* ............................. | 1 | 82 wks |
| 16 Jan 82 | ★ **LOVE SONGS** *CBS 10031* ...................... | 1 | 129 wks |
| 19 Nov 83 | **YENTL (original soundtrack)** *CBS 86302* ............ | 21 | 35 wks |
| 27 Oct 84 | **EMOTION** *CBS 86309* .......................... | 15 | 12 wks |
| 18 Jan 86 | ● **THE BROADWAY ALBUM** *CBS 86322* .............. | 3 | 16 wks |
| 30 May 87 | **ONE VOICE** *CBS 450 890–1* ...................... | 27 | 7 wks |
| 3 Dec 88 | **TILL I LOVED YOU** *CBS 462943 1* ................ | 29 | 13 wks |
| 25 Nov 89 | **A COLLECTION – GREATEST HITS ... AND MORE** | | | |
| | *CBS 465845 1* ................................. | 43 | 3 wks |

## STRINGS FOR PLEASURE   *UK, orchestra*                               *1 wk*

| | | | | |
|---|---|---|---|---|
| 4 Dec 71 | **BEST OF BACHARACH** *MFP 1334* .................. | 49 | 1 wk |

## Joe STRUMMER   *UK, male vocalist*                                   *1 wk*

| | | | | |
|---|---|---|---|---|
| 14 Oct 89 | **EARTHQUAKE WEATHER** *Epic 465347 1* ........... | 58 | 1 wk |

## STYLE COUNCIL   *UK, male vocal/instrumental duo*                    *93 wks*

| | | | | |
|---|---|---|---|---|
| 24 Mar 84 | ● **CAFE BLEU** *Polydor TSCLP 1* ...................... | 2 | 38 wks |
| 8 Jun 85 | ★ **OUR FAVOURITE SHOP** *Polydor TSCLP 2* ........... | 1 | 22 wks |
| 17 May 86 | ● **HOME AND ABROAD** *Polydor TSCLP 3* ............ | 8 | 8 wks |
| 14 Feb 87 | ● **THE COST OF LOVING** *Polydor TSCLP 4* ............ | 2 | 7 wks |
| 2 Jul 88 | **CONFESSIONS OF A POP GROUP** *Polydor TSCMC 5* .. | 15 | 3 wks |
| 18 Mar 89 | ● **SINGULAR ADVENTURES OF THE STYLE COUNCIL** | | | |
| | *Polydor TSCTV 1* ................................. | 3 | 15 wks |

## STYLISTICS  *US, male vocal group*                                         *139 wks*

| 24 Aug 74 | **ROCKIN' ROLL BABY**  *Avco 6466 012* ............... | 42 | 3 wks |
| 21 Sep 74 | **LET'S PUT IT ALL TOGETHER**  *Avco 6466 013* ........ | 26 | 14 wks |
| 1 Mar 75 | **FROM THE MOUNTAIN**  *Avco 9109 002* .............. | 36 | 1 wk |
| 5 Apr 75 | ★ **THE BEST OF THE STYLISTICS**  *Avco 9109 003* ....... | 1 | 63 wks |
| 5 Jul 75 | ● **THANK YOU BABY**  *Avco 9109 005* ................. | 5 | 23 wks |
| 6 Dec 75 | **YOU ARE BEAUTIFUL**  *Avco 9109 006* .............. | 26 | 9 wks |
| 12 Jun 76 | **FABULOUS**  *Avco 9109 008* ........................ | 21 | 5 wks |
| 18 Sep 76 | ★ **BEST OF THE STYLISTICS VOL. 2**  *H & L 9109 010* .... | 1 | 21 wks |

## STYX  *US, male vocal/instrumental group*                                   *24 wks*

| 3 Nov 79 | **CORNERSTONE**  *A & M AMLK 63711* .............. | 36 | 8 wks |
| 24 Jan 81 | ● **PARADISE THEATER**  *A & M AMLH 63719* ........... | 8 | 8 wks |
| 12 Mar 83 | **KILROY WAS HERE**  *A & M AMLX 63734* ............ | 67 | 6 wks |
| 5 May 84 | **CAUGHT IN THE ACT**  *A & M AMLM 66704* ......... | 44 | 2 wks |

## SUGARCUBES  *Iceland, male/female vocal/instrumental group*                 *9 wks*

| 7 May 88 | **LIFE'S TOO GOOD**  *One Little Indian TPLP 5* ........... | 14 | 6 wks |
| 14 Oct 89 | **HERE TODAY, TOMORROW, NEXT WEEK** | | |
| | *One Little Indian TPLP 15* .......................... | 15 | 3 wks |

## SUICIDAL TENDENCIES
*UK, male vocal/instrumental group*                                            *1 wk*

| 9 May 87 | **JOIN THE ARMY**  *Virgin V 2424* .................... | 81 | 1 wk |

## Donna SUMMER  *US, female vocalist*                                         *187 wks*

| 31 Jan 76 | **LOVE TO LOVE YOU BABY**  *GTO GTLP 008* ........ | 16 | 9 wks |
| 22 May 76 | **A LOVE TRILOGY**  *GTO GTLP 010* ................. | 41 | 10 wks |
| 25 Jun 77 | ● **I REMEMBER YESTERDAY**  *GTO GTLP 025* ......... | 3 | 23 wks |
| 26 Nov 77 | **ONCE UPON A TIME**  *Casablanca CALD 5003* .......... | 24 | 13 wks |
| 7 Jan 78 | ● **GREATEST HITS**  *GTO GTLP 028* ............... | 4 | 18 wks |
| 21 Oct 78 | **LIVE AND MORE**  *Casablanca CALD 5006* ............. | 16 | 16 wks |
| 2 Jun 79 | **BAD GIRLS**  *Casablanca CALD 5007* ................. | 23 | 23 wks |
| 10 Nov 79 | **ON THE RADIO – GREATEST HITS VOLS. 1 & 2** | | |
| | *Casablanca CALD 5008* .......................... | 24 | 22 wks |
| 1 Nov 80 | **THE WANDERER**  *Geffen K 99124* .................. | 55 | 2 wks |
| 31 Jul 82 | **DONNA SUMMER**  *Warner Bros. K 99163* ............. | 13 | 16 wks |
| 16 Jul 83 | **SHE WORKS HARD FOR THE MONEY** | | |
| | *Mercury MERL 21* ................................. | 28 | 5 wks |
| 15 Sep 84 | **CATS WITHOUT CLAWS**  *Warner Bros. 250806* ........ | 69 | 2 wks |
| 25 Mar 89 | **ANOTHER PLACE AND TIME**  *Warner Bros. WX 219* .... | 17 | 28 wks |

**SUNSHINE BAND** – *See KC and the SUNSHINE BAND*

## SUPERTRAMP  *UK/US, male vocal/instrumental group*                         *170 wks*

| 23 Nov 74 | ● **CRIME OF THE CENTURY**  *A & M AMLS 68258* ....... | 4 | 22 wks |
| 6 Dec 75 | **CRISIS? WHAT CRISIS?**  *A & M AMLH 68347* ......... | 20 | 15 wks |
| 23 Apr 77 | **EVEN IN THE QUIETEST MOMENTS** | | |
| | *A & M AMLK 64634* ............................. | 12 | 22 wks |
| 31 Mar 79 | ● **BREAKFAST IN AMERICA**  *A & M AMLK 63708* ....... | 3 | 53 wks |
| 4 Oct 80 | ● **PARIS**  *A & M AMLM 66702* ..................... | 7 | 17 wks |
| 6 Nov 82 | ● **FAMOUS LAST WORDS**  *A & M AMLK 63732* ......... | 6 | 16 wks |
| 25 May 85 | **BROTHER WHERE YOU BOUND** | | |
| | *A & M AMA 5014* ................................ | 20 | 5 wks |
| 18 Oct 86 | ● **THE AUTOBIOGRAPHY OF SUPERTRAMP** | | |
| | *A & M TRAMP 1* ................................. | 9 | 19 wks |
| 31 Oct 87 | **FREE AS A BIRD**  *A & M AMA 5181* .................. | 93 | 1 wk |

## SUPREMES  *US, female vocal group*  *180 wks*

| | | | | | |
|---|---|---|---|---|---|
| 5 Dec 64 | ● **MEET THE SUPREMES** | *Stateside SL 10109* ............ | **8** | 6 wks |
| 17 Dec 66 | **SUPREMES A GO-GO** | *Tamla Motown STML 11039* ...... | **15** | 21 wks |
| 13 May 67 | **SUPREMES SING MOTOWN** | | | |
| | | *Tamla Motown STML 11047* ........................ | **15** | 16 wks |
| 30 Sep 67 | **SUPREMES SING RODGERS AND HART** | | | |
| | | *Tamla Motown STML 11054* ........................ | **25** | 7 wks |
| 20 Jan 68 | ★ **GREATEST HITS** *Tamla Motown STML 11063* .......... | | **1** | 60 wks |
| 30 Mar 68 | ● **LIVE AT THE TALK OF THE TOWN** | | | |
| | | *Tamla Motown STML 11070* ........................ | **6** | 18 wks |
| 20 Jul 68 | **REFLECTIONS** *Tamla Motown STML 11073* ............ | | **30** | 2 wks |
| 1 Feb 69 | ● **LOVE CHILD** *Tamla Motown STML 11095* .............. | | **8** | 6 wks |
| 25 Sep 71 | **TOUCH** *Tamla Motown STML 11189* .................. | | **40** | 1 wk |
| 17 Sep 77 | ★ **20 GOLDEN GREATS** *Motown EMTV 5* .............. | | **1** | 34 wks |
| 21 Jan 89 | ● **LOVE SUPREME** *Motown ZL 72701* .................. | | **10** | 9 wks |

*See also Diana Ross and the Supremes with the Temptations; Supremes and the Four Tops. 20 Golden Greats and* Love Supreme *credited to Diana Ross and the Supremes.*

## SUPREMES and the FOUR TOPS
*US, female and male vocal groups*  *11 wks*

| | | | | |
|---|---|---|---|---|
| 29 May 71 | ● **MAGNIFICENT SEVEN** *Tamla Motown STML 11179* ..... | **6** | 11 wks |

*See also Supremes; Four Tops.*

## SURVIVOR  *US, male vocal/instrumental group*  *10 wks*

| | | | | |
|---|---|---|---|---|
| 21 Aug 82 | **EYE OF THE TIGER** *Scotti Bros SCT 85845* ............ | **12** | 10 wks |

**Walter SUSSKIND** – *See LONDON PHILHARMONIC CHOIR*

## SUTHERLAND BROTHERS and QUIVER
*UK, male vocal/instrumental group*  *11 wks*

| | | | | |
|---|---|---|---|---|
| 15 May 76 | **REACH FOR THE SKY** *CBS 69191* .................. | **26** | 8 wks |
| 9 Oct 76 | **SLIPSTREAM** *CBS 81593* ........................ | **49** | 3 wks |

## SWANS WAY  *UK, male/female vocal/instrumental group*  *1 wk*

| | | | | |
|---|---|---|---|---|
| 3 Nov 84 | **THE FUGITIVE KIND** *Balgier SWAN 1* .............. | **88** | 1 wk |

## Keith SWEAT  *US, male vocalist*  *21 wks*

| | | | | |
|---|---|---|---|---|
| 16 Jan 88 | **MAKE IT LAST FOREVER** *Elektra 960763 1* ........... | **42** | 21 wks |

## SWEET  *UK, male vocal/instrumental group*  *8 wks*

| | | | | |
|---|---|---|---|---|
| 18 May 74 | **SWEET FANNY ADAMS** *RCA LPI 5038* .............. | **27** | 2 wks |
| 22 Sep 84 | **SWEET 16 – IT'S ... IT'S ... SWEET'S HITS** | | |
| | *Anagram GRAM 16* .............................. | **49** | 6 wks |

## SWINGLE SINGERS  *US/France, male/female vocal group*  *18 wks*

| | | | | |
|---|---|---|---|---|
| 1 Feb 64 | **JAZZ SEBASTIAN BACH** *Philips BL 7572* ............ | **13** | 18 wks |

## SWING OUT SISTER
*UK, male/female vocal/instrumental group*  *32 wks*

| | | | | |
|---|---|---|---|---|
| 23 May 87 | ★ **IT'S BETTER TO TRAVEL** *Mercury OUTLP 1* ......... | **1** | 21 wks |
| 20 May 89 | ● **KALEIDOSCOPE WORLD** *Fontana 838293 1* .......... | **3** | 11 wks |

## SYBIL  *US, female vocalist*                                          *1 wk*

5 Sep 87   **LET YOURSELF GO**  *Champion CHAMP 1009* .........   92   1 wk

## SYLVESTER  *US, male vocalist*                                        *3 wks*

23 Jun 79   **MIGHTY REAL**  *Fantasy FTA 3009* ..................   62   3 wks

## David SYLVIAN  *UK, male vocalist*                                    *21 wks*

7 Jul  84 ● **BRILLIANT TREES**  *Virgin V 2290* ..................    4   14 wks
13 Sep  86   **GONE TO EARTH**  *Virgin VDL 1* ....................   24   5 wks
7 Nov  87   **SECRETS OF THE BEEHIVE**  *Virgin V 2471* ..........   37   2 wks
*See also David Sylvian and Holgar Czukay.*

## David SYLVIAN and Holgar CZUKAY
*UK/Germany, male vocal/instrumental duo*                                *1 wk*

2 Apr 88   **PLIGHT AND PREMONITION**  *Virgin VE 11* ..........   71   1 wk
*See also David Sylvian.*

## SYNTHPHONIC VARIATIONS
*UK, session musicians*                                                  *1 wk*

1 Nov 86   **SEASONS**  *CBS 450 149–1* .........................   84   1 wk

# *t*

## TALK TALK  *UK, male vocal/instrumental group*                        *59 wks*

24 Jul  82   **THE PARTY'S OVER**  *EMI EMC 3431* ...............   21   25 wks
25 Feb  84   **IT'S MY LIFE**  *EMI EMC 2400021* ..................   35   8 wks
1 Mar  86 ● **THE COLOUR OF SPRING**  *EMI EMC 3506* ..........    8   21 wks
24 Sep  88   **SPIRIT OF EDEN**  *Parlophone PCSD 105* ..............   19   5 wks

## TALKING HEADS
*US/UK, male/female vocal/instrumental group*                           *213 wks*

25 Feb  78   **TALKING HEADS '77**  *Sire 9103 328* ..................   60   1 wk
29 Jul  78   **MORE SONGS ABOUT FOOD AND BUILDINGS**
              *Sire K 56531* ......................................   21   3 wks
15 Sep  79   **FEAR OF MUSIC**  *Sire SRK 6076* ...................   33   5 wks
1 Nov  80   **REMAIN IN LIGHT**  *Sire SRK 6095* ...................   21   17 wks
10 Apr  82   **THE NAME OF THIS BAND IS TALKING HEADS**
              *Sire SRK 23590* ....................................   22   5 wks
18 Jun  83   **SPEAKING IN TONGUES**  *Sire K 923 8831* ...........   21   12 wks
27 Oct  84   **STOP MAKING SENSE**  *EMI TAH 1* ................   37   81 wks
29 Jun  85 ● **LITTLE CREATURES**  *EMI TAH 2* ................   10   65 wks
27 Sep  86 ● **TRUE STORIES**  *EMI EU 3511* ....................    7   9 wks
26 Mar  88 ● **NAKED**  *EMI EMD 1005* .........................    3   15 wks

## TANGERINE DREAM
*Germany, male instrumental group*                                      *77 wks*

20 Apr  74   **PHAEDRA**  *Virgin V 2010* ..........................   15   15 wks
5 Apr  75   **RUBYCON**  *Virgin V 2025* .........................   12   14 wks
20 Dec  75   **RICOCHET**  *Virgin V 2044* ........................   40   2 wks
13 Nov  76   **STRATOSFEAR**  *Virgin V 2068* ...................   39   4 wks
23 Jul   77   **SORCERER (film soundtrack)**  *MCA MCF 2806* .......   25   7 wks
19 Nov  77   **ENCORE**  *Virgin VD 2506* .........................   55   1 wk

Bruce Springsteen (left) and **STING** harmonize during the 1988 Amnesty International World Tour.

**DAVID SYLVIAN**, lead singer of Japan, had a brilliant 1984.

Marc Bolan (second from left) of **T. REX** displays the height of flared fashion.

| 1 Apr 78 | CYCLONE  *Virgin V 2097* | 37 | 4 wks |
| 17 Feb 79 | FORCE MAJEURE  *Virgin V 2111* | 26 | 7 wks |
| 7 Jun 80 | TANGRAM  *Virgin V 2147* | 36 | 5 wks |
| 18 Apr 81 | THIEF  *Virgin V 2198* | 43 | 3 wks |
| 19 Sep 81 | EXIT  *Virgin V 2212* | 43 | 5 wks |
| 10 Apr 82 | WHITE EAGLE  *Virgin V 2226* | 57 | 5 wks |
| 5 Nov 83 | HYPERBOREA  *Virgin V 2292* | 45 | 2 wks |
| 10 Nov 84 | POLAND  *Jive Electro HIP 22* | 90 | 1 wk |
| 26 Jul 86 | UNDERWATER SUNLIGHT  *Jive Electro HIP 40* | 97 | 1 wk |
| 27 Jun 87 | TYGER  *Jive Electro HIP 47* | 88 | 1 wk |

## TANK

*UK, male vocal/instrumental group*                                    *5 wks*

| 13 Mar 82 | FILTH HOUNDS OF HADES  *Kamaflage KAMLP 1* | 33 | 5 wks |

## TASTE

*Ireland, male vocal/instrumental group*                               *12 wks*

| 7 Feb 70 | ON THE BOARDS  *Polydor 583–083* | 18 | 11 wks |
| 9 Sep 72 | TASTE LIVE AT THE ISLE OF WIGHT  *Polydor 2383 120* | 41 | 1 wk |

## TAVARES

*US, male vocal group*                                                 *15 wks*

| 21 Aug 76 | SKY HIGH  *Capitol EST 11533* | 22 | 13 wks |
| 1 Apr 78 | THE BEST OF TAVARES  *Capitol EST 11701* | 39 | 2 wks |

## Andy TAYLOR

*UK, male vocalist/instrumentalist – guitar*                           *1 wk*

| 30 May 87 | THUNDER  *MCA MCG 6018* | 61 | 1 wk |

## James TAYLOR

*US, male vocalist*                                                    *111 wks*

| 21 Nov 70 | ● SWEET BABY JAMES  *Warner Bros. ES 1843* | 7 | 53 wks |
| 29 May 71 | ● MUD SLIDE SLIM AND THE BLUE HORIZON  *Warner Bros. WS 2561* | 4 | 41 wks |
| 8 Jan 72 | SWEET BABY JAMES (re-issue)  *Warner Bros. K 46043* | 34 | 6 wks |
| 18 Mar 72 | MUD SLIDE SLIM AND THE BLUE HORIZON (re-issue)  *Warner Bros. K 46085* | 49 | 1 wk |
| 9 Dec 72 | ONE MAN DOG  *Warner Bros. K 46185* | 27 | 5 wks |
| 4 Apr 87 | CLASSIC SONGS  *CBS/WEA JTV 1* | 53 | 5 wks |

## Roger TAYLOR

*UK, male vocalist/instrumentalist – drums*                            *9 wks*

| 18 Apr 81 | FUN IN SPACE  *EMI EMC 3369* | 18 | 5 wks |
| 7 Jul 84 | STRANGE FRONTIER  *EMI RTA 1* | 30 | 4 wks |

## Kiri TE KANAWA

*New Zealand, female vocalist*                                         *37 wks*

| 2 Apr 83 | CHANTS D'AUVERGNE VOL. 1  *Decca SXDL 7604* | 57 | 1 wk |
| 26 Oct 85 | BLUE SKIES  *London KTKT 1* | 40 | 29 wks |
| 13 Dec 86 | CHRISTMAS WITH KIRI  *Decca PROLP 12* | 47 | 4 wks |
| 17 Dec 88 | KIRI  *K-Tel NE 1424* | 70 | 3 wks |

Chants d'Auvergne Vol. 1 *credits the English Chamber Orchestra.* Blue Skies *credits the Nelson Riddle Orchestra.*

## TEARDROP EXPLODES
UK, male vocal/instrumental group                                    *41 wks*

| | | | | |
|---|---|---|---|---|
| 18 Oct 80 | **KILIMANJARO** | Mercury 6359 035 | 24 | 35 wks |
| 5 Dec 81 | **WILDER** | Mercury 6359 056 | 29 | 6 wks |

## TEARS FOR FEARS   UK, male vocal/instrumental duo        *158 wks*

| | | | | |
|---|---|---|---|---|
| 19 Mar 83 | ★ **THE HURTING** | Mercury MERS 17 | 1 | 65 wks |
| 9 Mar 85 | ● **SONGS FROM THE BIG CHAIR** | Mercury MERH 58 | 2 | 80 wks |
| 7 Oct 89 | ★ **THE SEEDS OF LOVE** | Fontana 838730 1 | 1† | 13 wks |

## TELEVISION   US, male vocal/instrumental group           *17 wks*

| | | | | |
|---|---|---|---|---|
| 26 Mar 77 | **MARQUEE MOON** | Elektra K 52046 | 28 | 13 wks |
| 29 Apr 78 | ● **ADVENTURE** | Elektra K 52072 | 7 | 4 wks |

## TEMPERANCE SEVEN   UK, male vocal/instrumental group  10 wks

| | | | | |
|---|---|---|---|---|
| 13 May 61 | **TEMPERANCE SEVEN PLUS ONE** | Argo RG 11 | 19 | 1 wk |
| 25 Nov 61 | **TEMPERANCE SEVEN 1961** | Parlophone PMC 1152 | 11 | 9 wks |

## TEMPLE CHURCH CHOIR
UK, male vocal/instrumental group                                    *3 wks*

| | | | | |
|---|---|---|---|---|
| 16 Dec 61 | ● **CHRISTMAS CAROLS** | HMV CLP 1309 | 8 | 3 wks |

**267**

*t*

## TEMPTATIONS   US, male vocal group                        *99 wks*

| | | | | |
|---|---|---|---|---|
| 24 Dec 66 | **GETTING READY** | Tamla Motown STML 11035 | 40 | 2 wks |
| 11 Feb 67 | **TEMPTATIONS GREATEST HITS** | | | |
| | Tamla Motown STML 11042 | | 26 | 40 wks |
| 22 Jul 67 | **TEMPTATIONS LIVE** | Tamla Motown STML 11053 | 20 | 4 wks |
| 18 Nov 67 | **TEMPTATIONS WITH A LOT OF SOUL** | | | |
| | Tamla Motown STML 11057 | | 19 | 18 wks |
| 20 Sep 69 | **CLOUD NINE** | Tamla Motown STML 11109 | 32 | 1 wk |
| 14 Feb 70 | **PUZZLE PEOPLE** | Tamla Motown STML 11133 | 20 | 4 wks |
| 11 Jul 70 | **PSYCHEDELIC SHACK** | Tamla Motown STML 11147 | 56 | 1 wk |
| 26 Dec 70 | **GREATEST HITS VOL. 2** | Tamla Motown STML 11170 | 35 | 12 wks |
| 29 Apr 72 | **SOLID ROCK** | Tamla Motown STML 11202 | 34 | 2 wks |
| 20 Jan 73 | **ALL DIRECTIONS** | Tamla Motown STML 11218 | 19 | 7 wks |
| 7 Jul 73 | **MASTERPIECE** | Tamla Motown STML 11229 | 28 | 3 wks |
| 8 Dec 84 | **TRULY FOR YOU** | Motown ZL 72342 | 75 | 5 wks |

*See also Diana Ross and the Supremes with the Temptations.*

## 10 C.C.   UK, male vocal/instrumental group              *197 wks*

| | | | | |
|---|---|---|---|---|
| 1 Sep 73 | **10 C.C.** | UK UKAL 1005 | 36 | 5 wks |
| 15 Jun 74 | ● **SHEET MUSIC** | UK UKAL 1007 | 9 | 24 wks |
| 22 Mar 75 | ● **THE ORIGINAL SOUNDTRACK** | Mercury 9102 50Q | 4 | 40 wks |
| 7 Jun 75 | ● **GREATEST HITS OF 10 C.C.** | Decca UKAL 1012 | 9 | 18 wks |
| 31 Jan 76 | ● **HOW DARE YOU?** | Mercury 9102 501 | 5 | 31 wks |
| 14 May 77 | ● **DECEPTIVE BENDS** | Mercury 9102 502 | 3 | 21 wks |
| 10 Dec 77 | **LIVE AND LET LIVE** | Mercury 6641 698 | 14 | 15 wks |
| 23 Sep 78 | ● **BLOODY TOURISTS** | Mercury 9102 503 | 3 | 15 wks |
| 6 Oct 79 | ● **GREATEST HITS 1972–1978** | Mercury 9102 504 | 5 | 21 wks |
| 5 Apr 80 | **LOOK HERE** | Mercury 9102 505 | 35 | 5 wks |
| 15 Oct 83 | **WINDOW IN THE JUNGLE** | Mercury MERL 28 | 70 | 2 wks |

*See also 10 C.C. and Godley and Creme.*

## 10 C.C. and GODLEY AND CREME

*UK, male vocal/instrumental group and instrumental duo*      *18 wks*

29 Aug 87 ● CHANGING FACES – THE VERY BEST OF 10 C.C. AND
           GODLEY AND CREME  *ProTV TGCLP 1* ..........   **4**   18 wks
*See also 10 C.C; Godley and Creme.*

## TEN CITY   *US, male vocal/instrumental group*      *12 wks*

18 Feb 89    FOUNDATION  *Atlantic WX 249* ...................   **22**   12 wks

## TEN POLE TUDOR   *UK, male vocal/instrumental group*      *8 wks*

9 May 81    EDDIE, OLD BOB, DICK & GARRY  *Stiff SEEZ 31* .....   **44**   8 wks

## 10,000 MANIACS   *US, male/female vocal/instrumental group*      *8 wks*

27 May 89    BLIND MAN'S ZOO  *Elektra EKT 57* .................   **18**   8 wks

## TEN YEARS AFTER   *UK, male vocal/instrumental group*      *73 wks*

21 Sep 68    UNDEAD  *Deram SML 1023* ........................   **26**   7 wks
22 Feb 69 ● STONEDHENGE  *Deram SML 1029* .................   **6**   5 wks
4 Oct 69 ● SSSSH  *Deram SML 1052* ...........................   **4**   18 wks
2 May 70 ● CRICKLEWOOD GREEN  *Deram SML 1065* ..........   **4**   27 wks
9 Jan 71 ● WATT  *Deram SML 1078* ...........................   **5**   12 wks
13 Nov 71    SPACE IN TIME  *Chrysalis CHR 1001* .................   **36**   1 wk
7 Oct 72    ROCK AND ROLL  *Chrysalis CHR 1009* .............   **27**   1 wk
28 Jul 73    RECORDED LIVE  *Chrysalis CHR 1049* ..............   **36**   2 wks

TENNILLE – *See CAPTAIN and TENNILLE*

## TERRAPLANE   *UK, male vocal/instrumental group*      *1 wk*

25 Jan 86    BLACK AND WHITE  *Epic EPC 26439* ...............   **74**   1 wk

Tammi TERRELL – *See Marvin GAYE and Tammi TERRELL*

## TESLA   *US, male vocal/instrumental group*      *2 wks*

11 Feb 89    THE GREAT RADIO CONTROVERSY  *Geffen WX 244*   **34**   2 wks

## TESTAMENT   *US, male vocal/instrumental group*      *3 wks*

28 May 88    THE NEW ORDER  *Megaforce 781849 1* ..............   **81**   1 wk
19 Aug 89    PRACTICE WHAT YOU PREACH  *Atlantic WX 297* ....   **40**   2 wks

## TEXAS   *UK, male/female vocal/instrumental group*      *27 wks*

25 Mar 89 ● SOUTHSIDE  *Mercury 838171 1* ....................   **3**   27 wks

## THAT PETROL EMOTION

*UK, male vocal/instrumental group*      *7 wks*

10 May 86    MANIC POP THRILL  *Demon FIEND 70* ..............   **84**   2 wks
23 May 87    BABBLE  *Polydor TPE LP 1* ........................   **30**   3 wks
24 Sep 88    END OF MILLENNIUM PSYCHOSIS BLUES
           *Virgin V 2550* ..................................   **53**   2 wks

## The THE  UK, male vocal/instrumental group                                    46 wks

| 29 Oct 83 | **SOUL MINING**  Some Bizzare EPC 25525 | ............... | 27 | 5 wks |
| 29 Nov 86 | **INFECTED**  Some Bizzare EPC 26770 | ................ | 14 | 30 wks |
| 27 May 89 | ● **MIND BOMB**  Epic 463319 1 | ....................... | 4 | 9 wks |

*Matt Johnson leads The The which is an informal group of his studio guests and friends.*


## THEATRE OF HATE  UK, male vocal/instrumental group                            9 wks

| 13 Mar 82 | **WESTWORLD**  Burning Rome TOH 1 | ............... | 17 | 6 wks |
| 18 Aug 84 | **REVOLUTION**  Burning Rome TOH 2 | ............... | 67 | 3 wks |


## THEN JERICO  UK, male vocal/instrumental group                                24 wks

| 3 Oct 87 | **FIRST (THE SOUND OF MUSIC)**  London LONLP 26 | ... | 35 | 7 wks |
| 4 Mar 89 | ● **THE BIG AREA**  London 828122 1 | .................... | 4 | 17 wks |


## THIN LIZZY
*Ireland/UK/US, male vocal/instrumental group*                                 212 wks

| 27 Sep 75 | **FIGHTING**  Vertigo 6360 121 | ...................... | 60 | 1 wk |
| 10 Apr 76 | ● **JAILBREAK**  Vertigo 9102 008 | ...................... | 10 | 50 wks |
| 6 Nov 76 | **JOHNNY THE FOX**  Vertigo 9102 012 | ................ | 11 | 24 wks |
| 1 Oct 77 | ● **BAD REPUTATION**  Vertigo 9102 016 | ............... | 4 | 9 wks |
| 17 Jun 78 | ● **LIVE AND DANGEROUS**  Vertigo 6641 807 | .......... | 2 | 62 wks |
| 5 May 79 | ● **BLACK ROSE (A ROCK LEGEND)**  Vertigo 9102 032 | .... | 2 | 21 wks |
| 18 Oct 80 | ● **CHINA TOWN**  Vertigo 6359 030 | .................. | 7 | 7 wks |
| 11 Apr 81 | ● **ADVENTURES OF THIN LIZZY**  Vertigo LIZTV 1 | ...... | 6 | 13 wks |
| 5 Dec 81 | **RENEGADE**  Vertigo 6359 083 | ..................... | 38 | 8 wks |
| 12 Mar 83 | ● **THUNDER AND LIGHTNING**  Vertigo VERL 3 | ........ | 4 | 11 wks |
| 26 Nov 83 | **LIFE**  Vertigo VERD 6 | ............................. | 29 | 6 wks |

*See also Phil Lynott and Thin Lizzy.*

## THIRD EAR BAND  UK, male instrumental group                                   2 wks

| 27 Jun 70 | **AIR, EARTH, FIRE, WATER**  Harvest SHVL 773 | ....... | 49 | 2 wks |


## THIRD WORLD  Jamaica, male vocal/instrumental group                           18 wks

| 21 Oct 78 | **JOURNEY TO ADDIS**  Island ILPS 9554 | ............... | 30 | 6 wks |
| 11 Jul 81 | **ROCKS THE WORLD**  CBS 85027 | .................... | 37 | 9 wks |
| 15 May 82 | **YOU'VE GOT THE POWER**  CBS 85563 | ............. | 87 | 3 wks |


## THIS MORTAL COIL
*UK, male/female instrumental group*                                            7 wks

| 20 Oct 84 | **IT'LL END IN TEARS**  4AD CAD 411 | ................ | 38 | 4 wks |
| 11 Oct 86 | **FILIGREE AND SHADOW**  4AD DAD 609 | ........... | 53 | 3 wks |

**Carla THOMAS** – *See Otis REDDING and Carla THOMAS*

**John Hugh THOMAS** – *See Aled JONES*


## Lillo THOMAS  US, male vocalist                                               7 wks

| 2 May 87 | **LILLO**  Capitol EST 2031 | .......................... | 43 | 7 wks |


## Ray THOMAS  UK, male vocalist                                                 3 wks

| 26 Jul 75 | **FROM MIGHTY OAKS**  Threshold THS 16 | ............. | 23 | 3 wks |

## Richard THOMPSON
*UK, male vocalist/instrumentalist – guitar*                                    *4 wks*

| | | | | |
|---|---|---|---|---|
| 27 Apr 85 | **ACROSS A CROWDED ROOM** *Polydor POLD 5175* .... | 80 | 2 wks |
| 18 Oct 86 | **DARING ADVENTURES** *Polydor POLD 5202* ......... | 92 | 1 wk |
| 29 Oct 88 | **AMNESIA** *Capitol EST 2075* ...................... | 89 | 1 wk |

## THOMPSON TWINS
*UK/New Zealand, male/female vocal/instrumental group*                          *120 wks*

| | | | | |
|---|---|---|---|---|
| 13 Mar 82 | **SET** *Tee TELP 2* .................................... | 48 | 3 wks |
| 26 Feb 83 | ● **QUICK STEP AND SIDE KICK** *Arista 204 924* ......... | 2 | 56 wks |
| 25 Feb 84 | ★ **INTO THE GAP** *Arista 205 971* ..................... | 1 | 51 wks |
| 28 Sep 85 | ● **HERE'S TO FUTURE DAYS** *Arista 207 164* ........... | 5 | 9 wks |
| 2 May 87 | **CLOSE TO THE BONE** *Arista 208 143* ................ | 90 | 1 wk |

## George THOROGOOD and the DESTROYERS
*US, male vocal/instrumental group*                                             *1 wk*

| | | | | |
|---|---|---|---|---|
| 2 Dec 78 | **GEORGE THOROGOOD AND THE DESTROYERS** *Sonet SNTF 781* .................................. | 67 | 1 wk |

## THREE DEGREES   *US, female vocal group*                                     *91 wks*

| | | | | |
|---|---|---|---|---|
| 10 Aug 74 | **THREE DEGREES** *Philadelphia International 65858* ........ | 12 | 22 wks |
| 17 May 75 | ● **TAKE GOOD CARE OF YOURSELF** *Philadelphia International PIR 69137* .................... | 6 | 16 wks |
| 24 Feb 79 | **NEW DIMENSIONS** *Ariola ARLH 5012* .............. | 34 | 13 wks |
| 3 Mar 79 | ● **A COLLECTION OF THEIR 20 GREATEST HITS** *Epic EPC 10013* ........................... | 8 | 18 wks |
| 15 Dec 79 | **3D** *Ariola 3D 1* .............................. | 61 | 7 wks |
| 27 Sep 80 | ● **GOLD** *Ariola 3D 2* ........................... | 9 | 15 wks |

## THROWING MUSES
*US/UK, male/female vocal/instrumental group*                                   *1 wk*

| | | | | |
|---|---|---|---|---|
| 4 Feb 89 | **HUNKPAPA** *4AD CAD 901* ...................... | 59 | 1 wk |

**TICH** – *See Dave DEE, DOZY, BEAKY, MICK and TICH*

## TIFFANY   *US, female vocalist*                                              *27 wks*

| | | | | |
|---|---|---|---|---|
| 27 Feb 88 | ● **TIFFANY** *MCA MCF 3415* ..................... | 5 | 21 wks |
| 17 Dec 88 | **HOLD AN OLD FRIEND'S HAND** *MCA MCF 3437* .... | 56 | 6 wks |

## TIGHT FIT   *UK, male/female vocal group*                                    *6 wks*

| | | | | |
|---|---|---|---|---|
| 26 Sep 81 | **BACK TO THE SIXTIES** *Jive HIP 1* ................. | 38 | 4 wks |
| 4 Sep 82 | **TIGHT FIT** *Jive HIP 2* ........................... | 87 | 2 wks |

**TIJUANA BRASS** – *See Herb ALPERT and the TIJUANA BRASS*

## TIK and TOK   *UK, male vocal/instrumental duo*                              *2 wks*

| | | | | |
|---|---|---|---|---|
| 4 Aug 84 | **INTOLERANCE** *Survival SUR LP 008* ............... | 89 | 2 wks |

## Tanita TIKARAM   *UK, female vocalist*                                       *44 wks*

| | | | | |
|---|---|---|---|---|
| 24 Sep 88 | ● **ANCIENT HEART** *WEA WX 210* .................. | 3 | 44 wks |

**TILBROOK** – *See DIFFORD and TILBROOK*

**JAMES TAYLOR** is shown with Carole King, whose song 'You've Got a Friend' was the lead track on his highest-placed LP.

**GEORGE THOROGOOD** and his group the Destroyers had one of America's all-time top fifty juke box favourites, 'Born to Be Bad', but only a one week life in the British album chart.

Opera star **KIRI TE KANAWA** had her greatest chart success with a collection of popular standards.

## TIMBUK THREE
*US, male/female vocal/instrumental duo* 4 *wks*

14 Feb 87 **GREETINGS FROM TIMBUK THREE** *IRS MIRF 1015* . 51 4 wks

## TIN MACHINE *US/UK, male vocal/instrumental group* 9 *wks*

3 Jun 89 ● **TIN MACHINE** *EMI-USA MTLS 1044* .............. 3 9 wks

**TOK** – *See TIK and TOK*

## TOM TOM CLUB
*US, female/male vocal/instrumental group* 1 *wk*

24 Oct 81 **TOM TOM CLUB** *Island ILPS 9686* ................. 78 1 wk

## TOMITA *Japan, male instrumentalist – synthesizer* 33 *wks*

7 Jun 75 **SNOWFLAKES ARE DANCING**
    *RCA Red Seal ARL 1 0488* .......................... 17 20 wks
16 Aug 75 **PICTURES AT AN EXHIBITION**
    *RCA Red Seal ARL 1 0838* .......................... 42 5 wks
7 May 77 **HOLST: THE PLANETS** *RCA Red Seal RL 11919* ....... 41 6 wks
9 Feb 80 **TOMITA'S GREATEST HITS** *RCA Red Seal RL 43076* ... 66 2 wks

## TOPOL *Israel, male vocalist* 1 *wk*

11 May 85 **TOPOL'S ISRAEL** *BBC REH 529* ................... 80 1 wk

## Bernie TORME *UK, male vocalist/instrumentalist – guitar* 3 *wks*

3 Jul 82 **TURN OUT THE LIGHTS** *Kamaflage KAMLP 2* ........ 50 3 wks

## Peter TOSH *Jamaica, male vocalist* 1 *wk*

25 Sep 76 **LEGALIZE IT** *Virgin V 2061* ........................ 54 1 wk

## TOTAL CONTRAST *UK, male vocal/instrumental duo* 3 *wks*

8 Mar 86 **TOTAL CONTRAST** *London LONLP 15* .............. 66 3 wks

## TOTO *US, male vocal/instrumental group* 39 *wks*

31 Mar 79 **TOTO** *CBS 83148* ............................... 37 5 wks
26 Feb 83 ● **TOTO IV** *CBS 85529* ............................ 4 30 wks
17 Nov 84 **ISOLATION** *CBS 86305* .......................... 67 2 wks
20 Sep 86 **FAHRENHEIT** *CBS 57091* ........................ 99 1 wk
9 Apr 88 **THE SEVENTH ONE** *CBS 460465 1* ................ 73 1 wk

## TOURISTS *UK, male/female vocal/instrumental group* 18 *wks*

14 Jul 79 **THE TOURISTS** *Logo GO 1018* .................... 72 1 wk
3 Nov 79 **REALITY EFFECT** *Logo GO 1019* .................. 23 16 wks
22 Nov 80 **LUMINOUS BASEMENT** *RCA RCALP 5001* .......... 75 1 wk

## Pete TOWNSHEND
*UK, male vocalist/instrumentalist – guitar*                                    *25 wks*

| 21 Oct 72 | **WHO CAME FIRST** *Track 2408 201* .................. | 30 | 2 wks |
| 3 May 80 | **EMPTY GLASS** *Atco K 50699* ...................... | 11 | 14 wks |
| 3 Jul 82 | **ALL THE BEST COWBOYS HAVE CHINESE EYES** | | |
| | *Atco K 50889* ................................... | 32 | 8 wks |
| 30 Nov 85 | **WHITE CITY** *Atco 25-2392-1* ...................... | 70 | 1 wk |

*See also Pete Townshend and Ronnie Lane.*

## Pete TOWNSHEND and Ronnie LANE
*UK, male vocal/instrumental duo*                                    *3 wks*

| 15 Oct 77 | **ROUGH MIX** *Polydor 2442 147* ...................... | 44 | 3 wks |

*See also Pete Townshend; Ronnie Lane and the Band Slim Chance.*

## TOYAH  *UK, female vocalist*                                    *97 wks*

| 14 Jun 80 | **THE BLUE MEANING** *Safari IEYA 666* .............. | 40 | 4 wks |
| 17 Jan 81 | **TOYAH TOYAH TOYAH** *Safari LIVE 2* .............. | 22 | 14 wks |
| 30 May 81 ● | **ANTHEM** *Safari VOOR 1* .......................... | 2 | 46 wks |
| 19 Jun 82 ● | **THE CHANGELING** *Safari VOOR 9* ................ | 6 | 12 wks |
| 13 Nov 82 | **WARRIOR ROCK – TOYAH ON TOUR** *Safari TNT 1* | 20 | 6 wks |
| 5 Nov 83 | **LOVE IS THE LAW** *Safari VOOR 10* ............... | 28 | 7 wks |
| 25 Feb 84 | **TOYAH! TOYAH! TOYAH!** *K-Tel NE 1268* .......... | 43 | 4 wks |
| 3 Aug 85 | **MINX** *Portrait PRT 26415* ........................... | 24 | 4 wks |

## TOY DOLLS  *UK, male vocal/instrumental group*                                    *1 wk*

| 25 May 85 | **A FAR OUT DISC** *Volume VOLP 2* .................. | 71 | 1 wk |

## T'PAU  *UK, female/male vocal/instrumental group*                                    *76 wks*

| 26 Sep 87 ★ | **BRIDGE OF SPIES** *Siren SIRENLP 8* ................ | 1 | 59 wks |
| 5 Nov 88 ● | **RAGE** *Siren SRNLP 20* ........................... | 4 | 17 wks |

## TRACIE  *UK, female vocalist*                                    *2 wks*

| 30 Jun 84 | **FAR FROM THE HURTING KIND** *Respond RRL 502* ... | 64 | 2 wks |

## TRAFFIC  *UK, male vocal/instrumental group*                                    *37 wks*

| 30 Dec 67 ● | **MR. FANTASY** *Island ILP 9061* .................. | 8 | 16 wks |
| 26 Oct 68 ● | **TRAFFIC** *Island ILPS 9081 T* ........................ | 9 | 8 wks |
| 8 Aug 70 | **JOHN BARLEYCORN MUST DIE** *Island ILPS 9116* .... | 11 | 9 wks |
| 24 Nov 73 | **ON THE ROAD** *Island ISLD 2* ........................ | 40 | 3 wks |
| 28 Sep 74 | **WHEN THE EAGLE FLIES** *Island ILPS 9273* .......... | 31 | 1 wk |

## TRANSVISION VAMP
*UK, male/female vocal/instrumental group*                                    *56 wks*

| 15 Oct 88 ● | **POP ART** *MCA MCF 3421* ........................ | 4 | 32 wks |
| 8 Jul 89 ★ | **VELVETEEN** *MCA MCG 6050* ...................... | 1 | 24 wks |

## TRAVELING WILBURYS
*US/UK, male vocal/instrumental group*                                    *35 wks*

| 5 Nov 88 | **THE TRAVELING WILBURYS VOLUME 1** | | |
| | *Wilbury WX 224* ................................ | 16 | 35 wks |

## Pat TRAVERS   US, male instrumentalist – guitar     *3 wks*

| 2 Apr 77 | MAKIN' MAGIC   *Polydor 2383 436* .................. | 40 | 3 wks |
|---|---|---|---|

## Randy TRAVIS   US, male vocalist     *2 wks*

| 6 Aug 88 | OLD 8 x 10   *Warner Bros. WX 162* ..................... | 64 | 2 wks |
|---|---|---|---|

## John TRAVOLTA   US, male vocalist     *6 wks*

| 23 Dec 78 | SANDY   *Polydor POLD 5014* ...................... | 40 | 6 wks |
|---|---|---|---|

## TREMELOES   UK, male vocal/instrumental group     *7 wks*

| 3 Jun 67 | HERE COME THE TREMELOES<br>*CBS SBPG 63017* ............................. | 15 | 7 wks |
|---|---|---|---|

## T. REX   UK, male vocal/instrumental group     *200 wks*

| 13 Jul 68 | MY PEOPLE WERE FAIR AND HAD SKY IN THEIR HAIR BUT NOW THEY'RE CONTENT TO WEAR STARS ON THEIR BROWS   *Regal Zonophone SLRZ 1003* ......... | 15 | 9 wks |
|---|---|---|---|
| 7 Jun 69 | UNICORN   *Regal Zonophone S 1007* ................... | 12 | 3 wks |
| 14 Mar 70 | A BEARD OF STARS   *Regal Zonophone SLRZ 1013* ....... | 21 | 6 wks |
| 16 Jan 71 | T. REX   *Fly HIFLY 2* ............................ | 13 | 24 wks |
| 7 Aug 71 | THE BEST OF T. REX   *Flyback TON 2* ............. | 21 | 7 wks |
| 9 Oct 71 | ★ ELECTRIC WARRIOR   *Fly HIFLY 6* ............... | 1 | 44 wks |
| 29 Mar 72 | ★ PROPHETS, SEERS AND SAGES THE ANGELS OF THE AGES/MY PEOPLE WERE FAIR . . .<br>*Fly Doubleback 0037 TOOFA 3/4* | 1 | 12 wks |
| 20 May 72 | ★ BOLAN BOOGIE   *Fly HIFLY 8* .................... | 1 | 19 wks |
| 5 Aug 72 | ● THE SLIDER   *EMI BLN 5001* ................... | 4 | 18 wks |
| 9 Dec 72 | A BEARD OF STARS/UNICORN   *Cube TOOFA 9/10* ... | 44 | 2 wks |
| 31 Mar 73 | ● TANX   *EMI BLN 5002* ..................... | 4 | 12 wks |
| 10 Nov 73 | GREAT HITS   *EMI BLN 5003* ..................... | 32 | 3 wks |
| 16 Mar 74 | ZINC ALLOY AND THE HIDDEN RIDERS OF TOMORROW<br>*EMI BLNA 7751* | 12 | 3 wks |
| 21 Feb 76 | FUTURISTIC DRAGON   *EMI BLN 5004* ............ | 50 | 3 wks |
| 9 Apr 77 | DANDY IN THE UNDERWORLD   *EMI BLN 5005* ..... | 26 | 3 wks |
| 30 Jun 79 | SOLID GOLD   *EMI NUT 5* .................. | 51 | 3 wks |
| 12 Sep 81 | T. REX IN CONCERT   *Marc ABOLAN 1* ............. | 35 | 6 wks |
| 7 Nov 81 | YOU SCARE ME TO DEATH   *Cherry Red ERED 20* ...... | 88 | 1 wk |
| 24 Sep 83 | DANCE IN THE MIDNIGHT   *Marc On Wax MARCL 501* . | 83 | 3 wks |
| 4 May 85 | ● BEST OF THE 20TH CENTURY BOY   *K-Tel NE 1297* ... | 5 | 21 wks |

*Prophets . . ./My People . . . is a double re-issue although* Prophets *had not previously been a hit.* Beard Of Stars/Unicorn *is a double re-issue. The first three albums and the two double re-issues are credited to* Tyrannosaurus Rex. Zinc Alloy . . . *and* Best Of The 20th Century Boy *are credited to Marc Bolan and T. Rex.* You Scare Me To Death *and* Dance In The Midnight *are credited to Marc Bolan.*

## TRIFFIDS   New Zealand, male vocal/instrumental group     *1 wk*

| 22 Apr 89 | THE BLACK SWAN   *Island ILPS 9928* ................ | 63 | 1 wk |
|---|---|---|---|

## TRIUMPH   Canada, male vocal/instrumental group     *8 wks*

| 10 May 80 | PROGRESSIONS OF POWER   *RCA PL 13524* ........ | 61 | 5 wks |
|---|---|---|---|
| 3 Oct 81 | ALLIED FORCES   *RCA RCALP 6002* ................ | 64 | 3 wks |

## TROGGS   UK, male vocal/instrumental group     *32 wks*

| 30 Jul 66 | ● FROM NOWHERE . . . THE TROGGS   *Fontana TL 5355* . | 6 | 16 wks |
|---|---|---|---|
| 25 Feb 67 | ● TROGGLODYNAMITE   *Page One POL 001* ............ | 10 | 11 wks |
| 5 Aug 67 | BEST OF THE TROGGS   *Page One FOR 001* .......... | 24 | 5 wks |

Image conscience Wendy James led **TRANSVISION VAMP** to a velveteen number one debut.

## TROUBADOURS DU ROI BAUDOUIN
*Zaire, male/female vocal group*      *1 wk*

| | | | |
|---|---|---|---|
| 22 May 76 | **MISSA LUBA** *Philips SBL 7592* ..................... | 59 | 1 wk |

## TROUBLE FUNK *US, male vocal/instrumental group*    *4 wks*

| | | | |
|---|---|---|---|
| 8 Nov 86 | **SAY WHAT!** *Fourth & Broadway DCLP 101* ............. | 75 | 2 wks |
| 5 Sep 87 | **TROUBLE OVER HERE, TROUBLE OVER THERE** *Fourth & Broadway BRLP 513* ......................... | 54 | 2 wks |

## Robin TROWER *UK, male instrumentalist – guitar*    *16 wks*

| | | | |
|---|---|---|---|
| 1 Mar 75 | **FOR EARTH BELOW** *Chrysalis CHR 1073* ............. | 26 | 4 wks |
| 13 Mar 76 | **LIVE** *Chrysalis CHR 1089* ......................... | 15 | 6 wks |
| 30 Oct 76 | **LONG MISTY DAYS** *Chrysalis CHR 1107* ............. | 31 | 1 wk |
| 29 Oct 77 | **IN CITY DREAMS** *Chrysalis CHR 1148* ............... | 58 | 1 wk |
| 16 Feb 80 | **VICTIMS OF THE FURY** *Chrysalis CHR 1215* .......... | 61 | 4 wks |

## TUBES *US, male vocal/instrumental group*    *7 wks*

| | | | |
|---|---|---|---|
| 4 Mar 78 | **WHAT DO YOU WANT FROM LIFE** *A & M AMS 68460* | 38 | 1 wk |
| 2 Jun 79 | **REMOTE CONTROL** *A & M AMLH 64751* ............ | 40 | 5 wks |
| 4 Jun 83 | **OUTSIDE INSIDE** *Capitol EST 12260* ................. | 77 | 1 wk |

**TUBEWAY ARMY** – *See Gary Numan*

## Ike and Tina TURNER
*US, male instrumentalist – guitar and female vocalist*    *1 wk*

| | | | |
|---|---|---|---|
| 1 Oct 66 | **RIVER DEEP – MOUNTAIN HIGH** *London HAU 8298* | 27 | 1 wk |

*See also Tina Turner.*

## Ruby TURNER *UK, female vocalist*    *17 wks*

| | | | |
|---|---|---|---|
| 18 Oct 86 | **WOMEN HOLD UP HALF THE SKY** *Jive HIP 36* ...... | 47 | 11 wks |
| 8 Oct 88 | **THE MOTOWN SONGBOOK** *Jive HIP 58* ............ | 22 | 6 wks |

## Tina TURNER *US, female vocalist*    *222 wks*

| | | | |
|---|---|---|---|
| 30 Jun 84 | ● **PRIVATE DANCER** *Capitol TINA 1* ................. | 2 | 146 wks |
| 20 Sep 86 | ● **BREAK EVERY RULE** *Capitol EST 2018* ............. | 2 | 49 wks |
| 2 Apr 88 | ● **LIVE IN EUROPE** *Capitol ESTD 1* .................. | 8 | 13 wks |
| 30 Sep 89 | ★ **FOREIGN AFFAIR** *Caiptol ESTU 2103* ............... | 1† | 14 wks |

*See also Ike and Tina Turner.*

## TURTLES *US, male vocal/instrumental group*    *9 wks*

| | | | |
|---|---|---|---|
| 22 Jul 67 | **HAPPY TOGETHER** *London HAU 8330* ............. | 18 | 9 wks |

## TWELFTH NIGHT *UK, male vocal/instrumental group*    *2 wks*

| | | | |
|---|---|---|---|
| 27 Oct 84 | **ART AND ILLUSION** *Music For Nations MFN 36* | 83 | 2 wks |

## TWIGGY *UK, female vocalist*    *11 wks*

| | | | |
|---|---|---|---|
| 21 Aug 76 | **TWIGGY** *Mercury 9102 600* ........................ | 33 | 8 wks |
| 30 Apr 77 | **PLEASE GET MY NAME RIGHT** *Mercury 9102 601* ..... | 35 | 3 wks |

## TWISTED SISTER  *US, male vocal/instrumental group*  20 wks

| | | | | |
|---|---|---|---|---|
| 25 Sep 82 | **UNDER THE BLADE** *Secret SECX 9* | | 70 | 3 wks |
| 7 May 83 | **YOU CAN'T STOP ROCK 'N' ROLL** *Atlantic A 0074* | | 14 | 9 wks |
| 16 Jun 84 | **STAY HUNGRY** *Atlantic 780156* | | 34 | 5 wks |
| 14 Dec 85 | **COME OUT AND PLAY** *Atlantic 78-1275-1* | | 95 | 1 wk |
| 25 Jul 87 | **LOVE IS FOR SUCKERS** *Atlantic WX 120* | | 57 | 2 wks |

**Tommy TYCHO** – *See David GRAY and Tommy TYCHO*

## TYGERS OF PAN TANG
*UK, male vocal/instrumental group*  20 wks

| | | | | |
|---|---|---|---|---|
| 30 Aug 80 | **WILD CAT** *MCA MCF 3075* | | 18 | 5 wks |
| 18 Apr 81 | **SPELLBOUND** *MCA MCF 3104* | | 33 | 4 wks |
| 21 Nov 81 | **CRAZY NIGHTS** *MCA MCF 3123* | | 51 | 3 wks |
| 28 Aug 82 | **THE CAGE** *MCA MCF 3150* | | 13 | 8 wks |

## Bonnie TYLER  *UK, female vocalist*  75 wks

| | | | | |
|---|---|---|---|---|
| 16 Apr 83 | ★ **FASTER THAN THE SPEED OF NIGHT** | | | |
| | *CBS 25304* | | 1 | 45 wks |
| 17 May 86 | **SECRET DREAMS AND FORBIDDEN FIRE** | | | |
| | *CBS 86319* | | 24 | 12 wks |
| 29 Nov 86 | **THE GREATEST HITS** *Telstar STAR 2291* | | 24 | 17 wks |
| 21 May 88 | **HIDE YOUR HEART** *CBS 460125 1* | | 78 | 1 wk |

## Judie TZUKE  *UK, female vocalist*  61 wks

| | | | | |
|---|---|---|---|---|
| 4 Aug 79 | **WELCOME TO THE CRUISE** *Rocket TRAIN 7* | | 14 | 17 wks |
| 10 May 80 | ● **SPORTS CAR** *Rocket TRAIN 9* | | 7 | 11 wks |
| 16 May 81 | **I AM PHOENIX** *Rocket TRAIN 15* | | 17 | 10 wks |
| 17 Apr 82 | **SHOOT THE MOON** *Chrysalis CDL 1382* | | 19 | 10 wks |
| 30 Oct 82 | **ROAD NOISE – THE OFFICIAL BOOTLEG** | | | |
| | *Chrysalis CTY 1405* | | 39 | 4 wks |
| 1 Oct 83 | **RITMO** *Chrysalis CDL 1442* | | 26 | 5 wks |
| 15 Jun 85 | **THE CAT IS OUT** *Legacy LLP 102* | | 35 | 3 wks |
| 29 Apr 89 | **TURNING STONES** *Polydor 839087 1* | | 57 | 1 wk |

# *U*

## UB 40  *UK, male vocal/instrumental group*  331 wks

| | | | | |
|---|---|---|---|---|
| 6 Sep 80 | ● **SIGNING OFF** *Graduate GRAD LP 2* | | 2 | 71 wks |
| 6 Jun 81 | ● **PRESENT ARMS** *DEP International LP DEP 1* | | 2 | 38 wks |
| 10 Oct 81 | **PRESENT ARMS IN DUB** | | | |
| | *DEP International LPS DEP 2* | | 38 | 7 wks |
| 28 Aug 82 | **THE SINGLES ALBUM** *Graduate GRADLSP 3* | | 17 | 8 wks |
| 9 Oct 82 | ● **UB 44** *DEP International LP DEP 3* | | 4 | 8 wks |
| 26 Feb 83 | **UB 40 LIVE** *DEP International LP DEP 4* | | 44 | 5 wks |
| 24 Sep 83 | ★ **LABOUR OF LOVE** *DEP International LP DEP 5* | | 1 | 76 wks |
| 20 Oct 84 | ● **GEFFREY MORGAN** *DEP International DEP 6* | | 3 | 14 wks |
| 14 Sep 85 | **BAGGARADDIM** *DEP International LP DEP 10* | | 14 | 23 wks |
| 9 Aug 86 | ● **RAT IN THE KITCHEN** *DEP International LP DEP 11* | | 8 | 20 wks |
| 7 Nov 87 | ● **THE BEST OF UB 40 VOL. 1** *Virgin UBTV 1* | | 3 | 45 wks |
| 23 Jul 88 | **UB40** *DEP International LPDEP 13* | | 12 | 12 wks |
| 9 Dec 89 | ● **LABOUR OF LOVE II** *DEP International LPDEP 14* | | 9† | 4 wks |

## UFO  UK, male vocal/instrumental group                                   48 wks

| | | | | |
|---|---|---|---|---|
| 4 Jun 77 | **LIGHTS OUT** *Chrysalis CHR 1127* | | 54 | 2 wks |
| 15 Jul 78 | **OBSESSION** *Chrysalis CDL 1182* | | 26 | 7 wks |
| 10 Feb 79 | ● **STRANGERS IN THE NIGHT** *Chrysalis CJT 5* | | 8 | 11 wks |
| 19 Jan 80 | **NO PLACE TO RUN** *Chrysalis CDL 1239* | | 11 | 7 wks |
| 24 Jan 81 | **THE WILD THE WILLING AND THE INNOCENT** *Chrysalis CHR 1307* | | 19 | 5 wks |
| 20 Feb 82 | ● **MECHANIX** *Chrysalis CHR 1360* | | 8 | 6 wks |
| 12 Feb 83 | **MAKING CONTACT** *Chrysalis CHR 1402* | | 32 | 4 wks |
| 3 Sep 83 | **HEADSTONE – THE BEST OF UFO** *Chrysalis CTY 1437* | | 39 | 4 wks |
| 16 Nov 85 | **MISDEMEANOUR** *Chrysalis CHR 1518* | | 74 | 2 wks |

## U.K.  UK, male vocal/instrumental group                                   3 wks

| | | | | |
|---|---|---|---|---|
| 27 May 78 | **U.K.** *Polydor 2302 080* | | 43 | 3 wks |

## U.K. SUBS  UK, male vocal/instrumental group                             26 wks

| | | | | |
|---|---|---|---|---|
| 13 Oct 79 | **ANOTHER KIND OF BLUES** *Gem GEMLP 100* | | 21 | 6 wks |
| 19 Apr 80 | **BRAND NEW AGE** *Gem GEMLP 106* | | 18 | 9 wks |
| 27 Sep 80 | ● **CRASH COURSE** *Gem GEMLP 111* | | 8 | 6 wks |
| 21 Feb 81 | **DIMINISHED RESPONSIBILITY** *Gem GEMLP 112* | | 18 | 5 wks |

## Tracey ULLMAN  UK, female vocalist                                       22 wks

| | | | | |
|---|---|---|---|---|
| 3 Dec 83 | **YOU BROKE MY HEART IN 17 PLACES** *Stiff SEEZ 51* | | 14 | 20 wks |
| 8 Dec 84 | **YOU CAUGHT ME OUT** *Stiff SEEZ 56* | | 92 | 2 wks |

## ULTRAVOX  UK/Canada, male vocal/instrumental group                      225 wks

| | | | | |
|---|---|---|---|---|
| 19 Jul 80 | ● **VIENNA** *Chrysalis CHR 1296* | | 3 | 72 wks |
| 19 Sep 81 | ● **RAGE IN EDEN** *Chrysalis CDL 1338* | | 4 | 23 wks |
| 23 Oct 82 | ● **QUARTET** *Chrysalis CDL 1394* | | 6 | 30 wks |
| 22 Oct 83 | ● **MONUMENT – THE SOUNDTRACK** *Chrysalis CUX 1452* | | 9 | 15 wks |
| 14 Apr 84 | ● **LAMENT** *Chrysalis CDL 1459* | | 8 | 26 wks |
| 10 Nov 84 | ● **THE COLLECTION** *Chrysalis UTV 1* | | 2 | 53 wks |
| 25 Oct 86 | ● **U-VOX** *Chrysalis CDL 1545* | | 9 | 6 wks |

## UNDERTONES  UK, male vocal/instrumental group                           47 wks

| | | | | |
|---|---|---|---|---|
| 19 May 79 | **THE UNDERTONES** *Sire SRK 6071* | | 13 | 21 wks |
| 26 Apr 80 | ● **HYPNOTISED** *Sire SRK 6088* | | 6 | 10 wks |
| 16 May 81 | **POSITIVE TOUCH** *Ardeck ARD 103* | | 17 | 6 wks |
| 19 Mar 83 | **THE SIN OF PRIDE** *Ardeck ARD 104* | | 43 | 5 wks |
| 10 Dec 83 | **ALL WRAPPED UP** *Ardeck ARD 1654281/3* | | 67 | 4 wks |
| 14 Jun 86 | **CHER O'BOWLIES: PICK OF UNDERTONES** *Ardeck EMS 1172* | | 96 | 1 wk |

**UNION GAP** – *See Gary PUCKETT and the UNION GAP*

## UNTOUCHABLES  US, male vocal/instrumental group                          7 wks

| | | | | |
|---|---|---|---|---|
| 13 Jul 85 | **WILD CHILD** *Stiff SEEZ 57* | | 51 | 7 wks |

## Midge URE  UK, male vocalist                                             18 wks

| | | | | |
|---|---|---|---|---|
| 19 Oct 85 | ● **THE GIFT** *Chrysalis CHR 1508* | | 2 | 15 wks |
| 10 Sep 88 | **ANSWERS TO NOTHING** *Chrysalis CHR 1649* | | 30 | 3 wks |

## URIAH HEEP   UK, male vocal/instrumental group

51 wks

| | | | |
|---|---|---|---|
| 13 Nov 71 | **LOOK AT YOURSELF**   *Island ILPS 9169* .............. | 39 | 1 wk |
| 10 Jun  72 | **DEMONS AND WIZARDS**   *Bronze ILPS 9193* .......... | 20 | 11 wks |
| 2 Dec 72 | **THE MAGICIAN'S BIRTHDAY**   *Bronze ILPS 9213* ...... | 28 | 3 wks |
| 19 May 73 | **LIVE**   *Island ISLD 1* ............................ | 23 | 8 wks |
| 29 Sep 73 | **SWEET FREEDOM**   *Island ILPS 9245* ................ | 18 | 3 wks |
| 29 Jun 74 | **WONDERWORLD**   *Bronze ILPS 9280* .............. | 23 | 3 wks |
| 5 Jul  75 ● | **RETURN TO FANTASY**   *Bronze ILPS 9335* .......... | 7 | 6 wks |
| 12 Jun 76 | **HIGH AND MIGHTY**   *Island ILPS 9384* ........... | 55 | 1 wk |
| 22 Mar 80 | **CONQUEST**   *Bronze BRON 524* ................... | 37 | 3 wks |
| 17 Apr 82 | **ABOMINOG**   *Bronze BRON 538* ................... | 34 | 6 wks |
| 18 Jun 83 | **HEAD FIRST**   *Bronze BRON 545* ................... | 46 | 4 wks |
| 6 Apr 85 | **EQUATOR**   *Portrait PRT 261414* .................... | 79 | 2 wks |

## USA FOR AFRICA
*US, male/female vocal/instrumental group*

5 wks

| | | | |
|---|---|---|---|
| 25 May 85 | **WE ARE THE WORLD**   *CBS USAID F1* .............. | 31 | 5 wks |

*This album contains tracks by various artists in addition to the title track.*

## U.T.F.O.   *US, male vocal group*

1 wk

| | | | |
|---|---|---|---|
| 16 Mar 85 | **ROXANNE ROXANNE (6 track version)**   *Streetwave 6 TRACK X KHAN 506* .................. | 72 | 1 wk |

## UTOPIA   *UK, male vocal/instrumental group*

3 wks

| | | | |
|---|---|---|---|
| 1 Oct 77 | **OOPS SORRY WRONG PLANET**   *Bearsville K 53517* ... | 59 | 1 wk |
| 16 Feb 80 | **ADVENTURES IN UTOPIA**   *Island ILPS 9602* ......... | 57 | 2 wks |

## U 2   *Ireland, male vocal/instrumental group*

720 wks

| | | | |
|---|---|---|---|
| 29 Aug 81 | **BOY**   *Island ILPS 9646* ............................ | 52 | 31 wks |
| 24 Oct 81 | **OCTOBER**   *Island ILPS 9680* ...................... | 11 | 41 wks |
| 12 Mar 83 ★ | **WAR**   *Island ILPS 9733* ......................... | 1 | 143 wks |
| 3 Dec 83 ● | **U2 LIVE: UNDER A BLOOD RED SKY**   *Island IMA 3* ... | 2 | 201 wks |
| 13 Oct 84 ★ | **THE UNFORGETTABLE FIRE**   *Island U2 5* .......... | 1 | 127 wks |
| 27 Jul  85 | **WIDE AWAKE IN AMERICA**   (import)   *Island 902791A* ... | 11 | 16 wks |
| 21 Mar 87 ★ | **THE JOSHUA TREE**   *Island U2 6* ................... | 1 | 113 wks |
| 20 Feb 88 | **THE JOSHUA TREE SINGLES**   *Island U2 PK 1* ........ | 100 | 1 wk |
| 22 Oct 88 ★ | **RATTLE AND HUM**   *Island U2 7* ................... | 1 | 47 wks |

# *v*

Frankie **VALLI** – *See FOUR SEASONS*

## VAN DE GRAAFF GENERATOR
*UK, male vocal/instrumental group*

2 wks

| | | | |
|---|---|---|---|
| 25 Apr 70 | **THE LEAST WE CAN DO IS WAVE TO EACH OTHER**   *Charisma CAS 1007* .................................. | 47 | 2 wks |

## VAN HALEN   *US/Holland, male vocal/instrumental group*

87 wks

| | | | |
|---|---|---|---|
| 27 May 78 | **VAN HALEN**   *Warner Bros. K 56470* .................. | 34 | 11 wks |
| 14 Apr 79 | **VAN HALEN II**   *Warner Bros. K 566116* ................ | 23 | 7 wks |

**MIDGE URE** shows his gift of a good set of teeth.

**LUTHER VANDROSS** got his body busy losing weight shortly after this photo was taken.

Bono of **U2** shows the desire to perform despite injury.

| | | | |
|---|---|---|---|
| 5 Apr 80 | **WOMEN AND CHILDREN FIRST** *Warner Bros. K 56793* | 15 | 7 wks |
| 23 May 81 | **FAIR WARNING** *Warner Bros. K 56899* | 49 | 4 wks |
| 1 May 82 | **DIVER DOWN** *Warner Bros. K 57003* | 36 | 5 wks |
| 4 Feb 84 | **1984** *Warner Bros. 92–3985* | 15 | 23 wks |
| 5 Apr 86 | **5150** *Warner Bros. WS 5150* | 16 | 18 wks |
| 4 Jun 88 | **OU812** *Warner Bros. WX 177* | 16 | 12 wks |

## Luther VANDROSS *US, male vocalist* — 197 wks

| | | | |
|---|---|---|---|
| 21 Jan 84 | **BUSY BODY** *Epic EPC 25608* | 42 | 8 wks |
| 6 Apr 85 | **THE NIGHT I FELL IN LOVE** *Epic EPC 26387* | 19 | 10 wks |
| 1 Nov 86 ● | **GIVE ME THE REASON** *Epic EPC 450134–1* | 3 | 99 wks |
| 21 Feb 87 | **NEVER TOO MUCH** *Epic EPC 32807* | 41 | 30 wks |
| 4 Jul 87 | **FOREVER, FOR ALWAYS, FOR LOVE** *Epic EPC 25013* | 23 | 16 wks |
| 16 Apr 88 | **BUSY BODY (re-issue)** *Epic 460183 1* | 78 | 4 wks |
| 29 Oct 88 ● | **ANY LOVE** *Epic 462908 1* | 3 | 22 wks |
| 11 Nov 89 | **BEST OF LUTHER VANDROSS – BEST OF LOVE** *Epic 465801 1* | 14† | 8 wks |

## VANGELIS *Greece, male instrumentalist – keyboards* — 139 wks

| | | | |
|---|---|---|---|
| 10 Jan 76 | **HEAVEN AND HELL** *RCA Victor RS 1025* | 31 | 7 wks |
| 9 Oct 76 | **ALBEDO 0.39** *RCA Victor RS 1080* | 18 | 6 wks |
| 18 Apr 81 ● | **CHARIOTS OF FIRE (film soundtrack)** *Polydor POLS 1026* | 5 | 97 wks |
| 5 May 84 | **CHARIOTS OF FIRE (re-issue)** *Polydor POLD 5160* | 39 | 10 wks |
| 13 Oct 84 | **SOIL FESTIVITIES** *Polydor POLH 11* | 55 | 4 wks |
| 30 Mar 85 | **MASK** *Polydor POLH 19* | 69 | 2 wks |
| 22 Jul 89 | **THEMES** *Polydor VGTV 1* | 11 | 13 wks |

*See also Jon and Vangelis.*

## VANILLA FUDGE *US, male vocal/instrumental group* — 3 wks

| | | | |
|---|---|---|---|
| 4 Nov 67 | **VANILLA FUDGE** *Atlantic 588–086* | 31 | 3 wks |

## VAPORS *UK, male vocal/instrumental group* — 6 wks

| | | | |
|---|---|---|---|
| 7 Jun 80 | **NEW CLEAR DAYS** *United Artists UAG 30300* | 44 | 6 wks |

## VARDIS *UK, male vocal/instrumental group* — 1 wk

| | | | |
|---|---|---|---|
| 1 Nov 80 | **100 MPH** *Logo MOGO 4012* | 52 | 1 wk |

## Frankie VAUGHAN *UK, male vocalist* — 20 wks

| | | | |
|---|---|---|---|
| 5 Sep 59 ● | **FRANKIE VAUGHAN AT THE LONDON PALLADIUM** *Philips BDL 7330* | 6 | 2 wks |
| 4 Nov 67 | **FRANKIE VAUGHAN SONGBOOK** *Philips DBL 001* | 40 | 1 wk |
| 25 Nov 67 | **THERE MUST BE A WAY** *Columbia SCX 6200* | 22 | 8 wks |
| 12 Nov 77 | **100 GOLDEN GREATS** *Ronco RTDX 2021* | 24 | 9 wks |

## Sarah VAUGHAN *US, female vocalist* — 1 wk

| | | | |
|---|---|---|---|
| 20 Mar 60 | **NO COUNT – SARAH** *Mercury MMC 14021* | 19 | 1 wk |

## Stevie Ray VAUGHAN and DOUBLE TROUBLE
*US, male vocal/instrumental group* — 1 wk

| | | | |
|---|---|---|---|
| 15 Jul 89 | **IN STEP** *Epic 463395 1* | 63 | 1 wk |

## Bobby VEE  *US, male vocalist*                                    46 wks

| 24 Feb | 62 | ● **TAKE GOOD CARE OF MY BABY**  *London HAG 2428* ... | 7 | 8 wks |
|---|---|---|---|---|
| 31 Mar | 62 | **HITS OF THE ROCKIN' 50'S**  *London HAG 2406* ........ | 20 | 1 wk |
| 12 Jan | 63 | ● **A BOBBY VEE RECORDING SESSION**  *Liberty LBY 1084* | 10 | 11 wks |
| 20 Apr | 63 | ● **BOBBY VEE'S GOLDEN GREATS**  *Liberty LBY 1112* ... | 10 | 14 wks |
| 5 Oct | 63 | **THE NIGHT HAS A THOUSAND EYES**  *Liberty LIB 1139* | 15 | 2 wks |
| 19 Apr | 80 | ● **THE BOBBY VEE SINGLES ALBUM** | | |
| | | *United Artists UAG 30253* ......................... | 5 | 10 wks |

*See also Bobby Vee and the Crickets.*


## Bobby VEE and the CRICKETS
*US, male vocalist and male vocal/instrumental group*              27 wks

| 27 Oct | 62 | ● **BOBBY VEE MEETS THE CRICKETS**  *Liberty LBY 1086* . | 2 | 27 wks |
|---|---|---|---|---|

*See also Bobby Vee; Crickets.*


## Suzanne VEGA  *US, female vocalist*                              110 wks

| 19 Oct | 85 | **SUZANNE VEGA**  *A & M AMA 5072* ................. | 11 | 71 wks |
|---|---|---|---|---|
| 9 May | 87 | ● **SOLITUDE STANDING**  *A & M SUZLP 2* ............. | 2 | 39 wks |


## Rosie VELA  *US, female vocalist*                                 11 wks

| 31 Jan | 87 | **ZAZU**  *A & M AMA 5016* ........................... | 20 | 11 wks |
|---|---|---|---|---|

## VELVET UNDERGROUND
*US, male/female vocal/instrumental group*                          4 wks

| 23 Feb | 85 | **V.U.**  *Polydor POLD 5167* ........................... | 47 | 4 wks |
|---|---|---|---|---|


## VENOM  *UK, male vocal/instrumental group* '                      2 wks

| 21 Apr | 84 | **AT WAR WITH SATAN**  *Neat NEAT 1015* ............. | 64 | 1 wk |
|---|---|---|---|---|
| 13 Apr | 85 | **POSSESSED**  *Neat NEAT 1024* ...................... | 99 | 1 wk |


## Anthony VENTURA ORCHESTRA
*Switzerland, orchestra*                                             4 wks

| 20 Jan | 79 | **DREAM LOVER**  *Lotus WH 5007* .................... | 44 | 4 wks |
|---|---|---|---|---|


## Tom VERLAINE  *US, male vocalist*                                 1 wk

| 14 Mar | 87 | **FLASH LIGHT**  *Fontana SFLP 1* ..................... | 99 | 1 wk |
|---|---|---|---|---|


## VIBRATORS  *UK, male vocal/instrumental group*                    7 wks

| 25 Jun | 77 | **THE VIBRATORS**  *Epic EPC 82907* ................. | 49 | 5 wks |
|---|---|---|---|---|
| 29 Apr | 78 | **V2**  *Epic EPC 82495* .............................. | 33 | 2 wks |


## VICE SQUAD  *UK, male/female vocal/instrumental group*           10 wks

| 24 Oct | 81 | **NO CAUSE FOR CONCERN**  *Zonophone ZEM 103* ...... | 32 | 5 wks |
|---|---|---|---|---|
| 22 May | 82 | **STAND STRONG STAND PROUD**  *Zonophone ZEM 104* | 47 | 5 wks |

## Sid VICIOUS  *UK, male vocalist*  8 wks

| 15 Dec 79 | **SID SINGS** *Virgin V 2144* .......................... | 30 | 8 wks |

**VIENNA PHILHARMONIC ORCHESTRA** – *See Aram KHATCHATURIAN/VIENNA PHILHARMONIC ORCHESTRA*

# VIENNA SYMPHONY ORCHESTRA
*Austria, orchestra*  4 wks

| 4 Apr 87 | **SYMPHONIC ROCK WITH THE VIENNA SYMPHONY ORCHESTRA** *Stylus SMR 730* ................... | 43 | 4 wks |

## VILLAGE PEOPLE  *US, male vocal group*  28 wks

| 27 Jan 79 | **CRUISIN'** *Mercury 9109 614* ...................... | 24 | 9 wks |
| 12 May 79 | **GO WEST** *Mercury 9109 621* ...................... | 14 | 19 wks |

## Gene VINCENT  *US, male vocalist*  2 wks

| 16 Jul 60 | **CRAZY TIMES** *Capitol T 1342* ..................... | 12 | 2 wks |

## Vinnie VINCENT  *US, male vocalist/instrumentalist – guitar*  2 wks

| 28 May 88 | **ALL SYSTEMS GO** *Chrysalis CHR 1626* .............. | 51 | 2 wks |

## VIOLENT FEMMES
*US, male/female vocal/instrumental group*  1 wk

| 1 Mar 86 | **THE BLIND LEADING THE NAKED** *Slash SLAP 10* ... | 81 | 1 wk |

## VIOLINSKI  *UK, male instrumental group*  1 wk

| 26 May 79 | **NO CAUSE FOR ALARM** *Jet JETLU 219* ............ | 49 | 1 wk |

## VISAGE  *UK, male vocal/instrumental group*  58 wks

| 24 Jan 81 | **VISAGE** *Polydor 2490 157* ......................... | 13 | 29 wks |
| 3 Apr 82 | ● **THE ANVIL** *Polydor POLD 5050* ................... | 6 | 16 wks |
| 19 Nov 83 | **FADE TO GREY – THE SINGLES COLLECTION** *Polydor POLD 5117* ......................... | 38 | 11 wks |
| 3 Nov 84 | **BEAT BOY** *Polydor POLH 12* ...................... | 79 | 2 wks |

## VIXEN  *US, female vocal/instrumental group*  1 wk

| 8 Oct 88 | **VIXEN** *Manhattan MTL 1028* ....................... | 66 | 1 wk |

# VOICE OF THE BEEHIVE
*UK/US, male/female vocal/instrumental group*  13 wks

| 2 Jul 88 | **LET IT BEE** *London LONLP 57* ..................... | 13 | 13 wks |

## Herbert VON KARAJAN  *Germany, male orchestra leader*  7 wks

| 26 Sep 70 | **BEETHOVEN TRIPLE CONCERTO** *HMV ASD 2582* .. | 51 | 2 wks |
| 16 Apr 88 | **THE ESSENTIAL KARAJAN** *Deutsche Grammophon HVKTV 1* ..................... | 51 | 5 wks |

*On the Beethoven concerto, the soloists were David Oistrakh (violin), Mstislav Rostropovich (cello) and Sviatoslav Richter (piano), with the Bertlin Philharmonic Orchestra – Germany, orchestra.*

## VOW WOW  *Japan/US, male vocal/instrumental group*  *1 wk*

18 Mar 89    **HELTER SKELTER**   *Arista 209691* ....................   **75**   1 wk

---

## VOYAGE  *UK/France, disco aggregation*  *1 wk*

9 Sep 78    **VOYAGE**   *GTO GTLP 030* ........................   **59**   1 wk

---

# *W*

**WAH!** – *See MIGHTY WAH!*

---

## John WAITE  *UK, male vocalist*  *3 wks*

10 Nov 84    **NO BREAKS**   *EMI America WAIT 1* ...................   **64**   3 wks

## Tom WAITS  *US, male vocalist*  *14 wks*

8 Oct 83    **SWORDFISHTROMBONE**   *Island ILPS 9762* .........   **62**   3 wks
19 Oct 85    **RAIN DOGS**   *Island ILPS 9803* ......................   **29**   5 wks
5 Sep 87    **FRANK'S WILD YEARS**   *Island ITW 3* ...............   **20**   5 wks
8 Oct 88    **BIG TIME**   *Island ITW 4* ..........................   **84**   1 wk

**WAILERS** – *See Bob MARLEY and the WAILERS*

---

## Rick WAKEMAN  *UK, male instrumentalist – keyboards*  *123 wks*

24 Feb 73 ● **THE SIX WIVES OF HENRY VIII**
     *A&M AMLH 64361* ............................   **7**   22 wks
18 May 74 ★ **JOURNEY TO THE CENTRE OF THE EARTH**
     *A&M AMLH 63621* .............................   **1**   30 wks
12 Apr 75 ● **THE MYTHS AND LEGENDS OF KING ARTHUR AND**
     **THE KNIGHTS OF THE ROUND TABLE**
     *A&M AMLH 64515 0022* ......................   **2**   28 wks
24 Apr 76 ● **NO EARTHLY CONNECTION**   *A&M AMLK 64583* ....   **9**   9 wks
12 Feb 77    **WHITE ROCK**   *A&M AMLH 64614* .................   **14**   9 wks
3 Dec 77    **CRIMINAL RECORD**   *A&M AMLK 64660* ...........   **25**   5 wks
2 Jun 79    **RHAPSODIES**   *A&M AMLX 68508* .................   **25**   10 wks
27 Jun 81    **1984**   *Charisma CDS 4022* ......................   **24**   9 wks
16 May 87    **THE GOSPELS**   *Stylus SMR 729* ....................   **94**   1 wk

*See also Kevin Peek and Rick Wakeman; Anderson Bruford Wakeman Howe.*

---

## Scott WALKER  *US, male vocalist*  *44 wks*

16 Sep 67 ● **SCOTT**   *Philips SBL 7816* ..........................   **3**   17 wks
20 Apr 68 ★ **SCOTT 2**   *Philips SBL 7840* ......................   **1**   18 wks
5 Apr 69 ● **SCOTT 3**   *Philips S 7882* ......................   **3**   4 wks
5 Jul 69 ● **SONGS FROM HIS TV SERIES**   *Philips SBL 7900* .......   **7**   3 wks
31 Mar 84    **CLIMATE OF HUNTER**   *Virgin V 2303* ..............   **60**   2 wks

*See also Walker Brothers.*

## WALKER BROTHERS  US, male vocal group    96 wks

| | | | | |
|---|---|---|---|---|
| 18 Dec 65 | ● **TAKE IT EASY**  Philips BL 7691 ...................... | **3** | 36 wks |
| 3 Sep 66 | ● **PORTRAIT**  Philips BL 7691 ........................ | **3** | 23 wks |
| 18 Mar 67 | ● **IMAGES**  Philips SBL 7770 ......................... | **6** | 15 wks |
| 16 Sep 67 | ● **WALKER BROTHERS' STORY**  Philips DBL 002 ...... | **9** | 19 wks |
| 21 Feb 76 | **NO REGRETS**  GTO GTLP 007 .................... | **49** | 3 wks |

*See also Scott Walker.*

## Bob WALLIS and his STORYVILLE JAZZMEN
*UK, male vocal/instrumental group*    1 wk

| | | | |
|---|---|---|---|
| 11 Jun 60 | **EVERYBODY LOVES SATURDAY NIGHT**  Top Rank BUY 023 ............................... | **20** | 1 wk |

## Joe WALSH  US, male vocalist    20 wks

| | | | |
|---|---|---|---|
| 17 Apr 76 | **YOU CAN'T ARGUE WITH A SICK MIND**  Anchor ABCL 5156 ............................... | **28** | 3 wks |
| 10 Jan 78 | **BUT SERIOUSLY FOLKS**  Asylum K 53081 ............ | **16** | 17 wks |

## WANG CHUNG  UK, male vocal/instrumental group    5 wks

| | | | |
|---|---|---|---|
| 21 Apr 84 | **POINTS ON THE CURVE**  Geffen GEF 25589 .......... | **34** | 5 wks |

**WAR** – *See Eric BURDON and WAR*

## Clifford T. WARD  UK, male vocalist    5 wks

| | | | |
|---|---|---|---|
| 21 Jul 73 | **HOME THOUGHTS**  Charisma CAS 1066 ............. | **40** | 3 wks |
| 16 Feb 74 | **MANTLE PIECES**  Charisma CAS 1077 ............... | **42** | 2 wks |

## Michael WARD  UK, male vocalist    3 wks

| | | | |
|---|---|---|---|
| 5 Jan 74 | **INTRODUCING MICHAEL WARD**  Philips 6308 189 ... | **26** | 3 wks |

## WARLOCK  Germany, male/female vocal/instrumental group    2 wks

| | | | |
|---|---|---|---|
| 14 Nov 87 | **TRIUMPH AND AGONY**  Vertigo VERH 50 ............ | **54** | 2 wks |

## Jennifer WARNES  US, female vocalist    12 wks

| | | | |
|---|---|---|---|
| 18 Jul 87 | **FAMOUS BLUE RAINCOAT**  RCA PL 90048 .......... | **33** | 12 wks |

## Dionne WARWICK  US, female vocalist    131 wks

| | | | |
|---|---|---|---|
| 23 May 64 | **PRESENTING DIONNE WARWICK**  Pye NPL 28037 .. | **14** | 10 wks |
| 7 May 66 | ● **BEST OF DIONNE WARWICK**  Pye NPL 28078 ........ | **8** | 11 wks |
| 4 Feb 67 | **HERE WHERE THERE IS LOVE**  Pye NPL 28096 ...... | **39** | 2 wks |
| 18 May 68 | ● **VALLEY OF THE DOLLS**  Pye NSPL 28114 ......... | **10** | 13 wks |
| 23 May 70 | **GREATEST HITS VOL. 1**  Wand WNS 1 ............. | **31** | 26 wks |
| 6 Jun 70 | **GREATEST HITS VOL. 2**  Wand WNS 2 ............. | **28** | 14 wks |
| 30 Oct 82 | ● **HEARTBREAKER**  Arista 204 974 .................. | **3** | 33 wks |
| 21 May 83 | **THE COLLECTION**  Arista DIONE 1 ................ | **11** | 17 wks |
| 29 Oct 83 | **SO AMAZING**  Arista 205 755 ...................... | **60** | 3 wks |
| 23 Feb 85 | **WITHOUT YOUR LOVE**  Arista 206 571 ............. | **86** | 2 wks |

*See also Stevie Wonder.*

**VANGELIS** had the top instrumental soundtrack of the 80s.

Blackie Lawless of **W.A.S.P.**, whose acronym stands for We Are Sexual Perverts.

Everybody loved **BOB WALLIS AND HIS STORYVILLE JAZZMEN** for one Saturday night.

## WAS (NOT WAS) *US, male vocal/instrumental group*      *6 wks*

| | | | |
|---|---|---|---|
| 9 Apr 88 | **WHAT UP DOG?** *Fontana SFLP 4* .................... | **47** | 6 wks |

## Geno WASHINGTON *UK, male vocalist*      *51 wks*

| | | | |
|---|---|---|---|
| 10 Dec 66 | ● **HAND CLAPPIN' – FOOT STOMPIN' – FUNKY BUTT –** | | |
| | **LIVE!** *Piccadilly NPL 38026* ...................... | **5** | 38 wks |
| 23 Sep 67 | ● **HIPSTERS, FLIPSTERS, AND FINGER POPPIN'** | | |
| | **DADDIES** *Piccadilly NSPL 38032* .................. | **8** | 13 wks |

## Grover WASHINGTON Jr
*US, male instrumentalist – saxophone*      *10 wks*

| | | | |
|---|---|---|---|
| 9 May 81 | **WINELIGHT** *Elektra K 52262* ...................... | **34** | 9 wks |
| 19 Dec 81 | **COME MORNING** *Elektra K 52337* .................. | **98** | 1 wk |

## W.A.S.P. *US, male vocal/instrumental group*      *20 wks*

| | | | |
|---|---|---|---|
| 8 Sep 84 | **W.A.S.P.** *Capitol EJ 2401951* ........................ | **51** | 2 wks |
| 9 Nov 85 | **THE LAST COMMAND** *Capitol WASP 2* ............. | **48** | 1 wk |
| 8 Nov 86 | **INSIDE THE ELECTRIC CIRCUS** *Capitol EST 2025* .... | **53** | 3 wks |
| 26 Sep 87 | **LIVE IN THE RAW** *Capitol EST 2040* ............... | **23** | 4 wks |
| 15 Apr 89 | ● **THE HEADLESS CHILDREN** *Capitol EST 2087* ....... | **8** | 10 wks |

## WATERBOYS *UK, male vocal/instrumental group*      *37 wks*

| | | | |
|---|---|---|---|
| 16 Jun 84 | **A PAGAN PLACE** *Ensign ENCL 3* ................... | **100** | 1 wk |
| 28 Sep 85 | **THIS IS THE SEA** *Ensign ENCL 5* ................... | **37** | 17 wks |
| 29 Oct 88 | **FISHERMAN'S BLUES** *Ensign CHEN 5* ............. | **13** | 19 wks |

## WATERFRONT *UK, male vocal/instrumental duo*      *3 wks*

| | | | |
|---|---|---|---|
| 12 Aug 89 | **WATERFRONT** *Polydor 837970 1* ................... | **45** | 3 wks |

## Roger WATERS *UK, male vocalist/instrumentalist – bass*      *18 wks*

| | | | |
|---|---|---|---|
| 12 May 84 | **THE PROS AND CONS OF HITCH-HIKING** | | |
| | *Harvest SHVL 240105* ............................... | **13** | 11 wks |
| 27 Jun 87 | **RADIO K.A.O.S.** *EMI KAOS 1* ...................... | **25** | 7 wks |

## Jody WATLEY *US, female vocalist*      *4 wks*

| | | | |
|---|---|---|---|
| 5 Sep 87 | **JODY WATLEY** *MCA MCG 6024* ................... | **62** | 2 wks |
| 27 May 89 | **LARGER THAN LIFE** *MCA MCG 6044* ............. | **39** | 2 wks |

**WAVES** – *See KATRINA and the WAVES*

## WAX *UK/US, male vocal/instrumental duo*      *3 wks*

| | | | |
|---|---|---|---|
| 12 Sep 87 | **AMERICAN ENGLISH** *RCA PL 71430* .............. | **59** | 3 wks |

## Jeff WAYNE *US/UK, orchestra and cast*      *230 wks*

| | | | |
|---|---|---|---|
| 1 Jul 78 | ● **WAR OF THE WORLD** *CBS 96000* ................. | **5†** | 230 wks |

*This album featured various artists but is commonly credited to Jeff Wayne, its creator and producer. See also Kevin Peek and Rick Wakeman.*

## WAYSTED  *UK, male vocal/instrumental group*  *5 wks*

| 8 Oct 83 | **VICES**  Chrysalis CHR 1438 | 78 | 3 wks |
| 22 Sep 84 | **WAYSTED**  Music For Nations MFN 31 | 73 | 2 wks |

## WEATHER PROPHETS
*UK, male vocal/instrumental group*  *2 wks*

| 9 May 87 | **MAYFLOWER**  Elevation ELV 1 | 67 | 2 wks |

## WEATHER REPORT  *US, male instrumental group*  *12 wks*

| 23 Apr 77 | **HEAVY WEATHER**  CBS 81775 | 43 | 6 wks |
| 11 Nov 78 | **MR. GONE**  CBS 82775 | 47 | 3 wks |
| 27 Feb 82 | **WEATHER REPORT**  CBS 85326 | 88 | 2 wks |
| 24 Mar 84 | **DOMINO THEORY**  CBS 25839 | 54 | 1 wk |

## Marti WEBB  *UK, female vocalist*  *32 wks*

| 16 Feb 80 | ● **TELL ME ON A SUNDAY**  Polydor POLD 5031 | 2 | 23 wks |
| 28 Sep 85 | **ENCORE**  Starblend BLEND 1 | 55 | 4 wks |
| 6 Dec 86 | **ALWAYS THERE**  BBC REB 619 | 65 | 5 wks |

**Ben WEBSTER** – *See Gerry MULLIGAN and Ben WEBSTER*

## WEDDING PRESENT
*UK, male vocal/instrumental group*  *11 wks*

| 24 Oct 87 | **GEORGE BEST**  Reception LEEDS 001 | 47 | 2 wks |
| 23 Jul 88 | **TOMMY**  Reception LEEDS 2 | 42 | 3 wks |
| 29 Apr 89 | **UKRAINSKI VISTUIP V JOHNA PEELA** RCA PL 74104 | 22 | 3 wks |
| 4 Nov 89 | **BIZZARO**  RCA PL 74302 | 22 | 3 wks |

## WEE PAPA GIRL RAPPERS
*UK, female vocal duo*  *3 wks*

| 5 Nov 88 | **THE BEAT, THE RHYME AND THE NOISE**  Jive HIP 67 | 39 | 3 wks |

## Bert WEEDON  *UK, male instrumentalist – guitar*  *26 wks*

| 16 Jul 60 | **KING SIZE GUITAR**  Top Rank BUY 026 | 18 | 1 wk |
| 23 Oct 76 | ★ **22 GOLDEN GUITAR GREATS**  Warwick WW 5019 | 1 | 25 wks |

**WELCH** – *See MARVIN, WELCH and FARRAR*

## WENDY and LISA  *US, female vocal duo*  *4 wks*

| 10 Oct 87 | **WENDY AND LISA**  Virgin V 2444 | 84 | 2 wks |
| 28 Mar 89 | **FRUIT AT THE BOTTOM**  Virgin V 2580 | 45 | 2 wks |

## WESTWORLD
*UK/US, male/female vocal/instrumental group*  *2 wks*

| 5 Sep 87 | **WHERE THE ACTION IS**  RCA PL 71429 | 49 | 2 wks |

## WET WET WET  *UK, male vocal/instrumental group*    *92 wks*

| | | | | |
|---|---|---|---|---|
| 3 Oct 87 | ★ **POPPED IN SOULED OUT**  *Precious  JWWWL 1* ........ | **1** | 71 wks |
| 19 Nov 88 | ● **THE MEMPHIS SESSIONS**  *Precious  JWWWL 2* ......... | **3** | 13 wks |
| 11 Nov 89 | ● **HOLDING BACK THE RIVER**  *Precious  842011 1* ....... | **2†** | 8 wks |

## WE'VE GOT A FUZZBOX AND WE'RE GONNA USE IT
*UK, female vocal/instrumental group*    *6 wks*

| | | | | |
|---|---|---|---|---|
| 26 Aug 89 | ● **BIG BANG**  *WEA  WX 282* ......................... | **5** | 6 wks |

## WHAM!  *UK, male/female vocal/instrumental duo*    *233 wks*

| | | | | |
|---|---|---|---|---|
| 9 Jul 83 | ★ **FANTASTIC**  *Inner Vision  IVL 25328* ................... | **1** | 116 wks |
| 17 Nov 84 | ★ **MAKE IT BIG**  *Epic  EPC 86311* ...................... | **1** | 72 wks |
| 19 Jul 86 | ● **THE FINAL**  *Epic  EPC 88681* ...................... | **2** | 45 wks |

## WHISPERS  *US, male vocal group*    *9 wks*

| | | | | |
|---|---|---|---|---|
| 14 Mar 81 | **IMAGINATION**  *Solar  SOLA 7* ..................... | **42** | 5 wks |
| 6 Jun 87 | **JUST GETS BETTER WITH TIME**  *Solar  MCF 3381* ..... | **63** | 4 wks |

## Alan WHITE  *UK, male instrumentalist – drums*    *4 wks*

| | | | | |
|---|---|---|---|---|
| 13 Mar 76 | **RAMSHACKLED**  *Atlantic  K 50217* .................. | **41** | 4 wks |

## Barry WHITE  *US, male vocalist*    *136 wks*

| | | | | |
|---|---|---|---|---|
| 9 Mar 74 | **STONE GON'**  *Pye  NSPL 28186* ..................... | **18** | 17 wks |
| 6 Apr 74 | **RHAPSODY IN WHITE**  *Pye  NSPL 28191* ............. | **50** | 1 wk |
| 2 Nov 74 | ● **CAN'T GET ENOUGH**  *20th Century  BT 444* ............ | **4** | 34 wks |
| 26 Apr 75 | **JUST ANOTHER WAY TO SAY I LOVE YOU**  *20th Century  BT 466* .............................. | **12** | 15 wks |
| 22 Nov 75 | **GREATEST HITS**  *20th Century  BTH 8000* ............. | **18** | 12 wks |
| 21 Feb 76 | **LET THE MUSIC PLAY**  *20th Century  BT 502* .......... | **22** | 14 wks |
| 9 Apr 77 | **BARRY WHITE'S GREATEST HITS VOL. 2**  *20th Century  BTH 8001* ........................... | **17** | 7 wks |
| 10 Feb 79 | **THE MAN**  *20th Century  BT 571* ................... | **46** | 4 wks |
| 21 Dec 85 | **HEART AND SOUL**  *K-Tel  NE 1316* ................. | **34** | 10 wks |
| 17 Oct 87 | **THE RIGHT NIGHT AND BARRY WHITE**  *Breakout  AMA 5154* .............................. | **74** | 6 wks |
| 2 Jul 88 | ● **THE COLLECTION**  *Mercury  BWTV 1* ............... | **5** | 16 wks |

## Karyn WHITE  *US, female vocalist*    *27 wks*

| | | | | |
|---|---|---|---|---|
| 11 Mar 89 | **KARYN WHITE**  *Warner Bros.  WX 235* ................ | **20** | 27 wks |

## Snowy WHITE  *UK, male vocalist/instrumentalist – guitar*    *5 wks*

| | | | | |
|---|---|---|---|---|
| 11 Feb 84 | **WHITE FLAMES**  *Towerbell  TOWLP 3* ................ | **21** | 4 wks |
| 9 Feb 85 | **SNOWY WHITE**  *Towerbell  TOWLP 8* ................ | **88** | 1 wk |

## Tony Joe WHITE  *US, male vocalist*    *1 wk*

| | | | | |
|---|---|---|---|---|
| 26 Sep 70 | **TONY JOE**  *CBS  63800* ......................... | **63** | 1 wk |

## WHITE LION  US, male vocal/instrumental group — 1 wk

| | | | | | |
|---|---|---|---|---|---|
| 1 Jul | 89 | **BIG GAME** *Atlantic WX 277* ........................ | **47** | 1 wk |

## WHITESNAKE  UK, male vocal/instrumental group — 141 wks

| | | | | | |
|---|---|---|---|---|---|
| 18 Nov | 78 | **TROUBLE** *EMI International INS 3022* ................. | **50** | 2 wks |
| 13 Oct | 79 | **LOVE HUNTER** *United Artists UAG 30264* ............. | **29** | 7 wks |
| 7 Jun | 80 | ● **READY AND WILLING** *United Artists UAG 30302* ...... | **6** | 15 wks |
| 8 Nov | 80 | ● **LIVE IN THE HEART OF THE CITY** *United Artists SNAKE 1* ........................... | **5** | 15 wks |
| 18 Apr | 81 | ● **COME AND GET IT** *Liberty LBG 30327* .............. | **2** | 23 wks |
| 27 Nov | 82 | ● **SAINTS 'N' SINNERS** *Liberty LBG 30354* ............ | **9** | 9 wks |
| 11 Feb | 84 | ● **SLIDE IT IN** *Liberty LBG 2400001* ................... | **9** | 7 wks |
| 11 Apr | 87 | ● **WHITESNAKE 1987** *EMI EMC 3528* ................ | **8** | 57 wks |
| 25 Nov | 89 | ● **SLIP OF THE TONGUE** *EMI EMD 1013* ............. | **10†** | 6 wks |

## Slim WHITMAN  US, male vocalist — 59 wks

| | | | | | |
|---|---|---|---|---|---|
| 14 Dec | 74 | **HAPPY ANNIVERSARY** *United Artists UAS 29670* ...... | **44** | 2 wks |
| 31 Jan | 76 | ★ **THE VERY BEST OF SLIM WHITMAN** *United Artists UAS 29898* ........................ | **1** | 17 wks |
| 15 Jan | 77 | ★ **RED RIVER VALLEY** *United Artists UAS 29993* | **1** | 14 wks |
| 15 Oct | 77 | ● **HOME ON THE RANGE** *United Artists UATV 30102* ..... | **2** | 13 wks |
| 13 Jan | 79 | **GHOST RIDERS IN THE SKY** *United Artists UATV 30202* | **27** | 6 wks |
| 22 Dec | 79 | **SLIM WHITMAN'S 20 GREATEST LOVE SONGS** *United Artists UAG 30270* ........................ | **18** | 7 wks |

## Roger WHITTAKER  Kenya, male vocalist — 110 wks

| | | | | | |
|---|---|---|---|---|---|
| 28 Jun | 70 | **I DON'T BELIEVE IN IF ANYMORE** *Columbia SCX 6404* ........................... | **23** | 1 wk |
| 3 Apr | 71 | **NEW WORLD IN THE MORNING** *Columbia SCX 6456* . | **45** | 2 wks |
| 6 Sep | 75 | ● **THE VERY BEST OF ROGER WHITTAKER** *Columbia SCX 6560* ........................... | **5** | 42 wks |
| 15 May | 76 | **THE SECOND ALBUM OF THE VERY BEST OF ROGER WHITTAKER** *EMI EMC 3117* ................... | **27** | 7 wks |
| 9 Dec | 78 | **ROGER WHITTAKER SINGS THE HITS** *Columbia SCX 6601* ........................ | **52** | 5 wks |
| 4 Aug | 79 | **20 ALL TIME GREATS** *Polydor POLTV 8* ............. | **24** | 9 wks |
| 7 Feb | 81 | **THE ROGER WHITTAKER ALBUM** *K-Tel NE 1105* ... | **18** | 14 wks |
| 27 Dec | 86 | **SKYE BOAT SONG AND OTHER GREAT SONGS** *Tembo TMB 113* ........................ | **89** | 1 wk |
| 23 May | 87 | **HIS FINEST COLLECTION** *Tembo RWTV 1* ........... | **15** | 19 wks |
| 23 Sep | 89 | **HOME LOVIN' MAN** *Tembo RWTV 2* ................. | **20** | 10 wks |

## WHO  UK, male vocal/instrumental group — 202 wks

| | | | | | |
|---|---|---|---|---|---|
| 25 Dec | 65 | ● **MY GENERATION** *Brunswick LAT 8616* ............. | **5** | 11 wks |
| 17 Dec | 66 | ● **A QUICK ONE** *Reaction 593-002* ..................... | **4** | 17 wks |
| 13 Jan | 68 | **THE WHO SELL-OUT** *Track 613-002* ................. | **13** | 11 wks |
| 7 Jun | 69 | ● **TOMMY** *Track 613-013/4* .......................... | **2** | 9 wks |
| 6 Jun | 70 | ● **LIVE AT LEEDS** *Track 2406-001* ................... | **3** | 21 wks |
| 11 Sep | 71 | ★ **WHO'S NEXT** *Track 2408-102* ...................... | **1** | 13 wks |
| 18 Dec | 71 | ● **MEATY, BEATY, BIG AND BOUNCY** *Track 2406-006* .. | **9** | 8 wks |
| 17 Nov | 73 | ● **QUADROPHENIA** *Track 2647-013* ................. | **2** | 13 wks |
| 26 Oct | 74 | ● **ODDS AND SODS** *Track 2406-116* ................. | **10** | 4 wks |
| 23 Aug | 75 | **TOMMY (film soundtrack version)** *Track 2657-007* ...... | **30** | 2 wks |
| 18 Oct | 75 | ● **THE WHO BY NUMBERS** *Polydor 2490-129* .......... | **7** | 6 wks |
| 9 Oct | 76 | ● **THE STORY OF THE WHO** *Polydor 2683-069* .......... | **2** | 18 wks |
| 9 Sep | 78 | ● **WHO ARE YOU** *Polydor WHOD 5004* ............. | **6** | 9 wks |
| 30 Jun | 79 | **THE KIDS ARE ALRIGHT** *Polydor 2675 174* ............. | **26** | 13 wks |
| 25 Oct | 80 | **MY GENERATION (re-issue)** *Virgin V 2179* ............. | **20** | 7 wks |
| 28 Mar | 81 | ● **FACE DANCES** *Polydor WHOD 5037* ................. | **2** | 9 wks |
| 11 Sep | 82 | **IT'S HARD** *Polydor WHOD 5066* ................. | **11** | 6 wks |
| 17 Nov | 84 | **WHO'S LAST** *MCA WHO 1* ...................... | **48** | 4 wks |

**WET WET WET** popped into the charts in 1987.

**THE WHO** are shown shortly before the death of drummer Keith Moon (left) in 1978.

| | | | |
|---|---|---|---|
| 12 Oct 85 | **THE WHO COLLECTION** *Impression IMDP 4* .......... | **44** | 6 wks |
| 19 Mar 88 | ● **WHO'S BETTER WHO'S BEST** *Polydor WTV 1* ........ | **10** | 11 wks |
| 19 Nov 88 | **THE WHO COLLECTION** *Stylus SMR 570* ............ | **71** | 4 wks |

*The two albums titled* The Who Collection *are different.*

## Jane WIEDLIN   *US, female vocalist*                           *3 wks*

| | | | |
|---|---|---|---|
| 24 Sep 88 | **FUR** *Manhattan MTL 1029* ......................... | **48** | 3 wks |

## WILD HORSES   *UK, male vocal/instrumental group*             *4 wks*

| | | | |
|---|---|---|---|
| 26 Apr 80 | **WILD HORSES** *EMI EMC 3324* ................... | **38** | 4 wks |

## Eugene WILDE   *US, male vocalist*                            *4 wks*

| | | | |
|---|---|---|---|
| 8 Dec 84 | **EUGENE WILDE** *Fourth & Broadway BRLP 502* ......... | **67** | 4 wks |

## Kim WILDE   *UK, female vocalist*                             *75 wks*

| | | | |
|---|---|---|---|
| 11 Jul 81 | ● **KIM WILDE** *RAK SRAK 544* .................... | **3** | 14 wks |
| 22 May 82 | **SELECT** *RAK SRAK 548* ...................... | **19** | 11 wks |
| 26 Nov 83 | **CATCH AS CATCH CAN** *RAK SRAK 165408* .......... | **90** | 1 wk |
| 17 Nov 84 | **TEASES AND DARES** *MCA MCF 3250* ............. | **66** | 2 wks |
| 18 May 85 | **THE VERY BEST OF KIM WILDE** *RAK WILDE 1* ...... | **78** | 4 wks |
| 15 Nov 86 | **ANOTHER STEP** *MCA MCF 3339* ................. | **73** | 5 wks |
| 25 Jun 88 | ● **CLOSE** *MCA MCG 6030* ....................... | **8** | 38 wks |

*Another Step changed label number during its chart run to MCA KIML 1.*

## Colm WILKINSON   *Ireland, male vocalist*                     *6 wks*

| | | | |
|---|---|---|---|
| 10 Jun 89 | **STAGE HEROES** *RCA BL 74105* ................... | **27** | 6 wks |

## Alyson WILLIAMS   *US, female vocalist*                       *21 wks*

| | | | |
|---|---|---|---|
| 25 Mar 89 | **RAW** *Def Jam 463293 1* ........................... | **29** | 21 wks |

## Andy WILLIAMS   *US, male vocalist*                           *439 wks*

| | | | |
|---|---|---|---|
| 26 Jun 65 | ● **ALMOST THERE** *CBS BPG 62533* ................. | **4** | 46 wks |
| 7 Aug 65 | **CAN'T GET USED TO LOSING YOU** *CBS BPG 62146* . | **16** | 1 wk |
| 19 Mar 66 | **MAY EACH DAY** *CBS BPG 62658* ................... | **11** | 6 wks |
| 30 Apr 66 | **GREAT SONGS FROM MY FAIR LADY** *CBS BPG 62430* | **30** | 1 wk |
| 23 Jul 66 | **SHADOW OF YOUR SMILE** *CBS 62633* .............. | **24** | 4 wks |
| 29 Jul 67 | **BORN FREE** *CBS SBPG 63027* ................... | **22** | 11 wks |
| 11 May 68 | ★ **LOVE ANDY** *CBS 63167* ......................... | **1** | 22 wks |
| 6 Jul 68 | ● **HONEY** *CBS 63311* ............................ | **4** | 17 wks |
| 26 Jul 69 | **HAPPY HEART** *CBS 63614* ....................... | **22** | 9 wks |
| 27 Dec 69 | **GET TOGETHER WITH ANDY WILLIAMS** *CBS 63800* | **13** | 12 wks |
| 24 Jan 70 | **ANDY WILLIAMS' SOUND OF MUSIC** *CBS 63920* .... | **22** | 10 wks |
| 11 Apr 70 | ★ **GREATEST HITS** *CBS 63920* .................... | **1** | 116 wks |
| 20 Jun 70 | ● **CAN'T HELP FALLING IN LOVE** *CBS 64067* ........ | **7** | 48 wks |
| 5 Dec 70 | ● **ANDY WILLIAMS SHOW** *CBS 64127* ............... | **10** | 6 wks |
| 3 Apr 71 | ★ **HOME LOVING MAN** *CBS 64286* ................. | **1** | 25 wks |
| 31 Jul 71 | **LOVE STORY** *CBS 64467* ...................... | **11** | 11 wks |
| 29 Apr 72 | **THE IMPOSSIBLE DREAM** *CBS 67236* ............. | **26** | 3 wks |
| 29 Jul 72 | **LOVE THEME FROM 'THE GODFATHER'** *CBS 64869* | **11** | 16 wks |
| 16 Dec 72 | **GREATEST HITS VOL. 2** *CBS 65151* ................ | **23** | 10 wks |
| 22 Dec 73 | ● **SOLITAIRE** *CBS 65638* ...................... | **3** | 26 wks |
| 15 Jun 74 | ● **THE WAY WE WERE** *CBS 80152* ................. | **7** | 11 wks |
| 11 Oct 75 | **THE OTHER SIDE OF ME** *CBS 69152* ................ | **60** | 1 wk |
| 28 Jan 78 | ● **REFLECTIONS** *CBS 10006* ...................... | **2** | 17 wks |
| 27 Oct 84 | **GREATEST LOVE CLASSICS** *EMI ANDY 1* .......... | **22** | 10 wks |

*Greatest Love Classics also credits the Royal Philharmonic Orchestra. See also Royal Philharmonic Orchestra.*

## Deniece WILLIAMS  *US, female vocalist*                              *12 wks*

21 May 77   **THIS IS NIECEY**  *CBS 81869* . . . . . . . . . . . . . . . . . . . .   **31**   12 wks
*See also Johnny Mathis and Deniece Williams.*

## Don WILLIAMS  *US, male vocalist*                              *136 wks*

10 Jul  76   **GREATEST HITS VOL. 1**  *ABC ABCL 5147* . . . . . . . . . .   **29**   15 wks
19 Feb  77   **VISIONS**  *ABC ABCL 5200* . . . . . . . . . . . . . . . . . . . . . .   **13**   20 wks
15 Oct  77   **COUNTRY BOY**  *ABC ABCL 5233* . . . . . . . . . . . . . . . .   **27**   5 wks
5 Aug  78 ● **IMAGES**  *K-Tel NE 1033* . . . . . . . . . . . . . . . . . . . . . . . . .   **2**   38 wks
5 Aug  78   **YOU'RE MY BEST FRIEND**  *ABC ABCD 5127* . . . . . . . .   **58**   1 wk
4 Nov 78   **EXPRESSIONS**  *ABC ABCL 5253* . . . . . . . . . . . . . . . . . .   **28**   8 wks
22 Sep  79   **NEW HORIZONS**  *K-Tel NE 1048* . . . . . . . . . . . . . . . . .   **29**   12 wks
15 Dec  79   **PORTRAIT**  *MCA MCS 3045* . . . . . . . . . . . . . . . . . . . . . .   **58**   4 wks
6 Sep  80   **I BELIEVE IN YOU**  *MCA MCF 3077* . . . . . . . . . . . . . . .   **36**   5 wks
18 Jul  81   **ESPECIALLY FOR YOU**  *MCA MCF 3114* . . . . . . . . . . . .   **33**   7 wks
17 Apr  82   **LISTEN TO THE RADIO**  *MCA MCF 3135* . . . . . . . . . . .   **69**   3 wks
23 Apr  83   **YELLOW MOON**  *MCA MCF 3159* . . . . . . . . . . . . . . . . . .   **52**   1 wk
15 Oct  83   **LOVE STORIES**  *K-Tel NE 1252* . . . . . . . . . . . . . . . . . .   **22**   13 wks
26 May  84   **CAFE CAROLINA**  *MCA MCF 3225* . . . . . . . . . . . . . . . .   **65**   4 wks

## Iris WILLIAMS  *UK, female vocalist*                              *4 wks*

22 Dec  79   **HE WAS BEAUTIFUL**  *Columbia SCX 6627* . . . . . . . . . . . .   **69**   4 wks

## John WILLIAMS  *UK, male instrumentalist – guitar*                   *31 wks*

3 Oct  70   **PLAYS SPANISH MUSIC**  *CBS 72860* . . . . . . . . . . . . . . . .   **46**   1 wk
17 Jun  78   **TRAVELLING**  *Cube HIFLY 27* . . . . . . . . . . . . . . . . . . . . .   **23**   5 wks
30 Jun  79 ● **BRIDGES**  *Lotus WH 5015* . . . . . . . . . . . . . . . . . . . . . . . .   **5**   22 wks
4 Aug  79   **CAVATINA**  *Cube HIFLY 32* . . . . . . . . . . . . . . . . . . . . . .   **64**   3 wks
*See also John Williams with the English Chamber Orchestra conducted by Daniel Barenboim; Cleo Laine and John Williams.*

## John WILLIAMS  *US, male conductor*                              *10 wks*

25 Dec  82   **ET – THE EXTRATERRESTRIAL**  *MCA MCF 3160* . . . .   **47**   10 wks

## John WILLIAMS with the ENGLISH CHAMBER ORCHESTRA conducted by Daniel BARENBOIM
*UK, male instrumentalist – guitar, with orchestra and male conductor*      *9 wks*

8 Feb  76   **RODRIGO: CONCERTO DE ARANJUEZ**  *CBS 79369* . .   **20**   9 wks
*See also John Williams (UK).*

## Wendy O. WILLIAMS  *US, female vocalist*                         *1 wk*

30 Jun  84   **W.O.W.**  *Music For Nations MFN 24* . . . . . . . . . . . . . . . . . .   **100**   1 wk

## Ann WILLIAMSON  *UK, female vocalist*                           *13 wks*

15 Feb  86   **PRECIOUS MEMORIES**  *Emerald Gem ERTV 1* . . . . . . . .   **16**   9 wks
6 Feb  88   **COUNT YOUR BLESSINGS**  *Emerald Gem ERTV 2* . . . . . .   **58**   4 wks

## Sonny Boy WILLIAMSON
*US, male vocalist/instrumentalist – guitar*

1 wk

20 Jun  64   **DOWN AND OUT BLUES**  *Pye NPL 28036* . . . . . . . . . . . .   **20**   1 wk

*W*

## Bruce WILLIS  *US, male vocalist*                                        *28 wks*

18 Apr 87 ● **THE RETURN OF BRUNO**  *Motown ZL 72571* .........  **4**  28 wks

## Mari WILSON  *UK, female vocalist*                                       *9 wks*

26 Feb 83  **SHOW PEOPLE**  *Compact COMP 2* ..................  **24**  9 wks
Show People *credits Mari Wilson with the Wilsations.*

## WIN  *UK, male/female vocal/instrumental group*                          *1 wk*

25 Apr 87  **UH! TEARS BABY**  *Swampland LONLP 31* .............  **51**  1 wk

**WINCHESTER CATHEDRAL CHOIR** – *See Andrew Lloyd Webber*

## WINDJAMMER  *US, male vocal/instrumental group*                          *1 wk*

25 Aug 84  **WINDJAMMER II**  *MCA MCF 3231* ..................  **82**  1 wk

**WINGS** – *See Paul McCartney*

## Johnny WINTER  *US, male/vocal instrumental group*                       *12 wks*

16 May 70  **SECOND WINTER**  *CBS 66321* .....................  **59**  2 wks
31 Oct 70  **JOHNNY WINTER AND ...**  *CBS 64117* .............  **29**  4 wks
15 May 71  **JOHNNY WINTER AND LIVE**  *CBS 64289* ...........  **20**  6 wks

## Ruby WINTERS  *US, female vocalist*                                      *16 wks*

10 Jun 78  **RUBY WINTERS**  *Creole CRLP 512* ..................  **27**  7 wks
23 Jun 79  **SONGBIRD**  *K-Tel NE 1045* .......................  **31**  9 wks

## Steve WINWOOD  *UK, male vocalist*                                       *117 wks*

9 Jul 77  **STEVE WINWOOD**  *Island ILPS 9494* ................  **12**  9 wks
10 Jan 81  **ARC OF A DIVER**  *Island ILPS 9576* .................  **13**  20 wks
14 Aug 82 ● **TALKING BACK TO THE NIGHT**  *Island ILPS 9777* ....  **6**  13 wks
12 Jul 86 ● **BACK IN THE HIGH LIFE**  *Island ILPS 9844* ...........  **8**  42 wks
7 Nov 87  **CHRONICLES**  *Island SSW 1* ......................  **12**  17 wks
2 Jul 88 ● **ROLL WITH IT**  *Virgin V 2532* .....................  **4**  16 wks

## WIRE  *UK, male vocal/instrumental group*                               *3 wks*

7 Oct 78  **CHAIRS MISSING**  *Harvest SHSP 4093* ................  **48**  1 wk
13 Oct 79  **154**  *Harvest SHSP 4105* ............................  **39**  1 wk
9 May 87  **THE IDEAL COPY**  *Mute STUMM 42* .................  **87**  1 wk

## WISHBONE ASH  *UK, male vocal/instrumental group*                        *75 wks*

23 Jan 71  **WISHBONE ASH**  *MCA MKPS 2014* .................  **34**  2 wks
9 Oct 71  **PILGRIMAGE**  *MCA MDKS 8004* ...................  **14**  9 wks
20 May 72 ● **ARGUS**  *MCA MDKS 8006* .........................  **3**  20 wks
26 May 73  **WISHBONE FOUR**  *MCA MDKS 8011* .............  **12**  10 wks
30 Nov 74  **THERE'S THE RUB**  *MCA MCF 2585* ............  **16**  5 wks
3 Apr 76  **LOCKED IN**  *MCA MCF 2750* ..................  **36**  2 wks
27 Nov 76  **NEW ENGLAND**  *MCA MCG 3523* .................  **22**  3 wks
29 Oct 77  **FRONT PAGE NEWS**  *MCA MCG 3524* .........  **31**  4 wks
28 Oct 78  **NO SMOKE WITHOUT FIRE**  *MCA MCG 3528* ........  **43**  3 wks
2 Feb 80  **JUST TESTING**  *MCA MCF 3052* .................  **41**  4 wks
1 Nov 80  **LIVE DATES II**  *MCA MCG 4012* ..................  **40**  3 wks
25 Apr 81  **NUMBER THE BRAVE**  *MCA MCF 3103* ............  **61**  5 wks
16 Oct 82  **BOTH BARRELS BURNING**  *A&M ASH 1* ..........  **22**  5 wks

# Bill WITHERS    US, male vocalist                                     10 wks

| 11 Feb 78 | **MENAGERIE**  CBS 82265 | 27 | 5 wks |
| 15 Jun 85 | **WATCHING YOU, WATCHING ME**  CBS 26200 | 60 | 1 wk |
| 17 Sep 88 | **GREATEST HITS**  CBS 32343 | 90 | 4 wks |

# WIZZARD    UK, male vocal/instrumental group                          11 wks

| 19 May 73 | **WIZZARD BREW**  Harvest SHSP 4025 | 29 | 7 wks |
| 17 Aug 74 | **INTRODUCING EDDY AND THE FALCONS**  Warner Bros. K 52029 | 19 | 4 wks |

# WOLFSBANE    US, male vocal/instrumental group                        1 wk

| 5 Aug 89 | **LIVE FAST DIE FAST**  Def American 838486 1 | 48 | 1 wk |

# Bobby WOMACK    US, male vocalist                                     15 wks

| 28 Apr 84 | **THE POET II**  Motown ZL 72205 | 31 | 8 wks |
| 28 Sep 85 | **SO MANY RIVERS**  MCA MCF 3282 | 28 | 7 wks |

See also Wilton Felder.

# WOMACK and WOMACK    US, male/female vocal duo                        52 wks

| 21 Apr 84 | **LOVE WARS**  Elektra 960293 | 45 | 13 wks |
| 22 Jun 85 | **RADIO M.U.S.I.C. MAN**  Elektra EKT 6 | 56 | 2 wks |
| 27 Aug 88 | ● **CONSCIENCE**  Fourth & Broadway BRLP 519 | 4 | 37 wks |

**295**

*w*

# WOMBLES
UK, male vocalist/arranger/producer, Mike Batt under group name       55 wks

| 2 Mar 74 | **WOMBLING SONGS**  CBS 65803 | 19 | 17 wks |
| 13 Jul 74 | **REMEMBER YOU'RE A WOMBLE**  CBS 80191 | 18 | 31 wks |
| 21 Dec 74 | **KEEP ON WOMBLING**  CBS 80526 | 17 | 6 wks |
| 8 Jan 77 | **20 WOMBLING GREATS**  Warwick PR 5022 | 29 | 1 wk |

# Stevie WONDER    US, male vocalist/multi-instrumentalist             325 wks

| 7 Sep 68 | **STEVIE WONDER'S GREATEST HITS**  Tamla Motown STML 11075 | 25 | 10 wks |
| 13 Dec 69 | **MY CHERIE AMOUR**  Tamla Motown STML 11128 | 17 | 2 wks |
| 12 Feb 72 | **GREATEST HITS VOL. 2**  Tamla Motown STML 11196 | 30 | 4 wks |
| 3 Feb 73 | **TALKING BOOK**  Tamla Motown STMA 8007 | 16 | 48 wks |
| 1 Sep 73 | ● **INNERVISIONS**  Tamla Motown STMA 8011 | 8 | 55 wks |
| 17 Aug 74 | ● **FULFILLINGNESS' FIRST FINALE**  Tamla Motown STMA 8019 | 5 | 16 wks |
| 16 Oct 76 | ● **SONGS IN THE KEY OF LIFE**  Tamla Motown TMSP 6002 | 2 | 54 wks |
| 10 Nov 79 | ● **JOURNEY THROUGH THE SECRET LIFE OF PLANTS**  Motown TMSP 6009 | 8 | 15 wks |
| 8 Nov 80 | ● **HOTTER THAN JULY**  Motown STMA 8035 | 2 | 55 wks |
| 22 May 82 | ● **ORIGINAL MUSIQUARIUM 1**  Motown TMSP 6012 | 8 | 17 wks |
| 22 Sep 84 | ● **WOMAN IN RED – SELECTIONS FROM ORIGINAL MOTION PICTURE SOUNDTRACK**  Motown ZL 72285 | 2 | 19 wks |
| 24 Nov 84 | **LOVE SONGS – 16 CLASSIC HITS**  Telstar STAR 2251 | 20 | 10 wks |
| 28 Sep 85 | ● **IN SQUARE CIRCLE**  Motown ZL 72005 | 5 | 16 wks |
| 28 Nov 87 | **CHARACTERS**  RCA ZL 72001 | 33 | 4 wks |

The Woman In Red *also features Dionne Warwick. See also Dionne Warwick; Diana Ross/Michael Jackson/ Gladys Knight/Stevie Wonder.*

## WONDER STUFF  *UK, male vocal/instrumental group*  *15 wks*

| | | | |
|---|---|---|---|
| 27 Aug 88 | **THE EIGHT LEGGED GROOVE MACHINE** | | |
| | *Polydor GONLP 1* .................................. | **18** | 7 wks |
| 14 Oct 89 ● **HUP**  *Polydor 841187 1* ............................ | | **5** | 8 wks |

## Roy WOOD  *UK, male vocalist/multi-instrumentalist*  *14 wks*

| | | | |
|---|---|---|---|
| 18 Aug 73 | **BOULDERS**  *Harvest SHVL 803* ..................... | **15** | 8 wks |
| 24 Jul 82 | **THE SINGLES**  *Speed SPEED 1000* .................. | **37** | 6 wks |

## WOODENTOPS  *UK, male vocal/instrumental group*  *6 wks*

| | | | |
|---|---|---|---|
| 12 Jul 86 | **GIANT**  *Rough Trade ROUGH 87* ..................... | **35** | 4 wks |
| 5 Mar 88 | **WOODENFOOT COPS ON THE HIGHWAY** | | |
| | *Rough Trade ROUGH 127* ........................... | **48** | 2 wks |

## Edward WOODWARD  *UK, male vocalist*  *12 wks*

| | | | |
|---|---|---|---|
| 6 Jun 70 | **THIS MAN ALONE**  *DJM DJLPS 405* ................ | **53** | 2 wks |
| 19 Aug 72 | **THE EDWARD WOODWARD ALBUM**  *Jam JAL 103* .. | **20** | 10 wks |

## WORKING WEEK
*UK, male/female vocal/instrumental group*  *10 wks*

| | | | |
|---|---|---|---|
| 6 Apr 85 | **WORKING NIGHTS**  *Virgin V 2343* ................. | **23** | 9 wks |
| 27 Sep 86 | **COMPANEROS**  *Virgin V 2397* ..................... | **72** | 1 wk |

## WORLD PARTY  *Ireland/UK, male vocal/instrumental group*  *4 wks*

| | | | |
|---|---|---|---|
| 21 Mar 87 | **PRIVATE REVOLUTION**  *Chrysalis CHEN 4* .......... | **56** | 4 wks |

**WORLD'S FAMOUS SUPREME TEAM** – *See Malcolm McLAREN*

## WRECKLESS ERIC  *UK, male vocalist*  *5 wks*

| | | | |
|---|---|---|---|
| 1 Apr 78 | **WRECKLESS ERIC**  *Stiff SEEZ 6* ................... | **46** | 1 wk |
| 8 Mar 80 | **BIG SMASH**  *Stiff SEEZ 21* ........................ | **30** | 4 wks |

## Klaus WUNDERLICH
*Germany, male instrumentalist – organ*  *19 wks*

| | | | |
|---|---|---|---|
| 30 Aug 75 | **THE HIT WORLD OF KLAUS WUNDERLICH** | | |
| | *Decca SPA 434* ................................... | **27** | 8 wks |
| 20 May 78 | **THE UNIQUE KLAUS WUNDERLICH SOUND** | | |
| | *Decca DBC 5/5* ................................... | **28** | 4 wks |
| 26 May 79 | **THE FANTASTIC SOUND OF KLAUS WUNDERLICH** | | |
| | *Lotus LH 5013* ................................... | **43** | 5 wks |
| 17 Mar 84 | **ON THE SUNNY SIDE OF THE STREET** | | |
| | *Polydor POLD 5133* ............................. | **81** | 2 wks |

## WURZELS  *UK, male vocal/instrumental group*  *25 wks*

| | | | |
|---|---|---|---|
| 3 Jul 76 | **COMBINE HARVESTER**  *One-Up OU 2138* .......... | **15** | 20 wks |
| 2 Apr 77 | **GOLDEN DELICIOUS**  *EMI Note NTS 122* ........... | **32** | 5 wks |

*See also Adge Cutler and the Wurzels.*

## Bill WYMAN  *UK, male vocalist/instrumentalist – bass*          *7 wks*

| 8 Jun | 74 | **MONKEY GRIP**  *Rolling Stones COC 59102* ............. | 39 | 1 wk |
| 10 Apr | 82 | **BILL WYMAN**  *A & M AMLH 68540* .................. | 55 | 6 wks |

## Tammy WYNETTE  *US, female vocalist*          *49 wks*

| 17 May | 75 | ● **THE BEST OF TAMMY WYNETTE**  *Epic EPC 63578* .... | 4 | 23 wks |
| 21 Jun | 75 | **STAND BY YOUR MAN**  *Epic EPC 69141* ............. | 13 | 7 wks |
| 17 Dec | 77 | ● **20 COUNTRY CLASSICS**  *CBS PR 5040* ............. | 3 | 11 wks |
| 4 Feb | 78 | **COUNTRY GIRL MEETS COUNTRY BOY**  *Warwick PR 5039* ................................ | 43 | 3 wks |
| 6 Jun | 87 | **ANNIVERSARY – 20 YEARS OF HITS**  *Epic 450 393–1* .. | 45 | 5 wks |

# *x*

## X MAL DEUTSCHLAND
*UK/Germany, male/female vocal/instrumental group*          *1 wk*

| 7 Jul | 84 | **TOCSIN**  *4AD CAD 407* ........................... | 86 | 1 wk |

## X-RAY SPEX  *UK, male/female vocal/instrumental group*          *14 wks*

| 9 Dec | 78 | **GERM FREE ADOLESCENTS**  *EMI International INS 3023* .......................... | 30 | 14 wks |

**297**

*γ*

## XTC  *UK, male vocal/instrumental group*          *45 wks*

| 11 Feb | 78 | **WHITE MUSIC**  *Virgin V 2095* ...................... | 38 | 4 wks |
| 28 Oct | 78 | **GO 2**  *Virgin V 2108* ............................... | 21 | 3 wks |
| 1 Sep | 79 | **DRUMS AND WIRES**  *Virgin V 2129* ................ | 34 | 7 wks |
| 20 Sep | 80 | **BLACK SEA**  *Virgin V 2173* ........................ | 16 | 7 wks |
| 20 Feb | 82 | ● **ENGLISH SETTLEMENT**  *Virgin V 2223* ............. | 5 | 11 wks |
| 13 Nov | 82 | **WAXWORKS – SOME SINGLES (1977–82)**  *Virgin V 2251* .................................... | 54 | 3 wks |
| 10 Sep | 83 | **MUMMER**  *Virgin V 2264* ......................... | 51 | 4 wks |
| 27 Oct | 84 | **THE BIG EXPRESS**  *Virgin V 2325* ................. | 38 | 2 wks |
| 8 Nov | 86 | **SKYLARKING**  *Virgin V 2399* ...................... | 90 | 1 wk |
| 11 Mar | 89 | **ORANGES AND LEMONS**  *Virgin V 2581* ............. | 28 | 3 wks |

# *γ*

## YARDBIRDS  *UK, male vocal/instrumental group*          *8 wks*

| 23 Jul | 66 | **YARDBIRDS**  *Columbia SX 6063* ..................... | 20 | 8 wks |

## YAZOO  *UK, female/male vocal/instrumental duo*          *83 wks*

| 4 Sep | 82 | ● **UPSTAIRS AT ERIC'S**  *Mute STUMM 7* .............. | 2 | 63 wks |
| 16 Jul | 83 | ★ **YOU AND ME BOTH**  *Mute STUMM 12* .............. | 1 | 20 wks |

**DWIGHT YOAKAM** was the best dressed country star of the late eighties.

Composer Andy Mackay celebrates with the three actress/singers of **ROCK FOLLIES**, the only number one TV soundtrack.

The soundtrack to **THE SOUND O♪ MUSIC** (Julie Andrews shown here) tied with 'South Pacific' in being number one in four different years, th♪ most ever.

## YAZZ  UK, female vocalist                                    32 wks

26 Nov 88 ● **WANTED**  *Big Life YAZZLP 1* ......................  3  32 wks

## YELLO  Switzerland, male vocal/instrumental duo             13 wks

21 May 83 **YOU GOTTA SAY YES TO ANOTHER EXCESS**
                *Stiff SEEZ 48* ......................................  65  2 wks
 6 Apr 85 **STELLA**  *Elektra EKT 1* ...........................  92  1 wk
 4 Jul 87 **ONE SECOND**  *Mercury MERH 100* ..................  48  3 wks
10 Dec 88 **FLAG**  *Mercury 836778 1* ..........................  56  7 wks

## Bryn YEMM  UK, male vocalist                                14 wks

 9 Jun 84 **HOW DO I LOVE THEE**  *Lifestyle LEG 17* .............  57  2 wks
 7 Jul 84 **HOW GREAT THOU ART**  *Lifestyle LEG 15* ...........  67  8 wks
22 Dec 84 **THE BRYN YEMM CHRISTMAS COLLECTION**
                *Bay BAY 104* ....................................  95  2 wks
26 Oct 85 **MY TRIBUTE – BRYN YEMM INSPIRATIONAL ALBUM**
                *Word WSTR 9665* ................................  85  2 wks

My Tribute . . . *also credits the Gwent Chorale.*

## YES  UK, male vocal/instrumental group                     200 wks

 1 Aug 70  **TIME AND A WORD**  *Atlantic 2400–006* ................  45   3 wks
 3 Apr 71 ● **THE YES ALBUM**  *Atlantic 2400–101* .................   7  29 wks
 4 Dec 71 ● **FRAGILE**  *Atlantic 2409–019* .........................   7  17 wks
23 Sep 72 ● **CLOSE TO THE EDGE**  *Atlantic K 50012* .............   4  13 wks
26 May 73 ● **YESSONGS**  *Atlantic K 60045* ......................   7  13 wks
22 Dec 73 ★ **TALES FROM TOPOGRAPHIC OCEANS**
                *Atlantic K 80001* ...............................   1  15 wks
21 Dec 74 ● **RELAYER**  *Atlantic K 50096* .......................   4  11 wks
29 Mar 75 **YESTERDAYS**  *Atlantic K 50048* ....................  27   7 wks
30 Jul  77 ★ **GOING FOR THE ONE**  *Atlantic K 50379* .............   1  28 wks
 7 Oct 78 ● **TORMATO**  *Atlantic K 50518* .......................   8  11 wks
30 Aug 80 ● **DRAMA**  *Atlantic K 50736* ........................   2   8 wks
10 Jan 81 **YESSHOWS**  *Atlantic K 60142* ......................  22   9 wks
26 Nov 83 **90125**  *Atco 790125* ..............................  16  28 wks
29 Mar 86 **9012 LIVE: THE SOLOS**  *Atco 790 474–1* ..............  44   3 wks
10 Oct 87 **BIG GENERATOR**  *Atco WEX 70* ...................  17   5 wks

## Dwight YOAKAM  US, male vocalist/instrumentalist – guitar    4 wks

 9 May 87 **HILLBILLY DELUXE**  *Reprise WX 106* ...............  51  3 wks
13 Aug 88 **BUENAS NOCHES FROM A LONELY ROOM**
                *Reprise WX 193* ..................................  87  1 wk

## Faron YOUNG  US, male vocalist                               5 wks

28 Oct 72  **IT'S FOUR IN THE MORNING**  *Mercury 6338 095*  27  5 wks

## Neil YOUNG  Canada, male vocalist                          167 wks

31 Oct 70 ● **AFTER THE GOLDRUSH**  *Reprise RSLP 6383* .........   7  68 wks
 4 Mar 72 ★ **HARVEST**  *Reprise K 54005* ........................   1  33 wks
27 Oct 73 **TIME FADES AWAY**  *Warner Bros. K 54010* .............  20   2 wks
10 Aug 74 **ON THE BEACH**  *Reprise K 54014* ...................  42   2 wks
 5 Jul  75 **TONIGHT'S THE NIGHT**  *Reprise K 54040* ............  48   1 wk
27 Dec 75 **ZUMA**  *Reprise K 54057* ...........................  44   2 wks
 9 Jul  77 **AMERICAN STARS 'N' BARS**  *Reprise K 54088* ........  17   8 wks
17 Dec 77 **DECADE**  *Reprise K 64037* .........................  46   4 wks
28 Oct 78 **COMES A TIME**  *Reprise K 54099* ....................  42   3 wks
14 Jul  79 **RUST NEVER SLEEPS**  *Reprise K 54105* ..............  13  13 wks

| 1 Dec 79 | **LIVE RUST** *Reprise K 64041* ....................... | 55 | 3 wks |
|---|---|---|---|
| 15 Nov 80 | **HAWKS AND DOVES** *Reprise K 54109* ............. | 34 | 3 wks |
| 14 Nov 81 | **RE-AC-TOR** *Reprise K 54116* ...................... | 69 | 3 wks |
| 5 Feb 83 | **TRANS** *Geffen GEF 25019* ....................... | 29 | 5 wks |
| 3 Sep 83 | **EVERYBODY'S ROCKIN'** *Geffen GEF 25590* ........ | 50 | 3 wks |
| 14 Sep 85 | **OLD WAYS** *Geffen GEF 26377* ..................... | 39 | 3 wks |
| 2 Aug 86 | **LANDING ON WATER** *Geffen 924 109-1* ............ | 52 | 2 wks |
| 4 Jul 87 | **LIFE** *Geffen WX 109* ............................ | 71 | 1 wk |
| 30 Apr 88 | **THIS NOTE'S FOR YOU** *WEA WX 168* ............. | 56 | 3 wks |
| 21 Oct 89 | **FREEDOM** *Reprise WX 257* ....................... | 17 | 5 wks |

Rust Never Sleeps, Live Rust, Re-ac-tor *and* Life *credited to Neil Young and Crazy Horse.*
Everybody's Rockin' *credited to Neil Young and the Shocking Pinks.* This Note's For You *credits the Blue Notes. See also Stills–Young Band; Crosby, Stills, Nash and Young.*

## Paul YOUNG *UK, male vocalist* 185 wks

| 30 Jul 83 | ★ **NO PARLEZ** *CBS 25521* .......................... | 1 | 119 wks |
|---|---|---|---|
| 6 Apr 85 | ★ **THE SECRET OF ASSOCIATION** *CBS 26234* ........ | 1 | 49 wks |
| 1 Nov 86 | ● **BETWEEN TWO FIRES** *CBS 450 150-1* ............. | 4 | 17 wks |

## Sydney YOUNGBLOOD *US, male vocalist* 8 wks

| 28 Oct 89 | **FEELING FREE** *Circa CIRCA 9* .................... | 23† | 8 wks |
|---|---|---|---|

## Y&T *US, male vocal/instrumental group* 15 wks

| 11 Sep 82 | **BLACK TIGER** *A & M AMLH 64910* ................. | 53 | 8 wks |
|---|---|---|---|
| 10 Sep 83 | **MEAN STREAK** *A & M AMLX 64960* ................. | 35 | 4 wks |
| 18 Aug 84 | **IN ROCK WE TRUST** *A & M AMLX 65007* ............ | 33 | 3 wks |

## 300

*z*

## Frank ZAPPA *US, male vocalist/multi-instrumentalist* 55 wks

| 28 Feb 70 | ● **HOT RATS** *Reprise RSLP 6356* ...................... | 9 | 27 wks |
|---|---|---|---|
| 19 Dec 70 | **CHUNGA'S REVENGE** *Reprise RSLP 2030* ............ | 43 | 1 wk |
| 6 May 78 | **ZAPPA IN NEW YORK** *Discreet K 69204* .............. | 55 | 1 wk |
| 10 Mar 79 | **SHEIK YERBOUTI** *CBS 88339* ..................... | 32 | 7 wks |
| 13 Oct 79 | **JOE'S GARAGE ACT 1** *CBS 86101* .................. | 62 | 3 wks |
| 19 Jan 80 | **JOE'S GARAGE ACTS 2 & 3** *CBS 88475* .............. | 75 | 1 wk |
| 16 May 81 | **TINSEL TOWN REBELLION** *CBS 88516* ............. | 55 | 4 wks |
| 24 Oct 81 | **YOU ARE WHAT YOU IS** *CBS 88560* ............. | 51 | 2 wks |
| 19 Jun 82 | **SHIP ARRIVING TOO LATE TO SAVE A DROWNING WITCH** *CBS 85804* ............................ | 61 | 4 wks |
| 18 Jun 83 | **THE MAN FROM UTOPIA** *CBS 25251* ............. | 87 | 1 wk |
| 27 Oct 84 | **THEM OR US** *EMI FZD 1* ........................ | 53 | 2 wks |
| 30 Apr 88 | **GUITAR** *Zappa ZAPPA 6* .......................... | 82 | 2 wks |

## Lena ZAVARONI *UK, female vocalist* 5 wks

| 23 Mar 74 | ● **MA** *Philips 6308 201* ............................. | 8 | 5 wks |
|---|---|---|---|

## Z.Z. TOP *US, male vocal/instrumental group* 178 wks

| 12 Jul 75 | **FANDANGO** *London SHU 8482* ...................... | 60 | 1 wk |
|---|---|---|---|
| 8 Aug 81 | **EL LOCO** *Warner Bros. K 56929* .................... | 88 | 2 wks |
| 30 Apr 83 | ● **ELIMINATOR** *Warner Bros. W 3774* .................. | 3 | 135 wks |
| 9 Nov 85 | ● **AFTERBURNER** *Warner Bros. WX 27* ................ | 2 | 40 wks |

# Various Artists

## ANONYMOUS COVER VERSIONS

| | | | | |
|---|---|---|---|---|
| 29 Feb 64 | **BEATLEMANIA** *Top Six TSL 1* | 19 | 1 wk |
| 7 Aug 71 | **HOT HITS 5** *MFP 5208* | 48 | 1 wk |
| 7 Aug 71 ★ | **HOT HITS 6** *MFP 5214* | 1 | 7 wks |
| 7 Aug 71 | **TOP OF THE POPS VOL. 17** *Hallmark SHM 740* | 16 | 3 wks |
| 7 Aug 71 ★ | **TOP OF THE POPS VOL. 18** *Hallmark SHM 745* | 1 | 12 wks |
| 7 Aug 71 | **MILLION SELLER HITS** *MFP 5203* | 46 | 2 wks |
| 21 Aug 71 | **SMASH HITS SUPREMES STYLE** *MFP 5184* | 36 | 3 wks |
| 2 Oct 71 ● | **TOP OF THE POPS VOL. 19** *Hallmark SHM 750* | 3 | 9 wks |
| 23 Oct 71 ● | **HOT HITS 7** *MFP 5236* | 3 | 9 wks |
| 6 Nov 71 | **SMASH HITS COUNTRY STYLE** *MFP 5228* | 38 | 1 wk |
| 13 Nov 71 ★ | **TOP OF THE POPS VOL. 20** *Hallmark SHM 739* | 1 | 8 wks |
| 27 Nov 71 | **NON STOP 20 VOL. 4** *Plexium PXMS 1006* | 35 | 2 wks |
| 4 Dec 71 | **SMASH HITS 71** *MFP 5229* | 21 | 3 wks |
| 11 Dec 71 ● | **HOT HITS 8** *MFP 5243* | 2 | 4 wks |
| 27 Sep 75 | **40 SINGALONG PUB SONGS** *K-Tel NE 509* | 21 | 7 wks |
| 6 Nov 76 | **FORTY MANIA** *Ronco RDT 2018* | 21 | 6 wks |

Compilation albums are listed alphabetically by label, for each label that has produced at least three hit compilations. Other hit compilations are listed together at the end of this section. Multi-artist Film Soundtacks, TV spin-offs, Original Cast Recordings and so on are then listed separately.

From 14 January 1989, a new Compilation Albums chart was established and all entries on this chart are listed in this section. A dotted line in each label section indicates when the new chart began. Some albums will have entries both above and below the line, indicating that they appeared in the main chart before 14 January 1989, and the Compilations chart thereafter. Various Artist albums of material not previously released as singles (e.g. Stage Cast Recordings) still qualify for the main chart.

## COMPILATIONS

### A & M

| | | | | |
|---|---|---|---|---|
| 2 May 87 | **PRINCE'S TRUST TENTH ANNIVERSARY BIRTHDAY PARTY** *A & M AMA 3906* | 76 | 3 wks |
| 22 Aug 87 | **THE PRINCE'S TRUST CONCERT 1987** *A & M PTA 1987* | 44 | 3 wks |
| 5 Dec 87 | **SPECIAL OLYMPICS – A VERY SPECIAL CHRISTMAS** *A & M AMA 3911* | 40 | 5 wks |
| 23 Dec 89 | **SPECIAL OLYMPICS – A VERY SPECIAL CHRISTMAS** *A & M AMA 3911* | 19 | 1 wk |

### Arcade

| | | | | |
|---|---|---|---|---|
| 29 Jul 72 ★ | **20 FANTASTIC HITS** *Arcade 2891 001* | 1 | 24 wks |
| 29 Nov 72 ● | **20 FANTASTIC HITS VOL. 2** *Arcade 2891 002* | 2 | 14 wks |
| 7 Apr 73 ● | **40 FANTASTIC HITS FROM THE 50'S AND 60'S** *Arcade ADEP 3/4* | 2 | 15 wks |
| 26 May 73 ● | **20 FANTASTIC HITS VOL. 3** *Arcade ADEP 5* | 3 | 8 wks |
| 15 Nov 75 ● | **DISCO HITS '75** *Arcade ADEP 18* | 5 | 11 wks |
| 26 Mar 77 | **ROCK ON** *Arcade ADEP 27* | 16 | 10 wks |
| 2 Jun 77 | **RULE BRITANNIA** *Arcade ADEP 29* | 56 | 1 wk |
| 23 Feb 80 | **FIRST LOVE** *Arcade ADEP 41* | 58 | 2 wks |

### Atlantic

| | | | | |
|---|---|---|---|---|
| 2 Apr 66 | **SOLID GOLD SOUL** *Atlantic ATL 5048* | 12 | 27 wks |
| 5 Nov 66 | **MIDNIGHT SOUL** *Atlantic 587–021* | 22 | 19 wks |

| | | | | |
|---|---|---|---|---|
| 14 Jun 69 | **THIS IS SOUL** *Atlantic 643–301* ..................... | | 16 | 15 wks |
| 25 Mar 72 | **THE NEW AGE OF ATLANTIC** *Atlantic K 20024* ....... | | 25 | 1 wk |
| 22 Jun 74 | **ATLANTIC BLACK GOLD** *Atlantic K 40550* ........... | | 23 | 7 wks |
| 3 Apr 76 | **BY INVITATION ONLY** *Atlantic K 60112* ............. | | 17 | 6 wks |
| 11 Apr 81 | **CONCERTS FOR THE PEOPLE OF KAMPUCHEA** | | | |
| | *Atlantic K 60153* .................................. | | 39 | 2 wks |
| 2 Feb 85 | **THIS IS SOUL** *Atlantic SOUL 1* ..................... | | 78 | 7 wks |
| 6 Jun 87 | ● **ATLANTIC SOUL CLASSICS** *Atlantic WX 105* ........ | | 9 | 23 wks |
| 18 Jun 88 | **ATLANTIC SOUL BALLADS** *Atlantic WX 98* .......... | | 84 | 2 wks |

*Beggars Banquet*

| | | | | |
|---|---|---|---|---|
| 21 Nov 81 | **SLIP STREAM** *Beggars Banquet BEGA 31* ............... | | 72 | 3 wks |
| 15 May 82 | **SEX SWEAT AND BLOOD** *Beggars Banquet BEGA 34* .... | | 88 | 1 wk |
| 11 Sep 82 | **THE BEST OF BRITISH JAZZ FUNK VOLUME 2** | | | |
| | *Beggars Banquet BEGA 41* ........................ | | 44 | 4 wks |

*CBS*

| | | | | |
|---|---|---|---|---|
| 20 May 67 | **THRILL TO THE SENSATIONAL SOUNDS OF SUPER** | | | |
| | **STEREO** *CBS PR 5* ........................... | | 20 | 30 wks |
| 28 Jun 69 | **THE ROCK MACHINE TURNS YOU ON** *CBS SPR 22* . | | 18 | 7 wks |
| 28 Jun 69 | **ROCK MACHINE I LOVE YOU** *CBS SPR 26* ......... | | 15 | 5 wks |
| 20 May 72 | ● **THE MUSIC PEOPLE** *CBS 66315* .................... | | 10 | 9 wks |
| 21 Oct 78 | ● **SATIN CITY** *CBS 10010* ......................... | | 10 | 11 wks |
| 2 Jun 79 | **THIS IS IT** *CBS 10014* ......................... | | 6 | 12 wks |
| 19 Apr 80 | **FIRST LADIES OF COUNTRY** *CBS 10018* ............ | | 37 | 6 wks |
| 21 Jun 80 | **KILLER WATTS** *CBS KW1* ....................... | | 27 | 6 wks |
| 4 Apr 81 | **BITTER SUITE** *CBS 22082* ...................... | | 55 | 3 wks |
| 16 Oct 82 | ● **REFLECTIONS** *CBS 10034* ....................... | | 4 | 91 wks |
| 22 Oct 83 | **IMAGINATIONS** *CBS 10044* ....................... | | 15 | 21 wks |
| 20 Apr 85 | **CLUB CLASSICS VOLUME 2** *CBS VAULT 2* .......... | | 90 | 2 wks |
| 14 Mar 87 | ● **MOVE CLOSER** *CBS MOOD 1* ................... | | 4 | 19 wks |
| 27 Jun 87 | **THE HOLIDAY ALBUM** *CBS MOOD 2* .............. | | 13 | 9 wks |
| 30 Apr 88 | ★ **NITE FLITE** *CBS MOOD 4* ........................ | | 1 | 26 wks |
| .......... | .................................................. | | | |
| 4 Mar 89 | ● **CHEEK TO CHEEK** *CBS MOOD 6* ................. | | 2 | 24 wks |
| 13 May 89 | ★ **NITE FLITE 2** *CBS MOOD 8* ...................... | | 1 | 26 wks |
| 30 Dec 89 | **LAMBADA** *CBS 466055 1* ........................ | | 19† | 1 wk |

*Champion*

| | | | | |
|---|---|---|---|---|
| 8 Nov 86 | **ULTIMATE TRAX VOLUME 1** *Champion CHAMP 103* .. | | 66 | 2 wks |
| 7 Mar 87 | **ULTIMATE TRAX VOLUME 2** *Champion CHAMP 1005* . | | 50 | 2 wks |
| 18 Jul 87 | **ULTIMATE TRAX 3 – BATTLE OF THE D.J.s** | | | |
| | *Champion CHAMP 1008* ........................... | | 69 | 2 wks |

*Decca*

| | | | | |
|---|---|---|---|---|
| 8 Feb 64 | **READY STEADY GO** *Decca LK 4577* ................. | | 20 | 1 wk |
| 28 Jun 69 | **THE WORLD OF BLUES POWER** *Decca SPA 14* ...... | | 24 | 6 wks |
| 5 Jul 69 | **THE WORLD OF BRASS BANDS** *Decca SPA 20* ....... | | 13 | 11 wks |
| 6 Sep 69 | ● **THE WORLD OF HITS VOL. 2** *Decca SPA 35* .......... | | 7 | 5 wks |
| 20 Sep 69 | **THE WORLD OF PROGRESSIVE MUSIC (WOWIE** | | | |
| | **ZOWIE)** *Decca SPA 34* ......................... | | 17 | 2 wks |
| 20 Sep 69 | **THE WORLD OF PHASE 4 STEREO** *Decca SPA 32* .... | | 29 | 2 wks |
| 7 Aug 71 | ● **THE WORLD OF YOUR 100 BEST TUNES** | | | |
| | *Decca SPA 112* .................................. | | 10 | 22 wks |
| 9 Oct 71 | ● **THE WORLD OF YOUR 100 BEST TUNES VOL. 2** | | | |
| | *Decca SPA 155* .................................. | | 9 | 13 wks |
| 27 Sep 75 | **THE WORLD OF YOUR 100 BEST TUNES VOL. 10** | | | |
| | *Decca SPA 400* .................................. | | 41 | 4 wks |
| 13 Dec 75 | **THE TOP 25 FROM YOUR 100 BEST TUNES** | | | |
| | *Decca HBT 1112* ................................. | | 21 | 5 wks |
| 26 Nov 83 | ● **FORMULA 30** *Decca PROLP 4* ...................... | | 6 | 17 wks |

*DJ International*

| | | | | |
|---|---|---|---|---|
| 20 Sep 86 | **THE HOUSE SOUND OF CHICAGO** | | | |
| | *DJ International LONLP 22* ......................... | | 52 | 12 wks |
| 18 Apr 87 | **THE HOUSE OF SOUND OF CHICAGO VOLUME 2** | | | |
| | *DJ International LONLP 32* ......................... | | 38 | 7 wks |
| 31 Oct 87 | **JACKMASTER VOLUME 1** *DJ International JACKLP 501* | | 36 | 4 wks |
| 13 Feb 88 | **JACKMASTER VOLUME 2** *DJ International JACKLP 502* | | 38 | 3 wks |

*EMI*

| | | | | |
|---|---|---|---|---|
| 21 Jun 69 | **IMPACT** *EMI STWO 2* ........................... | | 15 | 14 wks |
| 2 Jun 73 | ★ **PURE GOLD** *EMI EMK 251* ...................... | | 1 | 11 wks |

| | | | | | |
|---|---|---|---|---|---|
| 18 Nov | 78 | ★ **DON'T WALK BOOGIE** *EMI EMTV 13* .............. | 1 | 23 wks |
| 21 Apr | 79 | ● **COUNTRY LIFE** *EMI EMTV 16* ..................... | 2 | 14 wks |
| 2 Jun | 79 | **KNUCKLE SANDWICH** *EMI International EMYV 18* ..... | 19 | 6 wks |
| 15 Dec | 79 | **ALL ABOARD** *EMI EMTX 101* ..................... | 13 | 8 wks |
| 23 Feb | 80 | **METAL FOR MUTHAS** *EMI EMC 3318* .............. | 16 | 7 wks |
| 14 Jun | 80 | **METAL FOR MUTHAS VOL. 2** *EMI EMC 3337* ........ | 58 | 1 wk |
| 13 Mar | 82 | **20 WITH A BULLET** *EMI EMTV 32* ................. | 11 | 8 wks |
| 26 May | 84 | ● **THEN CAME ROCK 'N' ROLL** *EMI THEN 1* ........ | 5 | 15 wks |
| 5 Mar | 88 | ● **UNFORGETTABLE** *EMI EMTV 44* .................. | 5 | 21 wks |
| 22 Oct | 88 | **THE CLASSIC EXPERIENCE** *EMI EMTVD 45* ........ | 27 | 12 wks |
| 3 Dec | 88 | **HELLO CHILDREN...EVERYWHERE** *EMI EM 1307* | 59 | 5 wks |

| | | | | | |
|---|---|---|---|---|---|
| 14 Jan | 89 | ● **THE CLASSIC EXPERIENCE** *EMI EMTVD 45* ........ | 8† | 22 wks |
| 28 Jan | 89 | **UNFORGETTABLE** *EMI EMTV 44* .................. | 18 | 1 wk |
| 18 Mar | 89 | ★ **UNFORGETTABLE 2** *EMI EMTV 46* ................ | 1 | 15 wks |
| 30 Sep | 89 | ● **IS THIS LOVE** *EMI EMTV 47* ..................... | 2 | 8 wks |
| 18 Nov | 89 | ★ **THE 80'S ALBUM OF THE DECADE** *EMI EMTVD 48* .. | 1† | 7 wks |
| 9 Dec | 89 | ● **IT'S CHRISTMAS** *EMI EMTV 49* ................... | 3† | 4 wks |

### Epic
| | | | | | |
|---|---|---|---|---|---|
| 2 Jul | 83 | **DANCE MIX – DANCE HITS VOL. 1** *Epic EPC 25564* ... | 85 | 2 wks |
| 24 Sep | 83 | **DANCE MIX – DANCE HITS VOL. 2** *Epic DM 2* ....... | 51 | 3 wks |
| 3 Mar | 84 | **DANCE MIX – DANCE HITS VOL. 3** *Epic DM 3* ....... | 70 | 1 wk |
| 3 Mar | 84 | **ELECTRO SHOCK VOLTAGE** *Epic VOLT 1* ......... | 73 | 1 wk |
| 16 Jun | 84 | ● **AMERICAN HEARTBEAT** *Epic EPC 10045* .......... | 4 | 22 wks |
| 16 Jun | 84 | **DANCE MIX – DANCE HITS VOL. 4** *Epic DM 4* ....... | 99 | 1 wk |
| 8 Mar | 86 | ● **HITS FOR LOVERS** *Epic EPC 10050* ................ | 2 | 14 wks |

### FFRR
| | | | | | |
|---|---|---|---|---|---|
| 30 Jan | 88 | **THE HOUSE SOUND OF CHICAGO VOLUME 3** *FFRR FFRLP 1* ....................................... | 40 | 4 wks |
| 27 Aug | 88 | **THE HOUSE SOUND OF LONDON VOLUME 4** *FFRR FFRDP 4* ....................................... | 70 | 7 wks |
| 1 Oct | 88 | **BALEARIC BEATS VOLUME 1** *FFRR FFRLP 5* ....... | 58 | 2 wks |

### Hits
| | | | | | |
|---|---|---|---|---|---|
| 1 Dec | 84 | ★ **THE HITS ALBUM** *CBS/WEA HITS 1* .............. | 1 | 36 wks |
| 13 Apr | 85 | ★ **HITS 2** *CBS/WEA HITS 2* ..................... | 1 | 21 wks |
| 7 Dec | 85 | ● **HITS 3** *CBS/WEA HITS 3* ..................... | 2 | 21 wks |
| 29 Mar | 86 | ★ **HITS 4** *CBS/WEA/RCA/Arista HITS 4* ............ | 1 | 21 wks |
| 22 Nov | 86 | ★ **HITS 5** *CBS/WEA/RCA/Arista HITS 5* ............ | 1 | 25 wks |
| 25 Jul | 87 | ★ **HITS 6** *CBS/WEA/BMG HITS 6* .................... | 1 | 19 wks |
| 5 Dec | 87 | ● **HITS 7** *CBS/WEA/BMG HITS 7* .................... | 2 | 17 wks |
| 30 Jul | 88 | ● **HITS 8** *CBS/WEA/BMG HITS 8* .................... | 2 | 13 wks |
| 17 Dec | 88 | ● **THE HITS ALBUM** *CBS/WEA/BMG HITS 9* .......... | 5 | 4 wks |

| | | | | | |
|---|---|---|---|---|---|
| 14 Jan | 89 | ● **THE HITS ALBUM** *CBS/WEA/BMG HITS 9* .......... | 4 | 7 wks |
| 3 Jun | 89 | ★ **HITS 10** *CBS/WEA/BMG HITS 10* ................... | 1 | 13 wks |
| 2 Dec | 89 | ● **MONSTER HITS** *CBS/WEA/BMG HITS 11* ........... | 2† | 5 wks |

### Impression
| | | | | | |
|---|---|---|---|---|---|
| 16 Oct | 82 | **BEST FRIENDS** *Impression LP IMP 1* ................ | 28 | 21 wks |
| 3 Sep | 83 | **SUNNY AFTERNOON** *Impression LP IMP 2* .......... | 13 | 8 wks |
| 26 Nov | 83 | **PRECIOUS MOMENTS** *Impression LP IMP 3* ......... | 77 | 5 wks |
| 7 Apr | 84 | **ALWAYS AND FOREVER – THE COLLECTION** *Impression LP IMP 4* ............................. | 24 | 12 wks |
| 21 Jul | 84 | **WIPEOUT – 20 INSTRUMENTAL GREATS** *Impression LP IMP 5* ............................. | 37 | 3 wks |
| 28 Jul | 84 | **SUNNY AFTERNOON VOLUME TWO** *Impression LP IMP 7* ............................. | 90 | 1 wk |
| 22 Dec | 84 | **FRIENDS AGAIN** *Impression LP IMP 8* ............... | 91 | 1 wk |

### Island
| | | | | | |
|---|---|---|---|---|---|
| 26 Aug | 67 | **CLUB SKA '67** *Island ILP 956* ....................... | 37 | 19 wks |
| 14 Jun | 69 | **YOU CAN ALL JOIN IN** *Island IWPS 2* .............. | 18 | 10 wks |
| 29 Mar | 80 | **CLUB SKA '67 (re-issue)** *Island IRSP 4* .............. | 53 | 6 wks |
| 16 Jun | 84 | **CREW CUTS** *Island IMA 11* ....................... | 71 | 4 wks |
| 27 Oct | 84 | **CREW CUTS – LESSON 2** *Island IMA 14* ............. | 95 | 2 wks |
| 18 Jul | 87 | ● **THE ISLAND STORY** *Island ISL 25* ................. | 9 | 10 wks |

### Jack Trax
| | | | | | |
|---|---|---|---|---|---|
| 18 Jul | 87 | **JACK TRAX – THE FIRST ALBUM** *Jack Trax JTRAX 1* .. | 83 | 2 wks |
| 3 Oct | 87 | **JACK TRAX – THE SECOND ALBUM** *Jack Trax JTRAX 2* | 61 | 2 wks |
| 5 Mar | 88 | **JACK TRAX – THE FOURTH ALBUM** *Jack Trax JTRAX 4* | 49 | 4 wks |

## Jetstar

| | | | |
|---|---|---|---|
| 30 Mar 85 | **REGGAE HITS VOLUME 1** *Jetstar JETLP 1001* ......... | **32** | 11 wks |
| 26 Oct 85 | **REGGAE HITS VOLUME 2** *Jetstar JETLP 1002* ......... | **86** | 2 wks |
| 4 Jun 88 | **REGGAE HITS VOLUME 4** *Jetstar JETLP 1004* ......... | **56** | 7 wks |
| 17 Dec 88 | **REGGAE HITS VOLUME 5** *Jetstar JETLP 1005* ......... | **96** | 1 wk |
| 5 Aug 89 | **REGGAE HITS VOLUME 6** *Jetstar JETLP 1006* ......... | **13** | 6 wks |
| 23 Dec 89 | **REGGAE HITS VOLUME 7** *Jetstar JETLP 1007* ......... | **20** | 1 wk |

## K-Tel

| | | | |
|---|---|---|---|
| 10 Jun 72 | ★ **20 DYNAMIC HITS** *K-Tel TE 292* .................... | **1** | 28 wks |
| 7 Oct 72 | ★ **20 ALL TIME HITS OF THE 50'S** *K-Tel NE 490* ......... | **1** | 22 wks |
| 29 Nov 72 | ● **25 DYNAMIC HITS VOL. 2** *K-Tel TE 291* ............. | **2** | 12 wks |
| 2 Dec 72 | ★ **25 ROCKIN' & ROLLIN' GREATS** *K-Tel NE 493* ...... | **1** | 18 wks |
| 31 Mar 73 | ★ **20 FLASHBACK GREATS OF THE SIXTIES** *K-Tel NE 494* ..................................... | **1** | 11 wks |
| 21 Apr 73 | ● **BELIEVE IN MUSIC** *K-Tel TE 294* ................... | **2** | 8 wks |
| 8 Nov 75 | **GOOFY GREATS** *K-Tel NE 707* .................. | **19** | 7 wks |
| 13 Dec 75 | ● **40 SUPER GREATS** *K-Tel NE 708* .................. | **9** | 8 wks |
| 31 Jan 76 | ● **MUSIC EXPRESS** *K-Tel TE 702* .................. | **3** | 10 wks |
| 10 Apr 76 | ● **JUKE BOX JIVE** *K-Tel NE 709* ...................... | **3** | 13 wks |
| 17 Apr 76 | **GREAT ITALIAN LOVE SONGS** *K-Tel NE 303* ........ | **17** | 14 wks |
| 15 May 76 | **HIT MACHINE** *K-Tel TE 713* .................... | **4** | 10 wks |
| 5 Jun 76 | **EUROVISION FAVOURITES** *K-Tel NE 712* .......... | **44** | 1 wk |
| 2 Oct 76 | **SUMMER CRUISING** *K-Tel NE 918* ................. | **30** | 1 wk |
| 16 Oct 76 | ● **COUNTRY COMFORT** *K-Tel NE 294* .............. | **8** | 12 wks |
| 16 Oct 76 | ★ **SOUL MOTION** *K-Tel NE 930* ..................... | **1** | 14 wks |
| 4 Dec 76 | ● **DISCO ROCKET** *K-Tel NE 948* ................... | **3** | 14 wks |
| 11 Dec 76 | **44 SUPERSTARS** *K-Tel NE 939* ................... | **14** | 10 wks |
| 12 Feb 77 | ● **HEARTBREAKERS** *K-Tel NE 954* ................... | **2** | 18 wks |
| 19 Feb 77 | ● **DANCE TO THE MUSIC** *K-Tel NE 957* .......... | **5** | 9 wks |
| 7 May 77 | **HIT ACTION** *K-Tel NE 993* ....................... | **15** | 9 wks |
| 29 Oct 77 | **SOUL CITY** *K-Tel NE 1003* ....................... | **12** | 7 wks |
| 12 Nov 77 | ● **FEELINGS** *K-Tel NE 1006* ...................... | **3** | 24 wks |
| 26 Nov 77 | ★ **DISCO FEVER** *K-Tel NE 1014* ................... | **1** | 20 wks |
| 21 Jan 78 | **40 NUMBER ONE HTIS** *K-Tel NE 1008* ............... | **15** | 7 wks |
| 4 Mar 78 | ● **DISCO STARS** *K-Tel NE 1022* .................... | **6** | 8 wks |
| 10 Jun 78 | ● **DISCO DOUBLE** *K-Tel NE 1024* .................. | **10** | 6 wks |
| 8 Jul 78 | **ROCK RULES** *K-Tel RL 001* ........................ | **12** | 11 wks |
| 8 Jul 78 | **THE WORLD'S WORST RECORD SHOW** *Yuk/K-Tel NE 1023* ................................ | **47** | 2 wks |
| 19 Aug 78 | ● **STAR PARTY** *K-Tel NE 1034* ..................... | **4** | 9 wks |
| 4 Nov 78 | ● **EMOTIONS** *K-Tel NE 1035* ...................... | **2** | 17 wks |
| 25 Nov 78 | ● **MIDNIGHT HUSTLE** *K-Tel NE 1037* ................ | **2** | 13 wks |
| 20 Jan 79 | ★ **ACTION REPLAY** *K-Tel NE 1040* .................. | **1** | 14 wks |
| 7 Apr 79 | **DISCO INFERNO** *K-Tel NE 1043* ................... | **11** | 9 wks |
| 5 May 79 | **HI ENERGY** *K-Tel NE 1044* ...................... | **17** | 7 wks |
| 22 Sep 79 | **HOT TRACKS** *K-Tel NE 1049* ..................... | **31** | 8 wks |
| 24 Nov 79 | ● **NIGHT MOVES** *K-Tel NE 1065* ................... | **10** | 10 wks |
| 24 Nov 79 | **TOGETHER** *K-Tel NE 1053* ....................... | **35** | 8 wks |
| 12 Jan 80 | ● **VIDEO STARS** *K-Tel NE 1066* ................... | **5** | 10 wks |
| 26 Jan 80 | **THE SUMMIT** *K-Tel NE 1067* ..................... | **17** | 5 wks |
| 29 Mar 80 | ● **STAR TRACKS** *K-Tel NE 1070* ................... | **6** | 8 wks |
| 26 Apr 80 | **GOOD MORNING AMERICA** *K-Tel NE 1072* ......... | **15** | 12 wks |
| 17 May 80 | **HAPPY DAYS** *K-Tel ONE 1076* ................... | **32** | 6 wks |
| 17 May 80 | ● **MAGIC REGGAE** *K-Tel NE 1074* ................. | **9** | 17 wks |
| 14 Jun 80 | ● **HOT WAX** *K-Tel NE 1082* ...................... | **3** | 10 wks |
| 27 Sep 80 | ● **MOUNTING EXCITEMENT** *K-Tel NE 1091* .......... | **2** | 8 wks |
| 11 Oct 80 | ● **THE LOVE ALBUM** *K-Tel NE 1062* ............... | **6** | 16 wks |
| 25 Oct 80 | **AXE ATTACK** *K-Tel NE 1100* .................... | **15** | 14 wks |
| 15 Nov 80 | ● **CHART EXPLOSION** *K-Tel NE 1103* ............... | **6** | 17 wks |
| 3 Jan 81 | **NIGHTLIFE** *K-Tel NE 1107* ...................... | **25** | 9 wks |
| 14 Feb 81 | **HIT MACHINE** *K-Tel NE 1113* .................... | **17** | 6 wks |
| 21 Mar 81 | **RHYTHM 'N' REGGAE** *K-Tel NE 1115* ............. | **42** | 4 wks |
| 25 Apr 81 | ● **CHARTBUSTERS 81** *K-Tel NE 1118* ............... | **3** | 9 wks |
| 2 May 81 | **AXE ATTACK 2** *K-Tel NE 1120* .................. | **31** | 6 wks |
| 23 May 81 | ● **THEMES** *K-Tel NE 1122* ....................... | **6** | 15 wks |
| 29 Aug 81 | **CALIFORNIA DREAMING** *K-Tel NE 1126* ........... | **27** | 11 wks |
| 19 Sep 81 | **DANCE DANCE DANCE** *K-Tel NE 1143* ........... | **29** | 4 wks |
| 3 Oct 81 | **THE PLATINUM ALBUM** *K-Tel NE 1134* ............ | **32** | 11 wks |
| 10 Oct 81 | ● **LOVE IS ...** *K-Tel NE 1129* .................... | **10** | 15 wks |
| 21 Nov 81 | ★ **CHART HITS 81** *K-Tel NE 1142* .................... | **1** | 17 wks |
| 9 Jan 82 | ● **MODERN DANCE** *K-Tel NE 1156* .................. | **6** | 10 wks |

| | | | |
|---|---|---|---|
| 20 Feb 88 | **MAD ON HOUSE VOLUME 1** *Needle MADD 1* ......... | 81 | 2 wks |
| 14 May 88 | **HOUSE HITS** *Needle HOHI 88* .................... | 25 | 8 wks |

*Nouveau Music*

| | | | |
|---|---|---|---|
| 24 Sep 83 | **CLASSIC THEMES** *Nouveau Music NML 1001* ........... | 61 | 2 wks |
| 2 Jun 84 | **ESSENTIAL DISCO AND DANCE** | | |
| | *Nouveau Music NML 1010* ........................... | 96 | 1 wk |
| 30 Mar 85 | **DREAM MELODIES** *Nouveau Music NML 1013* ......... | 91 | 1 wk |

*Now!*

| | | | |
|---|---|---|---|
| 10 Dec 83 | ★ **NOW THAT'S WHAT I CALL MUSIC** *EMI/Virgin NOW 1* | 1 | 50 wks |
| 7 Apr 84 | ★ **NOW THAT'S WHAT I CALL MUSIC 2** | | |
| | *EMI/Virgin NOW 2* ................................ | 1 | 38 wks |
| 11 Aug 84 | ★ **NOW THAT'S WHAT I CALL MUSIC 3** | | |
| | *EMI/Virgin NOW 3* ................................ | 1 | 30 wks |
| 8 Dec 84 | ● **NOW THAT'S WHAT I CALL MUSIC 4** | | |
| | *EMI/Virgin NOW 4* ................................ | 2 | 43 wks |
| 1 Jun 85 | ● **NOW DANCE** *EMI/Virgin NOD 1* .................... | 3 | 14 wks |
| 17 Aug 85 | ★ **NOW THAT'S WHAT I CALL MUSIC 5** | | |
| | *EMI/Virgin NOW 5* ................................ | 1 | 21 wks |
| 30 Nov 85 | ★ **NOW – THE CHRISTMAS ALBUM** *EMI/Virgin NOX 1* . | 1 | 22 wks |
| 7 Dec 85 | ★ **NOW THAT'S WHAT I CALL MUSIC 6** | | |
| | *EMI/Virgin NOW 6* ................................ | 1 | 40 wks |
| 19 Jul 86 | ● **NOW – THE SUMMER ALBUM** *EMI/Virgin SUMMER 1* | 7 | 9 wks |
| 23 Aug 86 | ★ **NOW THAT'S WHAT I CALL MUSIC 7** | | |
| | *EMI/Virgin NOW 7* ................................ | 1 | 21 wks |
| 8 Nov 86 | ● **NOW DANCE '86** *EMI/Virgin NOD 2* ................. | 2 | 13 wks |
| 29 Nov 86 | **NOW THAT'S WHAT I CALL MUSIC '86** | | |
| | *EMI/Virgin/Polygram CDNOW 86* .................... | 65 | 4 wks |
| 6 Dec 86 | ★ **NOW THAT'S WHAT I CALL MUSIC 8** | | |
| | *EMI/Virgin/Polygram NOW 8* ....................... | 1 | 23 wks |
| 4 Apr 87 | ★ **NOW THAT'S WHAT I CALL MUSIC 9** | | |
| | *EMI/Virgin/Polygram NOW 9* ....................... | 1 | 26 wks |
| 3 Oct 87 | ● **NOW! SMASH HITS** *EMI/Virgin/Polygram NOSH 1* ...... | 5 | 10 wks |
| 5 Dec 87 | ★ **NOW THAT'S WHAT I CALL MUSIC 10** | | |
| | *EMI/Virgin/Polygram NOW 10* ...................... | 1 | 21 wks |
| 2 Apr 88 | ★ **NOW THAT'S WHAT I CALL MUSIC 11** | | |
| | *EMI/Virgin/Polygram NOW 11* ...................... | 1 | 17 wks |
| 23 Jul 88 | ★ **NOW THAT'S WHAT I CALL MUSIC 12** | | |
| | *EMI/Virgin/Polygram NOW 12* ...................... | 1 | 17 wks |
| 3 Dec 88 | ★ **NOW THAT'S WHAT I CALL MUSIC 13** | | |
| | *EMI/Virgin/Polygram NOW 13* ...................... | 1 | 6 wks |
| ................ | | | |
| 14 Jan 89 | ★ **NOW THAT'S WHAT I CALL MUSIC 13** | | |
| | *EMI/Virgin/Polygram NOW 13* ...................... | 1 | 15 wks |
| 1 Apr 89 | ★ **NOW THAT'S WHAT I CALL MUSIC 14** | | |
| | *EMI/Virgin/Polygram NOW 14* ...................... | 1 | 18 wks |
| 15 Jul 89 | ★ **NOW DANCE '89** *EMI/Virgin NOD 3* ................. | 1 | 14 wks |
| 26 Aug 89 | ★ **NOW THAT'S WHAT I CALL MUSIC 15** | | |
| | *EMI/Virgin/Polygram NOW 15* ...................... | 1 | 13 wks |
| 2 Dec 89 | ★ **NOW THAT'S WHAT I CALL MUSIC 16** | | |
| | *EMI/Virgin/Polygram NOW 16* ...................... | 1† | 5 wks |

*Philips*

| | | | |
|---|---|---|---|
| 9 Mar 63 | ● **ALL STAR FESTIVAL** *Philips DL 99500* .............. | 4 | 19 wks |
| 2 Jun 73 | ● **20 ORIGINAL CHART HITS** *Philips TV 1* ............. | 9 | 11 wks |
| 2 Jun 73 | **NICE 'N' EASY** *Philips 6441 076* .................... | 36 | 1 wk |
| 6 Aug 77 | **NEW WAVE** *Philips 5300 902* ...................... | 11 | 12 wks |

*Polydor*

| | | | |
|---|---|---|---|
| 10 Dec 66 | **STEREO MUSICALE SHOWCASE** *Polydor 104450* ...... | 26 | 2 wks |
| 9 Oct 71 | **THE A–Z OF EASY LISTENING** *Polydor 2661 005* ...... | 24 | 4 wks |
| 24 Feb 79 | **20 OF ANOTHER KIND** *Polydor POLS 1006* ........... | 45 | 3 wks |
| 19 May 79 | **BOOGIE BUS** *Polydor 9198 174* .................... | 23 | 11 wks |
| 3 May 80 | ● **CHAMPAGNE AND ROSES** *Polydor ROSTV 1* ........ | 7 | 14 wks |
| 30 Aug 80 | **I AM WOMAN** *Polydor WOMTV 1* ................... | 11 | 13 wks |
| 11 Oct 80 | **COUNTRY ROUND UP** *Polydor KOWTV 1* ........... | 64 | 3 wks |
| 18 Oct 80 | **MONSTERS OF ROCK** *Polydor 2488 810* ............. | 16 | 5 wks |
| 6 Dec 80 | **THE HITMAKERS** *Polydor HOPTV 1* ................ | 45 | 10 wks |
| 4 Apr 81 | ● **ROLL ON** *Polydor REDTV 1* ...................... | 3 | 13 wks |
| 17 Oct 81 | **MONSTER TRACKS** *Polydor HOPTV 2* ............... | 20 | 8 wks |
| 12 Jan 85 | **BREAKDANCE 2 – ELECTRIC BOOGALOO** | | |
| | *Polydor POLD 5168* ............................. | 34 | 20 wks |
| 12 Nov 88 | ● **THE PREMIER COLLECTION** *Polydor ALWTV 1* ...... | 3 | 9 wks |

| | | | | |
|---|---|---|---|---|
| 14 Jan 89 | ★ **THE PREMIER COLLECTION** *Polydor ALWTV 1* ...... | 1† | 30 wks |
| 4 Feb 89 | ★ **THE MARQUEE – 30 LEGENDARY YEARS** | | |
| | *Polydor MOTV 1* ................................. | 1 | 21 wks |

*Pye*

| | | | | |
|---|---|---|---|---|
| 9 May 59 | ● **CURTAIN UP** *Pye Nixa BRTH 0059* ................. | 4 | 13 wks |
| 23 Jun 62 | **HONEY HIT PARADE** *Pye Golden Guinea GGL 0129* ..... | 13 | 7 wks |
| 30 Nov 62 | **ALL THE HITS BY ALL THE STARS** | | |
| | *Pye Golden Guinea GGL 0162* ........................ | 19 | 2 wks |
| 7 Sep 63 | **HITSVILLE** *Pye Golden Guinea GGL 0202* .............. | 11 | 6 wks |
| 14 Sep 63 | **THE BEST OF RADIO LUXEMBOURG** | | |
| | *Pye Golden Guinea GGL 0208* ........................ | 14 | 2 wks |
| 23 Nov 63 | **HITSVILLE VOL. 2** *Pye Golden Guinea GGL 0233* ........ | 20 | 1 wk |
| 4 Jan 64 | **THE BLUES VOL. 1** *Pye NPL 28030* .................. | 15 | 3 wks |
| 22 Feb 64 | **FOLK FESTIVAL OF THE BLUES (LIVE RECORDING)** | | |
| | *Pye NPL 28033* .................................. | 16 | 4 wks |
| 30 May 64 | **THE BLUES VOL. 2** *Pye NPL 28035* .................. | 16 | 3 wks |
| 10 Feb 68 | **STARS OF '68** *Marble Arch MAL 762* ................ | 23 | 3 wks |
| 16 Oct 71 | **PYE CHARTBUSTERS** *Pye PCB 15000* .............. | 36 | 1 wk |
| 18 Dec 71 | **PYE CHARTBUSTERS VOL. 2** *Pye PCB 15001* ........ | 29 | 3 wks |

*Ronco*

| | | | | |
|---|---|---|---|---|
| 21 Oct 72 | ● **20 STAR TRACKS** *Ronco PP 2001* .................... | 2 | 13 wks |
| 23 Jun 73 | ★ **THAT'LL BE THE DAY** *Ronco MR 2002/3* .............. | 1 | 8 wks |
| 8 Nov 75 | **BLAZING BULLETS** *Ronco RTI 2012* ................ | 17 | 8 wks |
| 6 Dec 75 | **GREATEST HITS OF WALT DISNEY** *Ronco RTD 2013* . | 11 | 12 wks |
| 13 Dec 75 | **A CHRISTMAS GIFT** *Ronco P 12430* .................. | 39 | 5 wks |
| 24 Jan 76 | ● **STAR TRACKIN' 76** *Ronco RTL 2014* ................ | 9 | 5 wks |
| 8 Jan 77 | **CLASSICAL GOLD** *Ronco RTD 42020* ................ | 24 | 12 wks |
| 16 Jul 77 | **SUPERGROUPS** *Ronco RTL 2023* .................... | 57 | 1 wk |
| 26 Nov 77 | **BLACK JOY** *Ronco RTL 2025* ........................ | 26 | 13 wks |
| 18 Mar 78 | ● **BOOGIE NIGHTS** *Ronco RTL 2027* .................. | 5 | 7 wks |
| 18 Nov 78 | **BOOGIE FEVER** *Ronco RTL 2034* .................. | 15 | 11 wks |
| 9 Jun 79 | **ROCK LEGENDS** *Ronco RTL 2037* .................. | 54 | 3 wks |
| 3 Nov 79 | ● **ROCK 'N' ROLLER DISCO** *Ronco RTL 2040* .......... | 3 | 11 wks |
| 8 Dec 79 | **PEACE IN THE VALLEY** *Ronco RTL 2043* .............. | 6 | 18 wks |
| 22 Dec 79 | **MILITARY GOLD** *Ronco RTD 42042* .............. | 62 | 3 wks |
| 25 Oct 80 | **STREET LEVEL** *Ronco RTL 2048* .................... | 29 | 5 wks |
| 8 Nov 80 | ● **COUNTRY LEGENDS** *Ronco RTL 2050* .............. | 9 | 12 wks |
| 15 Nov 80 | **RADIOACTIVE** *Ronco RTL 2049* ..................... | 13 | 9 wks |
| 29 Nov 80 | **SPACE INVADERS** *Ronco RTL 2051* .................. | 47 | 3 wks |
| 6 Dec 80 | **THE LEGENDARY BIG BANDS** *Ronco RTL 2047* ...... | 24 | 6 wks |
| 9 May 81 | ★ **DISCO DAZE AND DISCO NITES** *Ronco RTL 2056 A/B* | 1 | 23 wks |
| 19 Sep 81 | ● **SUPER HITS 1 & 2** *Ronco RTL 2058 A/B* .............. | 2 | 17 wks |
| 24 Oct 81 | **COUNTRY SUNRISE/COUNTRY SUNSET** | | |
| | *Ronco RTL 2059 A/B* ............................ | 27 | 11 wks |
| 14 Nov 81 | **ROCK HOUSE** *Ronco RTL 2061* .................... | 44 | 4 wks |
| 12 Dec 81 | **MISTY MORNINGS** *Ronco RTL 2066* ............... | 44 | 5 wks |
| 12 Dec 81 | **MEMORIES ARE MADE OF THIS** *Ronco RTL 2062* ..... | 84 | 4 wks |
| 26 Dec 81 | ● **HITS HITS HITS** *Ronco RTL 2063* ............... | 2 | 10 wks |
| 24 Apr 82 | ● **DISCO UK & DISCO USA** *Ronco RTL 2073* ............ | 7 | 10 wks |
| 15 May 82 | ● **CHARTBUSTERS** *Ronco RTL 2074* .................. | 3 | 10 wks |
| 3 Jul 82 | ● **OVERLOAD** *Ronco RTL 2079* ..................... | 10 | 8 wks |
| 28 Aug 82 | **SOUL DAZE/SOUL NITES** *Ronco RTL 2080* ........... | 25 | 10 wks |
| 11 Sep 82 | ● **BREAKOUT** *Ronco RTL 2081* ........................ | 4 | 8 wks |
| 30 Oct 82 | **MUSIC FOR THE SEASONS** *Ronco RTL 2075* .......... | 41 | 10 wks |
| 27 Nov 82 | **CHART WARS** *Ronco RTL 2086* ................... | 30 | 7 wks |
| 27 Nov 82 | **THE GREAT COUNTRY MUSIC SHOW** *Ronco RTD 2083* | 38 | 7 wks |
| 18 Dec 82 | **THE BEST OF BEETHOVEN/STRAUSS/** | | |
| | **TCHAIKOWSKY/MOZART (4 LPs)** *Ronco RTL 2084* . | 49 | 10 wks |
| 25 Dec 82 | ★ **RAIDERS OF THE POP CHARTS** *Ronco RTL 2088* ..... | 1 | 17 wks |
| 19 Mar 83 | ● **CHART RUNNERS** *Ronco RTL 2090* ................. | 4 | 13 wks |
| 21 May 83 | ● **CHART ENCOUNTERS OF THE HIT KIND** | | |
| | *Ronco RTL 2091* ............................... | 5 | 10 wks |
| 18 Jun 83 | **LOVERS ONLY** *Ronco RTL 2093* .................... | 12 | 13 wks |
| 16 Jul 83 | **HITS ON FIRE** *Ronco RTL 2095* ..................... | 11 | 10 wks |
| 17 Sep 83 | ● **THE HIT SQUAD – CHART TRACKING** | | |
| | *Ronco RON LP 1* ................................. | 4 | 9 wks |
| 17 Sep 83 | **THE HIT SQUAD – NIGHT CLUBBING** | | |
| | *Ronco RON LP 2* ................................. | 28 | 7 wks |
| 12 Nov 83 | **HIT SQUAD – HITS OF '83** *Ronco RON LP 4* .......... | 12 | 11 wks |
| 17 Dec 83 | ● **GREEN VELVET** *Ronco RON LP 6* ................. | 6 | 17 wks |
| 7 Jan 84 | **CHART TREK VOLS. 1 & 2** *Ronco RON LP 8* ........ | 20 | 9 wks |
| 21 Jan 84 | ● **SOMETIMES WHEN WE TOUCH** *Ronco RON LP 9* ... | 8 | 14 wks |

| | | |
|---|---|---|
| 24 Mar 84 | **BABY LOVE** *Ronco RON LP 11* ..................... | 47 | 6 wks |
| 7 Apr 84 | **DREAMS AND THEMES** *Ronco RON LP 10* .......... | 75 | 2 wks |

Green Velvet *was re-issued on Telstar STAR 2252.*

*Serious*

| | | | |
|---|---|---|---|
| 7 Jun 86 | **UPFRONT 1** *Serious UPFT 1* ...................... | 17 | 10 wks |
| 23 Aug 86 | **UPFRONT 2** *Serious UPFT 2* ...................... | 27 | 6 wks |
| 1 Nov 86 | **UPFRONT 3** *Serious UPFT 3* ...................... | 37 | 5 wks |
| 31 Jan 87 | **UPFRONT 4** *Serious UPFT 4* ...................... | 21 | 5 wks |
| 28 Mar 87 | **SERIOUS HIP-HOP 2** *Serious SHOP 2* ............... | 95 | 1 wk |
| 28 Mar 87 | **UPFRONT 5** *Serious UPFT 5* ...................... | 21 | 6 wks |
| 23 May 87 | **UPFRONT 6** *Serious UPFT 6* ...................... | 22 | 6 wks |
| 4 Jul 87 | **BEST OF HOUSE VOLUME 1** *Serious BEHO 1* ........ | 55 | 12 wks |
| 15 Aug 87 | **UPFRONT 7** *Serious UPFT 7* ...................... | 31 | 4 wks |
| 12 Sep 87 | **BEST OF HOUSE VOLUME 2** *Serious BEHO 2* ........ | 30 | 7 wks |
| 17 Oct 87 | **HIP-HOP '87** *Serious HHOP 87* ................... | 81 | 1 wk |
| 17 Oct 87 | **UPFRONT 8** *Serious UPFT 8* ...................... | 22 | 6 wks |
| 14 Nov 87 | **BEST OF HOUSE VOLUME 3** *Serious BEHO 3* ........ | 61 | 3 wks |
| 12 Dec 87 | **BEST OF HOUSE MEGAMIX** *Serious BOIT 1* .......... | 77 | 4 wks |
| 19 Dec 87 | **UPFRONT 9** *Serious UPFT 9* ...................... | 92 | 1 wk |
| 20 Feb 88 | **DANCE MANIA VOLUME 2** *Serious DAMA 2* .......... | 59 | 2 wks |
| 12 Mar 88 | **BEST OF HOUSE VOLUME 4** *Serious BEHO 4* ........ | 27 | 8 wks |
| 9 Apr 88 | **UPFRONT 10** *Serious UPFT 10* .................... | 45 | 5 wks |
| 14 May 88 | **BEST OF HOUSE MEGAMIX VOLUME 2** *Serious BOIT 2* . | 73 | 2 wks |
| 29 Oct 88 | **ACID TRAX MEGAMIX VOLUME 1** *Serious DUIX 1* .... | 93 | 1 wk |
| .......... | | | |
| 18 Feb 89 | **UPFRONT '89** *Serious UPFT 89* ..................... | 15 | 1 wk |

*Starblend*

| | | | |
|---|---|---|---|
| 12 Nov 83 | **IN TOUCH** *Starblend STD 9* ...................... | 89 | 2 wks |
| 23 Jun 84 | **BROKEN DREAMS** *Starblend SLTD 1* ............... | 48 | 7 wks |
| 27 Apr 85 | **12 X 12 MEGA MIXES** *Starblend SLTD 1* .............. | 77 | 2 wks |
| 3 Aug 85 | **AMERICAN DREAMS** *Starblend SLTD 12* ............. | 43 | 8 wks |
| 21 Dec 85 | **CHRISTMAS AT THE COUNTRY STORE** *Starblend NOEL 1* .................................... | 94 | 1 wk |
| 12 Jul 86 | **DISCOVER COUNTRY/DISCOVER NEW COUNTRY** *Starblend DNC 1* .................................... | 60 | 3 wks |
| 16 Aug 86 | **HEARTBREAKERS** *Starblend BLEND 3* .............. | 38 | 8 wks |
| 20 Sep 86 | **ABSOLUTE ROCK 'N' ROLL** *Starblend SLTD 15* ....... | 88 | 1 wk |

*Street Sounds*

| | | | |
|---|---|---|---|
| 19 Feb 83 | **STREET SOUNDS EDITION 2** *Street Sounds STSND 002* . | 35 | 6 wks |
| 23 Apr 83 | **STREET SOUNDS EDITION 3** *Street Sounds STSND 003* . | 21 | 5 wks |
| 25 Jun 83 | **STREET SOUNDS EDITION 4** *Street Sounds STSND 004* . | 14 | 8 wks |
| 13 Aug 83 | **STREET SOUNDS EDITION 5** *Street Sounds STSND 005* . | 16 | 8 wks |
| 8 Oct 83 | **STREET SOUNDS EDITION 6** *Street Sounds STSND 006* . | 23 | 5 wks |
| 22 Oct 83 | **STREET SOUNDS ELECTRO 1** *Street Sounds ELCST 1* .. | 18 | 8 wks |
| 17 Dec 83 | **STREET SOUNDS EDITION 7** *Street Sounds STSND 007* . | 48 | 4 wks |
| 7 Jan 84 | **STREET SOUNDS ELECTRO 2** *Street Sounds ELCST 2* .. | 49 | 7 wks |
| 3 Mar 84 | **STREET SOUNDS HI ENERGY 1** *Street Sounds HINRG 16* | 71 | 1 wk |
| 10 Mar 84 | **STREET SOUNDS CRUCIAL ELECTRO** *Street Sounds ELCST 999* ......................... | 24 | 10 wks |
| 10 Mar 84 | **STREET SOUNDS EDITION 8** *Street Sounds STSND 008* . | 22 | 7 wks |
| 7 Apr 84 | **STREET SOUNDS ELECTRO 3** *Street Sounds ELCST 3* .. | 25 | 9 wks |
| 12 May 84 | **STREET SOUNDS EDITION 9** *Street Sounds STSND 009* . | 22 | 5 wks |
| 9 Jun 84 | **STREET SOUNDS ELECTRO 4** *Street Sounds ELCST 4* .. | 25 | 9 wks |
| 30 Jun 84 | **STREET SOUNDS UK ELECTRO** *Street Sounds ELCST 1984* ......................... | 60 | 4 wks |
| 21 Jul 84 | **LET THE MUSIC SCRATCH** *Street Sounds MKL 1* ...... | 91 | 3 wks |
| 11 Aug 84 | **STREET SOUNDS CRUCIAL ELECTRO 2** *Street Sounds ELCST 1000* ......................... | 35 | 6 wks |
| 18 Aug 84 | **STREET SOUNDS EDITION 10** *Street Sounds STSND 010* . | 24 | 6 wks |
| 6 Oct 84 | **STREET SOUNDS ELECTRO 5** *Street Sounds ELCST 5* .. | 17 | 6 wks |
| 10 Nov 84 | **STREET SOUNDS EDITION 11** *Street Sounds STSND 011* . | 48 | 4 wks |
| 9 Mar 85 | **STREET SOUNDS ELECTRO 6** *Street Sounds ELCST 6* .. | 24 | 10 wks |
| 9 Mar 85 | **THE ARTISTS VOLUME 1** *Street Sounds ARTIS 1* ....... | 65 | 4 wks |
| 18 May 85 | **STREET SOUNDS ELECTRO 7** *Street Sounds ELCST 7* .. | 12 | 7 wks |
| 18 May 85 | **STREET SOUNDS EDITION 12** *Street Sounds STSND 12* . | 23 | 4 wks |
| 13 Jul 85 | **STREET SOUNDS ELECTRO 8** *Street Sounds ELCST 8* .. | 23 | 5 wks |
| 13 Jul 85 | **THE ARTISTS VOLUME 2** *Street Sounds ARTIS 2* ....... | 45 | 4 wks |
| 17 Aug 85 | **STREET SOUNDS EDITION 13** *Street Sounds STSND 13* . | 19 | 9 wks |
| 17 Aug 85 | **STREET SOUNDS NY VS LA BEATS** *Street Sounds ELCST 1001* ......................... | 65 | 4 wks |

| | | | | | |
|---|---|---|---|---|---|
| 5 Oct 85 | STREET SOUNDS ELECTRO 9 | *Street Sounds ELCST 9* . . | 18 | 6 wks |
| 12 Oct 85 | THE ARTISTS VOLUME 3 | *Street Sounds ARTIS 3* . . . . . . . | 87 | 2 wks |
| 16 Nov 85 | STREET SOUNDS EDITION 14 | *Street Sounds STSND 14* . | 43 | 3 wks |
| 21 Dec 85 | STREET SOUNDS ELECTRO 10 | *Street Sounds ELCST 10* . | 72 | 6 wks |
| 21 Dec 85 | STREET SOUNDS EDITION 15 | *Street Sounds STSND 15* . | 58 | 8 wks |
| 29 Mar 86 | STREET SOUNDS HIP-HOP ELECTRO 11 | | | |
| | *Street Sounds ELCST 11* . . . . . . . . . . . . . . . . . . . . . . . . . . . | | 19 | 5 wks |
| 5 Apr 86 | STREET SOUNDS EDITION 16 | *Street Sounds STSND 16* . | 17 | 7 wks |
| 21 Jun 86 | JAZZ JUICE 2 | *Street Sounds SOUND 4* . . . . . . . . . . . . . . . . | 96 | 1 wk |
| 28 Jun 86 | STREET SOUNDS HIP-HOP ELECTRO 12 | | | |
| | *Street Sounds ELCST 12* . . . . . . . . . . . . . . . . . . . . . . . . . . . | | 28 | 4 wks |
| 19 Jul 86 | STREET SOUNDS EDITION 17 | *Street Sounds STSND 17* . | 35 | 5 wks |
| 6 Sep 86 | STREET SOUNDS HIP-HOP ELECTRO 13 | | | |
| | *Street Sounds ELCST 13* . . . . . . . . . . . . . . . . . . . . . . . . . . . | | 23 | 5 wks |
| 11 Oct 86 | STREET SOUNDS EDITION 18 | *Street Sounds STSND 18* . | 20 | 5 wks |
| 11 Oct 86 | JAZZ JUICE 3 | *Street Sounds SOUND 5* . . . . . . . . . . . . . . . . | 88 | 1 wk |
| 11 Oct 86 | STREET SOUNDS HIP-HOP ELECTRO 14 | | | |
| | *Street Sounds ELCST 14* . . . . . . . . . . . . . . . . . . . . . . . . . . . | | 40 | 3 wks |
| 15 Nov 86 | STREET SOUNDS HIP-HOP ELECTRO 15 | | | |
| | *Street Sounds ELCST 15* . . . . . . . . . . . . . . . . . . . . . . . . . . . | | 46 | 2 wks |
| 6 Dec 86 | STREET SOUNDS EDITION 19 | *Street Sounds STSND 19* . | 61 | 3 wks |
| 24 Jan 87 | STREET SOUNDS ELECTRO 3 | *Street Sounds ELCST 1002* | 41 | 3 wks |
| 7 Feb 87 | STREET SOUNDS ANTHEMS VOLUME 1 | | | |
| | *Street Sounds MUSIC 5* . . . . . . . . . . . . . . . . . . . . . . . . . . . | | 61 | 3 wks |
| 14 Feb 87 | STREET SOUNDS EDITION 20 | *Street Sounds STSND 20* . | 25 | 4 wks |
| 13 Jun 87 | STREET SOUNDS HIP-HOP ELECTRO 16 | | | |
| | *Street Sounds ELCST 16* . . . . . . . . . . . . . . . . . . . . . . | | 40 | 3 wks |
| 4 Jul 87 | STREET SOUNDS DANCE MUSIC '87 | | | |
| | *Street Sounds STSND 871* . . . . . . . . . . . . . . . . . . . . . . . | | 40 | 5 wks |
| 15 Aug 87 | STREET SOUNDS HIP-HOP 17 | *Street Sounds ELCST 17* | 38 | 3 wks |
| 15 Aug 87 | JAZZ JUICE 5 | *Street Sounds SOUND 8* . . . . . . . . . . . . . . . . | 97 | 1 wk |
| 12 Sep 87 | BEST OF WEST COAST HIP HOP | *Street Sounds MACA 1* . | 80 | 2 wks |
| 12 Sep 87 | STREET SOUNDS '87 VOLUME 2 | | | |
| | *Street Sounds STSND 872* . . . . . . . . . . . . . . . . . . . . . . . | | 47 | 3 wks |
| 24 Oct 87 | STREET SOUNDS HIP-HOP 18 | *Street Sounds ELCST 18* | 67 | 1 wk |
| 12 Mar 88 | STREET SOUNDS HIP-HOP 20 | *Street Sounds ELCST 20* | 39 | 4 wks |
| 19 Mar 88 | STREET SOUNDS 88–1 | *Street Sounds STSND 881* . . . . . . . | 73 | 2 wks |
| 4 Jun 88 | STREET SOUNDS HIP-HOP 21 | *Street Sounds ELCST 21* | 87 | 1 wk |

### Studio Two

| | | | | | |
|---|---|---|---|---|---|
| 21 Oct 67 | ● BREAKTHROUGH | *Studio Two STWO 1* . . . . . . . . . . . . . . | 2 | 11 wks |
| 4 Sep 71 | TOTAL SOUND | *Studio Two STWO 4* . . . . . . . . . . . . . . . . | 39 | 4 wks |
| 30 Oct 71 | STUDIO TWO CLASSICS | *Studio Two STWO 6* . . . . . . . . . | 16 | 4 wks |

### Stylus

| | | | | | |
|---|---|---|---|---|---|
| 3 Aug 85 | THE MAGIC OF TORVILL AND DEAN | *Stylus SMR 8502* | 35 | 9 wks |
| 17 Aug 85 | NIGHT BEAT | *Stylus SMR 8501* . . . . . . . . . . . . . . . . . . . . . | 15 | 8 wks |
| 24 Aug 85 | DISCO BEACH PARTY | *Stylus SMR 8503* . . . . . . . . . . . . . | 29 | 10 wks |
| 14 Dec 85 | VELVET WATERS | *Stylus SMR 8507* . . . . . . . . . . . . . . | 54 | 4 wks |
| 28 Dec 85 | CHOICES OF THE HEART | *Stylus SMR 8511* . . . . . . . . . . | 87 | 2 wks |
| 8 Mar 86 | ● NIGHT BEAT 2 | *Stylus SMR 8613* . . . . . . . . . . . . . . . . . . . . | 7 | 9 wks |
| 17 May 86 | LET'S HEAR IT FROM THE GIRLS | *Stylus SMR 8614* . . . | 17 | 10 wks |
| 1 Nov 86 | BLACK MAGIC | *Stylus SMR 619* . . . . . . . . . . . . . . . . . . . . . | 26 | 9 wks |
| 8 Nov 86 | ● HIT MIX '86 | *Stylus SMR 624* . . . . . . . . . . . . . . . . . . . . . . . . | 10 | 14 wks |
| 22 Nov 86 | CLASSICS BY CANDLELIGHT | *Stylus SMR 620* . . . . . . . | 74 | 4 wks |
| 14 Mar 87 | BANDS OF GOLD – THE SWINGING SIXTIES | | | |
| | *Stylus SMR 726* . . . . . . . . . . . . . . . . . . . . . . . . . . . . . . . . . | | 48 | 6 wks |
| 21 Mar 87 | BANDS OF GOLD – THE SENSATIONAL SEVENTIES | | | |
| | *Stylus SMR 727* . . . . . . . . . . . . . . . . . . . . . . . . . . . . . . . . . | | 75 | 4 wks |
| 28 Mar 87 | BANDS OF GOLD – THE ELECTRIC EIGHTIES | | | |
| | *Stylus SMR 728* . . . . . . . . . . . . . . . . . . . . . . . . . . . . . . . . . | | 82 | 1 wk |
| 11 Jul 87 | ● SIXTIES MIX | *Stylus SMR 733* . . . . . . . . . . . . . . . . . . . . . . | 3 | 44 wks |
| 24 Oct 87 | HIT FACTORY | *Stylus SMR 740* . . . . . . . . . . . . . . . . . . . . . | 18 | 17 wks |
| 21 Nov 87 | HIT MIX – HITS OF THE YEAR | *Stylus SMR 744* . . . . . . . | 29 | 11 wks |
| 2 Apr 88 | ● HIP HOP AND RAPPING IN THE HOUSE | | | |
| | *Stylus SMR 852* . . . . . . . . . . . . . . . . . . . . . . . . . . . . . . . . . | | 5 | 13 wks |
| 30 Apr 88 | THE WORLDS OF FOSTER AND ALLEN | | | |
| | *Stylus SMR 861* . . . . . . . . . . . . . . . . . . . . . . . . . . . . . . . . . | | 21 | 15 wks |
| 7 May 88 | SIXTIES MIX 2 | *Stylus SMR 855* . . . . . . . . . . . . . . . . . . . . . | 14 | 20 wks |
| 4 Jun 88 | BACK ON THE ROAD | *Stylus SMR 854* . . . . . . . . . . . . . . | 29 | 11 wks |
| 30 Jul 88 | ● THE GREATEST EVER ROCK 'N' ROLL MIX | | | |
| | *Stylus SMR 858* . . . . . . . . . . . . . . . . . . . . . . . . . . . . . . . . . | | 8 | 15 wks |
| 3 Sep 88 | ● RAP TRAX | *Stylus SMR 859* . . . . . . . . . . . . . . . . . . . . . . . | 3 | 13 wks |

| | | | | |
|---|---|---|---|---|
| 5 Feb 83 | | INSTRUMENTAL MAGIC *Telstar STAR 2227* .......... | 68 | 5 wks |
| 30 Apr 83 | | 20 GREAT ITALIAN LOVE SONGS *Telstar STAR 2230* . . | 28 | 6 wks |
| 4 Jun 83 | | IN THE GROOVE – THE 12 INCH DISCO PARTY | | |
| | | *Telstar STAR 2228* ............................... | 20 | 12 wks |
| 12 Nov 83 | | ROOTS REGGAE 'N' REGGAE ROCK *Telstar STAR 2233* | 34 | 6 wks |
| 19 Nov 83 | | SUPERCHART '83 *Telstar STAR 2236* ............... | 22 | 9 wks |
| 4 Feb 84 | ● | THE VERY BEST OF MOTOWN LOVE SONGS | | |
| | | *Telstar STAR 2239* ............................... | 10 | 22 wks |
| 26 May 84 | | DON'T STOP DANCING *Telstar STAR 2242* ........... | 11 | 12 wks |
| 13 Oct 84 | ● | HITS HITS HITS – 18 SMASH ORIGINALS | | |
| | | *Telstar STAR 2243* ............................... | 6 | 9 wks |
| 8 Dec 84 | | LOVE SONGS – 16 CLASSIC LOVE SONGS | | |
| | | *Telstar STAR 2246* ............................... | 20 | 12 wks |
| 15 Dec 84 | ● | GREEN VELVET *Telstar STAR 2252* ................. | 10 | 10 wks |
| 7 Sep 85 | | OPEN TOP CARS AND GIRLS IN T-SHIRTS | | |
| | | *Telstar STAR 2257* ............................... | 13 | 9 wks |
| 16 Nov 85 | ● | THE LOVE ALBUM *Telstar STAR 2268* ............. | 7 | 18 wks |
| 16 Nov 85 | ★ | THE GREATEST HITS OF 1985 *Telstar STAR 2269* ..... | 1 | 17 wks |
| 30 Nov 85 | | THE PRINCE'S TRUST COLLECTION *Telstar STAR 2275* | 64 | 5 wks |
| 7 Dec 85 | | PERFORMANCE – THE VERY BEST OF TIM RICE AND | | |
| | | ANDREW LLOYD WEBBER *Telstar STAR 2262* ..... | 33 | 7 wks |
| 7 Dec 85 | | MORE GREEN VELVET *Telstar STAR 2267* ........... | 42 | 5 wks |
| 18 Dec 86 | ● | THE CHART *Telstar STAR 2278* .................... | 6 | 12 wks |
| 1 Nov 86 | | ROCK LEGENDS *Telstar STAR 2290* .................. | 54 | 7 wks |
| 8 Nov 86 | ● | THE GREATEST HITS OF 1986 *Telstar STAR 2286* ..... | 8 | 13 wks |
| 8 Nov 86 | | LOVERS *Telstar STAR 2279* ........................ | 14 | 16 wks |
| 22 Nov 86 | | SIXTIES MANIA *Telstar STAR 2287* .................. | 19 | 22 wks |
| 6 Dec 86 | | MOTOWN CHARTBUSTERS *Telstar STAR 2283* ...... | 25 | 12 wks |
| 28 Mar 87 | | THE DANCE CHART *Telstar STAR 2285* .............. | 23 | 8 wks |
| 3 Oct 87 | | TRACKS OF MY TEARS *Telstar STAR 2295* ........... | 27 | 7 wks |
| 31 Oct 87 | | LOVE SONGS *Telstar STAR 2298* .................... | 12 | 24 wks |
| 21 Nov 87 | | THE GREATEST HITS OF 1987 *Telstar STAR 2309* ..... | 12 | 11 wks |
| 28 Nov 87 | | DANCE MIX '87 *Telstar STAR 2314* .................. | 39 | 10 wks |
| 28 Nov 87 | | ALWAYS AND FOREVER *Telstar STAR 2301* ......... | 41 | 10 wks |
| 28 Nov 87 | | SIXTIES PARTY MEGAMIX ALBUM *Telstar STAR 2307* | 46 | 7 wks |
| 26 Dec 87 | | THE GREATEST LOVE *Telstar STAR 2316* ........... | 11 | 40 wks |
| 26 Dec 87 | ● | LIFE IN THE FAST LANE *Telstar STAR 2315* .......... | 10 | 12 wks |
| 1 Oct 88 | | ... AND THE BEAT GOES ON *Telstar STAR 2338* ...... | 12 | 8 wks |
| 5 Nov 88 | | THE HEART AND SOUL OF ROCK 'N' ROLL | | |
| | | *Telstar STAR 2351* ............................... | 60 | 6 wks |
| 12 Nov 88 | | THE LOVE ALBUM '88 *Telstar STAR 2332* ............ | 51 | 9 wks |
| 19 Nov 88 | | THE GREATEST HITS OF 1988 *Telstar STAR 2334* ..... | 11 | 8 wks |
| 19 Nov 88 | | BEST OF HOUSE '88 *Telstar STAR 2347* .............. | 33 | 8 wks |
| 19 Nov 88 | | INSTRUMENTAL GREATS *Telstar STAR 2341* ........ | 79 | 5 wks |
| 3 Dec 88 | | HYPERACTIVE *Telsta STAR 2328* ................... | 78 | 4 wks |
| 3 Dec 88 | | BACK TO THE SIXTIES *Telstar STAR 2348* ........... | 47 | 6 wks |
| 17 Dec 88 | | MORNING HAS BROKEN *Telstar STAR 2337* ......... | 88 | 2 wks |
| 31 Dec 88 | | THE GREATEST LOVE 2 *Telstar STAR 2352* .......... | 37 | 2 wks |
| ........... | | ........................................................... | | |
| 14 Jan 89 | ● | THE GREATEST LOVE 2 *Telstar STAR 2352* .......... | 3 | 23 wks |
| 14 Jan 89 | ● | THE GREATEST HITS OF 1988 *Telstar STAR 2334* ..... | 8 | 8 wks |
| 14 Jan 89 | ● | THE GREATEST LOVE *Telstar STAR 2316* ........... | 7 | 29 wks |
| 14 Jan 89 | | BEST OF HOUSE 1988 *Telstar STAR 2347* ............. | 11 | 5 wks |
| 14 Jan 89 | | BACK TO THE SIXTIES *Telstar STAR 2348* ........... | 14 | 4 wks |
| 14 Jan 89 | | LOVE SONGS *Telstar STAR 2298* .................... | 18 | 2 wks |
| 25 Feb 89 | ★ | THE AWARDS *Telstar STAR 2346* ................... | 1 | 8 wks |
| 4 Mar 89 | ★ | DEEP HEAT *Telstar STAR 2345* ..................... | 1 | 15 wks |
| 22 Apr 89 | ● | DEEP HEAT – THE SECOND BURN *Telstar STAR 2356* | 2 | 13 wks |
| 15 Jul 89 | ● | PROTECT THE INNOCENT *Telstar STAR 2363* ....... | 9 | 9 wks |
| 15 Jul 89 | | RHYTHM OF THE SUN *Telstar STAR 2362* ........... | 12 | 4 wks |
| 22 Jul 89 | ● | DEEP HEAT 3 – THE THIRD DEGREE *Telstar STAR 2364* | 2 | 13 wks |
| 22 Jul 89 | ● | THIS IS SKA *Telstar STAR 2366* .................... | 6 | 10 wks |
| 23 Sep 89 | ★ | DEEP HEAT 4 – PLAY WITH FIRE *Telstar STAR 2388* .. | 1 | 11 wks |
| 14 Oct 89 | ● | MOTOWN HEARTBREAKERS *Telstar STAR 2343* ..... | 4† | 10 wks |
| 11 Oct 89 | ● | THE GREATEST LOVE 3 *Telstar STAR 2384* .......... | 4† | 8 wks |
| 18 Nov 89 | ● | NUMBER ONES OF THE EIGHTIES *Telstar STAR 2382* . | 2† | 7 wks |
| 18 Nov 89 | ● | THE GREATEST HITS OF 1989 *Telstar STAR 2389* ..... | 4† | 7 wks |
| 25 Nov 89 | ● | DEEP HEAT 1989 – FIGHT THE FLAME | | |
| | | *Telstar STAR 2380* ............................... | 4† | 6 wks |
| 25 Nov 89 | ● | HEAVEN AND HELL *Telstar STAR 2361* ............. | 9† | 6 wks |
| 9 Dec 89 | | SOFT ROCK *Telstar STAR 7397* .................... | 15† | 4 wks |

Green Velvet *was a re-issue of Ronco RON LP 6.*

## Towerbell

| | | | |
|---|---|---|---|
| 28 Sep 85 | THE TV HITS ALBUM *Towerbell TVLP 3* ............. | 26 | 13 wks |
| 8 Feb 86 ● | THE DANCE HITS ALBUM *Towerbell TVLP 8* ......... | 10 | 11 wks |
| 15 Mar 86 | THE CINEMA HITS ALBUM *Towerbell TVLP 9* ........ | 44 | 9 wks |
| 12 Apr 86 | THE TV HITS ALBUM TWO *Towerbell TVLP 10* ....... | 19 | 7 wks |
| 17 May 86 | SISTERS ARE DOIN' IT *Towerbell TVLP 11* ........... | 27 | 9 wks |
| 7 Jun 86 | TWO'S COMPANY *Towerbell TVLP 12* ............... | 51 | 5 wks |
| 28 Jun 86 | DANCE HITS II *Towerbell TVLP 13* ................. | 25 | 8 wks |
| 2 Aug 86 | THE ORIGINALS *Towerbell TBDLP 14* ............... | 15 | 9 wks |
| 9 Aug 86 | YOU'VE GOT TO LAUGH *Towerbell TVLP 15* ........ | 51 | 3 wks |

## Trojan

| | | | |
|---|---|---|---|
| 7 Aug 71 | TIGHTEN UP VOLUME 4 *Trojan TBL 163* ............. | 20 | 7 wks |
| 21 Aug 71 | CLUB REGGAE *Trojan TBL 159* .................... | 25 | 4 wks |
| 16 Jun 84 | 20 REGGAE CLASSICS *Trojan TRLS 222* ............. | 89 | 1 wk |

## TV

| | | | |
|---|---|---|---|
| 2 Oct 82 | MODERN HEROES *TV TVA 1* ................... | 24 | 7 wks |
| 9 Oct 82 | ENDLESS LOVE *TV TV 2* ..................... | 26 | 8 wks |
| 6 Nov 82 | FLASH TRACKS *TV PTVL 1* ..................... | 19 | 7 wks |
| 25 Dec 82 | PARTY FEVER/DISCO MANIA *TV TVA 5* ........... | 71 | 3 wks |

## Urban

| | | | |
|---|---|---|---|
| 14 Nov 87 | URBAN CLASSICS *Urban URBLP 4* .................. | 96 | 1 wk |
| 24 Sep 88 | URBAN ACID *Urban URBLP 15* .................... | 51 | 8 wks |
| 8 Oct 88 | ACID JAZZ AND OTHER ILLICIT GROOVES *Urban URBLP 16* .............................. | 86 | 3 wks |

## Vertigo

| | | | |
|---|---|---|---|
| 21 Jun 86 | HEAR 'N' AID *Vertigo VERH 35* .................... | 50 | 2 wks |
| 27 Aug 88 ★ | HOT CITY NIGHTS *Vertigo PROVTV 15* .............. | 1 | 14 wks |
| 4 Nov 89 ● | ROCK CITY NIGHTS *Vertigo RCNTV 1* ............. | 3† | 9 wks |

## Virgin

| | | | |
|---|---|---|---|
| 22 Nov 80 | CASH COWS *Virgin MILK 1* ....................... | 49 | 1 wk |
| 17 Apr 82 | MUSIC OF QUALITY AND DISTINCTION (VOLUME 1) *Virgin V 2219* ...................................... | 25 | 6 wks |
| 1 Jun 85 | MASSIVE *Virgin V 2346* .......................... | 61 | 3 wks |

## Warwick

| | | | |
|---|---|---|---|
| 29 Nov 75 | ALL-TIME PARTY HITS *Warwick WW 5001* ........... | 21 | 8 wks |
| 17 Apr 76 ● | INSTRUMENTAL GOLD *Warwick WW 5012* .......... | 3 | 24 wks |
| 29 May 76 | HAMILTON'S HOT SHOTS *Warwick WW 5014* ........ | 15 | 5 wks |
| 8 Jan 77 | SONGS OF PRAISE *Warwick WW 5020* .............. | 31 | 2 wks |
| 29 Jan 77 | HIT SCENE *Warwick PR 5023* ..................... | 19 | 5 wks |
| 11 Mar 78 ● | FONZIE'S FAVOURITES *Warwick WW 5037* .......... | 8 | 16 wks |
| 25 Nov 78 | LOVE SONGS *Warwick WW 5046* ................. | 47 | 7 wks |
| 2 Dec 78 | BLACK VELVET *Warwick WW 5047* ................ | 72 | 3 wks |
| 31 Mar 79 | LEMON POPSICLE *Warwick WW 5050* ............. | 42 | 6 wks |
| 7 Apr 79 | COUNTRY PORTRAITS *Warwick WW 5057* ......... | 14 | 10 wks |
| 10 Nov 79 | 20 SMASH DISCO HITS (THE BITCH) *Warwick WW 5061* | 42 | 5 wks |
| 16 Feb 80 | COUNTRY GUITAR *Warwick WW 5070* ............. | 46 | 3 wks |
| 14 Nov 81 | DISCO EROTICA *Warwick WW 5108* ................ | 35 | 8 wks |
| 10 Apr 82 | PS I LOVE YOU *Warwick WW 5121* ................ | 68 | 3 wks |
| 6 Nov 82 | HITS OF THE SCREAMING 60'S *Warwick WW 5124* .... | 24 | 10 wks |
| 22 Dec 84 | MERRY CHRISTMAS TO YOU *Warwick WW 5141* ..... | 64 | 2 wks |

—————— *Other Compilation Albums* ——————

| | | | |
|---|---|---|---|
| 10 Mar 62 | GREAT MOTION PICTURE THEMES *HMV CLP 1508* . | 19 | 1 wk |
| 24 Aug 63 | THE MERSEY BEAT VOLUME 1 *Oriole PS 40047* ...... | 17 | 5 wks |
| 16 May 64 | OUT CAME THE BLUES *Ace of Hearts AH 72* .......... | 19 | 1 wk |
| 11 Sep 66 | STARS CHARITY FANTASIA SAVE THE CHILDREN FUND *SCF PL 145* .................................. | 6 | 16 wks |
| 8 Apr 67 ● | HIT THE ROAD STAX *Stax 589005* .................. | 10 | 16 wks |
| 11 May 68 | BLUES ANYTIME *Immediate IMLP 014* ............... | 40 | 1 wk |
| 4 Dec 71 | BREAKTHROUGH *MFP 1334* ...................... | 49 | 1 wk |
| 22 Jan 72 ★ | CONCERT FOR BANGLADESH *Apple STCX 3385* ..... | 1 | 13 wks |
| 15 Mar 75 | SOLID SOUL SENSATIONS *Disco Diamond DDLP 5001* .. | 30 | 1 wk |
| 16 Aug 75 | NEVER TOO YOUNG TO ROCK *GTO GTLP 004* ..... | 30 | 5 wks |
| 6 Dec 75 | SUPERSONIC *Stallion SSM 001* .................... | 21 | 6 wks |
| 31 Jan 76 | REGGAE CHARTBUSTERS 75 *Cactus CTLP 114* ...... | 53 | 1 wk |

**313**

| | | | |
|---|---|---|---|
| 12 Nov 88 | **THE HIT FACTORY VOLUME 2** *Fanfare/PWL HF 4* .... | 16 | 9 wks |
| 17 Dec 88 | **NOEL – CHRISTMAS SONGS AND CAROLS** | | |
| | *Trax TRXLP 701* ................................. | 89 | 2 wks |
| 24 Dec 88 | **THE BEIDERBECKE COLLECTION** *Dormouse DM 20* .. | 89 | 2 wks |
| | .................................................. | | |
| 14 Jan 89 | **THE HIT FACTORY VOLUME 2** *Fanfare/PWL HF 4* .... | 13 | 3 wks |
| 14 Jan 89 | **THE BEIDERBECKE COLLECTION** *Dormouse DM 20* .. | 14 | 5 wks |
| 18 Feb 89 | **CAPITOL CLASSICS VOLUME 1** *Capitol EMS 1316* .... | 16 | 2 wks |
| 4 Mar 89 | ● **AND ALL BECAUSE THE LADY LOVES** ... *Dover ADD 6* | 2 | 10 wks |
| 15 Apr 89 | **THE SONGS OF BOB DYLAN** *Start STDL 20* .......... | 13 | 5 wks |
| 10 Jun 89 | ● **FFRR – SILVER ON BLACK** *London 8281551* ........... | 8 | 5 wks |
| 1 Jul 89 | **THIS IS GARAGE** *Cooltempo CTLP 12* ................ | 18 | 2 wks |
| 15 Jul 89 | ● **THE HIT FACTORY VOLUME 3** *Fanfare/PWL HF 8* .... | 3 | 10 wks |
| 22 Jul 89 | **DREAMS OF IRELAND** *Trax MODEM 1035* ........... | 19 | 1 wk |
| 5 Aug 89 | **THE 2 TONE STORY** *2 Tone CHRTT 5009* ........... | 16 | 5 wks |
| 19 Aug 89 | ● **HEART AND SOUL** *Heart And Soul HASTV 1* .......... | 2 | 12 wks |
| 16 Sep 89 | **WAREHOUSE RAVES** *Rumour RUMLD 101* ........... | 15 | 4 wks |
| 23 Sep 82 | ● **JUST SEVENTEEN – HEARTBEATS** *Fanfare FARE 1* .. | 3 | 6 wks |
| 14 Oct 89 | ● **ITALIA – DANCE MUSIC FROM ITALY** | | |
| | *deConstruction 64289* .............................. | 4 | 6 wks |
| 11 Nov 89 | ● **DANCE DECADE – DANCE HITS OF THE 80's** | | |
| | *London DDTV 1* .................................. | 8 | 6 wks |
| 2 Dec 89 | **THAT LOVING FEELING** *Dino DINTV 5* ............. | 11† | 5 wks |

# FILM SOUNDTRACKS

| | | | |
|---|---|---|---|
| 8 Nov 58 | ★ **SOUTH PACIFIC** *RCA RB 16065* .................... | 1 | 286 wks |
| 8 Nov 58 | ● **THE KING AND I** *Capitol LCT 6108* ................. | 4 | 103 wks |
| 8 Nov 58 | ● **OKLAHOMA** *Capitol LCT 6100* .................... | 4 | 90 wks |
| 6 Dec 58 | ● **CAROUSEL** *Capitol LCT 6105* ..................... | 8 | 15 wks |
| 31 Jan 59 | ● **GIGI** *MGM C 770* ............................... | 2 | 88 wks |
| 10 Oct 59 | ● **PORGY AND BESS** *Philips ABL 3282* ................ | 7 | 5 wks |
| 23 Jan 60 | ● **THE FIVE PENNIES** *London HAU 2189* .............. | 2 | 15 wks |
| 7 May 60 | ● **CAN CAN** *Capitol W 1301* ........................ | 2 | 31 wks |
| 28 May 60 | **PAL JOEY** *Capitol LCT 6148* ....................... | 20 | 1 wk |
| 23 Jul 60 | **HIGH SOCIETY** *Capitol LCT 6116* .................. | 16 | 1 wk |
| 5 Nov 60 | **BEN HUR** *MGM C 802* .......................... | 15 | 3 wks |
| 21 Jan 61 | **NEVER ON SUNDAY** *London HAT 2309* ............ | 17 | 1 wk |
| 18 Feb 61 | ● **SONG WITHOUT END** *Pye GGL 30169* ............. | 9 | 10 wks |
| 29 Apr 61 | ● **SEVEN BRIDES FOR SEVEN BROTHERS** *MGM C 853* | 6 | 22 wks |
| 3 Jun 61 | **EXODUS** *RCA RD 27210* ......................... | 17 | 1 wk |
| 11 Nov 61 | **GLENN MILLER STORY** *Ace Of Hearts AH 12* ......... | 12 | 7 wks |
| 24 Mar 62 | ★ **WEST SIDE STORY** *Philips BBL 7530* ................ | 1 | 175 wks |
| 28 Apr 62 | ● **IT'S TRAD DAD** *Columbia 33SX 1412* ............... | 3 | 21 wks |
| 22 Sep 62 | **THE MUSIC MAN** *Warner Bros. WB 4066* ............. | 14 | 9 wks |
| 3 Nov 62 | **PORGY AND BESS** *CBS APG 60002* ................. | 14 | 7 wks |
| 15 Jun 63 | **JUST FOR FUN** *Decca LK 4524* ..................... | 20 | 2 wks |
| 31 Oct 64 | ● **MY FAIR LADY** *CBS BPG 72237* .................. | 9 | 51 wks |
| 31 Oct 64 | **GOLDFINGER** *United Artists ULP 1076* ................ | 14 | 5 wks |
| 16 Jan 65 | ● **MARY POPPINS** *HMV CLP 1794* .................... | 2 | 82 wks |
| 10 Apr 65 | ★ **SOUND OF MUSIC** *RCA RB 6616* .................. | 1 | 381 wks |
| 30 Apr 66 | **FUNNY GIRL** *Capitol W 2059* ..................... | 19 | 3 wks |
| 11 Sep 66 | ● **DR ZHIVAGO** *MGM C 8007* ..................... | 3 | 106 wks |
| 22 Jul 67 | **CASINO ROYALE** *RCA Victor SF 7874* ............... | 35 | 1 wk |
| 29 Jul 67 | **A MAN AND A WOMAN** *United Artists SULP 1155* ...... | 31 | 11 wks |
| 28 Oct 67 | ● **THOROUGHLY MODERN MILLIE** *Brunswick STA 8685* | 9 | 19 wks |
| 9 Mar 68 | ● **THE JUNGLE BOOK** *Disney ST 3948* ................ | 5 | 51 wks |
| 21 Sep 68 | **STAR** *Stateside SSL 10233* ......................... | 36 | 1 wk |
| 12 Oct 68 | ● **THE GOOD, THE BAD AND THE UGLY** | | |
| | *United Artists SULP 1197* ........................... | 2 | 18 wks |
| 23 Nov 68 | ● **OLIVER** *RCA Victor SB 6777* ..................... | 4 | 107 wks |
| 23 Nov 68 | **CAMELOT** *Warner Bros. WS 1712* ................... | 37 | 1 wk |
| 8 Feb 69 | ● **CHITTY CHITTY BANG BANG** *United Artists SULP 1200* | 10 | 4 wks |
| 10 May 69 | **FUNNY GIRL** *CBS 70044* ......................... | 11 | 22 wks |
| 14 Jun 69 | ● **2001 – A SPACE ODYSSEY** *MGM CS 8078* ......... | 3 | 67 wks |
| 20 Dec 69 | ● **EASY RIDER** *Stateside SSL 5018* ................... | 2 | 67 wks |
| 24 Jan 70 | **JUNGLE BOOK (re-issue)** *Disney BVS 4041* .......... | 25 | 26 wks |
| 7 Feb 70 | ● **PAINT YOUR WAGON** *Paramount SPFL 257* .......... | 2 | 102 wks |
| 14 Mar 70 | **HELLO DOLLY** *Stateside SSL 10292* ................. | 45 | 2 wks |
| 18 Jul 70 | **WOODSTOCK** *Atlantic 2662 001* ................... | 35 | 19 wks |
| 24 Apr 71 | ● **LOVE STORY** *Paramount SPFL 267* ................. | 10 | 33 wks |
| 12 Feb 72 | ● **CLOCKWORK ORANGE** *Warner Bros. K 46127* ........ | 4 | 46 wks |

| Date | Title | Pos | Weeks |
|---|---|---|---|
| 8 Apr 72 | FIDDLER ON THE ROOF *United Artists UAD 60011/2* ... | 26 | 2 wks |
| 13 May 72 | 2001 – A SPACE ODYSSEY (re-issue) *MGM 2315 034* ... | 20 | 2 wks |
| 29 Nov 72 | SOUTH PACIFIC (re-issue) *RCA Victor SB 2011* ........ | 25 | 2 wks |
| 31 Mar 73 | CABARET *Probe SPB 1052* ......................... | 13 | 22 wks |
| 14 Apr 73 | LOST HORIZON *Bell SYBEL 8000* ................. | 36 | 3 wks |
| 22 Sep 73 | JESUS CHRIST SUPERSTAR *MCA MDKS 8012/3* ..... | 23 | 18 wks |
| 23 Mar 74 ● | THE STING *MCA MCF 2537* ..................... | 7 | 35 wks |
| 27 Apr 74 | AMERICAN GRAFFITI *MCA MCSP 253* ............. | 37 | 1 wk |
| 8 Jun 74 | A TOUCH OF CLASS *Philips 6612 040* ............... | 32 | 1 wk |
| 5 Oct 74 | SUNSHINE *MCA MCF 2566* ..................... | 47 | 3 wks |
| 5 Apr 75 | TOMMY *Polydor 2657 014* ......................... | 21 | 9 wks |
| 31 Jan 76 | JAWS *MCA MCF 2716* ............................ | 55 | 1 wk |
| 5 Mar 77 | MOSES *Pye 28503* ................................ | 43 | 2 wks |
| 9 Apr 77 ★ | A STAR IS BORN *CBS 86021* ..................... | 1 | 54 wks |
| 2 Jul 77 | THE BEST OF CAR WASH *MCA MCF 2799* .......... | 59 | 1 wk |
| 11 Mar 78 ★ | SATURDAY NIGHT FEVER *RSO 2658 123* .......... | 1 | 65 wks |
| 22 Apr 78 ● | THE STUD *Ronco RTD 2029* ...................... | 2 | 19 wks |
| 29 Apr 78 | CLOSE ENCOUNTERS OF THE THIRD KIND *Arista DLART 2001* ............................ | 40 | 6 wks |
| 6 May 78 | THE LAST WALTZ *Warner Bros. K 66076* .............. | 39 | 4 wks |
| 20 May 78 | THANK GOD IT'S FRIDAY *Casablanca TGIF 100* ....... | 40 | 5 wks |
| 27 May 78 | FM *MCA MCSP 284* ............................ | 37 | 7 wks |
| 8 Jul 78 ★ | GREASE *RSO RSD 2001* ......................... | 1 | 47 wks |
| 12 Aug 78 | SGT PEPPER'S LONELY HEARTS CLUB BAND *A&M AMLZ 66600* ............................ | 38 | 2 wks |
| 7 Oct 78 | CONVOY *Capitol EST 24590* ...................... | 52 | 1 wk |
| 30 Jun 79 | THE WORLD IS FULL OF MARRIED MEN *Ronco RTD 2038* ............................ | 25 | 9 wks |
| 14 Jul 79 | THE WARRIORS *A&M AMLH 64761* ................ | 53 | 7 wks |
| 6 Oct 79 | QUADROPHENIA *Polydor 2625 037* ................ | 23 | 16 wks |
| 5 Jan 80 | THE SECRET POLICEMAN'S BALL *Island ILPS 9601* .. | 33 | 6 wks |
| 9 Feb 80 | SUNBURN *Warwick RTL 2044* ..................... | 45 | 7 wks |
| 16 Feb 80 | GOING STEADY *Warwick WW 5078* ................ | 25 | 10 wks |
| 8 Mar 80 | THE ROSE *Atlantic K 50681* ...................... | 68 | 1 wk |
| 7 Jun 80 | THE GREAT ROCK 'N' ROLL SWINDLE *Virgin V 2168* | 16 | 11 wks |
| 19 Jul 80 ● | XANADU *Jet JET LX 526* .......................... | 2 | 17 wks |
| 16 Aug 80 ● | CAN'T STOP THE MUSIC *Mercury 6399 051* .......... | 9 | 8 wks |
| 6 Sep 80 ★ | FAME *RSO 2479 253* ............................ | 1 | 25 wks |
| 14 Feb 81 ● | DANCE CRAZE *2-Tone CHRTT 5004* ............... | 5 | 15 wks |
| 12 Dec 81 | THE SECRET POLICEMAN'S OTHER BALL *Springtime HAHA 6003* ........................... | 69 | 4 wks |
| 20 Mar 82 | THE SECRET POLICEMAN'S OTHER BALL (THE MUSIC) *Springtime HAHA 6004* ...... | 29 | 5 wks |
| 17 Jul 82 | THE SOUND OF MUSIC (re-issue) *RCA Ints 5134* ...... | 98 | 1 wk |
| 4 Sep 82 | ROCKY III *Liberty LBG 30351* ..................... | 42 | 7 wks |
| 4 Sep 82 | ANNIE *CBS 70219* ............................. | 83 | 2 wks |
| 11 Sep 82 | BRIMSTONE AND TREACLE *A&M AMLH 64915* .... | 67 | 3 wks |
| 12 Feb 83 | AN OFFICER AND A GENTLEMAN *Island ISTA 3* ..... | 40 | 14 wks |
| 25 Jun 83 | RETURN OF THE JEDI *RSO RSD 5023* ............. | 85 | 5 wks |
| 2 Jul 83 ● | FLASHDANCE *Casablanca CANH 5* ................. | 9 | 30 wks |
| 1 Oct 83 | STAYING ALIVE *RSO RSBG 3* .................... | 14 | 8 wks |
| 21 Apr 84 ● | FOOTLOOSE *CBS 70246* ......................... | 7 | 25 wks |
| 21 Apr 84 | AGAINST ALL ODDS *Virgin V 2313* ............. | 29 | 10 wks |
| 16 Jun 84 ● | BREAKDANCE *Polydor POLD 5147* ................. | 6 | 29 wks |
| 7 Jul 84 | BEAT STREET *Atlantic 780154* .................... | 30 | 13 wks |
| 18 Aug 84 | ELECTRIC DREAMS *Virgin V 2318* .............. | 46 | 7 wks |
| 29 Sep 84 | GHOSTBUSTERS *Arista 206 559* ................. | 24 | 25 wks |
| 16 Feb 85 | BEVERLY HILLS COP *MCA MCF 3253* ............. | 24 | 32 wks |
| 22 Jun 85 | A VIEW TO A KILL *Parlophone BOND 1* ............. | 81 | 1 wk |
| 11 Jan 86 | BACK TO THE FUTURE *MCA MCF 3285* ............ | 66 | 8 wks |
| 1 Feb 86 | MISTRAL'S DAUGHTER *Carrere CAL 221* .......... | 53 | 3 wks |
| 1 Feb 86 ● | ROCKY IV *Scotti Brothers SCT 70272* ............... | 3 | 22 wks |
| 5 Apr 86 | ABSOLUTE BEGINNERS *Virgin V 2386* ........... | 19 | 9 wks |
| 26 Apr 86 | OUT OF AFRICA *MCA MCF 3310* ................. | 81 | 2 wks |
| 5 Jul 86 | LABYRINTH *EMI America AML 3104* ................ | 38 | 2 wks |
| 11 Oct 86 ● | TOP GUN *CBS 70296* ............................ | 4 | 46 wks |
| 11 Apr 87 | THE BLUES BROTHERS *Atlantic K 50715* ........... | 59 | 26 wks |
| 2 May 87 | PLATOON *WEA WX 95* ........................... | 90 | 2 wks |
| 18 Jul 87 | BEVERLY HILLS COP 2 *MCA MCF 3383* ............ | 71 | 5 wks |
| 1 Aug 87 | THE LIVING DAYLIGHTS *Warner Bros. WX 111* ....... | 57 | 6 wks |
| 1 Aug 87 ● | WHO'S THAT GIRL *Sire WX 102* ................. | 4 | 25 wks |
| 22 Aug 87 | LA BAMBA *London LONLP 36* ...................... | 24 | 15 wks |
| 3 Oct 87 | FULL METAL JACKET *Warner Bros. 925 613-1* ......... | 60 | 4 wks |

**315**

| | | | | |
|---|---|---|---|---|
| 31 Oct | 87 | **DIRTY DANCING** *RCA BL 86408* .................. | 4 | 63 wks |
| 16 Jan | 88 | **FLASHDANCE (re-issue)** *Mercury PRICE 111* .......... | 93 | 2 wks |
| 20 Feb | 88 | **CRY FREEDOM** *MCA MCG 6029* ................... | 73 | 2 wks |
| 14 May | 88 | ● **MORE DIRTY DANCING** *RCA BL 86965* ............ | 3 | 27 wks |
| 24 Sep | 88 | ● **BUSTER** *Virgin V 2544* ........................... | 6 | 16 wks |
| 22 Oct | 88 | **GOOD MORNING VIETNAM** *A & M AMA 3913* ....... | 50 | 9 wks |
| | | | | |
| 14 Jan | 89 | ● **BUSTER** *Virgin V 2544* ........................... | 2 | 31 wks |
| 14 Jan | 89 | ● **DIRTY DANCING** *RCA BL 86408* .................. | 3† | 51 wks |
| 21 Jan | 89 | ● **GOOD MORNING VIETNAM** *A & M AMA 3913* ..... | 7 | 26 wks |
| 21 Jan | 89 | ● **THE BLUES BROTHERS** *Atlantic K 50715* ............ | 9 | 37 wks |
| 28 Jan | 89 | **THE LOST BOYS** *Atlantic 7817671* ................. | 13 | 15 wks |
| 4 Feb | 89 | ● **COCKTAIL** *Elektra EKT 54* ........................ | 2 | 15 wks |
| 4 Feb | 89 | **MORE DIRTY DANCING** *RCA BL 86965* ............ | 14 | 17 wks |
| 18 Mar | 89 | **SCANDAL** *Parlophone PCS 7331* ..................... | 13 | 3 wks |
| 22 Apr | 89 | **TOP GUN** *CBS 70296* ............................. | 12 | 16 wks |
| 13 May | 89 | **DIRTY DANCING – LIVE IN CONCERT** *RCA BL 90336* | 19 | 2 wks |
| 15 Jul | 89 | **LICENCE TO KILL** *MCA MCG 6051* ................ | 17 | 2 wks |
| 22 Jul | 89 | **GHOSTBUSTERS 2** *MCA MCG 6056* ............... | 15 | 4 wks |

The West Side Story *album on Philips BBL 7530 during its chart run changed label and number to CBS BPG 62058.*

## STAGE CAST RECORDINGS

**316**

| | | | | |
|---|---|---|---|---|
| 8 Nov | 58 | ● **MY FAIR LADY (BROADWAY)** *Philips RBL 1000* ...... | 2 | 129 wks |
| 24 Jan | 59 | ● **WEST SIDE STORY (BROADWAY)** *Philips BBL 7277* .. | 3 | 27 wks |
| 26 Mar | 60 | ● **AT THE DROP OF A HAT (LONDON)** | | |
| | | *Parlophone PMC 1033* ................................ | 9 | 1 wk |
| 26 Mar | 60 | ● **FINGS AIN'T WOT THEY USED TO BE (LONDON)** | | |
| | | *Decca LK 4346* .................................... | 5 | 11 wks |
| 2 Apr | 60 | ● **FLOWER DRUM SONG (BROADWAY)** *Philips ABL 3302* | 2 | 27 wks |
| 7 May | 60 | ● **FOLLOW THAT GIRL (LONDON)** *HMV CLP 1366* .... | 5 | 9 wks |
| 21 May | 60 | ● **MOST HAPPY FELLA (BROADWAY)** *Philips BBL 7374* . | 6 | 13 wks |
| 21 May | 60 | **MAKE ME AN OFFER (LONDON)** *HMV CLP 1333* .... | 18 | 1 wk |
| 28 May | 60 | ● **FLOWER DRUM SONG (LONDON)** *HMV CLP 1359* .. | 10 | 3 wks |
| 9 Jul | 60 | **MOST HAPPY FELLA (LONDON)** *HMV CLP 1365* .... | 19 | 1 wk |
| 30 Jul | 60 | **WEST SIDE STORY (BROADWAY)** *Philips SBBL 504* .. | 14 | 1 wk |
| 10 Sep | 60 | ● **OLIVER (LONDON)** *Decca LK 4359* ................. | 4 | 91 wks |
| 11 Mar | 61 | **KING KONG (SOUTH AFRICA)** *Decca LK 4392* ........ | 12 | 8 wks |
| 6 May | 61 | ● **MUSIC MAN (LONDON)** *JMH CLP 1444* ............ | 8 | 13 wks |
| 24 Jun | 61 | ● **SOUND OF MUSIC (BROADWAY)** *Philips ABL 3370* .. | 4 | 19 wks |
| 22 Jul | 61 | **BYE-BYE BIRDIE (LONDON)** *Philips ABL 3385* ....... | 17 | 3 wks |
| 22 Jul | 61 | **BEYOND THE FRINGE (LONDON)** *Parlophone PMC 1145* | 13 | 17 wks |
| 29 Jul | 61 | ● **SOUND OF MUSIC (LONDON)** *HMV CLP 1453* ....... | 4 | 68 wks |
| 9 Sep | 61 | ● **STOP THE WORLD I WANT TO GET OFF (LONDON)** | | |
| | | *Decca LK 4408* .................................... | 8 | 14 wks |
| 14 Jul | 62 | ● **BLITZ (LONDON)** *HMV CLP 1569* ................. | 7 | 21 wks |
| 18 May | 63 | **HALF A SIXPENCE (LONDON)** *Decca LK 4521* ........ | 20 | 2 wks |
| 3 Aug | 63 | **PICKWICK (LONDON)** *Philips AL 3431* ............. | 12 | 10 wks |
| 4 Jan | 64 | **MY FAIR LADY (BROADWAY)** *CBS BPG 68001* ...... | 19 | 1 wk |
| 22 Feb | 64 | **AT THE DROP OF ANOTHER HAT (LONDON)** | | |
| | | *Parlophone PMC 1216* ............................... | 12 | 11 wks |
| 3 Oct | 64 | ● **CAMELOT (BROADWAY)** *CBS APG 60001* .......... | 10 | 12 wks |
| 16 Jan | 65 | **CAMELOT (LONDON)** *HMV CLP 1756* ............. | 19 | 1 wk |
| 11 Mar | 67 | ● **FIDDLER ON THE ROOF (LONDON)** *CBS SBPG 70030* | 4 | 50 wks |
| 28 Dec | 68 | ● **HAIR (LONDON)** *Polydor 583–043* .................. | 3 | 94 wks |
| 30 Aug | 69 | **OLIVER (LONDON) (re-issue)** *Decca SPA 30* .......... | 23 | 4 wks |
| 6 Sep | 69 | **HAIR (BROADWAY)** *RCA SF 7959* ................. | 29 | 3 wks |
| 19 Feb | 72 | **GODSPELL (LONDON)** *Bell BELLS 203* ............. | 25 | 17 wks |
| 18 Nov | 78 | **EVITA (LONDON)** *MCA MCF 3257* ................ | 24 | 18 wks |
| 1 Aug | 81 | ● **CATS (LONDON)** *Polydor CATX 001* .............. | 6 | 26 wks |
| 6 Nov | 82 | **MACK AND MABEL (BROADWAY)** *MCA MCL 1728* .. | 38 | 7 wks |
| 7 Aug | 84 | **STARLIGHT EXPRESS (LONDON)** | | |
| | | *Starlight/Polydor LNER 1* ........................., .... | 21 | 9 wks |
| 15 Feb | 86 | **LES MISERABLES (LONDON)** | | |
| | | *First Night ENCORE 1* ............................. | 72 | 4 wks |
| 21 Feb | 87 | ★ **THE PHANTOM OF THE OPERA (LONDON)** | | |
| | | *Polydor PODV 9* ................................... | 1† | 119 wks |
| 16 Sep | 89 | ★ **ASPECTS OF LOVE (LONDON)** *Polydor 841126 1* ...... | 1† | 16 wks |

## STUDIO CAST RECORDINGS

| | | | | |
|---|---|---|---|---|
| 25 Jun 60 | **SHOWBOAT** *HMV CLP 1310* ........................ | 12 | 1 wk |
| 8 Feb 72 | ● **JESUS CHRIST SUPERSTAR** *MCA MKPS 2011/2* ..... | 6 | 20 wks |
| 22 Jan 77 | ● **EVITA** *MCA MCX 503* ........................... | 4 | 35 wks |
| 17 Jun 78 | **WHITE MANSIONS** *A&M AMLX 64691* .............. | 51 | 3 wks |
| 10 Nov 84 | ● **CHESS** *RCA PL 70500* ........................... | 10 | 16 wks |
| 18 May 85 | **WEST SIDE STORY** *Deutsche Grammophon 41525* ......... | 11 | 32 wks |
| 2 Nov 85 | **CHESS PIECES** *Telstar STAR 2274* ................... | 87 | 3 wks |
| 10 May 86 | **WEST SIDE STORY – HIGHLIGHTS** | | |
| | *Deutsche Grammophon 45963* ........................... | 72 | 6 wks |
| 17 May 86 | **DAVE CLARK'S 'TIME'** *EMI AMPH 1* ............... | 21 | 6 wks |
| 11 Oct 86 | ● **SOUTH PACIFIC** *CBS SM 42205* ................. | 5 | 24 wks |
| 27 Jun 87 | **MATADOR** *Epic VIVA 1* ........................ | 26 | 5 wks |
| 21 Nov 87 | **MY FAIR LADY** *Decca MFL 1* ................... | 41 | 12 wks |

## TV and RADIO SOUNDTRACKS and SPIN-OFFS

| | | | | |
|---|---|---|---|---|
| 13 Dec 58 | ● **OH BOY!** *Parlophone PMC 1072* ..................... | 9 | 14 wks |
| 4 Mar 61 | ● **HUCKLEBERRY HOUND** *Pye GGL 004* ............. | 10 | 12 wks |
| 30 Feb 63 | **THAT WAS THE WEEK THAT WAS** *Parlophone PMC 1197* | 11 | 9 wks |
| 28 Mar 64 | **STARS FROM STARS AND GARTERS** *Pye GGL 0252* . | 17 | 2 wks |
| 4 Nov 72 | **THE BBC 1922–1972 (TV AND RADIO EXTRACTS)** | | |
| | *BBC 50* ........................................ | 16 | 7 wks |
| 4 Jan 75 | **BBC TV'S BEST OF TOP OF THE POPS** | | |
| | *Super Beeb BELP 001* .......................... | 21 | 5 wks |
| 10 Apr 76 | ★ **ROCK FOLLIES** *Island ILPS 9362* ................... | 1 | 15 wks |
| 22 Oct 77 | **10 YEARS OF HITS – RADIO ONE** *Super Beeb BEDP 002* . | 39 | 3 wks |
| 8 Apr 78 | ● **PENNIES FROM HEAVEN** *World Records SH 266* ....... | 10 | 17 wks |
| 1 Jul 78 | **MORE PENNIES FROM HEAVEN** *World Records SH 267* . | 31 | 4 wks |
| 15 Dec 79 | **FAWLTY TOWERS** *BBC REB 377* ................. | 25 | 10 wks |
| 7 Feb 81 | **FAWLTY TOWERS VOLUME 2** *BBC REB 405* ........ | 26 | 7 wks |
| 14 Feb 81 | **HITCHHIKERS GUIDE TO THE GALAXY VOL. 2** | | |
| | *Original ORA 54* .............................. | 47 | 4 wks |
| 1 Aug 81 | **MUSIC OF COSMOS** *RCA RCALP 5032* ........... | 43 | 10 wks |
| 21 Nov 81 | **BRIDESHEAD REVISITED** *Chrysalis CDL 1367* ....... | 50 | 12 wks |
| 23 Oct 82 | **ON THE AIR – 60 YEARS OF BBC THEME MUSIC** | | |
| | *BBC REF 454* ................................. | 85 | 3 wks |
| 26 Nov 83 | **REILLY ACE OF THEMES** *Red Bus BUSLP 1004* ...... | 54 | 6 wks |
| 4 Feb 84 | **AUF WIEDERSEHEN PET** *Towerbell AUF 1* .......... | 21 | 6 wks |
| 18 Feb 84 | **THE TUBE** *K-Tel NE 1261* ..................... | 30 | 6 wks |
| 8 Sep 84 | **SONG AND DANCE** *RCA BL 70480* ................. | 46 | 4 wks |
| 18 May 85 | **VICTORY IN EUROPE – BROADCASTS FROM BBC** | | |
| | **CORRESPONDENTS** *BBC REC 562* .............. | 61 | 1 wk |
| 28 Sep 85 | **THE TV HITS ALBUM** *Towerbell TVLP 3* ............. | 26 | 13 wks |
| 26 Oct 85 | **MIAMI VICE** *BBC/MCA REMV 584* .............. | 11 | 9 wks |
| 16 Nov 85 | **THE EASTENDERS SING-A-LONG ALBUM** | | |
| | *BBC REB 586* ................................. | 33 | 10 wks |
| 23 Nov 85 | **TELLY HITS – 16 TOP TV THEMES** *Stylus BBSR 508* ... | 34 | 6 wks |
| 15 Feb 86 | ● **JONATHAN KING'S ENTERTAINMENT U.S.A.** | | |
| | *Stylus SMR 6812* ............................. | 6 | 11 wks |
| 12 Apr 86 | **THE TV HITS ALBUM TWO** *Towerbell TVLP 10* ........ | 19 | 7 wks |
| 5 Jul 86 | **TELLY HITS 2** *Stylus BBSR 616* ................... | 68 | 2 wks |
| 18 Oct 86 | **THE VERY BEST OF ENTERTAINMENT U.S.A.** | | |
| | **VOLUME 2** *Priority UPTVR 1* ................... | 44 | 4 wks |
| 1 Nov 86 | **SIMON BATES – OUR TUNE** *Polydor PROLP 10* ....... | 58 | 5 wks |
| 26 Dec 86 | ● **THE SINGING DETECTIVE** *BBC REN 608* .......... | 10 | 24 wks |
| 27 Jun 87 | **THE ROCK 'N' ROLL YEARS 1956–59** *BBC REN 631* .. | 80 | 2 wks |
| 27 Jun 87 | **THE ROCK 'N' ROLL YEARS 1960–63** *BBC REN 632* .. | 84 | 1 wk |
| 27 Jun 87 | **THE ROCK 'N' ROLL YEARS 1964–67** *BBC REN 633* .. | 71 | 2 wks |
| 27 Jun 87 | **THE ROCK 'N' ROLL YEARS 1968–71** *BBC REN 634* .. | 77 | 1 wk |
| 3 Oct 87 | **MOONLIGHTING** *MCA MCF 3386* ................. | 50 | 6 wks |
| 17 Oct 87 | **MIAMI VICE 2** *MCA MCG 6019* ................... | 71 | 4 wks |
| 28 Nov 87 | **THE CHART SHOW – DANCE HITS '87** *Chrysalis ADD 1* | 39 | 6 wks |
| 26 Mar 88 | **THE CHART SHOW – ROCK THE NATION** | | |
| | *Dover ADD 2* ................................. | 16 | 8 wks |
| 1 Oct 88 | ● **MOONLIGHTING 2** *WEA WX 202* ................... | 5 | 9 wks |
| 1 Oct 88 | **MIAMI VICE 3** *MCA MCG 6033* ..................... | 95 | 1 wk |

| | | | |
|---|---|---|---|
| 8 Oct 88 ● **ONES ON 1** *BBC REF 693* | 10 | 7 wks |
| 29 Oct 88 ● **SMASH HITS PARTY '88** *Dover ADD 5* | 6 | 11 wks |

| | | | |
|---|---|---|---|
| 14 Jan 89 **SMASH HITS PARTY '88** *Dover ADD 5* | 12 | 5 wks |
| 20 May 89 ● **THE CHART SHOW – ROCK THE NATION 2** | | |
| *Dover ADD 4* | 8 | 4 wks |
| 3 Jun 89 ● **THE CHART SHOW – DANCE MASTERS** *Dover ADD 7* | 4 | 7 wks |
| 17 Jun 89 ● **RAY MOORE – A PERSONAL CHOICE** *BBC STAR 2352* | 7 | 4 wks |
| 23 Sep 89 **TV TUNES** *K-Tel NE 1429* | 17 | 3 wks |
| 28 Oct 89 ★ **SMASH HITS PARTY '89** *Dover ADD 8* | 1† | 10 wks |

## MISCELLANEOUS

| | | | |
|---|---|---|---|
| 12 Sep 70 **EDINBURGH MILITARY TATTOO 1970** | | |
| *Waverley SZLP 2121* | 34 | 4 wks |
| 18 Sep 71 **EDINBURGH MILITARY TATTOO 1971** | | |
| *Waverley SZLP 2128* | 44 | 1 wk |
| 11 Dec 71 **ELECTRONIC ORGANS TODAY** *Ad-Rhythm ADBS 1* | 48 | 1 wk |
| 8 Dec 73 ● **MUSIC FOR A ROYAL WEDDING** *BBC REW 163* | 7 | 6 wks |
| 27 Dec 75 **STRINGS OF SCOTLAND** *Philips 6382 108* | 50 | 1 wk |
| 8 Aug 81 ★ **THE OFFICIAL BBC ALBUM OF THE ROYAL WEDDING** | | |
| *BBC REP 413* | 1 | 11 wks |
| 3 Jul 82 **JOHN PAUL II – THE PILGRIM POPE** *BBC REB 445* | 71 | 4 wks |
| 9 Aug 86 **ROYAL WEDDING** *BBC REP 596* | 55 | 1 wk |

# Most Weeks on

# Chart

The following table lists the 137 recording acts that have spent 150 weeks or more on the British albums chart from the first chart on 8 Nov 1958 up to and including the chart of 30 Dec 1989. It is, of course, possible for an act to be credited with two or more chart weeks in the same week if the act has more than one album on the chart in any one week.

|  | Weeks |
|---|---|
| BEATLES | 1082 |
| SIMON AND GARFUNKEL | 1034 |
| ELVIS PRESLEY | 1023 |
| DIRE STRAITS | 1014 |
| QUEEN | 841 |
| DAVID BOWIE | 829 |
| FLEETWOOD MAC | 744 |
| PINK FLOYD | 736 |
| U2 | 720 |
| CLIFF RICHARD | 684 |
| ROLLING STONES | 650 |
| ELTON JOHN | 617 |
| FRANK SINATRA | 613 |

*(plus 23 weeks with Count Basie)*

| | |
|---|---|
| PHIL COLLINS | 592 |
| ROD STEWART | 571 |
| BOB DYLAN | 552 |

*(plus 3 with the Grateful Dead)*

| | |
|---|---|
| MICHAEL JACKSON | 533 |

*(plus 58 weeks with Jackson Five, 10 weeks with Diana Ross, Gladys Knight and Stevie Wonder, and 24 weeks with Diana Ross)*

| | |
|---|---|
| MEAT LOAF | 525 |
| BEACH BOYS | 524 |
| ABBA | 506 |
| PAUL McCARTNEY/WINGS | 497 |
| CARPENTERS | 473 |
| NEIL DIAMOND | 473 |
| MIKE OLDFIELD | 471 |
| ANDY WILLIAMS | 439 |
| SHADOWS | 414 |
| TOM JONES | 411 |
| LED ZEPPELIN | 411 |
| MADONNA | 409 |
| STATUS QUO | 399 |
| BRUCE SPRINGSTEEN | 387 |
| THE SOUND OF MUSIC (Original Soundtrack) | 382 |
| JIM REEVES | 381 |
| GENESIS | 379 |
| BARBRA STREISAND | 377 |
| DIANA ROSS | 368 |

*(plus 45 weeks with Marvin Gaye, 10 weeks with Michael Jackson, Gladys Knight and Stevie Wonder, and 24 weeks with Michael Jackson)*

| | |
|---|---|
| JAMES LAST | 364 |
| ELECTRIC LIGHT ORCHESTRA | 348 |
| DURAN DURAN | 332 |
| UB40 | 331 |
| POLICE | 327 |
| STEVIE WONDER | 325 |

*(plus 10 weeks with Diana Ross, Gladys Knight and Michael Jackson)*

| | |
|---|---|
| BUDDY HOLLY | 319 |
| HERB ALPERT | 309 |
| EURYTHMICS | 309 |
| BARRY MANILOW | 308 |
| MOODY BLUES | 307 |
| MADNESS | 300 |
| JOHN LENNON | 297 |

MEATLOAF

**322**

**Donny Osmond** has racked up 104 weeks as a solo act, 103 as part of the Osmonds, and 19 with his sister Marie, a total of 226 weeks.

**Alison Moyet** has been on the chart for 135 weeks as a soloist and 83 as half of Yazoo, a total of 218 weeks.

**Graham Nash** has had 8 weeks on the chart as a soloist, 5 weeks as half of a duo with David Crosby, 14 weeks as one third of Crosby Stills and Nash, 79 weeks as one quarter of Crosby, Stills, Nash and Young and 106 weeks as one fifth of the Hollies, a total of 212 weeks.

**Steve Winwood** has clocked up 117 weeks on the chart as a solo act, 47 weeks as a member of the Spencer Davis Group, 37 playing in Traffic and 10 as part of Blind Faith, a total of 211 weeks.

**Vangelis** has 139 weeks of chart life as a soloist and 53 more as half of Jon and Vangelis, a total of 192 weeks.

**Mr. Acker Bilk** has scored 76 weeks as a soloist and with his Paramount Jazz Band, a further 61 weeks with Chris Barber, and 24 weeks with Kenny Ball and Chris Barber, a total of 161 weeks.

**David Sylvian** has 21 solo weeks on the chart, 1 in partnership with Holgar Czukay and 136 as a member of Japan, a total of 158 weeks.

**Marvin Gaye** has spent 93 solo weeks on the chart, 45 with Diana Ross, 9 with Smokey Robinson and 4 with Tammi Terrell, a total of 151 weeks.

**Boy George** has 6 solo weeks to his credit and 144 more as lead vocalist with Culture Club, a total of 150 weeks.

BOY GEORGE

# Most Weeks on Char
# in a Year

There has been fifty instances of one act clocking up 100 or more chart weeks in one year. Dire Straits' record score in 1986 is the equivalent of four albums on the chart every week throughout the year.

| | | |
|---|---|---|
| 217 | DIRE STRAITS . . . . . . . . . . . . . | 1986 |
| 198 | DAVID BOWIE . . . . . . . . . . . . | 1983 |
| 182 | DAVID BOWIE . . . . . . . . . . . . | 1973 |
| 177 | BRUCE SPRINGSTEEN . . . . . . | 1985 |
| 168 | U2 . . . . . . . . . . . . . . . . . . . . . . | 1985 |
| 167 | SIMON AND GARFUNKEL . . . | 1970 |
| 158 | DIRE STRAITS . . . . . . . . . . . . . | 1985 |
| 135 | TOM JONES . . . . . . . . . . . . . . . | 1968 |

U2

**323**

Simon and Garfunkel have racked up 100 chart weeks in a year five times. Dire Straits have done it four times, in consecutive years (1983 to 1986 inclusive). The Beatles, David Bowie and U2 have topped the century in three years, while Abba, Phil Collins, Madonna, Michael Jackson and Queen have done it twice.

ROBERT PLANT

# Most Weeks on Chart in Each Chart Year

| | | |
|------|--------|-------|
| 1958 | ELVIS PRESLEY | 16* |
| 1959 | FRANK SINATRA | 56* |
| 1960 | ELVIS PRESLEY | 51 |
| 1961 | ELVIS PRESLEY | 91* |
| 1962 | GEORGE MITCHELL MINSTRELS | 109* |
| 1963 | CLIFF RICHARD | 72 |
| 1964 | JIM REEVES | 115* |
| 1965 | BOB DYLAN | 112 |
| 1966 | BEACH BOYS | 95 |
| 1967 | HERB ALPERT | 101 |
| 1968 | TOM JONES | 135* |
| 1969 | SEEKERS | 66 |
| 1970 | SIMON AND GARFUNKEL | 167* |
| 1971 | ANDY WILLIAMS | 111 |
| 1972 | CAT STEVENS | 89 |
| 1973 | DAVID BOWIE | 182* |
| 1974 | DAVID BOWIE | 107 |
| 1975 | ELTON JOHN | 105 |
| 1976 | DEMIS ROUSSOS | 84 |
| 1977 | PINK FLOYD | 108 |
| 1978 | ABBA | 112 |
| 1979 | ELECTRIC LIGHT ORCHESTRA | 112 |
| 1980 | POLICE | 116 |
| 1981 | BARRY MANILOW | 92 |
| 1982 | JAPAN | 85 |
| 1983 | DAVID BOWIE | 198* |
| 1984 | DIRE STRAITS | 116 |
| 1985 | BRUCE SPRINGSTEEN | 177 |
| 1986 | DIRE STRAITS | 217* |
| 1987 | MADONNA | 127 |
| 1988 | MICHAEL JACKSON | 114 |
| 1989 | GUNS N' ROSES | 85 |

(* denotes record annual total at the time)

Elvis Presley and David Bowie have each been the year's chart champions three times, and Dire Straits have won twice. No other act has been chart champion more than once.

## Most Weeks on Chart in 1988

| | |
|-------|--------|
| 114 | MICHAEL JACKSON (+ 13 with Diana Ross, 2 with Jacksons) |
| 107 | FLEETWOOD MAC |
| 100 | PET SHOP BOYS |
| 82 | ERASURE |
| 75 | U2 |
| 70 | DIRE STRAITS |
| 70 | WHITNEY HOUSTON |

| Weeks | Artist |
|-------|--------|
| 60 | LUTHER VANDROSS |
| 60 | WET WET WET |
| 56 | ALEXANDER O'NEAL |

Michael Jackson topped the annual lists for the first time, having been out of the top ten acts of the year since 1984, but Fleetwood Mac, scoring their first annual century of weeks 21 years after their chart debut, and the Pet Shop Boys gave him a good run for his money. It was the sixth year in a row that at least three acts racked up 100 chart weeks, the longest such run in album chart history. Six of the previous year's top ten acts reappeared in 1988's top ten, the only newcomers apart from Michael Jackson being Erasure, Wet Wet Wet and Alexander O'Neal.

ELVIS PRESLEY

## Most Weeks on Chart in 1989

| | |
|-------|--------|
| 85 | GUNS N' ROSES |
| 73 | ERASURE |
| 68 | GLORIA ESTEFAN |
| 65 | DEACON BLUE |
| 58 | U2 |
| 54 | TRACY CHAPMAN |
| 54 | ROY ORBISON |
| 53 | KYLIE MINOGUE |
| 53 | SIMPLY RED |
| 51 | BOBBY BROWN |

For the first time since 1982, no act topped the 100 week mark. Guns N' Roses, thanks mainly to the new lease of life given to their 1987 release *Appetite For Destruction*, took heavy metal to the top of the annual charts for the first time. After such a comparatively steady 1988, in 1989 only Erasure and U2 (enjoying their 7th consecutive year among the elite) held over from the top acts of the year before, although Simply Red and Roy Orbison had been in the Top 10 before, Simply Red in 1987 and the late Roy Orbison a quarter of a century before, in 1964.

# Most Weeks on Chart by One Album

This is a list of all the albums that have spent a total of 100 weeks or more on the chart. Re-releases and re-issues are counted, provided that the re-issue is identical to the original release.

Three of these albums, *Jeff Wayne's War Of The Worlds*, *Phantom Of The Opera* and *Hearsay/All Mixed Up* were still on the chart at the end of 1989.

DIRTY DANCING spent 63 weeks on the main chart up to the beginning of 1989, and a further 51 weeks on the compilations chart, where it remained at the end of the year. No other album has totalled over 100 weeks on a combination of the two charts.

Five of the seven Dire Straits albums released to the end of 1989 are in this list. Three albums each by the Beatles, Phil Collins, Simon and Garfunkel, Michael Jackson and U2 have spent over 100 weeks on the chart, as well as two each by David Bowie, Duran Duran, Electric Light Orchestra, Whitney Houston, and Madonna. There have been three recent title holders for the record of longest stay on the chart – *The Sound Of Music*, Meat Loaf's *Bat Out Of Hell*, and finally, from 24 Oct 1987, Fleetwood Mac's *Rumours*, which has now enjoyed the equivalent of eight and a half years on our albums chart.

The sales of a record are not necessarily reflected in the length of its chart run. *Off The Wall* and *Thriller* have both had longer chart runs than Michael Jackson's best-seller in Britain, *Bad*, while Dire Straits' biggest seller, *Brothers In Arms*, still has some way to go before its chart life overtakes that of *Makin' Movies*.

# Most Hit Albums

An album is a hit if it spends only one week at number 100. Double, treble and quadruple albums count as only one hit. Re-issues do not count as a new hit.

62 ELVIS PRESLEY
53 JAMES LAST
49 FRANK SINATRA
*(plus 1 with Count Basie)*
45 CLIFF RICHARD
35 ROLLING STONES
32 BOB DYLAN
*(plus 1 with Grateful Dead)*
29 ELTON JOHN
28 SHIRLEY BASSEY
28 DIANA ROSS
*(plus 2 with Marvin Gaye, and 1 with Gladys Knight, Stevie Wonder and Michael Jackson)*
26 DAVID BOWIE
26 JIM REEVES
25 BEACH BOYS
25 BEATLES
24 NEIL DIAMOND
24 JOHNNY MATHIS
*(plus 1 with Natalie Cole, 1 with Deniece Williams and 1 with Henry Mancini)*
24 ANDY WILLIAMS
23 SHADOWS
23 STATUS QUO
21 JETHRO TULL
20 TOM JONES
20 WHO
20 NEIL YOUNG
*(plus 1 with Stills-Young Band and 3 with Crosby, Stills, Nash and Young)*
19 DEEP PURPLE
19 HAWKWIND
*(includes 1 as Hawklords)*
19 PAUL McCARTNEY/WINGS
19 ROD STEWART
*(plus 1 with the Faces)*
19 GARY NUMAN/TUBEWAY ARMY
*(plus 1 with Sharpe and Numan)*
19 SANTANA
*(Carlos Santana 3 more with various other partners)*
18 JIMI HENDRIX
*(plus 1 with Curtis Knight)*
17 BLACK SABBATH
17 QUEEN
16 MARC BOLAN/T. REX/TYRANNOSAURUS REX
16 JOHNNY CASH
16 ERIC CLAPTON
*(plus 1 with John Mayall and 1 with Cream)*
16 MIKE OLDFIELD
16 PINK FLOYD
16 BARBRA STREISAND
16 TANGERINE DREAM
15 HERB ALPERT
15 ALICE COOPER
15 GENESIS
15 VAN MORRISON
15 ROY ORBISON
15 SLADE

15 YES
14 CARPENTERS
14 ELVIS COSTELLO
*(includes 1 as the Costello Show)*
14 JOHN DENVER
*(plus 1 with Placido Domingo)*
14 DAVID ESSEX
14 KISS
14 MOODY BLUES
14 STRANGLERS
14 DON WILLIAMS
14 STEVIE WONDER
*(plus 1 with Diana Ross, Gladys Knight and Michael Jackson)*
13 FLEETWOOD MAC
13 BARRY MANILOW
13 MOTORHEAD
13 DONNA SUMMER
13 TEMPTATIONS
*(plus 3 with Diana Ross and the Supremes)*
13 UB40
13 WISHBONE ASH
12 ABBA
12 MAX BYGRAVES
12 CURE
12 HOLLIES
12 BUDDY HOLLY
12 JACKSONS
*(4 as Jackson Five including one with Michael Jackson, 8 as Jacksons)*
12 MICHAEL JACKSON
*(plus 1 with Diana Ross, Gladys Knight and Stevie Wonder, 1 with Jackson Five)*
12 BILLY JOEL
12 JOHN LENNON/PLASTIC ONO BAND
12 LONDON SYMPHONY ORCHESTRA
12 MANTOVANI
12 JOHN MAYALL
*(plus 1 with Eric Clapton)*
12 ROXY MUSIC
*(plus 2 with Bryan Ferry)*
12 URIAH HEEP
12 FRANK ZAPPA
11 BEE GEES
11 GEORGE BENSON
*(plus 1 with Earl Klugh)*
11 ELKIE BROOKS
11 RAY CONNIFF
11 BARBARA DICKSON
11 ELECTRIC LIGHT ORCHESTRA
11 EVERLY BROTHERS
*(Phil Everly 1 more solo)*
11 ENGELBERT HUMPERDINCK
11 JUDAS PRIEST
11 KINKS
11 BOB MARLEY AND THE WAILERS
11 JONI MITCHELL
11 RUSH
11 LEO SAYER
11 SIOUXSIE AND THE BANSHEES
11 10 C.C.
*(plus 1 with Godley and Creme)*
11 THIN LIZZY
*(plus 1 with Phil Lynott)*
11 BARRY WHITE
10 AC/DC

| | |
|---|---|
| 10 | JOAN ARMATRADING |
| 10 | BARCLAY JAMES HARVEST |
| 10 | BYRDS |
| 10 | VAL DOONICAN |
| 10 | EMERSON LAKE AND PALMER |
| | *(Emerson, Lake and Powell 1 more)* |
| 10 | FOSTER AND ALLEN |
| 10 | RORY GALLAGHER |
| 10 | JEAN-MICHEL JARRE |
| 10 | BERT KAEMPFERT |
| 10 | KING CRIMSON |
| 10 | LED ZEPPELIN |
| 10 | LEVEL 42 |
| 10 | GEORGE MITCHELL MINSTRELS |
| 10 | NANA MOUSKOURI |
| 10 | OLIVIA NEWTON-JOHN |
| 10 | ALAN PARSONS PROJECT |
| 10 | PUBLIC IMAGE LTD. |
| 10 | RAINBOW |
| 10 | CHRIS REA |
| 10 | SHOWADDYWADDY |
| 10 | SHAKIN' STEVENS |
| 10 | TALKING HEADS |
| 10 | DIONNE WARWICK |
| 10 | ROGER WHITTAKER |

Rick Wakeman has hit the charts 9 times, plus once more with Kevin Peek and again with Anderson Bruford Wakeman Howe. Simon and Garfunkel have had 9 hit albums. Paul Simon has 8 more solo hit albums and Art Garfunkel 6. Marvin Gaye has 8 hit albums to his credit and one each with Tammi Terrell, Diana Ross and Smokey Robinson, a total of 11. Vangelis has amassed 6 solo hit albums, plus 4 more with Jon Anderson.

CLIFF RICHARD

# Most Top Ten
# Hit Albums

The rules for this category are the same as for Most Hit Albums, except that the album must have made the Top Ten for at least one week.

| | |
|---|---|
| 36 | ELVIS PRESLEY |
| 29 | CLIFF RICHARD |
| 27 | ROLLING STONES |
| 27 | FRANK SINATRA |
| | *(plus 1 with Count Basie)* |
| 24 | BOB DYLAN |
| 18 | BEATLES |
| 18 | DAVID BOWIE |
| 17 | PAUL McCARTNEY/WINGS |
| 16 | ELTON JOHN |
| 16 | STATUS QUO |
| 15 | QUEEN |
| 15 | ROD STEWART |
| | *(plus 1 with the Faces)* |
| 13 | BEACH BOYS |
| 13 | PINK FLOYD |
| 13 | JIM REEVES |
| 13 | WHO |
| 12 | GENESIS |
| | *(Phil Collins 4 more solo, Mike Rutherford one as part of Mike & the Mechanics)* |
| 11 | TOM JONES |
| 10 | ELVIS COSTELLO |
| 10 | LED ZEPPELIN |
| 10 | SHADOWS |
| | *(plus 16 with Cliff Richard)* |
| 10 | ANDY WILLIAMS |
| 9 | BLACK SABBATH |
| 9 | DEEP PURPLE |
| 9 | ROXY MUSIC |
| | *(plus 2 with Bryan Ferry)* |
| 9 | YES |
| 8 | ABBA |
| 8 | DEPECHE MODE |
| 8 | FLEETWOOD MAC |
| 8 | JIMI HENDRIX |
| 8 | JOHNNY MATHIS |
| | *(plus 1 with Deniece Williams)* |
| 8 | MOODY BLUES |
| 8 | UB40 |
| 8 | STEVIE WONDER |
| 7 | BEE GEES |
| 7 | KATE BUSH |
| 7 | CARPENTERS |
| 7 | CREAM |
| | *(plus 1 with Eric Clapton)* |
| 7 | DIRE STRAITS |
| 7 | ELECTRIC LIGHT ORCHESTRA |
| 7 | EMERSON LAKE AND PALMER |
| 7 | BUDDY HOLLY AND THE CRICKETS |
| 7 | JOHN LENNON/PLASTIC ONO BAND |
| 7 | DIANA ROSS |
| | *(plus 1 with Marvin Gaye)* |
| 7 | SMITHS |
| | *(Morrissey one more solo)* |
| 7 | STRANGLERS |
| 7 | 10 C.C. |
| | *(plus 1 with Godley & Creme)* |
| 7 | THIN LIZZY |
| 7 | ULTRAVOX |
| 7 | WHITESNAKE |
| 6 | AC/DC |
| 6 | SHIRLEY BASSEY |
| 6 | BLONDIE |
| | *(Debbie Harry one more solo)* |

| | | | |
|---|---|---|---|
| 6 | MARC BOLAN/T. REX/ TYRANNOSAURUS REX | 5 | FREE |
| 6 | ERIC CLAPTON | 5 | JEAN-MICHEL JARRE |
| | *(plus 1 with Cream)* | 5 | BILLY JOEL |
| 6 | RUSS CONWAY | 5 | JACK JONES |
| 6 | CURE | 5 | KINKS |
| 6 | EURYTHMICS | 5 | LEVEL 42 |
| 6 | PETER GABRIEL | 5 | MADONNA |
| 6 | HOLLIES | 5 | BOB MARLEY and the WAILERS |
| 6 | ENGELBERT HUMPERDINCK | 5 | MEAT LOAF |
| 6 | IRON MAIDEN | 5 | NEW ORDER |
| 6 | JAM | 5 | MIKE OLDFIELD |
| 6 | JETHRO TULL | 5 | ORCHESTRAL MANOEUVRES IN THE DARK |
| 6 | MADNESS | 5 | PRINCE |
| 6 | BARRY MANILOW | 5 | RAINBOW |
| 6 | MANTOVANI | 5 | SANTANA |
| 6 | MARILLION | | *(plus 1 with Mahavishnu John McLaughlin)* |
| 6 | GEORGE MITCHELL MINSTRELS | 5 | SHOWADDYWADDY |
| 6 | GARY NUMAN/TUBEWAY ARMY | 5 | PAUL SIMON |
| 6 | ROY ORBISON | | *(plus 6 with Simon and Garfunkel)* |
| 6 | POLICE | 5 | SIMPLE MINDS |
| 6 | RUSH | 5 | SLADE |
| 6 | LEO SAYER | 5 | SPANDAU BALLET |
| 6 | SIMON AND GARFUNKEL | 5 | BRUCE SPRINGSTEEN |
| | *(Paul Simon 5 more solo, Art Garfunkel 2 more solo)* | 5 | BARBRA STREISAND |
| 6 | CAT STEVENS | 5 | STYLE COUNCIL |
| 6 | SUPREMES | 5 | SUPERTRAMP |
| | *(plus 1 with the Four Tops, plus 1 with Diana Ross and the Temptations)* | 5 | U2 |
| 5 | HERB ALPERT | | |
| 5 | MAX BYGRAVES | | |
| 5 | JOHNNY CASH | | |
| 5 | CULTURE CLUB | | |
| 5 | JOHN DENVER | | |
| 5 | NEIL DIAMOND | | |
| 5 | VAL DOONICAN | | |
| 5 | DURAN DURAN | | |
| 5 | EAGLES | | |
| 5 | ECHO AND THE BUNNYMEN | | |
| 5 | DUANE EDDY | | |
| 5 | EVERLY BROTHERS | | |
| 5 | BRYAN FERRY | | |
| | *(plus 2 with Roxy Music)* | | |

Steve Winwood has 3 solo Top Ten albums, 3 more as part of the Spencer Davis Group, 2 as a member of Traffic and one as one third of Blind Faith, a total of 9.

The only act to hit the chart ten times or more and to take every hit into the Top Ten is Led Zeppelin, who have scored ten Top Ten hits out of ten tries.

**329**

BRUCE SPRINGSTEEN

# Most Hits Without a Top Ten Hit

Only five acts have had ten or more hit albums without ever reaching the Top Ten. They are **Tangerine Dream** (16 hits), **Van Morrison** (15 hits), **Barclay James Harvest** (10 hits), **Alan Parsons Project** (10 hits) and **Public Image Ltd.** (10 hits). The Alan Parsons Project has never even hit the Top Twenty, their most successful album being their eighth hit, *Ammonia Avenue*, which reached number 24 in 1984. **Van Morrison** finally hit the Top Ten in April 1990, after the period covered by this book.

**James Last** has hit the Top Ten only four times out of 53 chart entries, a hit-making career which includes a run of 31 consecutive hit albums (his second to 32nd hits inclusive) which all missed the Top Ten. **Neil Young** has so far clocked up 18 hit albums since his last Top 10 hit. There have been 57 hit compilation albums on the **Street Sounds** label totalling 269 weeks on the charts, but the highest placing for any of them is 12 by *Street Sounds Electro* 7 in March 1985.

NEIL YOUNG

# Most Albums on the Chart in One Week

Dire Straits' total of 217 weeks on the chart in one year (1986) is the equivalent of an average of four albums in the Top 100 in every week of the year. Only four artists in the history of the albums chart have charted with at least seven albums in one week, as follows:

| | | |
|---|---|---|
| 14 albums in a chart of 60 | Elvis Presley | 10 Sep 1977 |
| 12 albums in a chart of 60 | Elvis Presley | 17 Sep 1977 |
| 11 albums in a chart of 60 | Elvis Presley | 1 Oct 1977 |
| 11 albums in a chart of 60 | Elvis Presley | 8 Oct 1977 |
| 10 albums in a chart of 100 | David Bowie | 16 Jul 1983 |
| 9 albums in a chart of 60 | Elvis Presley | 24 Sep 1977 |
| 9 albums in a chart of 100 | David Bowie | 11 Jun 1983 |
| 9 albums in a chart of 100 | David Bowie | 9 Jul 1983 |
| 8 albums in a chart of 20 | Jim Reeves | 26 Sep 1964 |
| 8 albums in a chart of 100 | David Bowie | 27 Aug 1983 |
| 7 albums in a chart of 20 | Jim Reeves | 29 Aug 1964 |
| 7 albums in a chart of 20 | Jim Reeves | 5 Sep 1964 |
| 7 albums in a chart of 20 | Jim Reeves | 3 Oct 1964 |
| 7 albums in a chart of 20 | Jim Reeves | 10 Oct 1964 |
| 7 albums in a chart of 60 | Elvis Presley | 15 Oct 1977 |
| 7 albums in a chart of 100 | David Bowie | 14 May 1983 |
| 7 albums in a chart of 100 | David Bowie | 21 May 1983 |
| 7 albums in a chart of 100 | David Bowie | 28 May 1983 |
| 7 albums in a chart of 100 | David Bowie | 4 Jun 1983 |
| 7 albums in a chart of 100 | David Bowie | 18 Jun 1983 |
| 7 albums in a chart of 100 | David Bowie | 30 Jul 1983 |
| 7 albums in a chart of 100 | David Bowie | 20 Aug 1983 |
| 7 albums in a chart of 100 | Bruce Springsteen | 15 Jun 1985 |

(nine consecutive weeks) to 10 Aug 1985

Of all these instances, only Elvis Presley on 10 Sep 1977 and Bruce Springsteen for four weeks from 6 Jul 1985 held the top spot. The most complete chart domination was by Jim Reeves on 26 Sep 1964, when he accounted for 40% of the albums chart. Bruce Springsteen's achievement in the summer of 1985 is the only example of an artist who has released as many as seven albums charting *all* his albums at once. Only Jim Reeves on 3 Oct 1964 and Elvis Presley on 10 Sep 1977 placed three albums in the Top Ten. In 1986, Dire Straits charted all six of their albums (one of which was a double album) for a total of 12 weeks. For seven of those weeks they held the number one spot.

# Least Successful Chart Act

Since 8 August 1981, when the chart was extended to a Top 100, eight acts have achieved the minor distinction of a chart career consisting of only one week at number 100. These acts, in chronological order, are:

| | | | | |
|---|---|---|---|---|
| 17 | Oct | 81 | RONNIE LAWS ................. | Solid Ground |
| 17 | Dec | 83 | SLEIGHRIDERS ............. | A Very Merry Disco |
| 11 | Feb | 84 | EUROPEANS ............................ | Live |
| 30 | Jun | 84 | WENDY O. WILLIAMS ................. | WOW |
| 30 | Mar | 85 | SECOND IMAGE ............ | Strange Reflections |
| 12 | Oct | 85 | ALIEN SEX FIEND ............ | Maximum Security |
| 29 | Nov | 86 | SHOP ASSISTANTS .............. | Shop Assistants |
| 3 | Oct | 87 | BOLSHOI ...................... | Lindy's Party |

There is also one compilation album which lasted at number 100 for just one week:

| | | | | |
|---|---|---|---|---|
| 26 | Nov | 83 | VARIOUS ARTISTS ...... | Twelve Inches Of Pleasure |

Before 8 August 1981 and since 14 January 1989, 19 acts achieved the lesser distinction of one week of chart life on the bottom rung of a smaller chart:

| | | | | Chart Size |
|---|---|---|---|---|
| 11 Jun | 60 | BOB WALLIS and his STORYVILLE JAZZMEN ................. Everybody Loves Saturday Night | | 20 |
| 18 Jun | 60 | SHELLEY MANNE ........................... My Fair Lady | | 20 |
| 25 Jun | 60 | KNIGHTSBRIDGE STRINGS..................... String Sway | | 20 |
| 17 Dec | 60 | BIG BEN BANJO BAND .............. More Minstrel Melodies | | 20 |
| 24 Dec | 60 | NEW WORLD THEATRE ORCHESTRA Let's Dance To The Hits Of The 30s and 40s | | 20 |
| 14 Jul | 62 | ERROL GARNER ......................... Close Up In Swing | | 20 |
| 9 Feb | 63 | SPOTNICKS.................................... Out-A-Space | | 20 |
| 18 Apr | 64 | HARRY SECOMBE, PETER SELLERS & SPIKE MILLIGAN ........ How To Win An Election | | 20 |
| 20 Jun | 64 | SONNY BOY WILLIAMSON.............. Down And Out Blues | | 20 |
| 29 Jul | 67 | MANITAS DE PLATA ...................... Flamenco Guitar | | 40 |
| 22 Jun | 68 | SOLOMON KING ....................... She Wears My Ring | | 40 |
| 17 Aug | 68 | O. C. SMITH....................... Hickory Holler Revisited | | 40 |
| 28 Feb | 70 | BOBBIE GENTRY & GLEN CAMPBELL .................... Bobbie Gentry And Glen Campbell | | 50 |
| 20 Jun | 70 | MOIRA ANDERSON ..................... These Are My Songs | | 50 |
| 28 Nov | 70 | SAVOY BROWN .............................. Lookin' In | | 50 |
| 13 Apr | 74 | DEKE LEONARD ............................. Kamikaze | | 50 |
| 1 Apr | 78 | CULTURE ........................... Two Sevens Clash | | 60 |
| 30 Sep | 78 | CERRONE ................................ Supernature | | 60 |
| 18 Mar | 89 | VOW WOW .............................. Helter Skelter | | 75 |

**331**

Six compilation albums have also spent just 1 week at the bottom of the smaller charts, as follows:

| | | | |
|---|---|---|---|
| 28 May | 60 | 'Pal Joey' Original Film Soundtrack | 20 |
| 23 Nov | 63 | Hitsville Vol 2 | 20 |
| 8 Feb | 64 | Ready Steady Go! | 20 |
| 11 May | 68 | Blues Anytime | 40 |
| 3 Nov | 79 | Mods Mayday 79 | 75 |
| 23 Dec | 89 | Reggae Hits Vol 7 | 20 |

(The last album was listed on the compilation chart only)

The ADICTS have spent one week at number 99 with their only hit album, *The Sound Of Music*, and one week on the bottom rung, number 75, with their only hit single, *Bad Boy*. This is the nearest to the ultimate least successful chart double so far.

# The Number One Albums 8 Nov 1958 to 30 December 1989

*Weeks*

8 Nov 58   SOUTH PACIFIC Film Soundtrack (RCA) . . . . . . . . . . . . . . . . . . . . . . . . . . . . . 70

12 Mar 60   THE EXPLOSIVE FREDDY CANNON Freddy Cannon (Top Rank) . . . . . . . . 1
19 Mar 60   SOUTH PACIFIC Film Soundtrack (RCA) . . . . . . . . . . . . . . . . . . . . . . . . . . . . 19
30 Jul 60   ELVIS IS BACK Elvis Presley (RCA) . . . . . . . . . . . . . . . . . . . . . . . . . . . . . . . . . 1
6 Aug 60   SOUTH PACIFIC Film Soundtrack (RCA) . . . . . . . . . . . . . . . . . . . . . . . . . . . . . 5
10 Sep 60   DOWN DRURY LANE TO MEMORY LANE 101 Strings (Pye) . . . . . . . . . . . . 5
15 Oct 60   SOUTH PACIFIC Film Soundtrack (RCA) . . . . . . . . . . . . . . . . . . . . . . . . . . . . 13

14 Jan 61   GI BLUES Elvis Presley (RCA) . . . . . . . . . . . . . . . . . . . . . . . . . . . . . . . . . . . . . 7
4 Mar 61   SOUTH PACIFIC Film Soundtrack (RCA) . . . . . . . . . . . . . . . . . . . . . . . . . . . . . 1
11 Mar 61   GI BLUES Elvis Presley (RCA) . . . . . . . . . . . . . . . . . . . . . . . . . . . . . . . . . . . . . 3
1 Apr 61   SOUTH PACIFIC Film Soundtrack (RCA) . . . . . . . . . . . . . . . . . . . . . . . . . . . . . 1
8 Apr 61   GI BLUES Elvis Presley (RCA) . . . . . . . . . . . . . . . . . . . . . . . . . . . . . . . . . . . . 12
1 Jul 61   SOUTH PACIFIC Film Soundtrack (RCA) . . . . . . . . . . . . . . . . . . . . . . . . . . . . . 4
29 Jul 61   BLACK AND WHITE MINSTREL SHOW George Mitchell Minstrels (HMV) . . 4
26 Aug 61   SOUTH PACIFIC Film Soundtrack (RCA) . . . . . . . . . . . . . . . . . . . . . . . . . . . . . 1
2 Sep 61   BLACK AND WHITE MINSTREL SHOW George Mitchell Minstrels (HMV) . . 1
9 Sep 61   SOUTH PACIFIC Film Soundtrack (RCA) . . . . . . . . . . . . . . . . . . . . . . . . . . . . . 1
16 Sep 61   BLACK AND WHITE MINSTREL SHOW George Mitchell Minstrels (HMV) . . 1
23 Sep 61   THE SHADOWS Shadows (Columbia) . . . . . . . . . . . . . . . . . . . . . . . . . . . . . . . 4
21 Oct 61   BLACK AND WHITE MINSTREL SHOW George Mitchell Minstrels (HMV) . . 1
28 Oct 61   THE SHADOWS Shadows (Columbia) . . . . . . . . . . . . . . . . . . . . . . . . . . . . . . . 1
4 Nov 61   21 TODAY Cliff Richard (Columbia) . . . . . . . . . . . . . . . . . . . . . . . . . . . . . . . . 1
11 Nov 61   ANOTHER BLACK AND WHITE MINSTREL SHOW George Mitchell
Minstrels (HMV) . . . . . . . . . . . . . . . . . . . . . . . . . . . . . . . . . . . . . . . . . . . . . . . 8

6 Jan 62   BLUE HAWAII Elvis Presley (RCA) . . . . . . . . . . . . . . . . . . . . . . . . . . . . . . . . . 1
13 Jan 62   THE YOUNG ONES Cliff Richard (Columbia) . . . . . . . . . . . . . . . . . . . . . . . . 6
24 Feb 62   BLUE HAWAII Elvis Presley (RCA) . . . . . . . . . . . . . . . . . . . . . . . . . . . . . . . . 17
23 Jun 62   WEST SIDE STORY Film Soundtrack (Philips/CBS) . . . . . . . . . . . . . . . . . . . . 5
28 Jul 62   POT LUCK Elvis Presley (RCA) . . . . . . . . . . . . . . . . . . . . . . . . . . . . . . . . . . . . 5
1 Sep 62   WEST SIDE STORY Film Soundtrack (CBS) . . . . . . . . . . . . . . . . . . . . . . . . . . . 1
8 Sep 62   POT LUCK Elvis Presley (RCA) . . . . . . . . . . . . . . . . . . . . . . . . . . . . . . . . . . . . 1
15 Sep 62   WEST SIDE STORY Film Soundtrack (CBS) . . . . . . . . . . . . . . . . . . . . . . . . . . . 1
22 Sep 62   THE BEST OF BALL, BARBER AND BILK Kenny Ball, Chris Barber and Acker
Bilk (Pye) . . . . . . . . . . . . . . . . . . . . . . . . . . . . . . . . . . . . . . . . . . . . . . . . . . . . . 1
29 Sep 62   WEST SIDE STORY Film Soundtrack (CBS) . . . . . . . . . . . . . . . . . . . . . . . . . . . 3
20 Oct 62   THE BEST OF BALL, BARBER AND BILK Kenny Ball, Chris Barber and Acker
Bilk (Pye) . . . . . . . . . . . . . . . . . . . . . . . . . . . . . . . . . . . . . . . . . . . . . . . . . . . . . 1
27 Oct 62   OUT OF THE SHADOWS Shadows (Columbia) . . . . . . . . . . . . . . . . . . . . . . . 3
17 Nov 62   WEST SIDE STORY Film Soundtrack (CBS) . . . . . . . . . . . . . . . . . . . . . . . . . . . 1
24 Nov 62   OUT OF THE SHADOWS Shadows (Columbia) . . . . . . . . . . . . . . . . . . . . . . . 1
1 Dec 62   ON STAGE WITH THE BLACK AND WHITE MINSTRELS George Mitchell
Minstrels (HMV) . . . . . . . . . . . . . . . . . . . . . . . . . . . . . . . . . . . . . . . . . . . . . . . 2
15 Dec 62   WEST SIDE STORY Film Soundtrack (CBS) . . . . . . . . . . . . . . . . . . . . . . . . . . . 1
22 Dec 62   OUT OF THE SHADOWS Shadows (Columbia) . . . . . . . . . . . . . . . . . . . . . . . 1
29 Dec 62   BLACK AND WHITE MINSTREL SHOW George Mitchell Minstrels (HMV) . . 2

12 Jan 63   WEST SIDE STORY Film Soundtrack (CBS) . . . . . . . . . . . . . . . . . . . . . . . . . . . 1
19 Jan 63   OUT OF THE SHADOWS Shadows (Columbia) . . . . . . . . . . . . . . . . . . . . . . . 2
2 Feb 63   SUMMER HOLIDAY Cliff Richard and the Shadows (Columbia) . . . . . . . . . . 14
11 May 63   PLEASE PLEASE ME Beatles (Parlophone) . . . . . . . . . . . . . . . . . . . . . . . . . . 30
7 Dec 63   WITH THE BEATLES Beatles (Parlophone) . . . . . . . . . . . . . . . . . . . . . . . . . . 21

2 May 64   ROLLING STONES Rolling Stones (Decca) . . . . . . . . . . . . . . . . . . . . . . . . . . 12
25 Jul 64   A HARD DAY'S NIGHT Beatles (Parlophone) . . . . . . . . . . . . . . . . . . . . . . . . 21
19 Dec 64   BEATLES FOR SALE Beatles (Parlophone) . . . . . . . . . . . . . . . . . . . . . . . . . . . 7

6 Feb 65   ROLLING STONES No. 2 Rolling Stones (Decca) . . . . . . . . . . . . . . . . . . . . . . . 3
27 Feb 65   BEATLES FOR SALE Beatles (Parlophone) . . . . . . . . . . . . . . . . . . . . . . . . . . . 1

MONKEES

```
21 Sep 68   DELILAH Tom Jones (Decca) ........................................... 1
28 Sep 68   BOOKENDS Simon and Garfunkel (CBS) ............................... 2
12 Oct 68   GREATEST HITS Hollies (Parlophone)................................. 6
23 Nov 68   THE SOUND OF MUSIC Soundtrack (RCA) .......................... 1
30 Nov 68   GREATEST HITS Hollies (Parlophone)................................ 1
 7 Dec 68   THE BEATLES Beatles (Apple) ........................................ 7

25 Jan 69   BEST OF THE SEEKERS Seekers (Columbia) ........................... 1
 1 Feb 69   THE BEATLES Beatles (Apple) ........................................ 1
 8 Feb 69   BEST OF THE SEEKERS Seekers (Columbia) ........................... 1
15 Feb 69   DIANA ROSS AND THE SUPREMES JOIN THE TEMPTATIONS Diana Ross/
            Supremes/Temptations (Tamla Motown) .............................. 4
15 Mar 69   GOODBYE Cream (Polydor) ........................................... 2
29 Mar 69   BEST OF THE SEEKERS Seekers (Columbia) ........................... 2
12 Apr 69   GOODBYE Cream (Polydor) ........................................... 1
19 Apr 69   BEST OF THE SEEKERS Seekers (Columbia) ........................... 1
26 Apr 69   GOODBYE Cream (Polydor) ........................................... 1
 3 May 69   BEST OF THE SEEKERS Seekers (Columbia) ........................... 1
10 May 69   ON THE THRESHOLD OF A DREAM Moody Blues (Deram) .............. 2
24 May 69   NASHVILLE SKYLINE Bob Dylan (CBS) ............................... 4
21 Jun 69   HIS ORCHESTRA, HIS CHORUS, HIS SINGERS, HIS SOUND Ray Conniff
            (CBS) .............................................................. 3
12 Jul 69   ACCORDING TO MY HEART Jim Reeves (RCA International) ............. 4
 9 Aug 69   STAND UP Jethro Tull (Island) ...................................... 3
30 Aug 69   FROM ELVIS IN MEMPHIS Elvis Presley (RCA) ....................... 1
 6 Sep 69   STAND UP Jethro Tull (Island) ...................................... 2
20 Sep 69   BLIND FAITH Blind Faith (Polydor)................................. 2
 4 Oct 69   ABBEY ROAD Beatles (Apple) ....................................... 11
20 Dec 69   LET IT BLEED Rolling Stones (Decca) ............................... 1
27 Dec 69   ABBEY ROAD Beatles (Apple) ........................................ 6

 7 Feb 70   LED ZEPPELIN 2 Led Zeppelin (Atlantic).............................. 1
14 Feb 70   MOTOWN CHARTBUSTERS VOL. 3 Various (Tamla Motown) ........... 1
21 Feb 70   BRIDGE OVER TROUBLED WATER Simon and Garfunkel (CBS) ......... 13
23 May 70   LET IT BE Beatles (Parlophone) .................................... 3
13 Jun 70   BRIDGE OVER TROUBLED WATER Simon and Garfunkel (CBS) ......... 4
11 Jul 70   SELF PORTRAIT Bob Dylan (CBS) .................................... 1
18 Jul 70   BRIDGE OVER TROUBLED WATER Simon and Garfunkel (CBS) ......... 5
22 Aug 70   QUESTION OF BALANCE Moody Blues (Threshold) ................... 3
12 Sep 70   COSMO'S FACTORY Creedence Clearwater Revival (Liberty) ............ 1
19 Sep 70   GET YOUR YA YAS OUT Rolling Stones (Decca) ...................... 2
 3 Oct 70   BRIDGE OVER TROUBLED WATER Simon and Garfunkel (CBS) ......... 1
10 Oct 70   PARANOID Black Sabbath (Vertigo) ................................. 1
17 Oct 70   BRIDGE OVER TROUBLED WATER Simon and Garfunkel (CBS) ......... 1
24 Oct 70   ATOM HEART MOTHER Pink Floyd (Harvest) ........................ 1
31 Oct 70   MOTOWN CHARTBUSTERS VOL. 4 Various (Tamla Motown) ........... 1
 7 Nov 70   LED ZEPPELIN 3 Led Zeppelin (Atlantic)............................. 3
28 Nov 70   NEW MORNING Bob Dylan (CBS)..................................... 1
 5 Dec 70   GREATEST HITS Andy Williams (CBS) ............................... 1
12 Dec 70   LED ZEPPELIN 3 Led Zeppelin (Atlantic)............................. 1
19 Dec 70   GREATEST HITS Andy Williams (CBS) ............................... 4

16 Jan 71†  BRIDGE OVER TROUBLED WATER Simon and Garfunkel (CBS) ......... 11
 3 Apr 71   HOME LOVING MAN Andy Williams (CBS) ........................... 2
17 Apr 71   MOTOWN CHARTBUSTERS VOL. 5 Various (Tamla Motown) ........... 3
 8 May 71   STICKY FINGERS Rolling Stones (Rolling Stones) ..................... 4
 5 Jun 71   RAM Paul and Linda McCartney (Apple) ............................. 2
19 Jun 71   STICKY FINGERS Rolling Stones (Rolling Stones) ..................... 1
26 Jun 71   TARKUS Emerson, Lake and Palmer (Island) ......................... 1
 3 Jul 71   BRIDGE OVER TROUBLED WATER Simon and Garfunkel (CBS) ......... 5
 7 Aug 71   HOT HITS 6 Various (MFP) .......................................... 1
14 Aug 71   EVERY GOOD BOY DESERVES FAVOUR Moody Blues (Threshold) ....... 1
21 Aug 71   TOP OF THE POPS VOL. 18 Various (Hallmark) ....................... 3
11 Sep 71   BRIDGE OVER TROUBLED WATER Simon and Garfunkel (CBS) ......... 1
18 Sep 71   WHO'S NEXT Who (Track)........................................... 1
25 Sep 71   FIREBALL Deep Purple (Harvest) .................................... 1
```

† This includes 8 weeks at number one when charts were not published due to a postal strike.

SLADE

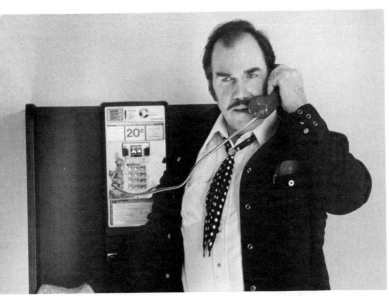

SLIM WHITMAN

29 Sep 79  OCEANS OF FANTASY Boney M (Atlantic/Hansa) ....................
6 Oct 79  THE PLEASURE PRINCIPLE Gary Numan (Beggars Banquet) .............
13 Oct 79*  EAT TO THE BEAT Blondie (Chrysalis) .............................
13 Oct 79*  REGGATTA DE BLANC Police (A & M) ........................
10 Nov 79  TUSK Fleetwood Mac (Warner Bros.) .............................
17 Nov 79  GREATEST HITS VOL. 2 Abba (Epic) ...........................
8 Dec 79  GREATEST HITS Rod Stewart (Riva) ..............................

12 Jan 80  GREATEST HITS VOL. 2 Abba (Epic) ...........................
19 Jan 80  PRETENDERS Pretenders (Real) ............................
16 Feb 80  THE LAST DANCE Various (Motown)..........................
1 Mar 80  STRING OF HITS Shadows (EMI) ............................
22 Mar 80  TEARS AND LAUGHTER Johnny Mathis (CBS).....................
5 Apr 80  DUKE Genesis (Charisma) ..............................
19 Apr 80  GREATEST HITS Rose Royce (Whitfield) ......................
3 May 80  SKY 2 Sky (Ariola).................................
17 May 80  THE MAGIC OF BONEY M Boney M (Atlantic/Hansa) ..............
31 May 80  McCARTNEY II Paul McCartney (Parlophone).....................
14 Jun 80  PETER GABRIEL Peter Gabriel (Charisma) .....................
28 Jun 80  FLESH AND BLOOD Roxy Music (Polydor) ......................
5 Jul 80  EMOTIONAL RESCUE Rolling Stones (Rolling Stones) ...............
19 Jul 80  THE GAME Queen (EMI) ...............................
2 Aug 80  DEEPEST PURPLE Deep Purple (Harvest) ......................
9 Aug 80  BACK IN BLACK AC/DC (Atlantic) .........................
23 Aug 80  FLESH AND BLOOD Roxy Music (Polydor) ......................
13 Sep 80  TELEKON Gary Numan (Beggars Banquet) ......................
20 Sep 80  NEVER FOR EVER Kate Bush (EMI) ........................
27 Sep 80  SCARY MONSTERS AND SUPERCREEPS David Bowie (RCA) ..........
11 Oct 80  ZENYATTA MONDATTA Police (A & M)........................
8 Nov 80  GUILTY Barbra Streisand (CBS) .........................
22 Nov 80  SUPER TROUPER Abba (Epic) .............................

24 Jan 81  KINGS OF THE WILD FRONTIER Adam and the Ants (CBS) .............
7 Feb 81  DOUBLE FANTASY John Lennon (Geffen) ......................
21 Feb 81  FACE VALUE Phil Collins (Virgin) ........................
14 Mar 81  KINGS OF THE WILD FRONTIER Adam and the Ants (CBS) .............
23 May 81  STARS ON 45 Starsound (CBS)...........................
27 Jun 81  NO SLEEP TIL HAMMERSMITH Motorhead (Bronze) ..................
4 Jul 81  DISCO DAZE & DISCO NITES Various (Ronco) ....................
11 Jul 81  LOVE SONGS Cliff Richard (EMI) .........................
15 Aug 81  THE OFFICIAL BBC ALBUM OF THE ROYAL WEDDING Soundtrack (BBC)
29 Aug 81  TIME Electric Light Orchestra (Jet) .......................
12 Sep 81  DEAD RINGER Meat Loaf (Epic) ..........................
26 Sep 81  ABACAB Genesis (Charisma) .........................
10 Oct 81  GHOST IN THE MACHINE Police (A & M) ......................
31 Oct 81  DARE Human League (Virgin) ...........................
7 Nov 81  SHAKY Shakin' Stevens (Epic) .........................
14 Nov 81  GREATEST HITS Queen (EMI) ...........................
12 Dec 81  CHART HITS '81 Various (K-Tel) .........................
19 Dec 81  THE VISITORS Abba (Epic) ............................

9 Jan 82  DARE Human League (Virgin) ...........................
30 Jan 82  LOVE SONGS Barbra Streisand (CBS) ......................
20 Mar 82  THE GIFT Jam (Polydor) .............................
27 Mar 82  LOVE SONGS Barbra Streisand (CBS) ......................
10 Apr 82  THE NUMBER OF THE BEAST Iron Maiden (EMI) .................
24 Apr 82  1982 Status Quo (Vertigo) ...........................
1 May 82  BARRY LIVE IN BRITAIN Barry Manilow (Arista) ................
8 May 82  TUG OF WAR Paul McCartney (Parlophone) ...................
22 May 82  COMPLETE MADNESS Madness (Stiff) ......................
5 Jun 82  AVALON Roxy Music (Polydor) ..........................
12 Jun 82  COMPLETE MADNESS Madness (Stiff) ......................
19 Jun 82  AVALON Roxy Music (Polydor) ..........................
3 Jul 82  THE LEXICON OF LOVE ABC (Neutron) ......................
24 Jul 82  =THE LEXICON OF LOVE ABC (Neutron) ......................
           =FAME Original Soundtrack (RSO) .......................

\* Two charts published this week because of a change in chart collation.

17 Aug 85 NOW! THAT'S WHAT I CALL MUSIC 5 Various Artists (EMI/Virgin) . . . . . .
21 Sep 85 LIKE A VIRGIN Madonna (Sire) . . . . . . . . . . . . . . . . . . . . . . . . . . . . . . . . . . . .
28 Sep 85 HOUNDS OF LOVE Kate Bush (EMI) . . . . . . . . . . . . . . . . . . . . . . . . . . . . . . .
12 Oct 85 LIKE A VIRGIN Madonna (Sire) . . . . . . . . . . . . . . . . . . . . . . . . . . . . . . . . . . . .
19 Oct 85 HOUNDS OF LOVE Kate Bush (EMI) . . . . . . . . . . . . . . . . . . . . . . . . . . . . . . .
26 Oct 85 THE LOVE SONGS George Benson (K-Tel) . . . . . . . . . . . . . . . . . . . . . . . . . .
2 Nov 85 ONCE UPON A TIME Simple Minds (Virgin) . . . . . . . . . . . . . . . . . . . . . . .
9 Nov 85 THE LOVE SONGS George Benson (K-Tel) . . . . . . . . . . . . . . . . . . . . . . . . . .
16 Nov 85 PROMISE Sade (Epic) . . . . . . . . . . . . . . . . . . . . . . . . . . . . . . . . . . . . . . . . . . . .
30 Nov 85 THE GREATEST HITS OF 1985 Various Artists (Telstar) . . . . . . . . . . . . . . . .
7 Dec 85 NOW! THAT'S WHAT I CALL MUSIC 6 Various Artists (EMI/Virgin) . . . . . .
21 Dec 85 NOW! – THE CHRISTMAS ALBUM Various Artists (EMI/Virgin) . . . . . . . . . .

4 Jan 86 NOW! THAT'S WHAT I CALL MUSIC 6 Various Artists (EMI/Virgin) . . . . . . .
18 Jan 86 BROTHERS IN ARMS Dire Straits (Vertigo) . . . . . . . . . . . . . . . . . . . . . . . . . .
29 Mar 86 HITS 4 Various Artists (CBS/WEA/RCA Ariola) . . . . . . . . . . . . . . . . . . . . . . .
26 Apr 86 STREET LIFE – 20 GREAT HITS Bryan Ferry/Roxy Music (EG) . . . . . . . . . . . .
31 May 86 SO Peter Gabriel (Virgin) . . . . . . . . . . . . . . . . . . . . . . . . . . . . . . . . . . . . . . . .
14 Jun 86 A KIND OF MAGIC Queen (EMI) . . . . . . . . . . . . . . . . . . . . . . . . . . . . . . . . . . .
21 Jun 86 INVISIBLE TOUCH Genesis (Charisma) . . . . . . . . . . . . . . . . . . . . . . . . . . . . . .
12 Jul 86 TRUE BLUE Madonna (Sire) . . . . . . . . . . . . . . . . . . . . . . . . . . . . . . . . . . . . . . .
23 Aug 86 NOW! THAT'S WHAT I CALL MUSIC 7 Various Artists (EMI/Virgin) . . . . . .
27 Sep 86 SILK AND STEEL Five Star (Tent) . . . . . . . . . . . . . . . . . . . . . . . . . . . . . . . . . .
4 Oct 86 GRACELAND Paul Simon (Warner Bros.) . . . . . . . . . . . . . . . . . . . . . . . . . . . . .
8 Nov 86 EVERY BREATH YOU TAKE – THE SINGLES Police (A & M) . . . . . . . . . . . .
22 Nov 86 HITS 5 Various Artists (CBS/WEA/RCA Ariola) . . . . . . . . . . . . . . . . . . . . . . .
6 Dec 86 NOW! THAT'S WHAT I CALL MUSIC 8 Various Artists (EMI/Virgin) . . . . . . .

17 Jan 87 THE WHOLE STORY Kate Bush (EMI) . . . . . . . . . . . . . . . . . . . . . . . . . . . . . .
31 Jan 87 GRACELAND Paul Simon (Warner Bros.) . . . . . . . . . . . . . . . . . . . . . . . . . . . . .
21 Feb 87 PHANTOM OF THE OPERA Original London Cast (Polydor) . . . . . . . . . . . . . .
14 Mar 87 THE VERY BEST OF HOT CHOCOLATE Hot Chocolate (RAK) . . . . . . . . . . .
21 Mar 87 THE JOSHUA TREE U2 (Island) . . . . . . . . . . . . . . . . . . . . . . . . . . . . . . . . . . . .
4 Apr 87 NOW! THAT'S WHAT I CALL MUSIC 9
Various Artists (EMI/Virgin/Phonogram) . . . . . . . . . . . . . . . . . . . . . . . . . . . . .
9 May 87 KEEP YOUR DISTANCE Curiosity Killed The Cat (Mercury) . . . . . . . . . . . . .
23 May 87 IT'S BETTER TO TRAVEL Swing Out Sister (Mercury) . . . . . . . . . . . . . . . . . .
6 Jun 87 LIVE IN THE CITY OF LIGHT Simple Minds (Virgin) . . . . . . . . . . . . . . . . . . .
13 Jun 87 WHITNEY Whitney Houston (Arista) . . . . . . . . . . . . . . . . . . . . . . . . . . . . . . . . .
25 Jul 87 INTRODUCING THE HARD LINE ACCORDING TO TERENCE TRENT
D'ARBY Terence Trent D'Arby (CBS) . . . . . . . . . . . . . . . . . . . . . . . . . . . . . . . .
1 Aug 87 HITS 6 Various Artists (CBS/WEA/BMG) . . . . . . . . . . . . . . . . . . . . . . . . . . . . .
29 Aug 87 HYSTERIA Def Leppard (Bludgeon Riffola) . . . . . . . . . . . . . . . . . . . . . . . . . . .
5 Sep 87 HITS 6 Various Artists (CBS/WEA/BMG) . . . . . . . . . . . . . . . . . . . . . . . . . . . . .
12 Sep 87 BAD Michael Jackson (Epic) . . . . . . . . . . . . . . . . . . . . . . . . . . . . . . . . . . . . . . .
17 Oct 87 TUNNEL OF LOVE Bruce Springsteen (CBS) . . . . . . . . . . . . . . . . . . . . . . . . . .
24 Oct 87 NOTHING LIKE THE SUN Sting (A & M) . . . . . . . . . . . . . . . . . . . . . . . . . . . . .
31 Oct 87 TANGO IN THE NIGHT Fleetwood Mac (Warner Bros.) . . . . . . . . . . . . . . . . .
14 Nov 87 FAITH George Michael (Epic) . . . . . . . . . . . . . . . . . . . . . . . . . . . . . . . . . . . . . .
21 Nov 87 BRIDGE OF SPIES T'Pau (Siren) . . . . . . . . . . . . . . . . . . . . . . . . . . . . . . . . . . .
28 Nov 87 WHENEVER YOU NEED SOMEBODY Rick Astley (RCA) . . . . . . . . . . . . . . .
5 Dec 87 NOW! THAT'S WHAT I CALL MUSIC 10 Various Artists
(EMI/Virgin/Polygram) . . . . . . . . . . . . . . . . . . . . . . . . . . . . . . . . . . . . . . . . . . .

16 Jan 88 POPPED IN SOULED OUT Wet Wet Wet (Precious) . . . . . . . . . . . . . . . . . . . .
23 Jan 88 TURN BACK THE CLOCK Johhny Hates Jazz (Virgin) . . . . . . . . . . . . . . . . . . .
30 Jan 88 INTRODUCING THE HARDLINE ACCORDING TO TERENCE TRENT
D'ARBY Terence Trent D'Arby (CBS) . . . . . . . . . . . . . . . . . . . . . . . . . . . . . . . .
26 Mar 88 VIVA HATE Morrissey (HMV) . . . . . . . . . . . . . . . . . . . . . . . . . . . . . . . . . . . . . .
2 Apr 88 NOW! THAT'S WHAT I CALL MUSIC 11 Various Artists
(EMI/Virgin/Polygram) . . . . . . . . . . . . . . . . . . . . . . . . . . . . . . . . . . . . . . . . . . .
23 Apr 88 SEVENTH SON OF A SEVENTH SON Iron Maiden (EMI) . . . . . . . . . . . . . . .
30 Apr 88 THE INNOCENTS Erasure (Mute) . . . . . . . . . . . . . . . . . . . . . . . . . . . . . . . . . . .
7 May 88 TANGO IN THE NIGHT Fleetwood Mac (Warner Bros.) . . . . . . . . . . . . . . . . .
21 May 88 LOVESEXY Prince (Paisley Park) . . . . . . . . . . . . . . . . . . . . . . . . . . . . . . . . . . .
28 May 88 TANGO IN THE NIGHT Fleetwood Mac (Warner Bros.) . . . . . . . . . . . . . . . . .
4 Jun 88 NITE FLITE Various Artists (CBS) . . . . . . . . . . . . . . . . . . . . . . . . . . . . . . . . . . .

**341**

y the end of the decade, the success of the *Now!* and *Hits* albums series distorted album sales to
ch an extent that the record industry decided to create two different charts, so from 14 January
89, the albums charts were split into a Top 75 'Artist Albums' and a Top 20 Compilation
lbums. The number one hits on the Compilation Albums chart during 1989 were as follows:

All albums were, of course, credited to 'Various Artists'.

# Most Number One Albums

| | |
|---|---|
| 12 | BEATLES |
| 9 | ROLLING STONES |
| 8 | ABBA |
| 8 | LED ZEPPELIN |
| 7 | PAUL McCARTNEY/WINGS |
| 7 | ROD STEWART |
| 6 | DAVID BOWIE |
| 6 | BOB DYLAN |
| 6 | ELVIS PRESLEY |
| 6 | QUEEN |
| 6 | CLIFF RICHARD |
| 5 | POLICE |
| 4 | GENESIS |
| 4 | ELTON JOHN |
| 4 | ROXY MUSIC |
| | *(1 with Bryan Ferry)* |
| 4 | SHADOWS |
| 4 | SIMPLE MINDS |
| 4 | STATUS QUO |
| 4 | U2 |
| 3 | BONEY M |
| 3 | KATE BUSH |
| 3 | PHIL COLLINS |
| 3 | DEEP PURPLE |
| 3 | DIRE STRAITS |

| | |
|---|---|
| 3 | FLEETWOOD MAC |
| 3 | JOHN LENNON |
| 3 | MADONNA |
| 3 | GEORGE MITCHELL MINSTRELS |
| 3 | MOODY BLUES |
| 3 | GARY NUMAN/TUBEWAY ARMY |
| 3 | PINK FLOYD |
| 3 | SLADE |
| 3 | BARBRA STREISAND |
| 3 | T. REX |
| 3 | ANDY WILLIAMS |

Simon and Garfunkel have 2 number on albums, and Paul Simon has scored 2 mo solo.

Diana Ross and the Supremes have 2 numb ones and one more with the Temptations.

Bryan Ferry has one solo number one to with the 4 Roxy Music chart-toppers, on all which he sang lead and on one of which he w given equal billing with Roxy Music as it al featured several solo Ferry tracks.

Sting has one solo number one album as well 5 as lead singer with Police.

Michael Jackson has only 2 number on albums, but he features on one more with t Jackson Five, which also features solo Micha Jackson tracks.

George Michael has one solo chart-toppi album and 2 more as half of Wham!

ROLLING STONES

# Most Weeks at Number One

| | |
|---|---|
| 163 | BEATLES |
| 115 | Cast of *SOUTH PACIFIC* Film Soundtrack |
| 70 | Cast of *THE SOUND OF MUSIC* Film Soundtrack |
| 49 | ABBA |
| 49 | ELVIS PRESLEY |
| 48 | SIMON and GARFUNKEL *(Paul Simon 9 more solo)* |
| 43 | ROLLING STONES |
| 29 | CLIFF RICHARD |
| 27 | ROD STEWART |
| 22 | CARPENTERS |
| 22 | BOB DYLAN |
| 21 | DIRE STRAITS |
| 21 | ELTON JOHN |
| 21 | SHADOWS |
| 20 | DAVID BOWIE |
| 19 | GEORGE MITCHELL MINSTRELS |
| 18 | Cast of *SATURDAY NIGHT FEVER* Film Soundtrack |
| 16 | PAUL McCARTNEY/WINGS |
| 15 | POLICE |
| 15 | BARBRA STREISAND |
| 14 | LED ZEPPELIN |
| 13 | BEACH BOYS |
| 13 | Cast of *GREASE* Film Soundtrack |
| 13 | Broadway Cast of *WEST SIDE STORY* |
| 13 | PHIL COLLINS |
| 13 | MICHAEL JACKSON *(plus 3 with Jackson Five)* |
| 13 | QUEEN |
| 13 | ROXY MUSIC |
| 12 | ADAM and the ANTS |
| 12 | KIDS FROM 'FAME' |
| 12 | BOB MARLEY and the WAILERS |
| 12 | T. REX |
| 10 | JOHN LENNON |
| 10 | MADONNA |
| 10 | DIANA ROSS and the SUPREMES *(plus 4 with the Temptations)* |
| 10 | STYLISTICS |
| 10 | SLIM WHITMAN |

List excludes individual appearances on compilation and soundtracks, except where the soundtrack is credited to one artist, for example Elvis Presley's 'Blue Hawaii'.

---

# Most Weeks at Number One by an Album In Total

| | | |
|---|---|---|
| 15 | SOUTH PACIFIC | Film Soundtrack |
| 70 | THE SOUND OF MUSIC | Film Soundtrack |
| 41 | BRIDGE OVER TROUBLED WATER | Simon and Garfunkel |
| 30 | PLEASE PLEASE ME | Beatles |
| 27 | SERGEANT PEPPER'S LONELY HEARTS CLUB BAND | Beatles |
| 22 | GI BLUES | Elvis Presley (Film Soundtrack) |
| 21 | WITH THE BEATLES | Beatles |
| 21 | A HARD DAY'S NIGHT | Beatles (Film Soundtrack) |
| 18 | BLUE HAWAII | Elvis Presley (Film Soundtrack) |
| 18 | SATURDAY NIGHT FEVER | Film Soundtrack |
| 17 | ABBEY ROAD | Beatles |
| 17 | THE SINGLES 1969–1973 | Carpenters |
| 14 | SUMMER HOLIDAY | Cliff Richard and the Shadows (Film Soundtrack) |
| 14 | BROTHERS IN ARMS | Dire Straits |
| 13 | WEST SIDE STORY | Film Soundtrack |
| 13 | JOHN WESLEY HARDING | Bob Dylan |
| 13 | GREASE | Film Soundtrack |
| 12 | THE ROLLING STONES | Rolling Stones |
| 12 | KINGS OF THE WILD FRONTIER | Adam and the Ants |
| 12 | THE KIDS FROM 'FAME' | The Kids From Fame |
| 12 | LEGEND | Bob Marley and the Wailers |
| 11 | BEATLES FOR SALE | Beatles |
| 11 | 20 ALL TIME HITS OF THE FIFTIES | Various Artists |
| 11 | ELTON JOHN'S GREATEST HITS | Elton John |
| 11 | GREATEST HITS | Abba |
| 10 | ROLLING STONES NO. 2 | Rolling Stones |
| 10 | 20 GOLDEN GREATS | Beach Boys |
| 10 | ARRIVAL | Abba |

# Most Consecutive Weeks at Number One by One Album

| | | |
|---|---|---|
| 70 | SOUTH PACIFIC Film Soundtrack | from 8 Nov 58 |
| 30 | PLEASE PLEASE ME Beatles | from 11 May 63 |
| 23 | SERGEANT PEPPER'S LONELY HEARTS CLUB BAND Beatles | from 10 Jun 67 |
| 21 | WITH THE BEATLES Beatles | from 7 Dec 63 |
| 21 | A HARD DAY'S NIGHT Beatles | from 25 Jul 64 |
| 19 | SOUTH PACIFIC Film Soundtrack | from 19 Mar 60 |
| 18 | THE SOUND OF MUSIC Film Soundtrack | from 1 Oct 66 |
| 18 | SATURDAY NIGHT FEVER Film Soundtrack | from 6 May 78 |
| 17 | BLUE HAWAII Elvis Presley | from 24 Feb 62 |
| 14 | SUMMER HOLIDAY Cliff Richard and the Shadows | from 2 Feb 63 |
| 13 | SOUTH PACIFIC Film Soundtrack | from 15 Oct 60 |
| 13 | BRIDGE OVER TROUBLED WATER Simon and Garfunkel | from 21 Feb 70 |
| 13 | GREASE Film Soundtrack | from 7 Oct 78 |
| 12 | GI BLUES Elvis Presley | from 8 Apr 63 |
| 12 | ROLLING STONES Rolling Stones | from 2 May 64 |
| 12 | LEGEND Bob Marley and the Wailers | from 19 May 84 |
| 11 | ABBEY ROAD Beatles | from 4 Oct 69 |
| 11 | BRIDGE OVER TROUBLED WATER Simon and Garfunkel | from 16 Jan 71 |
| 11 | THE SINGLES 1969–1973 Carpenters | from 9 Mar 74 |
| 11 | ELTON JOHN'S GREATEST HITS Elton John | from 23 Nov 74 |
| 10 | THE SOUND OF MUSIC Film Soundtrack | from 5 Jun 65 |
| 10 | THE SOUND OF MUSIC Film Soundtrack | from 16 Oct 65 |
| 10 | THE SOUND OF MUSIC Film Soundtrack | from 19 Feb 66 |
| 10 | JOHN WESLEY HARDING Bob Dylan | from 9 Mar 68 |
| 10 | 20 GOLDEN GREATS Beach Boys | from 24 Jul 76 |
| 10 | KINGS OF THE WILD FRONTIER Adam and the Ants | from 14 Mar 81 |
| 10 | BROTHERS IN ARMS Dire Straits | from 18 Jan 86 |

The run of 11 weeks by *Bridge Over Troubled Water* includes 8 weeks at number one when charts were not published because of a postal strike.

# Longest Climb to Number One

Four albums have taken more than one year from their original date of chart entry to climb to the number one position, as follows:

**3 years 298 days** (from 13 Jul 68 to 6 May 72)
Tyrannosaurus Rex *My People Were Fair And Had Sky In Their Hair, But Now They're Content To Wear Stars On Their Brows*

**2 years 67 days** (from 5 Jul 75 to 10 Sep 77)
Elvis Presley *40 Greatest Hits*

**1 year 321 days** (from 6 Sep 80 to 24 Jul 82)
Original Soundtrack *Fame*

**1 year 83 days** (from 14 Jul 73 to 5 Oct 74)
Mike Oldfield *Tubular Bells*

8 other albums have taken 30 weeks or more to reach the top spot, as follows:

| | | |
|---|---|---|
| *Rumours* | Fleetwood Mac | **49 weeks** |
| *The Freewheelin' Bob Dylan* | Bob Dylan | **48 weeks** |
| *Like A Virgin* | Madonna | **44 weeks** |
| *Black and White Minstrel Show* | George Mitchell Minstrels | **36 weeks** |
| *Born In The USA* | Bruce Springsteen | **36 weeks** |
| *Greatest Hits* | Andy Williams | **35 weeks** |
| *Band On The Run* | Wings | **33 weeks** |
| *And I Love You So* | Perry Como | **30 weeks** |

Tyrannosaurus Rex hit number one with the longest titled album ever to hit the top only after it was re-released in 1972 as a double album with *Prophets, Seers, Sages and the Angels Of The Ages*. Presley's album hit the top in the period immediately following his death. *Tubular Bells* spent 11 weeks at number two before climbing to the very top, and *Rumours* had spent 32 weeks in the Top Ten before hitting the number one slot. *The Freewheelin' Bob Dylan* climbed to the top in its seventh chart run.

JAMES LAST

# Most Hits Without a Number One Hit

| | |
|---|---|
| 53 | JAMES LAST (one no. 2 hit) |
| 28 | SHIRLEY BASSEY (one no. 2 hit) |
| 28 | DIANA ROSS (two no. 2 hits, and has hit number one twice with the Supremes and once with the Supremes and Temptations) |
| 24 | NEIL DIAMOND (one no. 2 hit) |
| 19 | HAWKWIND (one no. 9 hit) |
| 19 | SANTANA (two no. 6 hits) |
| 18 | JIMI HENDRIX (two no. 2 hits) |
| 16 | JOHNNY CASH (one no. 2 hit) |
| 16 | ERIC CLAPTON (three no. 3 hits, but has hit number one as part of both Cream and Blind Faith) |
| 16 | TANGERINE DREAM (whose biggest hit reached no. 12) |
| 15 | HERB ALPERT (one no. 2 hit) |
| 15 | VAN MORRISON (whose biggest hit reached no. 13) |

## Most Consecutive Number One Hit Albums

Sixteen different acts have hit the very top of the albums chart with three or more consecutive official album releases, as follows:

**11 BEATLES.** (From *Please Please Me* in 1963 to *Let It Be* in 1970. All the Beatles albums made while they were actively recording hit number one. During this run *A Collection Of Beatles Oldies, Magical Mystery Tour* (import) and *Yellow Submarine* all hit the charts, but only the *Oldies* album could be considered even vaguely as part of the official sequence of Beatles albums. If it is considered an official album release, then the Beatles have a best consecutive run of 7 number ones, and a smaller run of 4.)

**8 ABBA.** (From 1976 to 1982: *Greatest Hits* to *The Singles – The First Ten Years* inclusive.)

**8 LED ZEPPELIN.** (From 1970 to 1979: *Led Zeppelin 2* to *In Through The Out Door* inclusive.)

**6 ROD STEWART.** (From 1971 to 1976: *Every Picture Tells A Story* to *A Night On The Town* inclusive.)

**5 POLICE.** (From 1979 to 1986: *Reggatta De Blanc* to *Every Breath You Take – The Singles* inclusive. These were their final five albums.)

**5 ROLLING STONES.** (From 1969 to 1973: *Let It Bleed* to *Goat's Head Soup*. Their last two official releases on Decca and their first three on Rolling Stones Records.)

**4 BOB DYLAN.** (From 1968 to 1970: *John Wesley Harding* to *New Morning* inclusive.)

**4 ELTON JOHN.** (From 1973 to 1975: *Don't Shoot Me, I'm Only The Piano Player* to *Elton John's Greatest Hits* inclusive.)

**4 SIMPLE MINDS.** (From 1984 to 1989: *Sparkle In The Rain* to *Street Fighting Years* inclusive. Each album spent only one week at the top of the charts.)

**3 BONEY M.** (From 1978 to 1980: *Night Flight To Venus, Oceans Of Fantasy* and *The Magic Of Boney M.*)

**3 DAVID BOWIE.** (From 1973 to 1974: *Aladdin Sane, Pin-Ups* and *Diamond Dogs*.)

**3 GEORGE MITCHELL MINSTRELS.** (From 1961 to 1963, the first album chart hat-trick: *The Black And White Minstrel Show, Another Black And White Minstrel Show* and *On Stage With The George Mitchell Minstrels*.)

**3 GARY NUMAN.** (From 1979 to 1980: *Replicas, The Pleasure Principle* and *Telekon. Tubeway Army* was released before *Replicas*, even though it hit the charts later.)

**3 SLADE.** (From 1973 to 1974: *Slayed?, Sladest* and *Old New Borrowed And Blue*.)

**3 T. REX.** (From 1971 to 1972: *Electric Warrior, Prophets Seers And Sages The Angels Of The Ages/My People Were Fair And Had Sky In Their Hair But Now They're Content To Wear Stars On Their Brows* and *Bolan Boogie*. The second of the three was a double album re-issue, but it had never been issued in that format, and the first of the two albums had never been a hit before.)

**3 U2.** (From 1984 to 1988: *The Unforgettable Fire, The Joshua Tree* and *Rattle And Hum*.)

Police and the Rolling Stones both came onto the charts at number one five times in succession. Police also completed their hat-trick of number one singles by coming onto the chart at number one, a feat only once equalled. Led Zeppelin and Simple Minds have had four

consecutive albums debut at number one, while the Beatles, David Bowie and U2 have done it with three in a row.

# Straight in at Number One

After the first chart on 8 November 1958, no album made its chart debut at number one until the Beatles' fifth .album, *Help*, did so on 14 August 1965. However, it is now a fairly common event in the albums charts, much more so than in the singles charts. There was a period of seven consecutive weeks in September and October 1989 when a new album crashed into the charts at number one each week. Fourteen acts have achieved this feat at least three times, as follows:

DAVID BOWIE

6   DAVID BOWIE
    ROLLING STONES

5   BEATLES
    LED ZEPPELIN
    POLICE

4   ABBA
    GENESIS
    PAUL McCARTNEY
    SIMPLE MINDS
    U2

3   PHIL COLLINS
    DIRE STRAITS
    ELTON JOHN
    STATUS QUO

Paul McCartney has therefore achieved the feat nine times, five times with the Beatles and four times solo. Phil Collins has done it seven times, four times with Genesis and three times solo.

**348**

## The Top Twenty Albums Acts

A table showing the comparative achievements of the twenty most charted album acts of all time, who have each spent a total of over 500 weeks on the Albums charts.

| Act | Year First Charted | Total Weeks | Total Hits | Top Ten | No. Ones | Most Charted Album |
|---|---|---|---|---|---|---|
| BEATLES | 1963 | 1082 | 25 | 18 | 12 | *Sgt. Pepper's Lonely Hearts Club Band*: 164 wks |
| SIMON AND GARFUNKEL | 1966 | 1034 | 9 | 6 | 2 | *Bridge Over Troubled Water*: 303 wks |
| ELVIS PRESLEY | 1958 | 1023 | 92 | 36 | 6 | *Blue Hawaii* 71 wks |
| DIRE STRAITS | 1978 | 1014 | 7 | 7 | 3 | *Makin' Movies*: 249 wks |
| QUEEN | 1974 | 841 | 17 | 15 | 6 | *Greatest Hits*: 326 wks |
| DAVID BOWIE | 1972 | 829 | 26 | 18 | 6 | *The Rise And Fall Of Ziggy Stardust And The Spiders From Mars*: 168 wks |
| FLEETWOOD MAC | 1968 | 744 | 13 | 8 | 3 | *Rumours*: 443 wks |
| PINK FLOYD | 1967 | 736 | 16 | 13 | 3 | *Dark Side Of The Moon*: 296 wks |
| U2 | 1981 | 720 | 9 | 5 | 4 | *Live Under A Blood Red Sky*: 201 wks |
| CLIFF RICHARD | 1959 | 684 | 45 | 29 | 6 | *Love Songs*: 43 wks |
| ROLLING STONES | 1964 | 650 | 35 | 27 | 9 | *Rolling Stones*: 51 wks |
| ELTON JOHN | 1970 | 617 | 29 | 16 | 4 | *Greatest Hits* and *Goodbye Yellow Brick Road*: 84 wks |
| FRANK SINATRA | 1958 | 613 | 49 | 27 | 1 | *My Way*: 59 wks |
| PHIL COLLINS | 1981 | 592 | 4 | 4 | 3 | *Face Value*: 270 wks |
| ROD STEWART | 1970 | 571 | 19 | 15 | 7 | *Atlantic Crossing*: 88 wks |

PHIL COLLINS

BOB DYLAN

| | | | | | | |
|---|---|---|---|---|---|---|
| BOB DYLAN | 1964 | 552 | 32 | 24 | 6 | *Greatest Hits*: 83 wks |
| MICHAEL JACKSON | 1972 | 533 | 12 | 4 | 2 | *Off The Wall:* 173 wks |
| MEAT LOAF | 1978 | 525 | 7 | 5 | 1 | *Bat Out Of Hell*: 395 wks |
| BEACH BOYS | 1965 | 524 | 25 | 13 | 2 | *Best Of The Beach Boys*: 142 w |
| ABBA | 1974 | 506 | 12 | 8 | 8 | *Greatest Hits*: 130 wks |

Over the past two years since *British Hit Albums 3* was published, only Michael Jackson has moved into the Top 20 acts, at the expense of the Carpenters, who slip to number 22. All the top acts, except for Simon and Garfunkel, David Bowie, Frank Sinatra and the Beach Boys have appeared in the charts over the past two years. Michael Jackson has added most to his total in 1988 and 1989, a further 160 weeks. Fleetwood Mac (143 weeks), U2 (137) and Dire Straits (114) are the only other acts in the Top 20 to add at least 100 weeks over the final two years of the decade.

Fleetwood Mac, U2 and Phil Collins have all climbed four places within the Top 20 since the end of 1987, while the Rolling Stones, Frank Sinatra and the Beach Boys have each slipped three rungs.

Both Elvis Presley and Frank Sinatra featured in the very first albums chart. The most recent arrival to the charts of any of the Top 20 acts is by U2, whose first album chart action came in the week ending 29 August 1981.

Of the 20 leading acts, ten are British, seven are American, one is a transatlantic mixture (Fleetwood Mac), one is Irish and one Swedish. There are nine male solo acts, but no female soloists. The ladies in Fleetwood Mac and Abba make the only dent in the male supremacy of the albums charts. The highest ranked female soloist is Madonna, at number 29.

If we look at the top acts on the basis of the average number of weeks each hit album has spent in the charts (i.e. Total Weeks divided by Total Hits), six acts prove to have spent an average of more than one year on the charts with each album:

| | |
|---|---|
| PHIL COLLINS | 148.0 weeks on chart per album |
| DIRE STRAITS | 144.9 weeks on chart per album |
| SIMON AND GARFUNKEL | 114.9 weeks on chart per album |
| U2 | 80.0 weeks on chart per album |
| MEAT LOAF | 75.0 weeks on chart per album |
| FLEETWOOD MAC | 57.2 weeks on chart per album |

If Phil Collins had had as many hit albums as Elvis Presley, he would have spent 13,616 weeks on the charts. However, as every album he makes racks up almost three years on the chart, he may not feel the need to release his 92nd hit for some time to come.

At the other end of the scale, each album hit by Elvis Presley has lasted on average only 11.1 weeks on the chart, each Frank Sinatra hit lasts only 12.5 weeks, and each Cliff Richard album hangs around for no more than 15.2 weeks. Bob Dylan (17.3 weeks) and the Rolling Stones (18.6 weeks) are the only other acts to average fewer than 20 weeks of chart action per hit.

# The Authors

Of the obsolete configurations **PAUL GAMBACCINI**
has one album on 78 r.p.m. disc, *Schubert's 'Great'*
*Symphony in C Major* by the London Symphony Orchestra
conducted by Bruno Walter, one eight-track cartridge,
*Whatever's For Us* by Joan Armatrading, and many
thousands of vinyl albums, more than he needs for
historical purposes. His CD collection is expanding like
Alice after taking an Eat Me pill. Paul also has a DAT
machine in anticipation of the next technological
revolution, but no recorded tapes for it. He is thinking of
buying a time machine to enjoy all his recorded music
properly.

**JONATHAN RICE** is still known to his two co-authors
and his three friends as Jo, and to his children as Dad. (His
wife refers to him as Hey You.) He is, however, fed up
with being asked to write books for the Virago Press about
women in rock music and being confused with the lady
who writes children's books. He has therefore reverted to
the long playing version of his name and wishes it to be
known that the bloke who writes on cricket and did a
chapter in that immortal book, *Business In Japan*, is the
same Jonathan Rice. In the words of the Eurythmics,
makers of his favourite album of 1989, *We Too Are One*.

**TIM RICE** was born four years before the world's first
glimpse of the commercial long playing record, eleven
years before the publication of the first album chart in the
U.S., and fourteen before the debut of the U.K. best-
selling LP lists. On the 20th February 1971 an album he
wrote and produced with Andrew Lloyd Webber, the
original studio recording of 'Jesus Christ Superstar',
reached number one in those U.S. album charts and
dozens of albums featuring his songs in total or in part
have charted in America and Britain since. His co-authors
have, inexplicably, rejected his idea of including symbols
in this book to indicate exactly which ones he wrote.